Interpersonal Communication Research:

Advances Through Meta-Analysis

LEA's COMMUNICATIONS SERIES
Jennings Bryant and Dolf Zillmann, General Editors

Selected titles in Interpersonal Communication
(Rebecca G. Rubin, Advisory Editor) include:

For a complete list of titles in LEA's Communication Series, please contact Lawrence Erlbaum Associates, Publishers.

Interpersonal Communication Research:

Advances Through Meta-Analysis

Edited by

Mike Allen
University of Wisconsin–Milwaukee

Raymond W. Preiss
University of Puget Sound

Barbara Mae Gayle
University of Portland

Nancy A. Burrell
University of Wisconsin–Milwaukee

LAWRENCE ERLBAUM ASSOCIATES, PUBLISHERS
2002   Mahwah, New Jersey   London

Copyright © 2002 by Lawrence Erlbaum Associates, Inc.
All rights reserved. No part of this book may be reproduced in any
form, by photostat, microform, retrieval system, or any other
means, without prior written permission of the publisher.

Lawrence Erlbaum Associates, Inc., Publishers
10 Industrial Avenue
Mahwah, NJ 07430

Cover design by Kathryn Houghtaling Lacey

Library of Congress Cataloging-in-Publication Data

Interpersonal communication research : advances through
meta-analysis / edited by Mike Allen ... [et al.].
    p. cm.
Includes bibliographical references and index.
ISBN 0-8058-3131-2 (cloth : alk. paper)
ISBN 0-8058-3132-0 (pbk. : alk. paper)
1. Interpersonal communication. 2. Interpersonal
communication—Research.   I. Allen, Mike, 1959–
BF637.C45 I644   2001
153.6 —dc21
                                                    00-067768
                                                         CIP

Books published by Lawrence Erlbaum Associates are printed
on acid-free paper, and their bindings are chosen for strength
and durability.

Printed in the United States of America
10 9 8 7 6 5 4 3 2 1

Contents

v

IV: INTERACTIONAL ISSUES IN INTERPERSONAL COMMUNICATION

V: META-ANALYSIS AND INTERPERSONAL COMMUNICATION THEORY GENERATION

Preface

On Numbers, Narratives, and Insights Regarding Interpersonal Communication

Raymond W. Preiss and Mike Allen

The study of interpersonal communication is one of the more vibrant domains for social scientific theorizing and investigation. This interest is warranted, as the dyad has long been viewed as the nexus for message exchange and relationship evolution. As might be expected in an area dedicated to the study of the nuances and perplexities of social discourse, the complexity of the relational issues embedded in the interpersonal context is both intriguing and bewildering. Those interested in systematically understanding the richness of social life must address germinal issues: how and why individuals are attracted to certain others, how talk synchronizes perceptions and behaviors, or how and why individuals employ strategic messages to achieve relational outcomes. Of course, the list of "fundamental" issues is long and our journals provide a record of the conversations between scholars seeking adherence to various positions on that long list.

This book is about those conversations. Contributors approach their tasks from various perspectives and with numerous agendas. All of us, however, share the commitment to establish reliable generalizations about interpersonal communication in ways that can be properly described as "scientific." We search for stable, unbiased, predictable generalizations that operate within clearly defined interpersonal parameters (see Allen & Preiss,

1993, for a discussion of these qualities). Locating stable, unbiased, predictable generalizations has been complicated by the splintering of the macrodomain of interpersonal communication into subgroupings or rubrics that share common (or disparate) features. Issues of gender, conflict, communication competence, or group cohesion blur the oversimplified titles of our courses and force us to broadly consider the "long list" as we explore the ways human utterance functions interpersonally. We seek the generalizations that unify and explicate the interpersonal context.

This quest is a daunting task. Although every theory is assessed by its ability to produce meaningful generalizations, there are many theories to consider and many experimental findings to evaluate. Virtually every issue on the long list is contested and advocates offer important observations and key findings that are consistent with their perspectives. Faced with disparate theoretical approaches, assumptions, and methods, it is not surprising that progress has been uneven and that some theoretical questions resist interpretation. There is, it would seem, no lack of interpersonal communication research. There is, it is certain, little consensus on the interpersonal communication generalizations rooted in the experimental evidence.

We believe that social scientific progress in understanding interpersonal communication would be served best if the literature could be simultaneously expanded and summarized. Before people accept claims regarding the planetary origins of men and women, the literature on relational communication should be gathered and systematically summarized. These summaries would identify voids in the literature and draw attention to accepted issues that are supported by only a limited number of findings. In short, a comprehensive review of interpersonal communication would provide fertile soil for the next generation of studies. As research accumulated, the new primary research would be folded into ever-widening reviews of the issues explored in the investigations. Two methods for summarizing literature and reviewing findings are currently being used: narrative summaries and meta-analysis.

THE LOGIC OF NARRATIVE SUMMARIES

The narrative review or summary is the traditional verbal description of a body of literature (Pillemer, 1984) and the qualitative method for evaluating research on a given topic (Rosenthal, 1984). In most instances, the narrative reviewer will explicate a basic assumption or question and classify existing research using a vote-counting system (Did the studies on the roster of germane research detect a significant effect? Was the significant effect in the predicted direction? Were the significant effects attributable to a competing theory?).

The reader is asked to tally the votes (confirming or nonconfirming tests) and render a judgment regarding the question of interest.

The outcome of the narrative summary may range from strong support (a uniform confirming vote count) for some proposition to no support (the failure to detect confirming votes). Of course, interesting questions and the subtle texture of interpersonal communication issues will rarely produce a clear-cut vote count. If 60% or 70% of the votes confirm a proposition, the narrative reviewer must question the robustness of the relationship and provide a rationale for nonconfirming outcomes. If 30% or 40% of the votes are confirming, the reviewer must impugn the relationship and express the concern that little progress has been made in understanding such an important issue. In either outcome, more research will certainly be required.

The difficulty with the narrative review process involves the tendency for narrative reviewers to treat each qualifying vote as being 100% accurate. Because empirical findings are assessed probabilistically, it is a tautology that the findings of any one study may be the result of sampling error. Usually, narrative reviewers do not consider the possibility of Type I (false positive) or Type II (false negative) error as factors influencing trends in the primary research. Instead, experts tend to introduce intervening variables that explain apparent inconsistencies in the experimental record. In instances where discrepancies resist the philosopher's stone of the confounding variable, narrative reviewers may assess sample characteristics, research designs, or statistical methods as the source of contradictory findings. This produces a web of issues, theoretical and methodological, that deflect attention away from hypothesized relationships.

Of course, expert narrative summaries are essential components of the scientific enterprise, as they provide an avenue for subjective interpretation, reformulation, and reappraisal. If the goal is to assess evidence, however, this approach usually possesses the liability of nonrepresentativeness. In the course of making the case for an innovative interpretation or conclusion, the reviewer elevates certain studies as exemplars of the feature of interest. The difficulty here is that narrative reviews usually do not employ explicit rules or the methods used to locate primary evidence, how the reviewer determined which studies were germane to the analysis, and what criteria were used to determine whether or not an effect was present. The reader is asked to consider the exemplar studies in the context of a theoretical narrative or story that explains what the findings mean. Although reviewers make the case that the confirming evidence (the vote) is consistent with a novel interpretation, the reader is often not told why nonconfirming exemplars were excluded from the review.

The narrative summary offers an important venue for experts to advance their informed conclusions about a domain of literature. The risk is that in making the case for one interpretation, the ballot box for the vote count can be "stuffed" with nonrepresentative example studies. When nonconforming studies are mentioned, new variables may be introduced to explain discrepancies. The intervening variables may have been studied in only a limited number of investigations, and applying them to an entire domain runs the risk of overgeneralization. For these reasons, it is difficult for the vote-counting method used by narrative summaries to present a balanced portrayal of a large domain of literature.

THE LOGIC OF META-ANALYTIC SUMMARIES

The term *meta-analysis* (Hedges & Olkin, 1985; Hunter, Schmidt, & Jackson, 1982) refers to a cluster of research procedures for aggregating primary research findings and estimating the direction and magnitude of effects. By coding and transforming outcomes into a common metric, it is possible to combine results across studies, estimate average effects, and detect moderator variables. In this book, we use variance-centered forms of meta-analysis (Hunter & Schmidt, 1990). This procedure requires the calculation of a weighted average correlation that is tested for homogeneity of the sample. The homogeneity test, using chi-square, compares the expected variability in the sample of correlations to the actual variability in the observed correlations. A significant chi-square indicates the existence of greater variability than would be expected due to random sampling error. This would be a sign of the probable existence of a moderator variable and a reason to interpret the average effect cautiously.

These techniques quantify the magnitude of an effect across a body of research (Johnson, Mullen, & Salas, 1995) and may be used in a variety of strategic ways. Preiss and Allen (1995) suggested that meta-analyses can serve four functions in the review process. They grouped the meta-analytic procedures in a 2 × 2 matrix based on the researcher's goal (providing a historical record vs. hypothesis testing) and the scope of the review (resolving a specific question vs. summarizing a research domain). This scheme shows the utility of meta-analytic procedures in addressing questions encountered by researchers interested in interpersonal communication (see Fig. P1). Of course, the categories are extreme cases, and middle positions exist. They serve the purpose of illustrating the flexibility of meta-analysis as a research tool.

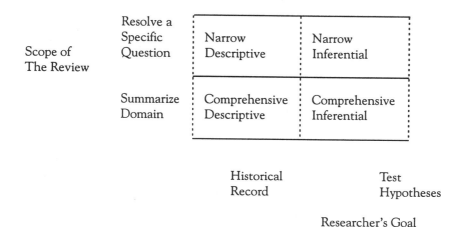

FIG. P1.   Approaches to meta-analysis.

Narrow-Descriptive Meta-Analysis

Meta-analyses in this category address a single question or assess a limited number of conceptual issues. Usually the answer or implications of the findings will radiate to a larger set of theoretical issues. An example in the area of interpersonal communication is the Allen and Burrell (chap. 8, this volume) meta-analysis on the effects of parents' sexual orientation on the adjustment of their children. The evidence on this narrow, substantive question has theoretical, legal, and policy-making ramifications.

This sort of meta-analysis is often used when earlier reviews (narrative or meta-analytic) have located unresolved inconsistencies and demonstrated how broad issues may by clarified by untangling a limited set of outcomes. Narrow-descriptive meta-analyses should be employed in ways that reflect the literature in the domain, not by restricting the definition of the domain. For example, if the interpersonal researcher was interested in the narrow question of the relation between shyness and loneliness, she or he would aggregate all instruments used to assess these variables, code for possible moderator variables resulting from the various measurement instruments, and report the results of the moderator search. Unless there are compelling theoretical reasons to do so, it would be less appropriate to restrict the domain by selecting a single, commonly used instrument measuring each variable and summarizing only the studies using that instrument. Of course, less desirable still would be aggregating studies using obscure, specialized instruments when accepted, standardized tools were available. In any event, theoretical justifications for all such decisions are essential and restricted definitions or capricious selection criteria merit cautious interpretation.

Narrow-Inferential Meta-Analysis

Although meta-analyses in this category address a single question or a limited number of conceptual issues, the goal of the meta-analysis is to test hypotheses. If the researcher establishes generalizations within a narrow set of conditions, additional theory development is possible and the scope of the findings may be increased. An example in the area of interpersonal communication is the Ah Yun (chap. 7, this volume) meta-analysis on the effects of attitude similarity on attraction. Virtually all interpersonal researchers have followed the discussion between scholars holding competing views on this issue. Ah Yun tests three hypotheses, searches for moderators, and offers methodological suggestions that would allow for tests of alternative interpretations.

Narrow-inferential meta-analyses are now commonly used to summarize the evidence in a given area. This popularity is probably due to the recent arrival of meta-analysis as a research tool. Because decades of narrative reviews have failed to resolve rather basic issues, meta-analytic investigations are being devised that set the stage for more sophisticated research. By establishing whether a relation exists and if so, under what conditions, the researcher establishes baseline summaries. We believe that, over time, progressively more complex issues will be examined meta-analytically.

Comprehensive-Descriptive Meta-Analysis

Early research using meta-analysis treated the empirical summary as a historical document (Glass, 1976, 1983). The logic here is that meta-analytic assessment constitutes a pragmatic tool, a historical report card of the research in a given area. Some of the early literature asserts that empirical aggregation is atheoretic, but that view has faded (see Preiss & Allen, 1995). When a comprehensive review of an entire body of research is conducted, the results have theoretical and pragmatic implications. The Hamilton and Mineo (chap., 16, this volume) review of the literature on argumentativeness and verbal aggressiveness is an example of this approach to meta-analysis. The contributors review a substantial body of literature focusing on an important theoretical relationship. They probe the theorized associations from several directions, assess instruments, and offer a critique of assumptions and applications.

The comprehensive-descriptive meta-analysis provides a historical record that is either consistent or inconsistent with theoretical expectations. This justifiably creates tensions that prompt reflection and reevaluation. A consistent history draws attention toward application and policy. For example, a hypothetical finding that communication skills training increases relational satisfaction would encourage counselors to employ this technique in their practices. An inconsistent record on this issue would force researchers and practitioners to reconsider and refine their views on the role of communication in the process of relationship maintenance. Comprehensive-descriptive meta-analyses are compelling because they usually embrace large bodies of literature on complex topics. The results may validate decades of practice or cast a shadow over commonly accepted maxims. For this reason comprehensive-descriptive reviews are inherently political and may significantly affect future research.

Comprehensive-Inferential Meta-Analysis

Perhaps the most ambitious enterprise, the comprehensive-inferential form of meta-analysis aggregates large bodies of literature and tests the assumptions and outcomes predicted by one or more theories. Usually these endeavors involve hundreds of studies, scores of moderators, and, often, the construction of mathematical models. Dindia's (chap., 10, this volume) reviews of self-disclosure, Allen's (chap., 13, this volume) work on comforting strategies, or Hample and Dallinger's (chap., 11, this volume) examination of compliance-gaining appeals might be classified in this category. Usually, comprehensive-inferential meta-analyses serve to consolidate bodies of literature and become the benchmark for new theoretical contributions. The act of isolating generalizations does not imply "correct answers." Rather, the stable findings become a platform for innovative interpretations and original insights.

THE ORGANIZATION OF THE BOOK

We believe that both narrative and meta-analytic reviews are vital to the scientific study of interpersonal communication. The risks associated with narrative reviews involve distorting average effects by considering example findings as being 100% accurate, building theoretical stories that ignore counterexamples, and introducing intervening variables that may obscure fundamental generalizations. In later chapters, Canary and Mattrey (chap., 20, this volume) and Fitzpatrick (chap., 21, this volume) point to risks associated with meta-analytic reviews. They address search procedures and coding decisions as a potential source of bias. The dynamic interplay of the narrative review and the meta-analytic review deepens understanding and enriches both approaches.

In selecting and arranging chapters in this volume, we were mindful of the issues addressed and the potential of chapters to establish significant generalizations about interpersonal communication. It became clear that meta-analytic methods were not novelties in investigations focusing on interpersonal communication. We also sought out issues that were fundamental to discussions underway in communication journals and that reflected current (or enduring) controversies. There was no shortage of potential candidates.

We present the issues using five general themes. In Part I, we set the stage for the independent meta-analyses. Two chapters make the case for using meta-analysis to address meaningful issues in the interpersonal communication literature. In Part II, we present an overview of individual characteristics in interpersonal communication and three meta-analyses reflecting this theme. Contributors discuss sex differences in self-esteem, sex differences in powerful language, and social skills. In Part III, literature emphasizing the dyadic approach to interpersonal communication is considered. In this part, we provide an overview and contributors present summaries on sexual orientation and children, similarity and attraction, self-disclosure, and compliance gaining. Part IV explores the interactional approach to interpersonal communication. Following an overview, meta-analyses are presented on comforting, social support, safe-sex interactions, argumentativeness, conflict styles, and sexual coercion. In Part V, contributors consider the impact of the meta-analyses on our understanding of interpersonal communication. Authors discuss pedagogy and textbooks, assess representations of the interpersonal communication literature, evaluate the prospects for future theory development, and chart the course for new investigations.

The issues summarized in these chapters reinforce Hamilton and Hunter's (1998) contention that meta-analysis is a necessary tool for theory construction. The conclusions reached by the contributors to this volume provide three invitations for future research. First, the findings may be baselines for new, primary investigations that may be integrated into more sophisticated meta-analyses. A second invitation is for scholars to empirically summarize the variables that are conceptually aligned with the findings of these meta-analyses. The goal here is to establish sets of interlocking generalizations that provide breadth of understanding about interpersonal communication. Finally, readers are invited to replicate and refine the summaries. Allen and Preiss (1993) offered preliminary guidelines for these replications and possible benefits, including testing mathematical models, enlarging samples, and generalizing results.

Meta-analysis is an inherently public enterprise. All meta-analysts explicitly state search procedures, study inclusion standards, coding rules, and aggregation formulas. Any informed reader of any theoretical or ideological persuasion is welcome to sort through the primary literature and add, recode, reformulate, or reinterpret it. When readers accept the invitations to replicate, interlock, and extend empirical summaries, we believe that interpersonal communication researchers will, indeed, see advances through meta-analysis.

REFERENCES

Allen, M., & Preiss, R. W. (1993). Replication and meta-analysis: A necessary connection. *Journal of Social Behavior and Personality, 8,* 9–20.

Glass, G. V. (1976). Primary, secondary, and meta-analysis of research. *Educational Researcher, 5,* 3–8.

Glass, G. V. (1983). Synthesizing empirical research: Meta-analysis. In S. A. Ward & L. J. Reed (Eds.), *Knowledge structure and use: Implications for synthesis and interpretation* (pp. 399–421). Philadelphia: Temple University Press.

Hamilton, M. A., & Hunter, J. E. (1998). A framework for understanding: Meta-analysis of the persuasion literature. In M. Allen & R. W. Preiss (Eds.), *Persuasion: Advances through meta-analysis* (pp. 1–28). Cresskill, NJ: Hampton.

Hedges, L. V., & Olkin, I. (1985). *Statistical methods of meta-analysis.* Orlando, FL: Academic Press.

Hunter, J. E., & Schmidt, F. (1990). *Methods for meta-analysis.* Newbury Park, CA: Sage.

Hunter, J. E., Schmidt, F. L., & Jackson, G. B. (1982). *Meta-analysis: Cumulating findings across research.* Beverly Hills, CA: Sage.

Johnson, B., Mullen, M., & Salas, E. (1995). Comparison of three major meta-analytic approaches. *Journal of Applied Psychology, 80,* 94–106.

Pillemer, D. (1984). Conceptual issues in research synthesis. *Journal of Special Education, 18,* 27–40.

Preiss, R. W., & Allen, M. (1995). Understanding and using meta-analysis. *Evaluation and the Health Professions, 18,* 315–335.

Rosenthal, R. (1984). *Meta-analytic procedures for social research.* Beverly Hills, CA: Sage.

I

Interpersonal Communication Research and Meta-Analysis

1

Meta-Analysis and Interpersonal Communication: Function and Applicability

Mike Allen and Raymond W. Preiss

Meta-analysis provides a technique that allows researchers to aggregate data and summarize existing reports. The technique is used to reduce or eliminate various sources of artifact and statistical error. Additionally, meta-analysis provides an ability to examine the impact of various design issues and various theoretical possibilities. In this chapter, we explain what meta-analysis is and the justification for using the procedure. Our goal in this chapter is to enhance understanding of meta-analysis so that reading subsequent chapters is easier. The discussion does not consider a number of technical issues relating to the mathematical or methodological features of meta-analysis, as those discussions do exist and can be found in various textbooks dealing with meta-analysis (e.g., Cooper & Hedges, 1994; Hunter & Schmidt, 1990).

WHY USE META-ANALYSIS?

The problem in the social sciences is the use of statistical inference to make decisions about whether the experimental or survey results are not due to random chance. Consider the simple issue of determining whether a coin

3

flip is biased by evaluating whether heads or tails is a more likely outcome. If we flipped the coin 100 times and the coin flip is fair, the outcome should be theoretically 50 heads and 50 tails. We could flip the coin 100 times and if all 100 flips come out either heads or tails, we would suppose the coin is biased; that is, more likely to produce one outcome over the other. The problem is that very seldom does the theoretically random result (50/50) or the completely biased (100% heads or tails) outcome ever occur. It is much more likely that the outcome will be somewhere between totally random and totally biased.

Suppose the outcome of our coin flip is 51 tails and 49 heads. The results depart from a perfectly random distribution (50 of each), but a person would probably not argue that the deviation constitutes evidence of bias. Similarly, a coin flip that generates a 99 to 1 outcome would probably make the case that the coin flip was biased. The key is that ultimately we will set up some decision rule that makes the distribution of heads and tails considered biased or acceptable. For example, any coin flip is biased if, when flipped 100 times, more than 66 heads or tails appear as an outcome. In a sense, the decision rule is arbitrary because a 66–34 split would be considered a fair coin flip, but a 67–33 split would be considered evidence of a biased coin flip. However, such a procedure is in fact the standard operating practice of the social sciences. The alpha (or Type I error rate) is considered at 5%, or more commonly as texts would say, the statistical test is considered significant at $p < .05$. This is a dividing line so that those associations falling on either side of .05, regardless of the magnitude of the difference, are considered as supporting or not supporting our experiment. In other words, the researcher in a social scientific article is saying that the probability of the observed statistic occurring due to random chance is less than (or greater than) 5%.

The goal of researchers is to have the outcome from their investigation match the empirical outcome that is considered to really exist. The comparison is between what the investigation produces using the significance rules and the outcome considered to be real or "true." There are four possible outcomes of an experiment or survey, regardless of the relation assessed (see Table 1.1). Of the four outcomes, two are consistent and two involve errors. No errors have been committed if the investigation finds an effect (rejects the null hypothesis) and there is in fact a relation. Similarly, no error has been made if the investigation concludes there is no relation (fails to reject the null hypothesis) and in fact no relation exists. The other two outcomes are considered errors because the outcome of the investigation is inconsistent with what really exists.

TABLE 1.1
Outcomes of Research

	State of Nature	
Action Concerning Hypothesis Testing	Hypothesis Is true	Hypothesis Is False
Accept experimental hypothesis	Correct decision	Type II error
Reject experimental hypothesis	Type I error	Correct decision

The first error, often called Type I, is a false positive result. The investigation concludes that there is a relation (rejects the null hypothesis) when none exists. Type I error occurs typically about 5% of the time or the equivalent of the alpha error rate just discussed. The amount of Type I error is set by the research community or the scholar and most tests of significance are calibrated to reflect this level of error. Type I error is serious because the investigator believes an association is present when one is not. Creating a theory or using the results to design further investigations involves a resource commitment that comes from a finding that does not exist. Type I errors occur randomly. This type of error cannot be predicted by examining the investigation design or by exploring the sample size. In science, if a thorough search has been conducted for Relation A and no evidence for A exists, it would be prudent for the scientist to conclude that the relation does not exist. If such an error was made, an educator using the scientific record would conclude that an educational procedure does not provide an improvement when it actually does.

The rate of occurrence of Type II error results from a combination of three factors: (a) the level of Type I error, (b) the size of the effect, and (c) the size of the sample. The maximum level of Type II error is 1 minus Type I error. If Type I error is set at .05 or 5%, the maximum level of Type II error is 95%. Seldom is the level of error that large because the larger the size of the effect and the larger the size of the sample, the more likely any given relation would be detected as significant (Cohen, 1987).

Larger effects are easier to detect. If you have two drugs and one drug A cures 10 out of 100 patients infected with a fatal disease but drug B cures 95 out of 100 patients infected with a fatal disease, it is easy to determine which of the two drugs is more effective. However, if A only cured 49 and B only cured 51, the difference that exists would be difficult to detect given the normal amount of sampling error associated with estimating any statistical parameter.

Larger sample sizes diminish the confidence interval, which makes smaller effects more likely to be significant at whatever probability level is chosen. Consider something like the calculation involved in the t test. The numerator is $M_1 - M_2$. For any two given mean values for each group, these values would remain the same regardless of the sample size. The t test takes that mean difference and divides it by the average weighted standard deviation corrected for sample size. The larger the sample size, the smaller the value in the denominator, which for any fixed numerator makes the value larger. The result is that for any given mean difference, the t statistic will, by definition, be larger and more likely to be significant. This premise for t can be found in any of the normal tests of significance used in statistical analysis. Increasing sample size both increases the accuracy of the estimate for any effect (by diminishing sampling error) and makes any given effect more likely to be significant.

The result of Type I and Type II errors is inconsistency in results across studies. This problem not only exists in the social sciences, but also plagued medicine until meta-analysis was introduced recently in that discipline. For example an individual can view a morning news program and find that eating X is supposed to reduce the risk of cancer, according to a prominent article in that month's medical journal. However, a person will hear a month later that a new study about X in a different medical journal reports no link between eating X and reductions in cancer. The result is that good advice emerging from medical research on dietary issues appears elusive given the number of contradictory studies. This same state of confusion often exists in interpersonal communication research, where studies appear to contradict each other, so that the greater the number of studies the greater the level of confusion.

Meta-analysis, by combining samples, essentially increases the power of detecting a small effect and reduces the level of Type II error. At the same time, if the averaging process generates an average effect that is zero or near zero, one can assess whether any current significant findings are the result of Type I error. The possibility does exist that a single finding from an investigation accepted as a milestone in achievement could turn out to be inconsistent with most of the existing literature. This is possible if a finding comes from a study considered "groundbreaking." For example, a study might be the first one to address some issue but the findings are subject to either Type I or Type II error and as a result are not replicated successfully, which leads to all sorts of complications. In the social sciences, there are often less than perfect designs or measurement techniques that should indicate that the level, particularly of Type II error, could be substantial (often over 50%).

WHAT META-ANALYSIS DOES

A typical meta-analysis is undertaken to respond to contradictory study results and consists of a sequence of steps that are taken to aggregate the findings of that body of research. A brief summary of the process for most meta-analyses is found in the following five steps: (a) defining the issue, (b) collecting the available literature, (c) converting and correcting statistical information, (d) averaging the available data, and (e) considering the variation in the observed effects. Contemporary meta-analysis basically involves these five steps, although the degree of difficulty within each step varies depending on the particular meta-analysis topic selected and the nature of the primary studies in the domain of available literature.

The first step is defining the problem or issue for consideration by establishing inclusion and exclusion criteria for data. A meta-analyst must define the variables or context in a manner that is consistent and relatively clear. The extant literature on a topic may not be as reflective in terms of defining or considering the issues. Consider the Sahlstein and Allen (chap. 4, this volume) meta-analysis that compares men and women on the basis of their level of self-esteem. Each variable, gender and self-esteem, must be defined. Gender can be defined using a variety of criteria; the authors in this case chose a biological definition. Most studies used self-report as a means of establishing gender. Such a choice is probably not unwarranted, but there can be many circumstances in which self-report data may be suspect. The definition of self-esteem in this chapter also includes the measurement of self-concept as an equivalent measure. The authors point out that in many investigations the variables are treated interchangeably despite several arguments that the two variables are conceptually distinct. This example points out that every meta-analysis creates definitions to explore the literature and such definitions may be at odds with some of the scholars in the area being explored. The critical feature is not the ability of the scholar to select the "ultimate" definition, but rather that the definition used be detailed and explicit enough to permit others to replicate the analysis. The possibility exists that a scholar could test the literature multiple times, using a different set of definitional criteria each time to compare results.

In the second step, the relevant empirical literature must be collected. This collection requires that the scholar search various indexes and existing literature reviews. Some material will be readily available from a variety of sources and some material will be difficult to obtain. The standard should never be whether the scholar has collected everything that exists, but rather whether the scope of the material included represents a fair search of the material and has generated enough information to conduct a valid analysis. The scholar needs to consider whether or not the method of generating information systematically excludes any sources of information that might produce unusual or different results for some reason. The search procedure may or may not include unpublished information, information published in a language other than that of the scholar, or information found in private reports, governmental studies, or corporate entities. The scholar should be clear on the nature of the search and provide enough details so that another person could replicate the analysis.

In the third step, each study is converted to a common metric and adjusted for various methodological artifacts as necessary. The results of any investigation can be converted into a correlation coefficient for use in a meta-analysis. That is, the chi-square, r, F, t, d, z, and so on, are converted into a correlation coefficient. Using the simple associative rules of math such that $a = b$, $a = c$, therefore $b = c$ indicates that all forms of statistics can be mathematically translated into each other, provided the necessary information is available for the transformation. The use of a common metric means that the size of associations can be directly compared across investigations, regardless of the particular statistical analysis employed.

In the fourth step, the data are then averaged. The averaging process is simply to take the estimate from each study, add up the contributions, and divide that total by the number of studies (weighted on the basis of sample size). Weighting by sample size is essential because the size of sampling error is related directly to the size of the sample. A large-sample study (10,000) has much less sampling error than a study with a small sample (20). Failure to weight by sample size means that the estimate of the small-sample study is given the same importance as the large-sample study. Weighting by sample size reduces Type II error, because one of the contributing factors is the size of the sample. The advantage of meta-analysis is that by combining sample sizes, the final estimate has the properties of the combined sample size. However, this quality is lost if the final estimate or average is not weighted by sample size.

The last step involves the assessment of variability in the initial findings and the possible sources of variation associated with features of the primary studies that may moderate the observed relation. The issue is a simple comparison, often using chi-square, between the theoretical level of variability among the studies due to sampling error versus the actual level of variability among the data sets. If sampling error serves as an explanation for variability, one can then estimate the level of variability that should exist. The basis of the chi-square statistic is the difference between the observed and the expected values and whether that difference is more than expected due to chance.

One way to conceptualize this step is to consider the random or systematic sources of variance present in the distribution of effects. Random sources of variability can be issues related to sampling error. The question in meta-analysis is whether the differences observed among studies are the result of simply random or systematic factors. Studies may be consistently different on some basis. For example, suppose studies were either conducted on college students or high school students. One could examine whether the difference, based on age, contributes to a difference in the outcome observed between investigations. The focus should be on the variability in the original data points and what sources of variability contribute to the observed difference among the various effects.

The advantage of meta-analysis lies in the ability to replicate the process. The requirements of a meta-analysis for explicitness in the definition of the concepts and the procedures for statistical analysis mean that other scholars can replicate the process. Scholars can disagree about the decisions of any particular meta-analysis and test the impact of those decisions in subsequent replications of the meta-analysis. The confidence in the outcome of any finding should grow as the number and variety of data sets expands and other replications or new meta-analyses on similar topics are performed.

INTERPERSONAL COMMUNICATION AND META-ANALYSIS

Research on interpersonal communication can and should contribute to the development of scientific findings. Yet, some scientific truths are created by fallible humans using methods based on probabilistic inferences and riddled with all sorts of potential for error. The problem of relying on interpersonal communication research, without some method of assessing Type I and Type II error, is that the results may not only produce inconsistent findings, but a chaotic theoretical approach to future research. Allen (1997) suggested that many narrative or box-score reviews that try to make sense of interpersonal communication research could end up simply perpetuating errors and capitalizing on chance. Additionally, attempts to explain inconsistencies in the interpersonal communication literature become more confused, especially when the number of studies becomes larger and larger. This happens because errors cannot be accounted for on the basis of methodological artifacts or some other type of examination of the investigations. Meta-analysis handles the issues of assessing the impact and the contribution to interstudy variability in outcome on the basis of random factors relating to sampling error.

Interpersonal communication scholars striving to formulate theories must also sift through all sorts of information riddled with Type I and Type II error. A sophisticated examination, comparison, or classification does not provide a good basis for analysis without a statistical method for elimination of error such as meta-analysis. A telling example of the quandaries faced by scholars summarizing large domains of complex research may be found in the similarity and attraction literature. Sixty years of accumulated literature resulted in competing theoretical camps and disagreements over germane processes and methodological approaches. Ah Yun's (chap. 9, this volume) meta-analysis provides compelling evidence of a strong association between attitude similarity and interpersonal attraction and advances the proposition that interaction early in the relationship weakens the attitude—attraction relationship. Thus, the meta-analysis consolidated the literature, addressed points of theoretical controversy, and provided avenues for additional research. A narrative review would find this level of synthesis difficult to achieve with any precision.

Once the results of interpersonal communication research are tested for error, scholars can begin to treat the findings as a much closer approximation to truth. Consider the example of the interpersonal consequences of self-disclosure. Dindia (chap. 10, this volume) draws on earlier meta-analyses, summarizes key theoretical issues (sex differences, self-disclosure and liking, and reciprocity), and concludes that self-disclosure is indeed a foundational issue in relational development and management. When interpersonal communication research findings can be demonstrated as consistent across a large set of investigations, the confidence in the findings grows, as does the predictability of generating various outcomes.

APPLICATION OF META-ANALYSIS

There are many approaches and possibilities for employing a meta-analytic review (Preiss & Allen, 1995). Occasionally, the results of a series of meta-analysis call into question an effort that is presumed to exist. For example, many scholars assumed that widespread differences in interpersonal communication were based on biological gender. That conclusion was called into question in communication by Canary and Hause (1993) and in the social sciences in general by Hyde and Plant (1995). Using meta-analysis on biological gender as a major basis for theorizing generated disappointing findings. The overall results led Allen (1998) to call for reconsidering both measurement and theoretical approaches. The meta-analyses in this volume on self-esteem (Sahlstein & Allen, chap. 10), power in language use (Timmerman, chap. 5), self-disclosure (Dindia, chap. 10), safe sex discussions (Allen, Emmers-Sommer, & Crowell, chap. 15), and interpersonal conflict (Gayle, Preiss, & Allen, chap. 18) confirm Allen's conclusion. The consistently small effects observed across many meta-analyses suggest that, when compared to traditional literature reviews, meta-analysis generates more accurate conclusions (Cook & Leviton, 1980; Wachter & Straf, 1990), even if the results are disquieting. The technique is adaptable and flexible, allowing scholars to summarize dozens, even hundreds, of interpersonal communication studies to develop or grapple with theoretical issues.

When applying the results of a meta-analysis, it is important to understand the distinction that clinical science deals with the individual and social science deals with the group. As social scientists, we wish to offer conclusions that address group tendencies. If the question is "Do men or women initiate relationships?" a meta-analysis on this topic would not assert that all men or all women initiate expressions of interest. The conclusion is simply that one of the two groups is first to begin the conversation. Predictions about individuals are not made, because the level of analysis is the group. This observation often leads to the assertion that the social sciences are "soft" or unable to offer robust generalizations. Hedges (1987) explored this assertion by variability found in the natural sciences (the "hard" sciences) and the social sciences. His meta-analysis found that there is actually slightly less variability in investigation outcomes in the social sciences. Variability, then, it not something unique to the social sciences, but rather is something that occurs in all sciences investigating group-level outcomes. The difference is that the hard sciences have, for many years, been using some form of data aggregation to compare and contrast the variability in findings (e.g., smokers vs. nonsmokers, drug trial vs. placebo, bombarding one element with electrons vs. bombarding a different element).

The results of other meta-analyses will slowly revolutionize and energize areas of interpersonal communication. The topic areas covered in this book such as social skills, sexual coercion, similarity and attraction, social support, and so forth, aid in the process of generating better theoretical understanding and lay the foundation for the next round of investigations. Over time, the number of meta-analyses related to a cluster of theoretical issues will increase and the implications will radiate within and across domains of literature. New primary studies will seek to build on generalizations rather than resolve error-laden patterns of conflicting results. In the past there was a sense of futility or hopelessness because few findings seemed to emerge after years and years of data collection on a topic. With meta-analysis, the interpersonal communication researcher is able to see the relational landscape clearly for the first time. In such glimpses of lucidity emerge the possibility of generating better theoretical positions and the next round of investigations.

REFERENCES

Allen, M. (1997, January). How I got tired of playing connect the dots. *Personal Relationship Issues, 4,* 8–10.

Allen, M. (1998). Methodological considerations when examining a gendered world. In D. Canary & K. Dindia (Eds.), *Handbook of sex differences & similarities in communication: Critical essays and empirical investigations of sex and gender in interaction* (pp. 427–444). Mahwah, NJ: Lawrence Erlbaum Associates.

Canary, D., & Hause, K. (1993). Is there any reason to research sex differences in communication? *Communication Quarterly, 41,* 129–144.

Cohen, J. (1987). *Statistical power analysis for the behavioral sciences* (rev. ed.). Hillsdale, NJ: Lawrence Erlbaum Associates.

Cook, T., & Leviton, L. (1980). Reviewing the literature: A comparison of traditional methods with meta-analysis. *Journal of Personality, 48,* 449–472.

Cooper, H., & Hedges, L. (1994). *The handbook of research synthesis.* New York: Russell Sage Foundation.

Hedges, L. (1987). How hard is hard science, how soft is soft science: The empirical cumulativeness of research. *American Psychologist, 42,* 443–455.

Hunter, J., & Schmidt, F. (1990). *Methods of meta-analysis: Correcting for artifact and bias in research findings.* Thousand Oaks, CA: Sage.

Hyde, J., & Plant, E. (1995). Magnitude of psychological gender differences: Another side to the story. *American Psychologist, 50,* 159–161.

Preiss, R., & Allen, M. (1995). Understanding and using meta-analysis. *Evaluation & the Health Professions, 18,* 315–335.

Wachter, K., & Straf, M. (1990). *The future of meta-analysis.* New York: Russell Sage Foundation.

2

Meta-Analysis in Context: A Proto-Theory of Interpersonal Communication

Charles R. Berger

As the chapters of this volume amply demonstrate, meta-analytic techniques serve a useful function in assessing the degree of empirical support for relations between variables and the extent to which these relations may be moderated by other factors. The utility of meta-analytic reviews for those with applied communication concerns is obvious. A public policy, a course of intervention, or a therapeutic strategy should not be based on variables that have no demonstrated relation with the outcome variables of interest. The studies concerned with communication apprehension persuasively make this point. Combinations of therapies for dealing with communication apprehension are more effective in reducing this potentially debilitating condition than is any one therapy by itself (Allen, Hunter, & Donohue, 1989). Obviously, results like these have immediate and important implications for those interested in developing programs to reduce the communication apprehension individuals experience in a wide variety of communication contexts. Other meta-analytic reviews cited in this volume report findings with similar immediate practical consequences.

The relevance of meta-analyses to the design and implementation of re-search-based practical interventions is transparent; less obvious, however, is the role meta-analytic study results may play in the theory development pro-cess. On this point, one might claim that theory building itself presupposes well-established empirical regularities about which to theorize, and that meta-analysis can provide evidence for the robustness of these regularities and the variables that might moderate them. At first blush, the claim that theory development critically depends on the demonstration of reliable re-lations between variables may seem self-evident. After all, why should one try to explain a relation between variables that is not well supported by em-pirical data? Or, even more extreme, why should one try to explain why two variables are consistently unrelated? Because many have noted the relative paucity of original theorizing by individuals identifying themselves as com-munication researchers (Berger, 1991; Berger & Chaffee, 1987), any tech-nique that is of potential utility for developing communication theory should be a welcome addition to those available to communication re-searchers. The question is how far meta-analytic studies can take us in the direction of developing communication theories.

In addition to the potential roles meta-analysis might play in both theory development and applied endeavors, it is possible that meta-analysis may expose gaps in existing bodies of research, and thus serve a heuristic func-tion in guiding future research efforts. However, an important point that is frequently missed in discussions of exposing so-called knowledge gaps is that the notion of a gap implies the existence of some kind of underlying sys-tematic perspective that serves as the template for judging whether or not a gap actually exists. In the absence of such a structure, it is impossible to ren-der judgments about the existence or nonexistence of such knowledge gaps. Unfortunately, the templates invoked to make such judgments frequently remain implicit; that is, researchers do not usually articulate a complete the-oretical framework when rendering such judgments. Thus, the claim that a knowledge gap exists and must be filled with further research is not fre-quently evaluated within any kind of broader conceptual system.

These issues are addressed within the domain of interpersonal communi-cation. To begin to deal with them, it is first necessary to advance a proto-theory of interpersonal communication that stipulates what substantive theories of interpersonal communication should seek to explain and how to go about the task of explanation. The proto-theory proposed is a partial re-sponse to Burleson's (1992) call for a philosophy of communication that problematizes neglected aspects of the communication process so that they will be examined in greater detail. The explication of a proto-theory should aid in this process. Once this proto-theory of interpersonal communication is formulated, it should be possible to evaluate the contribution the meta-analytic studies of interpersonal communication phenomena presented in this volume make toward the goal of developing more particularistic interpersonal communication theories. That is, given a proto-theory, it should be possible to evaluate the potential contribution of meta-analytic techniques to theory construction efforts. Although I focus on interpersonal communication in this chapter, the comparisons and evaluations should have potentially important implications for other domains of communication inquiry as well.

A PROTO-THEORY OF INTERPERSONAL COMMUNICATION

Proto-theory is not a substantive theory intended to explain particular communication phenomena; rather, it explicates a general prototype, plan, or blueprint for such substantive communication theories. Proto-theory adumbrates the relevant phenomena to be explained and the form an explanation for the phenomena might take. As such, it provides a general guide to theory development. The potential contribution of the meta-analysis studies germane to interpersonal communication will be evaluated within this proto-theoretic matrix.

Relevant Phenomena

It would be an act of utter folly to attempt to elucidate fully the incredible diversity of topics researched under the general rubric of interpersonal communication, let alone review exhaustively individual studies reported under each topic. Over the past two decades, considerable literatures have developed in such areas as communication and the development of interpersonal relationships, compliance-gaining strategies, communication and interpersonal conflict, bargaining and negotiation, comforting communication, communication and perspective taking, miscommunication, deceptive and equivocal communication, and computer-mediated communication. This already somewhat lengthy list is hardly exhaustive. Although detecting commonalities among this seeming melange of research topics and unifying them within the context of a proto-theory would appear to be a difficult task, it is this project that is undertaken in the following pages.

Fundamental Cognitive Processes.   For two or more individuals to engage each other in social interaction, whether the interaction is highly conflicted or warmly affectionate, certain fundamental conditions must be true. First, the individuals must have available at least some sensory channels. Usually, these modalities include visual, aural, olfactory, and tactile; however, communication is not rendered impossible when one or more of these channels are unavailable to interaction participants. Assuming all of these sensory channels are intact, for messages to be exchanged between or among interaction participants, still other preconditions must be met. Participants must have the neurological substrate necessary to support the development of cognitive structures and processes that enable them to processes these sensory inputs, whether these inputs are strings of speech sounds, facial expressions, or gestures. These structures and processes give rise to what is commonly referred to as comprehension, understanding, and interpretation. Of course, this is only half of the story. Cognitive structures and processes arising from this neurological substrate must subserve the linguistic productions that are realized in action by such motor activities as speech and gesticulation. The successful production of motor behaviors like speech and gestures presupposes that the requisite anatomical, physiological, and neurological conditions for the operation of these systems have been met. These processes produce the outputs that are commonly referred to by the denizens of the communication field as verbal and nonverbal messages.

At this juncture, it is worth noting at least three points concerning the preceding account. First, it is very difficult to imagine the possibility of social interaction without at least some of the preconditions being met. Take away all sensory inputs, or allow sensory inputs but suspend comprehension and understanding processes, and a hypothetical social actor would be at a total loss to understand the others present in the situation at any level. Alternatively, given comprehension and interpretative capabilities in the complete absence of message production abilities, including motor productions, the social interaction capacities of even the most understanding communicator would be severely diminished. These fundamental processes are indeed prerequisites for carrying out what is commonly called interpersonal communication.

Second, these fundamental message comprehension and production processes constitute at least one of the sought-after commonalities shared by the seemingly diverse list of interpersonal communication research topics listed earlier. Whether individuals are engaged in a romantic interlude, a discussion about the state of their marriage, interpersonal conflict, bargaining and negotiation, deceptive communication, or comforting each other, the neurological and cognitive processes adumbrated are in play. Unfortunately, as Burleson (1992) noted, with few exceptions (e.g., Berger, 1997; Greene, 1997; Hewes, 1995), interpersonal communication researchers have failed to take these basic message comprehension and production processes very seriously. Rather than problematize these fundamental processes and studying them as Burleson (1992) suggested, the complexities and nuances are frequently finessed by invoking such facile terms as *sense making, meaning making, message decoding,* and *message encoding.* It is as if the details of the fundamental processes that make communication between humans possible are either unimportant or should be studied by someone else. However, understanding these fundamental processes should promote a more complete understanding of interpersonal communication, including the potential individual processing constraints under which individuals are placed when interacting with each other.

Third, the focus on comprehension and production processes provides a potentially more catholic context from which to view the study of interpersonal communication. With few exceptions (e.g., Honeycutt's [1991] work on imagined interactions), most interpersonal communication theory and research begins at the point individuals come into close enough physical proximity so that they can sense each other in some way. They may exchange words or they may exchange glances, but something is exchanged. However, from the perspective of the individual actor, any encounter with another individual occurs within a much broader experiential context, much of which is provided by previous interactions with the environment, including other people. As individuals move about the physical world, their senses continuously pick up information from the environment. Some of these visual, aural, tactile, and olfactory inputs do not involve other people at all; they are purely nonsocial interactions with the environment. Against this broader experiential background, we visually encounter those who emit strings of sound we call speech, as well as a variety of other relevant stimuli. In some ways our experience of the world is primarily visual; one that is sometimes punctuated by the speech sounds of humans. From the perspective of developing interpersonal communication theories, it seems extremely unwise to ignore this broader experiential context.

Cognitive structures and processes not only enable message comprehension and interpretation as well as message production; they also guide goal-directed action beyond the generation of verbal and written discourse. When individuals encounter each other in face-to-face or mediated communication contexts, their interactions are purposive, even if the ostensible reason for their interaction is merely to pass time. The goals that individuals pursue in their encounters are represented hierarchically in cognitive structures (Dillard, 1990, 1997; Lichtenstein & Brewer, 1980), and the plans they use to guide their verbal and nonverbal actions in pursuing these goals are also represented cognitively (Berger, 1995, 1997). Whether these goals and plans are consciously formulated and implemented or primed and activated nonconsciously (Bargh, 1997; Langer, 1989, 1992), they serve to direct action during interpersonal encounters. Of course, during a particular encounter, goals and plans may transmute in a variety of ways; for example, a simple request for information from a complete stranger might mark the beginning of a close friendship or a romantic relationship. Regardless of the interaction's trajectory, goals and plans guide the actions of those involved.

Just as it is difficult to imagine the possibility of interpersonal communication in the absence of any sensory inputs or the capabilities of message comprehension and production, so too is it problematic to consider the possibility of interpersonal communication in the absence of cognitive representations of goals and plans. The ability to comprehend and produce verbal messages does not necessarily ensure the capability of organizing the broader range of actions necessary to achieve many goals. This latter ability is a critical prerequisite for the conduct of any interpersonal communication episode.

Affective Processes.   The preceding discussion has made clear the necessity for interpersonal communication theories to address the fundamental cognitive structures and processes that enable individuals to produce and understand each other's messages, but the nature of interpersonal communicative activity itself demands that affective processes also be accorded center stage in theorizing about interpersonal communication for a number of reasons (Planalp, 1999). First, some interpersonal communication episodes are organized around explicit efforts to alter affect. Individuals may seek to assuage others' fears or disappointments and otherwise comfort them (Burleson, 1987, 1994), or conversely, for a variety of reasons individuals may explicitly attempt to induce negative emotions like embarrassment in others (Petronio, Snyder, & Bradford, 1992).

Second, individuals may engage each other in social interaction to ascertain what emotion they should be feeling in a given context. Research germane to the social comparison of emotions (Festinger, 1954; Giles & Wiemann, 1987; Schachter, 1959; Schachter & Singer, 1962; Suls & Miller, 1977) has demonstrated that under certain conditions, individuals will alter affective states based on the observations of others in the same social context. These alterations in affect can result from verbal interaction, but can occur when only visual interaction is possible (Schachter, 1959). These socially driven alterations of affect are especially dramatic when individuals are uncertain of the situational appropriateness of their initial emotional responses. Individuals may devote lengthy conversations to discussions of how they ought to respond emotionally to specific circumstances (e.g., should one be angry or sad when their child performs poorly in a particular situation).

Third, the valence of affect is a fundamental element of the processes underlying relationship development and relationship decay (Clore & Ketelaar, 1997). The immense amount of research devoted to determining the antecedents and consequences of interpersonal attraction and liking attests to the central role that affective responses to others play in developing and deteriorating relationships. In general, we tend to interact with those to whom we are attracted and to avoid interaction if possible with those we dislike. There are, of course, exceptions to this seemingly obvious generalization (e.g., individuals who remain in apparently abusive relationships), but even such apparent counterexamples may not necessarily provide contrary evidence. Some individuals in abusive relationships may not only harbor extremely negative affect toward their abusive partner; they may also want very much to escape the relationship. However, the problem of exactly how to exit the relationship in a way that will forestall severe retaliation from the abuser may stand in the way.

Fourth, even in social situations where the focus of the participants is on issues other than those associated directly with affect (e.g., task-oriented and problem-solving interactions), emotional responses may assume a prominent role. When progress toward a goal is thwarted, negative affect may be generated and have to be managed (Berger, 1995, 1997; Planalp, 1999; Srull & Wyer, 1986). By contrast, when desired goals are achieved, participants may experience positive affect, which may or may not have to be managed depending on the future group goals. For example, the coach of an athletic team may have to bring players back down to earth very soon after a big win to prepare them for the next crucial game in a series. Individuals winning lotteries must continue to meet at least some of the mundane exigencies of life in spite of the initial euphoria.

Although sensory, comprehension, production, and planning processes are fundamental prerequisites for interpersonal communication, one can imagine interpersonal encounters that are very close to "affectless." The countless routine service encounters that are carried out in everyday commercial life tend to range from neutral to moderately positive in affective tone with the occasional negative encounter. Certainly, at least some of these mundane transactions border on affectless; that is, the goals of the particular encounter are met, but accomplished in a way that has few if any affective consequences for participants. However, because normally functioning humans are capable of recognizing and producing a wide range of affects, and because affect is an important feature of many social interactions and social relationships, it too must be considered a fundamental property of interpersonal communication.

Internal Representations of Critical Interaction Features.
The individual sensory, cognitive, planning, and affective processes just considered serve as a platform or scaffolding for interpersonal communication. Given these platforms and their interactions with the physical and social world, individuals are capable of developing internal representations of these worlds. From the point of view of the proto-theory of interpersonal communication, an important question is what features of social interactions tend to be extracted from these interactions with the physical and the social environment. Note that at this juncture our focus has shifted from the fundamental processes like perception that enable social interaction to questions regarding the content of the cognitive system itself. It seems inevitable that such a shift be made. Exclusive focus on fundamental processes does little to illuminate how the content of the cognitive system interacts with incoming sensory data to produce interpretations of social encounters.

A number of multidimensional scaling studies of social situations (Forgas, 1979) and social relationships (Wish, Deutsch, & Kaplan, 1976) have recovered similar dimensions that individuals appear to use routinely to characterize social relationships between people. First, these studies usually find a dimension associated with dominance, power, and control. This dimension resembles the potency factor reported in earlier studies of connotative meaning (Osgood, Suci, & Tannenbaum, 1957), and it is similar to the control dimension of interpersonal relationships posited by Schutz (1958). The dominance dimension has also emerged in studies of situational features that influence the selection of compliance-gaining strategies (Cody, Woelfel, & Jordan, 1983). Apparently, a significant feature of interpersonal interactions is the degree to which the participants are of relatively equal power or whether some interaction participants are relatively dominant and others are relatively submissive.

A second dimension revealed in some of these investigations concerns the degree to which the interaction is cooperative or competitive (Forgas, 1979; Wish et al., 1976). Closely related to this dimension is the friendly–hostility axis, such that cooperation is associated with friendliness and hostility is associated with competitiveness. Cooperativeness judgments may be in some ways related to those associated with dominance and submissiveness. By their very nature, competitive interactions activate control concerns because the idea of winning implies dominance, whereas the concept of losing implies submissiveness. However, it is possible for coopera-tive interactions to feature asymmetric power relationships. Teachers and students may cooperate such that students acquire knowledge from teach-ers; yet, because of the roles students and teachers typically play and be-cause teachers presumably have more knowledge about their subject than do their students, teachers assume a dominant position in relation to stu-dents. In spite of these power asymmetries, however, the relationship might still be characterized as cooperative. Thus, these exceptions suggest that the dominance–submissive and cooperative–competitive dimensions are not isomorphic, but may be related in some ways.

A third feature of social relationships and situations that has been found in a number of studies has to do with the degree to which the situation or re-lationships among the participants therein are formal or informal (Berger & Douglas, 1981; Forgas, 1979; Wish et al., 1976). Although it is possible that the control dimension is in some ways related to this dimension as well, with some formal situations involving power discrepancies and informal situa-tions implying more equality among participants, it is not coterminous with it. However, Wish et al. (1976) did find task-oriented interactions to be as-sociated with the formal pole of this dimension and socioemotional relation-ships to be located toward the informal end. Increases in formality potentiate increases in behavioral constraints. The actions deployed in for-mal interaction episodes may be dictated by formal protocols that must be strictly observed by participants. Such protocols may prescribe appropriate verbal and nonverbal actions for all participants (e.g., bowing in the appro-priate manner at the appropriate time and saying the proper words). Failure to observe these interaction conventions may result in the violator being perceived as incompetent and not well trained.

A fourth critical feature that has been demonstrated to have consider-able impact on interpersonal affect is that of perceived similarity. Heider's (1958) classic discussion of the perception of interpersonal relationships featured the importance of unit relationships between people like proximity and similarity. He argued that the proximity of individuals fostered percep-tions of similarity. Individuals tend to affiliate with and be attracted to those they perceive to be similar to themselves (Byrne, 1971; Duck, 1973; New-comb, 1961; Schachter, 1959). Of course, the bases on which similarity or dissimilarity is established may be highly varied; that is, individuals may be similar or dissimilar with respect to a wide variety of physical, demographic, and attitudinal attributes.

Finally, another dimension that has been found to characterize social re-lationships is that of superficial versus intense (Forgas, 1979; Wish et al.,

1976). Interactions with casual acquaintances define the former end of this continuum and interactions between counselors and their clients, spouses, or among teammates are associated with the latter. This dimension may be closely associated with the continuum labeled involved–uninvolved (Forgas, 1979) and may share affinities with the relational consequences dimension recovered in studies of persuasive communication situations (Cody & McLaughlin, 1980, 1985; Cody et al., 1983).

One way to view some of the dimensions recovered in these multidimensional scaling studies is in terms of goals. Such notions as control, cooperation, competition, affiliation, and inclusion may be thought of as relatively abstract goals individuals pursue in their interactions with others. In many cases, such goals as control, cooperation, and competition subserve specific instrumental goals; that is, to achieve a specific instrumental goal like enriching one's self, one may have to gain control over or cooperate with others. Goals like affiliation and inclusion that at first blush may appear to be primarily consummatory may in fact also be pursued to achieve particularistic instrumental goals (e.g., affiliating with powerful people and having informal relationships with them to curry their favor).

These fundamental dimensions or goals for organizing social interaction appear to be available to most people, and individual differences may serve to promote differential salience among them. For example, in his discussion of the power motive or need for power (n Power), Winter (1973) suggested that individuals with high levels of n Power not only see power as their goal in social situations; they tend to define their relationships with others in terms of power and control. There is ample evidence to support the view that individuals high in n Power tend to define their social interactions this way. It may be that for individuals with very high power motivation levels, exercising control is sometimes a consummatory goal. Presumably, individuals scoring high in need for affiliation (n Affiliation) are predisposed to view their interactions and relationships with others in ways that differ significantly from those of their counterparts high in n Power. These very different ways of approaching social interactions, based as they are on different goal orientations, should promote very different interaction styles.

As significant as the relationships between personality predispositions like those just discussed and the fundamental dimensions of social interaction may be, these dimensions may be rendered more or less salient by events that occur during the course of social encounters. Individuals may begin a given encounter with each other while mutually pursuing an affiliative goal or frame (Dillard, Solomon, & Samp, 1996), for example, "Let's chat" or "Let's have some fun together," only to find themselves engaged in a titanic power struggle by the end of the encounter. These dramatic and sometimes difficult-to-understand goal shifts during conversations may be explained by the automatic activation of different goals and plans. An offhand remark or a particular facial expression may be responsible for this activation. These subtle sources of activation may not be easily recalled; thus, those experiencing such dramatic changes during their conversations may remain puzzled by them, even after considerable retrospection (Bargh, 1997).

The important point here is that what encounters are about or what they mean to their participants is determined in part by the particular goals and plans individuals believe themselves and others to be pursuing during the encounter. It is these mutual inferences about goals and plans that help individuals imbue particular encounters with meaning. Of course, there is no guarantee that individuals will generate similar inferences about each other's goals and plans (Reddy, 1979), and there will always be some degree of inferential slippage between parties to the same social interaction. Inferential disjunctions between social interactants may themselves fuel considerable interpersonal conflict (Sillars, 1998). These potential problems notwithstanding, whether these goals and plans and the inferences that flow from them are activated by relatively enduring predispositions or by particular events that occur during encounters, they serve to drive individual understanding and interpretations of social behavior and they help shape the production of subsequent messages.

Interaction Processes. The cognitive turn in social psychology has promoted a massive retreat of many of its adherents from the world of social interaction to the world of the computer screen and the reaction time task. Even studies that go beyond examining the effects of experimental manipulations on various cognitive processing and judgment measures rarely examine potential effects within the context of ongoing social interaction. Although examining how rapidly individuals walk after being differentially primed with elderly or neutral words may be a clever demonstration of how priming influences individual behavior (Bargh, 1997), such studies provide little understanding of how priming effects may or may not be consequential in ongoing social interactions among individuals.

In stark contrast to those who approach the study of social interaction from a cognitive perspective are communication researchers who eschew psychologically oriented explanations of social interaction. For example, in discussing her extensive program of research on equivocal communication (Bavelas, Black, Chovil, & Mullett, 1990), Bavelas (1998) noted that frequently communication theorists invoke psychological processes to explain communication sequences. She argued that rather than ask why particular messages are produced, a question that orients its asker toward explanations rooted in psychological processes, communication researchers should ask how a particular message fits within a larger sequence of messages. This view is consistent with the perspective of interpersonal communication advanced by the Palo Alto group several decades ago (Watzlawick, Beavin, & Jackson, 1967), and one that is also reflected in the work on relational control (Mark, 1971; Rogers & Farace, 1975; Rogers-Millar & Millar, 1979).

The relational control perspective is predicated on the assumption that control and dominance are relationship properties that emerge from sequences of messages exchanged between people. Patterns of dominance and submission can be ascertained by examining how individual bids for dominance are responded to by other interactants. A postulate guiding this line of inquiry is that to understand control processes in social interaction, one does not have to invoke the kinds psychological processes adumbrated earlier. One only need study sequential patterns of one-up, one-down, and one-across conversational moves to understand how control processes work in social interactions.

Bavelas (1998) explicitly bifurcated the study of communication phenomena and mental life, and suggested that the study of hypothetical mental states be left "to cognitive and personality psychologists" (p. 188). However, it is difficult to square this general admonition with the notion that there may be considerable variation among receivers' interpretations of the degree to which a given sequence of messages is equivocal or clear. For example, when asked by a gift giver whether one likes the gift, a gift receiver who dislikes the gift might say, "Oh, it's not bad." By invoking a set of criteria generated by a particular theoretical stance, an analyst might deem such a message to be equivocal rather than clear. However, our hypothetical analyst's judgment notwithstanding, this same exchange might be judged to be quite clear by some participants in a given interaction. The individual's interpretation of the equivocal response to his or her question and any influence the interpretation might have on subsequent messages would be the result of the kinds of individual cognitive processes described earlier.

Moreover, if one explains the generation of such equivocal messages by recourse to such notions as politeness norms or face-saving concerns, one is implicitly recognizing the importance of individual cognitive processes. For, in the final analysis, such norms and concerns reside in the long-term memories of those who attend to them during their interactions with others. This is not to say that one cannot do social interaction research that brackets these mental processes in favor of in-depth analyses of message exchange sequences; however, if one's goal is a comprehensive understanding of social interaction processes, such individual interpretative processes cannot simply be ignored. The larger point to be made here is this: Psychologically oriented approaches to social behavior that essentially ignore social interaction in favor of individual cognitive and judgment processes are as limited as approaches to social interaction that eschew any significant explanatory role for individual psychological processes.

Unfortunately, the passage of a considerable amount of time has revealed that the spate of multidimensional scaling (MDS) studies of social relationships reported during the 1970s and early 1980s, a few of which were just considered, subsequently has done little to advance the development of interpersonal communication theory. Furthermore, these studies have motivated little if any further research. Consequently, the findings of these methodologically elegant studies have not been related to ongoing social interactions between people in any tangible way. Thus, the question of what differences these dimensions make when people engage in social interaction still remains.

This particular example may be diagnostic of an even larger issue. The general problem appears to be this: How can meaningful and potentially heuristic relationships be drawn between cognitive structures and processes on the one hand and patterns of social interaction on the other? Part of the answer to this question may involve trying to ascertain how goals and plans are played out during social interactions. To date, studies of strategic interaction generally have either examined the conditions that prompt individuals to select some strategies for attaining a goal over others, or how individuals who vary with respect to some individual difference characteristic say they would go about trying to achieve a particular goal (Boster, 1995). In the former case individuals have been asked to select strategies they would use from a list of strategies provided by the researcher, whereas in the latter case, individuals have provided answers to open-ended questions that have then been content analyzed. Under both of these research paradigms, individuals have responded to hypothetical scenarios and they have not attempted to achieve their goals while interacting with others. Miller (1987) noted this dearth of social interaction studies of compliance gaining when he observed:

> If persuasion researchers want to understand how compliance-gaining message strategies function in interpersonal settings—or, for that matter, how any symbolic inducement functions in any communicative setting—they must come to grips with the necessity of observing actual message exchanges. (p. 474)

Given the decided lack of research examining compliance gaining and other goals in the context of actual interactions between real people, Miller's (1987) admonition is still justified today. However, analyses of message exchanges between people do not, ipso facto, guarantee that relations between cognitive structures and processes and social interaction will be elucidated. One must approach such studies with at least a general research strategy. Such a strategy is mapped out in what follows.

One possible way to deal with this problem is to see whether the signatures of cognitive structures can be recovered from social interaction behavior. It is commonplace to conceive of such cognitive structures as plans and scripts as hierarchically organized conceptual representations of goal-directed action sequences. Abstract representations of actions tend to be found at the tops of these hierarchies, and these representations become more concrete at lower levels of the hierarchy (Berger, 1997; Lichtenstein & Brewer, 1980). This hierarchical property of plans has been used as the basis for formulating the hierarchy principle (Berger, 1997; Berger, Knowlton, & Abrahams, 1996). This line of research has demonstrated that when goal-directed action is thwarted and individuals wish to continue to pursue their goals, they tend to make less cognitively demanding lower level modifications to message plan hierarchies than more demanding alterations to higher level plan units. Thus, when individuals are asked to repeat geographic directions because they were not well understood, they rarely spontaneously alter the walk route of the second rendition of their directions. Rather, they are more likely to repeat the same walk route but increase their vocal amplitude (Berger, 1997; Berger & diBattista, 1993). Moreover, additional research has shown that alterations to higher level plan elements are indeed more cognitively demanding (Berger, 1997; Berger et al., 1996).

Other studies have demonstrated that individuals can recall goals and plans that they thought about during specific encounters with others (Waldron, 1990, 1997; Waldron & Applegate, 1994; Waldron, Caughlin, & Jackson, 1995; Waldron, Cegala, Sharkey, & Teboul, 1990). In these studies, after individuals have interacted for some period of time, they individually review videotape of their conversation. As they view the videotape, they are asked to indicate at what points in the conversation they can recall what they were thinking. When they can recall, they record the content of their thoughts. This procedure has revealed that thoughts about goals and plans are relatively common during conversations. For example, Waldron (1990) found that of some 2,273 thoughts individuals could recall after their conversations with others, 44% were concerned with the goals they were pursuing in the conversation and the plans they were using to pursue their goals.

As informative as this work is in spelling out the various roles plans play in message production and the potential beneficial effects of concrete planning (Waldron et al., 1995), it does not address directly the issue of how plan structure is reflected in social interaction structure. Furthermore, this work does not account for how individual-level plans are coordinated to achieve social interaction goals (Bruce & Newman, 1978; Carbonell, 1981; Waldron, 1997). Clearly, individuals can and do sometimes second-guess each other's goals and plans during their interactions (Hewes & Graham, 1989), and the inferences that arise from this second-guessing activity may be used to alter individual plans. How might these inferential processes be captured empirically?

Although such techniques as Markov modeling and lag-sequential analysis are available to detect patterns of sequential structure in social interaction, these techniques are not very informative about the hierarchical structure of social interaction. It is the goals interactants pursue and the plans they invoke to attain their goals that gives social interaction its structure (Dillard, 1997). The verbal and nonverbal acts manifested during social encounters are recruited and coordinated to achieve goals. These coordinated verbal and nonverbal acts are guided by plans. If these postulates are embraced, then the structure of individual plans ought to be manifested in various patterns of verbal and nonverbal action. Note that it is patterns of coordinated verbal and nonverbal action that should reflect plan structure, not individual verbal and nonverbal behaviors.

For example, in pursuing the goal of gaining compliance using a plan containing an abstract element like "providing positive incentives," the enactment of this plan element during the interaction might be accomplished by using both kind words (compliments and offers) and pleasant actions (pleasant vocal intonations, smiling, and touching). Conversely, social action guided by a compliance-gaining plan containing an abstract element like "threatening the other" might produce a coordinated pattern of verbal and nonverbal action characterized by threatening statements and actions. However, in both examples, the specific verbal and nonverbal behaviors used to realize these abstract plan elements in the social interaction arena could show considerable variation. There are a very large number of configurations of specific verbal and nonverbal actions that could be recruited to represent each of these abstractions at the level of social interaction. Thus, taken as a whole, these bundles of verbal and nonverbal behavior represent abstract interaction units, whereas the microactions that make up these bundles are the lower level units from which the larger units are constructed.

Of course, the preceding discussion presents a one-sided, individual-level view of the potential structural relations between plans and individual action. To socialize this perspective, it is necessary to take into account the plans of co-interactants and how those plans guide responses to those of the other. For example, the enactment of threat by one party to the interaction may be responded to in any number of different ways by the other party or parties, including compliance, counterthreat, or indifference. Presumably, these response patterns also would be guided by individual plans; however, these plans would be partially shaped by the nature of the initial threat enactment (e.g., its intensity or its duration) and the inferences flowing from observations of the initial threat. Obviously, as social interaction episodes like this one progress, individuals continue to accumulate remembrances of previous exchanges during the conversation. Moreover, they may develop an overarching conception of the conversation; for example, the conversation was about "borrowing money."

The view of social interaction just outlined is consistent with one advocated by Barker (1963). In Barker's ecologically oriented view, the stream of behavior can be analyzed in at least two distinct ways. First, natural units of behavior can be employed. In the case of children attending school, for example, relevant natural behavior units might be such activities as studying arithmetic, playing baseball, or being at recess. These molar activities can be broken down into successively more microscopic behavior units. Second, one might impose arbitrary units like time on the stream of behavior to divide it into segments. One might instead use intrusive methods like questionnaires or interviews that disrupt the natural flow of the behavior stream by forcing individuals to respond using less natural behavior units. These arbitrary units Barker termed *tesserae*. Barker argued that when arbitrary tesserae are imposed on the natural flow of the behavior stream, the interaction of the tesserae with natural behavior units inevitably creates distortions in the organization of natural behavior units. Consequently, he advocated that nonreactive research methods (Webb, Campbell, Schwartz, & Sechrest, 1966) and content analytic schemes that do not impose artificial tesserae on the temporal dimension of behavior be used to study behavior sequences.

Intensive and detailed observations of children engaged in everyday activities have revealed that behavior units sometimes exhibit two important properties (Barker, 1963). First, some behavioral units are organized around the pursuit of a goal or a set of goals. That is, naturally occurring behavioral units sometimes exhibit goal-directed properties. Second, molar behavioral units frequently manifest hierarchical organization in which smaller behavioral units are essential for the production of larger, more abstract units. In describing this property of the behavior stream, Barker (1963) asserted, "These facts point to a fundamental structural feature of the behavior stream: behavior units occur in enclosing–enclosed structures; small units form the components of larger units" (p. 11). In Barker's view, these enclosing–enclosed structures are hierarchically organized. In a similar vein, studies of how observers segment or unitize ongoing sequences of behavior have adduced evidence to support the notion that perceptions of behavioral units are also organized hierarchically (Newtson, 1973, 1976). Moreover, detailed analyses of goal-directed action sequences represented both visually and in written form have revealed that they too are hierarchically organized (Lichtenstein & Brewer, 1980). Research germane to action identification theory (Vallacher & Wegner, 1985) has shown the behavioral consequences of identifying actions at different levels of abstraction (Vallacher, Wegner, & Somoza, 1989). Even sequences of action or discourse that exhibit an apparently sequential or linear surface pattern may in fact be hierarchically organized.

Another way of thinking about such behavioral units is that streams of action are organized around goals and the plans used to reach them. Because action streams tend to be organized this way, we are able to use short-hand verbal labels to characterize lengthy and complex interaction sequences. How else could interactions played out in multiple episodes over lengthy time periods be reduced to such parsimonious characterizations as "She was trying to get him to talk," "They were negotiating," "They were fighting," "They were trying to make their marriage work," or "She was trying to persuade him"? Apparently, we ultimately understand complex interaction sequences based on our inferences about the goals individuals in them appear to be pursuing and the plans they seem to be using to attain them. This conclusion is consistent with that of Green (1989), who argued that understanding discourse is fundamentally dependent on our inferences about each other's goals and plans. Specifically she asserted, "Understanding a speaker's intention in saying what she said and the way she said it amounts to inferring the speaker's plan, in all of its hierarchical glory, although there is room for considerable latitude regarding the details" (p. 14). Consistent with this view, those concerned with how individuals arrive at definitions of the social situations in which they find themselves have argued that inferences concerning goals and plans are vital to the achievement of such definitions (Miller, Cody, & McLaughlin, 1994).

The preceding discussion suggests that one way to gain an understanding of the relations between cognitive structures and processes on the one hand and social interaction on the other is to determine how cognitive representations of goals and plans find their way into the stream of social interaction. Given Barker's (1963), Newtson's (1973, 1976), and Lichtenstein and Brewer's (1980) work, finding residues of these cognitive structures in ongoing behavior should not be as daunting a task as it might first seem. For, as we have seen, the stream of behavior itself sometimes exhibits a hierarchical structure that resembles that of a plan in the pursuit of a goal or a set of goals (Barker, 1963).

A Cautionary Note.   Before considering issues related to the explanation of the interpersonal communication phenomena already outlined, potential myopia associated with the preceding presentation should be noted and duly corrected. Clearly, in their everyday lives, individuals use plans to pursue many endeavors that do not have face-to-face interaction with others as their primary goal. Shopping at a supermarket, going to a bank, buying gas for a car, exercising, purchasing clothing, or chewing gum, and finding one's way to a specific location may involve interaction with others. However, the goals of obtaining food or money, exercising, buying clothing, chewing gum, or finding a specific location are not themselves intrinsically social. Social interaction may play an enabling role in attaining these goals, but only an enabling role. Moreover, the advent of what might be termed transactive technology is slowly eliminating the necessity of face-to-face interaction to satisfy at least some of these mundane goals (e.g., vending machines, automatic teller machines, credit card purchases at the gas pump, and credit card machines at supermarket checkout counters).

Goals and plans that guide specific interpersonal communication episodes may be embedded in still larger goal–plan structures, and only parts of these larger goal–plan structures may explicitly involve communicative activities (Berger, 1997). For example, a plan to achieve the highly abstract goal of personal happiness may involve social goals concerned with establishing and maintaining interpersonal relationships. However, the same large-scale plan might contain nonsocial goals and plans for realizing the regnant personal happiness goal. Such nonsocial goals as a large bank account, a new BMW 850, a house with an ocean view, and frequent trips to exotic places may also be an important part of the larger personal happiness plan. Thus, it is highly unrealistic to suppose that the goals and plans guiding actions in specific interpersonal encounters are independent of these larger structures and that the larger structures are not influenced by the subgoals and subplans embedded within them.

What Needs to Be Explained?

Given the cognitive and behavioral processes that make interpersonal communication possible, the question is what about these processes is in need of explanation. The view of interpersonal communication already outlined implies that when fundamental perceptual and cognitive processes are granted, individuals must have both relevant knowledge and performative skills to participate in social interaction episodes. Individuals must have a fund of knowledge about how social interaction works (procedural knowledge) and knowledge about the specific social actors who are part of a particular interaction (declarative knowledge) to pursue their goals. In addition, they must also have various motor skills that are used to realize this knowledge in action. An integral part of procedural knowledge is the goals individuals pursue and the plans they use to try to attain them.

Knowledge and Skill Acquisition.   Important questions about both knowledge and performative skills concern how they are acquired in the first place. Children learn how to participate in social interaction through both explicit and implicit learning. Children may be explicitly instructed by parents to wait their turn in conversations; however, in instructing a child to behave in this way, most parents probably do not and cannot explain the specific nonverbal signals that the child might use to gain control of the conversational floor from others. The child is usually provided with a general conversational convention (e.g., "It's not polite to interrupt others while they are speaking"), but the child is usually left to fill in the specifics of just how one should inject one's self into a conversation in a proper manner. Exactly how children fill in these details is not clear; however, it is probably the case that these details are not provided through explicit instruction.

With very few exceptions, interpersonal communication researchers have devoted very little attention to the acquisition of relevant knowledge and skills. Some studies have compared the cognitive complexity levels and perspective-taking skills of children and adults (Applegate, 1990; Burleson, 1987) and shown that cognitive complexity and perspective-taking ability both increase with age. Similarly, developmental psychologists have shown that children's plans for reaching goals become more complex as they grow older (Kreitler & Kreitler, 1987). However, even these studies have not determined how children's interactions with their environments influence their development in the cognitive complexity, perspective-taking, and plan domains. Thus, the details of how children acquire the knowledge and skills necessary to participate in social interaction remain to be spelled out.

Differential Knowledge and Skill Levels.   A second and related explanatory issue concerns the considerable variation in social skills that is observed within any particular age level. Clearly, even among adults, there are significant individual differences in the knowledge and skills necessary for the production of communicative activity that is effective in producing desired end states in a socially appropriate way. Why these knowledge and skill differences remain among adults even after considerable socialization is an issue worth addressing. However, there is at least one caution that needs to be heeded before undertaking such explanatory efforts. A search for effective communication skills that transcend the plethora of possible particularistic communication contexts may be futile.

What are commonly referred to as effective communication skills may be highly specific to particular goals. Thus, for example, the chief executive officer of a *Fortune* 500 company may be extremely effective in exercising social influence within that organizational context, only to be a dismal failure in inducing his junior high school age children to do their homework or study for tests. Even within the same general communication domain (e.g., formal organizations), individuals may show considerable variation in their abilities to achieve what are, at least in the abstract, apparently similar goals. Thus, a given manager may be highly influential in interactions with subordinates but not particularly influential in interactions with superiors. If this analysis is plausible, then it might be more productive to approach this problem from the perspective of expertise (Cantor & Kihlstrom, 1987) rather than questing after elusive general communication skills.

Altering Knowledge and Skill.   As noted earlier, even adults with many years' worth of experience interacting with others may encounter significant communication problems in specific interaction contexts. For example, individuals able to sustain long-term friendships with others may not be able to function well in the context of marriage, and individuals who have little difficulty making friends or communicating with their spouses may be utter failures when attempting to comfort others. Within the perspective presented here, these problems are important to study because of the potential opportunity to gain understanding of the knowledge and skills that are requisite for effective functioning in these various contexts. Once these knowledge and skill prerequisites are understood, the issue of how they can be acquired by individual communicators becomes tantamount. Devising strategies for inculcating this knowledge and skill into adults might also provide insights into how children acquire the same knowledge and skills.

From Interpersonal Communication to Interpersonal Relationships.

Over the past two decades, a considerable number of interpersonal communication researchers have devoted their energies to the study of the factors responsible for the development, maintenance, and decline of interpersonal relationships (Baxter & Montgomery, 1996; Duck, 1991). Understandably, this intense focus on the development of interpersonal relationships has tended to bias the study of relationships toward those that are more consequential and away from those that are less important. Thus, romantic, friendship, and family relationships have assumed center stage, whereas less intimate relationships (e.g., those that may be formed as part of everyday commercial transactions) have generally been overlooked. In fact, these latter interactions were termed *noninterpersonal relationships* by Miller and Steinberg (1975). Cappella (1987) questioned the wisdom of the interpersonal–noninterpersonal distinction when he noted that some potentially highly consequential relationships (doctor–patient, teacher–student) fall into the noninterpersonal category. This possibility notwithstanding, it is not unreasonable to assert that the study of interpersonal communication has in many ways become conflated with the study of the development of close, personal relationships.

As noted previously, as people seek to achieve goals in their everyday lives, a particular local goal currently being pursued may be embedded within a more abstract goal–plan framework. Thus, the pursuit of a specific close relationship may subserve a more regnant goal like personal happiness, one that may be satisfied by the achievement of nonrelationship goals as well. The abstract personal happiness goal may also be partially satisfied by the achievement of subgoals that involve communicative transactions with nonclose others (e.g., car dealers, financial consultants, etc.). Moreover, the abstract personal happiness goal may exert downward influence on these subgoals and help to define what constitutes satisfaction when they are achieved. Thus, examining these close relationship subgoals in isolation or ignoring the potential influence of noninterpersonal relationships is bound to distort the picture of how individuals carry out interpersonal communication in their everyday lives.

Another problem, similar to one noted earlier with respect to studies of strategic communication, is that in many instances those who study the development of close relationships do not directly examine interpersonal communication. All too frequently, individuals are interviewed or questioned about their relationships and asked to provide retrospective accounts of their experiences with their relationship partners. Rarely are parties to relationships observed as they interact with each other, although there are some exceptions represented in the marital communication literature (Burggraf & Sillars, 1987; Gottman, 1979, 1994; Sillars, 1998).

A prerequisite for understanding the multiple roles social interaction plays in the development, maintenance, and decay of social relationships is to study directly social interaction processes. Studying the residues of these social encounters by asking individuals to recall their experiences, sometimes long after they have taken place, simply does not provide the data necessary to link social interaction and relationship development processes. As discussed previously, cognitive representations of goals and plans may serve to structure goal-directed social interaction sequences. Thus, to understand how individuals' goals and plans for relationships are played out in their actions, these action streams must be studied directly. Then, the goal–plan structures identified in their actions can be related to the goal–plan cognitive structures that may have guided their actions. This approach to the study of social relationships should result in a more thorough understanding of how interpersonal communication and cognitive processes function in social relationships.

Clearly, some individuals experience communication-related difficulties when they attempt to execute close relationships; however, it is equally clear that some people encounter significant communication problems when involved in interpersonal relationships that are not at all close. The sources of these difficulties may vary as a function of relationship closeness; however, there may be some commonalities between close and nonclose relationships. For example, violations of expectations tied to work roles may be responsible for some communication problems in noninterpersonal work-related social contexts, whereas violations of expectations associated with marital and family roles (e.g., mother, father, wife, and husband) may be implicated in marital and family communication problems. Thus, violation of role expectations, regardless of the social context and intimacy level of the relationship, may fuel communication and relationship problems. Of course, the possibility that factors unique to close relationships and to noninterpersonal relationships may also contribute to these difficulties cannot be ignored. The important point is that a parochial focus on close relationships and their development serves to marginalize the communication problems individuals encounter in the many more numerous, nonclose relationships in which they participate as part of their everyday lives. The more catholic purview of interpersonal communication advocated in this proto-theory should provide at least a partial antidote to this currently more popular but myopic interpersonal communication perspective.

META-ANALYSIS AND PROTO-THEORY

Given this proto-theory of interpersonal communication, we now turn to an examination of the meta-analysis studies that have dealt with topics related to the research domain of interpersonal communication. The primary question addressed in the following discussion is the degree to which these groups of studies deal with the relevant phenomena and explanatory issues outlined in the proto-theory. Of course, many of the studies included in the meta-analyses reported in this volume were not designed with this proto-theory in mind. Nevertheless, it is still instructive to examine potential links between the proto-theory and the meta-analyses. These relations are examined with respect to the work reported on social skills.

Social Skills

This research domain concerns the degree to which individuals possess the skills necessary to achieve their goals in social situations. However, as Dillard and Spitzberg (1984) noted, there is considerable variance in how social skills are conceived ranging from cognitive to behavioral perspectives. Dillard and Spitzberg's meta-analysis revealed that several verbal (questions and compliments) and nonverbal (gestures and talk time) behaviors positively correlated with communication skill judgments in excess of .40. Conversely, adaptors and response latencies exhibited significant negative relations with social skill judgments. These results lead these researchers to conclude that being active and expressive during social interactions promotes increased judgments of social skill.

Although intuition suggests the validity of these relations between behavior and skill judgments in some social contexts, one can readily conceive of social situations in which inhibition of expressiveness to the point of silence might well be more effective in achieving goals. Knowing when not to say too much or to say anything may be as important as knowing what to say. Strategic use of longer response latencies in particular social situations might actually enhance communicative performance; for example, when individuals are already "hanging on every word" being uttered by a source. Moreover, other social exigencies may call for the enactment of behaviors that are not particularly positive and complimentary. Certain persuasion and negotiation goals may require a certain degree of curtness and negativity to be maximally effective (e.g., resisting physical abuse and sexual coercion, Emmers & Allen, 1995; Emmers-Sommer, chap. 17, this volume). A lengthy and positively toned response to such coercive attempts would indeed be perverse and probably not very skillful.

The proto-theory of interpersonal communication suggests a more catholic and potentially nuanced view of social skills. First, plans to achieve instrumental and communication goals may be evaluated with respect to their potential effectiveness in the absence of their behavioral enactment. Elements of abstract plans can be evaluated for their likely effectiveness and appropriateness before they are enacted (Berger, 1997). Based on such evaluations, individuals might conclude that a planned action like coercion would be less effective than offering positive incentives to achieve a particular persuasion goal. Moreover, these decisions to deploy or not to deploy these abstract plan elements could be made online, as interactions unfold, thus leading to the kind of cognitive editing studied by Hample and Dallinger (1991, chap. 11, this volume). Under this approach to social skill, messages that are foregone and suppressed become as important to study as those that are ultimately sent in determining what constitutes skilled performance. That is, what could have been said or done in the course of pursuing a goal but was not becomes highly significant.

Second, the correlational approach to assessing relations between social skill judgments and behaviors may itself be called into question. As proto-theory suggests, when individuals realize message plans at the level of social action, it is configurations of verbal and nonverbal actions taken together that make for skilled performances. By recognizing that too much of a good thing like expressiveness may undermine skill judgments, Spitzberg and Dillard (chap. 6, this volume) implicitly endorse the idea that configurations of behaviors are probably more important than individual behaviors in determining social skill levels. Moreover, the possibility that it is configurations of these behaviors that ultimately produce differences in social skill levels may explain the relatively attenuated correlations between individual behaviors and social skill judgments reported by Dillard and Spitzberg (1984). The notion of configuration carries with it the assumption that there are optimal levels of various verbal and nonverbal behaviors that produce effective performances. Clearly, heuristics like "more is better" or "less is better" with respect to particular verbal and nonverbal behaviors are far too simplistic to account for skilled communicative performances across the broad spectrum of social situations.

Finally, conceiving of social skills solely in terms of message and behavior production completely ignores the understanding and interpretation side of the social skills equation. The notion that skilled communicators have a deeper understanding of others than their less skilled counterparts is consistent with the constructivist work on comforting (Allen, 1989, chap. 13, this volume; Burleson, 1984, 1987, 1994). As the proto-theory advanced here suggests, to optimize one's plans for attaining goals during social interactions, an individual must first understand the goals fellow interactants are pursuing and the plans they are using to attain them. Given these assessments of interactions between one's goals and plans and those of others, astute communicators might well conclude that the time is not ripe for pursuing their own goals during a particular encounter. Or, such deft communicators might recognize that goals and plans might have to be modified before attempts are made to realize them in action. These possibilities suggest that a complete explanation for communication competence and skill must include message comprehension and interpretative processes on the one hand and message production processes on the other. The ability to display positive expressiveness during social interaction may prove completely ineffective if the goals and plans of others in the interaction are misunderstood.

CONCLUSION

Only a rough outline of a proto-theory of interpersonal communication could be sketched here. Although much of this outline remains to be fleshed out, this presentation has revealed how such a proto-theory, in combination with meta-analysis findings, might be used to detect significant gaps in our knowledge about interpersonal communication processes. Moreover, providing this proto-theoretic context for meta-analysis shows how some approaches to examining interpersonal communication phenomena might be potentially more fruitful than others. Of course, the basic postulates of the proto-theory presented here can and should be challenged. Nonetheless, this proto-theory of interpersonal communication addresses directly fundamental questions for which many would like answers; for example, why are some individuals more effective than others in achieving their goals during social interaction? The proto-theoretic purview presented here together with meta-analysis findings could prove to be a powerful combination for answering such critical questions.

REFERENCES

Allen, M. (1989, May). *A synthesis and extension of constructivist comforting research.* Paper presented at the annual conference of the International Communication Association, San Francisco, CA.

Allen, M., Hunter, J. E., & Donohue, W. A. (1989). Meta-analysis of self-report data on the effectiveness of public speaking anxiety treatment techniques. *Communication Education, 38,* 54–76.

Applegate, J. L. (1990). Constructs and communication: A pragmatic integration. In G. Neimeyer & R. Neimeyer (Eds.), *Advances in personal construct psychology* (Vol. 1, pp. 203–230). Greenwich, CT: JAI.

Bargh, J. A. (1997). The automaticity of everyday life. In R. S. Wyer, Jr. (Ed.), *Advances in social cognition* (Vol. 10, pp. 1–61). Mahwah, NJ: Lawrence Erlbaum Associates.

Barker, R. G. (1963). The stream of behavior as an empirical problem. In R. G. Barker (Ed.), *The stream of behavior: Explorations of its structure and content* (pp. 1–22). New York: Appelton-Century-Crofts.

Bavelas, J. B. (1998). Theoretical and methodological principles of the equivocation project. *Journal of Language and Social Psychology, 17,* 183–199.

Bavelas, J. B., Black, A., Chovil, N., & Mullett, J. (1990). *Equivocal communication.* Newbury Park, CA: Sage.

Baxter, L. A., & Montgomery, B. M. (1996). *Relating: Dialogues and dialectics.* New York: Guilford.

Berger, C. R. (1991). Communication theories and other curios. *Communication Monographs, 58,* 101–113.

Berger, C. R. (1995). A plan-based approach to strategic communication. In D. E. Hewes (Ed.), *The cognitive bases of interpersonal communication* (pp. 141–180). Hillsdale, NJ: Lawrence Erlbaum Associates.

Berger, C. R. (1997). *Planning strategic interaction: Attaining goals through communicative action.* Mahwah, NJ: Lawrence Erlbaum Associates.

Berger, C. R., & Chaffee, S. H. (1987). The study of communication as a science. In C. R. Berger & S. H. Chaffee (Eds.), *Handbook of communication science* (pp. 15–19). Newbury Park, CA: Sage.

Berger, C. R., & diBattista, P. (1993). Communication failure and plan adaptation: If at first you don't succeed, say it louder and slower. *Communication Monographs, 60,* 220–238.

Berger, C. R., & Douglas, W. (1981). Studies in interpersonal epistemology III: Anticipated interaction, self-monitoring and observational context selection. *Communication Monographs, 48,* 183–196.

Berger, C. R., Knowlton, S. W., & Abrahams, M. F. (1996). The hierarchy principle in strategic communication. *Communication Theory, 6,* 111–142.

Boster, F. J. (1995). Commentary on compliance-gaining message behavior research. In C. R. Berger & M. Burgoon (Eds.), *Communication and social influence processes* (pp. 91–113). East Lansing: Michigan State University Press.

Bruce, B., & Newman, D. (1978). Interacting plans. *Cognitive Psychology, 2,* 196–233.

Burggraf, C. S., & Sillars, A. L. (1987). A critical examination of sex differences in marital communication. *Communication Monographs, 54,* 276–294.

Burleson, B. R. (1984). Age, social-cognitive development, and the use of comforting strategies. *Communication Monographs, 51,* 140–153.

Burleson, B. R. (1987). Cognitive complexity. In J. C. McCroskey & J. A. Daly (Eds.), *Personality and interpersonal communication* (pp. 305–349). Newbury Park, CA: Sage.

Burleson, B. R. (1992). Taking communication seriously. *Communication Monographs, 59,* 79–86.

Burleson, B. R. (1994). Comforting messages: Features, functions, and outcomes. In J. A. Daly & J. M. Wiemann (Eds.), *Strategic interpersonal communication* (pp. 135–161). Hillsdale, NJ: Lawrence Erlbaum Associates.

Byrne, D. (1971). *The attraction paradigm.* New York: Academic Press.

Cantor, N., & Kihlstrom, J. F. (1987). *Personality and social intelligence.* Englewood Cliffs, NJ: Prentice Hall.

Cappella, J. N. (1987). Interpersonal communication: Definitions and fundamental questions. In C. R. Berger & S. H. Chaffee (Eds.), *Handbook of communication science* (pp. 184–238). Newbury Park, CA: Sage.

Carbonell, J. G. (1981). Counterplanning: A strategy-based model of adversary planning in real-world situations. *Artificial Intelligence, 16,* 295–329.

Clore, G., & Ketelaar, T. (1997). Minding our emotions: On the role of automatic, unconscious affect. In R. S. Wyer, Jr. (Ed.), *Advances in social cognition* (Vol. 10, pp. 105–120). Mahwah, NJ: Lawrence Erlbaum Associates.

Cody, M. J., & McLaughlin, M. L. (1980). Perceptions of compliance-gaining situations: A dimensional analysis. *Communication Monographs, 47,* 132–148.

Cody, M. J., & McLaughlin, M. L. (1985). The situation as a construct in interpersonal communication research. In M. L. Knapp & G. R. Miller (Eds.), *Handbook of interpersonal communication* (pp. 263–312). Beverly Hills, CA: Sage.

Cody, M. J., Woelfel, M. L., & Jordan, W. J. (1983). Dimensions of compliance-gaining situations. *Human Communication Research, 9,* 99–113.

Dillard, J. P. (1990). The nature and substance of goals in tactical communication. In M. J. Cody & M. L. McLaughlin (Eds.), *The psychology of tactical communication* (pp. 70–90). Clevedon, UK: Multilingual Matters.

Dillard, J. P. (1997). Explicating the goal construct: Tools for theorists. In J. O. Greene (Ed.), *Message production: Advances in communication theory* (pp. 47–69). Mahwah, NJ: Lawrence Erlbaum Associates.

Dillard, J. P., Solomon, D. H., & Samp, J. A. (1996). Framing social reality: The relevance of relational judgments. *Communication Research, 23,* 703–723.

Dillard, J. P., & Spitzberg, B. H. (1984). Global impressions of social skills: Behavioral predictors. In R. N. Bostrom (Ed.), *Communication yearbook 8* (pp. 446–463). Beverly Hills, CA: Sage.

Duck, S. (1973). *Personal relationships and personal constructs: A study of friendship formation.* London: Wiley.

Duck, S. (1991). *Understanding relationships.* New York: Guilford.

Emmers, T. M., & Allen, M. (1995, November). *Factors contributing to sexually coercive behaviors: A meta-analysis.* Paper presented at the annual conference of the Speech Communication Association, San Antonio, TX.

Festinger, L. (1954). A theory of social comparison processes. *Human Relations, 7,* 117–140.

Forgas, J. P. (1979). *Social episodes: The study of interaction routines.* London: Academic Press.

Giles, H., & Wiemann, J. M. (1987). Language, social comparison, and power. In C. R. Berger & S. H. Chaffee (Eds.), *Handbook of communication science* (pp. 350–384). Newbury Park, CA: Sage.

Gottman, J. M. (1979). *Marital interaction: Experimental investigations.* New York: Academic Press.

Gottman, J. M. (1994). *What predicts divorce: The relationship between marital process and marital outcomes.* Hillsdale, NJ: Lawrence Erlbaum Associates.

Green, G. M. (1989). *Pragmatics and natural language understanding.* Hillsdale, NJ: Lawrence Erlbaum Associates.

Greene, J. O. (Ed.). (1997). *Message production: Advances in communication theory.* Mahwah, NJ: Lawrence Erlbaum Associates.

Hample, D., & Dallinger, J. M. (1991, October). *The effects of situation on use or suppression of possible compliance gaining appeals.* Paper presented at the convention of the Organization Studying Communication, Language and Gender, Milwaukee, WI.

Heider, F. (1958). *The psychology of interpersonal relations.* New York: Wiley.

Hewes, D. E. (Ed.). (1995). *The cognitive bases of interpersonal communication.* Hillsdale, NJ: Lawrence Erlbaum Associates.

Hewes, D. E., & Graham, M. L. (1989). Second-guessing theory: Review and extension. In J. A. Anderson (Ed.), *Communication yearbook 12* (pp. 213–248). Newbury Park, CA: Sage.

Honeycutt, J. M. (1991). Imagined interactions, imagery and mindfulness/mindlessness. In R. Kunzendorf (Ed.), *Mental imagery* (pp. 121–128). New York: Plenum.

Kreitler, S., & Kreitler, H. (1987). Plans and planning: Their motivational and cognitive antecedents. In S. L. Friedman, E. K. Skolnick, & R. R. Cocking (Eds.), *Blueprints for thinking: The role of planning in cognitive development* (pp. 110–178). New York: Cambridge University Press.

Langer, E. J. (1989). *Mindfulness.* Reading, MA: Addison-Wesley.

Langer, E. J. (1992). Interpersonal mindlessness and language. *Communication Monographs, 59,* 324–327.

Lichtenstein, E. H., & Brewer, W. F. (1980). Memory for goal directed events. *Cognitive Psychology, 12,* 412–445.

Mark, R. A. (1971). Coding communication at the relationship level. *Journal of Communication, 21,* 221–232.

Miller, G. R. (1987). Persuasion. In C. R. Berger & S. H. Chaffee (Eds.), *Handbook of communication science* (pp. 446–483). Newbury Park, CA: Sage.

Miller, G. R., & Steinberg, M. (1975). *Between people: A new analysis of interpersonal communication.* Chicago: Science Research Associates.

Miller, L. C., Cody, M. J., & McLaughlin, M. L. (1994). Situations and goals as fundamental constructs in interpersonal communication research. In M. L. Knapp & G. R. Miller (Eds.), *Handbook of interpersonal communication* (2nd ed., pp. 162–198). Newbury Park, CA: Sage.

Newcomb, T. M. (1961). *The acquaintance process.* New York: Holt, Rinehart & Winston.

Newtson, D. (1973). Attribution and the unit of perception of ongoing behavior. *Journal of Personality and Social Psychology, 28,* 28–38.

Newtson, D. (1976). Foundations of attribution: The perception of ongoing behavior. In J. H. Harvey, W. J. Ickes, & R. F. Kidd (eds.), *New directions in attribution research* (Vol. 1, pp. 223–247). Hillsdale, NJ: Lawrence Erlbaum Associates.

Osgood, C. E., Suci, G. S., & Tannenbaum, P. H. (1957). *The measurement of meaning.* Urbana: University of Illinois Press.

Petronio, S., Snyder, E., & Bradford, L. (1992, October). *Planning strategies for the embarrassment of friends: An application and test of Berger's planning theory.* Paper presented at the annual conference of the Speech Communication Association, Chicago.

Planalp, S. (1999). *Communicating emotion: Social, moral, and cultural processes.* Paris: Cambridge University Press & Edition's de la Maison des Sciences de l'Homme.

Reddy, M. J. (1979). The conduit metaphor—A case of frame conflict in our language about language. In A. Ortony (Ed.), *Metaphor and thought* (pp. 284–324). London: Cambridge University Press.

Rogers, L. E., & Farace, R. B. (1975). Relational communication analysis: New measurement procedures. *Human Communication Research, 1,* 222–239.

Rogers-Millar, L. E., & Millar, F. E. (1979). Domineeringness and dominance: A transactional view. *Human Communication Research, 5*, 238–246.

Schachter, S. (1959). *The psychology of affiliation.* Stanford, CA: Stanford University Press.

Schachter, S., & Singer, J. L. (1962). Cognitive, social and physiological determinants of emotional state. *Psychological Review, 69*, 379–399.

Schutz, W. C. (1958). *Firo: A three-dimensional theory of interpersonal behavior.* New York: Holt, Rinehart & Winston.

Sillars, A. L. (1998). Mis(Understanding). In B. H. Spitzberg & W. R. Cupach (Eds.), *The dark side of close relationships* (pp. 73–102). Mahwah, NJ: Lawrence Erlbaum Associates.

Srull, T. K., & Wyer, R. S. (1986). The role of chronic and temporary goals in social information processing. In R. Sorrentino & E. T. Higgins (Eds.), *Handbook of motivation and cognition* (pp. 503–549). New York: Guilford.

Suls, J. M., & Miller, R. L. (Eds.). (1977). *Social comparison processes: Theoretical and empirical perspectives.* New York: Hemisphere.

Vallacher, R. R., & Wegner, D. M. (1985). *A theory of action identification.* Hillsdale, NJ: Lawrence Erlbaum Associates.

Vallacher, R. R., Wegner, D. M., & Somoza, M. (1989). That's easy for you to say: Action identification and speech fluency. *Journal of Personality and Social Psychology, 56*, 199–208.

Waldron, V. R. (1990). Constrained rationality: Situational influences on information acquisition plans and tactics. *Communication Monographs, 57*, 184–201.

Waldron, V. R. (1997). Toward a theory of interactive conversational planning. In J. O. Greene (Ed.), *Message production: Advances in communication theory* (pp. 195–220). Mahwah, NJ: Lawrence Erlbaum Associates.

Waldron, V. R., & Applegate, J. A. (1994). Interpersonal construct differentiation and conversational planning: An examination of two cognitive accounts for the production of competent verbal disagreement tactics. *Human Communication Research, 21*, 3–35.

Waldron, V. R., Caughlin, J., & Jackson, D. (1995). Talking specifics: Facilitating effects of planning on AIDS talk in peer dyads. *Health Communication, 7*, 179–204.

Waldron, V. R., Cegala, D. J., Sharkey, W. F., & Teboul, B. (1990). Cognitive and tactical dimensions of goal management. *Journal of Language and Social Psychology, 9*, 101–118.

Watzlawick, P., Beavin, J. H., & Jackson, D. D. (1967). *Pragmatics of human communication.* New York: Norton.

Webb, E. J., Campbell, D. T., Schwartz, R. D., & Sechrest, L. (1966). *Unobtrusive measures: Nonreactive research in the social sciences.* Chicago: Rand McNally.

Winter, D. G. (1973). *The power motive.* New York: The Free Press.

Wish, M., Deutsch, M., & Kaplan, S. J. (1976). Perceived dimensions of interpersonal relations. *Journal of Personality and Social Psychology, 33*, 409–420.

II

Individual Issues
in Interpersonal
Communication

3

An Overview of Individual Processes in Interpersonal Communication

Barbara Mae Gayle and Raymond W. Preiss

The importance that theorists and researchers attach to relational dynamics and social interaction is evident in the thousands of experiments and monographs devoted to these issues. For example, a database search of the term *interpersonal communication* resulted in 27,067 hits. Expanding the search to synonyms and related terms exponentially increases the archive of germane literature. Faced with the magnitude of this domain, we use this chapter to lay out our criteria for selecting the meta-analyses included in this book, identify the logic used to group and organize the meta-analyses, and provide the context for the first collection dealing with individual processes.

CRITERIA AND ORGANIZATION OF META-ANALYSES

Establishing selection criteria was a formidable task. The sheer volume of material, the complexity of interpersonal processes, and the nuances of interpersonal communication pose risks for both meta-analysts and those interested in placing the empirical reviews in context. Cooper and Rosenthal (1980) addressed the judgment calls that a meta-analytic reviewer must make when coding effects and interpreting findings, but the decisions that must be made when selecting and organizing meta-analyses has received less attention.

Hattie and Hansford (1984) and Preiss and Allen (1995) believed that areas merit empirical aggregation if they meet the criteria of uniqueness or suitability. A meta-analytic review may be considered unique if the area or question has never been empirically assessed, if earlier meta-analyses omitted key studies, or if conclusions grounded in existing meta-analyses are controversial or equivocal. A meta-analysis may also be considered unique if it explores a theoretical model or advances a potential moderator variable that clarifies theoretical approaches. When considering suitability, the primary issue of concern is variability. Although meta-analysis is an important tool for untangling a large number of apparently inconsistent experimental findings, it is also valuable when the goal is to estimate the magnitude of an effect in a domain of effects that are consistent in direction. The issue of magnitude may have important theoretical implications and result in mathematical models that clarify underlying processes.

We were mindful of both uniqueness and suitability when selecting and arranging the summaries found in later chapters. Because characteristics and behaviors of the participants are fundamental, we initially looked at issues associated with the individuals participating in interpersonal communication. We then examined the available empirical summaries exploring the dyad as the basic unit. Assessed in this area are issues such as attraction and self-disclosure. Finally, we looked to meta-analyses that examined the interaction itself as the central issue. Topics in this section include sexual communication and conflict management.

These three approaches—individual, dyadic, and interactional—serve as the framework and context for the empirical summaries selected for this book. These meta-analyses are in no way intended as exhaustive coverage of the salient issues in interpersonal communication. We do, however, hope to frame key controversies and point to new avenues of inquiry.

INDIVIDUAL PROCESSES

Understanding how relationships form and evolve is central to theorizing about interpersonal communication. Perceptions of and attributions about one's own behaviors and the actions of others are vital to this understanding. Giles and Street (1994) suggested that examining communicator characteristics helps explicate the motives, behaviors, and utterances that occur during the earliest stages of relationship formation. The most frequently occurring topics in this domain of literature include people's perceptions of others, their self-esteem or self-presentation, their need for affiliation or affinity, and their communicative skills or abilities. The purpose of this preview is to briefly discuss each of these areas, contextualize the three meta-analyses in this domain, and briefly summarize the theoretical significance of the findings.

Perceptions

Researchers have long observed that the way we process and interpret sensory data or perceive causality is based on observations of an other's actions and interpretations of the other's motives for acting in a certain way (Laing, Phillipson, & Lee, 1966). For example, Bahk (1993) believed that both perceived liking and perceived understanding affect an individual's ability to initiate a long-term relationship. Drawing on Heider's (1958) reasoning, Bahk suggested that people assume they know or can speculate about others' intentions or motivations. Individuals constantly make inferences or attributions, even though they may be inaccurate or misleading (Kelley, 1973). This attributional approach posits that people try to ascertain the causes of behavior and assign meanings systematically in ways that affect their own thoughts and feelings (Harvey & Weary, 1985). Furthermore, attribution researchers hold that individuals may not make objective or rationale interpretations, and are likely to maintain their interpretations regardless of contrary evidence (Burleson, 1986; Fincham, 1985; Reeder, 1985). Wood (1999), for example, found that survivors of violence in intimate relationships tend to "disassociate the men they love from the (same) men who inflict violence on them" by claiming that "he was not himself" (p. 5). These attributions are similar to perceptions of people in nonviolent relationships who explain the disagreeable behavior of their partners. It appears that individuals use idiosyncratic standards when forming attributions that assign blame, intentions, or motivations.

Research also suggests that relationship initiation and maintenance involve perceptions and attributions about the partner's communication. Vangelisti (1994) found that less damage is done to a relationship if individuals perceive that "the speaker did not 'mean' to hurt their feelings" (p. 77). Similarly, Metts (1994) concluded that positive interpretations about the other's justification of a particular action mitigated relational damage. Sillars (1982) discovered that individuals assume that their reasons for acting or feeling are much like other people's perceptions and they settle on one causal explanation rather than consider multiple interpretations. There is also evidence that individuals may commit the fundamental attribution error as they assign personal blame for an event rather than consider other possibilities. Sillars (1982) and Canary and Spitzberg (1990) documented several attribution biases associated with relationship formation and maintenance. Sillars (1982) found that a self-serving bias may develop due to people's preference for denying responsibility for an unfortunate action or failing to acknowledge responsibility for happier events. Parks (1994) concluded that "when the individual attributes communicative failures to negative characteristics of self such as character defects or a lack of social skills," troubled emotions result, but "when the failure can be attributed to transitory or controllable causes" (p. 607), individual emotions are more positive and manageable. Sillars (1980) discovered that in conflicts, individuals are more likely to attribute negative behaviors to their partners and positive behaviors to themselves. Canary and Spitzberg (1990) discovered that individuals make general attributions about their partner's competence based on the positiveness of the partner. Apparently, individuals are reluctant to change their attributions once made, and they have trouble considering that more than one explanation is possible or that their own behavior maybe problematic.

Manusov's (1990) study extended attribution principles to nonverbal behavior. Like researchers who studied attribution based on verbal communication, she found that "those who are more satisfied tend to make relationship-enhancing attributions, whereas those who are less satisfied create distress-maintaining casual explanations" (p. 114) about nonverbal communication. Individuals seem to make attributions based on both verbal and nonverbal messages, and these perceptions are related to significant relational outcomes.

The meta-analyses in this section approach perceptions and attributions in a straightforward way. Sahlstein and Allen (chap. 4) discuss sex differences and self-esteem from the perspective of gendered communication practices and socialization. The notion that mediated portrayals of gender affect perceptions and alter causal attributions is consistent with current theorizing in interpersonal communication. Also, the multidimensional conceptualization of these self-attributions provides opportunities to explore widening differences in these perceptions. The Timmerman (chap. 5) meta-analysis on power in language extends this idea of gender and attribution directly to communication behaviors. At issue is the use of message features that lead to attributions of power. The complexity of these perceptions can be seen in the coding systems for behaviors such as interruptions, attributions produced by hedges and tag questions, and politeness inferences based on the use of hostile verbs, civilities, and threats. Spitzberg and Dillard's (chap. 6) meta-analysis on social skills takes a somewhat different approach by identifying behaviors that index the skillfulness of the communicator. Molecular behaviors such as gaze, response latency, and feedback responses were associated with molar perceptions of skill. All three meta-analyses are unique and suitable from the perspective of perceptions and attributions.

Self-Esteem or Self-Presentation

Self-esteem refers to the way individuals view themselves in terms of their overall worth. Rosenberg (1979) theorized that self-esteem reflects the positive or negative feelings that people hold about themselves. Josephs (1991) claimed that one's self-esteem is a balance of an individual's conceptualization of her or his own value plus her or his need to be accepted by others. Greenberg, Pyszczynski, and Solomon (1986) believed that our culture provides the parameters we use to judge our self-worth, and that individuals use their own culture's criteria to judge their own overall value. Thus, it appears that individuals bring their constructed conceptualization of their self-worth to a relationship and that perception is reinforced or refined during interactions with others.

The perception of self-esteem has been associated with specific communication behaviors. Those individuals who have high self-esteem have been characterized as appreciating their own worth, being flexible and relaxed, and being open to criticism (Braden, 1992; Simmons, 1987). Individuals with high self-esteem have been found to be less easily influenced and more positively evaluated by others (Infante, 1976). Tedeschi and Norman (1985) noted that individuals with high self-esteem are more convinced that their real self corresponds to their conceptualization of an ideal self. Individuals with low self-esteem, on the other hand, lack confidence in their own ability, evaluate their own competency negatively, and expect failures (Baumeister, 1993). Low-self-esteem individuals are easily persuaded (Preiss & Gayle, 2000), perhaps because they are more apt to follow respected others (Infante, 1976). Communication seems to be a vital component of self-esteem processes. For example, Menees (1997) found that children of alcoholic parents who expressed their anger and frustration had higher self-esteem. Finally, several researchers established a link between jealousy and low self-esteem. Highly jealous individuals appear to possess lower levels of self-esteem (Mathes, Adams, & Davis, 1985) and lower levels of self-worth may lead to jealousy (Bringle, 1981).

Self-esteem is often considered a subset of self-concept. Turner (1987) suggested that one's self-concept, how we define or think about our capabilities, is based on a set of cognitive representations that induce levels of social comparison. Nicotera (1993) theorized that the self-concept provides information and expectations about how the self relates to the environment, claiming that "self-concept as it is developed, presented, and validated defines the nature and type of interpersonal relationships" (pp. 8–9). Thus, our self-concept affects how we communicate and with whom we become involved. Furthermore, the self-concept reflects how people see themselves in others' responses to their own behaviors and communication.

Nicotera (1993) reasoned that the way an individual's self-concept is supported results in different types and levels of relationships. Swann and Predmore (1985) maintained that relational partners have a mutual investment in stabilizing and supporting each other's self-concept. This is consistent with Goffman's (1959) view that our self-concept is not only what we believe about ourselves, but a comprehensive self-presentation that allows individuals to reaffirm privately held conceptions and manage their impressions of others (Shaw & Edwards, 1997). Burgoon (1994) claimed that impression management behaviors are aimed at avoiding social disapproval and enhancing others' feelings and attributions so that those perceptions more closely correspond to our ideal identity. Because individuals recognize they have a highly visible public self, most individuals monitor their own behaviors or actions (Snyder, 1979). High self-monitors are aware of the impression they make and are concerned about the appropriateness of their verbal and nonverbal skills (Giles & Street, 1994). These individuals are better able to express emotional states, possess greater encoding skills, initiate conversations, and are highly sensitive to feedback (Rhodewalt, 1986).

Taken together, the research on self-esteem, self-concept, and self-presentation suggests that an individual's perceptions of self influence her or his communicative interactions. The meta-analyses in this section make unique and suitable contributions to this characteristic of the interpersonal communication literature. Sahlstein and Allen's (chap. 4) analysis offers the provocative conclusion that sex-based differences in self-esteem may be increasing over time. Timmerman's (chap. 5) finding of a small, consistent pattern of powerlessness markers across coding categories can be interpreted as having roots in self-esteem. In this view, language-induced submissiveness is the result of socialization and marginalization. Finally, Spitzberg and Dillard's (chap. 6) meta-analysis isolates communication behaviors that convey impressions of competence and composure, and these behaviors are frequently associated with high self-esteem.

Affiliation or Affinity

A fourth theme in the interpersonal communication literature involves affiliation. Individuals possess a need to associate with, and be accepted by, others as well as to garner their potential partner's approval (Baumeister & Leary, 1995; Giles & Street, 1994). Indvik and Fitzpatrick (1986) argued that "affiliation refers to the emotional closeness and a high degree of sharing private information" (p. 3). These authors conceptualized four defining characteristics of affiliation: acceptance, openness, caring, and empathy. They also delineated affiliation from inclusion by defining *inclusion* as "attracting attention and interest and being differentiated from others" (Indvik & Fitzpatrick, 1986, p. 2). They theorized that inclusion is made up of five separate components: accessibility, similarity, evaluation, stimulation, and relational potential.

Regardless of how the process of association is conceptualized, it appears that both these attributes (affiliation and inclusion) occur during the bonding process and result in affinity or liking. According to Bell and Daly (1984), this "process by which individuals attempt to get others to like and feel positive toward them" (p. 91) is termed *affinity seeking*. Daly and Kreissen (1993) believed that affinity seeking is an integrated concept that (a) is an active process, (b) is strategic by nature, (c) engages people in making choices, and (d) encourages the use of affinity strategies through communication. In essence, affinity-seeking strategies are employed early in the relationship-building phase to ascertain the prospective partner's interest in establishing a relationship.

Affinity-seeking researchers often distinguish between two types of strategies. Individuals use one set of strategies to induce affiliation or inclusion and another set of strategies to test for reciprocated affinity (Baxter & Wilmot, 1984; Daly & Kreissen, 1993). Seven global strategies have been identified that elicit affiliation or liking (Bell & Daly, 1984; Daly & Kreissen, 1993). The controlling visibility strategy occurs when individuals differentiate, appear attractive, and establish autonomy by assuming control or conveying the impression of being in control. Appearing trustworthy and open and adhering to politeness norms are two other strategies used when seeking affinity or affiliation. Individuals may also reveal concern and caring through listening and supporting the other's self confidence, involve the other person by maximizing positive interactions, and involve the self by expressing a desire for a relationship. Finally, affinity may be sought by emphasizing similarities and equality.

Individuals have been found to implement "secret tests" to determine if the desire to build a relationship is actually reciprocated (Baxter & Wilmot, 1984). These eight global strategies involve confronting or directly assessing whether the other is interested in maintaining the relationship, sustaining or taking action to keep the relationship progressing, or withdrawing to ascertain if the other will assume responsibility for maintaining the relationship. Strategies like hazing or making the potential partner perform tasks and services, offering or setting up favorable situations for a potential part-ner to encounter, or increasing intimacy levels are also used. Finally, individ-uals might network by engaging a third party to help with relationship initiation or by diminishing their own reputation in hopes the potential partner will rescue the individual. Douglas (1987) claimed that individuals choose strategies based on social appropriateness as well as efficiency.

Researchers have identified the effectiveness of some affinity-seeking strategies. Roach (1998) found that in the workplace, theory "y" managers were perceived as using more affinity-seeking strategies that increased em-ployees' organizational identification. Bachman and Zakahi (2000) found that secure love schemes or adult attachment styles were positively corre-lated with commonalities, mutual trust, and concern and caring, whereas a clingy love schema was correlated with caring and closeness. Martin and Rubin (1998) found that individuals who were more controlling employed a greater range of strategies when seeking affinity. They also discovered that individuals who used a more expressive communicator style reported being more interpersonally competent and possessing a large affinity-seeking rep-ertoire. They found liking was associated with the awareness that affin-ity-seeking strategies have been employed.

The affiliation and affinity-seeking research suggests that individuals have both conscious and unconscious motivations in trying to obtain oth-ers' regard. Individuals employ specific strategies to entice others to like them and "test" others to see if they are interested in pursuing a relationship. One meta-analysis directly addresses the affiliation thesis. Spitzberg and Dillard (chap. 6) identify the skill areas of altercentrism (showing interest in and concern for the other party), expressiveness, and composure. These competencies are essential aspects of strategic interaction. The meta-analy-sis by Timmerman (chap. 5) also offers intriguing opportunities for theory development related to affiliation. Powerful language may provide a vehicle for affinity seeking, but we also note that less assertive speech provides op-portunities for secret tests, subtle maneuvers, and vivid contrasts in lan-guage use based on situational needs.

Communicative Skills or Abilities

Whenever individuals communicate, they choose language that reflects their basic beliefs about others and themselves. Jacobs (1994) suggested that "lan-guage is systematically organized in a variety of ways beyond the units of words and sentences all of which contribute to the information conveyed and the actions performed by a message" (p. 200). In other words, individuals may use language strategically to affect perceptions and impressions and to attempt to exert control during interactions (Bradac, Wiemann, & Schaefer, 1994; Jacobs, 1994). When researchers explore the relation between perceptions of social power or control and an individual's language style, aspects of powerful or powerless speech are often investigated. According to Bradac and Mulac (1984), powerless speech involves the use of "hedges, hesitations, intensifiers, deictic phrases, tag questions or instances of rising intonation imposed upon declarative sentences, and polite forms" (p. 2). A meta-analytic review by Burrell and Koper (1998) revealed that a powerful language style was perceived as more credible. Timmerman (chap. 5) investigates the relation between sex differences and the use of powerful and powerless language and her results help clarify the relation among language style, communicator credibility, and sex differences.

Other researchers exploring the relation between social power or control and an individual's language style have explored "the way one verbally and paraverbally interact to signal how literal meaning should be interpreted, filtered or understood" (Norton, 1978, p. 99). These researchers explored an individual's communicator style, which Norton (1978) conceptualized as being multidimensional. Communicators may engage in impression leaving or creating a lasting image, be contentious or challenging during a disagreement, or become open or revealing of their feelings. A communicator may be dominant or take charge, be dramatic and tell colorful stories, or be precise and document points with evidence. The remaining dimensions involve the communicator appearing relaxed, friendly or encouraging, attentive, and animated. Researchers have found that positive elements of communicator style are related to patients' satisfaction with their physician (Cardello, Ray, & Pettey, 1995) and supervisors' use of positive and expressive humor has been associated with her or his communicator style (Martin & Gayle, 1999). These lines of research are consistent with Norton's (1983) view that communicator style is a collection of learned behaviors that shape the way an individual is perceived.

The collections of behaviors construed as a style may result in clear impressions of the communicator. For example, individuals may be evaluated by how well they are perceived "to seek out meaningful interactions with others, render support, be relaxed, appreciate other's plight, and turn take appropriately" (Query, Parryk, & Flint, 1992, p. 80). Here an individual's communicator style is equated with perceived effectiveness, accuracy, and the clarity with which she or he is able to adapt to the needs and behaviors of others in any given situation (Parks, 1994; Spitzberg, 1994). On this level, the impression created is one of competence, and the meta-analyses in this section provide insights about the communicator skills or abilities theme evident in the interpersonal communication literature. Spitzberg and Dillard (chap. 6) directly assess the molecular behaviors that are associated with perceptions of communication competence. The large effect size observed between talk time and perception of skill level in naturalistic settings underscores the importance of communicator characteristics. This perception may be reverberating across meta-analyses, as powerless speakers (see Timmerman, chap. 5) and low-self-esteem communicators (see Sahlstein & Allen, chap. 4) may talk less than their powerful and high-self-esteem counterparts. These issues are ripe for future primary investigations.

CONCLUSION

Each of the areas discussed in this preview is more interrelated than distinctive. Meta-analysis is a valuable tool because it can summarize issues that cut across domains of literature and unify disparate findings. Each of the constructs in this unit deals with individual-level processes in interpersonal communication. From the vantage of perceptions, self-esteem or self-presentation, affiliation, and communicator skills, the meta-analyses summarize enduring issues, offer surprising insights, and pose new questions for future investigations. The ability to summarize findings and point to new avenues of research is an important benefit of meta-analysis. It offers interpersonal communication researchers an additional tool for theory development.

REFERENCES

Bachman, G., & Zakahi, W. R. (2000). Adult attachment and strategic relational communication: Love schemas and affinity-seeking. *Communication Reports, 13,* 12–19.

Bahk, C. (1993). Interpersonal perceptions of same-sex and opposite-sex friendships in the United States and Korea. In A. M. Nicotera (Ed.), *Interpersonal communication in friend and mate relationships* (pp. 79–106). Albany: State University of New York Press.

Baumeister, R. F. (1993). *Self-esteem: The puzzle of low self-regard.* New York: Plenum.

Baumeister, R. F., & Leary, M. R. (1995). The need to belong: Desire for interpersonal attachments as a fundamental human motivation. *Psychological Bulletin, 117,* 497–529.

Baxter, L. A., & Wilmot, W. W. (1984). Secret tests: Social strategies for acquiring information about the state of the relationship. *Human Communication Research, 11,* 171–201.

Bell, R. A., & Daly, J. A. (1984). The affinity-seeking function of communication. *Communication Monographs, 51,* 91–115.

Bradac, J. J., & Mulac, A. (1984). Attributional consequences of powerful and powerless speech styles in a crisis-intervention context. *Journal of Language and Social Psychology, 3,* 1–19.

Bradac, J. J., Wiemann, J. M., & Schaefer, K. (1994). The language of control in interpersonal communication. In J. A. Daly & J. M. Wiemann (Eds.), *Strategic interpersonal communication* (pp. 91–108). Hillsdale, NJ: Lawrence Erlbaum Associates.

Braden, N. (1992). *The power of self-esteem*. New York: Health Communications.

Bringle, R. G. (1981). Conceptualizing jealousy as a disposition. *Alternative Lifestyles, 4,* 274–290.

Burgoon, J. (1994). Nonverbal signals. In M. L. Knapp & G. R. Miller (Eds.), *Handbook of interpersonal communication* (pp. 229–285). Thousands Oaks, CA: Sage.

Burleson, B. R. (1986). Attribution schemes and causal inference in natural conversations. In D. G. Ellis & W. A. Donohue (Eds.), *Contemporary issues in language and discourse processes* (pp. 63–85). Hillsdale, NJ: Lawrence Erlbaum Associates.

Burrell, N. A., & Koper, R. J. (1998). The efficacy of powerful/powerless language on attitudes and source credibility. In M. Allen & R. Preiss (Eds.), *Persuasion: Advances through meta-analysis* (pp. 203–216). Cresskill, NJ: Hampton.

Canary, D. J., & Spitzberg, B. H. (1990). Attribution biases and associations between conflict strategies. *Communication Monographs, 57,* 139–151.

Cardello, L. L., Ray, E. B., & Pettey, G. E. (1995). The relationship of perceived physician communicator style to patient satisfaction. *Communication Reports, 8,* 27–37.

Cooper, H. M., & Rosenthal, R. (1980). Statistical versus traditional procedures for summarizing research findings. *Review of Educational Research, 52,* 291–302.

Daly, J. A., & Kreissen, P. O. (1993). Affinity-seeking. In J. A. Daly & J. M. Wiemann (Eds.), *Strategic interpersonal communication* (pp. 109–134). Hillsdale, NJ: Lawrence Erlbaum Associates.

Douglas, W. (1987). Affinity-testing in initial interactions. *Journal of Social and Personal Relationships, 4,* 3–16.

Fincham, F. D. (1985). Attributions in close relationships. In J. H. Harvey & G. Weary (Eds.), *Attribution: Basic issues and applications* (pp. 203–234). New York: Academic.

Giles, H., & Street, R. L. (1994). Communicator characteristics and behavior. In M. L. Knapp & G. R. Miller (Eds.), *Handbook of interpersonal communication* (pp. 103–161). Thousands Oaks, CA: Sage.

Goffman, E. (1959). *Presentation of self in everyday life*. Garden City, NY: Doubleday/Anchor.

Greenberg, J., Pyszczynski, T., & Solomon, S. (1986). The causes and consequences of a need for self-esteem. In R. Baumeister (Ed.), *Public self and private self* (pp. 189–212). New York: Springer-Verlag.

Harvey, J. H., & Weary, G. (1985). *Attribution: Basic issues and applications*. New York: Academic.

Hattie, J. A., & Hansford, B. C. (1984). Meta-analysis: A reflection on problems. *Australian Journal of Psychology, 26,* 239–254.

Heider, F. (1958). *The psychology of interpersonal relations*. New York: Wiley.

Indvik, J., & Fitzpatrick, M. A. (1986). Perceptions of inclusion, affiliation, and control in five interpersonal relationships. *Communication Quarterly, 34,* 1–11.

Infante, D. A. (1976). Persuasion as a function of the receiver's prior success or failure as a message source. *Communication Quarterly, 24,* 21–26.

Jacobs, S. (1994). Language and interpersonal communication. In M. L. Knapp & G. R. Miller (Eds.), *Handbook of interpersonal communication* (pp. 199–228). Thousands Oaks, CA: Sage.

Josephs, L. (1991). Character structure, self-esteem regulation, and the principle of identity maintenance. In R. Curtis (Ed.), *The relational self* (pp. 199–228). New York: Guilford.

Kelley, H. (1973). The process of causal attribution. *American Psychologist, 28,* 107–128.

Laing, R. D., Phillipson, H., & Lee, A. R. (1966). *Interpersonal perception.* New York: Springer.

Manusov, V. (1990). An application of attribution principles to nonverbal behavior in romantic dyads. *Communication Monographs, 57,* 104–118.

Martin, D., & Gayle, B. M. (1999). It isn't a matter of just being funny: Humor production by organizational leaders. *Communication Research Reports, 16,* 72–80.

Martin, M. M., & Rubin, R. B. (1998). Affinity-seeking and initial interactions. *The Southern Communication Journal, 63,* 131–143.

Mathes, E. W., Adams, H. E., & Davis, R. M. (1985). Jealousy: Loss of relationship rewards, loss of self-esteem, depression, anxiety, and anger. *Journal of Personality and Social Psychology, 48,* 1552–1561.

Menees, M. M. (1997). The role of coping, social support, and family communication in explaining the self-esteem of adult children of alcoholics. *Communication Reports, 10,* 9–19.

Metts, S. (1994). Relational transgressions. In W. R. Cupach & B. H. Spitzberg (Eds.), *The dark side of interpersonal communication* (pp. 217–240). Hillsdale, NJ: Lawrence Erlbaum Associates.

Nicotera, A. M. (1993). The importance of communication in interpersonal relationships. In A. M. Nicotera (Ed.), *Interpersonal communication in friend and mate relationships* (pp. 3–12). Albany: State University of New York Press.

Norton, R. W. (1978). Foundation of the communicator style construct. *Human Communication Research, 4,* 99–112.

Norton, R. W. (1983). *Communicator style: Theory, applications, and measures.* Beverly Hills, CA: Sage.

Parks, M. R. (1994). Communication competence and interpersonal control. In M. L. Knapp & G. R. Miller (Eds.), *Handbook of interpersonal communication* (pp. 589–620). Thousands Oaks, CA: Sage.

Preiss, R. W., & Allen, M. (1995). Understanding and using meta-analysis. *Evaluation & The Health Professions, 18,* 315–335.

Preiss, R. W., & Gayle, B. M. (2000, November). *Self-esteem and persuasion: A meta-analysis of studies involving message exposure.* Paper presented at the meeting of the National Communication Association, Seattle, WA.

Query, J. L., Parry, D., & Flint, L. J. (1992). The relationship among social support, communication competence, and cognitive depression for nontraditional students. *Journal of Applied Communication Research, 20,* 78–94.

Reeder, G. D. (1985). Implicit relations between dispositions and behaviors: Effects on dispositional attribution. In J. H. Harvey & G. Weary (Eds.), *Attribution: Basic issues and applications* (pp. 87–116). New York: Academic.

Rhodewalt, F. T. (1986). Self-presentation and the phenomenal self: On the stability and malleability of self-conceptions. In R. F. Baumeister (Ed.), *Public self and private self* (pp. 117–142). New York: Springer-Verlag.

Roach, K. D. (1998). Management view, power use, and affinity-seeking effects on college student employee identification. *Communication Research Reports, 15,* 354–364.

Rosenberg, M. (1979). *Conceiving of self.* New York: Basic.

Shaw, C. M., & Edwards, R. (1997). Self-concepts and self-presentations of males and females: Similarities and differences. *Communication Reports, 10,* 55–62.

Sillars, A. L. (1980). Attributions and communication in roommate conflicts. *Communication Monographs, 47,* 180–200.

Sillars, A. L. (1982). Attributions and communication: Are people "naïve scientists" or just naïve? In M. E. Roloff & C. R. Berger (Eds.), *Social cognition and communication* (pp. 73–106). Newbury Park, CA: Sage.

Simmons, R. G. (1987). Self-esteem in adolescence. In T. Honess & K. Yardley (Eds.), *Self and identity: Perspectives across lifespan* (pp. 172–192), New York: Routledge & Kegan Paul.

Snyder, M. (1979). Self-monitoring processes. In L. Berkowitz (Ed.), *Advances in experimental social psychology* (Vol. 12, pp. 85–128). New York: Academic.

Spitzberg, B. H. (1994). The dark side of incompetence. In W. R. Cupach & B. H. Spitzberg (Eds.), *The dark side of interpersonal communication* (pp. 25–50). Hillsdale, NJ: Lawrence Erlbaum Associates.

Swann, W. B., & Predmore, S. C. (1985). Intimates as agents of social support: Sources of consolation or despair? *Journal of Personality and Social Psychology, 49,* 1609–1617.

Tedeschi, J. T., & Norman, N. (1985). Social power, self presentation, and the self. In B. R. Schlenker (Ed.), *Self and identity* (pp. 293–322). New York: McGraw-Hill.

Turner, J. C. (1987). *Rediscovering the social group.* Oxford, UK: Blackwell.

Vangelisti, A. L. (1994). Messages that hurt. In W. R. Cupach & B. H. Spitzberg (Eds.), *The dark side of interpersonal communication* (pp. 53–82). Hillsdale, NJ: Lawrence Erlbaum Associates.

Wood, J. T. (1999). "That wasn't really him": Women's disassociation of violence from the men who enacted it. *Qualitative Research Reports in Communication, 1,* 1–7.

4

Sex Differences in Self-Esteem: A Meta-Analytic Assessment

Erin Sahlstein and Mike Allen

Communication is extremely important in the formation of one's sense of self. Our interactions with others and our exposure to culture and media inform and influence how we see ourselves. Nevertheless, we do not all have the same experience with the world and the people with whom we interact. Thus, our sense of self develops differently.

A prevalent and controversial topic of study today is how sense of self, or self-esteem, differs for males and females. How these differences are constructed and to what degree these differences exist are central questions that merit inquiry. The current research examining different levels of self-esteem has produced inconsistent results. This meta-analysis was conducted to aggregate the empirical outcomes of investigations examining sex differences in self-esteem.

LITERATURE REVIEW

Several definitions for self-esteem have been posited in the literature, but all have similar characteristics. Rosenberg (1972) defined self-esteem as a feeling of self-worth and fundamental respect for oneself. He characterized low self-esteem as a lack of respect for oneself and feelings of unworthiness, inadequacies, and deficiencies. Coopersmith (1967) referred to self-esteem as "the evaluation, which the individual makes and customarily maintains with regard to himself: it expresses an attitude of approval or disapproval, and indicates the extent to which the individual believes himself to be capable, significant, successful, and worthy" (p. 4). In general, these authors conclude that self-esteem represents a positive or negative personal evaluation of oneself.

The empirical literature examining the relation between self-esteem and sex differences generates controversial and often inconsistent conclusions. Despite the numerous studies on this subject, no definitive conclusion exists. Some studies report that males have significantly higher self-evaluations than females (e.g., Alpert-Gillis & Connell, 1989; Bohan, 1973; Dukes & Martinez, 1994; Richman, Clark, & Brown, 1985). Backes (1994) claimed: "Research indicates young adolescent females' self-concept is much lower than that of their male peers" (p. 19). In 1991, the American Association of University Women conducted a study of 3,000 adolescents ranging in ages from 9 to 15 and found a considerable gap in male and female self-esteem that widened as children grew older (Sadker & Sadker, 1994). Eccles et al. (1989) reported in a study of early adolescents that male self-esteem scores were higher than female scores.

Several other studies report no significant differences between male and female self-esteem (e.g., Alawyie & Alawyie, 1988; Lerner, Sorell, & Brackney, 1981; Maccoby & Jacklin, 1974; Mullis, Mullis, & Normandin, 1992; Osborne & LeGette, 1982; Williams & McGee, 1991). Maccoby and Jacklin (1974) reviewed several studies examining gender differences and concluded that males and females rate their overall self-images equally positive or negative. Research by Lerner et al. (1981) found results "consistent with empirical generalizations drawn from the sex differences literature from Maccoby and Jacklin" (p. 719).

Some other studies report female self-esteem as greater than male self-esteem (e.g., Cienki & Brooks, 1989; Kohr, Coldiron, Skiffington, Masters, & Blust, 1988; Spence, Helmreich, & Stapp, 1975; Whiteside, 1976). These results are quite controversial because they violate the expectation that females have lower self-esteem than males. Because the literature on self-esteem and sex differences provides inconsistent results, a more definitive conclusion would benefit future theory and research.

For some scholars, self-esteem represents a multidimensional construct including cognitive, social, and physical appearance dimensions that combine to create an overall or comprehensive self-evaluation. Richman et al. (1985) suggested that self-esteem constitutes a general feeling of self-worth constructed by the compilation of various area-specific feelings of self-worth. Women and men may evaluate each dimension differently, causing sex differences in subscales of self-esteem (Jackson, Hodge, & Ingram, 1994). Some research efforts find differences between the sexes on subscales of self-esteem (Chambliss, Muller, Hulnick, & Wood, 1978; Ezeilo, 1983; Osborne & LeGette, 1982; Richman et al., 1985; Ryan & Morrow, 1986), whereas others have found no significant differences (Alawyie & Alawyie, 1988; Klein, 1992). Jackson et al. (1994) argued that "a number of researchers have suggested that women and men draw from different domains of self-perceived strength to arrive at overall self-evaluation" (p. 616). A multidimensional conceptualization of self-esteem may explain why general self-esteem levels may be similar for males and females but different on various subdomains measuring self-esteem (i.e., physical appearance, communication skills, and academic achievement). The differences in domains may be the consequence of gender stereotypes in our culture and the different socialization processes for men and women.

Self-esteem is a product of communicating with other people and is constructed through interactions with others. Two possible reasons for sex differences in self-esteem may be the differential communication practices used by males versus females and the socialization of "men's talk" versus "women's talk." The first reason emerges from the possible differences in the messages sent to males and females and how these messages reflect different self-esteem levels. Sadker and Sadker (1994) claimed that the educational system in the United States is failing girls and causing lower levels of self-esteem. The different ways women and men are spoken to and treated may affect the construction of male and female self-esteem.

Self-esteem may also be explained by sex differences in communication. Women and men are socialized to communicate differently according to some scholars (Lakoff, 1975). Men are taught to be assertive, authoritative, and certain in their speech, whereas females are taught to be tentative, responsive, and inclusive in their speech. Men's speech is more powerful and women's speech is viewed as powerless. By definition, male and female types of speech help reinforce differences in confidence and esteem regarding how one communicates and what is being communicated. If men and women are taught to speak differently and these differences also help construct different images of the self, then this may be one area where the origins of self-esteem differences exist. For example, Grob and Allen (1995) found gender differences in a meta-analysis on the use of powerful and powerless language. Males used more powerful speech than females. Perhaps females used less powerful language as an indication of their level of self-esteem, and males, who may feel more confident in themselves overall, utilized more powerful language. Females may be socialized to speak in powerless ways, but the standard for confidence and authority is recognized by using powerful speech. Thus, women may find themselves in a confusing position where their self-esteem can be detrimentally affected. If females feel less confident in their physical appearance, cognitive ability, or social skill, then these feelings will be reflected in their communication with others.

Another major source of cultural and gender socialization takes place in the classroom (Wood, 1994). School is where children learn what is right and wrong, good and bad, and worthy and worthless. Wood (1994) argued that "The longer males attend school, the higher their self-esteem, achievement, and ambition; the longer females attend school, the lower their self-esteem and aspiration" (p. 248). Some scholars propose that the U.S. educational system has a hidden curriculum (Lee & Gropper, 1974) that favors males over females in various areas leading to gender stereotype reinforcement and lower self-esteem levels in women. The representation of women in higher education and positions of authority is low. The curriculum in our school system appears to be male biased, underrepresenting women and their part in history. Most important, our teachers are treating our children differently based on their sex. All three of these areas of the hidden curriculum are said to destroy female self-esteem and boost male self-perceptions. Sadker and Sadker (1994), in their book *Failing at Fairness: How America's Schools Cheat Girls*, argued that males have higher cognitive, social, and physical self-esteem because of our educational system. They argued females are treated differently in school and that the women of tomorrow cannot "afford" to be stripped of opportunities. Thus, differences in male and female self-esteem are presented as the outcome of unfair treatment in our school systems and society.

The mass media also affect gender socialization and stereotyping. The media have been blamed for decreasing female self-esteem, most notably in the domain of physical appearance. Attractiveness is central to female self-esteem, and the media play an integral part in constructing this emphasis. Women are barraged by messages valuing youth and beauty. Media's messages make women feel inferior to men and that their worthiness stems from their appearance (Wolf, 1991). Over their life span, females are constantly receiving messages about their looks that may have adverse effects on their self-esteem. Feelings of attractiveness, vital to female self-esteem, diminish drastically as girls reach adolescence and go on through high school (Sadker & Sadker, 1994). Decreasing female self-esteem may be an outcome of the constant bombardment of stereotypical sex-role portrayals on television (Herrett-Skjellum & Allen, 1995). Herrett-Skjellum and Allen's (1995) meta-analysis demonstrates that the majority of television content serves to reinforce traditional gender-role stereotypes. The propagation of the typical female submissive role in our society may influence young (and old) female viewers in causing them to feel cognitively inferior to males. Also, the media's physical portrayals of women are often idealistic and do not give women attainable role models (Wood, 1994). If the media indeed influences females in this way, one would expect lower female self-esteem, most notably on the dimension of physical attractiveness. The multiple facets of self-esteem may account for the inconsistency of results in various studies. If this body of research emphasizes different aspects of self-esteem, it is likely the findings would be varied and inconclusive.

If self-esteem differences between the sexes exist, then communication researchers should investigate how different messages can construct different levels of self-esteem in males and females. The need for a meta-analysis considering the relation between sex and self-esteem is extremely important considering the significant implications of the issue. The results of subsequent empirical studies on self-esteem and sex differences would merely replicate the existing varied conclusions; therefore, a meta-analysis is warranted. This review aggregates the available data to assess the overall relation between sex and level of self-esteem.

META-ANALYSIS TO EXAMINE SEX DIFFERENCES

Examining past research generates contradictory and inconsistent conclusions about whether males or females have higher self-esteem. Current, as well as past research, provides one of three conclusions: (a) There are no sex differences in self-esteem, (b) males have higher self-esteem, or (c) females have higher self-esteem. More studies comparing sex differences and self-esteem would add to the confusion and not resolve the inconsistency in findings. In this chapter, we examine the available research to locate an overall pattern to the sex difference and self-esteem question by using the technique of meta-analysis.

Literature Review Description

A computer search using a CD-ROM version of PSYCHLit, (from inception to June 1995) and ERIC (1966–June 1995) was conducted using the keywords *self-esteem, self-concept, gender,* and *sex.* The reference sections of each manuscript were also reviewed for relevant citations. The process gathered over 100 studies that were examined for relevancy in this report.

Manuscripts included in this meta-analysis met the following conditions: (a) The manuscript had to include a measurement of self-esteem or self-concept (a measurement was included if the measurement measured individuals' self-worth or feelings about the self); (b) the authors must have made a sex comparison between males and females on their levels of self-esteem; and (c) the authors must have provided sufficient statistical information to calculate the effect size of the sex difference.

Coding of Manuscripts

Each study was coded according to relevant information contained in the manuscript. Five codes were imposed on each study: (a) date of the study, (b) mean age of the sample, (c) race of the sample, (d) the measure(s) used to evaluate level of self-esteem, and (e) whether the measure was an overall effect or a subscale measurement. There were 20 different scales used across the 65 studies, some that reported effects for subscales of the measure. The subscales included in this analysis comprised three domains: cognitive, social, and physical appearance. If more subscales were reported, they were collapsed into one of the three main domains of the self-esteem. Table 4.1 is a summary of the studies contained in this report.[1]

RESULTS

The overall analysis included 124 cases with a sample of 379,217 and displays an average negative correlation ($r = -.009$) between males' and females' self-esteem, females having higher overall self-esteem. The effect however is heterogeneous, $\chi^2(123) = 1071.82, p < .05$.

Heterogeneity indicates the possibility of moderator variables that need further investigation. Subsequent analysis considering the date of the study showed a positive correlation ($r = .191$) for males. Therefore as the studies became more recent, male self-esteem was greater than female self-esteem.

Measures of Self-Esteem

The measures of comprehensive, cognitive, social, and physical appearance self-esteem were individually averaged for an overall effect. The comprehensive measure of self-esteem included the effects created by averaging across multiple scales and did not include subscale effects for cognitive, so-

---

[1]The studies used in this meta-analysis and the research that did not meet our criteria are not cited here due to space limitations. Anyone who wishes to obtain the complete references for this analysis may contact the Erin Sahlstein.

TABLE 4.1
Summary of Studies Included in Analysis

Author	Date	Overall Effect	Measures
Agrawal	1978	−.107	T
Alawyie	1985	.000	T, C, S, P
Allgood-Merton	1991	.169	T
Alpert-Gillis	1989	.200	T
Backes	1992	.085	T, C, S, P
Berrenberg	1989	.013	S
Bledsoe I	1961	−.013	T, P
Bledsoe II	1964	−.290	T
Bowler	1986	.106	T
Brack	1988	.281	T
Brenner	1992	.288	T
Brookover	1962	−.070	T
Butts	1963	.156	T
Calhoun	1986	.031	T
Campbell	1986	.000	T
Carlson I	1984	.000	T
Carlson II	1984	.000	T
Cate	1986	.066	T, C, S, P
Chambliss	1978	−.012	T, C, S, P
Cheung	1985	.000	T
Chiu	1990	.011	T
Cienki	1989	.009	T
Clark	1979	−.044	T
Coopersmith (Exp. 1)	1967	−.078	T
Coopersmith (Exp. 2)	1967	−.090	T
Dukes	1989	.103	T, S
Eccles	1989	.052	T
Edwins	1980	.159	T, C, S, P
Ezeilo	1983	.025	T, C, S, P
Feather	1985	.127	T
Flaherty	1980	.033	T, C, S
Fleming	1980	−.040	S
Gadzella	1984	−.430	T, C, S, P
Goldschmid	1968	.000	T
Gove	1975	.077	T
Hall	1979	.053	T
Heatherton	1991	.014	T, S, P

continued on next page

TABLE 4.1 (*continued*)

Author	Date	Overall Effect	Measures
Helmrich	1974	−.026	T
Hensley	1977	.050	T
Herbert	1969	.255	T
Hernandez	1984	−.292	T
Hong	1993	.078	T
Jackson (Exp. 1)	1994	.063	T, C, S, P
Jackson (Exp. 2)	1994	.137	T, C, S, P
Jones	1996	.257	T
Jong-Gierveld	1987	.100	T
Josephs (Exp. 1)	1992	.248	T
Josephs (Exp. 2)	1992	.142	T
Juhasz	1985	.071	T
Kahle	1976	.113	T, S
King	1981	−.135	T, P
Klein	1992	.000	T, P
Kohr	1984	−.026	C
L'Abate	1960	.126	T, C, S
Lamke	1982	.102	T
Lau	1989	.096	T, C, S, P
Lekarczyk	1969	−.105	T
Lerner	1977	.038	T
Long	1967	.102	T
Lortie-Lussier	1992	.000	T
Marron	1984	.164	T
Marsh (Exp. 1)	1981–87	.103	T, C, S, P
Marsh (Exp. 2)		.109	T, C, S, P
Marsh (Exp. 3)		.109	T, C, S, P
Marsh (Exp. 4)	1985	.041	T
Marsh (Exp. 5)	1991	.063	T
Marsh (Exp. 6)	1991	.000	T
Martinez	1987	−.011	T
Mintz	1986	.302	S
Mullis	1992	−.030	T
Nottelmann (Exp. 1)	1987	.152	T, C, S, P
Nottelmann (Exp. 2)	1987	.082	T, C, S, P
Nottelmann (Exp. 3)	1987	.119	T, C, S, P
O'Malley	1979	.044	T
Orlofsky I	1977	.063	T, C, S, P
Orlofsky II	1987	.131	T, C, S
Osborne	1982	.020	T, C, S, P

Author	Date	Overall Effect	Measures
Payne	1987	−.003	T
Pennebaker	1990	120.	T
Piers I	1964	−.029	T
Piers II	1977	.000	T
Prescott	1976	.032	P
Puglisi	1981	.056	T
Reynolds	1988	.000	T
Rice	1984	.055	T
Richman	1985	.030	T, C, S, P
Rosenberg	1975	.085	T
Rowlison	1988	−.060	T
Ryan	1986	.117	T, C, S, P
Ryff	1989	.102	T
Sethi	1986	.004	T
Simmons (Exp. 1)	1973	.160	T
Simmons (Exp. 2)	1976	.220	T
Simon	1975	.050	T
Spence	1975	−.049	T
Stein	1992	.117	T
Stoner	1978	.204	T, C, S, P
Tennen	1987	.000	T, S
Turner	1982	−.026	T, S
Watson	1987	.108	T
Whiteside	1976	−.150	T, S
Williams	1988	.037	T
Williams-Burns	1976	.092	T, C, S
Zeldow	1985	.052	T
Zuckerman I	1980	.000	T, C, P
Zuckerman II	1989	.000	T, C, S

T = total measure; S = social measure; C = cognitive measure; P = physical appearance measure.

cial, and physical domains. The comprehensive analysis included 64 cases ($N = 325,795$). The effect was negative, with females having higher self-esteem ($r = -.021$). The effect was significant, $\chi^2(63) = 2045.41$, $p < .05$. Analyses using date of study were performed. A positive correlation ($r = .051$) revealed males had higher self-esteem. As the studies became more recent, the gap between male and female self-esteem grew larger.

The cognitive subscale, which had 32 studies and a sample of 310,365 had an overall average negative effect ($r = -.026$) for females. The effect was heterogeneous, $\chi^2(31) = 186.63$, $p < .05$. Date of study was tested as a moderator variable and a positive correlation ($r = .095$) showed males had higher cognitive self-esteem as the studies became more recent.

Further analyses were conducted on the cognitive subscale without one large sample size's effect taken into account (Kohr et al., 1988). The study's sample ($N = 293,031$) was so large its effect was overpowering the results of the analysis. Without the large study, the overall effect was positive ($r = .024$) for males for the 31 studies included ($n = 17,334$). The chi-square was significant, $\chi^2(30) = 140.52$, $p < .05$. Not including the large study did not make a homogeneous sample. However, without the study by Kohr et al. (1988) dominating the analysis of the cognitive domain, the effect size was slightly positive for males, but the correlation was almost zero.

Analysis of the social self-esteem subscale was performed on 51 studies with a sample size of 39,487. The overall effect was positive for males ($r = .028$). The chi-square, $\chi^2(50) = 192.82$, $p < .05$, was significant and revealed heterogeneity across these samples. The possibility of moderator variables exists in this measurement of social self-esteem. Thus, analysis for date of study was performed and a slightly more positive correlation was revealed ($r = .117$).

Analyses were conducted on the third subscale, physical appearance. Twenty-eight studies with a sample size of 15,399 produced a positive effect ($r = .202$) displaying that males have higher self-esteem for their physical appearance than females. The chi-square, $\chi^2(27) = 110.83$, $p < .05$, was significant, indicating the possible presence of a moderating variable. Analysis correlating with the date of the study revealed a slightly higher positive correlation ($r = .310$). Males increased in self-esteem over females across time.

A second set of analyses was performed with respect to participant race and sex. Forty-two studies contained only White participants ($n = 20,762$). The correlation was slightly positive ($r = .057$) for males. However, the chi-square of 278.40 was significant ($p < .05$). Seventeen studies with Black participants were also analyzed ($n = 5,975$). A positive correlation ($r = .088$) was found with a nonsignificant chi-square of 16.95 ($p > .05$); thus the effect was homogeneous. Finally, analyses were performed on Native American participants ($n = 1,277$). There was a slightly positive correlation ($r = .043$), and the chi-square was nonsignificant, $\chi^2(8) = 38.55$, $p > .05$.

Age of the participant was also taken into consideration and tested. The mean age of the participants across all studies was 13.0 years. A positive correlation ($r = .316$) was found as participants aged. Therefore, as males and females get older, the gap between their levels of self-esteem widens. One possible explanation is that as females get older, they become more concerned with their looks and social status; therefore, their level of self-esteem may decrease as males' self-esteem increases with age. However, the correlation is only moderate.

DISCUSSION

The results reinforce some theoretical perspectives and stereotypical assumptions about gender differences in self-esteem. Each of the five analyses performed on the available data was consistent with the possible explanations presented by previous authors. The review of the existing literature indicated equivocal results among various studies. The main explanation for the mixed results may be the presence of a multifaceted self-esteem. Males and females differ in their levels of the specific spheres of self-esteem.

The overall effect showed females having slightly higher self-esteem than males. However, the effect was close to zero and indicated the possibility of intervening variables. Further analysis revealed that the date of the study might be one of the moderating variables. The more recently completed research studies demonstrated a larger effect, with male self-esteem being greater than female self-esteem. Moreover, other moderating variables should be expected if self-esteem is a multifaceted construct. The latter point was supported by the subsequent subanalyses.

The analyses performed on the comprehensive measures showed that females have higher self-esteem than males, but moderator variables were detected. Heterogeneity would be expected if one agrees that males and females differ in their cognitive, social, and physical appearance evaluations. After testing for the date-of-the-study moderator, the correlation became positive and males had higher self-esteem. If the overall measures tap all of the facets of self-esteem, one would expect males to score higher on cognitive and physical appearance self-esteem levels. Females would be expected to score higher on social self-esteem. The effects presented here do not support this line of reasoning.

The subscale analyses reflected sex differences in the three domains of self-esteem. Females were found to have higher cognitive self-esteem, whereas males had higher social and physical self-esteem. Some researchers argued that females receive unfair academic treatment and should have lower cognitive self-esteem; nevertheless, the empirical findings have been inconsistent (Jackson et al., 1994). Part of the reason for the inconsistent findings might be that cognitive self-esteem may be multifaceted, with subdomains of different academic subject areas.

Education may be failing females in the classroom as some researchers have argued, but the effect presented here did not reflect male domination. If schools serve the interests of some groups at the expense of others, there must be an exploration into how educators perpetuate or influence current social status differences and stereotypes (Sprague, 1992). This analysis did not support a male-dominated sex difference. Nevertheless, after excluding the effect of one extremely large study ($n = 293{,}031$), the effect became homogeneous and positive, with males having higher self-esteem. The correlation was small ($r = .024$) and therefore needs to be assessed with caution. After testing for date of the study, males seemed to show higher levels of cognitive self-esteem, and over the years the gap has widened. Our educational system may be having an effect by increasingly reinforcing male actions and ways of being over female behavior.

Males report slightly higher social self-esteem than females. This sex difference was inconsistent with the stereotypical view that women are more relationship oriented and socially competent. However, the existence of possible moderators was detected in the significant chi-square. Further analysis for date of study revealed an even larger positive correlation, with males having higher self-esteem.

The physical attractiveness domain displayed the predicted positive effect—males had higher self-esteem. With respect to study date, the effect became more positive. Therefore, male physical self-esteem has increased with respect to female physical self-esteem over the years. Other possible moderators could be influencing the results. These differences can be attributed to the socialization of females in our society. Although the effect was not extremely large, the difference between the two sexes is evident. Women do feel less confident with their physical image.

The media may be one of the largest influences on female self-esteem by perpetuating sex-role stereotypes. As implied by Herrett-Skjellum and Allen's (1995) meta-analysis of television, when females increase their levels of media intake and thus their exposure to gender stereotypes, female self-esteem decreases. Female role models on television and in movies place unfair expectations on women in our society. Males are exposed to a wide variety of role models and are given more range in what is considered an acceptable physical appearance, whereas women are bombarded with images of supermodels and *Baywatch* babes as samples of attractiveness in our society. The only real female examples on television are Oprah Winfrey, and Rosie O'Donnell, and even they have gone to great lengths to alter their appearances. The effects of media exposure on self-esteem need to be explored further.

These meta-analysis results are consistent with the conceptualization of self-esteem as multidimensional. By separating self-esteem research into three areas, it is clear men and women rate themselves differently. The conceptualization of a multifaceted self-esteem accounts for inconsistencies in results across studies. Additionally, the choice of measure may cause males or females to rate themselves higher or lower, depending on the scale's assessment (i.e., cognitive, social, or physical appearance).

These results do not provide answers or overwhelming support for future research on general sex differences; however, scholarship that leads to an increased understanding of how sex differences in cognitive, social, and physical self-esteem specifically form is in order. Although overall the data reported do not point to large differences between male and female self-esteem levels, experientially these differences can have important implications for the mental and physical health of individuals. Scholars in this discipline should give their increased attention to how communication is vital to the differentiated self-evaluation processes of males and females. Communication, in its varied forms, is how we come to know ourselves as well as others. Through processes of communication individuals (re)construct their self esteem through everyday talk and in their exposure to media. As Communication scholars we should be asking more questions concerning the role of communication in the process of constructing sex differences in specific self-evaluations (i.e., cognitively, socially, and physically). In the words of Sadker and Sadker (1994), "We believe that understanding these crucial issues will enable people to work for change" (p. xi).

REFERENCES

Alawyie, O., & Alawyie, C. Z. (1988). Self-concept development of Ghanaian school children. *Journal of Psychology, 122*, 139–145.

Alpert-Gillis, L. J., & Connell, J. P. (1989). Gender and sex-role influences on children's self-esteem. *Journal of Personality, 57*, 97–114.

Backes, J. (1994). Bridging the gender gap: Self-concept in the middle grades. *Schools in the Middle, 3*, 19–23.

Bohan, J. S. (1973). Age and sex differences in self-concept. *Adolescence, 8*, 379–384.

Chambliss, J., Muller, D., Hulnick, R., & Wood, M. (1978). Relationships between self-concept, self-esteem, popularity, and social judgments of junior high school students. *Journal of Psychology, 98*, 91–98.

Cienki, S. J., & Brooks, C. I. (1989). Self-esteem of high school students as a function of sex, grade, and curriculum orientation. *Psychological Reports, 64*, 191–194.

Coopersmith, S. A. (1967). *The antecedents of self-esteem*. San Francisco: Freeman.

Dukes, R. L., & Martinez, R. (1994). The impact of gender on self-esteem among adolescents. *Adolescence, 29*, 105–115.

Eagly, A. (1995). The science and politics of comparing women and men. *American Psychologist, 50*, 145–158.

Eccles, J. S., Wigfield, A., Flanagan, C. A., Miller, C., Reuman, D. A., & Yee, D. (1989). Self-concepts, domain values, and self-esteem: Relations and changes at early adolescence. *Journal of Personality, 57*, 283–310.

Ezeilo, B. N. (1983). Sex and urban–rural differences in self-concepts among Nigerian adolescents. *Journal of Psychology, 114,* 57–61.

Grob, L., & Allen, M. (1995, April). *Gender differences in powerful and powerless language: A meta-analytical review.* Paper presented at the annual meeting of the Central States Communication Association, St. Paul, MN.

Herrett-Skjellum, J., & Allen, M. (1995). *Television programming and sex stereotyping: A meta-analysis.* Manuscript submitted for publication.

Jackson, L. A., Hodge, C. N., & Ingram, J. M. (1994). Gender and self-concept: A reexamination of stereotypic differences and the role of gender attitudes. *Sex Roles, 30,* 615–630.

Klein, H. A. (1992). Temperament and self-esteem in late adolescence. *Adolescence, 27,* 689–694.

Kohr, R. L., Coldiron, R., Skiffington, E. W., Masters, J. R., & Blust, R. S. (1988). The influence of race, class, and gender on self-esteem for fifth, eighth, and eleventh grade students in Pennsylvania schools. *Journal of Negro Education, 57,* 467–481.

Lakoff, R. (1975). *Language and women's place.* New York: HarperCollins.

Lee, P. C., & Gropper, N. B. (1974). Sex-role culture and educational practice. *Harvard Educational Review, 44,* 369–407.

Lerner, R. M., Sorell, G. T., & Brackney, B. E. (1981). Sex differences in self-concept and self-esteem of late adolescents: A time-lag analysis. *Sex Roles, 7,* 709–722.

Maccoby, E. E., & Jacklin, C. N. (1974). *The psychology of sex differences.* Stanford, CA: Stanford University Press.

Mullis, A. K., Mullis, R. L., & Normandin, D. (1992). Cross-sectional and longitudinal comparisons of adolescent self-esteem. *Adolescence, 27,* 51–61.

Osborne, W. L., & LeGette, H. R. (1982). Sex, grade level, and social class differences in self-concept. *Measurement and Evaluation in Guidance, 14,* 195–201.

Richman, C. L., Clark, M. L., & Brown, K. P. (1985). General and specific self-esteem in late adolescent students: Race X gender X SES effects. *Adolescence, 20,* 555–556.

Rosenberg, M. (1972). *Society and the adolescent self-image.* Princeton, NJ: Princeton University Press.

Ryan, C. M., & Morrow, L. A. (1986). Self-esteem in diabetic adolescents: Relationship between age at onset and gender. *Journal of Consulting and Clinical Psychology, 54,* 730–731.

Sadker, M., & Sadker, D. (1994). *Failing at fairness: How America's schools cheat girls.* New York: Simon & Schuster.

Spence, J. T., Helmreich, R., & Stapp, J. (1975). Ratings of self and peers on sex-role attributes and their relationship to self-esteem and conceptions of masculinity and femininity. *Journal of Personality and Social Psychology, 32,* 29–39.

Sprague, J. (1992). Expanding the research agenda for instructional communication: Raising some unasked questions. *Communication Education, 41,* 1–25.

Whiteside, M. (1976). Age and sex differences in self-perception as related to ideal trait selections. *Adolescence, 11,* 585–592.

Williams, S., & McGee, R. (1991). Adolescents' perceptions of their strengths. *Journal of Youth and Adolescence, 20,* 325–337.

Wolf, N. (1991). *The beauty myth.* New York: Morrow.

Wood, J. T. (1994). *Gendered lives: Communication, gender and culture* (2nd ed.). Belmont, CA: Wadsworth.

5

Comparing the Production of Power in Language on the Basis of Sex

Lindsay M. Timmerman

In recent years the general public has developed a fascination with sex differences in communication. The extremely widespread popularity of Gray's (1992) book, *Men Are From Mars, Women Are From Venus*, is evidence of this interest. Gray has since developed seminars, produced daily calendars, and written several bestselling books further elaborating on the subject. Gray's main contention is that men and women are from different planets, and therefore speak totally different languages. His books purport to decode those languages for the opposite sex to enhance relational communication. Gray is the most popular writer on sex differences in language production, it is true, but it should be noted that more academic authors have also investigated this topic.

Deborah Tannen is a linguistics professor, and cites scholarly research in her books, but has achieved popular acclaim as well. Tannen's (1990) book, *You Just Don't Understand: Women and Men in Conversation*, was a slightly more academic slant on the same idea, that men and women come from different worlds. She followed up with *Talking From 9 to 5* (Tannen, 1994), which examined sex differences in communication at work. Both books were bestsellers. Although popular interest is recent, scholarly interest in the sex differences in language production is rooted in long-standing research, beginning with the work of Lakoff 25 years ago, and leading up to the efforts of Canary and Dindia (1998) and Hopper (1998) today.

LITERATURE REVIEW

Lakoff's two papers, *Language and Woman's Place* (1975a, 1975b) served as the catalyst for a substantial literature about men's and women's use of powerful and powerless language. Lakoff (1975a) claimed that "women experience linguistic discrimination in two ways: in the way they are taught to use language, and in the way general language use treats them" (p. 46). Lakoff's (1975a) hypothesis is that there are specific features that characterize women's speech, and that this language style actually keeps women in submissive positions and men in dominant roles. O'Barr (1982) also addressed this concern: "The tendency for more women to speak powerless language and for men to speak it less is due, at least in part, to the greater tendency of women to occupy relatively powerless social positions" (pp. 70–71). Whereas Lakoff (1975a, 1975b) identified women speaking a different language, O'Barr (1982) and his colleagues argued that individuals in lower status roles tend to use powerless language. In other words, the argument changes, as Lakoff (1975a) viewed women using primarily powerless features, whereas O'Barr concluded that both males and females would use powerless language in low-status roles (e.g., a janitor vs. a doctor).

Lakoff's (1975a, 1975b) work employs qualitative methodology, relying mostly on introspection. As she explained:

> I have examined my own speech and that of my acquaintances, and have used my own intuitions in analyzing it. I have also made use of the media: in some ways, the speech heard, e.g., in commercials or situation comedies on television mirrors the speech of the television-watching community. (Lakoff, 1975a, p. 46)

Lakoff (1975a) observed several differences between men's and women's speech, including: (a) vocabulary items (i.e., women have a greater repertoire of colors and use less harsh swear words), (b) empty adjectives (i.e., women use more words like *adorable, charming,* and *divine*), (c) question forms (i.e., women use tag questions and imperatives in question form, whereas men use declaratives), (d) polite forms (i.e., women say *please* and *thank you* more often than men), (e) hedges or forms of uncertainty (i.e., women use many phrases like *I guess, kinda,* and *I think*), (f) intensives (i.e., women use *really, so,* and *very* more frequently than men), and (g) hypercorrect grammar (i.e., women are less likely than men to use words like *ain't* or to shorten words like *doin'* or *runnin'*). These seven categories constitute some of the most common features that have been included in the construct of powerless language and examined over the past 25 years. A number of quantitative studies have been performed to test Lakoff's (1975a, 1975b) claims, and the findings on various linguistic features are considered in this section.

Floor Allocation

Taking the floor from another speaker, or maintaining one's turn rather than yielding to another, has been measured frequently over the years as powerful language. In fact, interruptions remain the single most researched feature of powerful and powerless language, with the general assumption that those who interrupt hold more power in a conversation. However, even with a substantial amount of literature on interruptions, the results remain inconclusive. Due to the extreme sex differences they found, Zimmerman and West's (1975) study is an often cited investigation of interruption behavior. They found that in 11 mixed-sex pairs, men performed 98% of all interruptions. West and Zimmerman (1983) performed a similar investigation, and found that in 5 mixed-sex dyads, men performed 75% of all interruptions. These percentages are extreme, but other researchers (Carli, 1990; Dindia, 1987; Mulac, Wiemann, Widenmann, & Gibson, 1988) have produced comparable results. Turner, Dindia, and Pearson (1995) found that men interrupt more than women in both same- and mixed-sex dyads do. Bilous and Krauss (1988) found that in mixed-sex pairs, men did more interrupting, but that it was the female same-gender pairs that interrupted one another more than the male same-gender pairs, to quite a large degree.

However, some empirical support contradicts these findings. Kollock, Blumstein, and Schwartz (1985) argued that "[i]nterruptions are clearly a sign of conversational dominance" (p. 40), but found no difference in the amount of interruptions between males and females in cross-sex pairs. Simkins-Bullock and Wildman (1991) found no differences in the amount of interruptions within mixed-sex dyads, or between male–male pairs and female–female pairs, supporting Kollock et al.'s (1985) findings. Interestingly, there is also support for the claim that women interrupt more than men do. Kennedy and Camden (1981) observed 35 graduate students over six 1-hour, mixed-sex group sessions. They found that women performed 157 (or 62%) of the 255 total interruptions. Dindia (1987) found women interrupting more than men in her study of 30 mixed-sex pairs. Clearly, results from studies investigating interruptions are inconsistent and inconclusive.

Certainty and Uncertainty

Generally, language that indicates a particular level of certainty about what the speaker is saying is considered "powerful" language. Research examining disclaimers, hedges, and tag questions explore uncertainty (powerlessness) in language production, and have also been subject to much empirical scrutiny, along with some controversy. Carli (1990) found women use a substantially larger amount of disclaimers than men do (up to 3.5 times more) in both same- and mixed-sex pairs. Other researchers (Entwisle & Garvey, 1972; Stutman, 1987) have replicated these results. Turner et al. (1995), however, found just the opposite—that men use more disclaimers than women in both same- and mixed-sex pairs. Similarly, the findings in this linguistic category are inconclusive.

Within the literature on hedges, a great deal of controversial evidence exists. Carli (1990) found that, similar to disclaiming behavior, women performed more hedges than men did, both in same-sex dyads and mixed-sex dyads. Mulac et al. (1988) found results that supported Carli's (1990) first finding, but not the second, as they reported men using more hedges in same-sex pairs than women. In an investigation of sex differences in children's language (comparing 20 children each in four age groups: 4 years, 8 years, 12 years, and 16 years), Staley (1982) found that in all age groups, males used more hedges than females. The only exception was the 12-year-old age group, which had just as strong an effect, but in the opposite direction, with girls using more hedges. An interesting side note is that the difference between the sexes was largest at age 16 (the oldest of the ages examined), which may indicate a learned behavior as time goes on. However, it was in the "unexpected" direction (boys hedging more than girls). Clearly, without further research, conclusions cannot be drawn.

Tag questions, as mentioned earlier, have been investigated in a number of studies as well. Besides Crosby and Nyquist (1977), Carli (1990) also found that women use more tag questions than men do, in both same- and mixed-sex pairs. McMillan, Clifton, McGrath, and Gale (1977) reported the same findings, with a slightly larger effect. The same researchers also reported that "imperative constructions in question form, ... defined as alternatives to simple and direct ways of ordering action" (p. 548) are used more by women than by men.

In some cases, researchers combine variables to indicate a "style" of speaking. For example, in three separate studies, Crosby and Nyquist (1977) coded for the use of female register, which is actually a combination variable that includes four powerless linguistic features: empty adjectives, tag questions, hedges, and the word *so*. They found that women rated higher in the use of female register than men. Overall, whether investigating hedges, tags, or combinations of these linguistic features, the research findings are contradictory.

Politeness and Impoliteness

Linguistic features that are considered displays of (im)politeness have also been examined as powerful or powerless. Hostile verbs (Gilley & Summers, 1970) were used more by men than women, and men were also found to do more swearing than women on a daily basis in everyday situations (Staley, 1978). In addition, men have been found to make threats more than women do (Scudder & Andrews, 1995). Civilities (saying *please, thank you, gladly, might I be able to have*, etc.) have been coded as powerless language, and have been found more in women's speech than in men's (Brouwer, Gerritsen, & DeHaan, 1979). Women have also been accused of a "fondness for hyperbole and ... use of adverbs of intensity" (Haas, 1979, p. 620), which is seen as powerless language. Empirical investigations comparing the use of intensifiers by men and women have supported this tendency (Carli, 1990; Crosby & Nyquist, 1977; McMillan et al., 1977; Mulac et al., 1988; Turner et al., 1995). Again, the findings in this area are hard to interpret.

As Deaux and Major (1987) noted, "in short, researchers attempting to document and replicate sex differences have often found them elusive, a case of 'now you see them, now you don't'" (p. 369). However, the need for clear-cut results is also evident. In a recent meta-analysis of powerful and powerless language, Burrell and Koper (1998) found that "powerful language is perceived as more credible than powerless language" (p. 248). Clearly, it is important in many situations to be perceived as credible or persuasive (e.g., teaching, parenting, sales, and legal contexts, to name a few). Burrell and Koper's finding indicates that women may be in the position of being perceived as less credible than men, and therefore less persuasive than men, simply as a result of the language they use. Because of the contradictory results and the important implications, a meta-analysis was performed to determine whether or not women speak less powerfully than men do.

METHOD

Sample

A thorough search of the research literature examining sex differences in the use of powerful and powerless language was conducted. The relevant literature was obtained through a search of journals in communication, social psychology, sociology, linguistics, and anthropology, as well as examination of social science indexes, including PSYCHLit (from inception through May 1998) and ERIC (1966–May 1998). The keywords that were used for the search were *powerful language, powerless language, gender and language, women and language, men and language*, and various combinations of those.

Three criteria were developed to determine whether a study would be included in the final analysis. Each study had to: (a) code for powerful and powerless language, (b) compare males' use with females' use of powerful and powerless language, and (c) include a language sample from actual language generated by a participant. These examples were then coded for powerful and powerless language features (as opposed to, e.g., a manipulated passage written by the researchers that was then rated by sex-role stereotypes). Basic information for each study is provided in Table 5.1.

Numerous studies were originally uncovered in the search, but not all of them were usable. Twenty-four studies did not meet the third criterion and were judged unusable due to manipulation of the dependent variable (Bell, Zahn, & Hopper, 1984; Bradac, Konsky, & Davies, 1976; Bradac, Konsky, & Elliott, 1976; Bradac & Mulac, 1984; Bradley, 1981; Carli, 1989; Conley, O'Barr, & Lind, 1978; Giles, Scholes, & Young, 1983; Giles, Wilson, & Conway, 1981; Gould & Stone, 1982; Haleta, 1996; Hall & Braunwald, 1981; Hogg, 1985; Hosman & Wright, 1987; Johnson & Vinson, 1987, 1990; Mulac, 1976; Mulac, Lundell, & Bradac, 1986; Newcombe & Arnkoff, 1979; Siegler & Siegler, 1976; von Baeyer, Sherk, & Zanna, 1981; Warfel, 1984; Wiley & Eskilson, 1985; Wright & Hosman, 1983). In addition, four studies were not included due to unrecoverable data—that is, findings were reported, but no usable data were evident in the article (Dubois & Crouch, 1975; Moore, Shaffer, Goodsell, & Baringoldz, 1983; Natale, Entin, & Jaffe, 1979; Sayers & Sherblom, 1987). Thirty studies were included in the final analysis, with a combined total sample of 3,012 participants.

Coding Studies

To streamline final analyses, the original 25 language features were collapsed into four categories: floor allocation, certainty–uncertainty, politeness–impoliteness, and style. It was hoped that more conclusive, concrete results would be uncovered by combining different linguistic features into groupings of behaviors with conceptual similarities.

The first category, floor allocation, included features such as interruptions, turn taking, starting a sequence, independent turns, and simultaneous speech. These language features were grouped together because they are all measures of taking or maintaining the floor in conversation. Catego-

TABLE 5.1
Description of Overall Analysis

Author	Year	N	Overall Correlation
Beattie	1981	55	−.105
Beck	1978	24	.482
Bilous	1988	60	−.260
Brouwer	1979	587	.080
Carli	1990	116	.261
Crosby (Exp. 1)	1977	64	.242
Crosby (Exp. 2)	1977	197	.072
Crosby (Exp. 3)	1977	90	.152
Dindia	1987	60	−.100
Entwisle	1972	665	.077
Gilley	1970	100	.268
Kennedy	1981	35	−.200
Kollock	1985	30	−.089
Martin	1983	40	.074
McMillan	1977	98	.449
Mulac	1980	63	.277
Mulac	1982	48	.110
Mulac	1985	12	.307
Mulac (Exp. 1)	1988	48	.038
Mulac (Exp. 2)	1988	48	.055
Pillon	1992	40	.315
Scudder	1995	142	.178
Simkins-Bullock	1991	78	.048
Staley	1978	26	.107
Staley	1982	55	.132
Stutman	1987	50	.100
Turner	1995	80	.085
West	1983	10	.700
Willis	1976	15	−.040
Zimmerman	1975	22	.716

Note. Only the first author is listed; see references for complete citation.

ries were coded as powerful language when used to either take the floor from another speaker or maintain the current speaking turn.

The second category, certainty–uncertainty, included the largest amount of language features (variables marked with a (+) are considered powerful when employed; those marked with a (−) are considered powerless): negations (+), such as "I'm not kidding"; justifiers (+), as in "I would say no, because ... "; qualifiers or disclaimers (–), such as "I'm not sure, but ... "; hedges (–), such as "I guess" or "kind of"; tag questions (–), as in "isn't that right?"; modal constructions (–), which are essentially identical to imperatives as questions (–), such as "Don't you think we should go to lunch now?"; fillers (–), as in "like" or "okay"; adverbials beginning a sentence (–), like "Really, I'd rather not ... "; and fillers beginning a sentence (–). All of the language features in this category indicated a particular level of (un)certainty about what the speaker was saying.

Politeness–impoliteness is the third category, and it included intensifiers (–), like "so" and "really"; verbal reinforcers (–), such as "yes" or "I see"; civilities (–), like "please" and "if you don't mind"; hostile verbs (+), as in "murdered" or "tortured"; threats (+); obscenities (+); and directives (+), such as "Think of another example." These variables were grouped together because they all represent a direct display of (im)politeness.

The fourth category, style, was comprised of variables culled from studies in which the researchers grouped several different linguistic features together to form one variable (i.e., the aforementioned female register, which included tag questions, empty adjectives, hedges, and the word so). Studies with variables that were not separable were also included in this category. The style category consisted of elaborated (+) versus restricted (–) codes, which is the difference between fully developing ideas and lacking specificity; female register (–); and dynamism (+), or being perceived as strong, active, loud, and aggressive.

Meta-Analysis Procedures

The procedure employed in this investigation involved converting available summary statistics (i.e., means, standard deviations, correlations, t statistics, F statistics) into correlational estimates for summarizing purposes. A positive correlation (a randomly assigned designation) indicated that men used more powerful language or women used more powerless language; a negative correlation indicated the reverse. The correlations were weighted for sample size and averaged.

A chi-square test for homogeneity was then performed on the summary data. If the chi-square test was nonsignificant, the average correlation was considered to be an accurate true score estimate. If, however, the chi-square test was significant, alternative methods of determining the average correlation were performed.

RESULTS

To assess the difference between males' and females' use of powerful and powerless language, an overall analysis of the summary correlation was estimated. The average effect was $r = +.105$ ($k = 30, N = 3,012$), indicating that overall, men used more powerful language than women did. However, results of the formal homogeneity test, $\chi^2(29) = 61.30, p < .05$, showed a significant amount of variance, indicating the presence of at least one moderator variable. Table 5.1 contains descriptive results for each study included in the meta-analysis.

In an effort to identify the moderator(s), each of the four categories was considered separately. Results for the subcategories can be found in Table 5.2. Floor allocation was included in 14 studies, employing a total of 604 participants. The effect was $r = +.067, \chi^2(13) = 27.82, p < .05$, with a significant amount of variance. The Zimmerman and West (1975) and West and Zimmerman (1983) studies had the largest correlations, and so were considered outliers and removed for the next set of analyses. When running the same statistics on floor allocation without these two studies, the effect was $r = +.025$ ($k = 12, n = 572$), and the variance was found to be trivial, $\chi^2(11) = 8.58, p > .05$. These indicate that men take the floor or maintain the floor more than women (and hence are using more powerful language).

Certainty–uncertainty was included in 10 studies, with a total sample size of 1,137. The effect was $r = +.087, \chi^2(9) = 27.66, p < .05$, indicating a significant amount of variance. The McMillan et al. (1977) study was an outlier here, having the largest correlation, and was removed for the next analysis. Without it, there were nine cases with a total of 1,039 participants. The effect was $r = +.054, \chi^2(8) = 14.68, p > .05$, indicating that men use more powerful (or "certain") language than women do.

Politeness–impoliteness was also included in 10 studies, employing a total of 1,191 participants. The effect was $r = +.162, \chi^2(9) = 17.10, p < .05$, indicating a significant amount of variance. Once again, McMillan et al. (1977) was an outlier, and without it, there were nine cases with 1,093 participants. The effect was $r = +.134, \chi^2(8) = 6.92, p > .05$, which indicates that women speak more politely than men—or, in other words, less powerfully.

The style category included 14 studies and 958 participants. The effect was $r = +.174, \chi^2(13) = 17.67, p > .05$, indicating that men speak more powerfully than women do.

The sex composition of the dyad was also considered as a possible moderator variable, and the same-sex pairs were analyzed apart from the mixed-sex

TABLE 5.2
Subcategory Results

Subcategory	K	N	R	χ^2
Floor allocation	14	604	.067	27.82*
Outliers removed	12	572	.025	8.58
Certainty	10	1,137	.087	27.66*
Outlier removed	9	1,039	.054	14.68
Politeness	10	1,191	.162	17.10*
Outlier removed	9	1,093	.134	6.92
Style	14	958	.174	17.67

Note. Additional analyses were run for floor allocation, certainty, and politeness.
*$p < .05$.

pairs. Seven studies ($n = 426$) investigated same-sex pairs, and the effect was $r = +.002$, $\chi^2(6) = 40.64$, $p < .05$, indicating a significant amount of variance. The Bilous and Krauss (1988) article was responsible for a large amount of variance, and was removed for the next analysis. The effect size without it ($n = 366$) was $r = +.126$, $\chi^2(5) = 2.56$, $p > .05$, which indicates that in same-sex pairs, men speak more powerfully than women do.

Fifteen studies incorporated mixed-sex pairs, using a total of 1,754 participants. The effect was $r = +.110$, $\chi^2 (14) = 18.94$, $p > .05$, indicating that men speak more powerfully than women do in mixed-sex pairs.

DISCUSSION

The existing literature regarding the use of powerful and powerless language by men and women has produced conflicting results. In the current investigation, results from 30 studies examining men's and women's powerful and powerless language use were subjected to meta-analysis. Results supported Lakoff's (1975a, 1975b) claim that men use more powerful language than women do, although all subcategories have small effect sizes. Interestingly, this means that taken together, these studies show that perhaps men and women are more similar than most findings would lead us to believe. The trend is present, however, and should not be ignored. In addition, the results indicate that there are moderator variables to consider, and analyses showed that men speak more powerfully to each other and to women, and they speak more powerfully across the board with respect to types of linguistic features.

Implications

Burrell and Koper's (1998) meta-analysis on powerful and powerless language and credibility found that "powerful language is perceived as *more credible* than powerless language" (p. 248). This finding impacts the current meta-analysis. Because men are using more powerful language than women are, men may be perceived as more credible than women, affirming Lakoff's (1975a, 1975b) fear that language is serving to keep women in submissive positions. Kramer (1974) echoed this concern: "all aspects of female speech, if they do indeed exist ... would indicate one way in which the sex roles are maintained" (pp. 20–21). Because there are many situations in which one would want to be perceived as credible, the findings presented here are particularly meaningful for interpersonal communication. As Kolb (1993) put it, women's "distinctive communication style that serves them well in other contexts may be a liability in negotiation" (p. 146). In fact, any time that women present ideas or attempt to influence others (e.g., in the classroom, at work, in personal relationships, etc.), they are in danger of being perceived as less credible and less persuasive than their male counterparts, solely due to the language they use. Staley (1982) found sex differences in children as young as 4 years old, which indicates that even as students, and at a very early age, girls may be perceived as less credible than boys.

Of course, another important implication of this meta-analysis is that powerful language is most definitely a skill that can be taught. We now have definitions of what language features are considered more powerful (and hence more credible), and we can use this knowledge to our benefit and teach women to communicate more powerfully when the situation may call for it. More and more women are getting degrees and joining the workforce, which means that women now commonly populate "men's places." Due to this change, women are finding themselves in direct competition with men, and being sensitive to linguistic differences may help equalize the sexes. That is to say, at times it is true that powerless language might be more appropriate (e.g., when negotiating with a party who does not want his or her authority challenged), but there are also times when powerful language is more appropriate (e.g., when perceived credibility is important). Teaching both men and women how to use various levels of power when they speak will likely be most useful to them.

Limitations

Although the conclusion that men speak more powerfully than women is supported here, it should be remembered that the effect sizes are small and therefore should be interpreted or generalized with caution. Although many of the individual studies found more sizable sex differences, taken together as a group there are smaller differences in language production. There are several issues that may be affecting these results, and perhaps more research in this area can shed some light on these limitations.

One issue that may require more careful consideration is message elicitation. Just under one third of the studies included in this analysis (Beck, 1978; Entwisle & Garvey, 1972; Gilley & Summers, 1970; Mulac, Incontro, & James, 1985; Mulac & Lundell, 1980, 1982; Mulac et al., 1988; Staley, 1978, 1982) placed a participant in a situation and required him or her to react (rather than interact), to code the language used. The rest of the studies (a clear majority) were interaction situations. This difference in message elicitation may have some moderating effects, in that being "in the moment" and interacting may have different effects on language production than simply reacting to stimuli in one's environment.

Another consideration is that almost all of the participants in this review were university students—generally the classic 18- to 22-year-old group. The are few exceptions (Brouwer et al., 1979; Crosby & Nyquist, 1977; Entwisle & Garvey, 1972; Staley, 1982; Stutman, 1987). Other environments may generate effects that would even be more significant, because at the university level we at least profess to be aware of sex discrimination and try to be "fair," considering the amount of bias that actually exists. In more real-world investigations (i.e., naturalistic observation in the workplace or in families), the differences between language production in men and women may actually be more pronounced.

The sample included in this review is also not very international or intercultural. Only two of the studies included in this analysis were performed on non-English-speaking participants (Brouwer et al., 1979; Pillon, Degauquier, & Duquesne, 1992), so we have no idea if these results would hold true in other countries, or in the United States if respondents used other languages. Romance languages (i.e., Spanish, French, and Italian), which give all objects an actual gender for the purpose of language, may, for example, have very interesting effects. In a related vein, power is a very different construct in some other countries (i.e., Asian politeness norms) that could have an effect on the correlations.

Future Research

It is necessary to investigate additional moderator variables to study further this area of communication. Type of language features should be explored more fully, so that we may determine which features are most important in various situations. For example, perhaps politeness forms are perceived as powerless language during persuasive efforts, but not during interpersonal interactions when there is no attempt at influence. The primary concern of future research in this area should be examining diverse contexts to examine the effects of using powerful and powerless language. In addition, the issue of message elicitation must be investigated, as the dynamics of the interaction may influence the use of powerful and powerless language. A third consideration is performing more naturalistic observation, as the effects may differ outside of the university boundaries. Naturally occurring language is an important feature to this area of study, but getting a representative sample of all populations (not just those involved in academia) could make a difference. Observing workplace negotiations, teaching practices, parenting strategies, and courtroom interactions would all be fruitful avenues for future inquiry on sex differences in language production. Ultimately, this meta-analysis has illuminated a small but perhaps crucial difference that exists between men's and women's language use.

REFERENCES

References marked with an asterisk indicate studies included in the meta-analysis.

*Beattie, G. W. (1981). Interruption in conversational interaction, and its relation to the sex and status of the interactants. *Linguistics, 19,* 15–35.

*Beck, K. (1978). Sex differentiated speech codes. *International Journal of Women's Studies, 1,* 566–572.

Bell, R. A., Zahn, C. J., & Hopper, R. (1984). Disclaiming: A test of two competing views. *Communication Quarterly, 32,* 28–36.

*Bilous, F. R., & Krauss, R. M. (1988). Dominance and accommodation in the conversational behaviors of same- and mixed-gender dyads. *Language and Communication, 8,* 183–194.

Bradac, J. J., Konsky, C. W., & Davies, R. A. (1976). Two studies of the effects of linguistic diversity upon judgments of communicator attributes and message effectiveness. *Communication Monographs, 43,* 70–79.

Bradac, J. J., Konsky, C. W., & Elliott, N. K. (1976). Verbal behavior of interviewees: The effects of several situational variables on verbal productivity, disfluency, and lexical diversity. *Journal of Communication Disorders, 9,* 211–225.

Bradac, J. J., & Mulac, A. (1984). A molecular view of powerful and powerless speech styles: Attributional consequences of specific language features and communicator intentions. *Communication Monographs, 51,* 307–319.

Bradley, P. H. (1981). The folk-linguistics of women's speech: An empirical examination. *Communication Monographs, 48,* 73–90.

*Brouwer, D., Gerritsen, M., & DeHaan, D. (1979). Speech differences between women and men: On the wrong track? *Language in Society, 8,* 33–50.

Burrell, N. A., & Koper, R. J. (1998). The efficacy of powerful/powerless language on attitudes and source credibility. In M. Allen & R. Preiss (Eds.), *Persuasion: Advances through meta-analysis* (pp. 203–216). Cresskill, NJ: Hampton.

Canary, D. J., & Dindia, K. (Eds.). (1998). *Sex differences and similarities in communication: Critical essays and empirical investigations of sex and gender in interaction.* Mahwah, NJ: Lawrence Erlbaum Associates.

Carli, L. L. (1989). Gender differences in interaction style and influence. *Journal of Personality and Social Psychology, 56,* 565–576.

*Carli, L. L. (1990). Gender, language, and influence. *Journal of Personality and Social Psychology, 59,* 941–951.

Conley, J., O'Barr, W., & Lind, E. (1978). The power of language: Presentational style in the courtroom. *Duke Law Journal,* 1375–1399.

*Crosby, F., & Nyquist, L. (1977). The female register: An empirical study of Lakoff's hypothesis. *Language in Society, 6,* 313–322.

Deaux, K., & Major, B. (1987). Putting gender into context: An interactive model of gender-related behavior. *Psychological Review, 94,* 369–389.

*Dindia, K. (1987). The effects of sex of subject and sex of partner on interruptions. *Human Communication Research, 13,* 345–371.

Dubois, B. L., & Crouch, I. (1975). The question of tag questions in women's speech: They don't really use more of them, do they? *Language in Society, 4,* 289–294.

*Entwisle, D. R., & Garvey, C. (1972). Verbal productivity and adjective usage. *Language and Speech, 15,* 288–298.

Giles, H., Scholes, J., & Young, L. (1983). Stereotypes of male and female speech: A British study. *Central States Speech Journal, 34,* 255–256.

Giles, H., Wilson, P., & Conway, T. (1981). Accent and lexical diversity as determinants of impression formation and employment selection. *Language Sciences, 3,* 91–103.

*Gilley, H., & Summers, C. (1970). Sex differences in the use of hostile verbs. *Journal of Psychology, 76,* 33–37.

Gould, R. J., & Stone, C. G. (1982). The "feminine modesty" effect: A self-presentational interpretation of sex differences in causal attribution. *Personality and Social Psychology Bulletin, 8,* 477–485.

Gray, J. (1992). *Men are from Mars, women are from Venus: A practical guide for improving communication and getting what you want in your relationship.* New York: HarperCollins.

Haas, A. (1979). Male and female spoken language differences: Stereotypes and evidence. *Psychological Bulletin, 86,* 616–626.

Haleta, L. L. (1996). Student perceptions of teachers' use of language: The effects of powerful and powerless language on impression formation and uncertainty. *Communication Education, 45,* 16–28.

Hall, J. A., & Braunwald, K. G. (1981). Gender cues in conversations. *Journal of Personality and Social Psychology, 40,* 99–110.

Hogg, M. A. (1985). Masculine and feminine speech in dyads and groups: A study of speech style and gender salience. *Journal of Language and Social Psychology, 4,* 99–112.

Hopper, R. (1998). *Gendering talk.* Unpublished manuscript.

Hosman, L. A., & Wright, J. W., II. (1987). The effects of hedges and hesitations on impression formation in a simulated courtroom context. *Western Journal of Speech Communication, 51,* 173–188.

Johnson, C., & Vinson, L. (1987). "Damned if you do, damned if you don't?": Status, powerful speech and evaluations of female witnesses. *Women's Studies in Communication, 10,* 37–44.

Johnson, C., & Vinson, L. (1990). Placement and frequency of powerless talk and impression formation. *Communication Quarterly, 38,* 325–333.

*Kennedy, C. W., & Camden, C. T. (1981). Gender differences in interruption behavior: A dominance perspective. *International Journal of Women's Studies, 4,* 18–25.

Kolb, D. M. (1993). Her place at the table: Gender and negotiation. In L. Hall (Ed.), *Negotiation: Strategies for mutual gain* (pp. 138–150). Newbury Park, CA: Sage.

*Kollock, P., Blumstein, P., & Schwartz, P. (1985). Sex and power in interaction: Conversational privileges and duties. *American Sociological Review, 50,* 34–46.

Kramer, C. (1974). Women's speech: Separate but unequal? *Quarterly Journal of Speech, 60,* 14–24.

Lakoff, R. (1975a). Language and woman's place. *Language in Society, 2,* 45–80.

Lakoff, R. (1975b). *Language and woman's place.* New York: Harper & Row.

*Martin, J. N., & Craig, R. T. (1983). Selected linguistic sex differences during initial social interactions of same-sex and mixed-sex student dyads. *Western Journal of Speech Communication, 47,* 16–28.

*McMillan, J. R., Clifton, A. K., McGrath, D., & Gale, W. S. (1977). Women's language: Uncertainty or interpersonal sensitivity and emotionality. *Sex Roles, 3,* 545–559.

Moore, S. F., Shaffer, L., Goodsell, D. A., & Baringoldz, G. (1983). Gender or situationally determined spoken language differences? The case of the leadership situation. *International Journal of Women's Studies, 6,* 44–53.

Mulac, A. (1976). Effects of obscene language upon three dimensions of listener attitude. *Communication Monographs, 43,* 300–307.

*Mulac, A., Incontro, C. R., & James, M. R. (1985). A comparison of the gender-linked language effect and sex-role stereotypes. *Journal of Personality and Social Psychology, 49,* 1099–1110.

*Mulac, A., & Lundell, T. L. (1980). Differences in perceptions created by syntactic-semantic productions of male and female speakers. *Communication Monographs, 47,* 111–118.

*Mulac, A., & Lundell, T. L. (1982). An empirical test of the gender-linked language effect in a public speaking setting. *Language and Speech, 25,* 243–256.

Mulac, A., Lundell, T. L., & Bradac, J. J. (1986). Male/female language differences and attributional consequences in a public speaking situation: Toward an explanation of the gender-linked language effect. *Communication Monographs, 53,* 115–129.

*Mulac, A., Wiemann, J. M., Widenmann, S. J., & Gibson, T. W. (1988). Male/female language differences in same-sex and mixed-sex dyads: The gender-linked language effect. *Communication Monographs, 55,* 315–335.

Natale, M., Entin, E., & Jaffe, J. (1979). Vocal interruptions in dyadic communication as a function of speech and social anxiety. *Journal of Personality and Social Psychology, 37,* 865–878.

Newcombe, N., & Arnkoff, D. B. (1979). Effects of speech style and sex of speaker on person perception. *Journal of Personality and Social Psychology, 37,* 1293–1303.

O'Barr, W. M. (1982). *Linguistic evidence: Language, power, and strategy in the courtroom.* New York: Academic Press.

*Pillon, A., Degauquier, C., & Duquesne, F. (1992). Males' and females' conversational behavior in cross-sex dyads: From gender differences to gender similarities. *Journal of Psycholinguistic Research, 21,* 147–172.

Sayers, F., & Sherblom, J. (1987). Qualification in male language as influenced by age and gender of conversational partner. *Communication Research Reports, 4,* 88–92.

*Scudder, J. N., & Andrews, P. H. (1995). A comparison of two alternative models of powerful speech: The impact of power and gender upon the use of threats. *Communication Research Reports, 12,* 25–33.

Siegler, D. M., & Siegler, R. S. (1976). Stereotypes of males' and females' speech. *Psychological Reports, 39,* 167–170.

*Simkins-Bullock, J. A., & Wildman, B. G. (1991). An investigation into the relationships between gender and language. *Sex Roles, 24,* 149–160.

*Staley, C. M. (1978). Male–female use of expletives: A heck of a difference in expectations. *Anthropological Linguistics, 20,* 367–380.

*Staley, C. M. (1982). Sex-related differences in the style of children's language. *Journal of Psycholinguistic Research, 11,* 141–158.

*Stutman, R. K. (1987). Witness disclaiming during examination. *Journal of the American Forensic Association, 23,* 96–101.

Tannen, D. (1990). *You just don't understand: Women and men in conversation.* New York: Ballantine.

Tannen, D. (1994). *Talking from 9 to 5: How women's and men's conversational styles affect who gets heard, who gets credit, and what gets done at work.* New York: Morrow.

*Turner, L. H., Dindia, K., & Pearson, J. C. (1995). An investigation of female/male verbal behaviors in same-sex and mixed-sex conversations. *Communication Reports, 8,* 86–96.

von Baeyer, C. L., Sherk, D. L., & Zanna, M. P. (1981). Impression management in the job interview: When the female applicant meets the male (chauvinist) interviewer. *Personality and Social Psychology Bulletin, 7,* 45–51.

Warfel, K. A. (1984). Gender schemas and perceptions of speech style. *Communication Monographs, 51,* 253–267.

*West, C., & Zimmerman, D. H. (1983). Small insults: A study of interruptions in cross-sex conversations between unacquainted persons. In B. Thorne, C. Kramarae, & N. Henley (Eds.), *Language, gender and society* (pp. 102–117). Rowley, MA: Newbury House.

Wiley, M. G., & Eskilson, A. (1985). Speech style, gender stereotypes, and corporate success: What if women talk more like men? *Sex Roles, 12,* 993–1007.

*Willis, F. N., & Williams, S. J. (1976). Simultaneous talking in conversation and sex of speakers. *Perceptual and Motor Skills, 43,* 1067–1070.

Wright, J. W., II, & Hosman, L. A. (1983). Language style and sex bias in the courtroom: The effects of male and female use of hedges and intensifiers on impression formation. *Southern Speech Communication Journal, 48,* 137–152.

*Zimmerman, D. H., & West, C. (1975). Sex roles, interruptions, and silences in conversation. In B. Thorne & N. Henley (Eds.), *Language and sex: Difference and dominance* (pp. 105–129). Rowley, MA: Newbury House.

6

Social Skills and Communication

Brian H. Spitzberg and James Price Dillard

What does it mean to be a skilled person? Ordinarily, when we think of skill, we think of ability, capability, and proficiency. A skilled architect is one knowledgeable in the trade, the terms, and the tasks of designing buildings. He or she is able to produce products such as blueprints that are relatively error-free and meet the demands of the clients and context. A skilled tennis player knows the rules and tactical requirements of the game, and he or she is able to demonstrate this knowledge on the court through consistent performance at a reasonably high level of success.

These notions of skill do not seem problematic. However, a brief review illustrates just how complicated they are. What constitutes consistency in performance? Even the best tennis players have "off" days and runs of bad luck. What constitutes knowledge of a trade? An architect who specializes only in hospitals may be proficient with health care structures, but incompetent with houses or schools. What constitutes a reasonably high level of success? Is success in tennis avoiding mistakes and following the rules, or is it defined by a high winning record against opponents: Any opponents, or only those of comparable talent? Clearly, what constitutes skill, even in well-defined contexts, is difficult to specify.

A similar difficulty arises with the concept of social skills. Social skills are often referred to as social competence or interpersonal competence or communication competence. Social skill usually implies high quality, or proficiency with social interaction and relationships. However, this intuitively appealing explanation tends to hide more than it reveals. This chapter examines the concept of social skills, the relations to communication, and the results of a meta-analytic approach to identifying these relations.

DEFINING SOCIAL SKILLS

Social skills are defined here as goal-directed actions in interpersonal contexts that are learnable, repeatable, and variable in their quality (see Spitzberg & Cupach, 1984, 1989). Some of these terms need explanation. First, skills are directed toward goals. *Goals* are objectives that represent preferred outcomes. Goals such as wanting to get a job offer or a date are rather clear and objective. Other goals are far more ambiguous in nature. A person may pursue a goal of meeting and establishing some rapport with an attractive person in class. This person may leave a conversation not exactly knowing whether or not rapport was achieved, partly because the goal itself has no obvious criteria to determine the degree to which it was accomplished. Nevertheless, all goals imply some continuum along which the skills directed toward them can be evaluated.

Second, the claim that social skills are *goal-directed* means that the action is in pursuit of objectives or preferred outcomes. This does not necessarily imply that the goals are achieved. Professional tennis players often miss on their first serves, and even occasionally double fault. An architect can leave some detail out of a blueprint. Such mistakes do not imply these professionals lack skills. The implication is that social skills must be defined separately from the actual accomplishments. The concept that skills can be identified independent of the outcomes is complex, especially in reference to social behavior. However, consider the context of seeking a date with someone. A person may engage in perfectly appropriate behavior when interacting with the object of attraction and still not actually get the date. The person displayed the skills necessary to get the date, but the other person simply was not attracted to the potential suitor.

Third, the terms *social* and *interpersonal* imply that the goal-directed nature of skills must be toward outcomes that are interpersonally interdependent. The goal of sharpening a pencil is not social in any significant sense, and therefore is irrelevant to the concept of social skills. On the other hand, needing to borrow a pencil clearly requires the use of request strategies, which in turn involve social, communicative behavior. Furthermore, this social behavior depends on the actions of another person. The goal cannot be achieved except through interaction with others.

The effectiveness, or goal success, of behavior can be viewed from two different levels: process and outcome. At the process level, the question is whether the appropriate behaviors are performed (e.g., did the tennis player engage in all the specific, correct actions involved in serving?). At the outcome level, the question is what the process accomplished (e.g., did the ball actually land in the right court, put the opponent in an awkward defensive position, or was it an ace?). Social skills refer to behaviors (i.e., process level) that are directed toward achieving some goal(s), but this does not require that the goals are always successfully accomplished. It is not uncommon, however, for social skills to be assessed at both the process and the outcome level. This practice is very important to understanding the meta-analysis described later in this chapter.

Fourth, social skills are learnable. This means that they can be specified, trained, reinforced, and improved. Social behavior may be genetically "hard-wired" to some extent. Research suggests that very small infants recognize their mother's face before others' faces, and that "peek-a-boo" is a template, or schema, for managing turn taking in interaction that later serves to facilitate the development of conversation skills (Foster, 1990). However, these innate skills are clearly expanded, refined, and repackaged into more elaborate sets and sequences of skills. Such learning occurs through both formal (e.g., parents teaching table manners and etiquette) and informal (e.g., watching a big brother or sister engage in an argument with a parent) processes.

Fifth, social skills are repeatable. Any person can get a tennis ball in the correct court on a serve by luck. The essence of skill is that the person can, with a high degree of consistency, go through the motions that get the ball into the appropriate court. What constitutes a high degree of consistency will vary by context and people's personal standards. This raises the last issue in defining social skills: quality.

Quality is the most problematic concept in defining social skills. What strikes one person as an appropriate opening or pick-up line will be viewed by another person as awkward, overly direct, or simply obnoxious (Kleinke, Meeker, & Staneski, 1986). The social skills literature generally identifies quality in terms of standards relevant to the context being studied. For example, if social skills are being studied in a heterosocial context in which a person is to make a good impression on a member of the opposite sex, quality may be evaluated by rating the person's attractiveness. If, on the other hand, a person's social skills are assessed in an assertion context (e.g., asking someone who just cut in line ahead of you to go to the back of the line), then effectiveness and appropriateness may serve as the best standards of evaluating quality.

Effectiveness is the degree to which actions have succeeded in their intention or in achieving preferred goals. *Appropriateness* is the degree to which actions fit, or are considered legitimate in, the context. Appropriate behavior tends to avoid violating any rules of the situation, although sometimes rules are violated in the process of establishing new rules. For example, a person may make a romantic move in a relationship that has always been platonic. In a sense, this behavior violates the rules of friendship, but in the process, it is redefining (or at least, attempting to redefine) the rules of the relationship.

Criteria of performance quality such as attractiveness, appropriateness, and effectiveness are obviously variable. This variability occurs in at least three distinct levels. Quality varies from low to high, by observer, and by context. The fact that a person can be described as socially skilled, very socially skilled, or barely socially skilled suggests this variability of quality. Social skillfulness is a continuum, ranging from low to high.

Quality also varies by observer. Such variances can be based on such issues as an observer's culture, sex, personality, expertise, and interactional role (e.g., participant or strictly observer). The fact that social skills vary by observer emphasizes both their social nature and the importance of viewing skills as both a behavioral and a perceptual phenomenon. Any comprehensive study of social skills must observe specific behaviors, as well as people's perceptions or evaluations of those behaviors.

Quality also varies by context. A tennis pro playing against beginners at a summer camp will perform quite differently than when in a Grand Slam tournament. Peoples' social behaviors do not occur in a vacuum, and the demands and complexities of a given context are likely to affect the quality of performance in significant ways.

One final implication of this analysis of quality is that quality is not determined objectively in behavior, but subjectively in evaluations. Is the tennis serve or the blueprint really about the exact line of movement in two or three dimensions? Or, is it about aesthetics, style, grace, smoothness, elegance, efficiency, and so forth? Obviously, one without the other makes the issue of quality irrelevant. The specific behaviors of interaction can be distinguished from the judgments about the quality of these behaviors. As such, behaviors can be viewed as relatively discrete, molecular types of actions. *Molecular* actions are specific, relatively discrete behaviors such as eye contact, questions, smiles, and talk time. Judgments of quality, in contrast, are more general and evaluative, and therefore, represent molar evaluations. *Molar* evaluations represent high-level or abstract judgments, such as evaluating the quality of a person's eye contact, questions, and so forth. The question for the investigation of social skills is whether certain molecular behaviors relate systematically to molar judgments of quality.

In general, socially skilled behavior refers to interaction behavior that is perceived to be competent (i.e., attractive, appropriate, or effective) in a given interpersonal context. This description provides two distinct elements for any study of social skills: molecular behaviors and molar perceptions. These two elements are both central to social skills research, and importantly, are conceptualized and operationalized as separate components.

THE IMPACT OF SOCIAL SKILLS

Social skills are the fabric of human relationships. Relationships exist in one of only two locations: mind or action. We often think about our relationships; we ponder, contemplate, worry about, mull over, reflect on, enjoy, and find both sorrow and delight in our relationships. However, as partners we are completely unable to pry open each other's heads and peer inside. All we ultimately know of others is their behaviors. For example, we know that trust affects relationships with others. Trust can be a set of beliefs or feelings about another person. But to the extent that this trust affects the relationship, it must affect it through one person's actions toward the other. The point is that all relationships are essentially comprised of the actions and interactions we make available to others.

If relationships are comprised of actions and interactions, it follows that the skillfulness (i.e., quality) with which these actions and interactions are performed determine the quality of life experienced in these relationships. Research from a variety of disciplines demonstrates that social skills are significant factors in predicting general health (Rook, 1992, 1998; Rook & Pietromonaco, 1987), learning disabilities (Swanson & Malone, 1992), and psychosocial problems such as depression and loneliness (Segrin, 1990, 1992, 1993, 1997; Segrin & Dillard, 1993). Social skills and competence also are related to perceptions of a person's physical attractiveness (Eagly, Ashmore, Makhijani, & Longo, 1991; Ritts, Patterson & Tubbs, 1992), and children's popularity and social status (Newcomb, Bukowski, & Pattee, 1993). People's abilities to marshal social support from others (Procidano, 1992; Röhrle & Sommer, 1994), manage conflicts, and achieve relationship satisfaction (Spitzberg, Canary, & Cupach, 1994) depend significantly on how competently they interact with others.

For some time, social skills were viewed as the primary basis of mental illness itself (e.g., Trower, 1980; Trower, Bryant, & Argyle, 1978). It was assumed that deficits in social skills facilitated negatively reinforcing social environments in which people increasingly found themselves ineffective in interacting with the normal world around them. Finally, research indicates that social skills training is highly effective in instilling higher levels of social skills (Beelmann, Pfingsten, & Lösel, 1994), and in reducing social phobias (Taylor, 1996) and psychiatric symptoms (Benton & Schroeder, 1990; Corrigan, 1991).

The nature of causality between social skills and such psychosocial phenomena is still not entirely clear. It could be that someone who is anxious, depressed, or lonely would lack motivation to perform social skills, or might literally get out of practice. For example, Spitzberg and Canary (1985) suggested that people who are chronically lonely may develop subsequently lower social skills. To date, however, the most carefully designed research by Segrin (1997) did not find that depression, loneliness, and anxiety led to reductions in social skills. The more reasonable conclusion is that over time, people with fewer or less consistent social skills find themselves with fewer resources for negotiating problematic relationships and achieving relational satisfaction. Further, deficits in social skills may actually create problems in relationships (e.g., being unable to assert oneself can allow problems to go unresolved). Such resulting problems, in turn, would be more difficult to resolve because of the lack of social skills.

The importance of social skills and the impact of our social relationships are difficult to underestimate. For example, research shows that experiencing abuse in our childhood and having small or inactive social relationship networks as adults have more harmful effects on our health and mortality than smoking, drinking, obesity, and health care practices! To the extent that social skills can enhance our relationships with family, friends, colleagues, and romantic partners, they quite literally provide one of the primary keys to health and happiness.

THE PROBLEM

If social skills are so important to the conduct of everyday relations with others, then it becomes essential that their nature be understood. For decades, research has vigorously pursued an extensive agenda investigating social skills. For obvious reasons, most of this research has come out of the clinical psychology and behavioral therapy literatures. Therapists need to know how to diagnose social skill deficits, how to instill new behaviors into clients' repertoires, what skills to include in the training, and how to assess outcomes of the training.

The basic model for these studies has been to present participants with some form of situation (e.g., hypothetical scenario, naturalistic encounter) and videotape their behavior in the situation. The taped behavior is then coded by third parties (blind to any experimental hypotheses) into relatively molecular social skill categories (e.g., amount of eye contact, frequency of gestures, number of questions asked, amount of talk time used, etc.). A different third-party group (also blind to experimental hypotheses) views the videotapes and rates the participants' social skillfulness. These ratings typically use molar-level (e.g., semantic differential) items ranging from attractive to unattractive, effective to ineffective, and appropriate to inappropriate. The coded molecular behaviors are then correlated to the molar ratings of social skillfulness to see what behaviors systematically predict impressions of social skills and competence.

There have been several problems with developing cumulative conclusions from the social skills research. First, social skills research evolved haphazardly. Different lines of research, often affiliated with particular disciplines, schools of psychiatry, clinics, or academic programs, tended to develop their own experimental designs, stimuli, scenarios, and assessment methods (Bellack, 1983). Consequently, one program might look at eye contact, whereas another would observe gestures. One group would look at both eye contact and gestures, whereas another would assess these and the use of questions. Although these different programs of research tended to share similar conceptions of social skills, and even tended to employ basically similar quasi-experimental designs, they often assessed different behaviors as types of social skills.

The second problem with attempts to derive cumulative conclusions from the social skills research concerns the differences in basic study design or population. Some researchers used hypothetical scenarios, whereas others used naturalistic situations. A hypothetical scenario, often called a role-play situation, would involve presenting a brief description of an imaginary, but typical, situation (e.g., returning a defective item for a refund, making a good impression on an opposite-sex stranger in a get-acquainted situation). Participants would be presented with the description, and then asked to behave as they normally would in such a situation. The person with whom they would be interacting was typically a confederate of the study. The confederates were often trained to behave in certain consistent ways so that differences across role plays would not be due to differences in confederate behavior. Other programs of research would focus more on naturalistic, or in vivo contexts. An in vivo study might ask clinic staff to engage outpatients in a taped interview or assertiveness situation in which the participant believed the context was part of ongoing clinic procedures rather than part of a study.

Research indicates that variations in methodology, sometimes even relatively subtle differences, can often significantly affect results. Differences in instructions (Martinez-Diaz & Edelstein, 1980; Nietzel & Bernstein, 1976), confederate behavior (Galassi & Galassi, 1976; Steinberg, Curran, Bell, Paxson, & Munroe, 1982), pretesting procedures (Mungas & Walters, 1979), selection instruments (Wallander, Conger, Mariotto, Curran, & Farrell, 1980), degree of rater involvement in the interaction (Gormally, 1982), and training (Corriveau et al., 1981) have all been found to influence participant behavior or rater evaluation of participant behavior.

The third problem with accumulating findings across studies in the social skills literature is that the findings appear to be inconsistent. For example, Conger and Farrell (1981) and Spence (1981) found talk time and eye contact to be related positively to ratings of social skillfulness, but Romano and Bellack (1980) failed to find such a relation. Such differences can result from numerous causes, including low statistical power, sampling error, and methodological differences such as those identified earlier. The problem of course, is that eyeballing such studies does not permit any obvious ways to determine which of these causes is responsible, much less how to compensate for such causes through normal literature review.

The comparability of these studies, therefore, is suspect. Yet, if social skills assessment and training are to progress, it is essential to know which skills are, in fact, consistently perceived to be competent, and just as important, which ones are not perceived to be competent. It was in this context that a meta-analysis of these studies was conducted. Meta-analysis assists in accounting for low power by accumulating participants across studies and can account for methodological differences as variables for analysis across research programs.

METHODS

A meta-analysis was conducted in three basic steps. First, a systematic search procedure was undertaken to produce a pool of studies for analysis. Second, the results of these studies were converted to a common effect size statistic, and the mean and variance of each distribution was computed. Third, the data were examined for any possible moderating variables that might account for variance in the distributions beyond what would be expected by chance.

Selection of Studies

Four criteria were established for inclusion of studies: Each study had to (a) be published, (b) use an English-speaking sample and be reported in English, (c) investigate adolescent or adult samples, and (d) relate frequency or duration counts of molecular behaviors to molar ratings of social skillfulness. A computer assisted search of *Psychological Abstracts* (circa 1982) was conducted. The first search employed the key methodological terms of *behavioral adjustment assessment, behavior adjustment analysis, coding, rating,* and *videotape,* resulting in 9,616 abstracts. The second search employed the key conceptual search terms of *social adjustment, social skill, social competence, interpersonal adjustment,* and *competence,* resulting in 2,233 abstracts. Cross-referencing these lists produced 132 articles. This residual pool was then stripped of dissertations ($n = 27$), foreign languages ($n = 4$), and children samples ($n = 23$), resulting in a pool of 78 studies between 1967 and 1982. However, only 4 of these specifically related molecular behaviors to ratings of social skills. In an effort to expand the sample, and given their relevance to the meta-analysis, current issues (1981–1982) of *Behavior Modification, Journal of Applied Behavior Analysis, Journal of Behavioral Assessment,* and *Journal of Consulting and Clinical Psychology* were examined. Finally, all back and current issues of *Behavior Therapy* were examined. The result of these procedures was a final sample of 18 studies presented in 14 articles.

Characteristics of the Studies

Some articles reported multiple studies in separate samples. In such cases, each separate sample was treated as a distinct data point. Sample sizes for the individual studies ranged from 10 to 93, with a mean of 46, totaling 824 participants across the 18 studies. Half of the studies formed groups ranging from low to high, thereby enhancing the range of skills represented. This practice tends to inflate effect sizes, but it was not possible to estimate the extent of this bias due to the relatively small number of studies involved.

Behavioral Predictors

A total of 12 molecular behaviors, 9 nonverbal and 3 verbal, were each common and measured similarly across at least three studies. These behaviors are briefly defined as follows: *Latency* is the number of seconds between the end of the previous person's statement and the beginning of the participant's response. *Gaze* is the number of seconds a participant appears to be looking toward the face of the other person. *Eye contact* is the amount of time a participant appears to be looking directly in the eyes of the other person. *Smiles* is the frequency of times participants display upturned corners of their lips, typically revealing their teeth. *Gestures* reflects the number (per minute) of gross hand or arm movements employed to facilitate, elaborate, or emphasize verbal utterances. *Head movements* is the number of times (per minute) the participant moves her or his head from side to side or up and down, other than postural shifts, which are used to indicate agreement or disagreement. *Adaptors*, commonly considered fidgeting, represent the number of times (per minute) a participant displays small movements of hands or fingers unrelated to speech (e.g., stroking, picking, scratching, playing with hair, tapping with object, etc.). *Volume* is the subjective loudness of a person's speech, typically rated on a 5-point scale ranging from x (very soft) to x (very loud). *Talk time* is the total amount of time spent speaking. *Questions* reflected the number of verbal utterances requesting information. *Compliments* were statements that made positive references to the other person. Finally, *minimal encourages* were the number of verbal feedback responses, typically indicating acknowledgment (e.g., "m-hm," "yes," "Really?" "Oh?," etc.).

Analysis

The effect size statistic selected for analysis was the Pearson correlation coefficient. When some other effect size was reported (i.e., t or F), it was converted to r (Hunter, Schmidt, & Jackson, 1982). When multiple effect sizes were reported for a given behavior, the effects were averaged (e.g., when multiple role plays were investigated for the same participant, the effect sizes were averaged across role plays). Distributions of effects were formed for each behavior, and the means and variances of these distributions were summarized and corrected for sampling error. The resulting variances were subjected to chi-square tests. This test ascertains whether the amount of variation is what would be expected by chance (i.e., sampling error). Given the high power of this test (Hunter et al., 1982), null results provide strong evidence that the differences between studies are not likely to be based on substantive or conceptual variables, and instead, are based on sampling error alone.

When a significant chi-square was found, the studies were examined for possible variables that could account for their differences. When possible, these variables were then used to code studies and further meta-analyses were conducted to estimate the homogeneity of the resulting categories and the differences in effect sizes between the categories. Such analysis helps identify possible moderator variables that influence the effect sizes.

Finally, reliability information was not sufficiently reported in all studies. Reliability estimates were therefore derived by converting the information provided, or by forming distributions of those estimates provided across studies (Nunnally, 1969). These estimates were then substituted when a given study provided no reliability information.

RESULTS

The results are summarized in Table 6.1. Social skill, the dependent variable, produced a mean reliability of .87 across 13 studies, which was the basis for correction of measurement error in the subsequent analyses.

In this initial analysis, the average correlation of molecular behaviors to third-party ratings of social skillfulness ranged from −.33 to .45. The average correlation across the 12 behaviors was .31, indicating a small but nontrivial effect. The average correlation was positive in all cases except response latency and use of adaptors. Thus, in general, an interactant's increased use of gaze, eye contact, smiles, gestures, head movements, greater volume, questions, compliments, and verbal encouragement tends to enhance others' views of this interactant's competence. The use of longer latency in responding to others' speaking turns and the use of nervous or unmotivated movements, such as scratching, tapping, and hair twirling, tends to impair one's competence in the eyes of others. The effects of most of these behaviors are relatively small, although in some instances, they account for very substantial amounts of variance in perceptions of social skills. For example, gestures, questions, and compliments each revealed moderate relations (i.e., .41 to .45) to perceptions of interactant competence.

There was one behavior, talk time, that revealed significant variance across studies, $\chi^2 (13) = 66.34, p < .001$, indicating that something was accounting for the differences across studies other than sampling error. The 14 studies examining talk time were examined for potential moderating variables. Two candidates appeared relevant: type of sample and type of situation. Samples were coded as either patient or nonpatient, based on whether the participants represented clinical populations or nonclinical populations. Situations were coded as either role play or in vivo (or unobtrusive, naturalistic).

Sample type (−.69) and situation type (.17) both correlated with social skill and with each other (−.42). Given that sample type and situation type were correlated to each other, it was reasoned that controlling for the most powerful variable (i.e., sample) might account for the effect of the other. However, both sample groups produced highly significant chi-squares, suggesting that both sample and situation type needed to be analyzed together. When the studies were separated (see Table 6.2), the resulting chi-square statistics were nonsignificant, indicating these variables interact to moderate the relation between behaviors and perceptions of social skill.

Talk time was strongly related to social skills ratings for nonpatient samples, but more so in naturalistic situations (.63) than role-play (.39) situa-

TABLE 6.1

Summary of Meta-Analysis Relating Behaviors to Social Skill Ratings

Behavior	Correlation of Behavior With Social Skill (r)	Standard Deviation of Rho (sr)	95% Confidence Interval		Number of (N)	Number of Studies (K)	Estimated Reliability	% Variance Attributable to Sampling Error	χ^2
			Lower Bound	Upper Bound					
Nonverbal									
Latency	-.33	.00	-.40	-.26	526	9	.99	100	4.31
Gaze	.35	.00	.23	.46	218	4	.98	100	2.46
Eye contact	.24	.00	.12	.46	268	5	.92	100	4.63
Smiles	.25	.00	.11	.38	189	9	.94	100	2.79
Gestures	.45	.00	.33	.57	170	4	.96	100	1.45
Head movements	.24	.00	.06	.41	110	3	.94	100	1.38
Adaptors	-.18	.00	-.36	.00	104	3	.99	100	2.81
Volume	.31	.00	.17	.44	184	5	.94	100	5.58
Talk time	.35	.25			635	14	.94	21	66.34*
Nonpatients/in vivo	.68	.00	.58	.77	137	7		100	5.27
Nonpatients/role play	.42	.04	.32	.51	289	6	.94	91	6.59
Verbal									
Questions	.41	.00	.32	.50	338	8	.92	100	7.05
Compliments	.41	.11	.28	.53	168	3	.94	52	5.78
Minimal encourages	.22	.11	.03	.40	100	4	.90	75	5.37

*$p < .001$.

TABLE 6.2
Effects of Talk Time on Social Skill Ratings

Situation	Sample	
	Patient	Nonpatient
Role play	$K = 0$	$r_{mean} = .39$
		$Sd_{mean} = .04$
In vivo	$r_{mean} = .08$	$r_{mean} = .63$
	$Sd_{mean} = .34$	$Sd_{mean} = .00$

tions. Further, talk time is unrelated to social skill ratings in patient samples in naturalistic situations (.08). There were no talk time studies of patients in role-play situations.

Finally, although there was a large ratio of error to observed variances ratio for compliments, suggesting variation that was not artifactual, the chi-square test was nonsignificant. Further analysis was not possible, given the small number of studies in this category.

DISCUSSION

The results of this study are both discouraging and encouraging. They are discouraging because (a) there appear to be a relatively small number of studies examining the relation between behavior and perceived skillfulness, and (b) more complex questions, such as the combined effects of behaviors, cannot be examined. For decades, therapists have employed social skills training as an integral component of treatment for a wide variety of interpersonal and psychological problems and as a source of personal enrichment. Yet, despite the enormous disciplinary and societal investments in such training, there has been surprisingly little research devoted to examining if the skills being trained are in fact effective in creating impressions of competence. By the early 1980s, only 14 articles could be located that specifically examined the relation between molecular behaviors and molar ratings of social skill. It would be easy to presume that the situation has improved significantly since the 1980s. However, a perusal of recent issues of many of the journals most represented in this meta-analysis reveals that studies have tended to move to the study of more specialized therapies for more specialized problems (e.g., social skills training for drug abusers, for juvenile delinquents, disabled persons, etc.). The more general question of which behaviors predict impressions of social skillfulness does not appear to have been a significant research priority.

The second discouraging result of this meta-analysis is the inability to examine the issue of combined effects. Specifically, behaviors do not occur in a vacuum. The meaning and significance of eye contact is likely to depend significantly on how it is framed within the entire behavioral performance a person provides. A compliment presented with no smiles, eye contact, gestures, or questions may be relatively inconsequential. A question asked with very low volume and long latency is just as likely to be viewed as incompetent. Given the nature of the design of the studies analyzed in this meta-analysis, there was no way to examine the combined effects of such behavior. Further, if the impact of a behavior depends on the behaviors that co-occur with it, clearly it is important to consider the behavior of the other person(s) in the interaction as well. Yet, almost no social skills research has analyzed the sequential or combined effects of confederate or partner behavior on the evaluation of a given person's skillfulness.

Despite these discouraging conclusions, however, it is clear that individual behaviors can have an impact on peoples' perceptions of competence. Indeed, it is somewhat surprising to consider that a given single type of behavior (e.g., head movements, questions, etc.) can significantly affect another person's impressions. In the entire context of a conversation or interaction episode, it is reassuring and intriguing that the mere frequency or duration of individual behaviors relate in systematic ways to perceived competence. To a large extent, this meta-analysis demonstrates that social skills training programs are on target. That is, the skills being assessed and trained appear to be related in valid ways to the primary criterion of interest—the impression that a person is a competent, socially skilled interactant.

There was only one unambiguously large effect, that of talk time among nonpatients in naturalistic (i.e., in vivo) contexts ($r = .68$). Such a substantial effect is remarkable for a gross-level measure such as talk time. The interaction between type of population and type of situation requires some explanation. First, patient samples may reveal a restriction of range in their verbal abilities. One of the factors that makes their condition serious enough to require clinical treatment may be limited verbalization. Such tendencies may be even more greatly restrained by role-play situations that may be so normative as to require only limited response. In contrast, "normal" interactants in relatively unstructured situations may have the most discretion to take the conversation wherever the situation and the participants desire.

Beyond the issue of the interaction between situation and sample types, the question remains why talk time should be important at all, and why it is so important in at least one particular context. One explanation may be that talk time is actually a composite measure, representing several behaviors simultaneously. To talk for extended periods of time, a person minimally needs to employ both verbal and nonverbal skills to manage turn taking, topic development, and conversational openings and closings. Regardless, it is an important finding that a single indicator, measured only by the amount of time a person spends speaking, accounts for 46% of the variance in perceptions of social skill. It suggests that a person cannot expect to make a positive impression through silence and passivity. Positive impressions appear to be made by holding the floor and having something (anything?) to say.

The strong positive correlation between talk time and social skill suggests a linear relation. However, this cannot be concluded decisively from this analysis. There was no way to adjust by proportion (i.e., how much time the interactant spoke relative to the total conversation length) or extreme range (i.e., whether or not there were extremely short talk durations and extremely long talk durations). Such an adjustment could permit a consideration of conversational narcissism, or the negative effect of dominating a conversation relative to the conversational partner. Research in other realms suggests that talk time is curvilinear to competence (Wheeless, Frymier, & Thompson, 1992). Specifically, interactants "who talk a great deal or very little are rated unfavorably and they are described as having predominantly unpleasant attributes. The most favorable evaluations are given to persons who contribute somewhat more than their share to the conversation" (Hayes & Meltzer, 1972, p. 554). Such a conclusion may also apply to all the other behaviors included in this meta-analysis (see Spitzberg, 1987, 1988, 1993, 1994, for discussion of curvilinearity and competence).

The size of the relations uncovered in this meta-analysis deserves further comment. The average correlation between any given behavior and ratings of social skillfulness was .31, accounting for just over 9% of the variance. This may not sound like a very substantial effect. However, another way of understanding this effect is to translate it into percentage improvement or success. Given the assumption $r = .31$ between the behaviors commonly taught in social skills programs and the perceptions others have of the interactant, a program that effectively taught such skills would be approximately equivalent to an improvement in perceived competence from 35% to 65% (Rosenthal, 1983). In essence, a person who actually learns to use more of the behaviors examined in this meta-analysis can expect substantial improvements in the average person's attribution of competence.

Finally, there is the issue of why: Why do these behaviors predict social skill? In examining the list of behaviors in Table 6.1, there appear to be four skill areas represented. *Composure* is the ability to appear calm, confident, and avoid signs of anxiety (e.g., latency, lack of eye contact, adaptors). *Altercentrism (alter* = other, *centrism* = to be centered on) is the ability to show interest in, concern for, and attention to the other person in the conversation (e.g., gaze, head movements, questions, compliments, etc.). *Expressiveness* is the ability to display animation in one's conversational behavior (e.g., smiles, gestures, volume, etc.). *Coordination* is the ability to manage turn taking, timing, entry, and exit in the conversation (e.g., latency, talk time, minimal encourages, etc.). There are other behaviors that fit into these categories, but extensive research shows these four clusters are significantly predictive of competence ratings, and may be fairly exhaustive as a taxonomy of social skills (see Spitzberg, 1995). When collapsed one level more (Spitzberg et al., 1994), it makes sense that there would need for a self dimension (i.e., an effectiveness, or expressiveness and composure), and an other-oriented dimension (i.e., appropriateness, or coordination and altercentrism).

Competence, therefore, is more likely to the extent that communicators pursue both self-interests and the interests of the other person(s) involved. Persons who want to initiate a romantic relationship with another need to appear composed and expressive if the other person is to perceive them as competent. Composure displays the suitor as confident and focused, and the expressiveness leaves vivid impressions and helps the other person know them. These skills help people pursue their own goals. However, unless the other person is made to feel important through coordination and altercentrism, attraction is unlikely to follow. Coordination shows a concern for making the interaction more comfortable, and the altercentrism gets the other person's interests involved in the conversation, and perhaps, the relationship. Thus, to be competent, interactants need to use their communication skills to promote both their own interests and the interests of the coparticipants.

ACKNOWLEDGMENT

This chapter is based on a study originally published with James P. Dillard as lead author (see Dillard & Spitzberg, 1984).

REFERENCES

References marked with an asterisk indicate studies included in the meta-analysis.

*Arkowitz, H., Lichtenstein, E., McGovern, K., & Hines, P. (1975). The behavioral assessment of social competence in males. *Behavior Therapy, 6,* 3–13.

Beelmann, A., Pfingsten, U., & Lösel, F. (1994). Effects of training social competence in children: A meta-analysis of recent evaluation studies. *Journal of Clinical Child Psychology, 23,* 260–271.

Bellack, A. S. (1983). Recurrent problems in the behavioral assessment of social skill. *Behaviour Research and Therapy, 21,* 29–41.

Benton, M. K., & Schroeder, H. E. (1990). Social skills training with schizophrenics: A meta-analytic evaluation. *Journal of Consulting and Clinical Psychology, 58,* 741–747.

*Conger, J. C., & Farrell, A. D. (1981). Behavioral components of heterosocial skills. *Behavior Therapy, 12,* 41–55.

Corrigan, P. W. (1991). Social skills training in adult psychiatric populations: A meta-analysis. *Journal of Behavior Therapy and Experimental Psychiatry, 22,* 203–210.

Corriveau, D. P., Vespucci, R., Curran, J. P., Monti, P.M., Wessberg, H. W., & Coyne, N. A. (1981). The effects of various rater training procedures on the perception of social skills and social anxiety. *Journal of Behavioral Assessment, 3,* 93–97.

Dillard, J. P., & Spitzberg, B. H. (1984). Global impressions of social skills: Behavioral predictors. In R. N. Bostrom (Ed.), *Communication yearbook 8* (pp. 446–463). Beverly Hills, CA: Sage.

*Dow, M. G., Glaser, S. R., & Biglan, A. (1981). The relevance of specific conversational behaviors to ratings of social skill: An experimental analysis. *Journal of Behavioral Assessment, 3,* 233–242.

Eagly, A. H., Ashmore, R. D., Makhijani, M. G., & Longo, L. C. (1991). What is beautiful is good, but … : A meta-analytic review of research on the physical attractiveness stereotype. *Psychological Bulletin, 110,* 109–128.

Foster, S. H. (1990). *The communicative competence of young children: A modular approach.* New York: Longman.

Galassi, M. D., & Galassi, J. P. (1976). The effects of role-playing variations on the assessment of assertive behavior. *Behavior Therapy, 7,* 343–347.

*Galassi, J. P., Hollandsworth, J. G., Jr., Radeki, J. C., Gay, M. L., Howe, M. R., & Evans, C. L. (1976). Behavioral performance in the validation of an assertiveness scale. *Behavior Therapy, 7,* 447–452.

*Glasgow, R. E., & Arkowitz, H. (1975). The behavioral assessment of male and female social competence in dyadic heterosexual interactions. *Behavior Therapy, 6,* 488–498.

Gormally, J. (1982). Evaluation of assertiveness: Effects of gender, rater involvement, and level of assertiveness. *Behavior Therapy, 13,* 219–225.

*Greenwald, D. P. (1977). The behavioral assessment of differences in social skill and social anxiety in female college students. *Behavior Therapy, 8,* 925–937.

Hayes, D. P., & Meltzer, L. (1972). Interpersonal judgments based on talkativeness: I. Fact or artifact? *Sociometry, 35,* 538–561.

Hunter, J., Schmidt, F., & Jackson, G. (1982). *Meta-analysis: Cumulating research findings across studies.* Beverly Hills, CA: Sage.

*Kern, J. M. (1982). The comparative external and concurrent validity of three role-plays for assessing heterosocial performance. *Behavior Therapy, 13,* 666–680.

Kleinke, C. L., Meeker, F. B., & Staneski, R. A. (1986). Preference for opening lines: Comparing ratings by men and women. *Sex Roles, 15,* 585–600.

*Martinez-Diaz, J. A., & Edelstein, B. A. (1980). Heterosocial competence: Predictive and construct validity. *Behavior Modification, 4,* 115–129.

*Minkin, N., Braukman, C. J., Minkin, B. L., Timbers, G. D., Timbers, B. J., Fixen, D. L., Phillips, E. L., & Wolf, M. M. (1976). The social validation and training of conversational skills. *Journal of Applied Behavior Analysis, 9,* 127–139.

Mungas, D. M., & Walters, H. A. (1979). Pretesting effects in the evaluation of social skills training. *Journal of Consulting and Clinical Psychology, 47,* 216–218.

Newcomb, A. F., Bukowski, W. M., & Pattee, L. (1993). Children's peer relations: A meta-analytic review of popular, rejected, neglected, controversial, and average sociometric status. *Psychological Bulletin, 113,* 99–128.

Nietzel, M. T., & Bernstein, D. A. (1976). Effects of instructionally mediated demand on the behavioral assessment of assertiveness. *Journal of Consulting and Clinical Psychology, 44,* 500.

Nunnally, J. (1969). *Psychometric theory* (2nd ed.). New York: McGraw-Hill.

Procidano, M. E. (1992). The nature of perceived social support: Findings of meta-analytic studies. In C. D. Spielberger & J. N. Butcher (Eds.), *Advances in personality assessment* (Vol. 9, pp. 1–26). Hillsdale, NJ: Lawrence Erlbaum Associates.

Ritts, V., Patterson, M. L., & Tubbs, M. E. (1992). Expectations, impressions, and judgments of physically attractive students: A review. *Review of Educational Research, 62,* 413–426.

Röhrle, B., & Sommer, G. (1994). Social support and social competencies: Some theoretical and empirical contributions to their relationship. In N. F. Nestmann & K. Hurrelmann (Eds.), *Social networks and social support in childhood and adolescence* (pp. 111–129). Berlin: de Gruyter.

*Romano, J. M., & Bellack, A. S. (1980). Social validation of a component model of assertive behavior. *Journal of Consulting and Clinical Psychology, 48,* 478–490.

Rook, K. S. (1992). Detrimental aspects of social relationships: Taking stock of an emerging literature. In H. O. F. Veiel & U. Baumann (Eds.), *The meaning and measurement of social support* (pp. 157–169). New York: Hemisphere.

Rook, K. S. (1998). Investigating the positive and negative sides of personal relationships: Through a lens darkly? In B. H. Spitzberg & W. R. Cupach (Eds.), *The dark side of close relationships* (pp. 369–393). Mahwah, NJ: Lawrence Erlbaum Associates.

Rook, K. S., & Pietromonaco, P. (1987). Close relationships: Ties that heal or ties that bind? In W. H. Jones & D. Perlman (Eds.), *Advances in personal relationships* (Vol. 1, pp. 1–35). Greenwich, CT: JAI.

Rosenthal, R. (1983). Meta-analysis: Toward a more cumulative social science. In L. Bickman (Ed.), *Applied social psychology annual* (Vol. 4, pp. 65–93). Beverly Hills, CA: Sage.

*Royce, W. S. (1982). Behavioral referents for molar ratings of heterosocial skill. *Psychological Reports, 50,* 139–146.

Segrin, C. (1990). A meta-analytic review of social skill deficits in depression. *Communication Monographs, 57,* 292–308.

Segrin, C. (1992). Specifying the nature of social skill deficits associated with depression. *Human Communication Research, 19,* 89–123.

Segrin, C. (1993). Social skills deficits and psychosocial problems: Antecedent, concomitant, or consequent? *Journal of Social and Clinical Psychology, 12,* 336–353.

Segrin, C. (1997). Social skills, stressful life events, and the development of psychosocial problems. *Journal of Social and Clinical Psychology, 18,* 14–34.

Segrin, C., & Dillard, J. P. (1993). The complex link between social skill and dysphoria. *Communication Research, 20,* 76–104.

*Spence, S. H. (1981). Validation of social skills of adolescent males in an interview conversation with a previously unknown adult. *Journal of Applied Behavior Analysis, 14,* 159–168.

Spitzberg, B. H. (1987). Issues in the study of communicative competence. In B. Dervin & M. J. Voight (Eds.), *Progress in communication sciences* (Vol. 8, pp. 1–46). Norwood, NJ: Ablex.

Spitzberg, B. H. (1988). Communication competence: Measures of perceived effectiveness. In C. H. Tardy (Eds.), *A handbook for the study of human communication: Methods and instruments for observing, measuring, and assessing communication processes* (pp. 67–106). Norwood, NJ: Ablex.

Spitzberg, B. H. (1993). The dialectics of (in)competence. *Journal of Social and Personal Relationships, 10,* 137–158.

Spitzberg, B. H. (1994). The dark side of (in)competence. In W. R. Cupach & B. H. Spitzberg (Eds.), *The dark side of interpersonal communication* (pp. 25–49). Hillsdale, NJ: Lawrence Erlbaum Associates.

Spitzberg, B. H. (1995). *The conversational skills rating scale: An instructional assessment of interpersonal competence.* Annandale, VA: Speech Communication Association.

Spitzberg, B. H., & Canary, D. J. (1985). Loneliness and relationally competent communication. *Journal of Social and Personal Relationships, 2,* 387–402.

Spitzberg, B. H., Canary, D. J., & Cupach, W. R. (1994). A competence-based approach to the study of interpersonal conflict. In D. D. Cahn (Ed.), *Conflict in personal relationships* (pp. 183–202). Hillsdale, NJ: Lawrence Erlbaum Associates.

Spitzberg, B. H., & Cupach, W. R. (1984). *Interpersonal communication competence.* Beverly Hills, CA: Sage.

Spitzberg, B. H., & Cupach, W. R. (1989). *Handbook of interpersonal competence research.* New York: Springer-Verlag.

*St. Lawrence, J. S. (1982). Validation of a component model of social skill with outpatient adults. *Journal of Behavioral Assessment, 4,* 15–26.

Steinberg, S. L., Curran, J. P., Bell, S., Paxson, M. A., & Munroe, S. M. (1982). The effects of confederate prompt delivery style in a standardized social stimulation test. *Journal of Behavioral Assessment, 4,* 263–272.

Swanson, H. L., & Malone, S. (1992). Social skills and learning disabilities: A meta-analysis of the literature. *School Psychology Review, 21,* 427–443.

Taylor, S. (1996). Meta-analysis of cognitive-behavioral treatments for social phobia. *Journal of Behavior Therapy and Experimental Psychiatry, 27,* 1–9.

Trower, P. (1980). Situational analysis of the components and processes of behavior of socially skilled and unskilled patients. *Journal of Consulting and Clinical Psychology, 48,* 327–339.

Trower, P., Bryant, B., & Argyle, M. (1978). *Social skills and mental health.* Pittsburgh, PA: University of Pittsburgh Press.

Wallander, J. L., Conger, A. J., Mariotto, M. J., Curran, J. P., & Farrell, A. D. (1980). Comparability of selection instruments in studies of heterosexual-social problem behaviors. *Behavior Therapy, 11,* 548–560.

Wheeless, L. R., Frymier, A. B., & Thompson, C. A. (1992). A comparison of verbal output and receptivity in relation to attraction and communication satisfaction in interpersonal relationships. *Communication Quarterly, 40,* 102–115.

III

Dyadic Issues
in Interpersonal
Communication

7

An Overview of Dyadic Processes in Interpersonal Communication

Barbara Mae Gayle and Raymond W. Preiss

As a way to approach interpersonal communication processes, we selected three general perspectives as the framework for this book. The first section emphasized individual characteristics and behaviors, and we now examine the empirical literature focusing on the dyad as a central issue in interpersonal communication. We were mindful of both the uniqueness and suitability criteria as we selected and arranged the empirical summaries in this section. In this overview, we make the case for dyadic processes, summarize some of the recent contributions in this area, and offer connections to the meta-analyses in this section. In Part III, we turn our attention to approaches that emphasize the interaction as a way to explain interpersonal communication processes and outcomes.

DYADIC PROCESSES

Dyadic communication is based upon the premise that "each participant affects and is affected by the other" (Wilmot, 1987, p. 38). As Duck and Pittman (1994) explained, it is

> through the daily activities of talk ... that two partners in a relationship achieve a comprehension of one another's psychology, an understanding of

roles and complementarity of behavior that reorganizes the relationship, and a realization of sharing that is itself an important message about the stability, nature, and futurity of the relationship (p. 682).

Thus, everyday interpersonal conversations are used to negotiate one's roles and identity, establish parameters in the relationship, maximize each person's needs, and acquire information about the partner.

Frequently occurring topics in the study of these dyadic issues involve an individual's identity construction, patterns of disclosure, aspects of attraction, relation uncertainty reduction strategies, need achievement, and relational influence. The meta-analyses in this section address issues concerning children's identity formation, the relationship between similarity of attitude and attraction, and the relational functions of self-disclosure. Also, a secondary data analysis explores the impact of the situation on utilizing compliance-gaining strategies. The purpose of this overview is to briefly discuss these commonly researched areas to provide the context for the three meta-analyses and one secondary data analysis. Each topic is reviewed, followed by a brief conceptual summary.

Relational and Personal Identity

Most researchers agree that interpersonal communication is an important aspect of dyadic processes. Central to dyadic exchanges are opportunities for self-discovery and change. Researchers believe that a person's identity is shaped and negotiated through her or his interactions with relational partners (McCall, 1987; Swann, 1987; Tajfel, 1981). Identity formation can occur in many contexts and across a diverse array of relationships. Thoits and Virshup (1997) suggested that identity formation is an ongoing process that is achieved through lasting relationships. They reasoned that one's role identity is established through interactions with relational partners who provide mutual exchanges of support. Over time, more and more of the partners' self-identity is thought to be integrated into the relationship, as opportunities for identity formation and reinforcement are encountered and managed.

Allen and Burrell (chap. 8) address a specific issue of identity construction: How the sexual identity of parents affects their children. The authors explore various research findings that lead to conflicting hypotheses regarding the impact of homosexual parenting on children's identity formation. Their research extends the dyadic perspective to an important social issue. Other meta-analyses in this section indirectly address identity formation. Dindia's (chap. 10) discussion on self-disclosure and liking and self-disclosure and reciprocity suggests a process of self-definition constructed through intimate exchanges. Ah Yun's (chap. 9) meta-analysis of the similarity and attraction literature indicates that the positive affect that occurs during interactions may affect the identity formation of relational partners.

Attraction

Theories of attraction attempt to explain the processes involved in relationship formation or maintenance. Researchers have explored three dimensions of attraction: social affinity, physical appearance, and task respect. Hatfield and Sprecher (1986) defined physical attractiveness as "one's conception of the ideal in appearance" (p. 5). Research on physical attraction reveals an overall preference for those who are physically attractive (Langlois, Roggman, Casey, Riesner-Danner, & Jenkins, 1987), a pattern of dating partners matching in terms of physical attraction (Feingold, 1988), and a tendency for physically attractive roommates to be more satisfied with their relationships (Carli, Ganley, & Pierce-Otay, 1991).

McCroskey and McCain (1974) argued that social attractiveness, in contrast to physical attractiveness, occurs when individuals enjoy interacting and want to spend time with their relational partner. Researchers found that people who are seen as humorous (Wanzer, Booth-Butterfield, & Booth-Butterfield, 1992) or are judged to be highly communicatively competent (Duran & Kelly, 1988) are viewed as more socially attractive, and those who are perceived as being verbally aggressive are seen as less socially attractive (Wanzer et al., 1992),

Johnson (1992) maintained that task attraction "deals with the perceived ability to work with another person" (p. 58). Individuals seem to base their judgments of this type of attraction on how competent a communicator the individual appears to be (Duran & Kelly, 1988; Johnson, 1992). Researchers have found that perceptions of task attraction are related to the versatility and responsiveness dimensions of communicator style and nonconfrontation and solution-orientation strategies of conflict management (Wheeless & Reichel, 1990). Perceptions of physical, social, and task attraction appear to affect relational initiation and maintenance.

The meta-analyses in this section reflect the dyadic approach to interpersonal communication. Ah Yun's (chap. 9) meta-analysis explores the extensively investigated topic of attitude similarity and attraction. Ah Yun provides a detailed account of the various approaches, competing theoretical explanations, and contradictory findings evident in this domain of literature. The positive average effect detected by the meta-analysis illustrates how interpersonal exchanges mediate perceptions of the participants. The Dindia (chap. 10) meta-analysis indirectly addresses the issue of interpersonal attraction by exploring the relation between liking and self-disclosure. She reports positive effect sizes that are consistent with fundamental dyadic processes such as reciprocity. Hample and Dallinger's (chap. 11) secondary data analysis suggests that the attraction to another individual maybe one of the relational situations that influence the choice of compliance-gaining tactics.

Relational Uncertainty

A dyadic process evident in judgments of interpersonal attraction involves uncertainty reduction. Uncertainty reduction theory (URT) is based on the assumption that as the amount of verbal or nonverbal affiliative communication increases, the level of uncertainty decreases (Berger, 1979; Berger & Calabrese, 1975). Researchers posit that high levels of uncertainty increase information-seeking behaviors and reciprocity rates, as participants learn about and predict their partner's behavior. If uncertainty reduction results in perceived attractiveness, verbal and nonverbal affiliative communication, intimacy levels, and liking tend increase (Berger & Calabrese, 1975). Personality and attitude similarities tend to reduce uncertainty, whereas differences tend to increase uncertainty (Berger, 1979). Berger and Calabrese (1975) theorized that uncertainty reduction is an important motive for communicating during three phases of initial interactions. In the entry phase, individuals exchange information on trivial topics and maintain low involvement. During the personal phase, individuals discuss their feelings, attitudes, and judgments and lay the foundation for a future relationship. In the exit phase, relational partners negotiate ways to allow the relationship to grow or they decide to stabilize or withdraw from the relationship.

Berger (1979, 1986) extended URT by advancing two types of uncertainty: cognitive and behavioral. He suggested that cognitive uncertainty is a generalized state, whereas behavioral uncertainty is felt as a result of a particular exchange. As individuals seek to establish deeper levels of relational intimacy, they must increase their knowledge about the partner. This requires individuals to move from a descriptive knowledge that accounts for others' current behavior; to predictive knowledge of the other's beliefs, attitudes, and feelings; to explanatory knowledge, where the individual can articulate the partner's behavior and motives. Individuals are thought to construct messages that facilitate uncertainty reduction, using passive strategies to unobtrusively observe the other, active strategies to seek information (perhaps from a third party), and interactive strategies to obtain information through direct exchanges (Berger, 1979).

Research indicates that URT is an important dyadic process. Parks and Adelman (1983) found that when an individual's family supports his or her romantic involvement, the individual reports less uncertainty about the relationship and are more committed to the partner. Neuliep and Ryan (1998) found that as fear and anxiety about interacting with someone from another culture increased, uncertainty about the other's future behavior increased. An exploration of home health care nurses' conversations with seriously ill patients revealed that nurses are "more reluctant to initiate conversations designed to reduce uncertainty about how a patient wants to be treated [concerning end-of-life issues] when conversations produce other uncertainties that may be even more threatening" (Hines, Badzek, Leslie, & Glover, 1998, p. 336). Brashers et al. (2000) discovered that individuals managing a diagnosis of HIV seek to both reduce uncertainty and maintain it. These authors concluded that uncertainty reduction is not necessarily a linear process and that avoidance of closure is also a viable uncertainty reduction strategy.

The meta-analyses and secondary analyses in this section indirectly address elements of the URT. Allen and Burrell (chap. 8) consider social stereotypes as an uncertainty reduction strategy used to judge the impact a parent's sexual practices may have on children. Hample and Dallinger (chap. 11) address the ways the situation can affect how certain an individual is that a compliance-gaining strategy will be effective. Dindia (chap. 10) and Ah Yun (chap. 9) directly address URT. Dindia's meta-analysis reveals how self-disclosure is used to reduce uncertainty and increase liking, and Ah Yun's summary addresses attitude similarity, which, if increased, leads to less uncertainty and greater attraction.

Disclosure Patterns

A fourth theme in the interpersonal communication literature involves disclosure patterns within the dyad. Dindia's (chap. 10) meta-analysis defines self-disclosure as "the process by which one person verbally reveals information about himself or herself (including thoughts, feelings, and experiences) to another person." She presents three meta-analyses on self-disclosure—sex differences, self-disclosure and liking, and reciprocity—to produce a comprehensive review of the self-disclosure research. Her findings related to sex stereotyping, relationship intimacy, and reciprocity have far-reaching theoretical implications for researchers interested in relational development.

Social penetration theory researchers view self-disclosure as a primary mechanism for regulating intimacy in interpersonal relationships. Altman and Taylor (1973) defined social penetration as "overt interpersonal behaviors which take place in social interaction and internal subjective processes which precede, accompany or follow overt exchange" (p. 5). They reasoned that self-disclosive exchanges result in "a subjective picture of what the other person is like, positive and negative feelings about the person, and an estimation of how the other individual would behave in a variety of situations" (p. 5). For example, Altman and Taylor suggested that in the initial relationship stages, partners might search for similarities as they promote a sense of trustworthiness needed for the relationship to progress to a more intimate level. Altman, Vinsel, and Brown (1981) concluded that relational partners engage in cycles of openness or closedness that vary in frequency (how often), amplitude (degrees of openness or closedness), regularity (patterns of openness and closedness), and duration (how long the cycle lasts). These cycles vary from couple to couple and involve a sense of equity in exchanges. Viable relationships withstand periods of stability and change and progress through a number of cycles and stages.

Taylor and Altman (1987) clarified social penetration theory by articulating four relationship development stages and delineating how individuals proceed from trivial to intimate exchanges within these stages. In the orientation stage, cautious and exploratory communication occurs in public arenas. In the exploration stage, thoughts and feelings are exchanged that reveal aspects of one's personality and private thoughts. As participants move to the affective exchange stage, even more about one's personality, feelings, and private thoughts are exchanged in a casual and freewheeling atmosphere. The final stable exchange stage is characterized by a continuous openness that allows partners to interpret and predict each other's behaviors and feelings. Taylor and Altman acknowledged that, for a relationship to grow, partners must negotiate inevitable conflicts and calculate the communication rewards involved in managing relational stress.

VanLear (1987, 1991) used longitudinal studies to investigate cyclical functions of the social penetration theory. VanLear (1987) found that there was a cycle of reciprocal exchanges over time as well as an equity norm related to the intimacy level of the disclosures. VanLear (1991) again supported the cyclical model and found that the short cycles were often part of larger fluctuations. He also noted that partners coincide in the amplitude and frequency of their disclosures.

Intercultural scholars have also employed social penetration theory. Although Gudykunst and Nishida (1983) identified more similarities than differences, they did find that Americans engage in more exchanges within their close friendships about their marriage; love, dating, and sex; and emotions than did their Japanese counterparts. Likewise, Korn (1993) found that Koreans and Americans have specific, stable topics that are explored within their close relationships. Americans tended to be more self-disclosive regarding separated or divorced parents, money, defensiveness about one's own beliefs, loans, conversing with others, sexual morality and birth control, and episodes of bravery. Korean partners, on the other hand, reported significantly more social penetration than Americans on family rules, the importance of education, and responsibility.

Overall, the research on self-disclosure and social penetration theory indicates that relational partners, at every stage of the relationship, have expectations about the amount and types of self-disclosure that are appropriate for the dyad. Clearly, Dindia's (chap. 10) meta-analysis in this section captures the essence of social penetration mechanisms. Consistent with Altman and Taylor's (1973) theorizing, Ah Yun's (chap. 9) meta-analysis on similarity and attraction addresses the idea that relational partners search for similarities in the initial stages of the relationship.

Social Exchange

A fifth theme in the interpersonal communication literature involves exchanges of messages as the basis of relational satisfaction. Researchers adopting the perspective of social exchange theory believe that individuals use a cost–benefit analysis in determining whether to continue or terminate their relationships (Blau, 1964; Homans, 1958; Thibaut & Kelley, 1959). Relational partners apply economic principles to minimize negative outcomes or costs such as time, money, and emotional energy and maximize relational rewards such as companionship, affection, and love (Foa & Foa, 1972; Walster, Berschied, & Walster, 1976).

Roloff (1981) argued that the "guiding force of interpersonal relationships is the advancement of both parties' self-interest" (p. 14). He claimed that each relational partner determines what is a fair exchange or what she or he expects of a particular relationship (Roloff, 1987). Thus, the nature of a satisfactory exchange and the terms for compliance or repayment will vary, based on the partner, the partner's past experiences, and the current relationship. These judgments are thought to result from a needs assessment, where partners negotiate the means for improving their relationships so that specific obligations are met or sanctions are invoked. Roloff (1987) suggested that these negotiations involve norms of reciprocity. Relational satisfaction is thought to be rooted in expectations of a fair distribution of relational resources, the equity of the exchanges, and the time allowed to satisfy needs.

Social exchange researchers have explored the tenets of the theory using a variety of relationship types. Cline and Musolf (1985) examined college students' relationships to test the efficacy of the social exchange model. They found that females made high intimacy investments with male partners, whereas males disclosed intimately only in short-term relationships. Cline and Musolf concluded that traditional sex-role socialization leads males and females to invest in relationships differently and expect different rewards. Canary and Stafford (1992) explored marital relationships. They found that partners' comparison level index or equity perceptions varied and that partners engaged in different relationship maintenance strategies. When wives reported their marriages were equitable, both husbands and wives reported greater use of positivity, assurance, and openness, and husbands reported greater use of social networks.

In organizational settings, Daniels and Spiker (1983) explored social exchange theory in terms of the superior's information adequacy on issues of organizational concern, the subordinate's relational satisfaction with her or his supervisor, and job satisfaction. Their results indicated that the information adequacy and job satisfaction model could be improved by accounting for the relational satisfaction and the loss of the superior's information. Cox and Kramer (1995) found that managers constantly engage in the process of calculating a cost–benefit ratio based on the employee's fit with organizational norms, expectations for performance, or the replacement costs. Positive ratios resulted in retaining the employee, whereas a "poor performance breakpoint" resulted in the employee being dismissed (Cox & Kramer, 1995, p. 179). Kramer (1993) observed support for social exchange processes in the adjustment of employees transferred to a new location. Transferees gathered their resources until they felt secure enough to negotiate their roles. However, Kramer did not detect the gradual deepening of relationships predicted by social exchange theory. For transferees, relationships developed and stabilized quickly.

Overall, research suggests that participants in ongoing relationships assess whether their needs are being met and how the dyad must adjust if the relationship is to continue. Although no meta-analysis in this section directly assesses the efficacy of social exchange theory, the basic principles can be identified indirectly. The motivation for self-disclosure described in Dindia's (chap. 10) meta-analysis, the positive affect underlying Ah Yun's (chap. 9) similarity and attraction meta-analysis, the costs and rewards inherent in establishing a strong homosexual parent–child relationship in Allen and Burrell's (chap. 8) meta-analysis, and the personal benefits derived from selecting the appropriate compliance-gaining strategies in Hample and Dallinger's (chap. 11) research all suggest that relationship negotiation is based on the self-interest of the parties involved.

Relational Influence

The final theme in the interpersonal communication literature stresses that individuals in dyadic exchanges are involved in a process of mutual influence. Dillard, Segrin, and Harden (1989) claimed that "an obvious and undisputable fact of social existence is that individuals attempt to influence others in order to achieve their own ends" (p. 19). These influence attempts might be active (to gain something from, or to change, another) or passive (having an impact on another) and elicit responses such as resistance, compliance, or withdrawal from the relationship (Dillard, 1990). Interpersonal influence appears to involve "regulative and persuasive attempts in face-to-face situations in which there is potential for feedback and reciprocal communication" (Newton & Burgoon, 1990, p. 478). Newton and Burgoon (1990) suggested that individuals attempt to attain instrumental goals, manage the relationship, and preserve desired identities. These maneuvers may involve considerable risk, as influence attempts occur between interdependent and interconnected partners.

Researchers have examined the way individuals enact their influence attempts. Dillard et al. (1989) advanced a goal–planning–action sequence based on the desired outcome and the costs to the relationship associated with the influence tactic or goal chosen. They suggested that individuals consider both primary goals that instigate the influence process and secondary goals that shape the verbal communication choices available. Dillard et al. (1989) proposed five types of secondary goals: identity, interactional, personal resources, relational resources, and arousal management. Newton and Burgoon (1990) found that content validation, self-assertions, and other accusations were the most common strategies, but greater communication satisfaction occurred when supportive tactics were employed. Males were more persuasive when using content validation and self-assertions and less persuasive using content invalidation and other accusations. Females were more persuasive using other-supported strategies and less persuasive using content invalidation. The research on interpersonal influence suggests that relational partners assess goals and strategically implement strategies to gain compliance.

In a situation that calls for persuasion, relational partners may elect to use messages or suppress them. Hample and Dallinger (chap. 11) address issues related to interpersonal influence or "the ways in which we try to get another person to comply with our wishes." In Study 1, they explore the suppression or endorsement of interpersonal persuasive appeals. In Study 2, they assess situational features that affect the decision-making processes individuals engage in when producing compliance-gaining appeals. Seven situational dimensions are identified that mediate the decision to endorse or suppress a potential persuasive appeal. Other meta-analyses in this section indirectly address interpersonal influence. In Ah Yun's (chap. 9) meta-analysis, the perception of attitudinal similarity is created, in part, through interpersonal influence attempts. Similarly, in Dindia's (chap. 10) meta-analysis on liking and self-disclosure, a partner might choose what to share to influence his or her relational partner's feelings of connectedness.

CONCLUSION

In this overview, we have tried to stress subtle distinctions between theories that share a great deal of intellectual space. Although recognizing the similarities, we believe that the dyadic nature of interpersonal communication can be illuminated by adopting the perspectives of relational and personal identity, attraction, relational uncertainty, disclosure patterns, social exchange, and interpersonal influence. Each theme highlights subtle features of relationships that lead to important outcomes. It is also fair to conclude that each theme emphasizes ongoing interpersonal processes that are fundamental to building, maintaining, or terminating relationships.

The goal of this preview was to offer a context for interpreting the meta-analyses in this section. Of course, each meta-analysis can stand alone as a summary of the domain of literature related to its topic. We believe that a longer view is also warranted. Meta-analytic findings have implications for the themes that have emerged over years, even decades, of research. The summaries in this section provide evidence that these dyadic communication themes are vital and robust. They summarize enduring issues, offer surprising insights, and pose interesting new questions for future investigation.

REFERENCES

Altman, L., & Taylor, D. A. (1973). *Social penetration: The development of interpersonal relationships.* New York: Holt, Rinehart & Winston.

Altman, L., Vinsel, A., & Brown, B. A. (1981). Dialectic conceptions in social psychology: An application to social penetration and privacy regulation. In L. Berkowitz (Ed.), *Advances in experimental social psychology* (Vol. 14, pp. 107–160). New York: Academic.

Berger, C. R. (1979). Beyond initial interactions: Uncertainty, understanding, and the development of interpersonal relationships. In H. Giles & R. N. St. Clair (Eds.), *Language and social psychology* (pp. 122–144). Oxford, UK: Basil Blackwell.

Berger, C. R. (1986). Uncertainty outcome values in predicted relationships: Uncertainty reduction theory then and now. *Human Communication Research, 13,* 34–38.

Berger, C. R., & Calabrese, R. J. (1975). Some explorations in initial interaction and beyond: Toward a development theory of interpersonal communication. *Human Communication Research, 1,* 99–112.

Blau, P. (1964). *Exchange and power in social life.* New York: Wiley.

Brashers, D. E., Neidig, J. L., Haas, S. M., Dobbs, L. K., Cardillo, L. W., & Russell, J. A. (2000). Communication in the management of uncertainty: The case of persons living with HIV or AIDS. *Communication Monographs, 67,* 63–84.

Canary, D. J., & Stafford, L. (1992). Relational maintenance strategies and equity in marriage. *Communication Monographs, 59,* 243–267.

Carli, L. L., Ganley, R., & Pierce-Otay, A. (1991). Similarity and satisfaction in roommate relationships. *Journal of Personality and Social Psychology, 17,* 419–426.

Cline, R. J., & Musolf, K. E. (1985). Disclosure as social exchange: Anticipated length of relationship, sex roles, and disclosure intimacy. *Western Journal of Speech Communication, 49,* 43–56.

Cox, S. A., & Kramer, M. W. (1995). Communication during employee dismissals: Social Exchange principles and group influences on employee exit. *Management Communication Quarterly, 9,* 156–190.

Daniels, T. D., & Spiker, B. K. (1983). Social exchange and the relationship between information adequacy and relational satisfaction. *Western Journal of Speech Communication, 47,* 118–137.

Dillard, J. P. (1990). A goal-driven model of interpersonal influence. In J. Dillard (Ed.), *Seeking compliance: The production of interpersonal influence messages* (pp. 41–56). Scottsdale, AZ: Gorsuch Scarisbrick.

Dillard, J. P., Segrin, C., & Harden, J. M. (1989). Primary and secondary goals in the production of interpersonal influence messages. *Communication Monographs, 56,* 19–38.

Duck, S., & Pittman, G. (1994). Social and personal relationships. In M. L. Knapp & G. R. Miller (Eds.), *Handbook of interpersonal communication* (pp. 676–695). Thousand Oaks, CA: Sage.

Duran, R. L., & Kelly, L. (1988). The influence of communicative competence on perceived task, social, and physical attraction. *Communication Quarterly, 36,* 41–49.

Feingold, A. (1988). Matching for attractiveness in romantic partners and same-sex friends: A meta-analysis and theoretical critique. *Psychological Bulletin, 104,* 226–235.

Foa, E., & Foa, U. (1972). Resource theory of social exchange. In J. Thibaut, J. Spence, & R. Carson (Eds.), *Contemporary topics in social psychology* (pp. 99–131). Morristown, NJ: General Learning Press.

Gudykunst, W. B., & Nishida, T. (1983). Social penetration in Japanese and American close friendships. In R. N. Bostrom (Ed.), *Communication yearbook 7* (pp. 592–611). Beverly Hills, CA: Sage.

Hatfield, E., & Sprecher, S. (1986). *Mirror, mirror ... The importance of looks in everyday life.* Albany: State University of New York Press.

Hines, S. C., Badzek, L., Leslie, N., & Glover, J. (1998). Managing uncertainty in conversations about treatment preferences: A study of home health care nurses. *Communication Research Reports, 15,* 331–339.

Homans, G. (1958). Social behavior as exchange. *American Journal of Sociology, 63,* 597–606.

Johnson, G. M. (1992). Subordinate perceptions of superior's communication competence and task attraction related to superior's use of compliance-gaining tactics. *Western Journal of Communication, 56,* 54–67.

Korn, C. J. (1993). Friendship formation and development in two cultures: Universal constructs in the United States and Korea. In A. M. Nicotera (Ed.), *Interpersonal communication in friend and mate relationships* (pp. 61–78). Albany: State University of New York Press.

Kramer, M. W. (1993). Communication about job transfers: Social exchange processes in learning new roles. *Human Communication Research, 20,* 147–174.

Langlois, J. H., Roggman, L. A., Casey, R. J., Riesner-Danner, L. A., & Jenkins, V. Y. (1987). Infant preferences for attractive faces: Rudiments of a stereotype? *Developmental Psychology, 23,* 363–369.

McCall, G. J. (1987). The self-concept and interpersonal communication. In M. E. Roloff & G. R. Miller (Eds.), *Interpersonal processes: New directions in communication research* (pp. 63–76). Newbury Park, CA: Sage.

McCroskey, J. C., & McCain, T. A. (1974). The measurement of interpersonal attraction. *Speech Monographs, 41,* 261–266.

Neuliep, J. W., & Ryan, D. J. (1998). The influence of intercultural communication apprehension and socio-communicative orientation on uncertainty reduction during initial cross-cultural interaction. *Communication Quarterly, 46,* 88–99.

Newton, D. A., & Burgoon, J. K. (1990). The use and consequence of verbal influence strategies during interpersonal disagreements. *Human Communication Research, 16,* 477–518.

Parks, M. R., & Adelman, M. B. (1983). Communication networks and the development of romantic relationships: An expansion of uncertainty reduction theory. *Human Communication Research, 10,* 55–79.

Roloff, M. E. (1981). *Interpersonal communication: The social exchange approach.* Beverly Hills, CA: Sage.

Roloff, M. E. (1987). Communication and reciprocity within intimate relationship. In M. E. Roloff & G. R. Miller (Eds.), *Interpersonal processes: New directions in communication research* (pp. 11–38). Newbury Park, CA: Sage

Swann, W. B., Jr. (1987). Identity negotiation: Where two roads meet. *Journal of Personality and Social Psychology, 53,* 1038–1051.

Tajfel, H. (1981). *Human groups and social categories: Studies in social psychology.* Cambridge, UK: Cambridge University Press.

Taylor, D. A., & Altman, I. (1987). Communication in interpersonal relationships: Social penetration processes. In M. E. Roloff & G. R. Miller (Eds.), *Interpersonal processes: New directions in communication research* (pp. 257–277). Newbury Park, CA: Sage.

Thibaut, J., & Kelley, H. (1959). *The social psychology of groups.* New York: Wiley.

Thoits, P. A., & Virshup, L. K. (1997). Me's and we's: Forms and functions of social identities. In R. D. Ashmore & L. Jessium (Eds.), *Self and identity* (pp. 106–126). Oxford, UK: Oxford University Press.

VanLear, C. A. (1987). The formation of social relationships: A longitudinal study of social penetration. *Human Communication Research, 13,* 299–322.

VanLear, C. A. (1991). Testing a cyclical model of communicative openness in relationship development: Two longitudinal studies. *Communication Monographs, 58,* 337–361.

Walster, E., Berschied, E., & Walster, G. (1976). New directions in equity research. In L. Berkowitz & E. Walster (Eds.), *Equity theory: Toward a general theory of social interaction* (pp. 1–42). New York: Academic.

Wanzer, M. B., Booth-Butterfield, M., & Booth-Butterfield, S. (1992). Are funny people popular? An examination of humor orientation, loneliness, and social attraction. *Communication Quarterly, 44,* 42–52.

Wilmot, W. W. (1987). *Dyadic communication*. New York: Random House.

Wheeless, L. R., & Reichel, L. S. (1990). A reinforcement model of the relationships of supervisor's general communication styles and conflict styles to task attraction. *Communication Quarterly, 38*, 372–387.

8

Sexual Orientation of the Parent: The Impact on the Child

Mike Allen and Nancy A. Burrell

The raising of a child represents one of the most important interactions between individuals that exists in society. The Supreme Court of the United States in various decisions (*Griswold v. Connecticut*, 1964) has recognized the right to raise a child as a fundamental question of freedom. The courts have recognized that parents are provided the right to determine choices for the child. The courts give parents wide latitude in determining how a child should be raised. A parent is permitted to determine religion, diet, schooling, and a whole host of other aspects of the upbringing of a child. The premise is that parents should be able to raise a child according to the beliefs and practices of their choosing. As long as the practices represent no direct and recognizable harm to the child, the courts have been reluctant to interfere with the right of a parent to raise a child according to the preference of the parent.

The question of the sexual practices of the parent come into question when a marriage ends in divorce, and about 50% of marriages in the United States do end in divorce (although recent evidence indicates that this rate may be dropping). One of the issues regarding the process of separation is how to determine the custody of children and visitation rights, a major issue for separating spouses. The divorce represents a relational change from husband and wife to a shared responsibility of mother and father. The divorce decree provides a framework for the dissolution of one set of relationships, while it must also provide a basis for a continued shared responsibility. The problem is separating one set of relational ties while maintaining and continuing another relationship. When the parents cannot agree on a suitable arrangement for custody, the courts must intervene and create an order that divides the responsibilities for the child(ren) among the parents. The order specifies which parent retains primary custody (unless custody is joint) as well as the physical placement of the child and resolves any other disagreements that require attention. Courts prefer that parents find satisfactory solutions to which both parties agree, but court-ordered judgments are required when the divorcing spouses do not agree.

When one parent is a homosexual, the resulting anger of the heterosexual parent creates the potential for a large impediment to finding a nonadjudicated solution to issues of custody and visitation. Many heterosexual partners would experience anger and resentment toward a divorcing homosexual partner. If the heterosexual spouse was unaware of the preference of the partner, the notification of the change in practice often would form the basis for the divorce. Divorcing couples often are angry with each other and seek methods of getting some measure of revenge. The heterosexual spouse may feel particularly betrayed after years of a relationship that is dissolving for reasons that the spouse cannot affect. The feeling of betrayal and accusations of dishonesty can create a situation in which the children become a focus for hurting the other party.

The issue of the sexual practices of the parent may be considered by the courts as a relevant issue in the determination of placement and visitation. The courts need to establish a custody arrangement that promotes the "best interests" of the child, while not abridging the rights of the parent to serve as a guiding force for the development of the person. The courts can choose to consider whether the sexual practices of the parent represent some factor that should affect the custody, placement, and visitation rights of the parent.

What the courts are seeking to determine is the impact of the environment in which the child will be exposed and raised. The courts are charged with the requirement of examining all relevant aspects of the environment and determining the "best" place and arrangement for the interests of the child. Such a charge is a broad one and the courts can consider a variety of elements in making the determination. The number of gay parents with children is estimated to be several million, indicating a great number of persons (both parents and children) potentially affected by the issue of parent sexual practices as a custody issue. The willingness or ability of the courts to examine this issue creates a basis of concern for millions of individuals in the United States.

This issue falls squarely in the field of communication and represents a set of issues that contain a number of theoretical and practical implications. The communication question is that the basis of determining the impact of parental sexual preference is based on the impact of interaction between the parent and child. Many of the studies examine or consider the issues based on the expectation that a continuing set of interactions between child and parent will generate various outcomes. The question before the courts is whether the sexual practices of the parent impact the interaction in a deleterious manner. The design of many of the studies examining the impact of the parental sexual practice involves the observation of the impact of how the sexual practices of the parent do or do not manifest themselves in the social interaction of the child. The examination involves an evaluation of how interaction with a type of individual generates various outcomes.

HOMOSEXUALS AND CUSTODY DECISIONS

Gay parents automatically lose custody and visitation in the courts in six states (Mississippi, Missouri, North Dakota, Oklahoma, South Dakota, and Virginia; see O'Dell, 1995). Parental homosexuality can serve as the basis for denial of visitation and custody of a child during a divorce in those states. Even in states that have statutes expressly forbidding the consideration of sexual preference of the parent, the judge may deem the acts of the parent as relevant in determining the "best interests" of the child (*Ketron v. Aguirre,* 1985; *Warren v. Warren,* 1980). Therefore even when the sexual choice or practice of the parent should not be considered as a basis for decision, the issues may be introduced at the discretion of the judge. The result is that the issue of the parent's sexual practice is introduced whenever the judge decides that the issue is relevant. Wide latitude of discretion for family court judges exists when considering the circumstances relevant to child custody. Statutory language can be avoided, ignored, or abused if the court considers the factor relevant. The statutory language in practice functions more as a guide to decision making rather than an absolute set of criteria that requires application or consideration.

In many states homosexual acts are illegal, and the court considers that a parent participating in illegal activities as part of a personal lifestyle is something detrimental to the interests of the child. The issues of homosexual practice become related to the degree that homosexuality is perceived as a criminal behavior of the parent by the judicial officer. The parent becomes a criminal in the eyes of the court when participating in homosexual activities. A criminal that is unlikely to reform can be viewed as inconsistent with the role of a parent (when viewed from a heterosexual perspective). The criminalization of homosexual acts serves as a basis for evaluation of the environment provided by the parent.

The criminalization of homosexuality comes from a moral stance about sexual practices. The U.S. Supreme Court in *Bowers v. Hardwick* (1986) ruled that, "The law, however, is constantly based on notions of morality ... [the justices of the court] are unpersuaded that the sodomy laws of some 25 states should be invalidated" (pp. 2846–2847). The court said that the arguments by the petitioners failed to provide a basis for rejecting the majority opinion that in a democracy matters of morality should be dismissed. The court in *Bowers* did not find that homosexuality constituted a fundamental right conferred by the constitution. The court argued that sexual practices are moral issues and fall within the purview of the legislature to determine whether or not such actions are criminal. The argument by the court explicitly rejected the claim that consensual behavior, even if private, escapes state regulation. The implication for child custody is that statutes making homosexuality a crime provide the basis for evaluations of the fitness of the homosexual parent because one is involved in criminal acts. The home and bedroom become the scene of an ongoing crime and therefore could be considered as unsuitable places for the upbringing of a child.

The family courts, given the discretion to consider all relevant behavior, can choose to include the parent's sexuality in making a determination of custody. The impact of the behavior is that judges (elected public officials or appointed by elected officials) are subject to popular opinion and personal bias. There are few restrictions or little oversight on the behavior of individual trial judges when it comes to determining the environment best suited for raising a child. Most appellate reviews are unlikely to reverse a decision made by a trial judge. Therefore, the decision, and the basis for that decision, is likely to be upheld on appeal. Family courts have a tradition of making custody and visitation decisions based on the individual needs of the child under consideration. Appellate courts are reluctant to second-guess the practices of most judges operating with the principles of improving children's lives. The net effect of the uncertain legal status of homosexuals and the discretion of justices creates a basis for decisions that would not tend to favor the homosexual parent.

The introduction of HIV as an infectious disease into society has probably increased the prejudice that the courts feel against homosexual parents (particularly gay men). HIV infection has raised the level of potential homophobic reactions to homosexuals by associating a disease with particular practices of that community. The stability of the environment is a factor, and if the parent is participating in actions that could put his or her health at serious risk, the judge may be predisposed to consider that as a factor in determining custody and visitation. This factor is one that the judge could introduce as a basis for making a custody determination. Custody determinations by a judicial officer can consider the level of risk to the health of a parent based on lifestyle, occupation, or any other factor that the court deems relevant.

A fear of the courts is that a homosexual parent may encourage homosexuality in the child. It is important to note that in a jurisdiction where homosexuality is a crime, the parent would be encouraging participation in an illegal behavior, which could be construed as a form of contributing to the delinquency of a minor. The courts would argue that the gay parent serves as a role model for the child and contact with the parent would encourage the child to pursue a life of homosexuality. The judicial officer would be taking a stance on the undesirability of homosexuality as a practice and the possibility of parental influence in this choice.

The court may feel that a child with a homosexual parent may not develop her or his full potential because of the stigma or social ostracism. A child with a gay parent may be teased, excluded, or subject to abuse at the hands of peer groups or other adults. The courts therefore believe that they are acting in the best interests of the child by protecting the child from the parent on the basis of how the parent's sexual preference will impact the child's development. The focus is not on parental rights; the focus becomes the best interests of the child. Judicial officers possess enormous discretion generally to determine what factors fall within the scope of that term. Once the issue of parental sexual orientation enters the court, the cornerstone of decision making becomes focused not on the parental rights, but on the interests of the child (such a consideration has been the basis for appellate court decisions; see S. v. S, 1980; S.E.G. v. R.A.G., 1987). The reference is to the stigma that the courts believe may exist for a child whose parent is a known homosexual. The courts are reluctant to grant custody to a parent when the stigma associated with some aspect of the parent's life may negatively impact the perception of that child by the community. Such an argument, although a part of the legal literature, appears relatively specious. Consider that the court in this view is not arguing that the parent's practices directly influence the child or create a risk. The court is arguing that the reactions of the community might create a hostile or negative environment for the child. Such a position, in our opinion, is unwarranted. The courts should not generally consider the popularity of the parent's religious or political convictions in the local community as the basis for a custody or placement decision. The argument about the impact on the child presupposes a community reaction that may or may not be documented and, even if true, creates a terrible precedent as a basis for the termination or limitation of parental rights.

The failure of a homosexual parent to disclose that fact at the time of the initial hearing poses a future risk. A court may consider any issue that changes the circumstances of the original custody decision. If the sexual practices of the parent were not disclosed at the initial hearing, then the other parent could decide later to challenge the hearing on the basis of new information regarding the sexual practices of the other parent. The judicial officer is also likely to view the failure to disclose this information originally as an indication of the desire to hide undesirable information. The failure to disclose further reduces the chances for a suitable child custody arrangement at a later date or risks the revocation or change of a custody arrangement. Because the failure to disclose this information may be used as a basis for some future action, the homosexual parent is faced with a very difficult decision at the time of the first custody decision. To disclose the practice risks loss of custody; however, the failure to disclose creates the possibility that at some future date the decision can be revisited and changed for failure to disclose.

Given that the reason for the divorce may be related to the sexual practices of one parent, the custody of the child is immediately at risk from the standpoint of the homosexual parent. The likelihood of disclosure by the other parent is high. Thus, the sexual practices of the homosexual parent could be used to barter or extort a more favorable custody arrangement for the heterosexual parent. If the sexual practices of the homosexual parent are the basis for the divorce, the judicial officer may view that as a factor influencing the custody decision. One factor in child custody issues is the stability offered by the various parents. A person that marries and has children has expressed a preference for heterosexual practices, and for a parent to express a change years later can be viewed as an indication of instability and interpreted as an indication of difficulty in handling relational issues. The marriage vow carries a sense of legal and moral commitment that the homosexual parent is now terminating. The judicial officer may consider this fact in terms of the ability of the parent to follow legal commitments required in the custody arrangement. Any view of this process in terms of changing views clearly undermines the ability of the homosexual parent to obtain favorable circumstances and may even work to deny basic custody or visitation rights in many circumstances.

The underlying dynamic creates a circumstance that forces disclosure, but such disclosure risks the parent's ability to gain custody, placement, or visitation. The dilemma is one that confronts thousands of gay parents as they approach an impending divorce and child custody hearing. The dilemma creates a very untenable situation if disclosure risks losing access to the child. Failure to disclose creates conditions that hang over the parent like the sword of Damocles, threatening one of the most important relationships that a person wishes to maintain.

There exists a set of other outcomes that the court may consider at risk: (a) cognitive development, (b) moral development, (c) general life satisfaction, and (d) ability to interact with others. Many of these outcomes are assessed by observing a child's social interaction with other children or the parent. The question is whether a child can interact with a homosexual parent in the same manner as with a heterosexual parent. The issue is whether being raised by a gay parent adversely impacts the child. These considerations are accessible and testable as empirical propositions within a social science paradigm.

RELEVANCE OF SOCIAL SCIENTIFIC INVESTIGATIONS

Social science seeks to determine to what degree a set of outcomes can be expected from a set of conditions. In terms of the issues surrounding parenting, is a child raised by a homosexual parent more likely to experience some type of negative outcome than a child raised by a heterosexual parent? The comparison is an important one because not all children raised by heterosexual parents grow up in desirable environments or reveal negative consequences. To expect that all children raised by homosexual or heterosexual parents will end up with a particular outcome is not realistic. Instead, scientific research examines the probability of various outcomes. Scientific investigations can simply examine the consequences or impact of various living conditions and whether parental sexual practices generate differences in outcome.

The legal analogy would be whether homosexual parents as a class of individuals should be expected to generate a relatively positive or negative influence on the development of the child. The arguments surrounding this impact involve a disagreement on the part of social scientists about what the data represent. The American Psychological Association (APA) argued before the Supreme Court that homosexual parents do not necessarily represent a negative influence on the development of a child. Cameron and Cameron (1997) argued that the APA *in amicus curae* (friend of the court) briefs to the Supreme Court misrepresented the scientific literature. Cameron and Cameron's paper is a critique of the briefs filed by the APA in support of granting homosexual parents custody, devoted to a critique of the available literature on various methodological grounds. The conclusion offered is that some studies do not support the conclusion maintained by the APA about the lack of harm due to homosexual parenting. These authors argued that the APA did not act consistent with scientific principles but were guided by other concerns in evaluating the evidence. However, Cameron and Cameron admitted that the literature is mixed: Some findings support the lack of a harmful effect and some point to negative outcomes. These authors argued overall that the findings are inconsistent and do not sustain the conclusion advanced by the APA. Many other social scientists (Bozett, 1989; Cramer, 1986; Kirkpatrick, 1987; Kleber, Howell, & Tibbits-Kleber, 1992; Nungesser, 1980; Patterson, 1992; Tasker & Golombok, 1997; Walters & Stinnett, 1971) support Cameron and Cameron's (1997) findings and conclude that the impact of a homosexual parent is relatively minimal in terms of negative consequences for the child. The conflict within the scientific community focuses on disagreements about the theoretical assumption level and the accuracy of the empirical description. This chapter is an examination of the latter rather than the former. Meta-analysis is designed to examine the issue surrounding the degree to which empirical consensus can be established.

The inconsistency among the outcomes of the empirical investigations serves as a basis for a more thorough and systematic review of the literature. The number of studies appearing in the APA brief and the Cameron and Cameron (1997) review is less than the number of investigations appearing in this report. This meta-analysis may or may not provide an exhaustive review, but it represents a larger effort than the existing narrative box score reviews of the literature. The key is that the review process of a meta-analysis provides a method of literature review capable of replication by others. The problem with the review of outcomes by Cameron and Cameron (1997) is the reliance on box score or significance test outcomes to determine the direction of the findings. Such procedures are fraught with the potential for error and the introduction of bias due to divergent perspectives, the very problem that the authors claimed is the problem in the APA position paper.

Cameron and Cameron (1997) argued that in submitting the legal brief, the APA failed as scientists in their responsibility to provide an objective representation of the data. Meta-analysis does not represent a truly objective method of analysis; but it does provide a method of literature summary that permits an assessment of the literature that others can replicate. If someone disagrees with the summary, or new data are available, the existing analysis can be replicated (and updated to include new and different data) to validate the analysis. The technique permits an intersubjective claim that is capable of independent testing and assessment. This intersubjectivity of the method means that others can independently assess the validity of the claims about the consistency of the evidence. If the empirical examples themselves are independent, then a consensus of observations can grow and inferences that represent scientific consensus about specific relations can be discussed.

From a scientific perspective, the issue of effect is a factual one. One should be able to compare children from households where some parents are heterosexual and homosexual. The question of whether a difference in outcome exists is a question that should be capable of empirical description and evaluation. This meta-analysis is simply a summary of the current data dealing with that comparison. It is an effort to assess whether differences exist in the current pool of empirical data.

This chapter considers one aspect of the process of making a determination in terms of the child's best interest. The courts do use social scientific evidence as a basis for consideration of issues. In the case of S. v. S. (1980) the appellate court wrote, "There is excellent scientific research on the effects of parental modeling on children. Speculating from such data, it is reasonable to suggest that Shannon [the daughter] may have difficulties in achieving a fulfilling heterosexual identity of her own in the future" (p. 66). This case is important because at the original trial the mother had won. The appellate court overturned this decision because, "the lower court erred in failing to apply the standards of the 'best interests of the child' and potential for endangering the physical, mental, moral, or emotional health of the child" (p. 66) warranted overturning the original decision. The court in this case took a general principle and then extrapolated that principle to the specific circumstances to create a conclusion.

The court was concerned that the continued interaction of the child with a homosexual parent represented a communication environment that would adversely effect the child. The court speculated from existing social scientific theory and evidence in an attempt to provide an application to the particulars of the pending case. Civil courts, of which family courts are a part, operate on the basis of preponderance of evidence rather than the criminal standard of proof beyond a reasonable doubt. A meta-analysis of the existing evidence, if consistent, should provide the basis of the preponderance of scientific evidence addressing this question.

METHODS

The literature was identified using the terms *gay parents* and *lesbian mothers*, using various databases that exist (COMINDEX, ERIC, PSYCHLit, Socabstracts). In addition, various reviews of the literature (Hitchens & Thomas, 1983; Maggiore, 1988, 1992) were examined for possible relevant studies for the analysis. This analysis is an expanded version of an earlier analysis by the authors (for additional search and statistical details followed by this updated report, see Allen & Burrell, 1996). Some research has been published since the original publication and review of these data and has been incorporated into this analysis (e.g., Green, Mandel, Hotvedt, Gray, & Smith, 1986; Javaid, 1993). Some additional material focused on the report of case studies from clinical work and could not be included in this analysis (Javaid, 1983). Meta-analysis should be viewed as an ongoing effort and additional data sets should be added to the analysis as they become available. Additional data sets work to strengthen, refine, and extend the original conclusion in a variety of important ways. This update points to the need to view research as a dynamic process of refinement and enlarging claims rather than a static creation of a claim that should simply be accepted.

Various elements of the existing studies required attention and were coded as potential moderator variables. One of the primary features of interest was the nature of the particular dependent variable considered in the investigation. Some dependent variables consider the cognitive, moral, or social development of the child. A potential problem exists because there are many different possible ways to measure a child's development. Each route of development should receive consideration and attention to explore the potential impact of the parent's sexual practices.

Statistical analysis was conducted using a variance-centered form of meta-analysis developed by Hunter and Schmidt (1990). The technique is designed to test whether the variability of the individual studies is the result of sampling error or the potential existence of some other feature that moderates or generates the differences in observed outcome. The homogeneity test examines the sample of effects compared to a hypothetical distribution where the differences between the observed effects are the result of random sampling error. The sum of the squared difference scores, weighted by sample size, form the basis of the chi-square statistic (Hedges & Olkin, 1985). A significant chi-square indicates that the level of total difference among the correlation is greater than what should exist due to random chance. A nonsignificant chi-square statistic indicates that the difference is not significantly greater than one would expect due to random differences. The important aspect to remember is that differences exist among the correlations and the question of a moderator focuses on the issue of whether those differences among the observed effects can be explained in terms of sampling error or some other feature.

RESULTS

The studies were separated on the basis of the perspective of the dependent variables. One set of dependent conditions comes from the perspective of an adult and another is from the perspective of the child. The rating of the behavior or aspects of the child's behavior came from self-reports made by the child or the observations of the parent or third parties.

Adult Perspective

The results from this perspective consider the following characteristics: (a) rating of child–child interaction, (b) sex role, (c) child's life satisfaction viewed by the parent, and (d) child's life satisfaction viewed by a teacher at school. When examining the overall average across all measures ($r = -.057$, $k = 13, N = 619$), the direction slightly favors the homosexual parent, but this difference is not significant.

The first set of results considers how an adult rates the quality of the interaction that a child has with other children. The designs of these investigations have observers evaluate the ability of the child in social interactions. The results demonstrate no differences between homosexual or heterosexual parents. The rating of child–child interaction ($r = -.119, k = 5, n = 284$) is in the homosexual parent direction.

The other sets of results mirror this finding. The ratings of sex role ($r = .012$) similarly show no difference between groups. This indicates that parents do not find the child's sex role a function of the parent's sexual practice. It is important to note that ratings by the parents ($r = -.081$) and the teacher ($r = .036$) demonstrate no difference as well. The last finding indicates that the child's display of general satisfaction is not predicated on the basis of the parent's sexual orientation (see Table 8.1).

Child Perspective

Measures from the perspective of the child consider: (a) sexual orientation (overall as well as broken down by boys and girls), (b) satisfaction with life (overall as well as broken down by boys and girls), and (c) cognitive development. The overall analysis across all measures demonstrates virtually no difference ($r = -.011$). Table 8.2 displays the complete set of results.

The results indicate that child's sexual orientation is not affected by the sexual orientation of the parent ($r = -.008$). This was true for both boys ($r = .005$) and girls ($r = -.034$). The results indicate that any argument about parental sexual practices as predictors of a child's sexual practices receives no empirical support.

TABLE 8.1
Examining Results From the Perspective of the Parent

	Overall	Rating of Child–Child Interaction	Sex Role	Rating by Parent	Rating by Teacher
k	13	5	7	4	4
n	619	284	353	179	167
Average r	−.057	−.119	.012	−.081	.036
χ^2	0.00	0.00	0.00	5.56	0.00
99% confidence interval					
Upper limit	.05	−.03	.15	.11	.23
Lower limit	−.16	−.27	−.13	−.27	−.16
Cohen's power estimate					
Large effect	.99	.99	.99	.99	.99
Medium effect	.99	.99	.99	.99	.99
Small effect	.79	.54	.59	.38	.35

The satisfaction with life scores indicate no differences between children of homosexual or heterosexual parents ($r = -.001$). The results indicate the sexual practices of the parent do not contribute either positively or negatively when comparing the scores of children in each group. Basically, a child is equally likely to feel satisfied or dissatisfied regardless of parental type. When broken down by gender of the child, the results show the same pattern for boys ($r = -.012$) and girls ($r = .038$). It is important to note that these results are from the perspective of the child and demonstrate no significant differences on the basis of parental sexual practice.

The final measure was that of cognitive development. Consistent with the other measures, cognitive development demonstrated no significant relation ($r = -.038$) to the parent's sexual orientation. This provides an indicator that the parent's sexual practices were not impacting on the child's cognitive development.

CONCLUSIONS

The results demonstrate no discernible difference in outcome on the basis of the parent's sexual practices. Results indicate that the influence of the par-

TABLE 8.2
Results From the Perspective of the Child

	Overall	Sexual Orientation			Lifestyle			Cognitive
		Overall	Boys	Girls	Overall	Boys	Girls	
k	15	12	6	7	8	5	5	4
n	775	664	206	263	490	156	163	308
Average r	−.001	−.008	.005	−.034	−.001	−.012	.038	−.038
χ^2	0.00	0.24	0.00	0.00	1.11	0.00	0.77	2.33
99% confidence interval								
Upper limit	.082	.092	.184	.125	.117	.194	.237	.109
Lower limit	−.103	−.108	−.174	−.192	−.115	−.217	−.164	−.184
Cohen's power estimate								
Large effect	.99	.99	.99	.99	.99	.99	.99	.99
Medium effect	.99	.93	.97	.99	.99	.92	.93	.98
Small effect	.88	.82	.41	.49	.43	.26	.27	.29

ent's heterosexuality or homosexuality is not related to any adverse outcome in the child's development. The results indicate no evidence for differential outcomes based on the parent's sexual orientation for any of the various issues studied to date. The results include a power analysis using Cohen's (1987) method to indicate that the probability of a large effect existing on the basis of undiscovered evidence is small. This inclusion is probably necessary because the database for the average correlations is relatively small and subject to a great deal of random sampling error. However, even the small databases provide a sense of clear impact and direction for evaluating overall effects. The power analysis indicates that there should be little expectation of large or moderate differences between parents on the basis of a homosexual or heterosexual classification.

The results also suggest that arguments about the possible negative consequences of a homosexual parent granted custody or visitation rights do not find empirical support. The use of the social learning theory or modeling as applied to the parent's sexual practices creating some type of influence on the child receives no empirical support. Parents may serve as a source of social learning for the child, but the relation appears to have no correlation with the parent's sexual orientation. The impact of the parent probably comes from some aspect of parenting skill that is not related to the homosexuality or heterosexuality of the parent. Research should continue to identify the relevant parental social practices that do impact children. The use of parental sexual practices as a substitute for more concrete understanding at this point appears unwarranted.

Courts have incorporated social scientific thinking in custody decisions. In S. v. S. (1980), for example, the courts accepted the premise of parental modeling as a basis for denying a gay parent custody. The issue is not whether the courts are using information generated by social scientists, but rather how that information should be incorporated within the context of the decision-making process. The problem that a judicial officer faces is that few guidelines appropriate for the interpretation and application of social scientific methods to understanding social issues exist. As the number of meta-analyses increases, the desire for policy-making institutions to incorporate that information as part of the consideration grows. The key element will be some method of developing a technique of sophisticated understanding that incorporates this new knowledge effectively into the decisions made by courts and legislatures.

This chapter suggests that homosexual parents should not be treated as part of a class that deserve group treatment, because this class or type of individual generates no negative consequences for children. This is not to say that some homosexual parents are unfit, any more than to say that all heterosexual parents are fit. The results of this chapter suggest that the conditions and circumstances of the individual parent should be considered in relation to the particular child or children. The important issue for the courts is to consider the suitability of a particular person as a parent for a child. The evidence accumulated to date fails to support an argument that a homosexual parent provides an unsuitable or risky environment.

None of the primary research studies appear in communication journals, books, or proceedings. However, if one examines the dependent measures for the studies, many of them are interaction measures of some quality of child–parent or child–child interaction. The focus on assessment of child development involves the evaluation of some aspect of the quality of communication behavior. Our results generate another methodological argument for focusing on behavioral performance as a means of determining the parent's ability. The key is that this examination of underlying relationships is largely not based on self-report data, which may reflect the biases of the parents or social mores introduced to the child. Instead, the methodological reliance on direct behavioral observations indicates that the differences are not reflected in observer assessments of interaction. This research points to a fruitful area where communication scholars have great potential to make meaningful contributions to an important social issue involving a question about communicative interaction.

One limitation of this area of research is the lack of subsequent adult or long-term data. The current effects point to the outcomes for childhood but do not necessarily indicate the life span effects, if any, of a home environment with a homosexual parent. Currently, one data set has addressed this issue (Bailey, Bobrow, Wolfe, & Mikach, 1995), dealing only with the sexual orientation of the adult son. The data seem to point to a higher homosexual tendency in adult sons, but whether this is due to genetic or environmental influences is unclear. If the difference is genetic or biologically based, then the fact that adult sons of homosexual fathers show a greater tendency toward homosexuality is simply the outcome of genetic selection. Even if the home environment contributed, the argument must involve an ethical stance about the desirability of homosexuality prior to the critique. Such ethical judgments are beyond the purview of this chapter.

Another issue to consider is the distinction between the existence of a homosexual parent and custody or visitation for that parent. The argument made to deny visitation or custody by a homosexual parent must rely on the particulars of the impact that contact has with the child. Arguing, for example, that a child will suffer from teasing or ostracism from other children and families because a parent is gay can occur even if the homosexual parent has no visitation or custody rights. To deny a parent the right of custody because of the potential reactions of others means that any parent whose actions or beliefs are unpopular could have those beliefs serve as a basis for the denial or termination of parental rights. Permitting judges to determine whether the actions or beliefs of a parent are unpopular enough to invoke a reaction from others is to discriminate against the ability of a parent to practice fundamental freedoms because of the potential for community reaction. It is frightening that a judge can act not on the basis of some proven right, but on the basis of what reactions may or may not occur. Such a position renders the parent's sexual orientation meaningless because it is the community that passes judgment on the parent, not as a parent, but as a person.

This area of investigation suggests the vitality and necessity of communication scholars in expanding the vision of their research. Interaction between individuals forms the basis for many everyday life assessments. Much of the evidence in this chapter considers the outcome of various communication processes. Although this process has been the focus of some scholarship (see, e.g., Sypher & Applegate, 1984), the discipline lags behind. Another aspect of child development considers the arguments about whether a child should be engaged in day care or home care. Many parents worry that sending a child to day care rather than having a parent stay at home undermines the child's development. A recent meta-analysis (Dindia, Schuh, & Allen, 1998) demonstrated no differences between children who received home care and those who were in day care. The primary dependent variables considered the issues of the child's ability to interact with parents and other children. At the heart of these studies was a consideration of the quality of communication, but none of the studies appeared in communication journals or were authored by members of communication departments. The noninvolvement of the communication discipline is probably due to the lack of recognition that child development is typically characterized as the development of social skills. The characterization of the environment and development of a child as a process of communication provides a basis for participation in an important area of research.

Child development research indicates a connection between assumptions about the nature of parental inputs into the child's development. The assessment of that process focuses on the child's ability to communicate or interact with others. However, this connection does not seem to involve an assumption that the sexual practices of the parent impact that development. The issue that Cameron and Cameron (1996, 1997) implicitly pointed to is some aspect of parenting related to the parent's sexual practices. The current data fail to suggest the significance of such a relation. The methodological issue claimed is that the current data do not consider the long-term implications of the sexuality of the parent. Most of the current studies do not consider whether the parental impact, although benign to the child during the formative years, manifests itself when the child eventually becomes an adult. Such follow-up data are unclear and not well developed.

Another issue raised by Cameron and Cameron (1996, 1997) is the feelings an adult child may generate toward the homosexual parent. The issue is whether over the longer term a child develops feelings of resentment or loss toward the gay parent. Cameron and Cameron (1997) cited evidence of surveyed adult children who express resentment against the gay parent for the "lifestyle." The evidence is difficult to assess however, because no baseline is provided. To determine whether this emotional feeling represents a problem, there would need to be a baseline comparison to persons raised by a heterosexual parent. There are many children raised by heterosexual parents who might feel resentment against the "lifestyle" of their parents. Whether this resentment is caused by the parent's sexual practices or a manifestation of normal differences caused by a generational gap is unclear. The emotional feelings are not converted into any other expression or outcome, so again it is unclear whether such feelings were felt by the child and impacted the transition to becoming an adult. Without some basis for comparison or evidence of impact it is difficult to assess the evidence. Future research should be conducted to develop these areas. Another option is some type of intervention to ameliorate these feelings, similar to other types of interventions currently used in families.

Although direct behavioral data are commendable, another aspect deserves additional consideration: the child's mental or emotional feelings. Such data may or may not be directly observable as behavior, but the importance of the child's emotions and attitudes deserves attention. Such data collection efforts are more suited to the use of self-report data measurement instruments. This analysis suggests that the particular method of data collection produces little difference in outcome. The method of analysis did not create divergent findings; the investigators generated those.

The consideration of child custody provides a difficult issue for society. The assumption of parental rights is something that the courts are reluctant to reverse. This finding continues to support the conclusion that biological parents, regardless of heterosexual or homosexual practices, should not have their rights to custody or visitation terminated or restricted. This study suggests that parents need to be evaluated in terms of the particular practices that they provide to a child. The information provided about the impact of the parent's sexual practices (heterosexual or homosexual) failed to provide a clear basis for custody preference on the basis of what impact such practices have on the child's development.

REFERENCES

References marked with an asterisk indicate studies included in the meta-analysis.

Allen, M., & Burrell, N. (1996). Comparing the impact of homosexual and heterosexual parents on children: Meta-analysis of existing research. *Journal of Homosexuality, 32*, 19–35.
Bailey, J., Bobrow, D., Wolfe, M., & Mikach, S. (1995). Sexual orientation of adult sons of gay fathers. *Developmental Psychology, 31*, 124–139.
Bowers v. Hardwick, 106 S. Ct. 2841 (1986).
Bozett, F. (1989). Gay fathers: A review of the literature. *Journal of Homosexuality, 18*(1–2), 137–162.
*Cameron, P., & Cameron, K. (1996). Homosexual parents. *Adolescence, 31*, 757–776.

Cameron, P., & Cameron, K. (1997). Did the APA misrepresent the scientific literature to courts in support of homosexual custody? *Journal of Psychology, 131,* 313–332.

Cohen, J. (1987). *Statistical power analysis for the behavioral sciences* (2nd ed.). Hillsdale, NJ: Lawrence Erlbaum Associates.

Cramer, D. (1986). Gay parents and their children: A review of research and practical implications. *Journal of Counseling and Development, 64,* 504–507.

Dindia, K., Schuh, R., & Allen, M. (1998, November). *Day care versus home care: A meta-analytic review.* Paper presented at the National Council on Family Relations convention, Milwaukee, WI.

*Flaks, D., Ficher, I., Masterpasqua, F., & Joseph, G. (1995). Lesbians choosing motherhood: A comparative study of lesbian and heterosexual parents and their children. *Developmental Psychology, 31,* 105–114.

*Golombok, S., Spencer, A., & Rutter, M. (1983). Children in lesbian and single parent households: Psychosexual and psychiatric appraisal. *Journal of Child Psychology and Psychiatry, 24,* 551–572.

*Golombok, S., & Tasker, F. (1996). Do parents influence the sexual orientation of their children? Findings from a longitudinal study of lesbian families. *Developmental Psychology, 32,* 3–11.

*Green, R. (1978). Sexual identity of 37 children raised by homosexual or trans-sexual parents. *American Journal of Psychiatry, 135,* 692–697.

*Green, R., Mandel, J., Hotvedt, M., Gray, J., & Smith, L. (1986). Lesbian mothers and their children: A comparison with solo parent heterosexual mothers and their children. *Archives of Sexual Behavior, 15,* 167–184.

Griswold v. Connecticut, 381 U.S. 479 (1964).

*Harris, M., & Turner, P. (1986). Gay and lesbian parents. *Journal of Homosexuality, 12,* 101–113.

Hedges, L., & Olkin, I. (1985). *Statistical methods for meta-analysis.* Orlando, FL: Academic.

Hitchens, D., & Thomas, A. (Eds.). (1983). *Lesbian mothers and their children: An annotated bibliography of legal and psychological materials.* San Francisco: Lesbian Rights Projects.

*Hoeffer, B. (1979). *Lesbian and heterosexual single mothers' influence on their children's acquisition of sex-role traits and behavior.* Unpublished doctoral dissertation, University of California-San Francisco, San Francisco.

*Hoeffer, B. (1981). Children's acquisition of sex-role behavior in lesbian-mother families. *American Journal of Orthopsychiatry, 51,* 536–544.

*Huggins, S. (1989). A comparative study of self-esteem of adolescent children of divorced lesbian mothers and divorced heterosexual mothers. *Journal of Homosexuality, 18,* 123–135.

Hunter, J., & Schmidt, F. (1990). *Methods of meta-analysis: Correcting error and bias in research findings.* Beverly Hills, CA: Sage.

Javaid, G. (1983). Sexual development of the adolescent daughter of a homosexual mother. *Journal of the American Academy of Child Psychiatry, 22,* 196–201.

*Javaid, G. (1993). The children of homosexual and heterosexual single mothers. *Child Psychiatry and Human Development, 23,* 235–248.

Ketron v. Aguirre, 692 S.W.2d 261 (Ark. App. 1985).

Kirkpatrick, M. (1987). Clinical implications of lesbian mother studies. *Journal of Homosexuality, 14,* 201–211.

*Kirkpatrick, M., Smith, C., & Roy, R. (1981). Lesbian mothers and their children: A comparative survey. *American Journal of Orthopsychiatry, 51,* 545–559.

Kleber, D., Howell, R., & Tibbits-Kleber, A. (1992). *The impact of parental homosexuality in child custody cases: A review of the literature.* Paper from the Lesbian Mothers Defense Fund, Seattle, WA.

*Kweskin, S., & Cook, A. (1982). Heterosexual and homosexual mothers' self-described sex-role behavior and ideal sex-role behavior in children. *Sex Roles, 8,* 967–975.

Maggiore, D. (1988). *Lesbianism: An annotated bibliography and guide to the literature, 1976–1986.*. Metuchen, NJ: Scarecrow Press.

Maggiore, D. (1992). *Lesbianism: An annotated bibliography and guide to the literature, 1976–1991.* Metuchen, NJ: Scarecrow Press.

*Mucklow, B. (1978). *Adult response to child behavior and self-concept: Lesbian and traditional mothers.* Unpublished master's thesis, Colorado State University, Fort Collins, CO.

Nungesser, L. (1980). Theoretical bases for research on the acquisition of social sex-roles by children of lesbian mothers. *Journal of Homosexuality, 5,* 177–187.

O'Dell, L. (1995, April 22). Court rules against custody for lesbian mother. *Milwaukee Journal Sentinel,* p. 3A.

*Ostrow, D. (1978). *Children of Urania: Gay parents redefining the family.* Unpublished bachelor's thesis, Hampshire College, Montreal, Canada.

Patterson, C. (1992). Children of lesbian and gay parents. *Child Development, 63,* 1025–1042.

*Puryear, D. (1978). *A comparison between the children of lesbian mothers and the Children of heterosexual mothers.* Unpublished doctoral dissertation, California School of Professional Psychology, Berkeley, CA.

*Rand, C., Graham, D., & Rawlings, E. (1982). Psychological health and factors the court seeks to control in lesbian mother custody trials. *Journal of Homosexuality, 8,* 27–39.

S. v. S., 608 S.W.2d 64 (Ky. App., 1980).

S.E.G. v. R.A.G., 735 S.W.2d 164 (Mo. App. 1987).

*Scallon, A. (1982). *An investigation of paternal attitudes and behavior in homosexual and nongay fathers.* Unpublished doctoral dissertation, California School of Professional Psychology, Los Angeles.

*Schwartz, J. (1985). *An exploration of personality traits in daughters of lesbian mothers.* Unpublished doctoral dissertation, California School of Professional Psychology, San Diego, CA.

Sypher, H., & Applegate, J. (Eds.). (1984). *Communication by children and adults: Social cognitive and strategic processes.* Beverly Hills, CA: Sage.

*Tasker F., & Golombok, S. (1997). *Growing up in a lesbian family: Effects on child development.* New York: Guilford.

Walters, J., & Stinnett, N. (1971). Parent–child relationships: A decade review of research. *Journal of Marriage and Family, 33,* 70–111.

Warren v. Warren, 386 So.2d 1166. (Ala. Cir. App., 1980).

9

Similarity and Attraction

Kimo AhYun

Some posit that the most established and well-known finding in the interpersonal literature is that attitude similarity creates interpersonal attraction (Berscheid & Walster, 1983; Cappella & Palmer, 1990; De Wolfe & Jackson, 1984; Parks & Adelman, 1983). However, others contend that this belief is unfounded (Sunnafrank, 1992) and Bochner (1991) went so far as to pronounce the issue dead. Clearly, extreme differences exist in the perceived effect that attitude similarity has on interpersonal attraction.

Although several narrative accounts have explored the effect that attitude similarity has on interpersonal attraction (Byrne, 1969; Byrne, Clore, & Smeaton, 1986; Byrne & Griffitt, 1973; Simons, Berkowitz, & Moyer, 1970), these summaries are limited to historical reviews of the progression of research in this area. As such, these accounts offer little assistance in determining the effect that attitude similarity has on interpersonal attraction.

In an effort to explore the differences in opinion with regard to the effect that attitude similarity has on interpersonal attraction, *Communication Monographs* invited scholars (Byrne, 1992; Sunnafrank, 1992) holding different views to discuss their ideas. Byrne (1992) maintained in his article that attitude similarity increases interpersonal attraction, whereas Sunnafrank (1992) countered in his article by arguing that the effect of attitude similarity on interpersonal attraction disappears in normal developing relationships. Unfortunately, these articles did little to bridge the gap in ideological differences. In fact, research on the relation between attitude similarity and interpersonal attraction continues without apparent resolve (Tan & Singh, 1995).

Exploring discrepancies in the research between attitude similarity and interpersonal attraction across studies should be of interest to interpersonal scholars. Given that interpersonal attraction is a key determinant in whether people seek to pursue relationships with one another, understanding important antecedent factors such as attitude similarity will assist in explaining why some relationships succeed and others fail.

This chapter illuminates some of the issues in the attitude similarity debate by employing a meta-analytic approach to the attitude similarity literature. Specifically, this review presents the uncorrected and corrected effect size (correlation coefficient) between attitude similarity and interpersonal attraction. The review considers the effect that differences in the manipulation of attitude items across studies have on the relation between attitude similarity and interpersonal attraction and tests the extent to which initial interaction moderates the effect that attitude similarity has on interpersonal attraction. The chapter offers suggestions for future research that should be conducted to assess the nature of the relation between attitude similarity and interpersonal attraction.

In addition to providing a more detailed account of the research concerning the effect of attitude similarity on interpersonal attraction, using a meta-analytic approach is warranted for several reasons. First, at the individual study level, sampling error exerts a significant toll on findings (Hunter & Schmidt, 1990). Meta-analysis aids in overcoming sampling error by combining findings from many studies and weighting them by their sample size. As such, the effect size obtained from a meta-analysis is a more accurate estimate of the actual effect size than findings from any individual study. Second, meta-analysis allows for a summed effect size that is corrected for error of measurement. Given that error of measurement systematically lowers the correlation, meta-analysis allows for the cumulation of studies as if they had perfect measurement. Finally, meta-analysis enables the identification of moderating variables in the literature. If there is variance in the effect sizes across studies, meta-analysis provides the tools to determine if these differences are artifactual (Hunter & Schmidt, 1990). If the differences are not artifactual, potential moderating variables can be examined by dividing studies into appropriate conditions.

LITERATURE REVIEW

As early as the 4th century BC, Aristotle (trans., 1932) suggested that friends regard the same things as good and evil. Working from the similarity principle introduced by Aristotle, several researchers successfully tested this proposition (Hunt, 1935; Kirkpatrick & Stone, 1935; Newcomb & Svehla, 1937; Schiller, 1932; Schooley, 1936).

By 1960, research concerning attitude similarity and close relationships merely examined the extent to which people in close relationships (e.g., spouses and friends), held similar attitudes. In an attempt to broaden the understanding of the potential effects of attitude similarity, Newcomb (1961) studied the effect of attitude similarity on attraction longitudinally. In his study, Newcomb assembled groups of housemates and asked them to complete attitude questionnaires. By collecting interpersonal attraction data on all housemates toward one another at several time points, his findings revealed that attitude similarity predicted attraction in later relational stages, but not early ones.

Contemporary research concerning attitude similarity and interpersonal attraction has followed a similar pattern (Bond, Byrne, & Diamond, 1968; Byrne, 1992; Byrne, Ervin, & Lamberth; 1970; Byrne & Griffitt, 1966; Byrne, Griffitt, & Golightly, 1966; Cherry, Byrne, & Mitchell, 1976; Curran & Lippold, 1975; Griffitt, 1969). Typically, participants completed a host of questions designed to represent their attitudes. Items used to assess attitudes measured issues such as school desegregation, politics, gardening, birth control, dating, and the advisability of freshmen having cars on campus (Byrne & Rhamey, 1965). About 1 week after participants completed attitude questionnaires, they were asked to evaluate their interpersonal attraction toward a bogus stranger given a list of the same attitude items that the stranger supposedly completed previously. To induce varying levels of attitude similarity, answers from the bogus stranger's attitude items were varied such that they were highly similar (e.g., six similar and two dissimilar) or highly dissimilar (e.g., two similar and six dissimilar) to the participant's responses to the same attitude items. Finally, participants reported judgments of interpersonal attraction toward the bogus stranger.

According to Byrne and Griffitt (1973), interpersonal attraction is an individual's affective evaluation of another and interest in interpersonal attraction has received attention from communication scholars for two primary reasons. First, interpersonal attraction is positively related to the extent to which people communicate with others. Consequently, interpersonal attraction is one antecedent to predict communication partners that people have. Second, interpersonal attraction is positively related to the amount of influence that others have on us in interpersonal exchanges. As such, interpersonally attractive others can potentially play an influential role in our behaviors. Given the significance of interpersonal attraction in our lives, research concerning this variable is important.

Predominantly, researchers have measured interpersonal attraction through the sum of two 7-point Likert-type items taken from Byrne's Interpersonal Judgment Scale (Byrne, 1971). The interpersonal attraction items ask individuals to report the extent to which they (a) like a target person, and (b) would enjoy working with a target person. After conducting and reviewing a host of studies using the bogus stranger technique in which attitude similarity was induced, Byrne and Nelson (1965) proposed a linear function of $Y = 5.44X + 6.62$ to describe the effect of attitude similarity (X) on attraction (Y). Byrne and Nelson's proposed linear function of the effect of attitude similarity and interpersonal attraction is important, because it reveals that attitude similarity systematically exerts a strong positive effect on interpersonal attraction.

A series of studies that followed the introduction of Byrne and Nelson's (1965) proposed linear function appeared to offer support (Bond et al., 1968; Byrne et al., 1970; Byrne & Griffitt, 1966a; Byrne et al., 1966; Cherry et al., 1976; Curran & Lippold, 1975; Griffitt, 1969). Consequently, Byrne (1992) reported that a lawlike relation exists between attitude similarity and interpersonal attraction. However, some studies have reported findings that are inconsistent with the linear function just proposed (Curran & Lippold, 1975; Sunnafrank, 1983, 1984, 1985, 1986; Sunnafrank & Miller, 1981).

There are two major arguments against the lawlike relation that has been proclaimed between attitude similarity and interpersonal attraction. The first posits that communication is a moderator that eliminates the effect that attitude similarity has on interpersonal attraction (Sunnafrank, 1984, 1985, 1986; Sunnafrank & Miller, 1981), by making attitudinally dissimilar others appear more interpersonally attractive during interaction processes. Specifically, this argument maintains that attitude dissimilarity can be an aversive force in new relationships. More specifically, individuals perceive that an interaction with an attitudinally dissimilar other would prevent them from achieving a stable communication interaction prior to interacting with them. However, when provided with an interaction opportunity, the interaction is typically pleasant and as a result, the aversive effect that attitude dissimilarity has on interpersonal attraction is not present.

A second argument to this claim is the repulsion hypothesis (Rosenbaum, 1986). According to the repulsion hypothesis, attitude similarity does not heighten interpersonal attraction, because similarity is expected. However, the discovery of attitude dissimilarity is unexpected and aversive, resulting in interpersonal repulsiveness that decreases interpersonal attractiveness. In particular, this argument reveals that attitude similarity has no effect on interpersonal attraction and attitude dissimilarity has a negative effect on interpersonal attraction.

In short, the repulsion hypothesis suggests that the important relation is not between attitude similarity and interpersonal attraction, but between attitude dissimilarity and interpersonal repulsion. Although some research has been conducted to test the repulsion hypothesis (Rosenbaum, 1986), at present an insufficient amount of evidence is available to confirm it as a plausible explanation. In particular, the testing of the repulsion hypothesis requires that a no-attitude-information condition exist. That is, a condition must exist in which a person receives no information about the attitudes of another. Because people have a tendency to make assumptions about the attitudes of others when they have no information about another, it has been argued that it is impossible to create a no-attitude-information condition (Byrne, 1992).

THEORY AND HYPOTHESES

Strength of the Attitude Similarity Manipulation

According to Byrne's (1969) reinforcement affect model of attraction, people have more positive affective responses toward people holding similar attitudes, because they like people who view the world in the same way. In short, Byrne's reinforcement affect model suggests a positive linear relation between perceived attitude similarity and interpersonal attraction. If Byrne's model is accurate, then variation in perceived similarity should be directly related to the degree to which people assess the interpersonal attractiveness of another. More specifically, given that there are differences in the degree to which people are presented as attitudinally similar, the greater the percentage of agreement, the greater the effect it should have on interpersonal attraction.

A second reason to expect that the greater percentage of agreement in the attitude similarity manipulation will be positively related to its corresponding effect size is with regard to restriction in range. Because restriction in the range of an independent variable systematically attenuates the effect on the dependent variable, it follows that as the range or percentage of agreement between the attitude similarity and dissimilarity variable increases, it will produce a greater effect on the dependent variable of interpersonal attraction. Given the apparent relation between the percentage of agreement used in the attitude similarity manipulation and its effect on a person's judgment of interpersonal attraction, the following hypothesis is offered.

H₁: As the difference in percentage between attitude similar and dissimilar conditions increases across studies, so will the correlation between attitude similarity and interpersonal attraction.

Number of Attitude Items

One reason to expect that the number of attitude items used in a study will influence the extent to which others are perceived as interpersonally attractive is the idea that some issues are more important to people than others. For example, an extremely religious person who is disinterested in sports will weigh attitude similarity on the belief that God exists as more important than the belief that Big Ten basketball teams are generally better than Pac Ten basketball teams.

The idea that people give more weight to important issues has been addressed by research. For example, Bowman and Fishbein (1978) examined individuals' attitudes toward an Oregon nuclear safeguard initiative. This study revealed that an indicator of voting behavior was the weight that people placed on reasons to vote for or against the initiative. That is, the stronger the weight of a belief about the initiative, the greater effect it had on a person's overall voting decision.

So why should it be expected that the number of items used in a study will explain varying effect sizes of interpersonal attraction found across studies? One possible explanation is that as the number of attitude items increases in a study, so does the opportunity for people to agree or disagree on an issue that is important to them. Additionally, if attitudes are revealed on issues that a person regards as important, then he or she is likely to use this information to form a stronger judgment of interpersonal attraction than another who fails to uncover information about a topic that is important to him or her.

A second reason that more attitude items might result in a greater corresponding interpersonal attraction judgment concerns the reliability phenomena. That is, as the number of items increase in a measure, so does its subsequent reliability of that measure. Consequently, when two variables are correlated with one another and the reliability of one of those variables increases, by definition, so will the correlation between those two variables.

Because considerable variance exists in the number of attitude items used across studies examined in this meta-analysis (7 to 56) and that information quantity can be expected to effect interpersonal judgments of others, the following hypothesis is presented:

H$_2$: As the number of attitude items used in a study increases so will the correlation between attitude similarity and interpersonal attraction.

Initial Interpersonal Interaction

Several studies (Sunnafrank, 1983, 1984; Sunnafrank & Miller, 1981) have varied the design from the typical bogus stranger technique employed in the attitude similarity–interpersonal attraction research by adding the variable of interaction. For example, Sunnafrank (1983, 1984) first had participants complete attitude inventories. Subsequently, attitude similar or dissimilar partners were formed and provided with the attitude inventory completed by their partner. After reading their partner's attitude inventory items, couples were brought together and they engaged in a 5-min get-acquainted interaction. On completion of the 5-min interaction, interactants were separated and asked to complete measures of interpersonal attraction toward their partner. Each of the dyads used here were same-sex pairs.

In another series of studies researching the effect that interaction has on the relation between attitude similarity and interpersonal attraction, Curran and Lippold (1975) had participants complete attitude similarity measures, but did not make them aware of each others' answers. Based on the completed measures, participants were apportioned into either attitude similar or dissimilar conditions. Subsequently, partners were provided with sufficient funds to go on a 30-min "Coke date," where they were given the chance to interact with one another outside of the laboratory setting. After their Coke date, they were asked to complete a measure of interpersonal attraction toward their partner. Each of the Coke date dyads were opposite-sex partners.

Two key elements in the preceding studies make them different from Byrne's (1969) typical bogus stranger research technique. The first is the presence of interaction. The second is that there were true attitude agreements or disagreements with real others. Consequently, the question here is whether these differences will moderate the relation between attitude similarity and interpersonal attraction.

The first reason to expect that initial interaction will influence the effect that attitude similarity has on interpersonal attraction is because in normal initial interactions, attitudes are usually not uncovered. Given the lack of attitude information, it cannot be used as a judgment of interpersonal attraction. In their work on the types of information revealed in initial interactions, Berger and Calabrese (1975) introduced their proposed stages of interaction. According to them, the first stage that people encounter is the entry phase. In this phase, people are governed by social norms and rules that limit conversation to low-risk topics such as demographic information. Although attitude information may be explored in this phase, it is not information typically central to a person and tends to focus on low-involvement issues.

A second reason to expect that initial interpersonal attraction will lower the effect that attitude similarity has on interpersonal research concerns the conversational goals and societal norms that governs people's actions. More specifically, in initial face-to-face interactions, people are generally pleasant. Consequently, the positive effects of initial interactions may work to suppress potential negative feelings that people may hold toward attitudinally discrepant others. In their research on initial interactions, Burleson and Denton (1992) suggested that people engaged in initial interactions are just trying to enjoy the interaction. Because most people dislike confrontation, people are likely to highlight similarities and downplay dissimilarities, which could potentially inflate perceived similarity by partners.

The effect of initial interpersonal interaction on the relation between attitude similarity and interpersonal attraction can be examined in two ways. First, limited interactions (e.g., interactions lasting fewer than 30 min) create situations where few attitude issues are uncovered, and even if they are uncovered, social norms cause people to downplay these dissimilarities. Consequently, in initial interpersonal interactions, the effect of attitude similarity on interpersonal attraction should be lower than when no interaction is present, because forces are acting to mitigate the effect of attitudinal disagreements. Therefore, the following hypothesis is presented:

H_{3a}: Communication between people will moderate the effect of attitude similarity on interpersonal attraction in initial interactions, such that the correlation between them will decrease.

Although the effect of attitude similarity on interpersonal attraction will be attenuated in initial interpersonal interactions due to social forces such as initial interaction norms and the lack of attitudinal information, these factors will be overcome as interaction increases. In particular, if Berger and Calabrese (1975) were correct in their idea that time elapsed in a relationship will result in more attitudinal knowledge of others and if attitude similarity is indeed an indicator of interpersonal attraction, then the effect of attitude similarity, at least in the initial stages of interaction, should be positively related to judgments of interpersonal attraction. Therefore, the following hypothesis is forwarded:

H_{3b}: The effect of attitude similarity on interpersonal attraction will increase as time elapses in initial interpersonal interactions.

METHODS

Relevant studies were obtained by initially starting with the Byrne and Sunnafrank's articles published in *Communication Monographs* in 1992. All relevant articles from the bibliographies of these articles were obtained and the bibliographies of these studies were searched. The bibliography searching process continued until no further germane articles were obtained. Using the method of the bibliography search yielded a diverse number of sources, including *Communication Monographs, Human Communication Research, Human Relations, Journal of Applied Social Psychology, Journal of Experimental Research in Personality, Journal of Personality, Journal of Personality and Social Psychology, Journal of Research in Personality, Journal of Social Psychology, Psychological Reports, Social Cognition,* and *The Western Journal of Communication.*

Additionally, the Social Science Citation Index, Dissertation Abstracts, and computer-based searches in PSYCINFO (psychology literature) and ACAD (Expanded Academic Index) were searched using the keywords *attitude similarity, value similarity, belief similarity, liking, attraction,* and *interpersonal attraction.* The initial search yielded 134 studies that could potentially be used in this meta-analysis. The list of obtained studies through the process used might not be a complete coverage of all studies, but given the large number of studies collected, it is unlikely that the omitted studies would change the general conclusions of this aggregation.

Criteria for Study Inclusion

To be included in this meta-analysis, the study had to focus on the relation between attitude similarity and interpersonal attraction. Examples of studies that were excluded given the criterion established included those measuring the effect of personality similarity (Atkinson & Schein, 1986) or use of noninterpersonal attraction measures as the dependent variable (Coombs & Chang, 1981). Forty-two of the studies collected were excluded by this criterion.

Each study also was required to include original data. Articles reviewing or rereporting data were not included in the selection process (Byrne, 1992). Seven studies collected were excluded by this criterion.

Studies failing to provide sufficient information to allow computation of the correlation between attitude similarity and interpersonal attraction were excluded. For example, Curran's (1973) study was excluded from analysis. Although he researched attitude similarity and interpersonal attraction, he did not provide sufficient statistical information necessary to reproduce the correlation coefficient. Five studies were excluded by this criterion. Given these criteria to include studies in this meta-analysis, 80 studies remained, leaving 92 effect sizes for the analyses (complete list available from author).

Meta-Analytic Methods

Hunter, Schmidt, and Jackson (1982) presented the general meta-analytic approach used in this chapter. Essentially, the procedures advanced by Hunter et al. involves the estimation of effect sizes between the variables being examined. After each of the effect sizes for individual studies are obtained, they are weighted by sample size and cumulated.

To provide a standard measure across studies, each of the findings were transformed into correlation coefficients. The primary source for transforming F values to correlations was Hunter's FTOR program (Hunter, 1991). When transforming other statistics (e.g., t tests) the formulas presented by Hunter et al. (1982) were used. The full meta-analysis was performed using Hunter's VGBARE program (Hunter, 1993).

Most studies used Byrne's (1969) two-item measure to assess interpersonal attraction. However, the reliability of these two items vary. Reported reliabilities are as low as .75 (Sunnafrank, 1986) and as high as .90 (Sunnafrank, 1985). The most commonly reported alpha is .85. Given that the mean between the highest and lowest report of alpha for these items (82.5) is extremely close to the reliability presented by Byrne (1969), .85 was used as the reliability estimate for Byrne's (1969) two-item interpersonal attraction measure. Several studies used only Byrne's (1969) liking question to measure interpersonal attraction. For these studies, Spearman–Brown's prophecy formula for estimating the reliability of shortened scales from a scale with a known reliability was employed (Brown, 1910; Spearman, 1910). Using Spearman–Brown's prophecy formula, a reliability of .74 was calculated as the reliability for only the liking item.

The reported reliabilities for studies not using Byrne's (1969) two-item interpersonal attraction measure were employed to correct their effect sizes for attenuation due to error of measurement. In cases where no reliability measure was presented and there was insufficient information to calculate an estimate of the reliability measure, then perfect measurement was assumed. Only 2 of the 92 effect sizes used in this study required the assumption of perfect measurement.

RESULTS

Attitude Similarity Effect Size

To estimate the effect of attitude similarity on interpersonal attraction across all of the effect sizes used in this meta-analysis ($k = 92$), the correlations computed for each of the individual studies were averaged. The overall uncorrected and weighted effect size for the relation between attitude similarity and interpersonal attraction is $r = .46$ ($k = 91$, $SD = .19$, $n = 10,588$). When corrected for attenuation due to error of measurement, the weighted effect size is $.51$ ($k = 91$, $SD = .22$, $n = 10,588$). Because corrected correlations have larger standard errors than corrected ones, a $.95$ confidence interval was calculated around the uncorrected effect size and each end was subsequently corrected for error of measurement. For these data, the estimated confidence interval for the corrected correlation is p ($.46 \leq$ MeanRho $\leq .56$) $= .95$.

Attitude Similarity Percentage of Agreement and Effect Size

Hypothesis 1 predicted a positive relation between the percentage of agreement difference between the most similar and dissimilar attitude conditions and the study effect sizes. To test this hypothesis a correlation was obtained between the uncorrected effect sizes, with the percentage difference between the largest attitude similarity condition less the smallest attitude similarity condition. For example, for a study using 12 attitude items and defining attitude similarity as having 9 of 12 items similar and attitude dissimilarity as having 3 of 12 items, the percentage of agreement was calculated. In this particular case, the percentage of attitude similarity was calculated as $.75$ ($9 \div 12$) and attitude dissimilarity was calculated as $.25$ ($3 \div 12$). As such, the percentage of difference in this example is $.50$ ($.75 - .25$). For these data, the correlation between the percentage of difference of attitude similarity conditions across studies and the uncorrected effect sizes is $.48$ and $.53$ when corrected for error of measurement ($k = 65$, $n = 7,282$).

There were slightly fewer studies used for the analyses here than all of the studies used in this meta-analysis ($k = 92$), because (a) data from interaction studies ($k = 11$) were not used in this analysis, and (b) some of the studies did not report the data needed to calculate strength ($k = 16$). Interaction studies were analyzed separately, because if interaction attenuates the relation between attitude similarity and interpersonal attraction, then their lower effect sizes would blur the test of the relation between manipulation strength and its effect size, because it is believed that the effect size in these studies will be zero. Given these findings, the percentage of agreement of attitude items had the expected effect on the correlation between attitude similarity and interpersonal attraction.

Number of Attitude Items and Effect Size

Hypothesis 2 stated that there would be a positive relation between the number of items employed in the attitude manipulation and the effect size across studies. For these data, the correlation between number of attitude items used in a study and effect size was .05 ($k = 76, n = 8,572$).

There were slightly fewer studies used for the analyses here than all of the studies used in this meta-analysis ($k = 92$), because (a) data from interaction studies ($k = 11$) were not used in this analysis, and (b) some of the studies did not report the number of attitude items used ($k = 5$). Given the low correlation between the number of attitude items used in a study and the effect size found in the study findings, this hypothesis is not supported.

Initial Interaction as a Moderating Variable

The full meta-analysis of all effect sizes used in this study had a large standard deviation and less than 10% of the variance across these studies could be attributed to sampling error. Consequently, there is evidence that there is at least one moderating variable in these data. Hypothesis 3a predicted that interaction moderates the effect of attitude similarity on interpersonal attraction, such that the effect size would be lower in interaction studies than studies having no interaction. Because all of the studies ($k = 92$) used in this meta analysis could be coded with respect to interaction, none of them were excluded to test Hypothesis 3. To test Hypothesis 3a, a subgroup analysis was performed.

The subgroup analysis testing Hypothesis 3a was a comparison of the corrected and weighted effect sizes for studies in which interaction was present or absent. For these data, the subgroup analysis for the no-interaction studies yielded $r = .58$ ($k = 81, n = 8,572$). In comparison, the interaction studies yielded $r = .18$ ($k = 11, n = 2,016$). This comparison reveals that absent interaction, attitude similarity exerts a strong effect on interpersonal attraction, but when interaction is present, attitude similarity exerts a weaker effect on interpersonal attraction.

Hypothesis 3b predicted that the effect of attitude similarity on interpersonal attraction would increase in the course of an initial interpersonal interaction. To test Hypothesis 3b, a subgroup analysis breaking the interaction conditions into either initial interaction only (5 min) or beyond initial interaction (approximately 30 min) was calculated. For these data, the average effect size for initial interaction studies is $r = .04$ ($k = 5, n = 362$) and $r = .21$ ($k = 6, n = 1,654$) for beyond initial interaction studies.

A final test to examine the effect that interaction has on the effect size of attitude similarity and interpersonal attraction studies was conducted by coding no interaction, initial interaction only, and beyond initial interaction studies with the values of 1 ($k = 81, n = 8,572$), 2 ($k = 6, n = 1,654$), and 3 ($k = 5, n = 362$), respectively. The correlation of the new study groupings (1, 2, or 3) with the effect size is $r = -.69$ and $r = -.73$ when corrected for error of measurement. Given these findings, the data show that initial interactions that are 30 or fewer min lessen the effect that attitude similarity has on interpersonal attraction and that as time elapses, at least from 5 to 30 min, the effect of attitude similarity on interpersonal attraction increases.

DISCUSSION

Overall Similarity Effect Size

The average corrected effect studies ($r = .51$) for all studies employed here showed a strong positive relation between attitude similarity and interpersonal attraction. Given that the correlation between the uncorrected and corrected correlation was large ($r = .99$), there was no evidence that error of measurement was a factor in differences across studies.

Percentage of Agreement

Given the high correlation between the strength of the attitude manipulation and effect sizes across studies ($r = .53$ when corrected for error of measurement), there is strong evidence to suggest that perceived percentage agreement of items exerts a strong influence on interpersonal attraction. Two reasons suggest that a positive relation would be found between percentage of agreement and interpersonal attraction. The first reason stated that as attitude similarity increased, so would positive affective responses toward people holding similar attitudes, which would lead to greater interpersonal attraction (Byrne, 1969). Although no direct test could be made to determine if attitudinally similar others had greater affective responses to others in comparison to attitudinally dissimilar others, the effect of greater interpersonal attraction was found. Consequently, although this model was not entirely affirmed, the evidence found is insufficient to discount it as an explanation.

The second reason supporting the relation between percentage of agreement and greater interpersonal attraction stated that as range restriction decreased across attitude similar conditions, there would be a greater effect on interpersonal attraction. Given the high correlation uncovered between the percentage of agreement and interpersonal attraction, support is provided for this explanation.

Attitude Items and Effect Size

The correlation between the number of attitude items used in each study and the effect size ($r = .05$) was minimal. The evidence suggests that the two variables are not related in a positive linear manner as hypothesized.

Two reasons supported the idea that the number of attitude items used in a study would influence the interpersonal attraction effect sizes across studies. The first indicated that people weight the importance of issues differentially. Consequently, the greater the number of attitude items that are used in a study, the more likely that an important one would be found, causing a more extreme judgment on interpersonal attraction. The findings did not support the proposed relation.

The second reason was a simple methodological explanation stating that as the number of attitude items increased, so would the reliability of this variable. Assuming that a relation exists between attitude similarity and interpersonal attraction, greater reliability of either of the variables would by definition result in a larger correlation between the two variables. No evidence was found to support this rationale.

Given the low correlation between the number of attitude items and interpersonal attraction effect sizes across studies, one of two conclusions can be drawn. First, the preceding rationales used to predict a positive linear effect between the use of a greater number of attitude items and stronger judgments of interpersonal attraction could be flawed. That is, the idea of issue importance and the reliability phenomenon are incorrect in this context.

A second conclusion that can be drawn is that factors within this meta-analysis prevented an accurate test of the relation between the number of attitude items and effect sizes across studies. In particular, the limited variance in number of attitude items across studies could have prevented an accurate test of this relation. Given strong support that there was a weak test of the relation between the number of attitude items and interpersonal attraction effect sizes in the studies used for this meta-analysis, any conclusions drawn from these findings should be taken with caution.

Interaction as a Moderator

Two tests were employed to examine the effect that interaction has on the relation between attitude similarity and interpersonal attraction. Not only did the subgroup analysis of interaction present or absent in studies reveal extreme differences in average effect sizes ($r = .18$ and $r = .58$), but the correlation of varied interaction levels with the effect size also showed evidence that interaction affects the relation between attitude similarity and interpersonal attraction ($r = .04$, $r = .21$, $r = .58$). Because a majority of the studies were done without any interaction, there was a substantial difference in the number of studies used for the comparison. However, given the extreme differences in average effect sizes across studies, it seems reasonable to conclude that interaction, at least in the early stages of relationships, lessens the effect that attitude similarity has on interpersonal attraction.

Future Research

Although the effect that attitude similarity has on interpersonal attraction has been examined in more than 100 studies, we have advanced little in our understanding of these variables except that in bogus stranger situations attitude similarity has a strong effect on interpersonal attractiveness and that initial interactions moderate the effect of attitude similarity. Clearly, a research program is needed to enhance our understanding in this domain.

One area of research that has generated considerable controversy in attitude similarity concerns the effect of initial interactions. Within this chapter, it is suggested that people are operating within particular rules and norms in initial interactions. Future research should test whether initial interaction norms operate to suppress the effect of attitude similarity on interpersonal attraction in newly formed relationships.

In addition to testing types of conversations, research should also be conducted on interactions over longer time periods than have previously been used. In particular, the research on initial interactions has had participants engage in conversations between 5 min (Sunnafrank, 1985) and 30 min (Curran & Lippold, 1975) long. Although this research has been useful in helping us understand the effect of initial interactions in the short term, it does little to help us understand how attitude similarity influences interpersonal attraction in relationships that are more enduring.

An interesting finding in this meta-analysis is that as the time of interaction increases, so did the effect that attitude similarity has on interpersonal attraction. Although these findings are limited to comparing the 5-min interaction ($r = .04$) with the 30-min interaction ($r = .21$) conditions, they do add interesting insight into the attitude similarity effect.

To obtain a more complete understanding of the effect that attitude similarity exerts on interpersonal attraction over time, research needs to examine interaction relationships greater than the 30-min maximum that has been used. This research would determine if the attitude similarity effect on interpersonal attraction remained stable after a certain period of time or if it fluctuated.

A second area of interest in the attitude similarity debate that has received considerable recognition involves an alternative explanation of the traditional attitude similarity effect on interpersonal attractiveness. As stated earlier, Rosenbaum's (1986) repulsion hypothesis maintains that attitude similarity does not increase interpersonal attraction, but that attitude dissimilarity decreases interpersonal attraction. If people are repulsed by people who are attitudinally dissimilar, then it would provide a completely different perspective on the effect that attitude similarity has on interpersonal attraction. To test the repulsion hypothesis, Rosenbaum replicated the traditional attitude similarity study (which includes only attitudinally similar and dissimilar conditions) and added a no-information control condition.

In his research, Rosenbaum (1986) apportioned participants into attitude similar, dissimilar, or no-attitude-information conditions. His research revealed that there were no significant mean differences between the attitude similar and no attitude conditions with respect to the interpersonal attractiveness of a bogus stranger. Additionally, the results showed that the attitude dissimilar others were rated a significantly less interpersonally attractive than both the attitude similar and no-attitude-information conditions. Although Rosenbaum's findings were consistent with his predictions, some researchers (Byrne, 1992) have argued that it is impossible to have a no-information control condition. That is, it has been argued that in the absence of attitudinal information about others, people assume that the anonymous person shares similar attitudes to them.

How might one go about forming a true no-information control group? The first step would be to create individuals that participants believe that they cannot make inferences about their attitudes. For example, a researcher might provide participants with a description of another in which limited information is provided (e.g., only name and nondescriptive background information). In this case, the lack of information about another could potentially heighten the realization that there is insufficient information to make attitudinal predictions. Once a no-inference condition is established, further testing of the repulsion hypothesis can be undertaken.

A third area of research that should be conducted is testing the theories to explain why some variables, such as interaction, influence the relation between attitude similarity and interpersonal attraction. For example, Sunnafrank (1985, 1986, 1992) consistently argued across several articles that initial interaction moderates the relation between attitude similarity and interpersonal attraction because without interaction people feel that their goals of achieving predictable, controllable, and stable environments are difficult to achieve. Consequently, in noninteraction research, participants rate attitude dissimilars as interpersonally unattractive because they perceive them as a threat to their interaction goals, whereas attitude similars are rated as interpersonally attractive, because they are perceived as interaction goal facilitators. However, once people interact, Sunnafrank (1992) argued that people realize that they can achieve these interpersonal goals and, consequently, the effect of attitude similarity is eliminated.

CONCLUSIONS

As early as the 4th century BC, Aristotle suggested that friends regard the same things as good and evil. Taken literally, Aristotle (trans., 1932) would agree with Byrne's (1969) notion that attitude similarity influences interpersonal attraction or conversely, that close relationships induce similar attitudes. Thousands of years have passed since Aristotle's revelation, but researchers are still questioning the conditions under which this statement is true. Although this chapter provides one step toward sorting out what we know about the relation between attitude similarity and interpersonal attraction, there remain many unanswered questions.

Communication scholars interested in interpersonal communication should find this chapter especially interesting. In particular, it reveals that communication, especially in initial interactions, plays an important role in assessments of interpersonal attraction. Specifically, this research suggests that the process by which people make judgments about the interpersonal attraction of others does not rely on potential discrepancies in attitudes.

A second reason that interpersonal communication scholars should find interest in this meta-analysis is the theoretical explanations that have been provided to describe the effect that interpersonal interaction has on the relation between attitude similarity and interpersonal attraction. In particular, this analysis provides new explanations, such as politeness theory, and nonverbal cues displayed in interpersonal interactions to explain why people make certain interpersonal attraction judgments.

Exploring the potential effect that politeness theory and the use of nonverbal communication has on the relation between attitude similarity and interpersonal attraction is important to understanding interpersonal attraction in the early stages of newly formed relationships. Specifically, if politeness and nonverbal cues moderate the relation between attitude similarity and attraction, then it implies that individuals are not only heavily influenced by social norms, but among other things, are actively engaged in balancing their desire to maintain a stable and tension-free relationship with the potentially aversive effect of attitude discrepancy that they may share with another.

REFERENCES

References marked with an asterisk indicate studies included in the meta-analysis.

Aristotle. (1932). *The rhetoric* (L. Cooper, Trans.). New York: Appleton-Century-Crofts. (Original work published 330 BC)

*Aronson, J. S., Davis, M. C., & Jones, L. C. (1983). Sequential effects of attitudinal stimuli. *Journal of Social Psychology, 119,* 257–260.

*Arrowood, A. J., & Short, J. A. (1973). Agreement, attraction, and self-esteem. *Canadian Journal of Behavioral Science, 5,* 242–252.

Atkinson, D. R., & Schein, S. (1986). Similarity in counseling. *The Counseling Psychologist, 14,* 319–357.

Berger C. R., & Calabrese, R. J. (1975). Some explorations in initial interactions and beyond: Toward a developmental theory in interpersonal communication. *Human Communication Research, 1,* 99–112.

Berscheid, E., & Walster, E. (1983). *Interpersonal attraction.* Reading, MA: Addison-Wesley.

*Bleda, P. R. (1973). Attitude similarity–dissimilarity and attraction in the middle eastern culture. *The Journal of Social Psychology, 91,* 153–154.

Bochner, A. P. (1991). On the paradigm that would not die. In J. A. Anderson (Ed.), *Communication yearbook 14* (pp. 484–491). Newbury Park, CA: Sage.

*Bond, M., Byrne, D., & Diamond, M. J. (1968). Effect of occupational prestige and attitude similarity on attraction as a function of assumed similarity of attitude. *Psychological Reports, 23,* 1167–1172.

Bowman, C. H., & Fishbein, M. (1978). Understanding public reaction to energy proposals: An application of the Fishbein model. *Journal of Applied Social Psychology, 8,* 319–340.

*Brink, J. H. (1977). Effect of interpersonal communication on attraction. *Journal of Personality and Social Psychology, 35,* 783–790.

Brown, W. (1910). Some experimental results in the correlation of mental abilities. *British Journal of Psychology, 3,* 296–322.

Burleson, B. R., & Denton, W. H. (1992). A new look at similarity and attraction in marriage: Similarities in social-cognitive and communication skills as predictors of attraction and satisfaction. *Communication Monographs, 59,* 268–287.

Byrne, D. (1992). The transition from controlled laboratory experimentation to less controlled settings: Surprise! Additional variables are operative. *Communication Monographs, 59,* 190–198.

*Byrne, D. (1961a). Interpersonal attraction and attitude similarity. *Journal of Abnormal and Social Psychology, 62,* 713–715.

*Byrne, D. (1961b). Interpersonal attraction as a function of affiliation need and attitude similarity. *Human Relations, 3,* 283–289.

Byrne, D. (1969). Attitudes and attraction. In L. Berkowitz (Ed.), *Advances in experimental psychology* (pp. 178–224). New York: Academic.

Byrne, D. (1971). *The attraction paradigm.* New York: Academic.

*Byrne, D., Baskett, G. D., & Hodges, L. H. (1971). Behavioral indicators of interpersonal attraction. *Journal of Applied Social Psychology, 1,* 137–149.

*Byrne, D., & Clore, G. L. (1967). Effectance arousal and attraction. *Journal of Personality and Social Psychology, 6,* 1–18.

*Byrne, D., Clore., G. L., & Griffitt, W. (1967). Response discrepancy versus attitude similarity–dissimilarity as determinants of attraction. *Psychonomic Science, 7,* 397–398.

Byrne, D., Clore, G. L., & Smeaton, G. (1986). The attraction hypothesis: Do similar attitudes affect anything? *Journal of Personality and Social Psychology, 6,* 1167–1170.

*Byrne, D., & Ervin, C. R. (1969). Attraction toward a negro stranger as a function of prejudice, attitude similarity, and the stranger's evaluation of the subject. *Human Relations, 22,* 397–404.

*Byrne, D., Ervin, C. R., & Lamberth, J. (1970). Continuity between the experimental study of attraction and real-life computer dating. *Journal of Personality and Social Psychology, 16,* 157–165.

*Byrne, D., Gouaux, C., Griffitt, W., Lamberth, J., Murakawa, N., Prasad, M., Prasad, A., & Ramirez, M. (1971). The ubiquitous relationship: Attitude similarity and attraction. *Human Relations, 24,* 201–207.

*Byrne, D., & Griffitt, W. (1966a). A developmental investigation of the law of attraction. *Journal of Personality and Social Psychology, 4,* 699–702.

*Byrne, D., & Griffitt, W. (1966b). Similarity versus liking: A clarification. *Psychonomic Science, 6,* 295–296.

Byrne, D., & Griffitt, W. (1973). Interpersonal attraction. *Annual Review of Psychology, 24,* 317–336.

*Byrne, D., Griffitt, W., & Golightly, C. (1966). Prestige as a factor in determining the effect of attitude similarity–dissimilarity on attraction. *Journal of Personality, 34,* 434–444.

*Byrne, D., Griffitt, W., Hudgins, W., & Reeves, K. (1969). Attitude similarity–dissimilarity and attraction: Generality beyond the college sophomore. *Journal of Social Psychology, 79,* 155–161.

*Byrne, D., London, O., & Griffitt, W. (1968). The effect of topic importance and attitude similarity–dissimilarity on attraction in an intrastranger design. *Psychonomic Science, 11,* 303–304.

*Byrne, D., London, O., & Reeves, K. (1968). The effects of physical attractiveness, sex, and attitude similarity on interpersonal attraction. *Journal of Personality, 36,* 259–271.

*Byrne, D., & Nelson, D. (1965). Attraction as a linear function of proportion of positive reinforcements. *Journal of Personality and Social Psychology, 6,* 659–663.

*Byrne, D., & Rhamey, R. (1965). Magnitude of positive and negative reinforcements as a determinance of attraction. *Journal of Personality and Social Psychology, 2,* 884–889.

*Cappella, J. N., & Palmer, M. T. (1990). Attitude similarity, relational history, and attraction: The mediating effects of kinesic and vocalic behaviors. *Communication Monographs, 57,* 161–183.

*Cherry, F., Byrne, B., & Mitchell, H. E. (1976). Clogs in the bogus pipeline: Demand characteristics and social desirability. *Journal of Research in Personality, 10,* 69–75.

*Clore, G. L., & Baldridge, B. (1970). The behavior of item weights in attitude-attraction research. *Journal of Experimental Social Psychology, 6,* 177–186.

*Clore, G. L., & Gormly, J. B. (1974). Knowing, feeling, and liking: A psychophysiological study of attraction. *Journal of Research in Personality, 8,* 218–230.

*Condon, J. W., & Crano, W. D. (1988). Inferred evaluation and the relationship between attitude similarity and interpersonal attraction. *Journal of Personality and Social Psychology, 54*, 789–797.

Coombs, L. C., & Chang, M. (1981). Do husbands and wives agree? Fertility attitude and later behavior. *Population and Environment, 4*, 109–127.

Curran, J. P. (1973). Examination of various interpersonal attraction principles in the dating dyad. *Journal of Experimental Research in Personality, 6*, 347–356.

*Curran, J. P., & Lippold, S. (1975). The effects of physical attraction and attitude similarity on attraction in dating dyads. *Journal of Personality, 43*, 528–539.

*Davis, J. M. (1984). Attraction to a group as a function of attitude similarity and geographic distance. *Social Behavior and Personality, 12*, 1–6.

*De Wolfe, T. E., & Jackson, L. A. (1984). Birds of a brighter feather: Level of moral reasoning and similarity of attitude as determinants of interpersonal attraction. *Psychological Reports, 54*, 789–797.

*Erwin, P. G. (1981). The role of attitudinal similarity and perceived acceptance evaluation in interpersonal attraction. *The Journal of Psychology, 100*, 133–136.

*Erwin, P. G. (1982). The role of attitudinal similarity and direct acceptance evaluations in attraction. *The Journal of Psychology, 111*, 97–100.

*Franklin, B. J. (1971). Attitude similarity–dissimilarity, dogmatism, and interpersonal attraction. *Psychology, 37*, 4–11.

*Gonzales, M. H., Davis, J. M., Loney, G. L., LuKens, C. K., & Junghans, C. M. (1983). Interactional approach to interpersonal attraction. *Journal of Personality and Social Psychology, 6*, 1192–1197.

*Good, L. R., & Good, K. C. (1972). Role of vindication motivation in the attitude similarity–attraction relationship. *Psychological Reports, 31*, 769–770.

*Good, L. R., & Nelson, D. A. (1971). Effects of person–group and intragroup attitude similarity on perceived group attractiveness and cohesiveness. *Psychonomic Science, 25*, 215–217.

*Gormly, A. V., & Clore, G. L. (1969). Attraction, dogmatism, and attitude similarity–dissimilarity. *Journal of Experimental Research in Personality, 4*, 9–13.

*Gouaux, C. (1971). Induced affective states and interpersonal attraction. *Journal of Personality and Social Psychology, 20*, 37–43.

*Gouaux, C., & Summers, K. (1973). Interpersonal attraction as a function of affective state and affective change. *Journal of Research in Personality, 7*, 254–260.

Griffitt, W. B. (1969). Personality similarity and self-concept as determinants of interpersonal attraction. *Journal of Social Psychology, 78*, 137–146.

*Hoyle, R. H. (1993). Interpersonal attraction in the absence of explicit attitudinal information. *Social Cognition, 11*, 309–320.

Hunt, A. (1935). A study of the relative value of certain ideals. *Journal of Abnormal and Social Psychology, 30*, 222–228.

Hunter, J. E., (1993). *VGBARE: A program to do bare bones meta-analysis on r.* East Lansing: Michigan State University, Department of Psychology.

Hunter, J. E., (1991). *FTOR: A program to convert F to r.* East Lansing: Michigan State University, Department of Psychology.

Hunter, J. E., & Schmidt, F. L. (1990). *Methods of meta-analysis.* Newbury Park, CA: Sage.

Hunter, J. E., Schmidt, F. L., & Jackson, G. B. (1982). *Meta-analysis: Cumulating research findings across studies.* Beverly Hills, CA: Sage.

*Insko, C. A., & Wetzel, C. (1974). Preacquaintance attraction as an interactive function of the proportion and number of similar attitudes. *Representative Research in Social Psychology, 5*, 27–33.

*Jackson, L. A., & Mascaro, G. M. (1971). Interpersonal attraction as a function of attitude similarity dissimilarity and attitude extremity. *Psychonomic Science, 23*, 187–188.

*Jamieson, D. W., Lyndon, J. E., & Zanna, M. P. (1987). Attitude and activity preference similarity: Differential bases of interpersonal attraction for low and high self-monitors. *Journal of Personality and Social Psychology, 53*, 1052–1060.

*Johnson, C. D. (1971). Competence motivation and interpersonal evaluation. *Bulletin of Psychonomic Society, 4*, 199–200.

*Johnson, J., & Johnson, D. W. (1972). The effects of other's actions, attitude similarity, and race on attraction toward others. *Human Relations, 2*, 121–130.

*Kaplan, M. F. (1972). Interpersonal attraction as a function of relatedness of similar and dissimilar attitudes. *Journal of Experimental Research in Personality, 6*, 17–21.

*Kaplan, M. F., & Olcsak, P. V. (1970). Attitude similarity and direct reinforcement as determinants of attraction. *Journal of Experimental Research in Personality, 4*, 186–189.

Kirkpatrick, C., & Stone, S. (1935). Attitude measurement and the comparison of generations. *Journal of Applied Psychology, 5*, 564–582.

*Kleck, R. E., & Rubenstein, C. (1975). Physical attractiveness, perceived attitude-similarity, and interpersonal attraction in an opposite-sex encounter. *Journal of Personality and Social Psychology, 31*, 107–114.

*Layton, B. D., & Insko, C. A. (1974). Anticipated interaction and the similarity–attraction effect. *Sociometry, 2*, 149–162.

*Lydon, J. E., Jamieson, D. W., & Zanna, M. P. (1988). Interpersonal similarity and the social intellectual dimensions of first impressions. *Social Cognition, 4*, 269–286.

*McGinley, H. (1980). A test for artifactual effects in an attitude similarity/interpersonal attraction study. *Bulletin of the Psychonomic Society, 16*, 137–139.

*McGinley, H., Nicholas, K., & McGinley, P. (1978). Effects of body position and attitude similarity on interpersonal attraction and opinion change. *Psychological Reports, 42*, 127–138.

*McGinley, H., & Reiner, M. (1979). Contingency awareness and interpersonal attraction. *Bulletin of the Psychonomic Society, 13*, 175–178.

Newcomb, T. M. (1961). *The acquaintance process.* New York: Holt, Rinehart, & Winston.

Newcomb, T., & Svehla, G. (1937). Intra-family relationships in attitude. *Sociometry, 1*, 659–667.

*Olczak, P. V., & Goldman, J. A. (1975). Self-actualization as a moderator of the relationship between attitude similarity and attraction. *The Journal of Psychology, 89*, 195–202.

*Orpen, C. (1984). Attitude similarity, attraction, and decision-making in the employment interview. *The Journal of Psychology, 117*, 111–120.

*Palmer, D. L., & Kalin, R. (1985). Dogmatic responses to belief dissimilarity in the "bogus stranger" paradigm. *Journal of Personality and Social Psychology, 48*, 171–179.

*Pander, J., & Rastogi, R. (1978). Intolerance of ambiguity and response to attitude similarity–dissimilarity. *Psychologia, 21*, 104–106.

Parks, M. R., & Adelman, M. B. (1983). Communication networks and the development of romantic relationships: An expansion of uncertainty reduction theory. *Human Communication Research, 10*, 55–79.

*Posavac, E. J., & Pasko, S. J. (1971). Interpersonal attraction and confidence of attraction ratings as a function of number of attitudes and attitude similarity. *Psychonomic Science, 23,* 433–435.

*Rosenbaum, M. E. (1986). The repulsion hypothesis: On the nondevelopment of relationships. *Journal of Personality and Social Psychology, 51,* 1156–1166.

*Sachs, D. H. (1975). Belief similarity and attitude similarity as determinants of interpersonal attraction. *Journal of Research in Personality, 9,* 57–65.

*Santee, R. T. (1976). The effect on attraction of attitude similarity as information about interpersonal reinforcement contingencies. *Sociometry, 39,* 153–156.

Schiller, B. (1932). A quantitative analysis of marriage selection in a small group. *Journal of Social Psychology, 3,* 297–319.

Schooley, M. (1936). Personality resemblances among married couples. *Journal of Abnormal and Social Psychology, 31,* 340–347.

*Scott, W. C. (1973). The linear relationship between interpersonal attraction and similarity: An analysis of the "unique stranger" technique. *Journal of Social Psychology, 91,* 117–125.

*Shaikh, T., & Kanekar, S. (1993). Attitudinal similarity and affiliation need as determinants of interpersonal attraction. *Journal of Social Psychology, 134,* 257–259.

*Shuntich, R. J. (1976). Some effects of attitudinal similarity and exposure of attraction and aggression. *Journal of Research in Personality, 10,* 155–165.

Simons, H. W., Berkowitz, N. N., & Moyer, J. (1970). Similarity, credibility, and attitude change. *Psychological Bulletin, 73,* 1–16.

*Singh, R. (1973). Attraction as a function of similarity in attitudes and personality characteristics. *Journal of Social Psychology, 91,* 87–95.

*Singh, R. (1974). Reinforcement and attraction: Specifying the effects of affective states. *Research in Personality, 8,* 291–305.

*Singh, R. (1975). Reinforcement, affect, and interpersonal attraction. *Psychologia, 18,* 142–148.

*Smeaton, G., Byrne, D., & Murmen, S. K. (1989). The repulsion hypothesis revisited: Similarity irrelevance or dissimilarity bias? *Journal of Personality and Social Psychology, 56,* 54–59.

*Smith, R. E., Meadow, B. L., & Sisk, T. K. (1970). Attitude similarity, interpersonal attraction, and evaluative social perception. *Psychonomic Science, 18,* 226–227.

Spearman, C. (1910). Correlation calculated from faulty data. *British Journal of Psychology, 3,* 271–295.

*Stroebe, W., Insko, C. A., & Layton, B. (1971). Effects of physical attractiveness, attitude similarity, and sex on various aspects of interpersonal attraction. *Journal of Personality and Social Psychology, 18,* 79–91.

*Sunnafrank, M. (1983). Attitude similarity and interpersonal attraction in communication processes: In pursuit of an ephemeral influence. *Communication Monographs, 50,* 273–284.

*Sunnafrank, M. (1984). A communication-based perspective on attitude similarity and interpersonal attraction in early acquaintance. *Communication Monographs, 51,* 372–380.

*Sunnafrank, M. (1985). Attitude similarity and interpersonal attraction during early communicative relationships: A research note on the generalizability of findings to opposite-sex relationships. *Western Journal of Speech Communication, 49,* 73–80.

*Sunnafrank, M. (1986). Communicative influences on perceived similarity and attraction: An expansion of the interpersonal goals perspective. *Western Journal of Speech Communication, 50,* 158–170.

Sunnafrank, M. (1992). On debunking the attitude similarity myth. *Communication Monographs, 59,* 164–179.

*Sunnafrank, M., & Miller, G. R. (1981). The role of initial conversations in determining attraction to similar and dissimilar strangers. *Human Communication Research, 8,* 16–25.

Tan, D. Y., & Singh, R. (1995). Attitude and attraction: A developmental study of the similarity–attraction and dissimilarity–repulsion hypotheses. *Personality and Social Psychology Bulletin, 21,* 975–986.

*Tesch, F. E., Huston, T. L., & Indenbaum, E. A. (1973). Attitude similarity, attraction, and physical proximity in a dynamic space. *Journal of Applied Social Psychology, 3,* 63–72.

*Tesser, A. (1971). Evaluative and structural similarity of attitudes as determinants of interpersonal attraction. *Journal of Personality and Social Psychology, 18,* 92–96.

*Touhey, J. C. (1974). Situated identities, attitude similarity, and interpersonal attraction. *Sociometry, 37,* 363–374.

*Williams, S., Ryckman, R. M., Gold, J. A., & Lenney, E. (1982). The effects of sensation seeking and misattribution of arousal on attraction toward similar and dissimilar strangers. *Journal of Research in Personality, 16,* 217–226.

*Yabrudi, P. F., Diaz, M., & Lufty, L. N. (1978). The effects of attitude similarity–dissimilarity, religion, and topic importance on interpersonal attraction among Lebanese university students. *The Journal of Psychology, 106,* 167–71.

10

Self-Disclosure Research: Knowledge Through Meta-Analysis

Kathryn Dindia

Self-disclosure refers to the process by which one person verbally reveals information about himself or herself (including thoughts, feelings, and experiences) to another person (Derlega, Metts, Petronio, & Margulis, 1993). Self-disclosure is the focus of much quantitative research because it is a key to the development and maintenance of relationships.

Three issues have dominated the quantitative research on self-disclosure: (a) sex differences in self-disclosure, (b) self-disclosure and liking, and (c) reciprocity of self-disclosure. Meta-analyses have been conducted on sex differences in self-disclosure (Dindia & Allen, 1992), self-disclosure and liking (Collins & Miller, 1994), and reciprocity of self-disclosure (Dindia & Allen, 1995). The purpose of this chapter is to summarize the results of the three meta-analyses, and to compare and contrast the results of the three meta-analyses for a comprehensive review of the research on self-disclosure.

SEX DIFFERENCES IN SELF-DISCLOSURE

There are more studies on sex differences in self-disclosure than on any other issue regarding self-disclosure. Jourard (1971) was the first to hypothesize that men disclose less than women. Dindia and Allen (1992) conducted a meta-analysis of sex differences in self-disclosure. The results of the meta-analysis were that women disclosed more than men; however, the difference was small, $r = .09$ ($d = .18, k = 205, N = 23,702$), and the effect size was heterogeneous, meaning that the effect sizes varied more than could be expected due to chance across the studies.

Hill and Stull (1987), in a narrative review of the literature, noted inconsistent findings in research on sex differences in self-disclosure. They argued that various situational factors may account for inconsistencies in sex differences in self-disclosure. Specifically, they argued that a number of situational factors have been found to affect self-disclosure (e.g., sex of target and relationship to target) and that these factors may interact with sex of the disclosure to mediate sex differences in self-disclosure. Thus, Dindia and Allen (1992) tested sex of target, relationship to target, measure of self-disclosure (as well as publication date and status), and interactions among sex of target, relationship to target, and measure of self-disclosure as potential moderators of sex differences in self-disclosure.

Year of publication did not moderate sex differences in self-disclosure. Sex differences have not decreased in the past 30 years. Similarly, whether or not a study was published did not moderate sex differences in self-disclosure. There was no evidence that studies finding sex differences were more likely to be published than studies finding no difference.

Measure of self-disclosure (self-report, other report, observational measure of self-disclosure) moderated sex differences in self-disclosure. Both self-report and observational measures of self-disclosure showed small sex differences ($r = .085, d = .17$, and $r = .11, d = .22$, respectively). However, when participants were reporting on another person's self-disclosure to them (disclosure received), they reported that women disclosed moderately more than men ($r = .22, d = .44$). Dindia and Allen (1992) interpreted this as a result of gender stereotypes. We perceive that we receive more self-disclosure from women than men because there is a stereotype that women self-disclose more than men.

Sex of target (male, female, same sex, opposite sex) moderated sex differences in self-disclosure. Women disclosed more to women than men disclosed to women ($r = .12, d = .24$); women disclosed more to women than men disclosed to men ($r = .155, d = .31$); women disclosed more to men than men disclosed to women ($r = .04, d = .08$); but women did not disclose more to men than men disclosed to men ($r = .015, d = .03$, confidence interval includes 0; see Table 10.1). In addition, sex differences in self-disclosure were significantly greater to female and same-sex partners than to opposite-sex and male partners.

TABLE 10.1
**Moderating Effect of Sex of Recipient on Sex Differences
in Self-Disclosure**

Comparison	d	Conclusion
W to M vs. M to M	.03 (CI inc 0)	No sex differences to male recipients
W to M vs. M to W	.08	Very small sex differences to opposite-sex recipients
W to W vs. M to W	.24	Small sex differences to female recipients
W to W vs. M to M	.31	Small sex differences to same-sex recipients

Note: Effect sizes for differences above the dotted line are significantly less than effect sizes for differences below the dotted line.

There was a significant interaction effect between relationship to target and measure of self-disclosure. Measure of self-disclosure (self-report vs. observation) did not moderate sex differences in self-disclosure to intimates. In intimate relationships, both self-report and observational data indicate that women disclose slightly more than men ($r = .105$, $d = .21$, and $r = .115$, $d = .23$, respectively). However, measure of self-disclosure moderated sex differences when the target was a stranger. Men reported that they self-disclose to strangers similarly to women ($r = -.01$, $d = -.02$, not significantly different from 0). However, observational studies of self-disclosure to a stranger found that women disclose slightly more than men ($r = .085$, $d = .17$), and the effect size was not significantly different from the effect size for self-report and observational measures of self-disclosure to intimates. Dindia and Allen (1992) interpreted the zero effect size for self-report measures of self-disclosure to strangers as a spurious result based on invalid self-report measures of self-disclosure when the target person is a stranger (individuals cannot validly report their level of self-disclosure to a generalized stranger).

Thus, the results of the meta-analysis of sex differences in self-disclosure indicate that women disclose more than men. However, sex differences in self-disclosure are small and are moderated by sex of recipient. Sex is not a stable individual difference variable that consistently predicts level of self-disclosure across sex of partner.

SELF-DISCLOSURE AND LIKING

Interest in the relation between self-disclosure and liking began with the work of Jourard (1959), who found a positive relation between self-report measures of self-disclosure to and liking for a partner. Since then, a number of studies have been conducted on the relation between self-disclosure and liking.

Three questions have been asked regarding the relation between self-disclosure and liking. First, does an individual's self-disclosure to a partner lead to the partner's liking of the individual? It has been argued that self-disclosure is rewarding to the recipient and therefore causes the recipient to like the disclosure. This particular relation is referred to as the *disclosure-liking hypothesis*. The second question is whether liking another person leads to disclosure to that person: Do people disclose to people they like? Finally, does disclosure to another person lead to liking for that person? It has been argued that self-disclosure to another individual is personally rewarding and therefore leads to liking of the recipient. Collins and Miller (1994) conducted meta-analyses of these three relations between self-disclosure and liking.

The first effect, that of an individual's self-disclosure on a partner's liking, has been of greatest theoretic interest. Studies examining this effect make up the bulk of the studies on self-disclosure and liking. Collins and Miller (1994) examined 94 studies testing this effect. The results were that higher levels of disclosure were associated with greater liking for the disclosure ($r = .14, d = .28, k = 94$), a small effect size. However, the results were not homogenous and several moderator variables were tested.

Collins and Miller (1994) categorized studies into correlational studies and experimental studies (further divided into strong and weak experiments) and tested whether this moderated the relation between self-disclosure and liking. The results were a large effect size for correlational studies ($r = .40, d = .85, k = 6$) and small effect sizes for experimental studies ($r = .14, d = .27, k = 57$ and $r = .10, d = .19, k = 31$ for strong and weak experiments, respectively). Although the effect sizes were small in experimental studies, they indicate a causal relation; disclosure causes liking.

Collins and Miller (1994) also tested whether type of study moderated the disclosure–liking relation. The results indicated that the largest effect size was for relationship surveys (the same subgroup as correlational studies) involving people in ongoing relationships ($r = .40, d = .85, k = 6$). Acquaintance studies (one subset of experimental studies) involving participants who interacted (or believed they were interacting) with a partner in a laboratory setting found a significantly smaller effect size, but the effect was still significantly different from zero ($r = .19, d = .38, k = 54$). Impression formation studies (a further subset of experimental studies) involving participants who observed or read about a target who disclosed at either a high or low level found a small but significant effect size that was smaller than that for acquaintance studies or relationship survey studies ($r = .10, d = .19,$

$k = 28$). Field studies (another subset of experimental studies) that involved disclosure between strangers in public places found a significant negative effect, indicating that higher levels of disclosure were related to less liking ($r = -.15, d = -.31, k = 6$). The effect size was homogenous and was significantly different from the other categories of studies. Collins and Miller interpreted the negative effect size as a result of an individual disclosing to a stranger in public, which may be viewed as extremely inappropriate and a violation of social norms.

Collins and Miller (1994) also tested whether sex of disclosure, sex of recipient, and the interaction of sex of disclosure and sex of recipient moderated the disclosure–liking relations. The results indicate that the disclosure–liking relation is stronger for female than male disclosures ($r = .15, d = .30, k = 53$, and $r = .05, d = .11, k = 24$) and the effect size for male disclosures did not differ significantly from zero. However, the results for both groups were heterogeneous, indicating that sex of disclosure, by itself, does not moderate the disclosure–liking relation. The results indicated little evidence of differences in the disclosure–liking relation for male versus female recipients of disclosure. The results for the interaction effect of sex of disclosure and sex of recipient were significant. The effect size for self-disclosure on liking was highest for female–female dyads ($d = .485, r = .236, n = 33$) and second for male–male dyads ($d = .247, r = .123, n = 15$). In both cases the effect size was significantly different from zero. The effect sizes for female–male dyads and male–female dyads were not significantly different from zero (female–male dyads, $d = -.265, r = -.132, n = 2$; male–female dyads, $d = .098, r = .049, n = 2$). However, these results must be viewed with caution given that two cells contained only two observations, the difference between the two cells with larger observations did not reach significance, and the results for three of the four cells were heterogeneous. Thus, no conclusions can be drawn about the interaction effect of sex of disclosure and sex of recipient.

Collins and Miller (1994) tested whether the level of disclosure moderated the disclosure–liking relation. They did not find evidence that high disclosure, relative to low disclosure, leads to less liking. However, they indicated that their finding is limited given the small number of studies on which it was based ($k = 7$) and the difficulty in comparing disclosure levels from one study to the next.

Whether self-disclosure was perceived as personalistic was also tested as a moderator. People can perceive another person's self-disclosure as personalistic (revealed only to the disclosee) or nonpersonalistic (revealed to many people). Collins and Miller (1994) found that the effect size for self-disclosure where a personalistic attribution was made was $r = .22$ ($d = .45, k = 10$) whereas the effect size for nonpersonalistic attributions was $r = .11$ ($d = .23, k = 12$). Although the difference was not statistically significant, it was in the predicted direction. Collins and Miller (1994) concluded that "these studies provide some evidence that the relation between disclosure and liking may be stronger if the recipient believes that the disclosure was given because of something unique or special about him- or herself" (p. 20).

Collins and Miller (1994) also conducted a meta-analysis of whether we disclose more to people we like (here the question is "Does liking cause disclosure?" instead of "Does disclosure cause liking?"). The results of the meta-analysis indicated that we disclose more to people we like ($r = .34, d = .72, k = 31$), a moderately large effect size; but the results were heterogeneous. The studies were again divided into correlational studies and experimental studies. The results were that the effect sizes for strong and weak experiments did not differ from each other ($r = .22, d = .45, k = 8$ and $r = .14, d = .28, k = 7$, respectively) but both were significantly smaller than the effect size for correlational studies ($r = .48, d = 1.11, k = 16$). The significant, yet smaller, effect size for experimental studies indicates a causal relation; liking causes disclosure.

The only other moderator that could be tested was sex of disclosure. The results indicated little evidence that men and women differ in their tendency to disclose to people they like.

Finally, Collins and Miller (1994) tested whether we like people as a result of disclosing to them. The meta-analysis was based on only five studies, all of them categorized as strong experiments, so the results should be interpreted with caution. The mean effect size was $r = .16$ ($d = .32$), a moderately small effect size, indicating a positive relation between disclosure and subsequent liking for the target. People who were induced to disclose at a higher level tended to like their partner more than people who did not disclose or who disclosed at lower levels. However, the results were heterogeneous so again the results should be interpreted with caution. Collins and Miller (1994) speculated that whether the participant believed he or she acted freely may have moderated the effect size. However, the authors examined the studies and found no reason to believe that the studies that showed no effect differed on this dimension compared with studies that showed an effect.

Thus, the results of Collins and Miller's (1994) meta-analyses of the disclosure–liking relation confirm that we like people who self-disclose to us, we disclose more to people we like, and we like others as a result of having disclosed to them (although the last finding should be interpreted with caution). In general the effect sizes for the disclosure–liking relation were small for experimental studies and large for correlational studies. The significant effect sizes for experimental studies, although small, are important because they indicate a causal relation; self-disclosure causes liking and liking causes self-disclosure. The significant effect sizes for correlational studies are important because they indicate that self-disclosure and liking are related not for just strangers but for intimates. The results also indicate that self-disclosure that is perceived as personalistic may lead to liking more than self-disclosure that is perceived as nonpersonalistic. Finally, level of self-disclosure (high vs. low intimacy) did not moderate the self-disclosure–liking relation; however, this final result should be interpreted with caution due to the small number of studies reviewed and lack of comparable levels of self-disclosure between studies.

RECIPROCITY OF SELF-DISCLOSURE

Dindia and Allen (1995) conducted a meta-analysis of reciprocity of self-disclosure. Because this meta-analysis has not been published elsewhere, it is reviewed here in more detail than the preceding meta-analyses.

Jourard (1971) originated the idea that self-disclosure is reciprocal: "In ordinary social relationships, disclosure is a reciprocal phenomenon. Participants in dialogue disclose their thoughts, feelings, actions, etc., to the other and are disclosed to in return. I called this reciprocity the 'dyadic effect': disclosure begets disclosure" (p. 66). Several theories and perspectives have been used to predict and explain reciprocity of self-disclosure. Trust-attraction is one explanation for reciprocity of self-disclosure. It has been argued that disclosing intimate information makes the recipient feel trusted. This creates attraction and leads the recipient to return disclosure as a sign of liking and a willingness to trust the original disclosure. Another explanation is social exchange. Receiving disclosure is a rewarding experience. Because the recipient has received something of value, he or she feels obligated to return something of similar value (Archer, 1979). Similarly, Gouldner's (1960) notion of a norm of reciprocity has been used to explain reciprocity of self-disclosure. Derlega et al. (1993) attributed reciprocity of self-disclosure to the more global constraints of conversational norms. That is, when a speaker self-discloses, the recipient must be responsive to the disclosure's vulnerability and to the conversational demand to be topically relevant. Reciprocity of self-disclosure addresses both these conversational constraints.

Dindia and Allen (1995) conducted a meta-analysis of 67 studies involving 5,173 participants on reciprocity of self-disclosure. The average weighted effect size for reciprocity of self-disclosure was $r = .32$ ($d = .69$), a moderately large effect size. However, the effect size was not homogenous χ^2

(66) = 289.46, $p \le .05$, indicating that the variation of the effect sizes across studies was not solely due to sampling error. One outlier was removed from the analysis and all subsequent analyses and the results for 66 studies involving 5113 participants was $r = .335$ ($d = .70$) χ^2 (65) = 248.74, $p \le .05$. Still, the effect size was not homogenous across studies. Thus, methods of testing of reciprocity and measure of self-disclosure were analyzed to determine their moderating effects on reciprocity of self-disclosure.

Method of Testing Reciprocity of Self-Disclosure

Reciprocity of self-disclosure has been operationally defined and tested using several methods.

Experimental Studies. The most common test of reciprocity of self-disclosure is whether an experimenter's or confederate's self-disclosure has a positive effect on a participant's self-disclosure (which is tested using t test or one-way analysis of variance). Typically, a participant is exposed to one of two experimental conditions of self-disclosure: high or low disclosure. The participant's disclosure in response to the confederate's disclosure is the dependent variable.

The generalizability of the results from these studies has been seriously questioned. As stated by Chelune (1979), "Investigators have used superficial, perfunctory remarks in the low disclosure condition and explicit, personal comments on highly private topics … for the high disclosure conditions" (p. 14). The results of these studies may not generalize to real-life conversations.

On the other hand, experimental studies are powerful in that it is possible to infer a causal relation; one person's self-disclosure causes another person's self-disclosure. However, it should be noted that the results of these studies only provide evidence of a one-way effect (A's self-disclosure causes B's self-disclosure). Strictly speaking, they do not provide evidence of reciprocity (mutual positive influence—A's self-disclosure causes B's self-disclosure and B's self-disclosure causes A's self-disclosure).

Correlational Studies. Reciprocity of self-disclosure is also tested with the correlation between two persons' self-disclosure (Hill & Stull, 1982). A significant positive correlation is interpreted as reciprocity of self-disclosure. This test of reciprocity typically involves a nonexperimental laboratory study in which self-disclosure is observed, or a questionnaire study in which self-disclosure is measured through self or other report data.

A criticism leveled against using the correlation between partners' self-disclosure as a test of reciprocity is that it confuses base rates of self-disclosure with reciprocity of self-disclosure. For example, two persons' self-disclosure may be related due to similar personality traits (e.g., Kate and John are both high or low disclosures) rather than one's self-disclosure elicits the other's self-disclosure, and vice versa. Correlation confounds individual differences in self-disclosure with reciprocity of self-disclosure. This is not a problem in laboratory studies where participants are randomly assigned partners (and are not likely to be similar in their openness), but it is very problematic in self-report studies in which individuals report on their self-disclosure to a family member, friend, spouse, and so on.

Sequential Analysis. Sequential analysis has been used to test reciprocity of self-disclosure. Whether an individual's self-disclosure elicits a partner's self-disclosure in the subsequent turn (or near subsequent turn), and vice versa, is tested. Sequential analysis can be used to test whether influence is mutual or two-way (reciprocity). Only a few studies have been conducted testing reciprocity of self-disclosure using sequential analysis (Dindia, 1982, 1988; Spencer, 1993; Strassberg, Gabel, & Anchor, 1976; Van Lear, 1987).

A different problem arises when using sequential analysis to test reciprocity of self-disclosure. An individual may reciprocate self-disclosure at a later point in the conversation, or even in a later conversation.

> The dyadic effect is assumed to be a time-bound process in which people mutually regulate their disclosure to one another, at some agreed upon pace. But, little more is said about temporal aspects of reciprocity. The rate at which it occurs, how it ebbs and flows, factors which accelerate or retard reciprocity of exchange are not discussed in detail. (Altman, 1973, p. 250)

Thus, reciprocity of self-disclosure may occur in a manner other than one person's self-disclosure increasing the probability of a partner's self-disclosure in the subsequent turn. Reciprocity of self-disclosure may not occur on a tit-for-tat basis ("My most embarrassing moment was … " and "My most embarrassing moment was … "). It may be that an individual's self-disclosure has a positive effect on a partner's self-disclosure, and vice versa, in some general sense that is not manifested on a turn-by-turn basis.

Social Relations Analysis. Miller and Kenny (1986) provided another method for testing reciprocity of self-disclosure. Miller and Kenny differentiated two types of reciprocity of self-disclosure: individual reciprocity and dyadic reciprocity. *Individual reciprocity* refers to the extent to which individuals who generally disclose are generally disclosed to in conversation. Individual reciprocity measures the correlation between individual differences in self-disclosure. *Dyadic reciprocity* refers to self-disclosure that is unique to the particular relationship, controlling for individual differences in self-disclosure. Dyadic reciprocity refers to the extent to which people adjust their disclosure to their partner (how much they disclose to their partner above or below how much they disclose in general). Dyadic reciprocity refers to the correlation between partners' unique adjustment in self-disclosure to each other. Of all the tests of reciprocity of self-disclosure, Miller and Kenny's dyadic reciprocity most closely matches Jourard's (1971) conceptual definition of reciprocity of self-disclosure.

Consequently, studies were coded as (a) experimental studies, (b) correlational studies, (c) sequential analysis studies, or (d) social relations analysis (dyadic reciprocity) studies. The results for experimental studies were a moderate effect size, $r = .296$ ($d = .62, k = 48, N = 4,038$), but the effect size was not homogenous across studies. The effect size for correlational studies was very large, $r = .561$ ($d = 1.36, k = 13, N = 808$), but the results were not homogenous. The effect size for studies employing sequential analysis was $r = .061$ ($d = .12, k = 5, N = 146$), a small, homogenous effect size. The effect size for studies employing social relations analysis was very large ($r = .508, d = 1.18, k = 4, N = 120$), and the effect size was homogenous.

Thus, how reciprocity of self-disclosure is tested moderates reciprocity of self-disclosure. Correlational studies and studies employing social relations analysis found large effect sizes. That studies employing social relations analysis (which control for individual differences in self-disclosure) found large effect sizes indicates that reciprocity is not just the result of partners who are similar in their overall levels of self-disclosure being paired with one another. Experimental studies found a moderate effect of one person's self-disclosure on another person's self-disclosure. Although the results may not be generalizable beyond the laboratory situation, they indicate a causal relation; one person's self-disclosure causes the other person's self-disclosure. The results for studies employing sequential analysis indicate that reciprocity does not occur on a turn-by-turn basis.

Measure of Self-Disclosure

Self-disclosure can be measured using observational or perceptual data. Two types of reciprocity of self-disclosure are studied with perceptual data. First, there is what is referred in the literature to as perceived reciprocity or intrasubjective perceptions of self-disclosure. Intrasubjective perceptions of self-disclosure refer to the perceptions of one person; that is, whether one person perceives his or her self-disclosure with the partner as reciprocal. Specifically, it refers to the correlation between an individual's perception of his or her self-disclosure to a partner (disclosure given) and the same individual's perception of the partner's self-disclosure to the individual (disclosure received).

Second, there is what is referred to as actual reciprocity or intersubjective perceptions of self-disclosure. Intersubjective perceptions refer to perceptions between persons. Specifically, it refers to the correlation between an individual's perception of his or her self-disclosure to a partner (A's perception of A's disclosure to B) and the partner's perception of his or her self-disclosure to the individual (B's perception of B's disclosure to A). Although this is labeled actual reciprocity, the term is a misnomer because it is still based on perceptions of self-disclosure and does not indicate whether actual self-disclosure is reciprocal.

Studies were divided on the basis of whether they employed an observational versus self-report measure of self-disclosure. Self-report studies were subsequently divided into three subsets: studies in which only the dependent variable is measured by self-report data (i.e., an experimental study where the independent variable [self-disclosure] is manipulated and the effect of an experimenter's self-disclosure on a person's self-reported perceived or intended self-disclosure is measured), nonexperimental studies employing intrasubjective perceptions of self-disclosure, and nonexperimental studies employing intersubjective perceptions of self-disclosure.

The results indicate that the effect size increases as one moves from objective observational data to more and more subjective data: observational measures of self-disclosure, $r = .283$ ($d = .59, k = 51, N = 3,420$); self-report measure of dependent variable (self-disclosure), $r = .349$ ($d = .745, k = 11, N = 1,207$); intersubjective perceptions of self-disclosure, $r = .566$ ($d = 1.37, k = 10, N = 600$); intrasubjective perceptions of self-disclosure, $r = .747$ ($d = 2.25, k = 5, N = 423$). All the effect sizes were heterogeneous except for the effect size for intrasubjective perceptions of self-disclosure.

Interaction of Method of Testing Reciprocity and Measure of Self-Disclosure

Dindia and Allen (1995) could not test the interaction effect between method of testing reciprocity and measure of self-disclosure because not all levels of each variable were crossed. Nonetheless, because of the lack of homogeneity, experimental studies were further divided on the basis of whether they employed an observational measure of self-disclosure versus a self-report measure of self-disclosure and correlational studies were divided on the basis of whether they employed an observational measure of self-disclosure or intrasubjective or intersubjective perceptions of self-disclosure.

The effect size for experimental studies employing observational measures of self-disclosure was smaller than the effect size for experimental studies employing self-report measures of self-disclosure ($r = .271, d = .563, k = 39, N = 2,919$ and $r = .349, d = .745, k = 11, N = 1,207$, respectively). The results for correlational studies indicated that as you move from observations of self-disclosure to more and more subjective data (intersubjective perceptions of self-disclosure to intrasubjective perceptions of self-disclosure) the effect size for reciprocity of self-disclosure gets larger ($r = .376, d = .811, k = 6, N = 348; r = .566, d = 1.37, k = 10, N = 600; r = .747, d = 2.25, k = 5, N = 423$, respectively). However, it should be noted that even when the effect sizes were differentiated by method of testing reciprocity and measure of self-disclosure, the resulting effect sizes were still heterogeneous (except for intrasubjective perceptions of self-disclosure in correlational studies), indicating that there are probably other variables that moderate reciprocity of self-disclosure.

Strangers Versus Intimates

Altman (1973) hypothesized that reciprocity of self-disclosure decreases as a relationship develops. According to Altman, the norm of reciprocity is important in the early stages of a relationship but the obligation to reciprocate diminishes in later stages. Alternatively, Hill and Stull (1982) argued that reciprocity does not decrease as a relationship develops, but that the time frame over which reciprocity occurs increases. According to Hill and Stull, as members of a relationship develop trust they do not need to reciprocate self-disclosure in a given encounter because they trust each other to reciprocate in the future. From this perspective, reciprocation is just as important in intimate relationships as between strangers, but the time frame over which reciprocity occurs is extended. Thus, according to Altman (1973), intimates should reciprocate self-disclosure less than strangers. According to Hill and Stull, intimates should reciprocate self-disclosure as much as strangers; however, reciprocity will not occur during a given conversation but over an extended period of time.

Dindia and Allen (1995) studied level of relationship, strangers versus intimates, as a potential moderator of reciprocity of self-disclosure. The majority of studies examined reciprocity of self-disclosure between strangers ($k = 52, N = 4,215$). The heterogenous effect size for these studies was $r = .317$ ($d = .67$). Only five studies ($N = 206$) examined reciprocity of self-disclosure for intimates (spouses or friends). The heterogenous effect size for intimates was $r = .437$ ($d = .97$). Thus, it appears that intimates reciprocate self-disclosure as much as strangers.

Given the small number of studies testing reciprocity of self-disclosure for intimates, it is impossible to test the competing hypotheses regarding reciprocity of self-disclosure for intimates. However, one of the studies (Dindia, Fitzpatrick, & Kenny, 1997) used social relations analysis to systematically analyze the effect of level of relationship on reciprocity of self-disclosure, within conversations, using observational data. The results were that there were no differences in reciprocity of self-disclosure for spouses versus opposite-sex strangers. In particular, Dindia et al. (1997) found that spouses, as well as strangers, reciprocate high-intimacy evaluative self-disclosure within conversations. This is in contrast to predictions by both Altman (1973), who predicted that intimates will not reciprocate self-disclosure, and Hill and Stull (1982), who predicted that intimates will reciprocate self-disclosure but over an extended period of time.

In summary, the results of the meta-analysis on reciprocity of self-disclosure indicate that self-disclosure is reciprocal. In general, the effect sizes range from moderate to very large, except for studies employing sequential analysis, which found no effect. The moderate to large effect sizes that were heterogeneous suggest that "reciprocity is 'normative,' meaning it is a common and expected occurrence but is not invariant or automatic" (Derlega et al., 1993, 37).

The effect size for reciprocity of self-disclosure was larger in correlational studies than in experimental studies. It is important to note that the moderate effect size for experimental studies indicates a causal relation, disclosure causes disclosure. The effect size for reciprocity of self-disclosure was also very large for studies employing social relations analysis. This indicates that the unique adjustment that one person makes in response to another person's self-disclosure is reciprocal. Taken together, the results provide strong evidence for reciprocity of self-disclosure.

The results for the studies employing sequential analysis indicate that self-disclosure is not reciprocal on a "tit for tat" basis. One person's self-disclosure does not increase the probability of the partner's self-disclosure in the subsequent utterance. Thus, the interpersonally competent response to self-disclosure may not be to immediately reciprocate self-disclosure. As Berg and Archer (1980) noted, "informal observations suggest that self-disclosures are met with a variety of responses. Indeed, a common reaction to hearing about an intimate problem in another's life is to express concern or empathy" (pp. 246–247). Berg and Archer conducted an experiment in which they examined participants' perceptions of an individual based on the individual's response to a self-disclosure. They (1980) found that the most favorable impressions of the respondent were formed when the respondent expressed concern for a disclosure rather than when the respondent returned any level of self-disclosure.

Although self-disclosure does not appear to be reciprocal on a turn-by turn basis, it does appear to be reciprocal within conversations. All the experimental studies and the correlational studies employing observational measures of self-disclosure were tests of reciprocity within a single conversation. Similarly, two studies employing social relations analysis (Dindia et al., 1997; Wright & Ingraham, 1985, 1986) found reciprocity of self-disclosure within conversations and Dindia et al. (1997) found this was true for spouses as well as strangers.

The effect size for reciprocity of self-disclosure depends on how self-disclosure is measured. The more subjective the measure of self-disclosure, the larger the effect size for reciprocity of self-disclosure. Thus, people may believe that self-disclosure is reciprocal more than it actually is.

The results of the meta-analysis also indicate that intimates as well as strangers reciprocate self-disclosure. However, this should be interpreted with caution, as only five studies tested reciprocity of self-disclosure for intimates and the resulting effect size was heterogeneous.

DISCUSSION

The purpose of this chapter was to summarize meta-analyses on sex differences in self-disclosure, self-disclosure and liking, and reciprocity of self-disclosure, and to compare and contrast the results of the meta-analyses for a comprehensive review of the research. The results of the meta-analyses suggest several theoretical and methodological implications.

A comparison of the results among the three meta-analyses has potential implications for how one views self-disclosure. Self-disclosure has been viewed as a personality trait and as an interpersonal process. The personality trait perspective views self-disclosure as an enduring characteristic or attribute of an individual. Studies cast within this perspective attempt to identify high and low disclosers and correlate individual differences in self-disclosure with demographic and biological characteristics (sex), sociocultural differences, and other personality traits (Archer, 1979). The interpersonal process perspective assumes that it is the process that occurs when individuals interact with each other, rather than the characteristics of either or both participants, that affects self-disclosure. The results of the meta-analyses provide support for the interpersonal process perspective of self-disclosure. The effect sizes for reciprocity of self-disclosure and the disclosure–liking relation were larger than the effect size for sex differences in self-disclosure.

The results of the three meta-analyses also have implications for the issue of self-disclosure and relationship development. There has been much theory and research on the role of self-disclosure in relationship development. The results of the meta-analyses support the idea that self-disclosure processes are similar in the beginning stages of relationships to those in more advanced relational stages. There were similarly small sex differences in self-disclosure for both strangers and intimates, self-disclosure was reciprocal between both strangers and intimates, and there was some evidence that reciprocity of self-disclosure occurs within conversations for both strangers and intimates. Unfortunately, the meta-analyses of self-disclosure and liking did not explicitly test the moderating effect of level of relationship. Correlational studies, which exclusively involved people in ongoing relationships, had larger effect sizes than experimental studies, which exclusively involved strangers. However, this was only one of several differences between correlational and experimental studies and thus the difference in effect sizes cannot be attributed to level of relationship.

Another issue is the validity of different measures of self-disclosure. The meta-analysis on sex differences in self-disclosure found that self-report and observational measures of self-disclosure yielded similar effect sizes. However, studies employing other-report measures (individuals are asked how much others disclose to them) found significantly larger effect sizes than studies employing self-report or observational measures of self-disclosure. The authors argued that other-report measures may be most susceptible to stereotypes of gender differences. The same meta-analysis found that self-report measures of self-disclosure to strangers yielded significantly different effect sizes than self-report measures of self-disclosure to friends, spouses, and parents, and observational measures of self-disclosure to strangers and friends, spouses, and parents. The meta-analysis of reciprocity of self-disclosure found that self-report measures of self-disclosure yielded higher effect sizes than observational measures of self-disclosure. When intrasubjective (one persons' perceptions of disclosure given and received) and intersubjective (two person's perceptions of disclosure given or received) perceptions of self-disclosure were compared, intrasubjective perceptions of self-disclosure have a larger effect size than intersubjective perceptions. The meta-analysis on self-disclosure and liking did not test for the moderating effect of measure of self-disclosure.

These results indicate that one must pay attention to how one measures self-disclosure. People have generalizations, schemas, or stereotypes about self-disclosure. People believe that women disclose more than men, that self-disclosure causes liking, that liking causes self-disclosure, and that self-disclosure is reciprocal. In general, the research indicates that these generalizations are true. However, these generalizations may affect our perceptions of self-disclosure and hence it might be best to use observational measures of self-disclosure. When self-report measures are used, it is important to use intersubjective perceptions of self-disclosure (i.e., ask each partner to rate self-disclosure given and received).

The results of the three meta-analyses also have implications for gender differences. Gender was examined as a main effect in the meta-analysis on sex differences in self-disclosure and as a moderator variable in the meta-analysis on self-disclosure and liking. The meta-analysis on reciprocity of self-disclosure did not test the moderating effect of gender. Gender had a small main effect on self-disclosure. It also had an effect on the disclosure–liking relation (but not the liking–disclosure relation) but it did not, by itself, moderate the disclosure–liking relation. Thus, it appears that sex does not exert a large or stable influence on the process of self-disclosure.

The knowledge gained from these three meta-analyses indicates that the importance placed on self-disclosure in the interpersonal communication literature and the personal relationships literature is not unfounded. Self-disclosure appears to be a key variable in the process of relationship development and maintenance. Self-disclosure is reciprocal for both strangers and intimates. Self-disclosure causes liking, and vice versa, and this appears to be true for both strangers and intimates. Although women disclose slightly more than men, and the disclosure–liking relation appears to be slightly stronger for female than male disclosures, in general, it appears that the process of self-disclosure is more similar than different for men and women.

REFERENCES

Altman, I. (1973). Reciprocity of interpersonal exchange. *Journal for the Theory of Social Behavior, 3,* 249–261.

Archer, R. L. (1979). Anatomical and psychological sex differences. In G. J. Chelune & Associates (Eds.), *Self disclosure: Origins, patterns, and implications of openness in interpersonal relationships* (pp. 80–109). San Francisco: Jossey-Bass.

Berg, J. H., & Archer, R . L. (1980). Disclosure or concern: A second look at liking for the norm breaker. *Journal of Personality, 48,* 245–257.

Chelune, G. J. (1979). Measuring openness in interpersonal communication. In G. J. Chelune & Associates (Eds.), *Self-disclosure: Origins, patterns, and implications of openness in interpersonal relationships* (pp. 1–27). San Francisco: Jossey-Bass.

Collins, N. L., & Miller, L. C. (1994). The disclosure–liking link: From meta-analysis toward a dynamic reconceptualization. *Psychological Bulletin, 116,* 457–475.

Derlega, V. J., Metts, S., Petronio, S., & Margulis, S. T. (1993). *Self-disclosure.* Newbury Park, CA: Sage.

Dindia, K. (1982). Reciprocity of self-disclosure: A sequential analysis. In M. Burgoon (Ed.), *Communication yearbook 6* (pp. 506–530). Beverly Hills, CA: Sage.

Dindia, K. (1988). A comparison of several statistical tests of reciprocity of self-disclosure. *Communication Research, 15,* 726–752.

Dindia, K., & Allen, M. (1992). Sex-differences in self-disclosure: A meta-analysis. *Psychological Bulletin, 112,* 106–124.

Dindia, K., & Allen, M. (1995, June). *Reciprocity of self-disclosure: A meta-analysis.* Paper presented at the International Network on Personal Relationships conference, Williamsburg, PA.

Dindia, K., Fitzpatrick, M. A., & Kenny, D. A. (1997). Self-disclosure in spouse and stranger dyads: A social relations analysis. *Human Communication Research, 23,* 388–412.

Gouldner, A. W. (1960). The norm of reciprocity: A preliminary statement. *American Sociological Review, 25,* 161–178.

Hill, C. T., & Stull, D. E. (1982). Disclosure reciprocity: Conceptual and measurement issues. *Social Psychology Quarterly, 45,* 238–244.

Hill, C. T., & Stull, D. E. (1987). Gender and self-disclosure: Strategies for exploring the issues. In V. J. Derlega & J. H. Berg (Eds.), *Self-disclosure: Theory, research, and therapy* (pp. 81–100). New York: Plenum.

Jourard, S. M. (1959). Self-disclosure and other-cathexis. *Journal of Abnormal and Social Psychology, 59,* 428–431.

Jourard, S. M. (1971). *The transparent self* (rev. ed.). New York: Van Nostrand Reinhold.

Miller, L. C., & Kenny, D. A. (1986). Reciprocity of self-disclosure at the individual and dyadic levels: A social relations analysis. *Journal of Personality and Social Psychology, 50,* 713–719.

Spencer, T. (1993, November). *Testing the self-disclosure reciprocity hypothesis within the context of conversational sequences in family interaction.* Paper presented at the annual meeting of the Speech Communication Association, Miami, FL.

Strassberg, D. S., Gabel, H., & Anchor, K. N. (1976). Patterns of self-disclosure in parent discussion groups. *Small Group Behavior, 7,* 369–378.

Van Lear, C. A. (1987). The formation of social relationships: A longitudinal study of social penetration. *Human Communication Research, 13,* 299–322.

Wright, T. L., & Ingraham, L. J. (1985). The simultaneous study of individual differences and relationship effects in social behavior in groups. *Journal of Personality and Social Psychology, 48,* 1041–1047.

Wright, T. L., & Ingraham, L. J. (1986). Partners and relationships influence self-perceptions of self-disclosures in naturalistic interactions. *Journal of Personality and Social Psychology, 50,* 631–635.

11

The Effects of Situation on the Use or Suppression of Possible Compliance-Gaining Appeals

Dale Hample and Judith M. Dallinger

Scholars in the communication discipline have always understood that people should say different sorts of things in different situations, even assuming that the same primary goal is in force. We request favors from friends differently than we ask strangers, we comfort loved ones differently than a therapist counsels a client, and we persuade a child differently than a political candidate addresses a nominating convention. This chapter is concerned with interpersonal persuasion—the ways in which we try to get another person to comply with our wishes. Here, too, we would expect that we would approach a romantic intimate differently than a supervisor, that we would phrase things differently under stress, and that the history of our relationship with the other person would make a difference in our choice of communication and persuasive strategies.

As we might expect, therefore, interest in situational effects has been evident from the earliest days of work on compliance-gaining tactics and strategies (G. R. Miller, Boster, Roloff, & Seibold, 1977). Many situational variables have been studied, and individual experimental reports have offered conclusions about the effects of these variables on people's choice of compliance-gaining tactics. Unfortunately, there are several quite substantial barriers to generalizing any of those conclusions (D. O'Keefe, 1990).

Without exception, those studies have been vulnerable to some persuasive criticisms initially made by Jackson and Backus (1982), given more detail by Jackson (1992), and brought up to date by Brashers and Jackson (1999). These investigations of compliance gaining typically use one example of each situation condition. For instance, a study crossing two situation variables (e.g., personal relationship and formality) might have one experimental stimulus reworded into four versions to represent combinations of high and low values on each of the variables. The experimenter might write a base message asking for a favor face to face, and then alter the instructions so that some people are told to direct their persuasion to either a friend or a stranger, in either a formal or informal setting. A variant design for this problem has been to have four different base situations, with each situation representing one concordance of values on the situation variables (e.g., leaving a phone message for a friend from work, speaking face to face with a stranger in a bar, etc.).

Both designs are extremely problematic with regard to the generalizability of their conclusions. The one-situation-revised design may not generalize to other base situations because it is virtually inconceivable that only the variables manipulated in the study are relevant to situational effects. One unstudied variable might in fact be interacting with those in the design, making the reported effects misleading in comparison to other situations. Suppose the base situation were a university library's study area: This setting involves quiet, has onlookers, and includes reasonably comfortable tables and chairs. Would this situation necessarily produce the same effects for intense persuasive appeals as a situation in which two runners approached the end of their 10-kilometer race? Experimenters using this sort of design hope that the manipulated variables will have the same effects in any situation, but this is more a hope than an assurance. The four-situations design seems to offer more chance of generalizing to situations in general, but in fact does not. This design fails even to demonstrate that the manipulated variables actually affect a single base situation systematically. The hope in this design is, again, that only the manipulated variables make any difference, and this is, again, implausible.

Readers may be aware that Jackson's methodological critiques have been controversial (see the brief summary and bibliography in Brashers & Jackson, 1999), but the disagreements have mostly focused on the design implications of her parallel criticisms about using single messages to represent categories of messages. The arguments have been about the feasibility of designs that successfully sample message domains, and whether meta-analysis is a reasonable community research strategy in the search for generalization.

None of these disagreements, so far as we know, seriously refute the basic logical criticisms of either of the situation designs that dominate the compliance-gaining research.

As a consequence of these design problems, the effort to justify generalizations about the effects of situation on the production of persuasive messages is unusually daunting. The leading contributions in this vein have been from Cody and McLaughlin, particularly their large-scale reviews of literature on situation as it relates to interpersonal communication in general (Cody & McLaughlin, 1985; L. C. Miller, Cody, & McLaughlin, 1994). They originally concluded that the main perceptible differences in interpersonal situations are intimacy, friendliness, pleasantness, situational apprehension, involvement, and dominance (Cody & McLaughlin, 1985), and offered a somewhat different list, the one used here and presented momentarily, in their more recent review (L. C. Miller et al., 1994).

Cody has also undertaken several studies that focus on persuasive communication in particular (Cody & McLaughlin, 1980; Cody, Woelfel, & Jordan, 1983). Both Cody et al. (1983) and L. C. Miller et al. (1994) settled on seven situational dimensions that seem to summarize people's perceptions. These factors are the ones used in this study; scale items used to operationalize these dimensions are in Table 11.1. The first variable is *personal benefits*, which refers to whether the persuader expects to profit in some way if the persuasive appeal is successful. *Situation apprehension* indexes the degree of unease the persuader feels in that particular situation. Third is *resistance to persuasion*, which represents the persuader's estimate of whether the target will be hard or easy to sway. *Rights* refers in particular to the persuader's perceived right to attempt persuasion in that circumstance. Fifth is the *intimacy* of the relationship implicated in the persuasive situation. The *dominance* factor is worded to measure whether the target normally dominates the persuader. Last, the *relational consequences* scales assess the persuader's perception that the effort to persuade could have long term effects on the persuader–target relationship.

Cody et al. (1983) reported confirmatory factor analyses for two situations, one intimate and one nonintimate. Although their results are clear, one might wish that the data summarized more than a pair of situations. This weakness in the data record is repaired by Study 1 of this chapter.

ENDORSING OR SUPPRESSING PERSUASIVE APPEALS

We have conducted a series of studies on cognitive editing of arguments (see Hample & Dallinger, 1990). Our basic premise is that, in a situation that calls out a persuasive appeal, persuaders often have more than one option. Either because he or she has a repertoire of appropriate messages that can be

TABLE 11.1
Scales for Measurement of Situation Dimensions.

Personal Benefits (high score means "no personal benefits")

8. I will benefit personally from this persuasion.

10. I personally gain if successful in this situation.

11. I personally benefit from this persuasion.

20. I personally would get a lot out of it if I were successful in this situation.

26. It would be to my personal advantage if I were successful in this situation.

Situation Apprehension (high score means "no situational apprehension")

3. I would feel nervous in this situation.

4. I would feel tense in this situation.

6. I would feel apprehensive in this situation.

17. I would feel uneasy in this situation.

Resistance to Persuasion (high score means "great resistance to persuasion")

2. I think that the person in this situation would be very agreeable to this persuasion.

7. I feel that the person in this situation would not be resistant to my persuasion.

13. I could talk the person in this situation into doing this very easily.

14. I would have no trouble in persuading the person in this situation.

Right to Persuade (high score means "great right to persuade")

9. I am not warranted in making this request.

22. I do not have a right to make this request.

23. I have no justification for making this request.

27. I have no reasonable grounds for making this request.

Intimacy (high score means "highly intimate situation")

1. This situation involves an impersonal relationship.

5. This situation involves a personally meaningless relationship.

21. This situation involves a shallow relationship.

25. This situation involves a superficial relationship.

Dominance (high score means "other is not dominant over me")

15. The person in this situation controls many of my behaviors.

16. The person in this situation has authority over me.

18. I am usually submissive to the person in this situation.

24. The person in this situation usually dominates me.

Relational Consequences (high score means "no relational consequences")

12. This persuasion has long-term consequences on the relationship between the person in the situation and myself.

19. This persuasion has future consequences for the relationship between the person in the situation and myself.

used intact or revised slightly to fit the circumstances, or because he or she is capable of generating more than one pertinent appeal, several potential messages are relevant to the production process. One or more of these messages might be used, and the others suppressed.

Hample and Dallinger's research program began by trying to identify the reasons people use to explain the suppressions (Hample, 1984). These reasons are the editorial criteria, or standards, that appear relevant to the message production process. The usual design of the cognitive editing studies involves giving respondents a situation, a list of possible messages (based on Marwell & Schmitt's [1967] typology), and a set of response scales summarizing the most common editorial choices. These response scales are *endorsement*, the decision to use the proffered message; *effectiveness*, rejecting the message on the grounds that it would not work; *too negative to use*, rejecting the message because it seems too distasteful or pressuring; *harm to self*, rejecting the message to protect own face; *harm to other*, rejecting the message because it is too face-threatening to the target; *harm to relationship*, rejecting the message to protect the intepersonal relationship between persuader and target; *truth*, rejecting the message on the grounds that it is false or impossible; *relevance*, rejecting the message because it does not seem pertinent, either to the persuader or the target; and a *residual* category of suppression reasons.

Most of the research program has concentrated on associating individual difference variables with preferences for the different editorial criteria. This work, along with the early studies generating the editorial standards, is reviewed in Hample and Dallinger (1990). A secondary analysis of the cumulated data, done to determine whether there are any systematic sex differences in editorial criteria usage, was also conducted (Dallinger & Hample, 1994).

Almost from the beginning of the research program, Jackson and Backus's (1982) analysis of situational effects was taken into account. All but the first of the studies made use of several stimulus situations. These were included to increase the generalizability of the individual differences results. The situations were not constructed in a systematic effort to vary any situational features, however. Dummy coding of the different situations in each study made it possible to report the size of the situation's effects in the editorial decisions, but not to interpret it in a theoretically interesting way.

The use of similar designs in many of the studies makes it possible to cumulate the data into a secondary data analysis (studies that cannot be cumulated in this way include Hample, 1984, 1991, 2000; Hample & Dallinger, 1985, 1992). The various situations used in those studies can be scaled (regrettably, using a different sample of respondents than those participating in the original studies) with the Cody et al. (1983) situation dimension items. The entire data set can then be reanalyzed to determine what situational differences affected the original respondents' editorial choices.

In this chapter, we report the results of two studies that should permit an answer to our research question: What are the effects of situations' dominance, intimacy, projected personal benefits, perceived relational consequences, expected resistance, right to persuade, and apprehension on the decision to endorse or suppress a potential persuasive appeal?

Study 1 generates scale values for the situations, and Study 2 undertakes the secondary data analysis.

STUDY 1: SCALING SITUATIONS

This initial study has two purposes: (a) to replicate the Cody et al. (1983) effort to scale the dimensions on which persuasive situations differ, and (b) to generate actual scale values for the situations used in the cognitive editing research program.

Method

Respondents.   Data were gathered from 200 undergraduates enrolled in communication classes at Western Illinois University. Of these, 99 (49.5%) were men, and 101 (50.5%) were women. Their median age was 20.5, and 75.5% were juniors or seniors. Participation was voluntary, and a few declined to fill out the questionnaires.

Procedure.   Each respondent completed a booklet that asked for some demographic information, followed by four situations. Each situation was accompanied by the 27 Cody et al. (1983) scales designed to assess the dimensions on which persuasive situations differ. The study included a total of 25 situations that were randomly distributed throughout the booklets. The booklet took about half an hour to complete.

Situations. The situations were those used in the cognitive editing research program and in other persuasion research we have conducted. With one exception, the situation descriptions are a few sentences long and end with an explicit statement of persuasive goal (e.g., to get a landlord to return an apartment deposit). The exception is B. J. O'Keefe's (1988) group leader problem, which is more detailed. O'Keefe's situation, however, was never used in the cognitive editing program. Because other researchers may wish to use these situations, they are listed in Table 11.2, along with the number of respondents who responded to each stimulus, and the situations' scores on the situation dimensions.

Scales. Cody et al. (1983) only published one end of their bipolar scales. These half-items were reworked into 5-point Likert scales, and appear in Table 11.1, listed according to the dimensions they represent. The Table 11.1 ordering corresponds to that in Table 11.3 (i.e., Table 11.3's Domin1 is the first dominance scale in Table 11.1).

Results

Reliabilities. All seven scales demonstrated reasonable reliability. Cronbach's alphas are as follows: for dominance, .78; for intimacy, .76; for personal benefit, .90; for relational consequences, .71; for resistance, .81; for rights to persuade, .79; and for situational apprehension, .88. Very minor improvements in reliability would have been obtained by dropping the second resistance item (from .81 to .82), and the first right to persuade item (from .79 to .81). However, we decided to retain the items on the grounds that they loaded well in the factor analysis, their deletions offer only minor increments to the alphas, and their retention might help to standardize the situation scales.

Factor Structure. We conducted a principal components analysis with varimax rotation, and forced a seven-factor solution (the seventh factor has an eigenvalue greater than 1, and the eighth is less than 1 anyway). The results are remarkably clean and correspond exactly to the expected factor structure. The loadings are given in Table 11.3, and the correlations among the dimensions (calculated by adding together item scores) are given in Table 11.4.

With a single minor exception, no scale has a loading of as much as .30 on any factor except its appropriate one. The loadings themselves are all greater than .60, with more than half greater than .80.

TABLE 11.2

**Situations Used in Study 1, Along With Their Scores
on the Situational Dimensions**

(Situation 1) You would like to spend the weekend of Christmas with your parents, but your spouse doesn't really want to do that, so you are trying to talk him/her into it ($N = 30$). (Dallinger et al., 1990)

	Per Ben	Sit App	Resist	Rights	Domin	Intimacy	Rel Con
M	12.25	12.47	11.50	15.80	14.23	16.07	5.33
SD	3.88	4.32	2.92	2.89	3.73	3.21	1.95

(Situation 2) You have an older car which has problems regularly, and you are tired of having it continually repaired. You would like to buy a new or used car to replace it, but your spouse thinks that it's less expensive and just a better idea in general to keep the old one. You are trying to talk him/her into getting the new one ($N = 26$). (Dallinger et al., 1990)

	Per Ben	Sit App	Resist	Rights	Domin	Intimacy	Rel Con
M	10.89	14.46	11.23	15.89	13.35	16.15	5.96
SD	4.14	3.43	2.89	2.64	3.06	2.60	1.89

(Situation 3) During the last year, you have become more and more aware that your spouse has poor eating habits. Therefore, you would like to convince him/her to eliminate snacks and eat healthier foods at regular mealtimes ($N = 31$). (Dallinger et al., 1990)

	Per Ben	Sit App	Resist	Rights	Domin	Intimacy	Rel Con
M	13.32	15.03	12.26	15.55	15.13	16.71	4.13
SD	3.77	4.08	3.68	3.59	3.20	3.68	1.88

(Situation 4) It is about two weeks before Christmas break and you need a ride home. You live in Chicago and your friend lives in Rockford. You would like your friend to give you a ride to Chicago on his/her way home (and thus drive about 50 miles out of his/her way) ($N = 36$). (Dallinger & Hample, 1989b)

	Per Ben	Sit App	Resist	Rights	Domin	Intimacy	Rel Con
M	10.94	11.03	13.17	12.50	14.14	14.44	5.94
SD	5.28	3.51	3.24	2.93	3.23	2.68	1.77

(Situation 5) You are interested in taking a class in how to make stained glass windows from the Leisure Learning Center, but you would really like to have company doing it. The class meets in the union one night for each of 6 weeks. You want to talk your friend into taking this class with you (N = 29). (Dallinger & Hample, 1989b)

	Per Ben	Sit App	Resist	Rights	Domin	Intimacy	Rel Con
M	11.31	15.79	10.90	14.48	16.41	14.86	6.41
SD	3.83	3.52	2.91	3.73	2.53	3.51	1.74

(Situation 6) Your younger sister is graduating from high school this spring and she says she doesn't plan to attend college because she is tired of going to school. You feel that it is really important for her to start college next fall, and you are trying to talk her into doing it (N = 31). (Dallinger & Hample, 1989b)

	Per Ben	Sit App	Resist	Rights	Domin	Intimacy	Rel Con
M	14.71	14.77	12.87	15.16	16.45	16.61	4.90
SD	5.80	3.16	3.40	3.33	2.94	3.33	1.97

(Situation 7) You are sure that you are getting the flu because you really feel awful, but you realize that you have a book due at the library TODAY. You don't want to walk it over there so you want to get your roommate to return it for you (N = 29). (Dallinger & Hample, 1989a; Hample & Dallinger, 1987a)

	Per Ben	Sit App	Resist	Rights	Domin	Intimacy	Rel Con
M	11.45	15.17	9.66	15.48	16.38	14.86	6.82
SD	4.25	3.63	2.81	2.50	2.29	2.40	2.07

(Situation 8) You are taking a class in which a group project accounts for a major part of the grade. You have a friend who is also taking the class, so you want to talk him/her into working on this project with you (N = 33). (Dallinger & Hample, 1989a; Hample & Dallinger, 1987a)

	Per Ben	Sit App	Resist	Rights	Domin	Intimacy	Rel Con
M	12.33	15.27	8.79	15.27	15.70	13.82	6.18
SD	4.54	3.56	2.96	2.58	3.37	3.37	1.94

continued on next page

TABLE 11.2 *(continued)*

(Situation 9) You are shopping with one of your friends and s/he has just tried on a really nice looking suit which you think would be great for his/her job interviews, which will be coming up soon. S/he can't decide whether or not to buy it and you want to talk him/her into getting it ($N = 29$). (Dallinger & Hample, 1989a; Hample & Dallinger, 1987a)

	Per Ben	Sit App	Resist	Rights	Domin	Intimacy	Rel Con
M	17.72	15.41	9.62	14.41	15.62	15.45	6.83
SD	4.00	3.62	3.11	2.67	3.31	2.95	1.95

(Situation 10) You have been dating the same person now for about two years and you are thinking about getting engaged. Christmas vacation is coming up soon and you want your boyfriend/girlfriend to come home with you. S/he initially disagrees but you are still trying to convince him or her ($N = 30$). (Hample & Dallinger, 1987e)

	Per Ben	Sit App	Resist	Rights	Domin	Intimacy	Rel Con
M	10.50	12.40	11.23	16.30	14.03	17.07	4.67
SD	4.89	4.90	3.66	3.08	3.12	2.97	2.58

(Situation 11) You have been living with your roommate in an apartment for several months. You generally take turns cleaning the place up and now it is his/her turn, but the apartment is in a real mess and s/he hasn't done any cleaning for several days. You want him/her to clean up ($N = 30$). (Hample & Dallinger, 1987e)

	Per Ben	Sit App	Resist	Rights	Domin	Intimacy	Rel Con
M	10.93	12.90	11.17	16.93	15.30	14.70	5.27
SD	4.56	3.77	3.11	2.29	3.28	3.11	2.12

(Situation 12) You have been living in an apartment with two friends for the school year and now, since school is over for the year, you are getting ready to move out. The landlord has come over to inspect the place, and you are trying to convince him to return your deposit money. Your roommates had to work so they aren't there with you ($N = 33$). (Hample & Dallinger, 1987e)

	Per Ben	Sit App	Resist	Rights	Domin	Intimacy	Rel Con
M	8.61	10.88	12.55	16.03	12.91	11.24	6.46
SD	3.55	4.25	3.18	3.22	3.58	3.78	2.12

(Situation 13) Neither you nor your friend does a lot of exercise, and you want to start jogging. You'd rather have some company when you do it, so you want him or her to go jogging with you (N = 33). (Hample & Dallinger, 1987b)

	Per Ben	Sit App	Resist	Rights	Domin	Intimacy	Rel Con
M	9.61	16.91	10.29	15.03	15.97	15.09	7.00
SD	4.56	2.89	4.02	3.39	3.16	2.79	2.25

(Situation 14) You are working on a big paper for a class that is due tomorrow, and neither you nor your roommate has any typing paper. Since you don't have time to go get any yourself, you want your roommate to go over to the bookstore and pick some up (N = 33). (Hample & Dallinger, 1987b)

	Per Ben	Sit App	Resist	Rights	Domin	Intimacy	Rel Con
M	10.03	14.06	10.85	13.97	14.97	14.70	6.42
SD	4.65	3.83	3.24	2.98	3.37	2.78	2.05

(Situation 15) It is the first semester of your roommate's senior year and so far, he or she hasn't done anything about trying to find a job for after graduation. You want him or her to get started—writing a resume, finding potential employers, getting placement papers in order (N = 34). (Hample & Dallinger, 1987b)

	Per Ben	Sit App	Resist	Rights	Domin	Intimacy	Rel Con
M	18.06	11.53	11.47	13.47	15.39	15.47	5.58
SD	4.67	3.40	3.17	2.94	2.11	2.76	2.03

(Situation 16) Your close friend has been really depressed for about the last month because s/he broke up with his/her boyfriend/girlfriend. You have noticed that s/he can't study or concentrate on schoolwork, and you are worried, so you want him/her to go see a counselor (N = 35). (Hample & Dallinger, 1987c)

	Per Ben	Sit App	Resist	Rights	Domin	Intimacy	Rel Con
M	15.86	12.74	13.83	14.74	14.80	15.97	5.14
SD	4.02	3.80	2.31	2.37	2.84	2.73	1.65

continued on next page

TABLE 11.2 (*continued*)

(Situation 17) You really want to go to see a particular movie, and you want your friend to come with you, even though you know that s/he rarely goes to see this kind of movie (N = 33). (Hample & Dallinger, 1987c)

	Per Ben	Sit App	Resist	Rights	Domin	Intimacy	Rel Con
M	13.63	14.79	11.63	14.52	15.50	14.61	6.94
SD	4.63	2.64	2.38	2.88	2.94	2.59	1.85

(Situation 18) It is the end of the school year and you and several of your friends want to have a party out at Lake Argyle to celebrate. Since you know that lots of other groups are planning to go out too, you want your friend to go out in the early afternoon and spend several hours alone saving a place for your party (N = 35). (Hample & Dallinger, 1987c)

	Per Ben	Sit App	Resist	Rights	Domin	Intimacy	Rel Con
M	13.23	12.63	13.66	11.56	15.74	13.03	6.34
SD	5.46	4.53	4.19	4.18	2.63	4.00	2.17

(Situation 19) Your little sister, who is 7 years old, has come to visit you for the weekend. It is Saturday morning and suddenly you have a chance to go out with someone you would really like to date, so you want your roommate to babysit your sister for the evening so you can go out (N = 38).

	Per Ben	Sit App	Resist	Rights	Domin	Intimacy	Rel Con
M	11.50	10.71	12.89	12.05	14.63	14.79	5.29
SD	5.81	3.76	3.01	3.38	3.91	2.97	1.94

(Situation 20) You want your friend to go camping with you for the weekend, and although it won't cost much money, s/he doesn't really like camping, so you are trying to talk him/her into going with you (N = 31).

	Per Ben	Sit App	Resist	Rights	Domin	Intimacy	Rel Con
M	11.90	14.78	12.71	14.61	16.45	16.47	6.41
SD	4.06	3.71	3.13	3.03	2.82	2.57	1.70

(Situation 21) Your roommate has a habit of swearing all of the time. It really doesn't bother you much, but you feel that s/he is giving other people a really bad impression of himself/herself, so you want to get him/her to stop swearing ($N = 38$).

	Per Ben	Sit App	Resist	Rights	Domin	Intimacy	Rel Con
M	16.34	11.32	13.74	13.05	15.55	14.18	5.05
SD	4.56	3.80	2.78	4.10	3.09	3.30	1.89

(Situation 22) Imagine that you have been assigned to a group project in one of your classes. The class is in your major and it is important to you to get a good grade in this class. Your final grade will depend to a great extent on how well the group project turns out. You were assigned to your group by the instructor, who also designated you to be the leader of your group. Each person will receive two grades for the project: an overall grade to the group based on the overall quality of the project report and an individual grade based on each person's contribution to the group effort. Your duties as group leader will include telling the instructor what grade you think each individual in the group deserves based on their individual contributions.

One group member (whose name is Ron) has been causing some problems. Ron seldom makes it to group meetings on time and entirely skipped one meeting without even calling anyone in advance to let the group know. When Ron missed that meeting, two of the group members wanted you to have the instructor remove Ron from your group, although another member persuaded the group to give him another chance. At the next meeting Ron arrived late but apologized for missing the previous meeting and mentioned something about family problems. Ron did volunteer to do all the background research on one important aspect of the group's topic, saying he had a special interest in that part of the project.

The group project is due next week. The group planned to put together the final draft of its report at a meeting scheduled for tomorrow afternoon. Ron calls you up today and says he doesn't have his library research done and can't get it finished before the meeting. He says he just needs more time ($N = 18$). (B. J. O'Keefe, 1988)

	Per Ben	Sit App	Resist	Rights	Domin	Intimacy	Rel Con
M	12.67	10.11	12.79	14.78	16.37	10.78	5.94
SD	4.10	3.90	3.46	3.21	3.00	2.02	2.21

(Situation 23) You have a friend who has been smoking for years and you're trying to get him/her to stop ($N = 34$). (Hample & Dallinger, 1998)

	Per Ben	Sit App	Resist	Rights	Domin	Intimacy	Rel Con
M	13.50	12.88	16.00	14.21	15.74	15.35	5.24
SD	4.88	3.79	3.36	3.01	3.41	3.00	2.19

continued on next page

TABLE 11.2 (*continued*)

(Situation 24) You are working on a big project for a class, which will count for a large portion of the course grade. Of the four people in the group, one member has not been showing up for group meetings or doing any part of the work for the project. You are trying to get him/her to do his/her part ($N = 17$). (Hample & Dallinger, 1998)

	Per Ben	Sit App	Resist	Rights	Domin	Intimacy	Rel Con
M	11.47	13.77	11.94	15.24	15.65	10.18	5.59
SD	4.20	4.79	2.82	3.68	4.21	3.45	2.43

(Situation 25) You have decided that it would be fun to go to Padre Island for spring break. You have a friend who can afford to go and has no other plans, but s/he is not quite sure that is what s/he wants to do. You are trying to convince him/her to go with you ($N = 32$). (Hample & Dallinger, 1998)

	Per Ben	Sit App	Resist	Rights	Domin	Intimacy	Rel Con
M	10.50	16.13	9.53	15.32	16.69	16.16	6.09
SD	4.57	3.09	2.69	2.99	2.71	2.86	2.18

Scale Values for Situations.   Values on each of the seven dimensions were obtained for each of the situations in our sample by the normal means of adding together the scores for each item. These values are displayed in Table 11.2.

Discussion

We consider that our results successfully replicate those of Cody et al. (1983). Reliabilities are adequate, and the dimensional structure of the scales is quite clear. The fact that our results summarize data for 25 more situations may give other researchers additional confidence in the scales.

STUDY 2: SECONDARY DATA ANALYSIS

We now come to the core of this chapter, the effort to say how (or whether) differences in situations affect how people undertake interpersonal persuasion. The other chapters in this book are traditional meta-analyses, in which the statistical results of earlier studies are cumulated, for example, by averaging several studies' correlations between two variables. Although what we do

Table 11.3

Factor Loadings of Situation Scales, Summed Across All Situations, With Eigenvalues and Percentage of Total Variance Accounted For

	Personal Benefit	Situation Apprehension	Resistance	Right to Persuade	Dominance	Intimacy	Relational Consequences
Domin1					.77		
Domin2					.81		
Domin3		.30			.67		
Domin4					.75		
Intim1						.69	
Intim2						.77	
Intim3						.73	
Intim4						.74	
Perben1	.82						
Perben2	.89						
Perben3	.87						
Perben4	.81						
Perben5	.82						
Relcon1							.86
Relcon2							.82
Resist1			.74				
Resist2			.68				
Resist3			.85				
Resist4			.83				
Rights1				.62			
Rights2				.84			
Rights3				.82			
Rights4				.75			
Sitapp1		.86					
Sitapp2		.88					
Sitapp3		.77					
Sitapp4		.72					
Eigenvalue	5.52	3.76	2.76	1.94	1.70	1.36	1.12
% Variance	20.5	13.9	10.2	7.2	6.3	5.0	4.2

Note. Loadings less than .30 are omitted from the table for clarity.

TABLE 11.4

Correlations Among the Dimensions of Situation

	Dominance	Intimacy	Personal Benefit	Relational Consequences	Resistance	Right to Persuade
Dominance						
Intimacy	.103***					
Personal benefit	.194***	.324***				
Relational consequences	.284***	−.292***	−.037			
Resistance	−.342***	−.019	.061*	−.536***		
Right to persuade	−.065**	.095***	−.292***	−.207***	−.369***	
Situation apprehension	.726***	.207***	.076**	.433***	−.667***	.253***

Note. $N = 1,692$.

*$p < .05$. **$p < .01$. *** $p < .001$.

here is certainly in the spirit of meta-analysis, our procedure is somewhat different. Instead of analyzing prior studies' results, we are reanalyzing the raw data from those investigations, thus performing a secondary data analysis. This has the advantage of permitting us to do new types of analyses that were not possible or anticipated in the original studies. Secondary data analysis is quite common in other fields, as when sociologists search for relations in U.S. Census databases, or when political scientists reexplore decades of public opinion polls, or when economists try to reconstruct a nation's economic history. Traditional meta-analysis is largely constrained by what the original investigators thought to test and report. By cumulating the raw data of earlier compliance-gaining investigations, and adding the information from Study 1, we are able to conduct statistical tests that are only possible in retrospect.

Having obtained values for each of the situations on all seven of the Cody et al. (1983) scales, we are able to reevaluate the data from nine earlier studies (Dallinger & Hample, 1989a, 1989b, 1991; Dallinger, Hample, & Myers, 1990; Hample & Dallinger, 1987a, 1987b, 1987c, 1987d, 1987e, 1998). Those studies used dummy variables (e.g., Situation 1 would be coded as either present or absent) to represent the different situations. The studies often reported situational effects, but those results were not substantively interpretable, precisely because we did not know on what systematic variables the situations differed. We could only say, for instance, that the three situations in a particular study had somewhat different effects, but we could not say why, because we did not know in what theoretically interesting ways the situations varied. This secondary data analysis permits a theoretically meaningful analysis of the features of situation that affect people's decisions to endorse or suppress persuasive messages.

Method

The raw data from the nine studies were cumulated. In all, 21 situations appear in the full data set (all but numbers 19–22 in Table 11.2). For each situation, its scores on the situation dimensions in Table 11.2 were inserted into the cumulated data set. The number of respondents for each situation ranges from 41 to 166, with a mean subsample size of 81.

The data set includes responses from 1,692 participants, of whom 953 (56%) were men and 737 (44%) were women. With the exception of the respondents in Dallinger et al. (1990), which used married couples recruited from the community, all the participants were enrolled in communication courses at Western Illinois University. Of the students, 62% were juniors or seniors. The mean age of our sample was 22.9; the median age, which is essentially unaffected by the married couples sample, was 21.

Results

Our primary results are shown in Table 11.5, which reports the results of a canonical analysis relating the frequency with which repondents used each editorial code to the situation's scores on the Cody et al. (1983) scales. Canonical correlations (R_c) indicate the correlations between two sets of variables. Just as an ordinary correlation shows the association between two variables, a canonical correlation measures the association between whatever one set of variables has in common and whatever a second set of variables has in common. These things in common (or variates) are what are actually correlated. Complex data sets may have more than one pair of things in common; these are called *roots*. Roots are interpreted by noticing carefully what individual variables have the highest loadings, or correlations, with the variate.

As Table 11.5 shows, in this analysis three roots were significant, all having modest effect sizes. Altogether, the three canonical roots account for 15.9% of the variance in the canonical variates. Univariate analyses of vari-

TABLE 11.5

Canonical Structure Matrix for Associations Between Editing Standards and Situation Dimensions

	Root 1	Root 2	Root 3
Endorse***	−.867	.016	−.275
Ineffective***	−.295	−.349	.507
Too negative***	.421	−.072	.363
Harm self***	.242	.424	−.197
Harm other***	.453	−.001	−.690
Harm relationship**	.265	.105	−.130
False**	.236	.273	−.082
Irrelevant	−.092	.346	.122
Residual***	.177	−.456	−.045
Dominance***	.275	−.700	−.317
Intimacy*	.197	.074	.295
Personal benefit***	.316	−.161	−.387
Relational consequences***	.591	.087	−.303
Resistance***	−.642	−.226	.435
Right to persuade***	−.401	.346	−.467
Situational apprehension***	.486	−.429	−.402
R_c	.318***	.215***	.110*

Note. The asterisks after the variables represent the results of univariate analyses of variance. The degrees of freedom for the editorial standards' tests are 9, 1682, and are 7, 1684 for the situation dimension tests. The overall test for the canonical analysis results is Pillais $F = 4.85$, $df = 63, 11774$, $p = .000$.

*$p < .05$. **$p < .01$. ***$p < .001$.

ance indicate that all the situation dimensions participate significantly in the roots, as do all the editorial criteria except relevance.

The first root is dominated by the decision to endorse, which is primarily predicted by the relational consequences and resistance dimensions. The prominence of endorsement in this root suggests that these are the results that will be of most interest to compliance-gaining researchers, who only use endorsement as a dependent variable. People are least likely to endorse possible arguments when the situation is one that has great relational consequences and little expected resistance. These are sensible results: People are more selective in choosing appeals when the matter is relationally delicate and when the target is expected to be especially pliable anyway. Only the most attractive strategies are used in sensitive circumstances; persuaders need not use any risky appeals because of the anticipated persuasibility of the target. The high loading for the harm to other criterion is also consistent with the results for the resistance dimension: Low anticipated resistance permits more sensitivity to the other's face.

The second root is less clear, in part because of the importance of the residual category to it. Dallinger et al. (1990) suggested that the prominence of this criterion in their study indicated that married couples had cooperatively developed idiosyncratic rules for suppressing possible arguments, but no other study has generated either important results for this criterion or persuasive explanations of it. Of the situational dimensions, dominance is clearly the most important. In trying to persuade someone who is typically dominant over the persuader, people are unusually attentive to own face and make great use of the harm to self standard. They are less concerned with the effectiveness of their appeals. This pattern suggests the possibility that people do not try too hard to succeed when faced with a dominant target, and focus more on minimizing their face losses in such circumstances.

The third root is mainly constituted by loadings for the effectiveness and harm to other criteria, which are broadly predicted by all the situation dimensions. Persuaders concentrate on effectiveness to the exclusion of harm to other under these circumstances: when the target is not dominant, when the situation holds out the possibility of great personal benefit, when considerable resistance is expected, when the persuader's right to persuade is unclear, and when the persuader has some apprehension about the task. This pattern generally suggests that persuaders will be unusually task-oriented when they face the difficult prospect of obtaining quite valued outcomes. The loadings for intimacy and relational consequences complicate this picture: The same task orientation appears when the situation is intimate and has noticeable relational implications. Perhaps intimacy and relational consequences are features of situation that can generate the possibility of personal benefits. In our data set (see Table 11.4), the personal benefits scale correlates with intimacy ($r = .32, p < .001$), but not with relational consequences ($r = -.04, ns$). The role of relational consequences in the third root therefore remains unclear, but the other results consistently suggest the circumstances under which persuaders will take on an effectiveness orientation to the possible detriment of other's face.

Discussion

Our results show that the situation dimensions are meaningfully related to the endorsement and suppression choices our repondents made on questionnaires. With the exception of the relevance standard, which has not often been significantly associated with individual differences variables (see Hample & Dallinger, 1990), all the editorial codes are affected by the nature of the situation. Similarly, all the situation dimensions proved to be statistically relevant.

Among the editorial criteria, we obtained the weakest results for relevance, truth, and harm to relationship. These three standards have also been the most difficult to predict using individual differences variables. Hample and Dallinger (1990) speculated that the problem with predicting truth and relevance is that these are common possessions of every competent adult, and they are omnirelevant. In spite of their persistent involvement in utter or suppress decisions, truth and relevance seem to have little variability from person to person or situation to situation. This limited variability may be due to the researchers' intention to provide lists of plausible persuasive appeals on the questionnaires; it may be that there have been few marginally relevant or marginally true appeals in the studies, and therefore, little opportunity for either individual predispositions or situational stimuli to call out differences on these two criteria. With regard to the harm to relationship standard, Hample and Dallinger (1992) showed that it is very closely associated with the harm to self and harm to other criteria. They speculated that harm to relationship is nearly redundant with harm to other in respondents' eyes. If so, it may be that the greater concreteness of "harm to other" leads to that criterion absorbing most of the experimental effects.

The chief disappointment in our results has to do with the modest effect size of the canonical variates' associations in Table 11.5. This, however, was forseeable. Our design necessitated applying consensual situation perceptions to individual editorial decisions. The effect sizes reported here should be viewed as lower bounds for the true effect sizes. Presumably, a study that associated individual situation perceptions with individual editorial behavior would result in larger estimates of the importance of situation to persuasive choices.

CONCLUSIONS

This chapter has been intended to serve two purposes: to illustrate secondary data analysis, and to offer conclusions about the effects of situation in interpersonal persuasion.

Secondary data analysis has certain advantages over traditional meta-analysis, because the original data are available in all their detail. Meta-analysts have to work with data summaries, in the form of reductive statistics. That is, a meta-analyst takes, say, a series of correlations as his or her input data for the meta-analysis, but a secondary data analyst has the raw data and can recalculate the correlation. If only the average correlation from a group of studies were of interest, secondary data analysis would offer no advantage and involve more trouble. However, if issues beyond those discussed in the original reports are to be explored, secondary data analysis may offer more opportunity than does meta-analysis. If this study had been meta-analytic, all we would have been able to add to the original reports would have been a more secure estimate of the size of situation's effects; we would not have been able to provide the details and explanations that we feel are the substantive value of this report. This study was only possible, however, because we actually have access to all the raw data. This is an argument for researchers not only preserving and documenting their raw data, but also being willing to share it.

In the course of presenting the results of our second study, we have already discussed the details of our findings, and will not repeat them here. We wish to emphasize, however, that our findings are sensible and securely based on a large sample. They constitute new information that was unavailable even to anyone who closely read every one of the original papers. Persuasion is a common component of interpersonal relationships and encounters, and the way we go about trying to influence others depends in part on the situation. We may take the situation as given, or try to reframe it so as to change its values on the perceptual dimensions studied here. Either way, we will react to the situation, just as we react to our personal goals and to the other person.

REFERENCES

Brashers, D. E., & Jackson, S. (1999). Changing conceptions of "message effects:" A 24-year overview. *Human Communication Research, 25,* 457–477.

Cody, M. J., & McLaughlin, M. L. (1980). Perceptions of compliance-gaining situations: A dimensional analysis. *Communication Monographs, 47,* 132–148.

Cody, M. J., & McLaughlin, M. L. (1985). The situation as a construct in interpersonal communication research. In M. L. Knapp & G. R. Miller (Eds.), *Handbook of interpersonal communication* (pp. 263–312). Beverly Hills, CA: Sage.

Cody, M. J., Woelfel, M. L., & Jordan, W. J. (1983). Dimensions of compliance-gaining situations. *Human Communication Research, 9,* 99–113.

Dallinger, J. M., & Hample, D. (1989a). Biological and psychological gender effects upon cognitive editing of arguments. In B. E. Gronbeck (Ed.), *Spheres of argument* (pp. 563–568). Annandale, VA: Speech Communication Association.

Dallinger, J. M., & Hample, D. (1989b, May). *Cognitive editing of arguments and interpersonal construct differentiation.* Paper presented at the annual meeting of the International Communication Association, San Francisco.

Dallinger, J. M., & Hample, D. (1991). Cognitive editing of arguments and interpersonal construct differentiation: Refining the relationship. In F. H. van Eemeren, R. Grootendorst, J. A. Blair, & C. A. Willard (Eds.), *Proceedings of the Second International Conference on Argumentation* (pp. 567–574). Dordrecht, Netherlands: Stichting International Centrum voor de Studie van Argumentatie en Taalbeheersing.

Dallinger, J. M., & Hample, D. (1994). The effects of gender on compliance gaining strategy endorsement and suppression. *Communication Reports, 7,* 43–49.

Dallinger, J. M., Hample, D., & Myers, K. A. (1990, June). *Spouses' understandings of marital conflict.* Paper presented at the annual meeting of the International Communication Association, Dublin, Ireland.

Hample, D. (1984, April). *Roads not taken, arguments not made.* Paper presented at the annual meeting of the Central States Communication Association, Chicago.

Hample, D. (1991, May). *Cognitive editing in the production of conversational utterances.* Paper presented at the annual meeting of the International Communication Association, Chicago.

Hample, D. (2000). Cognitive editing of arguments and reasons for requests: Evidence from think-aloud protocols. *Argumentation and Advocacy, 37,* 98–108.

Hample, D., & Dallinger, J. M. (1985). Unused compliance gaining strategies. In J. R. Cox, M. O. Sillars, & G. B. Walker (Eds.), *Argument and social practice* (pp. 675–691). Annandale, VA: Speech Communication Association.

Hample, D., & Dallinger, J. M. (1987a). Argument editing choices and argumentative competence. In J. W. Wenzel (Ed.), *Argument and critical practices* (pp. 455–464). Annandale, VA: Speech Communication Association.

Hample, D., & Dallinger, J. M. (1987b). Cognitive editing of argument strategies. *Human Communication Research, 14,* 123–144.

Hample, D., & Dallinger, J. M. (1987c, November). *The effects of Machiavellianism, social desirability, gender, and grade point average on cognitive editing of arguments.* Paper presented at the annual meeting of the Speech Communication Association, Boston.

Hample, D., & Dallinger, J. M. (1987d). The judgment phase of invention. In F. H. van Eemeren, R. Grootendorst, J. A. Blair, & C. A. Willard (Eds.), *Argumentation: Perspectives and approaches* (pp. 225–234). Dordrecht, Holland: Foris.

Hample, D., & Dallinger, J. M. (1987e). Self-monitoring and the cognitive editing of arguments. *Central States Speech Journal, 38,* 152–165.

Hample, D., & Dallinger, J. M. (1990). Arguers as editors. *Argumentation, 4,* 153–169.

Hample, D., & Dallinger, J. M. (1992). The use of multiple goals in cognitive editing of arguments. *Argumentation and Advocacy, 28,* 109–122.

Hample, D., & Dallinger, J. M. (1998). On the etiology of the rebuff phenomenon: Why are persuasive messages less polite after rebuffs? *Communication Studies, 49* 305–321.

Jackson, S. (1992). *Message effects research: Principles of design and analysis.* New York: Guilford.

Jackson, S., & Backus, D. (1982). Are compliance-gaining strategies dependent on situational variables? *Central States Speech Journal, 33,* 469–479.

Marwell, G., & Schmitt, D. R. (1967). Dimensions of compliance-gaining behavior: An empirical analysis. *Sociometry, 30,* 350–364.

Miller, G. R., Boster, F. J., Roloff, M. E., & Seibold, D. (1977). Compliance-gaining message strategies: A typology and some findings concerning effects of situational differences. *Communication Monographs, 44,* 37–51.

Miller, L. C., Cody, M. J., & McLaughlin, M. L. (1994). Situations and goals as fundamental constructs in interpersonal communication research. In M. L. Knapp & G. R. Miller (Eds.), *Handbook of interpersonal communication* (2nd ed., pp. 162–198). Thousand Oaks, CA: Sage.

O'Keefe, B. J. (1988). The logic of message design: Individual differences in reasoning about communication. *Communication Monographs, 55,* 80–103.

O'Keefe, D. (1990). *Persuasion: Theory and research.* Newbury Park, CA: Sage.

IV

Interactional Issues in Interpersonal Communication

12

An Overview of Interactional Processes in Interpersonal Communication

Barbara Mae Gayle and Raymond W. Preiss

Researchers interested in ongoing interpersonal processes often choose to examine message exchanges and sequences of messages. This approach has the advantage of capturing relationship dynamics that may not be apparent in investigations guided by individual or dyadic perspectives. Of course, no single approach adequately accounts for important relationship intricacies. The overviews to earlier sections provided a general context for meta-analyses on individual issues (self-esteem, communication competency, and language usage) and dyadic issues (identity, attraction, self-disclosure, and influence).

We now turn our attention to the interactional processes involved in ongoing relational exchanges between two parties. In this section, we provide a profile of the interactional perspective and review issues that have evolved in the literature guided by this approach. As with earlier sections, our summary is intended to provide the general context for the meta-analyses selected for this section. Although hardly exhaustive, the issues of relational support, conversational processes, and mutuality of control illustrate the virtues of the interactional approach.

INTERACTIONAL PROCESSES

When viewed from an interactional perspective, interpersonal relationships "are redundant, interlocked cycles of messages, continually negotiated and co-defined" (Millar & Rogers, 1987, p. 118). Communicative exchanges between two partners reflect the dynamics of the relationship, the current definition of the situation, and the intended or feared consequences the exchange may have on the trajectory of the relationship. The interactional approach stresses the interdependency of the partners and how a series of behaviors, utterances, and reactions may have immediate and cumulative effects. Frequently occurring themes in the interactional approach to interpersonal communication concern relational support and maintenance (e.g., commitment, comforting messages, and social support), conversational processes (e.g., confirming or disconfirming messages, facework, and argumentativeness), and mutuality of control (e.g., control, dominance, and conflict). The six meta-analyses in this section address several of these themes: comforting behaviors, social support, verbal aggression, safe sex negotiation, conflict, and sexual coercion. After briefly discussing the areas of relational support, conversational processes, and mutual control, we provide a conceptual summary of these meta-analyses.

Relational Support

Individuals in close interpersonal relationships have expectations concerning the level of affection and commitment anticipated, the candor and honesty of positions stated, and the degree of relational support conveyed during the exchange. These expectations are managed through interactions that meet the day-to-day challenges of maintaining close personal connections. Duck and Wood (1995) noted that "relational challenges of all sorts are practical and palpable experiences that are played out in complex contexts shaped by large historical and cultural influences as well as by relational history and the projected future and also by present activities and goals" (p. 5). Thus, normal interactions between partners sometimes require addressing the mundane, as well as the unique, challenges to the well-being of the relationship.

Most relational partners assume that expressions of affection will be part of the dialogue in their relationships. Dickens and Perlman (1981) claimed that liking or affection was a basic foundation of an ongoing relationship. Usually messages of affection involve "intentional and overt enactment or expression of feelings of closeness, care, and fondness for the relational partner" (Floyd & Moorman, 1998, p. 145). These expressions of affection are "important for the development of personal relationships not only because [they] can reduce uncertainty about the state of the relationship, but also because [they] cause relational partners to feel valued and cared for" (Floyd & Moorman, 1997, p. 279).

Mutually exchanged expressions of affection usually signal some form of relational commitment or desire to continue the relationship (Canary & Stafford, 1994). Commitment requires a deliberative choice to maintain the relationship (Acker & Davis, 1992) and is heightened by an individual's decision to invest time, energy, and resources in that relationship (Lund, 1985). According to Rusbult and Buunk (1993), relational commitment is influenced by relational satisfaction, length of the relationship, concern for one's partner, the quality and availability of alternatives, and the size of the relational investments made or to be required. Lund (1985) found that commitment is one of the better predictors of relational longevity. Fitzpatrick and Badzinski (1994) noted that commitment "to another's well-being" (p. 729) is a hallmark of affection.

One way relational partners contribute to each other's psychological well-being is through the use of comforting messages in times of emotional distress (Dolin & Booth-Butterfield, 1993). Burleson (1994) defined these verbal message strategies as "alleviating or lessening the emotional distresses experienced by others … arising from a variety of everyday hurts and disappointments" (p. 136). He believed that, although relational partners providing the comforting message may "experience some benefit or self-gain as a result of their efforts" (p. 137), the primary goal is the comfort of the other person. In his research, Burleson found that successful comforting strategies reveal a greater involvement with the partner and her or his problems, are nonevaluative, focus on possible causes for the distress, legitimize the partner's feelings, and help the partner gain perspective. Albrecht, Burleson, and Goldsmith (1994) maintained that the person-centeredness of effective comforting messages make them more consoling and encouraging.

Dolin and Booth-Butterfield (1993) expanded the conceptualization to include nonverbal behaviors. They identified 12 nonverbal strategies that were routinely used as comforting strategies. Hugs, proxemics, facial expressions, attentiveness, and increased touch were used during comforting more than 34% of the time. Bullis and Horn (1995) confirmed 11 of the 12 strategies Dolin and Booth-Butterfield (1993) isolated and detected 5 new strategies. Bullis and Horn (1995) found that hugs, proxemics, attentiveness, and increased touch were all used at least 30% of the time during comforting episodes. Thus, research suggests there are both verbal and nonverbal aspects to comforting messages.

Allen (chap. 13) explores the relation among comforting messages, cognitive complexity, perspective taking, and the age of the comforter. His goal is to test the theoretical models that emerged from the comforting research. Allen's results provide evidence regarding the constructivist interpretation of comforting behavior and the knowledge and motivation to produce comforting messages. Cognitive differentiation and abstraction appear to play important roles in this process, and Allen suggests avenues for future research related to the constructivist account of comforting messages.

In another meta-analysis in this section, Burrell (chap. 14) addresses the concept of social support. Like comforting behavior, social support is seen as intricately linked to an individual's well-being after experiencing adversity (Cutrona, 1996). The act of being supportive can be conceptualized as verbal and nonverbal strategies designed to promote emotional, physical, and relational benefits (Albrecht et al., 1994). Viewed as an interaction, social support is a communicative process through which support is solicited or enacted in the context of specific relationships by individuals or groups of individuals (Albrecht et al., 1994; Cutrona, 1996). This interactional approach is consistent with Woodward, Rosenfeld, and May's (1996) conclusion that social support may be tangible (e.g., assisting with a particular task), informational (e.g., providing information about available resources), or emotional (e.g., providing comforting words).

Burrell provides a meta-analytic summary of research on divorced couples. After narratively reviewing theoretical and methodological issues, she finds evidence that former husbands and wives receive different sources and types of social support. Her results suggest that divorce is not a single event, but a series of events that are influenced by the availability of social support networks. This pattern is similar to Woodward et al.'s (1996) finding of sex differences in the use of social support systems in sororities and fraternities.

In summary, research in the area of relational support suggests an interactive process in which relational partners both seek support and provide it. This process involves both verbal and nonverbal aspects of communication that are used to sustain or maintain interpersonal relationships. Like comforting behaviors, social support conveys concern for the other's psychological well-being at a time of stress or crisis. Unlike comforting, however, social support usually involves access to a larger social network. The meta-analyses indicate that individuals and networks of individuals can play an important role in this interactional process.

Conversational Processes

Partners engage in many conversations that vary widely in scope, quality, and goals, but a frequently occurring purpose is to establish rapport. They may encourage emotional attachment, increase personal knowledge about each other, or build a supportive relational climate. In these conversations, individuals "strive to preserve and promote other's face wants with the expectation that other actors will do the same for them" (Lim, 1990, p. 75). Conversational processes, then, involve elements of preserving interactants' self-image (e.g., facework), responding to a partner's recognition needs (e.g., confirming or disconfirming messages), and interpreting relational episodes (e.g., turning points, transgressions). Although discussions provide many opportunities to advance these (and other) goals, interactions may also simultaneously work toward multiple goals.

Brown and Levinson's (1987) politeness theory illustrates the utility of conversational processes in managing relational goals. Building on Goffman's (1967) supposition that individuals seek to maintain positive regard through social interactions, Brown and Levinson (1987) distinguished between positive and negative regard and face. They conceptualized positive face as an interactant's need for her or his partner to approve, appreciate, and honor the self-image she or he projects. Negative face was viewed as the desire of a partner to be free from intrusion and imposition and maintain her or his freedom to act. Brown and Levinson maintained that one's face needs are granted or not granted by a partner during unfolding conversations.

Many communicative acts may intentionally or inadvertently run counter to the face needs of one's partner. The result is a face-threatening act (FTA), which Lim and Bowers (1991) argued is mediated by the relationship between the individuals, their status differences, or the intrusiveness of the FTA. Lim (1990) suggested that politeness may be used to repair FTAs by adapting the conversation to emphasize relational obligations and consideration for both partners' face needs. This is consistent with Cupach and Metts's (1994) reasoning that individuals negotiate face-saving (self-oriented) and face-giving (other-oriented) communicative behaviors. Facework can involve protecting one's self-image (defensive facework), helping to maintain another's positive self-image (protective facework), minimizing damage to one or one's partner's face through language choice (preventive facework), or apologizing for or explaining about face loss (corrective facework; Metts, 1997; Tracy, 1990).

Scholars exploring the construct of interpersonal facework have investigated the implementation of face-saving messages. Rogan and Hammer

(1994) found that in hostage negotiations, negotiators were concerned with perpetrators' face needs and avoided attacking their self-concept while stressing positive face needs. Perpetrators tended to engage in self-enhancement to restore or promote their self-image. Cupach and Imahori (1993) investigated how Americans and Japanese handled social predicaments. They found no differences between the two groups in the social predicaments faced, but did detect evidence that how individuals coped with FTAs depended on the agent of the social transgression and the circumstances surrounding it. In terms of responses, Americans employed devices such as humor, accounts, and aggression, whereas Japanese participants used apologies and remediation in face-threatening situations. Finally, Leichty and Applegate (1991) revealed that speakers used more face support if they had less power and less face support if they were familiar with their partner and if the request was small.

Taken together, the facework research suggests that as relational commitment increases, the obligation to show concern for one's own face and the partner's face increases. Facework markers are interwoven into the interactions between partners. This is consistent with Goffman's (1967) observation that individuals desire to sustain both relational partners' facework. One meta-analysis in this section deals with face-saving interactions as heterosexual partners negotiate conversations about safe sex practices. Allen, Emmers-Sommer, and Crowell (chap. 5) explore the decisions partners make concerning when, how, and where to discuss sexual practices. Conversations on this important and sensitive topic reflect choices designed to protect one's own and the partner's self-image. These interactions can be effective in coordinating intimate situations, as individuals who do discuss these topics are more likely to engage in safe sex practices.

One way to sustain face needs during sensitive and risky conversations involves the use of confirming messages. Confirming interactions display responsiveness to the partner's feelings through the use of appropriate conversational and relational skills (Cissna & Siebury, 1981; Wilmot, 1987). Much like social support or comforting, confirming is a process through which an individual recognizes, acknowledges, and endorses her or his partner in ways that lead the partner to value her or his self-worth (Cissna & Siebury, 1981). On the other hand, disconfirming messages can involve indifference, imperviousness, or disqualification in ways that make partners feel unworthy or manipulated (Wilmot, 1987).

One extensively studied pattern of disconfirming messages is verbal aggression. Infante and Wigley (1986) defined verbal aggressiveness as a "personality trait that predisposes persons to attack the self-concepts of other people instead of, or in addition to, their positions on topics" (p. 61). Verbal aggression has been linked to such disconfirming communication behaviors as threats and warnings (Infante, Myers, & Buerkel, 1994; Rudd, Burant, & Beatty, 1994). Bayer and Cegala (1992) maintained that verbally aggressive relational partners tend to perceive opposition from others as an assault and respond communicatively with messages that damage the partner's face through embarrassment, anger, or hurt feelings. In contrast, argumentativeness has been defined as the tendency to engage in discussions about controversial ideas and topics, to easily support one's viewpoint without malice, and to refute the opposition's ideas (Infante & Rancer, 1996; Infante, Trebing, Shepherd, & Seeds, 1984). Bayer and Cegala (1992) found that parents who were more verbally argumentative employed a parenting style that has been associated with increases in children's social, cognitive, and emotional development.

The Hamilton and Mineo (chap. 16) meta-analysis in this section investigates the relation between argumentativeness and verbal aggression. By exploring the dimensionality of the argumentativeness scale and the assumption that argumentativeness inhibits verbal aggression, Hamilton and Mineo's results provide a critique of key theoretical and methodological issues. Moreover, they present eight meta-analyses related to issues frequently associated with argumentativeness and verbal aggressiveness. Results on the unidimensionality of the argumentativeness instrument and evidence on the constructive learning process thought to produce argumentativeness and lower verbal aggression provide intriguing opportunities for future research.

Another way to look at conversational processes is to examine the types of messages exchanged by relational partners (positive or negative in orientation) and how these messages serve to sustain or alter perceptions of the relationship. Because ongoing interactions provide opportunities for partners to assess relational growth and evolution, researchers have described episodes resulting in relationship change as turning points (Barge & Musambira, 1992; Baxter & Bullis, 1986; Bullis & Bach, 1989). Turning point research tries to isolate specific events or occurrences that prompt a change in the trajectory of the relationship. Often these turning points are explored by examining the reminiscences of relational partners.

Baxter and Bullis (1986) found that over 55% of all turning points involved explicit talk about the nature and status of the relationship. Among other findings, they reported that partners agree on over 50% of the turning points, that relational conversations vary based on the type of change event, and that turning points differ in the amount of commitment change that is observed. More relational conversations occurred during turning points involving relational exclusivity, making up after an argument or disagreement, agreeing to a serious commitment, and engaging in the first passionate exchanges. Less relational conversation occurred in turning points that involved getting to know the other person and during physical separations. Baxter and Bullis concluded that relationship talk was not uniform across all turning point types and that relational partners selectively engage in conversations about their relationships.

Conversational processes that may result in turning points are evident in several of the meta-analyses in this section. For example, Baxter and Bullis (1986) reported four categories of turning points associated with passion. The Allen et al. (chap. 15) meta-analysis in this section explores relational talk about using condoms during the first sexual encounter. They found that relational talk was associated with safe sex practices, an outcome suggesting a turning point. They also report that women were more likely to initiate a safe sex dialogue. Of course, conversational processes such as comforting, social support, and conflict, all topics of meta-analyses in this section, may mark relational turning points.

Mutuality of Control

A final theme involving interactional processes emphasizes the ways relational partners struggle to negotiate the parameters of the relationship that play out in day-to-day interactions. These discussions may explicitly or implicitly involve issues of control and dominance or the management of disagreements. Ideally, the interactions lead to mutual acceptance or general agreement about specific decisions and the way in which those decisions are reached. This mutuality refers to partners having a shared understanding of the way their relationship works (Acitelli, 1993).

One specific kind of mutuality, control mutuality, reflects consensus in the relationship about who is to take charge of specific relational issues. Indvik and Fitzpatrick (1986) noted that control involves relational partners' ability to influence one another. Canary and Stafford (1994) defined control mutuality as the "extent to which couples agree on who has the right to influence the other and establish relational goals" (p. 6). They believed that information about control mutuality, along with trust, liking, and commitment, can be used to assess the nature of an interpersonal relationship and its stability.

To investigate how partners share or distribute control, researchers examined bids for relational control or dominance, acceptance of others' control or domination, or a transitory type of control or domination that seeks to neutralize influence by either partner (Berger, 1994). Important topics in this area include legitimacy or the acceptance of one's partner's right to be controlling or domineering, exclusivity or the partner's commitment to the relationship regardless of control issues, and dependence or the recognition of the partners' interdependence in establishing control (Indvik & Fitzpatrick, 1986). Individuals in a relationship can exert control in ways that are adaptive and collaborative or they can manipulate both verbal and nonverbal messages to increase their own control of the interaction. Canary and Stafford (1994) maintained that a lack of "control mutuality or unilateral control is displayed in domineering behaviors" (p. 6) that are less productive for long-term relationships.

Dominance has been conceptualized as encompassing both verbal and nonverbal behaviors that are "recognized and interpreted by observers as part of an interactant's attempt to increase his/her control of an interaction" (Brandt, 1980, p. 32). Relational dominance has been characterized as "an emergent property of social interaction" and as having an immediate "relational impact" at the time the behavior was enacted during some "critical moment in the interaction" (Palmer & Lack, 1993, p. 167). This suggests that dominance or control can be a product of the interaction between relational partners where one partner demonstrates her or his ability to exercise power, as well as a product of the other partner's reactions to the dominance (Berger, 1994). This reaction informs the perpetrator about her or his own ability to exercise control or domination. Outcomes of this process might include legitimate power (the right to influence others based on one's status or role), linguistic power (providing reasonable explanations for the right to influence others), expert power (having specialized knowledge), referent power (others wanting to identify with the person), reward power (having the ability to meet others' needs), or coercive power (the ability to shape others' behavior; Berger, 1994).

The Emmers-Sommer (chap. 17) meta-analysis on sexual coercion supports Berger's (1994) theorizing on the reciprocal nature of social power and control. Results on the perceptual aspects of sexual coercion indicate that men and women agree on the nature of important features of the coercive episode. Both men and women perceived sexual coercion as more justifiable for women who initiated the date, went to a man's apartment, had a previous intimate relationship with the man, or consumed alcohol. In these situations, women tended to understand, if not endorse, men using control, power, and dominance to force sexual intercourse. Males' reactions to women's attempts to resist sexual coercion appear to be shaped by traditional sexual scripts. Women's verbal and nonverbal protests are viewed as being disingenuous and a motivation to continue the sexual pursuit. The Emmers-Sommer meta-analysis explores controversies regarding who has the right to exert control, the acceptance of control or dominance by a relational partner, and the use of coercive control and intimidation in sexual episodes.

Sexual coercion is a particularly onerous example of the conflicts that may arise in relationships. Disagreements about appropriate use of influence and the means and ends justifying force and coercion are not always likely to be resolved to the satisfaction of one or both parties. Retzinger (1995) noted that "conflict does not always resolve differences, unify persons or groups or result in constructive change, sometimes it is destructive, erodes relationships, and ends in violence" (p. 26). Conflicts may result in enduring disagreements and profound emotions that warrant, in the view of one or both parties, the termination of the relationship.

In less severe, manageable conflicts, the study of interpersonal communication has frequently examined ways to keep problematic events from terminating the partnership. The goal is often to extend the relationship and keep the "response to a lapse in the bond between" partners constructive (Retzinger, 1995, p. 23). This may involve the use of strategies to manage the conflict or explore the rationales individuals use for enacting certain behaviors. Cloven and Roloff (1995) found that the anticipation of a conflictual exchange can alter the response of the individuals involved. For example, Witteman (1992) found that nonintimate individuals were more likely to blame their partner for causing a conflict and were more likely to hold negative feelings about the partner than were individuals involved in an intimate relationship. Regardless of the intimacy level, however, Schutz (1999) discovered that partners tended to blame the other for initiating the conflict and sought to legitimize their own reaction by pointing to the partners' past infractions as evidence of responsibility for the current conflict. It appears that individuals focus more on their own feelings or needs than those of their partners. As the conflict evolves, the strategies that are employed to cope with conflictual exchange may vary according to the patterns of interactions established during their relationship (Sillars & Wilmot, 1993).

In addition to examining attributions of blame, researchers have explored the types of interpersonal conflict management strategies partners employ. Kluwer, de Dreu, and Buunk (1998) found that both male and female partners reported using "cooperative tactics to a greater extent and competitive tactics to a lesser extent than their opposite sex opponent" (p. 646), especially when the partners were involved in an intimate relationship. Witteman (1992) also found that partners in intimate relationships reported using more solution-oriented strategies, whereas those in nonintimate relationships engaged in more controlling or competitive strategies. Emmers-Sommer (1999) reported a similar pattern regardless of the intimacy level of the relationship. Same-sex friends, opposite-sex friends, and romantic partners engaged in integrative strategies and, following a negative or conflictual event, these partners reported a higher level of relational intimacy. Messman and Mikesell (2000) focused on sex differences and strategy use rather than relationship type and strategy use. They found that women used more distributive and integrative strategies than men. Researchers investigating conflict are still exploring who uses what strategy in which situation.

A meta-analysis in this section addresses the use of conflict management strategies by men and women in intimate and nonintimate relationships. Gayle, Preiss, and Allen (chap. 18) examine the evidence for commonly held beliefs that men use controlling or competitive strategies in nonintimate relationships and withdrawal strategies in intimate conflicts, and women use compromising strategies in nonintimate relationships and coercive strategies in intimate relationships. They found that extraneous variables such as stereotypical attitudes and gender-role enactments may influence the contradictory pattern of effects in the primary studies. In addition to finding small effect sizes for sex differences in conflict management selection, Gayle et al. point to emotional affect, situational constraints, and relational factors as areas meriting additional study. Much more research into interactional conflict processes is warranted.

In general, the research on control, dominance, and conflict reveals the necessity of a shared vision of the way a relationship is enacted. Partners negotiate the range of relational issues, including who has the right to exert influence, who may control relational resources, what goals and outcomes are preferred, and how conflicts or disagreements may be managed.

CONCLUSION

This overview summarizes a sample of topics and issues associated with the interactional approach to interpersonal communication. Researchers taking this view emphasize how cycles of messages allow relational realities to be codefined and understood. Themes evident in interactional processes include relational support, conversational processes such as politeness, facework, and confirmation; and mutuality of control. The issue covered in this section might well be viewed from an individual or dyadic perspective. It seems clear, however, that the framework of ongoing, unfolding relationship development provides insights that are not emphasized by other approaches. The six meta-analyses in this section address aspects of these dynamic relational processes by exploring comforting communication, social support, safe sex communication, argumentativeness, sexual coercion and resistance, and interpersonal conflict.

REFERENCES

Acitelli, L. K. (1993). You, me, and us: Perspectives on interpersonal awareness. In S. Duck (Ed.), *Individuals in relationships* (pp. 144–174). Newbury Park, CA: Sage.

Acker, M., & Davis, M. H. (1992). Intimacy, passion, and commitment in adult romantic relationships: A test of the triangular theory of love. *Journal of Social and Personal Relationships, 9,* 21–50.

Albrecht, T. L., Burleson, B. R., & Goldsmith, D. (1994). Supportive communication. In M. L. Knapp & G. W. Miller (Eds.), *Handbook of interpersonal relationships* (pp. 417–449). Thousand Oaks, CA: Sage.

Barge, J. K., & Musambira, G. W. (1992). Turning points in chair/faculty relationship. *Journal of Applied Communication Research, 20,* 54–77.

Baxter, L. A., & Bullis, C. (1986). Turning points in developing romantic relationships. *Human Communication Research, 12,* 469–493.

Bayer, C. L., & Cegala, D. J. (1992). Trait verbal aggressiveness and argumentativeness: Relations with parenting style. *Western Journal of Communication, 56,* 301–310.

Berger, C. R. (1994). Power, dominance, and social interaction. In M. L. Knapp & G. R. Miller (Eds.), *Handbook of interpersonal communication* (pp. 450–507). Thousand Oaks, CA: Sage.

Brandt, D. R. (1980). A systematic approach to the measurement of dominance in human face-to-face interaction. *Communication Quarterly, 28,* 31–43.

Brown, P., & Levinson, S. (1987). *Politeness: Some universals in language usage.* New York: Cambridge University Press.

Bullis, C., & Bach, B. W. (1989). Are mentor relationships helping organizations? An exploration of developing mentee–mentor–organizational identifications using turning points analysis. *Communication Quarterly, 37,* 199–213.

Bullis, C., & Horn, C. (1995). Get a little closer: Further examinations of nonverbal comforting strategies. *Communication Reports, 8,* 10–17.

Burleson, B. R. (1994). Comforting messages: Features, functions, and outcomes. In J. A. Daly & J. M. Wiemann (Eds.), *Strategic interpersonal communication* (pp. 135–161). Hillsdale, NJ: Lawrence Erlbaum Associates.

Canary, D. J., & Stafford, L. (1994). Maintaining relationships through strategic and routine interactions. In D. J. Canary & L. Stafford (Eds.), *Communication and relational maintenance* (pp. 3–22). New York: Academic.

Cissna, K. N. L., & Siebury, E. (1981). Patterns of interactional confirmation and disconfirmation. In C. Wilder-Mott & J. H. Weakland (Eds.), *Rigor and imagination: Essays from the legacy of Gregory Bateson* (pp. 253–282). New York: Praeger.

Cloven, D. H., & Roloff, M. E. (1995). Cognitive tuning effects of anticipating communication on thought about an interpersonal conflict. *Communication Reports, 8,* 1–9.

Cupach, W. R., & Imahori, T. T. (1993). Managing social predicaments created by others: A comparison of Japanese and American facework. *Western Journal of Communication, 57,* 431–444.

Cupach, W. R., & Metts, S. (1994). *Facework.* Thousand Oaks, CA: Sage.

Cutrona, C. E. (1996). *Social support in couples.* Thousand Oaks, CA: Sage.

Dickens, W. J., & Perlman, D. (1981). Friendship over the lifecycles. In S. Duck & R. Gilmore (Eds.), *Personal relationships: Vol. 2. Developing personal relationships* (pp. 911–922). New York: Academic.

Dolin, D. J., & Booth-Butterfield, M. (1993). Reach out and touch someone: Analysis of nonverbal comforting responses. *Communication Quarterly, 41,* 383–393.

Duck, S., & Wood, J. T. (1995). For better, for worse, for richer, for poorer: The rough and smooth of relationships. In S. Duck & J. T. Wood (Eds.), *Confronting relationship challenges* (pp. 1–23). Thousand Oaks, CA: Sage.

Emmers-Sommer, T. M. (1999). Negative relational events and event responses across relationship type: Examining and comparing the impact of conflict strategy-use on intimacy in same-sex friendships, opposite-sex friendships, and romantic relationships. *Communication Research Reports, 16,* 286–295.

Fitzpatrick, M. A., & Badzinski, D. M. (1994). All in the family: Interpersonal communication in kin relationships. In M. L. Knapp & G. W. Miller (Eds.), *Handbook of interpersonal relationships* (pp. 726–771). Thousand Oaks, CA: Sage.

Floyd, K., & Moorman, M. T. (1997). Affectionate communication in nonromantic relationships: Influences of communication, relational and contextual factors. *Western Journal of Communication, 61,* 279–298.

Floyd, K., & Moorman, M. T. (1998). The measurement of affectionate communication. *Communication Quarterly, 46,* 144–162.

Goffman, E. (1967). *Interaction ritual essays on face-to-face behavior.* Garden City, NY: Anchor Books, Doubleday.

Indvik, J., & Fitzpatrick, M. A. (1986). Perceptions of inclusion, affiliation, and control in five interpersonal relationships. *Communication Quarterly, 34,* 1–13.

Infante, D. A., Myers, S. A., & Buerkel, R. A. (1994). Argument and verbal aggression in constructive and destructive family and organizational disagreements. *Western Journal of Communication, 58,* 73–84.

Infante, D. A., & Rancer, A. S. (1996). Argumentativeness and verbal aggression: A review of recent theory and research. In B. R. Burleson (Ed.), *Communication yearbook 19* (pp. 319–352). Thousand Oaks, CA: Sage.

Infante, D. A., Trebing, J. D., Shepherd, P. E., & Seeds, D. E. (1984). The relationship of argumentativeness to verbal aggression. *The Southern Speech Communication Journal, 50,* 67–77.

Infante, D. A., & Wigley, C. J., III. (1986). Verbal aggressiveness: An interpersonal model and measure. *Communication Monographs, 53,* 61–69.

Kluwer, E. S., de Dreu, C. K. W., & Buunk, B. P. (1998). Conflict in intimate vs. non-intimate relationships: When gender role stereotyping overrides biased self–other judgment. *Journal of Social and Personal Relationships, 15,* 637–650.

Leichty, G., & Applegate, J. L. (1991). Social-cognitive and situational influences on the use of face-saving persuasive strategies. *Human Communication Research, 17,* 451–484.

Lim, T. S. (1990). Politeness behavior in social influence situations. In J. P. Dillard (Ed.), *Seeking compliance: The production of interpersonal influence messages* (pp. 75–86). Scottsdale, AZ: Gorsuch Scarisbrick.

Lim, T. S., & Bowers, J. W. (1991). Facework: Solidarity, approbation, and tact. *Human Communication Research, 17,* 415–450.

Lund, M. (1985). The development of investment and commitment scales for predicting continuity of personal relationships. *Journal of Social and Personal Relationships, 2,* 3–23.

Messman, S. J., & Mikesell, R. L. (2000). Competition and interpersonal conflict in dating relationships. *Communication Report, 13,* 21–34.

Metts, S. (1997). Face and facework: Implications for the study of personal relationships. In S. Duck (Ed.), *Handbook of personal relationship* (2nd ed., pp. 373–390). New York: Wiley.

Millar, F. E., & Rogers, L. E. (1987). Relational dimensions of interpersonal dynamics. In M. E. Roloff & G. R. Miller (Eds.), *Interpersonal processes: New directions in communication research* (pp. 117–139). Newbury Park, CA: Sage.

Palmer, M. T., & Lack, A. M. (1993). Topics, turns, and interpersonal control using serial judgment methods. *The Southern Communication Journal, 58,* 156–168.

Retzinger, S. M. (1995). Shame in anger in personal relationships. In S. Duck & J. T. Wood (Eds.), *Confronting relational challenges* (pp. 22–42). Thousand Oaks, CA: Sage.

Rogan, R. G., & Hammer, M. R. (1994). Crisis negotiations: A preliminary investigation of facework in naturalistic discourse. *Journal of Applied Communication Research, 22,* 216–231.

Rudd, J. E., Burant, P. A., & Beatty, M. J. (1994). Battered women's compliance-gaining strategies as a function of argumentativeness and verbal aggression. *Communication Research Reports, 11,* 13–22.

Rusbult, C. E., & Buunk, B. P. (1993). Commitment processes in close relationships: An interdependency analysis. *Journal of Social and Personal Relationships, 10,* 175–204.

Schutz, A. (1999). It was your fault: Self-serving biases in autobiographical accounts of conflicts in married couples. *Journal of Social and Personal Relationships, 16,* 193–208.

Sillars, A. L., & Wilmot, W. W. (1993). Communication strategies in conflict and mediation. In J. A. Daly & J. M. Wiemann (Eds.), *Strategic interpersonal communication* (pp. 163–190). Hillsdale, NJ: Lawrence Erlbaum Associates.

Tracy, K. (1990). The many faces of facework. In H. Giles & W. P. Robinson (Eds.), *Handbook of language and social psychology* (pp. 209–223). Chichester, UK: Wiley.

Wilmot, W. W. (1987). *Dyadic communication.* New York: Random House.

Witteman, H. (1992). Analyzing interpersonal conflict: Nature of awareness, type of initiating event, situational perceptions, and management styles. *Western Journal of Communication, 56,* 248–280.

Woodward, M. S., Rosenfeld, L. B., & May, S. K. (1996). Sex differences in social support in sororities and fraternities. *Journal of Applied Communication Research, 24,* 260–272.

13

A Synthesis and Extension of Constructivist Comforting Research

Mike Allen

From the late 1970s constructivist theory proposed analyzing messages and relationships based on the cognitive trait of cognitive complexity as a predictor of various message features and outcomes (Littlejohn, 1989). This chapter provides a synthesis of some the available research and the test of a causal model consistent with the predictions of this theory. The goal of this chapter is to take the existing data consistent with the theory and combine the data to conduct a test of the underlying tenets.

There is much debate about the measurement of cognitive complexity using the Role Category Questionnaire (RCQ; Allen, Mabry, Banski, & Preiss, 1991; Allen, Mabry, Banski, Carter, & Stoneman, 1990; Beatty, 1987; Beatty & Payne, 1984, 1985; Burleson, Applegate, & Neuwirth, 1981; Burleson, Waltman, & Samter, 1987; Kellermann, Burrell, & Allen, 1987; Powers, Jordan, & Street, 1979). Even among constructivists there is disagreement about how to measure cognitive complexity (Fransella & Bannister, 1977, 1979; D. O'Keefe & Sypher, 1981), and how to interpret cognitive complexity within a theory of communication (Applegate, Burke, Burleson, Delia, & Kline, 1985; B. O'Keefe & Delia, 1982). The measurement issues remain at this date unresolved and the implications of using the RCQ remain unclear.

This chapter does not resolve or provide any direct evidence on the measurement issues. The basic value of constructivist theory, despite the nagging issues of measurement, is the ability of the research to demonstrate consistent relations to the quality of message production. This chapter synthesizes and tests existing literature using one set of theoretical presuppositions and data about the quality of comforting messages individuals offer each other. The purpose is twofold: (a) to establish that results are consistent across a number of experiments, and (b) to provide a theoretical test of one model advanced based on those results. The test encourages the development of alternative models and explanations for the original data, even though it garners evidence supporting one possible explanation. The resolution of disputes between competing explanations requires more sophisticated evidence and further testing.

CONSTRUCTIVIST THEORY ABOUT COMFORTING STRATEGIES

Constructivist theory suggests effective comforting strategies depend on individual differences between people (Burleson, 1984b). Constructivists argue that individuals high in perspective taking and cognitive complexity comfort others more effectively than individuals with low levels of perspective taking and cognitive complexity. The constructivist theory about comforting behavior has two components: knowledge and motivation (Samter & Burleson, 1984). Knowledge can be divided into four types of information: (a) listener knowledge, (b) topic knowledge, (c) rhetorical knowledge, and (d) metacommunicative knowledge. Knowledge involves understanding the language and relationships such that a person can produce messages capable of achieving goals. In the case of a situation where a message sender wants to comfort another person, the expectation is that the message would provoke some positive emotional response on the part of the message receiver. The characterization of this would be empathy, sympathy, support, comfort, or other statements that improve the emotional state of a distressed person.

Motivation is based on a desire and a willingness to comfort (Samter & Burleson, 1984). Constructivist research primarily focuses on knowledge and the data on motivation are sparse. The rest of this chapter addresses the knowledge necessary for successful comforting behavior. Constructivist research typically does not consider the question of whether a person will provide support but investigates the action people use to provide support once a decision is made to offer support. The research designs establish a situation where a friend has encountered some negative event and instruct the participant to provide an appropriate message. The goal for the message is established as an obligation to provide a message, which is different from real-life settings, where the goal and expectations for a message may not be so clearly defined.

Research by Stiff, Dillard, Somera, Kim, and Sleight (1988) provides a theoretical explanation for motivation for comforting communication. These authors suggested a connection between motivation and knowledge such that the motivation to reach a comforting goal is linked to the knowledge necessary to be effective. Knowledge without the motivation may not be entirely effective and motivation without knowledge is ineffective.

Constructivism assumes a person possesses cognitive complexity before entering a situation. This means cognitive complexity is developed prior to a situation and is employed rather than developed in a particular interaction. A central hypothesis of constructivism is, "variations in messages cause or generate variations in construct system characteristics" (B. O'Keefe & Delia, 1982, p. 55), which indicates that one's cognitive system is an evolving structure that is changed as a result of interaction with the environment. However in any one communicative encounter, it is reasonable to assume a person's relative level of cognitive complexity does not change. If rapid or large changes in cognitive complexity were routine, most of the research involving cognitive complexity would be invalid because the measurement of cognitive complexity would occur before or after the targeted behavior in experiments. The possibility of rapid changes seems empirically denied by high test–retest correlations (particularly those waiting weeks or months between the tests) of measurement assessment (D. O'Keefe & Sypher, 1981). Because the position of rapidly changing scores has no empirical support and the existence of high test–retest reliabilities has been demonstrated for the RCQ (the principal measurement instrument of communication scholars measuring cognitive complexity; D. O'Keefe & Sypher, 1981), the assumption is that changes in an individual's level of cognitive complexity occur gradually and are not ongoing during some single communication encounter.

The assumption of constructivist research that a radical change in an individual's level of cognitive complexity is unlikely during a comforting encounter establishes cognitive complexity as a preexisting condition to any situation. However, age appears to be a predictor of the cognitive complexity of children, with older children being more cognitively complex than younger children. This finding is consistent with the theories about cognitive development that suggest that as an individual grows older cognitive complexity should increase (Turiel, 1978; Vygotsky, 1962, 1978). Burleson

(1982b, 1984b) stated that age is really a sum of more important characteristics relating to development. He suggested that age is an indication of cognitive development because a crucial point to this theory is that progression is natural and will occur with experience (Burleson, 1981). In a very real sense, age or experience causes the development of the cognitive system. Experiments have operationalized age as the year in school (Burleson, 1984a), which seems a reasonable indicator of both age and some measure of environmental exposure. Assuming a child is given a relatively normal environment, the expectation exists that the child's cognitive system will mature (one measure of this is the level of cognitive complexity). This suggests that any situation will naturally assist, longer term, in the development of the cognitive system.

Constructivist research has concentrated on demonstrating that those individuals with more highly developed cognitive structures will produce superior comforting strategies (and messages in general). Crockett (1982) argued that people with greater cognitive complexity possess more highly developed cognitive systems. He claimed that even if there is not a more highly developed hierarchical system for a more sophisticated dimensional structure, the sophistication of each dimension is greater when the number of elements in that dimension increases (this corresponds to more descriptions listed on a measurement device like the RCQ). This viewpoint is similar, in may ways, to the developmental view of interpersonal relationships that suggests that interpersonal relationships are based on each individual's learning psychological information about each other that differentiates a person from a stereotype (G. Miller & Steinberg, 1975). As people "learn" about other individuals, information increases, as does the ability to differentiate one person from another. The more sophisticated or developed a cognitive system is, the more likely an individual can be differentiated from other people and treated as a unique entity.

This view of interpersonal relationship development corresponds to the constructivist position that individuals with greater cognitive complexity better understand another person's feelings because they have a greater capacity to understand a different perspective (Burleson, 1984a). When engaged in an interaction requiring comforting messages, the cognitively complex person can provide more comfort because he or she knows what the other person is feeling (Samter, Burleson, & Murphy, 1987). More important, cognitively complex individuals have a greater understanding of the perspectives of others and can provide superior responses to other individuals. Additionally, the cognitive complex person will have a wider repertoire of strategies available. If nothing else, the cognitively complex person can keep trying strategies until one strategy or tactic succeeds. High levels of cognitive complexity are desirable because highly complex individuals are able to communicate more effectively and understand people and situations in a much more sophisticated manner.

Cognitive complexity can be divided into two components: cognitive differentiation and cognitive abstractness. *Cognitive differentiation* indicates the number of dimensions (or individual terms) providing a crude sense of the cognitive organizational system breadth. As previously indicated, Crockett (1982) assumed that the larger the number of constructs, the more differentiated the cognitive system. In practice, researchers believe that the higher the score (as generated by the RCQ), the more developed the cognitive system.

Cognitive abstractness denotes the quality of the elements in the cognitive system (Burleson, 1983). The more abstract the system, the greater the flexibility to appropriately handle a variety of situations. Burleson (1983) generated a system for coding the descriptions generated by the RCQ for abstractness, demonstrating that abstractness (construct quality) is unrelated to construct differentiation (the quantity of constructs). The abstractness deals with the sense of whether the descriptive properties address or consider underlying motivations or features. Suppose I describe John as "a person who gives flowers to his wife." This is an observable behavior that indicates one method of how my system makes judgments. This statement would be considered less abstract than if I wrote, "John is a kind person that thinks of the well-being of his family." The second statement would be considered more abstract because the reference is to an underlying understanding of the person's motivation, whereas the first statement only indicates a specific behavior from which one can infer a value.

Cognitive complexity, as a personality characteristic, should enable highly complex people to generate qualitatively better comforting messages. That is, when people are in a situation requiring the generation of comforting messages, they will generate more successful comforting messages if they have a higher level of cognitive differentiation or cognitive abstractness (as measured by the RCQ). This means that the higher the cognitive complexity, the greater the ability to take the perspective of the person in need of comfort (called the affective perspective-taking ability). Cognitive complexity (both abstraction and differentiation) should predict the ability of a person to "feel" for the other person (affective perspective taking) and the ability to generate highly comforting messages.

The final implication is that older children should possess greater levels of cognitive complexity (abstractness and differentiation) and therefore a greater level of affective perspective taking and a greater ability to generate highly comforting messages. The ability to take the perspective of another person should add to the ability to generate higher quality comforting messages. The goal of the message should be to provide comfort to the message recipient; that is, the effectiveness is based on the ability of the message to achieve certain outcomes from the perspective of the other person. A person able to understand the perspective of the message target should be able to provide a message more able to meet the needs of the other individual.

The results of this entire body of theory can be demonstrated by the causal model in Fig. 13.1. In the figure, age is the cause of both construct abstractness and construct differentiation. Construct abstractness and construct differentiation cause affective perspective taking and the ability to generate effective comforting messages, and perspective taking contributes to the ability to improve quality messages. It is this model, as represented in Fig. 13.1, that is tested in this chapter.

CURRENT TESTS OF THE CONSTRUCTIVIST MODEL

Typically, tests of the constructivist model have involved some type of multiple regression or partial correlation where the dependent measure has been the quality of comforting message. The predictor variables usually include some measure of the individual generating the messages' cognitive complexity (measured either by differentiation or abstractness). Other predictors, when included, are treated as independent or predictor variables in the equation. The path diagram in Fig. 13.2 shows an example of a model tested by multiple regression (Burleson, 1984a). In this model the dependent variable, comforting message quality, is predicted by a combination of the following variables: (a) age, (b) construct differentiation, (c) construct abstractness, and (d) perspective-taking ability. Another feature common to constructivist comforting research is to partial the relation between cognitive complexity

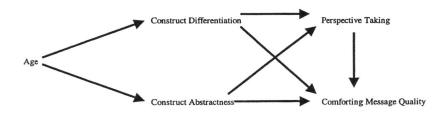

FIG. 13.1   Diagram of model.

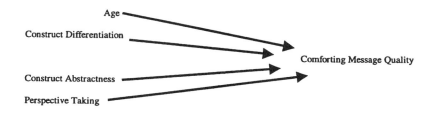

FIG. 13.2   Current operationalized test of the model.

and comforting message quality for the effect of age. This model is substantively different from the model that appears in Fig. 13.1. The impact of this partial correlation procedure is explored in the next section.

The partialing of age as a variable from these relations constitutes a problem when age is a variable that is partialed before examining other relations. If any variable partialed is a cause of either variable and is correlated with the other causal variable, "partial correlation is inappropriate, as it may result in partialing to much of the relation" (Pedhazur, 1982, pp. 110–111). The example is given of a variable x and a variable y that both cause variable z. In the case of constructivist comforting theory, the sequence would be age (x) and cognitive complexity (y), abstractness and differentiation, causing the quality of the comforting message (z). The result is that the conclusions presented in the literature, "without regard to the theoretical considerations about the pattern of relations among them may amount to a distortion of reality and result in misleading or meaningless results" (Pedhazur, 1982, p. 110). In this particular case, the theory and the data suggest a more comprehensive and exact model of the underlying processes. Duncan (1975) claimed that, "the numerical result is intelligible in terms of the model, while the one for the partial correlation is misleading" (p. 23). His conclusion is, "that when we attempt to reason from the values of two correlations to the value of a third, we must actually be working with an implicit causal model" (p. 13). A better solution for comforting research would be to make explicit the implicit causal models and test the explicit model.

Additionally, previous research used multiple regression with one dependent variable. Duncan (1975) and Heise (1975) pointed out that the use of multiple regression assumes a specific causal model. The critical assumption that the predictor variables are additive (Heise, 1975; Monge, 1980) is not met if there are causal relations among the predictor variables. The result is that the multiple regression will generate standardized coefficients that reflect one specific theoretical model. In this chapter, I argue that a different theoretical model is implied by the literature and therefore argue against the use of multiple regression techniques in prior studies. The set of theoretical assumptions inherent in the multiple regression does not seem to match the theoretical assumptions outlined in the text. Operational slippage occurs between the conceptualization of the theory and the specific models operationalized in the statistical tests.

More sophisticated techniques are required when there exist "extended systems of propositions" (McPhee & Babrow, 1987, p. 350). Given the theoretical emphasis of constructivism and the amount of writing devoted to outlining the theoretical tenets, causal modeling is warranted. Burleson (1987) suggested the need for more sophisticated techniques to understand the underlying processes at work, going beyond simply correlating cognitive complexity with certain types of behavior. Therefore, the application of path model diagrams using more causal modeling matching the underlying theoretical assumptions becomes justified.

TESTING THE THEORY USING EXISTING DATA

The current data from prior constructivist research can be used to test the proposed theoretical model. The test would differ from current analyses of the data using multiple regression models by using many predictor variables for one dependent variable. The test involves two steps: (a) an accumulation of data using meta-analysis, and (b) a test of the theoretical model using the average observed correlations derived from the first step.

The difference between this test and previous tests of the theory is the use of indirect relations among the variables rather than assuming only the direct relations incorporated as a part of multiple regression. For example, affective perspective taking becomes a dependent variable in this model as opposed to a causal or predictor variable in the previous tests using multiple regression. The connection of age to the quality of the comforting message is not direct in the proposed model; age functions as the exogenous variable that creates input for the system.

The model tested is not the only model that will fit the available data; many possible models would probably be consistent with the model. Testing a model, however, should be a process that evaluates models generated by existing theories rather than post hoc or ad hoc attempts to fit models to data. Models will always need to be refined, as the data do not conform to expectations; the question is the degree to which new models are similar to existing models. The construction of mathematically acceptable alternative models from the current data is possible, but the acceptance or rejection of any particular configuration should be based on the underlying theoretical presuppositions for those models. No claim will be made that the model tested here is the "definitive" model for constructivist comforting research. This is one interpretation the data suggests, but other interpretations can be and should be tested. The goal of this test is to serve as a starting point for the process of model building rather than offering a final word on the interpretation of the available data.

METHODS

The data analysis consists of two steps: (a) summarizing past research into average effect sizes and establishing the homogeneity of results from experiment to experiment, and (b) testing the proposed model using the summarized results.

Summarizing the Past Research

This summary of the previous literature was accomplished using the Schmidt–Hunter variance-centered form of meta-analysis (Bangert-Drowns, 1986; Hunter, Schmidt, & Jackson, 1982). This form of meta-analysis uses the metric of the correlation coefficient and tests the sample of correlations for homogeneity using a chi-square statistic. This technique has been shown by Monte Carlo simulations to be an acceptable method of detecting the existence of heterogeneity caused by possible moderator variables (Osburn, Callender, Greener, & Ashworth, 1983; Spector & Levine, 1987). The Schmidt–Hunter technique establishes that 75% of the observed variability should be due to random sampling error (as established by the average correlation). The chi-square test was included because it is an even more powerful test for variability.

One possible concern is that multiple effect sizes taken from the same data set are not independent. This may create conditions that adversely effect the estimation of the mean effect size or change the observed variance in the observed average correlation. A Monte Carlo simulation shows that the mean effect size and the associated estimates of the variance are unaffected even when nonindependent samples are used (Tracz, 1984). In principle, the use of multiple correlations from a single study in meta-analysis is no different than a single study using the same sample to estimate all the correlations for multiple regression. If independence is a problem for meta-analysis, then independence is a problem for all procedures using any sample to derive multiple mathematical estimates. This means that individual investigations obtaining estimates are affected by this problem of nonindependence of estimates because the correlation matrix (or covariance matrix) used to generate the results is generated from the same sample. The real issue is whether multiple samples achieve consistent results and the test for homogeneity (in the meta-analysis) of the observed correlations is an assessment of that issue.

A literature search was made of all constructivist literature for relevant data on comforting behavior. This included a manual search of all National Communication Association journals, all regional journals (Central States Communication Association, Eastern Communication Association, Southern States Communication Association, Western Communication Association), all International Communication Association journals, *Communication Yearbook*, and *Communication Research*, from 1970 to 1998. Additionally, the reference sections were searched for additional manuscripts. In addition, the *Index to Communication Studies through 1995* was searched using the keywords, *comfort, role category questionnaire, perspective taking,* and *constructivism.*

Testing the Causal Model

The proposed causal model was tested using the corrected correlation matrix with the least squares solution found in PATH (Hamilton & Hunter, 1986). This is an updated version of PACKAGE (Hunter, Cohen, & Nicol, 1982). The use of a least-squares solution has been a standard practice in many causal modeling efforts in communication research (McPhee & Babrow, 1987; K. Miller, Stiff, & Ellis, 1988; Stiff et al., 1988). The corrected correlations were used whenever sufficient reliability information was available to correct for error of measurement due to attenuation. It should be noted that intercoder reliability (a different form of reliability) was high for all measures using the results of some type of coding by observers.

The model is tested mathematically by taking the observed correlations and treating the correlations involved directly in one path as constrained. The technique then creates an expected correlation for the unconstrained correlations that would fit the model (taking into consideration the fixed or constrained correlations). There now exists an expected correlation matrix that can be compared to the observed correlation matrix (Duncan, 1975). This provides the basis of a chi-square test for goodness of fit between the expected correlations and the observed correlations. An insignificant chi-square means that the observed data do not significantly depart from the theoretical model.

RESULTS

Summary of Past Research

The summary of past research on the 10 relevant correlations of interest revealed a total of 18 estimations. A range from one to three estimates for each possible correlation existed. A summary of all the averaged correlations and the associated homogeneity tests is found in Table 13.1. When less than three estimates are available, no homogeneity test can be performed. The results show that all averaged correlations are homogenous with the exception of the correlation between construct differentiation and construct abstractness. Two of the correlations ($r = .35$ and $r = .48$) are higher than the other two observed correlations ($r = .13$ and $r = .19$). No explanation could be found to account for the difference. The problem is that the homogeneity may indicate the existence of two or more different groups. However, be-

TABLE 13.1
Summary of Available Data

	1	2	3	4	5
1. Age					
2. Construct differentiation					
k	3				
N	355				
Average r	.465				
Var. r	.0062				
3. Construct abstractness					
k	3	4			
N	355	472			
Average r	.445	.268			
Var. r	.0051	.0265			
4. Perspective taking					
k	2	5	2		
N	231	384	231		
Average r	.663	.555	.621		
Var. r		.0627			
5. Comforting message quality					
k	1	2	2	3	
N	137	547	207	434	
Average r	.593	.270	.422	.477	
Var. r				.0547	

cause all correlations are positive, the difference is found between groups where the direction of the correlation is the same, but the magnitude would differ between the two groups. A decision was made to use the average correlation because it represents the average across groups and the rest of the correlations were also averaged in the same manner. This averaging obtains the best estimate possible of the underlying population correlation and the average correlations were used for the subsequent path analysis.

Test of the Causal Model

The first model tested was that proposed by the original hypothesis and it generated a significant chi-square, $\chi^2(7) = 18.53$, $p < .05$. This indicates that the proposed model did not work as originally hypothesized. The data indicated that eliminating the direct connections between construct abstractness and construct differentiation to comforting skill message would improve the model. The analysis of differences between reproduced correlations and original correlations suggests that addition of a direct path from age to perspective taking and from construct differentiation to construct abstractness was necessary.

The consideration of the change in diagram must be justified on the basis of theoretical argument. The changes in the model argue that construct differentiation and construct abstractness affect message quality but only as a result of the ability to take a perspective. This is consistent with the original model in content by focusing the connection on how the organization of the cognitive system operates to change one's ability to take a different perspective. The addition of a path from age to perspective taking indicates that there are probably other changes, in addition to changes in construct differentiation and construct abstraction, that occur with age to predict perspective taking. The last path is less obvious. The argument that differentiation would predict or cause abstractness could simplify the function of the impact needed to create a means to organize and reorganize a cognitive system as it becomes larger and more sophisticated. The larger the number of elements, the greater the necessity of generating means of organizing the series of judgments that the system entails. The new model was subsequently tested.

The chi-square goodness-of-fit test for the overall model indicates that the matrix of correlations predicted by the model deviates from the observed matrix of correlations by an amount attributable to sampling error $\chi^2(5) = 8.7$, $p > .05$. This indicates that the hypothesized model is not inconsistent with the data. All of the path coefficients in the model are significant. See Fig. 13.3 for a visual depiction of this information. This indicates

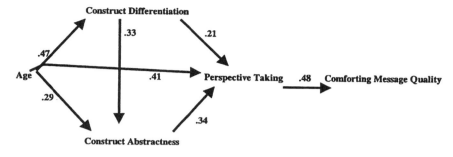

FIG. 13.3   Final model (all path coefficients are significant, $p < .05$).

that constructivist theory provides an adequate explanation for the observed data. No other models were tested, although the ability to construct and test additional models does exist. The statistical tests do not validate the theoretical model, but they confirm that no inconsistency exists between the theoretical model and the observed data. There may exist other models that will fit the data mathematically, but no comprehensive theoretically driven alternative to the current set of findings exists.

CONCLUSIONS

The first conclusion to be drawn is that constructivist theory provides an adequate account of the available data. The difference between previous assessments and this report is the shift from multiple regression models to more complex structural equation models assuming multivariate dependency among the variables. The shift answers the challenge made by Burleson (1987) for more sophistication and makes the available data subject to a single unifying explanation consistent with the assumptions of constructivism. Basically, the developmental argument that persons over time and by experience understand the perspective of another person permits the quality of messages to improve. The role of cognitive complexity becomes that of a structure that develops over time for individuals, but like many features develops differently for each person. Persons with greater levels of development understand the perspective of others better and therefore may generate higher quality messages.

One important issue at this stage of research is the need to draw a comparison between this model of comforting behavior and one other model proposed (Stiff et al., 1988). The Stiff et al. (1988) model is interested in the process of motivation in actually producing comforting behavior. Their final dependent variable was the willingness to volunteer time doing administrative tasks for a social service organization. (See Fig. 4 in the original Stiff et al. study for a representation of the model.) This model differs from assessing a person's cognitive system and whether that cognitive ability increases one's ability to produce high-quality comforting behavior. The Stiff et al. model examines as a dependent measure the willingness of a person to volunteer. The constructivist model predicts the quality of that participation. As Burleson and Samter (1984) recognized, there is a difference between knowledge about how to comfort and the motivation or willingness to engage in comforting behavior.

An examination of the two models reveals one crucial point of convergence. One of the variables in this investigation of constructivist comforting data is affective perspective taking. Both construct differentiation and construct abstractness predicted this personality feature. In the Stiff et al. (1988) model, the initial variable in the sequence is perspective taking, which starts the sequence predicting the willingness to volunteer to work for a prosocial institution. This suggests that the two parts of comforting behavior (knowledge and motivation) may both be connected to one underlying feature, cognitive complexity (as measured by cognitive differentiation and construct abstractness). These findings may mean the constructivism research has understated the importance that cognitive complexity plays in comforting behavior because it predicts both knowledge and eventually motivation.

The next step in comforting research should be to engage in testing some combination of the process involving knowledge and motivation. This would require experiments testing both the knowledge of an individual about how to comfort and the motivation or willingness to engage in such behavior. Both sets of information are required for a complete understanding of this important communicative event. The feature making this project possible should be a requirement of future research—the reporting of complete correlation matrices. This permits future researchers to consider and test other possibilities. Many of the investigations used in this report only reported one correlation, the use of multivariate techniques or multiple regression, without reporting a complete correlation matrix, which severely restricts the ability to incorporate data.

One controversy, still unresolved, is the relation between emotional empathy and prosocial behaviors. Two separate meta-analyses have been conducted with conflicting results. Underwood and Moore (1982) found no relation between empathy and prosocial behavior in a meta-analysis of the literature. Eisenberg and Miller (1987) however, in a later meta-analysis, found low to moderate relations existing between empathy and prosocial behaviors. The later meta-analysis claimed the divergent findings of the earlier meta-analysis were the result of the inclusion of methodological differences between groups of studies not considered in the early meta-analysis. Thus, the need exists to define and reexamine assumptions when trying to build a complete theory of the motivational aspects of comforting behavior.

Burleson (1987) suggested that more detailed accounts are required to understand the place of individual differences like cognitive complexity in communication behavior. This effort has been an attempt to advance the understanding of constructivist theory by retesting the original data using a specific theoretical model. The next step should be to complete the process and examine the connection between motivation and knowledge. The underlying processes by which knowledge is gained during the developmental process of childhood should be examined. The data point to the importance of age as a factor in the development of a sophisticated cognitive system, which leads to a more sophisticated understanding of the world. Nothing in the data presented in this analysis explains how this process takes place over time. Knowledge of this process would permit a specific application of constructivist theory by educators, medical practitioners, and parents.

Future research also should address one concern raised by Burleson (1984c)—whether or not the findings are domain specific. Does the same distinction between motivation and knowledge exist in areas of persuasion, compliance gaining, and interpersonal communication? The division may only exist in the area of comforting behavior and any generalization of this theoretical model should consider what areas of communicative behavior could be included. The results of this chapter suggest a direction for future research in areas like persuasion, compliance gaining, and other interaction contexts where an individual adapts a message to a particular person or audience.

Many potential areas for intervention exist where the ability to take the perspective of the target and generate high-quality messages would be beneficial. Consider suicide hotlines, drug counseling, treatment of depression, and other circumstances where one person needs to provide another with an appropriate message designed to facilitate some outcome. The term *sensitivity* has taken on a negative connotation when dealing with training individuals to consider the perspective of another person, but in a world where confrontations and communication misinterpretations can result in sexual harassment, date rape, police brutality, and other escalations, the need for individuals to be able to appreciate the perspective of another is essential.

Constructivism in the decade of the 1990s was not so much disproved as it was simply abandoned without much effort to replace or synthesize the existing efforts. Causal modeling, when combined with meta-analysis, allows researchers to go beyond the limitations of any one data set and generate new understandings across data sets. Constructivism represents an interesting and useful possibility for the examination of human communication. Other scholars should test the assumptions of this model and gather more data because the data pool for this synthesis is extremely limited. Other possible theoretical interpretations exist for these data and those should be considered as well. The goal of synthesizing and representing results among studies within a unifying theoretical framework offers much promise.

REFERENCES

References marked with an asterisk indicate studies included in the meta-analysis.

Allen, M., Mabry, E., Banski, M., Carter, P., & Stoneman, M. (1990). A thoughtful reappraisal of measuring cognition using the Role Category Questionnaire. *Communication Reports, 3,* 49–57.

Allen, M., Mabry, E., Banski, M., & Preiss, R. (1991). Valid and constructive thoughts: Continuing the dialog about the RCQ. *Communication Reports, 4,* 120–125.

*Applegate, J. (1982). The impact of construct system development on communication and impression formation in persuasive context. *Communication Monographs, 49,* 277–289.

Applegate, J., Burke, J., Burleson, B., Delia, J., & Kline, S. (1985). In I. Siegel (Ed.), *Parental belief systems: The psychological consequences for children* (pp. 107–142). Hillsdale, NJ: Lawrence Erlbaum Associates.

Bangert-Drowns, R. (1986). Review of developments in meta-analytic method. *Psychological Bulletin, 99,* 388–399.

Beatty, M. (1987). Erroneous assumptions underlying Burleson's critique. *Communication Quarterly, 35,* 329–333.

Beatty, M., & Payne, S. (1984). Loquacity and quantity of constructs as predictors of social perspective taking. *Communication Quarterly, 32,* 207–209.

Beatty, M., & Payne, S. (1985). Is construct differentiation loquacity? *Human Communication Research, 11,* 605–612.

Burleson, B. (1981). A cognitive-developmental perspective on social reasoning processes. *Western Journal of Speech Communication, 45,* 133–147.

*Burleson, B. (1982a). The affective perspective-taking process: A test of Turiel's role-taking model. In M. Burgoon (Ed.), *Communication yearbook 6* (pp. 473–488). Beverly Hills, CA: Sage.

Burleson, B. (1982b). The development of comforting communication skills in childhood and adolescence. *Child Development, 53,* 1578–1588.

*Burleson, B. (1983). Social cognition, empathic motivation, and adults' comforting strategies. *Human Communication Research, 10,* 295–304.

*Burleson, B. (1984a). Age, social-cognitive development, and the use of comforting strategies. *Communication Monographs, 51,* 140–153.

Burleson, B. (1984b). Comforting communication. In H. Sypher & J. Applegate (Eds.), *Communication by children and adults* (pp. 63–105). Beverly Hills, CA: Sage.

Burleson, B. (1984c). Role-taking and communication skills in childhood: Why they aren't related and what can be done about it. *Western Journal of Speech Communication, 48*, 155–170.

Burleson, B. (1987). Cognitive complexity. In J. McCroskey & J. Daly (Eds.), *Personality and interpersonal communication* (pp. 305–350). Beverly Hills, CA: Sage.

Burleson, B., Applegate, J., & Neuwirth, C. (1981). Is cognitive complexity loquacity? A reply to Jordan, Powers, and Street. *Human Communication Research, 7*, 212–225.

*Burleson, B., & Samter, W. (1984, November). *Individual differences in the perception of comforting messages: An exploratory investigation.* Paper presented at the annual Speech Communication Association Convention, Chicago.

Burleson, B., & Samter, W. (1985a). Consistencies in theoretical and naïve evaluations of comforting messages. *Communication Monographs, 51*, 140–153.

*Burleson, B., & Samter, W. (1985b). Individual differences in the perception of comforting messages: An exploratory investigation. *Central States Speech Journal, 36*, 39–50.

*Burleson, B., & Samter, W. (1990). Effects of cognitive complexity on the perceived importance of communication skills in friends. *Communication Research, 17*, 165–182.

Burleson, B., Waltman, M., & Samter, W. (1987). More evidence that cognitive complexity is not loquacity: A reply to Beatty and Payne. *Communication Quarterly, 35*, 317–328.

Crockett, W. (1982). The organization of construct systems. In J. Mancuso & J. Adams-Webber (Eds.), *The construing person* (pp. 62–95). New York: Praeger.

*Delia, J., & Clark, R. (1977). Cognitive complexity, social perception, and the development of listener-adapted communication in six-, eight-, ten-, twelve-year-old boys. *Communication Monographs, 24*, 326–345.

*Delia, J., Kline, S., & Burleson, B. (1979). The development of persuasive communication strategies in kindergartners through twelfth graders. *Communication Monographs, 46*, 241–256.

*Delia, J., O'Keefe, B., & O'Keefe, D. (1982). The constructivist approach to communication. In F. Dance (Ed.), *Human communication theory* (pp. 148–191). New York: Harper & Row.

Duncan, O. (1975). *Introduction to structural equation models.* New York: Academic.

Eisenberg, N., & Miller, P. (1987). The relation of empathy to prosocial and related behaviors. *Psychological Bulletin, 101*, 91–119.

Fransella, F., & Bannister, D. (1977). *A manual for repertory grid techniques.* San Francisco: Jossey-Bass.

Fransella, F., & Bannister, D. (Eds.). (1979). *Constructs of sociality and individuality.* New York: Academic.

*Hale, C., & Delia, J. (1976). Cognitive complexity and social perspective-taking. *Communication Monographs, 43*, 195–203.

Hamilton, M., & Hunter, J. (1986). *PACKAGE: An updated version of routines for doing confirmatory factor and path analysis.* Unpublished manuscript, Department of Communication, University of Connecticut, Storrs, CT.

Heise, D. (1975). *Causal analysis.* New York: Wiley.

Hunter, J., Cohen, S., & Nicol, T. (1982). *PACKAGE: A system of routines to do correlational analysis, including path analysis, confirmatory factor analysis, and exploratory factor analysis.* Unpublished manuscript, Department of Psychology, Michigan State University, East Lansing, MI.

Hunter, J., Schmidt, F., & Jackson, S. (1982). *Meta-analysis: Cumulating research findings across studies.* Beverly Hills, CA: Sage.

Kellermann, K., Burrell, N., & Allen, M. (1987, May). *The role category questionnaire: A measure in search of a construct?* Paper presented at the International Communication Association Convention, Montreal, Canada.

Littlejohn, S. (1989). *Theories of human communication* (3rd. ed.). Belmont, CA: Wadsworth.

McPhee, R., & Babrow, A. (1987). Causal modeling in communication research: Use, disuse, and misuse. *Communication Monographs, 54*, 344–366.

Miller, G., & Steinberg, M. (1975). *Between people.* Chicago: Science Research Associates.

Miller, K., Stiff, J., & Ellis, B. (1988). Communication and empathy as precursors to burnout among human service workers. *Communication Monographs, 55*, 250–265.

Monge, P. (1980). Multivariate multiple regression. In P. Monge & J. Cappella (Eds.), *Multivariate techniques in human communication research* (pp. 14–56). New York: Academic.

O'Keefe, B., & Delia, J. (1982). Impression formation and message production. In M. Roloff & C. Berger (Eds.), *Social cognition and communication* (pp. 33–72). Beverly Hills, CA: Sage.

*O'Keefe, B., Murphy, M., Meyers, R., & Babrow, A. (1989). The development of persuasive communication skills: The influence of developments in interpersonal constructs on the ability to generate communication-relevant beliefs and level of persuasive strategy. *Communication Studies, 40*, 29–40.

O'Keefe, D., & Sypher, H. (1981). Cognitive complexity measures and the relationship of cognitive complexity to communication: A critical review. *Human Communication Research, 8*, 72–92.

Osburn, H., Callender, J., Greener, J., & Ashworth, S. (1983). Statistical power of tests of the situational specificity hypothesis in validity generalization studies: A cautionary note. *Journal of Applied Psychology, 68*, 115–122.

Pedhazur, E. (1982). *Multiple regression in behavioral research* (2nd Ed). New York: Holt, Rinehart, & Winston.

Powers, W., Jordan, W., & Street, R. (1979). Language indices in the measurement of cognitive complexity: Is complexity loquacity? *Human Communication Research, 6*, 69–73.

*Rubin, R., & Henzl, S. (1984). Cognitive complexity, communication competence, and verbal ability. *Communication Quarterly, 32*, 263–270.

Samter, W., & Burleson, B. (1984). Cognitive and motivational influences on spontaneous comforting behavior. *Human Communication Research, 11*, 231–260.

*Samter, W., Burleson, B., & Basden-Murphy, L. (1989). Behavioral complexity is in the eye of the beholder: Effects of cognitive complexity and message complexity on impressions of the source of comforting messages. *Human Communication Research, 15*, 612–629.

Samter, W., Burleson, B., & Murphy, L. (1987). Comforting conversations: The effects of strategy type on evaluations of messages and message producers. *Southern Speech Communication Journal, 52*, 263–284.

Spector, R., & Levine, E. (1987). Meta-analysis for integrating study outcomes: A Monte Carlo study of its susceptibility to type I and type II errors. *Journal of Applied Psychology, 72*, 3–9.

*Stiff, J., Dillard, J., Somera, L., Kim, H., & Sleight, C. (1988). Empathy, communication, and prosocial behavior. *Communication Monographs, 55*, 198–213.

Tracz, S. (1984). *The effect of violation of the assumption of independence when combining correlation coefficients in a meta-analysis.* Unpublished doctoral dissertation, Southern Illinois University, Carbondale, IL.

Turiel, E. (1978). Distinct conceptual and developmental domains: Social convention and morality. In C. Keasey (Ed.), *Nebraska symposium on motivation* (pp. 21–52). Lincoln: University of Nebraska Press.

Underwood, B., & Moore, E. (1982). Perspective-taking and altruism. *Psychological Bulletin, 91,* 143–173.

Vygotsky, L. (1962). *Thought and language.* Cambridge, MA: MIT Press.

Vygotsky, L. (1978). *Mind in society.* Cambridge, MA: Harvard University Press.

14

Divorce: How Spouses Seek Social Support

Nancy A. Burrell

An obvious outcome of a broken relationship is divorce, which causes major distress in a family. Both children and parents are directly affected by the seriousness of a divorce:

> In recent years, America's divorce rate has actually been in decline. When it peaked in the early 1980's, the Centers for Disease Control and Prevention estimated that half of all marriages would end in divorce. Now that number is down to four in ten. Still, the rate is far higher than it was in the 1940's, 1950's and 1960's. (Holt, 1999, pp. L-1,4)

The decision to divorce is almost universally accepted as an unfortunate yet regrettable necessity, regardless of the potential for both community and societal disapproval, as evidenced by the relative ease of obtaining a divorce (Kitson & Raschke, 1981). The decision to divorce "represents merely a practical concession to the frailty of mankind, caught in a web of social relationships and cultural expectations that often impose intolerable pressure on the individual personality" (Murdock, 1950, p. 201). Rather than focusing on the systemic needs of the family, divorcing spouses center on their individual needs (e.g., self-esteem, health, and well-being). Moreover, research increasingly focuses on the process of divorce. Many scholars argue that developing new relationships and cultivating interpersonal resources are pivotal to the process of divorce (McKenry & Price, 1991; Pett, 1982; Spanier & Casto, 1979). The purpose of this chapter is to review some of the issues related to social support for divorcing spouses as they attempt to re-create balance in their lives through workplace, family, social, and other interpersonal relationships. The central question for this chapter and meta-analysis, do spouses draw on social support networks differently, focuses on potential gender differences during the process of divorce.

LITERATURE REVIEW

Numerous educators, therapists, and researchers have focused on the trauma associated with divorce (McKenry & Price, 1991). Many reasons exist for distress among divorced families. One reason for distress is tied to the loss of the other spouse or parent. Even after a painful and conflictual marriage, individuals continue to feel attachment to the ex-spouse and sadness and loneliness at his or her absence (Stinson, 1991). Another problem leading to stress and anxiety after divorce is the tremendous amount of responsibility placed on the single parent. Single parents suffer from task, emotional, and responsibility overload. The sheer number of tasks and problems related to household maintenance, economic and occupational difficulties that one person must address day-to-day is overwhelming (Vaux, 1988). Single-parent families eat more fast food and pickup meals and children are likely to have erratic bedtimes and are more often late to school (Stinson, 1991). A third problem faced by primarily mothers and children following divorce is economic. On average, men's economic position improves following divorce whereas women's financial status worsens (Stinson, 1991). Even in middle-class families, mothers and children experience a significant decline in their standard of living that occurs rapidly following separation (Stinson, 1991).

Marital dissolution is widely recognized as a significant disruptive force in the lives of families. The postdivorce adjustment period is the time immediately following the termination of a marriage (Thiessen, Avery, & Joanning, 1981). This period is described as the time when family members experience confusion, depression, self-doubt, and depreciation. Variables that affect the postadjustment period include the divorcee's age, income, prior marital relationship, who initiated the divorce, self-esteem, and social support system (Thiessen et al., 1981).

Numerous investigations have indicated that for a variety of populations, interventions designed to improve communication skills are critical in the initiation, development, and maintenance of interpersonal relationships (Satir, 1972; Schauble & Hill, 1976; Wood, 1999). For example, several researchers designed a training program to provide recent divorcees with communication skills to increase the possibility of developing and maintaining a positive social support system (Thiessen et al., 1981). Results comparing the experimental and control groups indicated that participants in the experimental group increased in divorce adjustment and empathy skills but did not improve in perceived social support or self-disclosure skills when contrasted with the control group (Thiessen et al., 1981). These researchers account for their results because they are based on a small sample size, participants were women and only recently divorced or separated, and the results reflect only a short-term assessment of the variables. Thiessen et al. (1981) suggested that perhaps the training would have been more meaningful and would have had more impact with the passing of time. Perhaps women needed more time to adjust to their divorces and would have been more receptive to improving their communicative skills.

Clearly, divorce causes numerous types of stress for those going through it. Bilge and Kaufman (1983) argued that "Increasing marital instability, escalating divorce rates, and the resulting dissolution of myriad nuclear families have left roughly 20% of all U.S. children under 18 years of age—some 12,000,000 of them in one-parent households" (p. 59). However, one-parent family systems are no more detrimental to the development and adjustment of children than other family forms, and divorce and separation can leave children unharmed in single-parent systems. Single-parent households are not "pathological" or "incomplete" but rather are created by situational contingencies to which individuals must adapt (Bilge & Kaufman, 1983). In short, it is not the family form but rather the support system and means of socialization that have the greatest influence on children (Cutrona, 1996).

Various social support networks can alleviate the stress caused by divorce for both parents and children. A person's social support network includes those people with whom he or she interacts on a regular basis (e.g., friends, neighbors, coworkers, and family members). Members of the social network are potential sources of support. Some research indicates that individuals with helpful support networks characterize them as small and deriving from their spouse and close family relationships (McFarlane, Norman, Streiner, & Roy, 1984). Conversely, individuals describing the least helpful social support also reported significantly more stressful events in the past 5 years and significantly more childhood crises (McFarlane et al., 1984). In contrast, other researchers conclude that although a large social network does not ensure that the key functions of social relationships will be provided for the person in need, there is generally a significant positive relation between, for example, network size and perceived social support (Cutrona, 1996).

Defining Social Support

Social support has various definitions, but all are based on the assumption that people must rely on one another to meet certain basic needs. Some scholars believe "social support is the fulfillment by others of basic ongoing requirements for well being" (Cutrona, 1996, p. 3). Other researchers view social support as transactions occurring after the onset of adversity (Cutrona, 1996; Rook, 1984). According to Schwarzer and Leppin (1989, p. 1), social support has become an "omnibus term" referencing different aspects of social relationships based on such global conceptualizations as "social support is the resources provided by others" (Cohen & Syme, 1985, p. 4). To appreciate the various views of social support, it is important to track the conceptual development of this construct historically.

Two central papers by Cassel (1976) and Cobb (1976) motivated interdisciplinary research in social support. Cassel (1976) concluded the best way to prevent illness was for individuals to increase their social support rather than to simply decrease their stress. Similarly, Cobb (1976) viewed social support as a form of information leading to several potential outcomes, such as being (a) loved and valued, (b) a part of a reciprocal network, and (c) cared for by others. Furthermore, Cobb conceived of social support as a buffer that was used during crises rather than improving one's ability to cope day to day. Finally, results from a meta-analysis suggest that lack of social support is related to ill health. Furthermore, social support and health are more closely associated for women than for men (Schwarzer & Leppin, 1989).

Another source of interest in social support came from community psychologists. These researchers were interested in support services and agencies that could provide assistance to individuals who were unable to cope with various stressors. This research indicated that emotional support given by health care personnel improved recipients' health (Auerbach & Kilmann, 1977; Whitcher & Fisher, 1979). In addition, the political climate of the 1960s challenged individuals to contribute to the betterment of their community, state, and nation. Community psychologists tracked programs such as Head Start and the War on Poverty that were designed and implemented as family interventions at a national level to provide the necessary social support services that a growing segment of society needed.

A third orientation to social support was based on child development. Bowlby's (1969, 1979, 1980) investigations framed in attachment theory conceived of social support as a personality variable that began in early, intimate relationships. Viewing social support from this perspective "demonstrates its stability over time, its perception of being available for access by the individual and the relationships that serve as support providers" (Sarason, Sarason, & Pierce, 1990, p. 11). Regardless of the orientation, the need for theoretical perspectives to frame how social support affects health and adjustment is critical. What follows is a brief discussion of the various operationalizations and theories used to investigate and to account for social support.

Operationalizing Social Support

How researchers define social support is directly related to how it is measured. For example, when the quality of the relationship over time is emphasized, measuring social support through self-report is the primary method. Obviously, the individual who has experienced a specific relationship is best qualified to assess whether the relationship meets his or her needs over time and during a crisis. This method has been criticized based on the potential for bias from the support recipient (Procidano & Heller, 1983). It may be, for example, that the "introverted" personality or "depressed" mood may bias the self-report about a specific relationship. In other words, an aggressive and physically violent spouse may report his wife as frequently providing help-intended behaviors when in reality she has given no social support whatsoever because she has been living in a shelter out of state for the past 6 months.

Another way to get at perceived social support is to ask the target person or recipient of the support how likely a potential provider will actually give social support. The question becomes how accurately the target person will assess the potential provider's ability to meet specific needs in a crisis. For example, researchers may ask a group of recently divorced spouses how likely various family members would be to provide child care, grocery money, or personal time to problem solve. The availability of support resources when needed is known as *perceived social support* (Cutrona, 1996; Dunkel-Schetter & Bennett, 1990). Researchers looking at perceived social support argue about the importance of believing that others will provide help if necessary (Leppin & Schwarzer, 1990).

To avoid self-report bias, inherent subjectivity, and the potential for inaccuracy, other researchers have looked at actual transactions of social support, better known as *received social support* (Barrera & Ainlay, 1983). The target is still asked to report on various indexes of support, but the transactions are more objective in that respondents are asked to recall specific events, their frequency, and in what specific time frame the actions occurred. Barrera and Ainlay (1983) examined the structural components of social support and found four factors: (a) directive guidance (e.g., providing advice, giving feedback), (b) nondirective support (e.g., unconditional availability, expressions of intimacy), (c) positive social interaction (e.g., joking, engaging in diversionary actions), and (d) tangible assistance (e.g., providing shelter, sharing tasks). Clearly, not as much is left to the imagination as the events to recall are framed more concretely. Received social support as a measure, however, is not without its critics. The critical indictment is simply that the frequency of reported supportive behaviors does not account for the quality of supportive behaviors and actions. In short, many of these actions may be perceived as demeaning, inappropriate, and undesired (Turner, Frankel, & Levin, 1983; Wortman & Lehman, 1985). Dunkel-Schetter and Bennett (1990) provided a detailed account of the strengths and weaknesses of received social support.

More recently researchers have developed coding schemes to track what people say and do to show support and concern (Cutrona, Suhr, & MacFarlane, 1990). Typically, individuals (e.g., relational partners, married couples) are asked to participate in videotaped interactions designed to elicit supportive behaviors. After the interactions, relational partners fill out a variety of questionnaires tracking perceived social support, marital adjustment, and personality and depressive symptoms. Use of these observational techniques is designed to catalogue specific verbal and nonverbal behaviors that are indexes of caring, concern, and support (see, e.g., Cutrona & Suhr, 1992). An application for this research is to develop interventions designed to improve social support when individuals are experiencing depression, loneliness, and distress (Cutrona, 1996). Practitioners involved in marital and family therapy, divorce counselors, health care-providers could utilize research on designing effective support interventions. What follows is a discussion summarizing typical theoretical approaches that researchers may use to account for social support.

Theoretical Approaches

When social support is seen as a necessary and valued commodity, resource theory is the theoretical frame. A basic tenet of resource theory is that power is attributed to those who can provide the greatest amount of valued or desired commodities and resources to meet specific needs and desires. Divorcing spouses may look to close friends, colleagues, and extended family members for support because they are lonely, frightened about not being able to buy groceries, or angry about being unable to cope with day-to-day parenting problems. Clearly, the social support sought is an important resource for emotional and possibly physical well-being. Embattled spouses may perceive social support as a necessary and highly valued source of power when one spouse has more sympathetic and responsive friends, coworkers, and family members than the other.

Another way to think about social support is as a personality characteristic. That is, perceived social support could be considered a personality variable in that it remains relatively stable over time (Sarason, Pierce, & Sarason, 1990). Using Bowlby's (1980) work on attachment theory, early childhood experiences shape the development and quality of adult relationships. In other words, as infants, we become attached to specific individuals and our future relationships are based on those very early relational experiences and attachments. For example, siblings may observe parents as placing great value on large family gatherings to celebrate holidays, birthdays, and various rites of passage across the life span of the family. These children, having observed and experienced social support from an extended family, as young adults begin dating and eventually marry individuals from similarly large families.

Other scholars have looked at social support in the development of relational schemas (e.g., prescribed behavioral routines, sets of expectations, and scripted scenarios; Baldwin, 1992; Berscheid, 1994; Planalp, 1987). The assumption driving this perspective is that as we enter into intimate relationships, we have a series of expectations or rules about being a relational partner. For example, when someone assures a distraught mother, communicates concern, or offers to help with child care, the recipient frames these supportive acts not only as a means to ease the immediate situation, but also as contributing to the recipient's view of her relationship with the support provider. Another part of a relational schema is whether or not someone can be called on for support and is capable of providing the necessary support. Clearly, an important aspect of intimate relationships, specifically marriage, is the expectation of being emotionally supported. Scholars have suggested that the survival of intimate relationships is linked with partners being responsive in times of need (Baxter, 1986; Cutrona, 1996).

Although this is not an exhaustive discussion of how social support has been framed theoretically by scholars, important characteristics of intimate relationships are closely linked with social support (e.g., trust, interdependence, love, and commitment). When spouses decide to divorce, they reach out to various members of their social networks. Mutual friends of the divorcing couple are sometimes asked to take sides based on their relational history and loyalty. Furthermore, grandparents, aunts and uncles, and even cousins are called on to rally around the feuding spouses. Even coworkers and their spouses become support providers when the process of divorce becomes overwhelmingly ugly for embattled spouses.

Moreover, scholars have argued that in some ways marriage constrains whereas divorce liberates both men and women to cultivate new relationships (Fischer, 1982; Gerstel, 1988b). In other words, over time relational partners may put limits on specific friendships of their partner, child care may interfere with maintaining social ties, or career paths may necessitate cultivating work relationships over nurturing neighborhood and familial ties. A pending divorce forces spouses to reevaluate current and past relationships. In adjusting to divorce, spouses must ask themselves to whom they can turn or count on for help with child care, financial advice, emotional support, career choices, and household maintenance. To cope with divorce, both men and women are motivated to renew old friendships and relationships and cultivate new ones. The question really becomes whether men and women rely on different social support networks and what the implications and consequences are if there are differences. To address this question the following meta-analysis was conducted.

METHOD

Literature Search Method

A search was made of PSYCHLit and ERIC using the terms *social support* and *divorce*. From the articles obtained, references were identified that contributed to additional, relevant citations. In addition, reviews of the social support literature (Cutrona, 1996; Gerstel, 1988a; Goetting, 1981; Gottlieb, 1983, 1988; House, 1987; Johnston & Campbell, 1986; Leavy, 1983; McKenry & Price, 1991) contributed to identification of sources. To be included in this report, a manuscript had to meet the following criteria: (a) the manuscript had to contain quantitative information, (b) the manuscript had to explore the relation between gender and type of social support received, and (c) there had to be enough information to calculate an effect size. A complete bibliography of manuscripts excluded and the reasons for exclusion is available from the author.

Coding

Manuscripts were coded to identify the source of social support. Categories for source of support included family, lovers, friends, and social. The family category included parents, siblings, children, relatives, in-laws, and kin. The lover category refers to current romantic partners including cohabiting individuals, boyfriends, girlfriends, and fiances. Friends were those individuals who had an ongoing relationship with the divorcing spouse. Studies operationalized in this category were coworkers, friends, and acquaintances. The final category was social, which included all other sources of support such as clubs, social activities, community, network density, and network size. When multiple terms occurred within a category, effect sizes were averaged so that only one representation per category was entered. For example, in the family category, if there were separate estimates for parents, brothers, and sisters of the divorcing spouse, the effect size was averaged across the types so that one effect was entered for that specific source of support (family).

Statistical Analysis

The analysis took place in three stages: transformation, averaging, and heterogeneity testing. The variance-centered technique of meta-analysis developed by Hunter and Schmidt (1990) was employed in this review. Transformation involves the process of converting statistical information to a common metric. The metric employed in this review is the correlation coefficient. All studies had the statistical information transformed into a correlation coefficient using the procedures outlined by Hunter and Schmidt.

A second step, the averaging process, computes a weighted average using the sample size of the individual effect as the weight. Theoretically, estimates of the overall effect with larger sample sizes should be more accurate than estimates of the effect with smaller sample sizes. Weighting by sample size simply reflects the improved accuracy of estimation of the population effect that studies with larger sample sizes possess. For example, a study with a sample size of 1,000 generates a correlation coefficient with half of the sampling error that a study with 200 participants generates.

Finally, the third step, testing for homogeneity, examines whether the inconsistency in observed effects can be attributed to sampling error. A chi-square test compares the observed variability to the expected variability due to sampling error. A nonsignificant chi-square indicates that the sample of correlations can be considered homogenous. Homogeneity simply means that the average correlation coefficient is the best estimate of the population parameter and that no moderator variable probably exists. A significant chi-square indicates heterogeneity among the effects. Heterogeneity means that the average effect should be interpreted cautiously. Heterogeneity indicates the possible existence of moderator variables. An adequate solution to heterogeneity is a system that creates subgroups that are all homogenous within a group but heterogeneous between groups. For example, Allen, D'Allesio, and Bregezel (1995) found that an average effect of the relation between exposure to pornography and aggressive behavior was heterogeneous. However, reclassification of effects based on the content of the material (violent, nonviolent, nude pictures) generated a solution that was homogenous.

RESULTS

This chapter compares the various sources of social support (family, lovers, friends, social) during the process of divorce.

Family

The first type of social support looked at family as a source of social support. Women are more likely to use their families ($r = -.166, k = 26, N = 9,258$). An examination finds that the effects are heterogeneous, $\chi^2 (25) = 63.25, p < .05$. The average correlation indicates that women receive more social support from families than men.

However, the effects should be interpreted cautiously because the average effect is based on a sample of correlations that may have at least one moderator variable. This effect using R. Rosenthal's (1984) Binomial Effect Size Display (BESD) indicates that women receive 38% more social support then men. A subanalysis compared elements within the family as a potential source of moderator variable. Six studies examined the social support provided to parents by adult children. Women received even more social support than the average effect would indicate ($r = -.232, N = 2,345$). This effect was computed using a homogenous sample of correlations $\chi^2 (5) = 4.72, p > .05$. In other words, these findings demonstrate that women rely more heavily on their adult children (60%, using BESD) than men for social support during the divorce process.

The second moderator variable centered on studies that considered parents as a source of social support. The average effect ($r = -.162, k = 5, N = 1,911$) indicates that women receive more social support from their parents than men. The observed effect is based on a homogenous set of effects, $\chi^2 (4) = 7.21, p > .05$. This average effect reflects the general tendency of women to receive 38% more social support from their families than men.

Lovers

The second category involves the social support that men and women receive from their romantic partners and lovers. The two studies in this category generate a positive correlation ($r = .101, N = 1,473$), based on a homogenous set of effects ($t = 1.37, p > .05$). In contrast to the family findings, men receive 22% more social support from their romantic partners and lovers than women.

Friends

This category involves friends, coworkers, and acquaintances when comparing spouses' social support during divorce. Women received more social support from friends than men ($r = -.174, k = 13, N = 3,177$). An examination of the distribution of effects finds heterogeneity across the sample, χ^2 $(12) = 35.48, p < .05$. In contrast to the findings for lovers, women received 40% more social support from their friends than men. An analysis was made excluding coworkers and acquaintances and using only studies that included friends. Across the six studies the average effect increased ($r = -.295, N = 2,093$) and was homogenous, $\chi^2 (5) = 6.25, p > .05$. Friends (excluding coworkers and acquaintances) provided more social support (85%) to women than men.

Social

This category includes clubs, social activities, community, social participation, network density, and network size. Men received more social support from this source than women did ($r = .083, k = 6, N = 2,467$) based on a homogenous set of effects, $\chi^2 (5) = 1.07, p > .05$. In other words, men are receiving 17% more social support from their social networks than women based on the BESD.

DISCUSSION

Results are easily summarized in that women received more social support from their families and friends, whereas men received more support from lovers and social networks. Of great importance to the following discussion are two well-documented patterns. First, women are more likely than men to obtain custody of the children. Second, women are far more likely than men to experience reductions in income (Gerstel, 1988a). These two patterns create different experiences that result in varying kinds of opportunities for social ties and relationships for men and women. What follows are a series of explanations regarding these findings. The results of this meta-analysis indicate relations but do not explain why they exist. This discussion provides an interpretation of those relations as well as the theoretical and practical implications.

Findings indicate that women tend to rely more on maintaining kinship ties than men. These results are consistent with Gerstel's (1988a) findings that men are more likely than women to diminish their reliance on kin over time. Because more women than men are the custodial parent, it may be necessary to rely on close relatives to help with child care, babysitting, and home maintenance chores. It may also be that the previous marriage prevented close kinship ties and that after the divorce, women are more comfortable reaching out to their immediate family members for support. In other words, rather than continuously fight about time spent with the in-laws, because of the divorce, it seems only natural to renew those familial relationships. It could also be that women are socialized to value and maintain links to their families. Research has demonstrated that wives rather than husbands call, write, visit, and keep in touch with their kin (O'Donnell, 1985; C. Rosenthal, 1985). On the basis of such findings, it makes sense that divorced women would look to their families for social support. On the other hand, it may be due to financial constraints: Because women may not have the luxury of joining a health club or playing in a tennis or golf league, they may be forced to stay at home rather than to form new social acquaintances and networks.

To further account for the gender differences in social support, it may be that men look more to links outside their immediate families because divorce to them connotes failure. Men may be embarrassed and view their failure at marriage as disconfirmation of their self-worth. Perhaps men tend to shut down communicatively and refuse to discuss their relational failure with their immediate family. Moreover, men may seek support outside the family by spending more time at the club, renewing old acquaintances socially, playing poker, and so on. By contrast, women may want to analyze and reanalyze what went wrong relationally and turn inward to their families and close friends. Finally, women may wish to talk about their relational failures and might feel more comfortable sorting out the details with their families.

Along the same line, men may wish to receive social support but not talk about their divorce—the reasons, the trauma, and their loss of face. Romantic partners and newly formed social networks would be ideal providers of support from this vantage point. This is not to say that women do not receive support from lovers and romantic partners, but rather this is a relative assessment to men. Men may also receive support from their families and adult children as well as close friends. Again, this is a relative comparison and does not assess the importance of social support sources.

Furthermore, this chapter does not indicate the need for social support but merely the relative source of social support. It may be the case that men need more social support from their families and adult children and women may need social support from their lovers and romantic partners. The point here is that regardless of the specific source of social support, both men and women may need to expand their total social support networks to enable their adjustment to the changed relational status and to move on with their lives. When viewing social support as a resource, there may be a need to upgrade or diversify social support. Men and women may need to extend their social support networks to heal as a future spouse, parent, and community member.

Social support programs and interventions are designed and implemented by professionals in social work, community mental health, public health, and community psychology. These interventions vary in scale, complexity, specification of process, correspondence to theory or research findings, and clarity of objectives (Vaux, 1988). Interventions and support groups vary from focused group orientation procedures to highly personalized, counseling sessions where self-disclosure and personal risk taking are highlighted (Cutrona, 1996; Pearson, 1990).

The literature on social support, however, makes it clear that the availability and utilization of support must be assessed when working with divorcing families (Cutrona, 1996; Pearson, 1990; Vaux, 1988). There are several reasons for this. First, it is clear that social support can have the effect of lessening some of the stressors associated with divorce. The availability of a relative who can provide child care to a custodial mother may give her the freedom to work more hours or to socialize in some other form of leisure activity (Gerstel, 1988b; Goetting, 1981). This freedom from child care may promote the mother's psychological adjustment and sense of well-being, which in turn might help her be a better parent. In short, clinicians involved in supporting families through the process of divorce should actively encourage family members to expand rather than constrict their networks of available support and advise them to take advantage of a variety of support systems. Divorcing spouses need to be shown that the utilization of support represents good coping behavior (Twaite, Silitsky, & Luchow, 1998).

Future meta-analyses might look at the diversity of sources of social support and the relationship to satisfactory adjustment. Reliance on specific sources of social support may not indicate better adjustment. We know that open family systems encourage interaction and information exchange with those outside the system, whereas closed family systems constrain and highly restrict outside interaction (Galvin & Brommel, 1995). Divorce may indicate more open or closed relational systems. Husbands or wives may need to close down their support systems, adjust to the finality of divorce, then open themselves up relationally, or just the opposite. Additional meta-analyses could provide insight into the role of social support in the development of new relationships, the quality and renewal of old relationships, and adjustment patterns of divorcing spouses over time. Clearly, the challenge is ours.

REFERENCES

References marked with an asterisk indicate studies included in the meta-analysis.

*Albrecht, S. (1980). Reactions and adjustment to divorce: Differences in the experiences of males and females. *Family Relations, 29,* 59–68.

Allen, M., D'Allesio, D., & Bregezel, K. (1995). A meta-analysis summarizing the effects of pornography II: Aggression after exposure. *Human Communication Research, 22,* 258–283.

Auerbach, S. M., & Kilmann, P. R. (1977). Crisis intervention: A review of outcome research. *Psychological Bulletin, 84,* 1189–1217.

*Baker, M. (1984). Women helping women: The transition from separation to divorce. *Conciliation Courts Review, 22,* 53–63.

Baldwin, M. W. (1992). Relational schemas and the processing of social information. *Psychological Bulletin, 112,* 461–484.

Barrera, M., & Ainlay, S. L. (1983). The structure of social support: A conceptual and empirical analysis. *Journal of Community Psychology, 11,* 133–143.

Baxter, L. A. (1986). Gender differences in the heterosexual relationship rules embedded in breakup accounts. *Journal of Social and Personal Relationships, 3,* 289–306.

Berscheid, E. (1994). Interpersonal relationships. *Annual Review of Psychology, 45,* 79–129.

Bilge, B., & Kaufman, G. (1983). Children of divorce and one-parent families: Cross-cultural perspectives. *Family Relations, 32,* 59–71.

Bowlby, J. (1969). *Attachment and loss: Vol. 1. Attachment.* New York: Basic Books.

Bowlby, J. (1979). The making and breaking of affectional bonds. *British Journal of Psychiatry, 130,* 201–210.

Bowlby, J. (1980). *Attachment and loss: Vol. 3. Loss: Sadness and depression.* New York: Basic Books.

*Caldwel, R., & Bloom, B. (1982). Social supports: Its structure and impact on marital disruption. *American Journal of Community Psychology, 10,* 647–667.

*Cargan, L., & Whitehurst, R. (1990). Adjustment differences in the divorced and the redivorced. *Journal of Divorce and Remarriage, 14,* 49–78.

Cassel, J. (1976). The contribution of social environment in host resistance. *American Journal of Epidemiology, 104,* 107–123.

*Chiriboga, D., Coho, A., Stein, J., & Roberts, J. (1979). Divorce, stress and the social supports: A study in helpseeking behavior. *Journal of Divorce, 13,* 75–94.

*Clark-Stewart, A., & Bailey, B. (1989). Adjusting to divorce: Why do men have it easier? *Journal of Divorce, 13,* 75–94.

Cobb, S. (1976). Social support as a moderator of life stress. *Psychosomatic Medicine, 38,* 300–314.

Cohen, S., & Syme, S. L. (1985). Issues in the study and application of social support. In S. Cohen & S. L. Syme (Eds.), *Social support and health* (pp. 3–22). New York: Academic.

Cutrona, C. E. (1996). *Social support in couples.* Thousand Oaks, CA: Sage.

Cutrona, C. E., & Suhr, J. A. (1992). Controllability of stressful events and satisfaction with spouse support behaviors. *Communication Research, 19,* 154–176.

Cutrona, C. E., Suhr, J. A., & MacFarlane, R. (1990). Interpersonal transactions and the psychological sense of support. In S. Duck & R. Silver (Eds.), *Personal relationships and social support* (pp. 30–45). London: Sage.

Dunkel-Schetter, C., & Bennett, T. (1990). Differentiating the cognitive and behavioral aspects of social support. In B. Sarason, I. Sarason, & G. Pierce (Eds.), *Social support: An interactional view* (pp. 267–296). New York: Wiley.

Fischer, C. (1982). *To dwell among friends*. Chicago: University of Chicago Press.

Galvin, K. M., & Brommel, B. J. (1995). *Family communication: Cohesion and change* (4th ed.). New York: HarperCollins.

Gerstel, N. (1988a). Divorce and kin ties: The importance of gender. *Journal of Marriage and the Family, 50*, 209–219.

Gerstel, N. (1988b). Divorce, gender, and social integration. *Gender & Society, 2*, 343–367.

*Gerstel, N., Riessman, C., & Rosenfield, S. (1985). Explaining the symptomatology of separated and divorced women and men: The role of material conditions and social networks. *Social Forces, 64*, 84–101.

Goetting, A. (1981). Divorce outcome research. *Journal of Family Issues, 2*, 350–378.

Gottlieb, B. H. (1983). Social support as a focus for integrative research in psychology. *American Psychologist, 38*, 278–287.

Gottlieb, B. H. (Ed.). (1988). *Marshaling social support: Formats, processes and effects*. Newbury Park, CA: Sage.

*Hammond, R., & Muller, G. (1992). The late-life divorced: Another look. *Journal of Divorce and Remarriage, 17*, 135–150.

House, J. S. (1987). Social support and social structure. *Sociological Forum 2*, 135–146.

Hunter, J. E., & Schmidt, F. L. (1990). *Methods of meta-analysis: Correcting error and bias in research findings*. Newbury Park, CA: Sage.

Johnston, J. R., & Campbell, L. E. (1986). Tribal warfare: The involvement of extended kin and significant others in custody and access disputes. *Conciliation Courts Review, 24*, 1–16.

*Kitson, G., & Holmes, W. (1992). *Portrait of divorce: Adjustment to marital breakdown*. New York: Guilford.

Kitson, G. C., & Raschke, H. J. (1981). Divorce research: What we know; what we need to know. *Journal of Divorce, 4*(3), 1–37.

*Kurdek, L., & Bisk, D. (1983). Dimensions and correlates of mothers' divorce experiences. *Journal of Divorce, 6*, 1–24.

Leavy, R. L. (1983). Social support and psychological disorder: A review. *Journal of Community Psychology, 11*, 3–21.

Leppin, A., & Schwarzer, R. (1990). Social support and physical health: An updated meta-analysis. In J. Weinman & S. Maes (Eds.), *Theoretical and applied aspects of health psychology* (pp. 185–202). London: Harwood.

McFarlane, A. H., Norman, G. R., Streiner, D. L., & Roy, R. G. (1984). Characteristics and correlates of effective and ineffective social supports. *Journal of Psychosomatic Research, 28*, 501–510.

McKenry, P. C., & Price, S. J. (1991). Alternatives for support: Life after divorce—A literature review. *Journal of Divorce & Remarriage, 15*(3–4) 1–19.

Holt, M. (1999, February 28). Divorce reform: States search for ways to strengthen marriage. *Milwaukee Journal Sentinel*, pp. L-1, 4.

Murdock, G. P. (1950). Family stability in non-European cultures. *Annals of the American Academy of Political and Social Science, 272*, 195–201.

O'Donnell, L. (1985). *The unheralded majority*. Lexington, MA: Lexington.

Pearson, R. E. (1990). *Counseling and social support: Perspectives and practice*. Beverly Hills, CA: Sage.

*Pett, M. (1982). Predictors of satisfactory social adjustment of divorced single parents. *Journal of Divorce, 5*, 1–17.

Planalp, S. (1987). Interplay between relational knowledge and events. In R. Burnett, P. McGhee, & D. D. Clarke (Eds.), *Accounting for relationships: Explanations, representation and knowledge* (pp. 175–191). New York: Methuen.

Procidano, M., & Heller, K. (1983). Measures of perceived social support from friends and family. *American Journal of Community Psychology, 11,* 1–24.

*Raschke, H. (1977). The role of social participation in postseparation and post divorce adjustment. *Journal of Divorce, 1,* 129–140.

Rook, K. S. (1984). Promoting social bonding: Strategies for helping the lonely and socially isolated. *American Psychologist, 39,* 1389–1407.

Rosenthal, C. (1985). Kinkeeping in the familial division of labor. *Journal of Marriage and the Family, 47,* 965–974.

Rosenthal, R. (1984). *Meta-analytic procedures for social research.* Beverly Hills, CA: Sage.

Sarason, B., Pierce, G., & Sarason, I. (1990). Social support: The sense of acceptance and role of relationships. In B. Sarason, I. Sarason, & G. Pierce (Eds.), *Social support: An interactional view* (pp. 97–128). New York: Wiley.

Sarason, B., Sarason, I., & Pierce, G. (Eds.). (1990). *Social support: An interactional view.* New York: Wiley.

Satir, V. (1972). *Peoplemaking.* Palo Alto, CA: Science & Behavior Books.

Schauble, P., & Hill, C. (1976). A laboratory approach to treatment in marriage counseling: Training in communication skills. *Family Coordinator, 25,* 277–284.

Schwarzer, R., & Leppin, A. (1989). Social support and health: A meta-analysis. *Psychology & Health, 3,* 1–15.

Spanier, G. B., & Casto, R. (1979). Adjustment to separation and divorce: An analysis of 50 cast studies. *Journal of Divorce, 2,* 241–253.

*Spanier, G., & Hanson, S. (1982). The role of extended kin in the adjustment to marital separation. *Journal of Divorce, 5,* 33–48.

*Spanier, G., & Lachman, M. (1980). Factors associated with adjustment to marital separation. *Sociological Focus, 13,* 369–381.

*Spicer, J., & Hampe, G. (1975). Kinship interaction after divorce. *Journal of Marriage and the Family, 37,* 113–119.

Stinson, K. (1991). *Adolescents, family and friends.* New York: Praeger.

Thiessen, J. D., Avery, A. W., & Joanning, H. (1981). Facilitating postdivorce adjustment among women: A communication skills training approach. *Journal of Divorce, 4*(2), 35–44.

Turner, R. J., Frankel, B. G., & Levin, D. M. (1983). Social support: Conceptualization, measurement, and implications for mental health. In J. R. Greenley (Ed.), *Research in community and mental health* (pp. 67–111). Greenwich, CT: JAI.

Twaite, J. A., Silitsky, D., & Luchow, A. K. (1998). *Children of divorce.* Northvale, NJ: Aronson.

Vaux, A. (1988). *Social support, theory, research, and intervention.* New York: Praeger.

Whitcher, S. J., & Fisher, J. D. (1979). Multidimensional reaction to therapeutic touch in a hospital setting. *Journal of Personality and Social Psychology, 36,* 87–96.

Wood, J. (1999). *Relational communication: Continuity and change in personal relationships* (2nd ed.). Belmont, CA: Wadsworth.

Wortman, C. B., & Lehman, D. R. (1985). Reactions to victims of life crises: Support attempts that fail. In I. G. Sarason & B. R. Sarason (Eds.), *Social support: Theory, research and applications* (pp. 463–489). The Hague, The Netherlands: Martinus Nijhoff.

*Wright, C., & Maxwell, J. (1991). Social support during adjustment to later-life divorce: How adult children help parents. *Journal of Divorce and Remarriage, 15,* 21–48.

15

Couples Negotiating Safer Sex Behaviors: A Meta-Analysis of the Impact of Conversation and Gender

Mike Allen, Tara M. Emmers-Sommer, and Tara L. Crowell

In 1981, AIDS was first diagnosed in the United States. Since then, more than 250,000 Americans have died of AIDS and by the year 2000 it was estimated that 40 million people worldwide would be diagnosed as HIV positive [CDC], 1994. HIV represents a potentially fatal health risk for every sexually active person in the world.[1] Fortunately, until a cure or vaccine is found, an individual's risk of HIV infection due to sexual transmission can be greatly reduced through the use of condoms. Despite the effectiveness of consistent and careful condom use, many sexually active Americans are still engaging in unprotected sexual activities. Bruce, Shrum, Trefethen, and Slovik (1990) indicated that 97% of young adults are knowledgeable about HIV and how to curtail transmission but many persons still engage in risky sexual behaviors.

---

[1]The two other principle methods of transmission are blood transfusions and needle sharing among intravenous drug users.

The fundamental concern for HIV prevention via sexual transmission is getting partners to discuss methods of risk reduction. Barriers to a couple's discussion of issues relating to reducing HIV infection risk create some challenges. These problems include the perception that insisting on using a condom constitutes a form of accusation against the partner concerning sexual infidelity or other behavior that would put the partner at risk. Consider that for most married couples, the discussion would seem out of place unless there was a known infection or risk by one of the partners. Married couples usually assume monogamy, or at least that the partner is not engaging in behavior that puts the other person at risk. Females have the possibility in the context of a heterosexual relationship of arguing that a condom provides a safe alternative to pregnancy prevention without the health risks of other methods. However, homosexuals, as well as heterosexual men, do not necessarily have that same option in providing a reason for a change in sexual behavior when involved in a committed relationship. A part of the concern about relying on monogamy is that persons may and do conceal either HIV seropositivity or participation in risky behaviors (either currently or in the recent past). Stebleton and Rothenberger (1993) found that 36% of men and 21% of women at a Midwestern university reported being sexually unfaithful to their partner, that 75% of men and 33% of women "never did ask" partners about past sexual history, and that men admitted they lied to sexual partners more often than women. Cochran and May (1990) reported that both men and women have lied to a partner to obtain sex and frequently reported that they would actively or passively deceive a dating partner. The use or insistence on the use of a condom may constitute an admission of previous undesirable behavior or an unspoken accusation against the other person.

In response, several countries and states have considered enacting laws that require disclosure to domestic partners of HIV test results. In Texas, for example, it is against the law for an HIV-infected person to purposely have sex with others to spread the disease. The problem with unprotected sex is that one person literally trying to kill the other can now use sex as a weapon. Even if sex is not intended as a weapon, one domestic partner's behavior may have permanent consequences for the other partner. The need for protection and trust goes beyond the emotional part of a relationship and impinges on physical safety. The need for communication between the couple becomes not just a matter of convenience but a matter of safety.

The willingness to ask questions about prior sexual behavior is difficult given taboos most people have about discussing prior sexual behavior with a potential partner. Baxter and Wilmot (1985) found that past relationships, other present relationships, sexual habits, and sexual experiences are often considered taboo topics in relational development. Whether the onset of HIV infection can significantly alter that dynamic in a relationship remains unclear (particularly for heterosexuals). The barrier means that one source of information (assuming that a member of a dyad would be honest or that they have even been tested and know their HIV status) is unavailable to a partner. However, the failure to consider issues of sexuality potentially put a person's health at risk. The result is a sense of privacy or a desire of not wanting to know about the prior sexual history of the other person. The current social expectations about conversation make such discussions for most couples inappropriate, awkward, and difficult to conduct. The notion that one should not "kiss and tell" means that people may not want to reveal specific or full information. The couple may tacitly agree therefore not to discuss past relationships, an unspoken relational conversational rule reinforced through social practice.

The problem of even attempting to discuss the subject requires an element of timing. To bring up the topic too soon in a conversation, date, or relationship may assume or promote the possibility of a sexual interaction when none is intended or the status of a relationship is still ambiguous. To discuss the topic may create an assumption by one partner that sexual relations will occur, which is not shared by the other member of the dyad. Merely including the topic in a discussion with someone generates a topic, the introduction of which may be or may seem to be inappropriate. The problem focuses on dealing with the nature of timing and confidence as well as dealing with the impact that a disclosure may have on the emerging relationship. The literature on date rape indicates that a primary consideration is a misperception between males and females about the sexual implications of any conversation (Abbey, 1987). A female introducing the topic of safer sex risks misinterpretation, because her partner may assume an interest in sexual interaction when none is intended.

Currently, little information exists about how couples deal with this issue. In many situations couples may not handle this issue and ignore the existence of safer sex issues in personal relationships and put themselves at risk. People may not talk about safe sex issues because they do not believe themselves at risk. Adelman (1991, 1992) examined how couples create conversations and games to handle issues of safe sexual practices. The couple about to engage in sex must find a method of introducing the practice of safer sexual conduct without offending the other person or implicitly violating an assumption that either person shares about the conduct of the relationship. The goal of educational intervention is to generate a routine behavior that individuals can adopt that permits the introduction of the safe sex topic and the adoption of safe sex practices. The embarrassment and difficulty of introducing the topic creates a difficult situation when designing an educational program or intervention intended to promote discussion between partners about this issue.

One problem of bringing up the topic or insisting on the use of a condom is that it can become either an admission or an accusation. For the person insisting on the use of a condom, the admission may constitute a self-disclosure of potential risk behavior ("I have been promiscuous") that may infect the other person. Within the context of a relationship, providing information about previous or other ongoing relationships that the person would prefer not to discuss for strategic reasons can be problematic. To insist on the use of a condom may function as an accusation about the beliefs or the behaviors of the other person ("I don't believe you are faithful"). The other person is implicitly accused of engaging in risk behaviors that require some preventive measure. In either circumstance, the net result of including a discussion about using a condom may bring a potentially serious set of issues to the relationship. Ignoring the topic may place a higher value on the relationship as opposed to emphasizing health concerns. Metts and Fitzpatrick (1992) argued that condom use is discontinued after the partners develop relational commitment and trust. Then, if the partner wants to discuss the issue of condom use, the underlying message that "I do not trust you" gets communicated. The problem of voicing an implicit accusation of mistrust may be the reduced discussion and subsequent use of condoms. The lack of using a condom by a couple then becomes a sign of trust, but at the same time it is a potential increase in risk.

In addition to relational issues, contextual or situational features may influence the discussion of sexual practices between partners. Within the context of places or arenas of discussion like the family or the school, the discussion of sexual practices may create a series of potential problems. Schools typically are not going to encourage adolescents to develop a script about handling sexual interactions. Many parents, as well as schools, do not want to be viewed as encouraging sexual interaction. Many schools fear a negative reaction from the public more than the potential for adolescents' infection with HIV. As of 1994, 16 states still did not require HIV and AIDS education programs. In addition, many states do not have mandates on AIDS instruction, and therefore, school districts have "local option" in choosing what to teach (including nothing) about HIV and AIDS. The failure of families, schools, and churches to provide a basis for discussion has contributed to the current crisis. Homosexual practices are simply not a part of the discussion. Unks (1996) posited that schools and media do not focus on the merits of teaching about a fatal disease but on the worthiness and morality of the homosexual "lifestyle." He pointed out that

> It is illogical to expect young people to change behavior on information alone, even if the information included knowledge of their own HIV status. … Comprehensive HIV prevention should include information, exploration of values and attitudes, skill building, and access to services, including condom availability. (Unks, 1996, p.)

Metts and Fitzpatrick (1992) claimed that many engage in the risky business of "know your partner" as a means to reduce risk. However, the problem is that the necessary conversation that must take place to know one's partner is not likely to occur.

Another factor is drug and alcohol use associated with sexual interaction. The use of drugs or alcohol may mean that persons are not in full control of their thoughts and are not able to fulfill an intended and planned sequence of behavior. The result is that well-intentioned behavior may be forgotten or excused on the basis of some type of drug use. Intravenous drug use, as well as increased number of sexual partners, is associated with HIV infection. The impact of using drugs or alcohol is to diminish the use of preventive HIV measures, with the need for prevention being highest for persons in these particular circumstances. The paradox created is that the persons most in need of behavioral change are those persons most resistant to the educational efforts. In addition, the circumstances under which the needed behavior occurs can be conditions that often are the most difficult in which to implement that particular change. This creates an enormous challenge for those involved in education who are trying to create a behavioral routine for the conditions least likely to permit their implementation.

A critical feature of any attempt at developing safer behavioral practices is generating patterns of behavior that minimize risk. For the sexually active individual, the requirement is a pattern of sexual practices that include AIDS risk-reduction techniques. The current pattern of sexual interaction scripts is often predicated on a lack of planning and foresight because sexual encounters are often not viewed as something a person should plan. The need to feel the "spontaneity" of the event creates a barrier to successful planning that would generate minimal-risk sexual behaviors. The issue is that many times an individual may feel a desire not to have a conversational plan or script developed because such a plan means confronting one's sexual desires and behaviors. The first step in any educational intervention is literally convincing a person that the development of a script does not involve the development of some type of antisocial or undesirable practice.

Compliance-gaining research focuses on how communication strategies are used to accomplish behavioral outcomes and examines how communication strategies can be used to create the motivation to engage in a behavior. In this case, the goal is for one member of the dyad to engage in a particular behavior. The problem is whether these activities are viewed as one person gaining compliance or whether the actions are considered negotiated behaviors between two individuals. Viewing this as a "negotiated" behavior indicates that each person will generate reasons for a particular action. In a negotiation there exists the possibility for compromise or alternatives. In compliance gaining, the goal is a behavior that is evaluated as a desirable or necessary outcome to judge the effectiveness of the message. Individuals must be convinced that the use of a condom is not simply a behavior that is negotiated, but a behavior that should be viewed as something that is nonnegotiable. Thus, educators need to help people view this interaction as not only important, but essential, in creating effective interactions that lead to safer sex practices.

Communication research demonstrates that the initial view of an interaction may be changed as a result of ongoing communication. This is particularly true for situations involving efforts at persuasion or compliance gaining. For some efforts, the goal of a communicator may be to create a change in perceptions to increase the effectiveness of the outcome. The question related to sexual behavior is the development of a communication script or pattern that will increase the probability of condom use.

Little work has examined about the perceptual framework of sexual interaction to illustrate whether each member of the dyad feels as though the interaction uses negotiation or compliance gaining. Insistence on a particular sexual act or form of sexual act represents something that can create real problems for a relationship, depending on the view that each member has of the dynamics of that relationship. The need for one member of the dyad to insist on a particular method of sexual behavior creates some potentially antagonistic dynamics in a developing relationship. Some important considerations for framing the issues of safe sexual practices warrant investigation.

Gender remains an important consideration in sexual issues. Many define the role of women in a sexual encounter as being responsible for pregnancy prevention, and the role of women typically involves the regulation and conduct of sexual behavior that the man accepts or rejects. One feature of interest is the degree to which both men and women accept or reject responsibility for the use of a condom. Unlike pregnancy, both partners are at risk from the other and this represents a joint responsibility that has implications for both individuals. The question is to what degree both members of a heterosexual dyad accept responsibility for practicing safer sexual behaviors.

METHODS

Literature Search

This project is part of a long-term series of meta-analyses dealing with the issues surrounding AIDS education and prevention (Allen & Emmers-Sommer, 1998). The current database contains more than 2,200 citations of the behavioral literature dealing with AIDS education and prevention. A copy of the complete bibliography as well a coding information is available from the first author. The issues involve considerable attempts across the globe to encourage the reduction of risk behaviors in a variety of contexts. Three different persons examined the titles of the articles in the database and determined the suitability for this analysis. No mere bibliography or reference accumulation, even with more than 2,200 references, can begin to tap the reservoir of potential manuscripts that exist. Currently, the unowned material listed in the bibliography will, when obtained, add at least another 2,500 manuscripts to this effort. The immense size of this literature combined with the numerous indexes that must be searched and number of manuscripts not contained in any index means that any literature search will always be inefficient. The number of manuscripts in foreign journals and those published in a language other than English presents a great challenge when assembling this database. Both interlibrary loan at the international level or attempts to purchase manuscripts, as well as problems in generating an accurate translation of the material, represent unusual and lengthy delays for this project.

To be included in the current analysis an investigation had to contain quantitative information dealing with couples' negotiation of safer sex behaviors. The data had to deal with the willingness of a member of a dyad considering sexual intercourse to address the issues of safer sex, including: (a) use of a condom, (b) past sexual practices, (c) past drug use, or (d) issues relating to a discussion of the serious risk of HIV infection. The critical focus had to concern some aspect of discussing the issues or the failure to discuss the issue of safe sex or HIV with the potential sexual partner. The goal of this meta-analysis is to examine the content of interpersonal communications on safe sex practices. Some manuscripts, although meeting the content standards, could not be used due to deficient or incomplete statistical reporting that did not permit the recovery of an effect size (Eldridge et al., 1997; Engelbert, Flora, & Nass, 1995; Freimuth, Hammond, Edgar, McDonald, & Fink, 1992; Gordon & Carey, 1996; Hobfall, Jackson, Lavin, Britton, & Shepherd, 1993; Kalichman, Rompa, & Coley, 1997; Malow & Ireland, 1996; Walter et al., 1993a; Zimmerman & Olson, 1994) dealing

TABLE 15.1

List of Studies and Effects in the Meta-Analysis

Author	Effect	Sample Size	Variable
Abraham	.050	351	Gender
Basen-Engquist	−.070	60	Conversation
Bryan	.185	198	Conversation
Chen	.126	202	Conversation
Cline	−.201	588	Gender
Cohen	−.248	509	Gender
Deren	.282	106	Conversation
DiClemente	.357	112	Conversation
Edgar	−.100	75	Gender
	−.071	204	Gender
F. Fisher	.125	290	Conversation
W. Fisher	.274	39	Conversation
	.421	62	Conversation
	.316	50	Conversation
	.375	33	Conversation
Goldman	−.288	602	Gender
Grimley	−.206	95	Gender
	.206	95	Conversation
Helweg	.000	239	Gender
Herold	.105	169	Gender
Johnson	.388	108	Conversation
Kasen	−.190	274	Gender
Kinnick	−.030	834	Gender
Knaus	−.191	184	Gender
Magura	.348	211	Conversation
Malow (1993)	.394	136	Conversation
Malow (1994)	.363	235	Conversation
Marín	.420	594	Conversation
Overby	.302	72	Conversation
Reel	−.062	261	Gender
Rye	.249	74	Conversation
Sacco	−.216	229	Gender
	−.195	465	Gender
Sheer	.150	290	Conversation
Shoop	.322	89	Conversation
Valdiserri	.050	759	Conversation
Waldron	.210	120	Conversation
Walter (1993)	.311	531	Gender

Walter (1994)	−.273	926	Gender
Wilson	−.110	971	Conversation
Wulfert	.000	403	Conversation
Yesmont	−.254	249	Gender
	.180	177	Conversation
	.244	25	Conversation

Note. For gender, a negative correlation indicates the women are more likely to discuss safer sex issues.

with other forms of interaction (patient–doctor; Vanderford, Smith, & Harris, 1992), dealing with determining reactions to existing messages or sequencing of behaviors (Edgar & Fitzpatrick, 1993; Sheer, 1995), not considering the conversation's implications (e.g., Maticka-Tyndale, 1991; Neuwirth & Dunwoody, 1989; Weisse, Turbiasz, & Whitney, 1995; Winett et al., 1992), or using qualitative methods (Adelman, 1991, 1992; Wight, 1994; Willig, 1994). No study was excluded on the basis of sexual preference; however, although there are an enormous number of studies examining homosexual (particularly males') safer sex practices, no study focused on conversational issues. Therefore, the entire database consists of studies that only included heterosexual participants.

Statistical Analysis

The statistical analysis was conducted using a variance-centered form of meta-analysis developed by Hunter and Schmidt (1990). This analysis assembles the available data, and then transforms the observed effects into a common metric (in this case r). The transformed data are then averaged to establish an overall effect. Then, the overall effect is subjected to some examination of the variability.

RESULTS

Conversation

The average effect across 26 studies demonstrates that persons talking about condoms prior to sex are more likely $(r = .156, N = 5,511,$ variance $= .0107)$ than nontalkers to use condoms. The effect was heterogeneous, $\chi^2(25, N = 5,511) = 192.23, p < .05,$ indicating the possible existence of a moderator variable. The size of the effect indicates that persons talking about HIV infection and condom use with a potential sexual partner are more likely to use condoms than nontalking couples. This confirms the argument that there exists a need to develop a behavioral script about the discussion of condoms as part of the sexual act that promotes the use of condoms. The average correlation indicates, using the Binomial Effect Size Display, a 38% increase in the probability of condom usage if such a conversation occurs. The results suggest that educational intervention should focus on developing conversational scripts addressing safe sex practices.

Gender

There were 18 studies comparing the willingness of men and women to engage in safer sexual communication. The average effect demonstrates that women are more likely ($r = -.124, N = 6,785$, variance $= .0103$) than men to engage in this behavior. The effect was heterogeneous, $\chi^2(17, N = 6,785) = 197.01, p < .05$, indicating the possible existence of a moderator variable. Nine of the 10 effects were negative, indicating that the effect is fairly consistent in favoring women. The moderator variable may distinguish between larger and smaller effects rather than differentiating on the basis of direction of the effect, as 9 of the 10 studies favored female conversation. The average effect indicates that educational interventions are probably more likely to be effective with females and efforts should consider the relative failure of males to engage or initiate such conversations.

CONCLUSIONS

The findings provide an important backdrop for understanding why couples choose to discuss and not discuss various issues within a relationship. The key to any educational effort designed to improve the willingness of couples to engage in open discussions prior to sexual behavior requires an understanding of the factors both inhibiting and promoting a discussion of HIV infection and transmission. Any method attempting to decrease the willingness of persons to engage in risky behaviors must assess increased conversations between partners as one possibility. A meta-analysis of educational interventions (Soglolow et al., 1998) indicates that safe sex does increase after educational efforts.

A problem remains when dealing with moral and social stigmas regarding taboo topics. The problem with discussion of sexual behavior or the conditions of sexual behavior is that sexual talk carries with it assumptions about the nature of the relationship that must exist prior to the discussion. No amount of educational effort is likely to change the basic set of assumptions about the nature of relationships generated by social mores. The educational efforts must work within those cultural assumptions by capitalizing on the values held by the individuals that are reflected in their behavioral practices. The notion of sensitivity and diversity in an educational intervention creates the need for assessment to find the best means of increasing the effectiveness of the educational program.

Another factor is that women are more likely to want to discuss sexual issues than men. This indicates that the educational efforts and information issues may be more effective among women than men. The reason may be social mores in the United States that require the female to assume more responsibility for the conduct of sexual relationships. Such behavior may not be the same for other cultures or situations in which the conduct of sexual behavior is not a responsibility of the female. Conversely, in societies in which there is a greater emphasis on female control, any educational efforts should target females. Additional research needs to link HIV and AIDS risk-reduction behaviors to assumptions about sexual roles. The results do not necessarily indicate an increase in safer sex behavior, however, because even if a woman may be more willing to initiate the behavior, her male partner may resist or refuse to comply. Thus, one member of the dyad is seeking compliance from the other member. The issue of sexual coercion becomes relevant because the discussion occurs within the context of essentially an admission by the woman that sex is acceptable under certain conditions. The question is what stance society would have regarding a woman saying no to sex without a condom under conditions of physical or psychological coercion.

One potential research variable for future consideration involves increasing the level of individual assertiveness, particularly on sexual issues. Assertive individuals are able to speak their minds and they act in their own best interests without denying or infringing on the rights of others. From an interactionist perspective, assertiveness is likely to be a key variable in the complex social interaction of discussing condom use (Treffke, Tiggemann, & Ross, 1992). Ross (1988) suggested that the ability to raise the issue of condom use in sexual encounters without fear of rebuff is the most important component of a general assertive personality style. Many researchers have found assertive communication strategies successful in safer sex negotiation and compliance gaining (e.g., Edgar, Freimuth, Hammond, McDonald, & Fink, 1992; Freimuth et al., 1992; Yesmont, 1992). Specifically, African American women who took "sexual assertiveness" classes were twice as likely to use condoms consistently afterward than those who took a standard 2-hour AIDS information course taught in a clinic. Among other things, the assertiveness classes taught how to put a condom on a partner, how to express sexual desires firmly, and how to cope with sexual situations when one or both participants have been drinking. Thus, it is expected that individuals, and especially a woman's level of assertiveness, should have a direct impact on communication regarding condom use and hence actual condom use.

This pool of research studies did not include homosexuals or intravenous drug users as an explicit grouping. Some high-risk populations are not included in this set of data. Because intravenous drug users are engaged in another set of behaviors that may involve risk, this indicates that one potential set of the group's behaviors are unknown. The risk of transmission comes from the intravenous drug user's potential to infect the other person, and the lover may not know about the use of such substances.

The lack of an identified homosexual population in the study means that one specific group with a unique risk potential is not included in this analysis. The homosexual male community may have developed a norm through socialization that makes such conversation unnecessary. Consider that in virtually any bar for gay men there is a bowl of free condoms next to the peanuts, as well as AIDS and HIV informational posters and pamphlets that are conspicuous. Virtually all heterosexual bars have condoms for sale in the restrooms. The social patterns may be such that sexual behavior provides a script or expectation that involves a condom for gay men and not for heterosexual couples. This process of accepting the need for condoms may be one that could be incorporated for heterosexuals as well. However, empirical studies need to be conducted on the development and application of safe sex practices and discussions by gay men.

One limitation to the simple application of these findings involves the issue of not considering the ethnographic trap inherent in a meta-analysis. The *ethnographic trap* refers to the inability to simply take the findings of any particular meta-analysis and apply them to some cultural setting. The findings of any meta-analysis involve establishing the degree of connection between abstract theoretical entities called variables. The manifestation of those variables in any given society requires an understanding of how that social system enacts the properties of those variables. Such knowledge is cultural, situated in the shared experiences of the community and the use of common symbols and meanings that defines that community. The key to successful application is the translation and application of the general findings of the meta-analysis to meet the symbolic requirements and needs of the particular language community. This implies a connection between various levels of knowledge, which is explained elsewhere (Allen & Silver, 1997). The truly successful implementation of any program of education that seeks a change in fundamental social behavior will require a great deal of consideration about the various needs of the community for which it is intended. The current lack of sophisticated efforts of combining such levels of knowledge generates a potential pitfall that is often unaddressed.

An examination of several interpersonal communication textbooks reveals little information about AIDS or HIV communication in relationships. This is surprising given the importance of the topic, especially to college students on U.S. campuses. The need to reduce the risk of infection by the use of condoms or abstinence is high, and still textbooks fail to mention this topic. The finding is surprising because the topic is obviously relevant to a variety of issues in interpersonal communication (intimacy, relational escalation, self-disclosure, turning points, relational history, etc.). The communication surrounding safer sex introduces the need to consider a variety of sexual preferences and practices in a manner that increases the likelihood of open discussion by partners in an interpersonal relationship. The failure to include these topics after more than a decade of research and given the need of the readers of the text for such information deserves continued discussion and exploration. The failure of interpersonal communication textbooks to include what should become a fundamental consideration currently and in the future proves troublesome. Given the growing body of research available on this topic, the ability to incorporate the material exists.

Educational efforts must not only target increasing knowledge about the nature of HIV infection and the methods of reducing risk. The educational efforts must involve a method of examining how each partner can create a behavioral routine to permit a conversational dynamic encouraging the discussion of sexual matters in a meaningful manner. If educational efforts focus simply on increasing knowledge about the risk of HIV without creating the knowledge necessary to create a behavioral routine that permits members of dyads to identify mechanisms to communicate about this risk, efforts will probably fail. Styker et al. (1995) argued, "Social and behavioral sciences have pointed out effective HIV prevention programs; the prospects for altering the course of the HIV epidemic will turn on whether we have the courage to implement them and the fortitude to sustain them" (p. 282).

REFERENCES

References marked with an asterisk indicate studies included in the meta-analysis. In the case where a data set appears in more than one manuscript, the earliest representation is indicated in the text and table.

Abbey, A. (1987). Misperceptions of friendly behavior as sexual interest: A survey of naturally occurring incidents. *Psychology of Women Quarterly, 11,* 173–194.
*Abraham, C., Sheeran, P., Spears, R., & Abrams, D. (1992). Health beliefs and promotion of HIV-preventive intentions among teenagers: A Scottish perspective. *Health Communication, 11,* 363–370.
- Adelman, M. (1991). Play and incongruity: Framing safe-sex talk. *Health Communication, 3,* 139–155.

Adelman, M. (1992). Sustaining passion: Eroticism and safe-sex talk. *Archives of Sexual Behavior, 21*, 481–494.

Allen, M., & Emmers-Sommer, T. (1998, April). *AIDS Research: An agenda for meta-analysis.* Report presented at the Central States Communication Association Convention, Chicago.

Allen, M., & Silver, C. (1997, April). *Quantitative and qualitative approaches to knowledge: Proposing a method of functional integration for the relationship between empirical methods.* Paper presented at the Central States Communication Association Convention, St. Louis, MO. (ERIC Document Reproduction Service No. ED 405 628)

*Basen-Engquist, K. (1992). Psychosocial predictors of "safer sex" behaviors in young adults. *AIDS Education and Prevention, 4*, 120–134.

Baxter, L. A., & Wilmot, W. W. (1985). Taboo topics in close relationships. *Journal of Social and Personal Relationships, 2*, 253–269.

Bruce, K., Shrum, J., Trefethen, C., & Slovik, L. (1990). Students' attitudes about AIDS, homosexuality, and condoms. *AIDS Education and Prevention, 2*, 220–234.

*Bryan, A., Aiken, L., & West, S. (1996). Increasing condom use: Evaluation of a theory-based intervention to prevent sexually transmitted diseases in young women. *Health Psychology, 15*, 371–382.

*Chen, T. (1997, May). *College students' media exposure to AIDS/Interpersonal communication about AIDS and their perceptions and adaptive responses towards AIDS prevention: Does "talking about AIDS" really help?* Paper presented at the International Communication Association Convention, Montreal, Canada.

*Cline, R., Freeman, K., & Johnson, S. (1990). Talk among sexual partners about AIDS: Factors differentiating those who talk from those who do not. *Communication Research, 17*, 792–808.

*Cline, R., Johnson, S., & Freeman, K. (1992). Talk among sexual partners about AIDS: Interpersonal communication risk reduction or risk enhancement? *Health Communication, 4*, 39–56.

Cochran, S., & Mays, V. (1990, March 15). Sex, lies, and HIV. *New England Journal of Medicine, 322*, 774–775.

*Cohen, D., & Dent, C. (1992). The validity of self-reported condom use. *American Journal of Public Health, 82*, 1563–1564.

*Deren, S., Shedlin, M., & Beardsley, M. (1996). HIV-related concerns and behaviors among Hispanic women. *AIDS Education and Prevention, 8*, 335–343.

*DiClemente, R. (1991). Predictors of HIV-preventive sexual behavior in a high-risk adolescent population: The influence of perceived peer norms and sexual communication on incarcerated adolescents' consistent use of condoms. *Journal of Adolescent Health, 12*, 385–390.

*Edgar, T., & Fitzpatrick, M. (1993). Expectations for sexual interaction: A cognitive test of the sequencing of sexual communication behaviors. *Health Communication, 5*, 239–261.

*Edgar, T., Freimuth, V., Hammond, S., McDonald, D., & Fink, E. (1992). Strategic sexual communication: Condom use resistance and response. *Health Communication, 4*, 83–104.

Eldridge, G., St. Lawrence, J., Little, C., Shelby, M., Brasfield, T., Service, J., & Sly, K. (1997). Evaluation of an HIV risk reduction intervention for women entering inpatient substance abuse treatment. *AIDS Education and Prevention, 9*(Supp. A), 62–76.

Engelbert, M., Flora, J., & Nass, C. (1995). AIDS knowledge: Effects of channel involvement and interpersonal communication. *Health Communication, 7*, 73–91.

*Fisher, J., Fisher, W., Williams, S., & Malloy, T. (1994). Empirical tests of an information-motivation-behavioral skills model of AIDS-preventive behavior with gay men and heterosexual university students. *Health Psychology, 13,* 238–250.

*Fisher, W., Fisher, W., & Rye, B. (1995). Understanding and promoting AIDS-preventive behavior: Insights from the theory of reasoned action. *Health Psychology, 14,* 255–264.

Freimuth, V., Hammond, S., Edgar, T., McDonald, D., & Fink, E. (1992). Factors explaining intent, discussion and use of condoms in first-time sexual encounters. *Health Education Research, 7,* 203–215.

*Goldman, J., & Harlow, L. (1993). Self-perception variables that mediate AIDS-preventive behavior in college students. *Health Psychology, 12,* 489–498.

Gordon, C., & Carey, M. (1996). Alcohol's effects on requisites for sexual risk reduction in men: An initial experimental investigation. *Health Psychology, 15,* 56–60.

*Grimley, D., Prochaska, J., Velicer, W., & Prochaska, G. (1995). Contraceptive and condom use: Adoption and maintenance: A stage paradigm approach. *Health Education Quarterly, 22,* 20–35.

*Helweg-Larsen, M., & Collins, B. (1994). The UCLA multidimensional condom attitudes scale: Documenting the complex determinants of condom use in college students. *Health Psychology, 13,* 224–237.

*Herold, E., & Mewhinney, D. (1993). Gender differences in casual sex and AIDS prevention: A survey of dating bars. *Journal of Sex Research, 30,* 36–42.

Hobfall, S., Jackson, A., Lavin, J., Britton, P., & Shepherd, J. (1993). Safer sex knowledge, behavior, and attitudes of inner-city women. *Health Psychology, 12,* 481–488.

Hunter, J., & Schmidt, J. (1990). *Methods of meta-analysis: Correcting error and bias in research findings.* Newbury Park, CA: Sage.

*Johnson, E., Hinkle, Y., Gilbert, D., & Gant, L. (1992). Black males who always use condoms: Their attitudes, knowledge about AIDS, and sexual behavior. *Journal of the National Medical Association, 84,* 341–352.

Kalichman, S., Rompa, D., & Coley, B. (1997). Lack of positive outcomes from a cognitive-behavioral HIV and AIDS prevention intervention for inner-city men: Lessons from a controlled pilot study. *AIDS Education and Prevention, 9,* 299–313.

*Kasen, S., Vaughan, R., & Walter, H. (1992). Self-efficacy for AIDS preventive behaviors among tenth grade students. *Health Education Quarterly, 19,* 187–202.

*Kinnick, B., Smart, D., Bell, D., Blank, W., Gray, T., & Schoeber, J. (1989). As assessment of AIDS-related knowledge, attitudes, and behaviors among selected college and university students. *AIDS & Public Policy Journal, 4,* 112–119.

*Magura, S., Shapiro, J., Siddiqui, Q., & Lipton, D. (1990). Variables influencing condom use among intravenous drug users. *American Journal of Public Health, 80,* 82–84.

*Maibach, E., & Flora, J. (1993). Symbolic modeling and cognitive rehearsal: Using video to promote AIDS prevention self-efficacy. *Communication Research, 20,* 517–545.

*Malow, R., Corrigan, S., Cunningham, S., West, J., & Pena, J. (1993). Psychosocial factors associated with condom use among African-American drug abusers in treatment. *AIDS Education and Prevention, 5,* 244–253.

Malow, R., & Ireland, S. (1996). HIV risk correlates among non-injection cocaine dependent men in treatment. *AIDS Education and Prevention, 8,* 226–235.

*Malow, R., West, J., Corrigan, S., Pena, J., & Cunningham, S. (1994). Outcome of psychoeducation for HIV risk education. *AIDS Education and Prevention, 6,* 113–125.

*Marín, B., Gómez, C., Tshann, J., & Gregorich, S. (1997). Condom use in unmarried Latino men: A test of cultural constructs. *Health Psychology, 16,* 458–467.

Maticka-Tyndale, E. (1991). Sexual scripts and AIDS prevention: Variations in adherence to safer-sex guidelines by heterosexual adolescents. *Journal of Sex Research, 28,* 45–66.

Metts, S., & Fitzpatrick, M. (1992). Thinking about safer sex: The risky business of "know your partner" advice. In T. Edgar, M. Fitzpatrick, & V. Freimuth (Eds.), *AIDS: A communication perspective* (pp. 1–19). Hillsdale, NJ: Lawrence Erlbaum Associates.

Neuwirth, K., & Dunwoody, S. (1989). The complexity of AIDS-related behavioral change: The interaction between communication and noncommunication variables. *AIDS & Public Policy, 4,* 20–30.

*Overby, K., & Kegeles, S. (1994). The impact of AIDS on an urban population of high-risk female minority adolescents: Implications for Intervention. *Journal of Adolescent Health, 15,* 216–227.

*Reel, B., & Thompson, T. (1994). A test of the effectiveness of strategies for talking about AIDS and condom use. *Journal of Applied Communication Research, 22,* 127–140.

Ross, M. (1988). Prevalence of classes of risk behaviors for HIV infection in a randomly selected Australian population. *Journal of Sex Research, 25,* 441–450.

*Rye, B. (1990). *Affective and cognitive predictors of AIDS preventive behaviors among female university students.* Unpublished master's thesis, University of Western Ontario, London, Canada.

*Sacco, W., Rickman, R., Thompson, K., Levine, B., & Reed, D. (1993). Gender differences in AIDS-relevant condom attitudes and condom use. *AIDS Education and Prevention, 5,* 311–326.

*Sheer, V. (1995). Sensation seeking predispositions and susceptibility to a sexual partner's appeals for condom use. *Journal of Applied Communication Research, 23,* 212–229.

*Sheer, V., & Cline, R. (1994). The development and validation of a model explaining sexual behavior among college students: Implications for AIDS communication campaigns. *Human Communication Research, 21,* 280–304.

*Shoop, D., & Davidson, P. (1994). AIDS and adolescents: The relation of parent and partner communication to adolescent condom use. *Journal of Adolescence, 17,* 137–148.

Sogolow, E., Semaan, S., Johnson, W., Neumann, M., Ramirez, G., Sweat, M., & Doll, L. (1998). *Effects of US-based HIV interventions on safer sex: Meta-analyses, overall and for populations, age groups, and settings* (International Conference on AIDS, Abstract No. 14283). Atlanta, GA: Centers for Disease Control.

*Stebleton, M., & Rothenberger, J. (1993). Truth or consequences: Dishonesty in dating and HIV/AIDS—related issues in college population. *Journal of American College Health, 42,* 51–54.

Stryker, J., Coates, T., DeCarlo, P., Haynes-Sanstad, K., Shriver, M., & Makadon, H. (1995). Prevention of HIV infection: Looking back, looking ahead. *Journal of the American Medical Association, 273,* 1143–1148.

Treffke, H., Tiggerman, M., & Ross, M. (1992). The relationship between attitude, assertiveness, and condom use. *Psychology and Health, 6,* 45–52.

Unks, G. (1996). Will schools risk teaching about the risk of AIDS? *The Clearinghouse, 69*(4), 205–211.

*Valdiserri, R., Arena, V., Proctor, D., & Bonati, F. (1989). The relationship between women's attitudes and condoms and their use: Implications for condom promotion programs. *American Journal of Public Health, 79,* 499–500.

Vanderford, M., Smith, D., & Harris, W. (1992). Value identification in narrative discourse: Evaluation of an HIV education demonstration project. *Journal of Applied Communication Research, 20,* 123–160.

*Waldron, V., Caughlin, J., & Jackson, D. (1995). Talking specifics: Facilitating effects of planning on AIDS talk in peer dyads. *Health Communication, 7,* 249–266.

*Walter, H., Vaughan, R., Gladis, M., Ragin, D., Kasen, S., & Cohall, A. (1993a). Factors associated with AIDS-related behavioral intentions among high school students in an AIDS epicenter. *Health Education Quarterly, 20,* 409–420.

*Walter, H., Vaughan, R., Gladis, M., Ragin, D., Kasen, S., & Cohall, A. (1993b). Factors associated with AIDS-related behaviors among high school students in an AIDS epicenter. *American Journal of Public Health, 82,* 528–532.

*Walter, H., Vaughan, R., Ragin, D., Cohall, A., & Kasen, S. (1994). Prevalence and correlates of AIDS-related behavioral intentions among urban minority high school students. *AIDS Education and Prevention, 6,* 339–350.

Weisse, C., Turbiasz, A., & Whitney, D. (1995). Behavioral training and AIDS risk reduction: Overcoming barriers to condom use. *AIDS Education and Prevention, 7,* 50–59.

Wight, D. (1994). Assimilating safer sex: Young heterosexual men's understanding of "safer sex." In P. Aggleton, P. Davies, & G. Hart (Eds.), *AIDS: Foundations for the future* (pp. 97–109). London: Taylor & Francis.

Willig, C. (1994). Marital discourse and condom use. In P. Aggleton, P. Davies, & G. Hart (Eds.), *AIDS: Foundations for the future* (pp. 110–121). London: Taylor & Francis.

*Wilson, T., Jaccard, J., Endias, R., & Minkoff, H. (1993). Reducing the risk of HIV infection for women: An attitudinal analysis of condom-carrying behavior. *Journal of Applied Social Psychology, 23,* 1093–1110.

Winett, R., Anderson, E., Moore, J., Sikkema, K., Hook, R., Webster, D., Taylor, C., Dalton, J., Ollendick, T., & Eisler, R. (1992). Family/media approach to HIV prevention: Results with a home-based, parent–teen video program. *Health Psychology, 11,* 203–206.

*Wulfert, E., & Wan, C. (1995). Safer sex intentions and condom use viewed from a health belief, reasoned action, and social cognitive perspective. *Journal of Sex Research, 32,* 299–311.

*Yesmont, G. (1992). The relationship of assertiveness to college students' safer sex behaviors. *Adolescence, 27,* 253–272.

Zimmerman, R., & Olson, K. (1994). AIDS-related risk behavior and behavior change in a sexually active, heterosexual sample: A test of three models of prevention. *AIDS Education and Prevention, 6,* 189–205.

16

Argumentativeness and Its Effect on Verbal Aggressiveness: A Meta-Analytic Review

Mark A. Hamilton and Paul J. Mineo

A Fanciful History of the Dawn of Reason

Two furry Neanderthals, Vag and Arg, were facing off, brandishing their clubs and snarling. Arg knew he could never beat Vag in a fight, but then he remembered that he had achieved some success in the past resolving disputes without resorting to violence. He attempted that technique in this momentous encounter, saying to Vag, "Wait! Can we talk about this?" Vag was somewhat surprised by Arg's suggestion, so he decided to listen, although he remained wary. Oddly enough, after some discussion, Vag decided that it wouldn't make sense to smash Arg over the head if he didn't have to, and he went away strangely relieved.

Some days later, Arg heard a ruckus and went to investigate. He found Vag and another Neanderthal, Meeg, shouting at each other. Vag was making some sense, but mostly he was hurling insults and threats at Meeg. Meeg finally gave in and left, shaking his head, grumbling under his breath. Afterward, Vag proudly boasted to Arg that he had beaten Meeg with words, just like Arg had taught him.

Arg was deeply troubled. Meeg plainly had not left satisfied with the encounter. Arg thought that this would surely lead to more conflict between Vag and

Meeg in the future. This was not how Arg thought his talking strategy should be used. It should be used to arrive at a mutually acceptable solution; it should not be used to "beat" people. Arg decided he had better find a way to clearly distinguish between talking to achieve cooperative solutions and talking as just another way of bullying people because some people, like Vag, had clearly confused the two.

Arg wanted a convincing way to make his point, so he invented meta-analysis.

Argumentativeness theory (Infante, 1987) proposes that sources choose between messages that are argumentative and those that are verbally aggressive (Infante, 1981, 1982, 1985; Infante & Rancer, 1982, 1993). Argumentative messages attack the positions that others take on given issues, whereas verbally aggressive messages attack the self-concepts of others rather than their positions (Infante & Rancer, 1982). As Dowling and Flint (1990) noted, the theory depicts this choice as dichotomous: A source must choose between attacking issues or people. A central proposition of argumentativeness theory is that by developing procedures that foster enlightened debate, researchers can provide recommendations for the control of verbal aggression (Infante, Hartley, Martin, Higgins, Bruning, & Hur, 1992; Infante, Trebing, Shepherd, & Seeds, 1984). We refer to this hypothesized causal chain as the *constructive learning process*. Advocates of the theory believe that the accumulation of knowledge about argumentation has been a defining feature of the communication discipline and that this pursuit should play an important part in the discipline's future (Infante & Rancer, 1996). If the advocates are correct about the constructive learning process, then the theory has important social, political, and interpersonal ramifications.

Argumentativeness theory (Infante & Rancer, 1982) identifies personality and situational variables that determine how likely people are to choose argumentative or verbally aggressive messages. The theory specifies two motivational factors: one that leads people to approach arguments and the other that leads them to avoid arguments. These motivational factors are thought to be key antecedents of whether an individual engages in arguments with others or falls back on pernicious, verbally aggressive attacks.

In this chapter, we pose two important questions for argumentativeness theory. The first research question concerns the dimensionality of the argumentativeness scale. Suppose that the scale consists of a single dimension that measures the general personality trait of motivation to argue. Argumentativeness theorists represent the general trait of argumentativeness with the abbreviation ARG_{gt}. All individuals could be rated as high to low on this one motive. Conversely, suppose that the scale consists of two or more independent dimensions that measure different motivations to argue. Individuals could be clustered along these multiple dimensions. If the scale were found to be multidimensional, then it would make sense for researchers to classify people into different types of argumentatives as Infante and Rancer (1996) suggested. Typing individuals in this way would provide a coarse means of capturing the interaction of the ARG_{ap} and ARG_{av} factors on important criterion variables. If the scale were found to be unidimensional, however, then it would make little sense for researchers to classify people into a variety of types. That would require selecting arbitrary cutoff points along the single dimension.

We begin by reviewing the conceptualization and operationalization of argumentativeness, exposing what appears to be a logical inconsistency in the theory that stems from the theory's proposal of a general trait of argumentativeness. Argumentativeness theorists represent the motivation to approach arguments with the abbreviation ARG_{ap}, and the motivation to avoid arguments with the abbreviation ARG_{av}. The general trait of argumentativeness is computed as the difference between scores on the approach-argument scale and scores on the avoid-argument scale as follows:

$$ARG_{gt} = ARG_{ap} - ARG_{av} \qquad [1]$$

Computation of a single trait score is the correct procedure if the general trait scale can be shown to be unidimensional; that is, the scale measures one and only one underlying trait. In a unidimensional scale, scores on the approach-argument scale would be negatively correlated with scores on the avoid-argument scale. That is, a person who is high on the general trait of argumentativeness would tend to agree with items indicating that he or she is motivated to approach arguments and disagree with items indicating that he or she is motivated to avoid arguments. Conversely, a person who is low on general trait argumentativeness would tend to disagree with items indicating that he or she is motivated to approach arguments and agree with items indicating that he or she is motivated to avoid arguments.

Yet argumentativeness theorists claim that the ARG_{ap} scale is independent of the ARG_{av} scale. In other words, scores on the ARG_{ap} scale are uncorrelated with scores on the ARG_{av} scale. If they are correct, then the ARG_{gt} scale would contain several distinct subscales, making it multidimensional. Thus, argumentativeness theory claims that the ARG_{gt} scale is both unidimensional and multidimensional. This inconsistency can be addressed by examining the correlation between the ARG_{ap} and ARG_{av} scales: A moderately negative correlation between the two scales would be prima

facie evidence for a unidimensional scale, whereas a zero correlation between the two scales would be prima facie evidence for a multidimensional
scale. Meta-analysis allowed us to estimate the correlation between the
ARG_{ap} and ARG_{av} scales.

The second research question concerns the value of argumentation in society: Does the motivation to argue inhibit verbal aggressiveness or not?
The main focus of argumentativeness theory is what we have dubbed the
constructive learning process. The theory proposes that argumentation
training enhances argumentativeness and that argumentativeness, in turn,
inhibits verbal aggressiveness. The chief practical implication of the theory
is that instructing people in argumentation should lower the level of verbal
aggression in society. Unfortunately, there is virtually no empirical evidence
that ARG_{gt} has a large negative effect on verbal aggressiveness. The lack of a
strong negative correlation between ARG_{gt} and verbal aggressiveness can,
however, be explained by the fact that argumentativeness theory does not
predict that ARG_{gt} will have a direct effect on verbal aggressiveness. Instead, the theory proposes that the effect of ARG_{gt} on verbal aggressiveness
is indirect, mediated by several variables. This mediating process would diminish the inhibitory effect of ARG_{gt} on verbal aggressiveness down to a
near-zero level. In fact, Infante and Wigley (1986) found that ARG_{gt} and
verbal aggressiveness were correlated at −.04. In the meta-analysis, we show
that the slight negative correlation reported by Infante and Wigley is the exception rather than the rule. All other studies show a modest positive correlation between ARG_{gt} and verbal aggressiveness. The startling implication
of the meta-analytic finding is that by enhancing the motivation to argue,
current programs of argumentation training may actually be increasing the
level of verbal aggressiveness in society. It is as if in our parable of Arg and
Vag, Arg discovered to his dismay that teaching Vag how to argue did not reduce Vag's desire to hurt others, but merely provided Vag with a new means
to implement his hurtful motives. In fact, our little fable foreshadows a key
finding of our meta-analysis—that increasing a person's confidence in his or
her ability to argue increases his or her verbal aggressiveness.

MOTIVATION TO ARGUE

Argumentativeness is a person's motivation to argue. Infante and Rancer
(1982) defined argumentativeness as a stable trait that predisposes a source to
identify controversies, advocate positions on controversial issues, and verbally attack the positions that others take. Their theory of argumentativeness
was closely patterned after the achievement motivation theory of Atkinson
(1964). In Atkinson's model, the achievement motive was defined as "a ca-

pacity for taking pride in accomplishment" (p. 241). Winning an argument may be considered a form of interpersonal accomplishment. Infante and Rancer (1982) described engaging in argument as an "exciting intellectual challenge, a competitive situation" (p. 72).

In his motivation theory, Atkinson (1964, 1974) proposed that achievement performance is a function of the motivation to achieve success, M_S, and the motivation to avoid failure, M_{AF}. He conceptualized M_S as the motivation to approach challenging tasks and M_{AF} as the motivation to avoid challenging tasks. These two motives combine to predict performance on challenging tasks, with M_S operationalized as need for achievement (n Ach) and M_{AF} operationalized as test anxiety. Similarly, Infante and Rancer (1982) identified two sets of motives associated with arguing: the motivation to approach arguments and the motivation to avoid arguments. In Atkinson's model, M_S and M_{AF} are independent of one another, and together the two motives create internal conflict in achievement situations. He referred to this clash of motives as an approach–avoidance conflict or an excitation–inhibition conflict. Infante and Rancer (1982) used precisely the same language to describe the conflict between ARG_{ap} and ARG_{av}. As evidence that M_S and M_{AF} are independent, Atkinson referred to studies that show that n Ach is uncorrelated with test anxiety. Following suit, Infante and Rancer (1982) assumed that ARG_{ap} and ARG_{av} are independent of one another. We depict this assumption in Fig. 16.1. M_S may potentially increase ARG_{ap} and decrease ARG_{av}. Conversely, M_{AF} may potentially decrease ARG_{ap} and increase ARG_{av}. Past achievement does appear to increase ARG_{gt}.[1]

The Dimensionality of the Argumentativeness Scale

Argumentativeness theorists suggest three components to the ARG_{gt} scale (Infante & Rancer, 1982). The first component is orientation toward situations in which arguing may occur. An approach orientation is founded on the perception that argument is an intellectual challenge, a competitive situation that involves winning points and defending positions. The theory is less clear about how those with an avoidance orientation perceive situations in which arguing may occur. We suspect that this orientation component is largely a function of competitiveness. The second component is affective re-

---

[1]Grade point average (GPA) could be taken as an indicator of n Ach. Infante (1982) reported that the effect of college GPA on ARG_{gt} was .43. Infante and Rancer (1982) found that communication apprehension correlated .41 with ARG_{av}. These two findings are consistent with the model shown in Fig. 16.1. However, Infante and Rancer also found that communication apprehension correlated .45 with ARG_{ap}—a finding inconsistent with the model in Fig. 16.1.

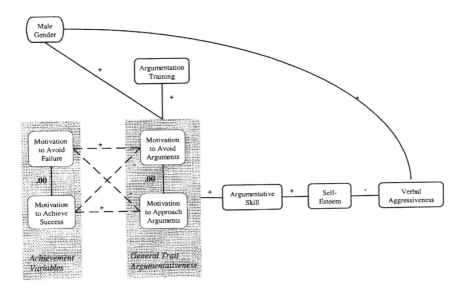

FIG. 16.1.   Model proposed by argumentativeness theory.

sponse to arguing. Those who have an approach orientation experience feel-ings of excitement as they anticipate arguing, as well as feelings of invigoration, satisfaction, and a sense of accomplishment following an argu-ment. Those who have an avoidance orientation experience anxiety as they anticipate arguing, as well as unpleasant feelings following an argument. The theory does not indicate the nature of these unpleasant feelings. They could be guilt or recrimination, hostility, sadness, or fear. The third motiva-tion concerns individuals' confidence in their ability to argue.

Testing the Unidimensionality of the Argumentativeness Scale.
Hunter (1980) described three criteria for testing the unidimen- sionality of a scale: homogeneity of content, internal consistency, and parallelism. Homo-geneous content requires that any content themes that exist within a scale should form a second-order factor. To be internally consistent, the items should correlate with one another to approximately the same degree, or the items should show a strong–weak gradient if the items vary considerably in quality. If the items are of approximately equal quality, then the correlation matrix among the items should be relatively flat (all correlations are roughly equal). If the items differ considerably in quality, then the correlations among

the items should form a pattern that reflects a gradient.[2] To be parallel, the items should correlate with variables that are external to the scale to approximately the same degree, or the items can vary along a strong–weak gradient in their relation to the external variable. If the items on the scale are all of approximately equal quality, then the items will all correlate with outside variables to approximately the same degree. If the items vary considerably in quality along a strong–weak gradient, then the strongest items should show the largest correlations with the external variables, and the weakest items the smallest correlations with the external variables. Parallelism is the most powerful tool in identifying nonunidimensional items on a scale (Hunter, 1980).

Argumentativeness theorists (Infante, 1981, 1986; Infante & Rancer, 1982, 1985; Rancer & Infante, 1985) recommend calculating the difference between ARG_{ap} and ARG_{av} as a measure of ARG_{gt} as shown in Equation 1. This general recommendation is appropriate only on the assumption that the argumentativeness scale is unidimensional. Rarely do they recommend treating ARG_{ap} and ARG_{av} as distinct variables in relation to other variables, as would be necessary if ARG_{ap} and ARG_{av} represented independent motivations to argue. With their recommendations in mind, we examined the content of the ARG_{gt} scale. The 20 items were inspected for content themes that might reveal two or more dimensions. The second criterion we applied to the ARG_{gt} scale was internal consistency. Use of Equation 1 implies that the items on the ARG_{gt} scale are internally consistent. It is possible that argumentativeness researchers have confused a strong–weak gradient on the scale with multidimensionality. As we show later, a number of researchers have discarded ARG_{gt} items in an effort to boost the scale's reliability. The third and most important criterion was parallelism. Use of Equation 1 implies that the items on the argumentativeness scale are parallel.

Consequences of a Multidimensional Argumentativeness Scale.
If the ARG_{gt} scale is multidimensional, then motivation to argue should be mapped onto a two-dimensional grid. If this is the case, then argumentativeness theorists should use the term *general orientation* rather than *general trait*. More important, treating a multidimensional general orientation scale as a unidimensional, general trait scale could substantially decrease the correlation of argumentativeness with other variables.

Advocates of argumentativeness theory are persistently unclear about the dimensionality of the ARG_{gt} scale. They imply that ARG_{gt} is unidimensional when they routinely employ the formula in Equation 1 to compute ARG_{gt}

---

[2]The technical name for this pattern is a *Guttman simplex.*

scores. Yet they make three claims that suggest multidimensionality. First, they state that there are distinct content themes among the ARG_{gt} items. Second, they state that ARG_{ap} and ARG_{av} are independent. Third, they state that ARG_{ap} and ARG_{av} should be considered separately when comparing whether two cultures vary in ARG_{ap} (Infante & Rancer, 1996). This is tantamount to claiming that the ARG_{gt} scale does not meet the three criteria for unidimensionality. If ARG_{ap} and ARG_{av} are uncorrelated and "interact" to produce ARG_{gt}, then the interaction between ARG_{ap} and ARG_{av} should be taken into account in any statistical analysis performed.

Typologies of Argumentatives.   Argumentativeness researchers have sometimes converted the continuous scores on the ARG_{ap} and ARG_{av} into categories. To cover the full two-dimensional area produced by the interaction of the ARG_{ap} and ARG_{av} scales shown in Fig. 16.2, the theorists suggest five categories of argumentatives occurring with approximately equal frequency. The five argumentative groups are highs (high approach with low avoidance), lows (low approach with high avoidance), apathetic moderates (low approach with low avoidance), conflicted moderates (high approach with high avoidance), and neutral moderates (those who are near the neutral point on the ARG_{ap} and ARG_{av} scales). The categorical scheme illustrated in Fig. 16.2 is necessary if researchers are to capture the nature of the interaction between the ARG_{ap} and ARG_{av} scales.

The five groups are located along two axes, as shown in Fig. 16.2. The primary axis runs through the low, neutral moderate, and high clusters. The primary axis represents the influence of the general trait of argumentativeness. Low argumentatives are anxious about engaging in arguments, and feel no compulsion to argue. High argumentatives are compelled to argue and experience little anxiety about engaging in argument. If the argumentativeness items form a unidimensional scale, then most people will fall into one of these three clusters.

A second axis runs through the apathetic moderate, neutral moderate, and conflicted moderate clusters. The secondary axis represents emotional involvement with arguing. The conflicted moderates are emotionally involved with arguing. On the one hand, they are compelled to argue, driven perhaps by competitiveness. On the other hand, they are anxious about arguing, perhaps gripped by the fear of failure. The apathetic moderates are emotionally uninvolved with arguing. They feel no compulsion to argue and no anxiety over arguing. If the argumentativeness items are multidimensional, forming two or more subscales, then chances are that as many people will fall into either the apathetic moderate and conflicted moderate clusters

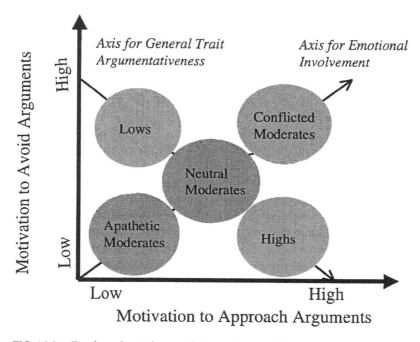

FIG. 16.2.   Five hypothesized types of orientation toward argumentativeness.

as fall into the low and high clusters. That is, we would expect that the five clusters should be of approximately equal size.

Choosing the Appropriate Analysis for the Argumentativeness Items

Suppose that the ARG_{ap} and ARG_{av} scales are uncorrelated. The appropriate statistic would be to treat the two motivations as distinct variables to determine their effects on criterion variables. If argumentativeness were to be used to predict a criterion variable, then multiple regression would allow the researcher to examine the main effect for ARG_{ap}, the main effect for ARG_{av}, and the interaction term represented by the product of ARG_{ap} and ARG_{av} scores as predictors of relevant criterion variables. If argumentativeness were to be used as a criterion variable, then discriminant analysis would allow the researcher to examine the effect of relevant predictor variables on membership in the five clusters shown in Fig. 16.2.

It can be misleading to combine heterogeneous subscales to form a summative scale that is then correlated with other variables of interest

(Briggs, 1992). If ARG$_{ap}$ and ARG$_{av}$ are uncorrelated, they may correlate differently with important predictor or criterion variables. If a multidimensional scale is summarized with a single score, it will be prone to reduced correlations with these important variables when researchers average across the disparate subscales. Suppose that a team of researchers employs a sample of 200 undergraduates. They find that their predictor variable X correlates −.26 with the ARG$_{av}$ and .00 with the ARG$_{ap}$. The average across the two argument scales computed as the general trait score, −.13, would not achieve statistical significance ($p > .05$). If the correlations of X with the ARG$_{ap}$ and ARG$_{av}$ scales are reported, then the correct conclusion can be retrieved. If, however, the difference formula is used to obtain ARG$_{gt}$, and only the correlation between X and ARG$_{gt}$ is reported, then the correct conclusion is lost. The researcher and perhaps the reader would incorrectly conclude that there is no relation between X and ARG$_{gt}$. Thus, the question of whether the ARG$_{gt}$ scale is unidimensional or multidimensional has serious consequences for argumentativeness theory. If the ARG$_{ap}$ and ARG$_{av}$ subscales were found to be uncorrelated, then most of the literature on argumentativeness would be of questionable value because it reports correlations with ARG$_{gt}$ rather than ARG$_{ap}$ or ARG$_{av}$.

THE EFFECT OF ARGUMENTATIVENESS ON VERBAL AGGRESSIVENESS

Drawing on the work of Zillmann (1979) and Geen (1990), we define *human aggression* as an activity that an aggressor intentionally directs toward intended victims that inflicts destruction on those victims or their property. Three features of this definition have implications for the study of aggressive communication. First, aggressive behavior is intended to harm the victim, which rules out accidental damage and implies a striving toward self-assertion (Storr, 1968). The intended harm can range from mild, as in competitive activities, to severe, as in life-and-death struggles. Second, destruction can vary by degree, ranging from partial to complete. There should be at least a moderately positive correlation between damage intended and damage inflicted. Third, damage can be inflicted directly to the victim or indirectly to the victim's property (Boelkins & Heiser, 1970), suggesting a *directness of attack* continuum.[3] In their narrative review of the

---

[3]In an effort to develop a model of aggressive communication, Infante and Rancer (1996) characterized argumentativeness as a form of aggression. If we were to accept an attack on another's position as an act of aggression, however, we would need to define a person's position on important social issues as their intellectual property. However, this definition seemed only to apply to copyright lawyers, so we rejected their characterization of argumentation as an act of aggression.

argumentativeness literature, Infante and Rancer (1996) concluded that males score are higher on both ARG_{gt} and verbal aggressiveness than females. We included their gender-based predictions in that portion of argumentativeness theory tested in our meta-analysis (see Fig. 16.1).

The Constructive Learning Process

The constructive learning process depicted in Fig. 16.1 proposes that argumentation training has a chilling effect on verbal aggressiveness. Rancer, Kosberg, and Silvestri (1992) proposed that training in argumentation enhances argumentativeness, argumentativeness enhances positive outcomes during argument, positive outcomes during argument enhance self-esteem, and self-esteem lowers verbal aggression. Indeed, Infante and Rancer (1996) claimed that teachers could reduce the level of verbal and physical aggression in society by developing students' argumentativeness. ARG_{gt} enhances positive outcomes of argument by improving argumentation skills, such that ARG_{gt} increases argumentation skill, and argumentation skill increases positive outcomes from argument. Argumentativeness theory also hypothesizes that argumentation skill inhibits verbal aggressiveness. The variable of positive outcomes from argument has rarely if ever been measured. To simplify the model shown in Fig. 16.1, we deleted the positive outcomes variable, and note that it is supposed to mediate the effect of argumentation skill on self-esteem. Thus, the model shown in Fig. 16.1 posits that argumentation training is connected to verbal aggressiveness through the four-step causal chain.

To develop a hypothesized model from which we could work, we sought to estimate the size of each of the effects in the model shown in Fig. 16.1. The effect of argumentation training on ARG_{gt} is actually small. Despite the small size of this effect, Infante and Rancer (1996) optimistically highlighted it as the most notable social ramification of their theory. They emphasized that the promotion of argumentativeness is a major justification for the past, present, and future existence of the communication discipline. Data from Infante (1982) indicate that high school debate training had a slight positive effect on ARG_{gt}; $r(710) = .12$. Data from Sanders, Wiseman, and Gass (1994) suggest that argumentation instruction decreases ARG_{gt}; $r(357) = -.04$. The weighted correlation averaged across these two studies is $r(1,067) = .07$. The Sanders et al. study contains a potential problem with respect to argumentativeness—the control group consisted of those enrolled in an interpersonal communication course. The course in interpersonal communication may have stressed the advantages of open communication, including arguing to resolve conflict. Thus the Infante result may be more accurate, or their training program may simply be more effective.

The Sanders et al. (1994) data show a positive effect of argumentation training on self-reported argumentation skills, $r(357) = .15$. Their data also show a negative effect of argumentation training on verbal aggressiveness, $r(357) = -.13$. Rancer et al. (1992) found that self-esteem correlates $-.01$ with ARG_{gt} and $-.09$ with verbal aggressiveness. We needed to make two assumptions to provide some initial estimates of the path coefficients for the hypothetical model in Fig. 16.1. The first assumption concerned the self-reported argumentation skill variable. Rancer et al. reported that ARG_{gt} is positively correlated with ratings of personal competence ($r = .15$) and personal power ($r = .36$). In addition, they reported that verbal aggressiveness is negatively correlated with competence ($r = -.09$) and personal power ($r = -.01$). Suppose that competence and power ratings indicate self-confidence. Based on this supposition, we averaged across the competence and power ratings to estimate the correlation of confidence in argumentation skill with ARG_{gt}, $r(132) = .25$, and with verbal aggressiveness, $r(132) = -.05$.

Our second assumption concerned the relation between ARG_{gt} and verbal aggressiveness. Prior to conducting our meta-analysis, we assumed a correlation of $-.04$ between ARG_{gt} and verbal aggressiveness, as reported by Infante and Wigley (1986). Our hypothetical model predicted that argumentation training increases ARG_{gt} ($\rho = .07$), ARG_{gt} increases confidence in argumentation skill ($\rho = .25$), confidence increases self-esteem ($\rho = .56$), and self-esteem inhibits verbal aggressiveness ($\rho = -.09$). We applied the product rule of causal modeling to the data used to test our working model. The predicted correlation between ARG_{gt} and verbal aggressiveness in this model is $-.01$. This value is well within sampling error of the $-.04$ value we assumed as the observed correlation between ARG_{gt} and verbal aggressiveness. Hence, the hypothesized model seemed promising. Our preliminary test of the working model revealed two unanticipated effects.

First, it appears that argumentation training inhibits verbal aggressiveness ($\rho = -.13$) through a process mediated by none of the variables identified by argumentativeness theory. The size of this effect is small. However, the effect of argumentation training on verbal aggressiveness via the process proposed in Fig. 16.1 (with ARG_{gt}, confidence in argumentative skill, and self-esteem as the mediating variables) is zero. Hence, the discovery of a parallel inhibition process suggests that argumentativeness plays a trivial role in the reduction of verbal aggressiveness, and that other variables that have yet to be identified play a more integral role.

Second, it appears that ARG_{gt} has a small negative effect ($\rho = -.14$) on self-esteem that is mediated by a variable other than argumentation skill. Argumentativeness theory suggests that ARG_{gt} bolsters people's self-esteem by increasing their confidence in their ability to argue. Suppose, however, that the consequences of ARG_{gt} are not all positive. ARG_{gt} may decrease a person's interpersonal attractiveness. Self-esteem depends, in part, on appearing attractive to others. It may therefore be that more argumentative individuals are less popular; that is, ARG_{gt} could inhibit self-esteem by decreasing attractiveness.

METHODS

Two sets of meta-analyses were conducted. The first set addressed the first research question concerning the unidimensionality of the ARG_{gt} scale. Four meta-analyses were performed in this set. We began by estimating the correlation between the ARG_{ap} and ARG_{av} scales, but only five studies were available. Fortunately, many more studies provided reliability estimates for the ARG_{ap} scale, the ARG_{av} scale, and the ARG_{gt} scale. These reliabilities allowed us to estimate the correlation between the ARG_{ap} and ARG_{av} scales. Hence, our second and third meta-analyses examined the average interitem correlation on the ARG_{ap} subscale and the average interitem correlation on the ARG_{av} subscale, respectively. The final meta-analysis in this set examined the average interitem correlation on the ARG_{gt} scale, where the ARG_{av} items had been reverse coded so that they would have positive part–whole correlations. The results of the latter four meta-analyses were combined to determine whether the ARG_{ap} and ARG_{av} scales should be kept separate and treated as independent scores or combined as a measure of ARG_{gt}.

The second set of meta-analyses addressed the second research question concerning the correlation between ARG_{gt} and verbal aggressiveness. Four meta-analyses were performed in this set. Our fifth meta-analysis estimated the reliability of the verbal aggressiveness scale, and our sixth the effect of ARG_{gt} on verbal aggressiveness. A large degree of variability across samples in either of these two meta-analyses would suggest the presence of moderator variables. If the average correlation between ARG_{gt} and verbal aggressiveness were negative, this would support the proposed constructive learning process. If the average correlation were positive, however, this would suggest that argumentativeness theory should be revised. The seventh and eighth meta-analyses estimated the effect of male gender on argumentativeness and verbal aggressiveness, respectively.

Samples

Relevant studies for our two sets of meta-analyses were obtained from re-view articles and a keyword search of PsychInfo. The meta-analytic proce-dures used followed the variance-centered method recommended by Hunter and Schmidt (1990). We determined the weighted average correla-tion (r) for the total number of participants (TN). When three or more sam-ples were available, we calculated the standard deviation of the correlation for the sample of studies (SD_r), the standard deviation of the correlation es-timated for the population of studies (SD_p), and the percentage of variance explained by sampling error. We also calculated a chi-square test for hetero-geneity to detect variance beyond that expected from sampling error, and 90% confidence intervals around the mean correlation.

Procedures for Estimating Internal Consistency

Researchers have used several different versions of the ARG_{gt} scale. The most common is the full 20-item scale proposed by Infante and Rancer (1982). Shorter versions were also used, including 10-item and 8-item forms. The standard score coefficient alphas were reported by most re-searchers. Coefficient α reliability estimates depend on the number of items on the scale and the average within-scale correlations, $\bar{r}_{ws}$. The number of nonredundant within-scale correlations, i, is calculated as follows:

$$i \quad \frac{n \ (n \ 1)}{2} \tag{2}$$

where n is the number of items. Applying Equation 2, the 10-item ap-proach-argument or avoid-argument scales would yield 45 nonredundant correlations for the calculation of $\bar{r}_{ws}$. By contrast, for the 4-item ARG_{ap} and ARG_{av} scales, there would be a mere 6 nonredundant correlations used to calculate $\bar{r}_{ws}$.

Provided with the alpha reliability and the number of items in a given study, we could work backward to calculate $\bar{r}_{ws}$. Thus, we could compare the $\bar{r}_{ws}$ across samples regardless of the number of items used in a particular study. We used meta-analysis to summarize across studies and then estimate the $\bar{r}_{ws}$ across studies for the approach-argument items, the $\bar{r}_{ws}$ for the avoid-argument items, and the $\bar{r}_{ws}$ for the general trait items. We then used these three values to estimate the average between-scale correlations, $\bar{r}_{bs}$, in the ARG_{gt} scale.

The reader might object that the values of $\bar{r}_{ws}$ for studies that used the short forms of the general trait scale should not be compared to the values of

$\bar{r}_{ws}$ for studies that used the long forms because the ratio of $\bar{r}_{ws}$ to $\bar{r}_{bs}$ will be substantially larger for the long form than the short form.[4] However, researchers who used the short forms of the ARG_{gt} scale did not randomly eliminate items. Instead, a number of these researchers (Blickle, 1995; Blickle, Habasch, & Senft, 1998) tested for heterogeneous items, and then eliminated those that had the lowest quality. That is, they discarded the items that had the weakest correlations with the other items on the scale. Presumably, this would substantially boost the $\bar{r}_{ws}$ for the short-form studies, raising it to the level of the long-form studies.

We assumed that the smaller within-scale to between-scale ratio for the short forms was offset by the boost in the within-scale correlations when the low-quality items were eliminated. Consider a few examples of researchers who eliminated low-quality items. Kazoleas (1993) reduced the 20-item scale down to 12 items and his $\bar{r}_{ws}$ was a rather large .35. Infante and Gordon (1985) used a 10-item scale that had an $\bar{r}_{ws}$ of .31. Infante (Infante & Gordon, 1987) used an even shorter 5-item scale with an $\bar{r}_{ws}$ of .31. Finally, Boster, Levine, and Kozleas (1993) reduced the 20-item scale down to 13 items and their $\bar{r}_{ws}$ was .30.

RESULTS

Argumentativeness

We employed three criteria to assess the degree of unidimensionality of the ARG_{gt} scale: homogeneity of item content, internal consistency, and parallelism.

Homogeneity of Content. The ARG_{gt} scale may contain a small subscale (Items 16 and 18) that measures argumentative skill (Blickle et al., 1998). Blickle et al. (1998) used the Argumentativeness Competence Form (Trapp, Yingling, & Wanner, 1987) as a measure of argumentative skill. In fact, Blickle (1995) conducted a confirmatory factor analysis of the ARG_{gt} scale and concluded that the two argumentative skill items formed a separate factor. To determine whether there was evidence of an argumentation

---

[4]For the 20-item general trait scale, there would be 90 nonredundant within-scale correlations (45 from the approach-argument scale and 45 from the avoid-argument scale) and 100 nonredundant between-scale correlations (approach items correlated with avoid items). Thus, for the 20-item scale, the ratio of within-scale to between-scale correlations is .90. For the 8-item general trait scale, there would be 12 nonredundant within-scale correlations (6 from the approach-argument scale and 6 from the avoid-argument scale) and 64 nonredundant between-scale correlations. Thus, for the 8-item scale, the ratio of within-scale to between-scale correlations is .19.

skill subscale among the argumentativeness items, we regenerated the correlation matrix from Suzuki and Rancer (1994) based on the factor-loading matrix they provided. Our reanalysis indicated that Items 16 and 18 were only slightly correlated in the Suzuki and Rancer data, and this was the case for both the U.S. and Japanese samples. In fact, the alpha reliabilities for the argumentative skill scale in the Suzuki and Rancer data would be .11 for the U.S. sample and .26 for the Japanese sample. Although Blickle's (1995) argumentation skill scale did not replicate, his study differs from the Suzuki and Rancer (1994) study in that Blickle et al. (1998) randomly intermixed items on the survey. Nearly all other studies present the ARG_{gt} and verbal aggressiveness scales intact, encouraging response set, as evidenced by the lower reliabilities on the Blickle et al. (1998) argumentativeness scale scores. Other subscales might exist within the argumentativeness items, one related to hostility guilt (Items 1 and 5) and another to curiosity (Items 2 and 15). These clusters might show higher correlations with standard measures of hostility guilt and Need for Cognition (Cacioppo & Petty, 1982) than they do with the ARG_{av} and ARG_{ap} scales, respectively.

We detected other potential content themes in the ARG_{ap} and ARG_{av} scales. On the ARG_{ap} scale, the majority of the items should be a function of n Ach or more specifically competitiveness (Items 4, 7, 9, 11, 13, 17, and 20). Infante and Rancer (1982) stated that motives that inhibit argument are based in the anxiety associated with arguing. We found that such items could be grouped into two themes: anxiety over consequences such as retribution (Items 3, 6, 8, 10, and 12), and active avoidance (Items 14 and 19). Item 14 may correlate highly with empathy scales. Given that our content analysis uncovered seven content themes, it was quite possible that the ARG_{gt} scale could be multidimensional.

Internal Consistency.   We began by estimating the correlation between the ARG_{ap} and ARG_{av} scales. We could locate only five sample correlations. Infante and Rancer (1982) reported a correlation of .07 ($N = 692$). Suzuki and Rancer (1994) reported correlations of −.39 for their U.S. sample ($N = 755$) and −.34 for their Japanese sample ($N = 716$). Blickle (1995, Study 1) reported a correlation of −.64 ($N = 140$), and Rancer, Whitecap, Kosberg, and Avtgis (1997) reported a correlation of −.51 ($N = 296$) The average weighted correlation was −.28, $k = 5$, $TN = 2,557$. There was massive variance across studies, $SD_r = .22$, and $SD_\rho = .22$, $\chi^2(4) = 50.23$, $p <$ .0001, so much so that it seemed implausible given the hypothesized trait-like quality of responses to the ARG_{ap} with ARG_{av} scales. The lone positive correlation was the $r = .07$ obtained by Infante and Rancer (1982).

With the .07 value excluded, $\bar{r} = -.41$, and the variance across samples dropped sharply to $SD_r = .08$. Thus, the .07 value is 6 SD away from the mean correlation.[5]

Next, we performed the meta-analysis on the $\bar{r}_{ws}$ values for ARG_{ap}. The $\bar{r}_{ws}$ values for the samples used in the meta-analysis can be found in Table 16.1. The average $\bar{r}_{ws}$ for ARG_{ap} was .39, $k = 17$, $TN = 5,746$. There was substantial variance across samples, with $SD_r = .07$, and $SD_\rho = .05$. Sampling error explained 44% of the variance across samples, $\chi^2(16) = 38.90$, $p < .001$. The 90% confidence interval ranged from .32 to .46. To put these findings in perspective, a 10-item ARG_{ap} scale with an $\bar{r}_{ws}$ of .39 would have an alpha reliability of .87. Thus, the typical 10-item ARG_{ap} scale has rather good reliability.

Next, we performed the meta-analysis on the $\bar{r}_{ws}$ values for ARG_{av}. The $\bar{r}_{ws}$ values for the samples used in the meta-analysis can be found in Table 16.1. The average $\bar{r}_{ws}$ for ARG_{av} was .33, $k = 17$, $TN = 5,746$. There was little variance across samples, with $SD_r = .06$, and $SD_\rho = .03$. Sampling error explained 73% of the variance across samples, $\chi^2(16) = 23.30$, $p = .11$. The 90% confidence interval ranged from .29 to .37. A 10-item ARG_{av} scale with an $\bar{r}_{ws}$ of .33 would have a coefficient alpha reliability of .83. The typical 10-item ARG_{ap} scale would thus have adequate reliability.

Once we had estimates of the correlation between the ARG_{ap} and ARG_{av} scales ($\bar{r} = -.28$), and the $\bar{r}_{ws}$ for ARG_{ap} (.39) and ARG_{av} (.33), we could then estimate what the $\bar{r}_{ws}$ would be for a 20-item ARG_{gt} measure as follows:

$$\bar{r}_{ws} = .39 * 45 + .33 * 45 + 100 * .28 = .32 \qquad (3)$$

where the $\bar{r}_{ws}$ values for ARG_{ap} and ARG_{av} are weighted by the number of nonredundant within-scale correlations in the matrix, and the $\bar{r}_{bs}$ for the ARG_{ap} with ARG_{av} correlations is weighted by the number of nonredundant between-scale correlations in the matrix.

---

[5]Infante and Rancer (1982) reported that the .07 value was obtained from an oblique factor analysis. The ARG_{ap} with ARG_{av} correlations from the other studies were negative. They used the OBLIMIN procedure within SPSS to estimate the correlation between the two factors (D. A. Infante, personal communication, August, 15, 1998). The OBLIMIN program reverses the sign of the correlation it reports between factor scores. It may be that Infante and Rancer mistakenly reported the reverse-coded factor score correlation rather than the factor correlation. Thus, the actual correlation between the ARG_{ap} with ARG_{av} scales may have been $r = -.07$. We ran a simulation using the DOS version of SPSS to compare the factor correlations reported by the OBLIMIN routine to those obtained from raw score correlations. In each case, the OBLIMIN estimated correlation was less than the raw score correlation, suffering a 16% attenuation. Thus, we believe the actual correlation between ARG_{ap} with ARG_{av} in the Infante and Rancer (1982) study may have been more like $r = -.08$.

TABLE 16.1

**Average Interitem Correlations and Number of Items Within
the Argument Approach and Argument Avoidance Scales**

Study	N	ARG_{ap}		ARG_{av}	
		$\bar{r}_{ws}$	N Items	$\bar{r}_{ws}$	N Items
Blickle 1995 (1)	140	.36	10	.37	10
Canary et al., 1988	434	.33	10	.27	10
Dowling & Flint, 1990	564	.41	10	.33	10
Infante & Gordon, 1985	216	.42	10	.36	10
Infante & Rancer, 1982	692	.50	10	.38	10
Klopf et al., 1991 (Finns)	247	.43	10	.36	10
Klopf et al., 1991 (U.S.)	154	.36	10	.33	10
Nicotera & Rancer, 1994	175	.55	4	.45	4
Onyekwere et al., 1991	240	.44	10	.40	10
Nicotera et al., 1990	164	.40	10	.42	10
Prunty et al., 1990	321	.32	10	.26	10
Rancer et al., 1986	31	.29	10	.25	10
Rancer et al., 1992	132	.42	10	.31	10
Roach, 1992	203	.40	10	.37	10
Sanders et al., 1994	357	.38	10	.35	10
Stewart & Roach, 1993	526	.26	10	.31	10
Suzuki & Rancer, 1994 (Japan)	716	.33	10	.22	10
Suzuki & Rancer, 1994 (U.S.)	755	.39	10	.33	10
Total	5,746	.39		.33	

Our last meta-analysis in this set was conducted to obtain an observed value for $\bar{r}_{ws}$ on the ARG_{gt} scale. The $\bar{r}_{ws}$ values for the samples used in the meta-analysis can be found in Table 16.2. The average $\bar{r}_{ws}$ for ARG_{gt} was .27, $k = 12$, $TN = 2,362$. There was little variance across samples, with $SD_r = .05$, and $SD_\rho = .00$. Sampling error explained 100% of the variance across samples. To put these findings in perspective, a 20-item ARG_{gt} scale with an $\bar{r}_{ws}$ of .27 would have a coefficient alpha reliability of .88. The difference between the predicted value for the ARG_{gt} $\bar{r}_{ws}$ (.32) and the obtained value for the ARG_{gt} $\bar{r}_{ws}$ (.27) was only

.05. The small size of this error suggests that the assumptions that went into the reliability analysis were well founded, and that the estimated correlation of $-.28$ between the ARG_{ap} and ARG_{av} scales is relatively accurate. Correcting this correlation for the average alphas obtained from our meta-analyses (.87 for ARG_{ap} and .83 for ARG_{av}) yields a correlation of $-.33$ between ARG_{ap} and ARG_{av}. This finding is consistent with a unidimensional ARG_{gt} measure derived from the ARG_{ap} and ARG_{av} subscales.

External Consistency.   If the ARG_{ap} and ARG_{av} scales are part of a homogenous, unidimensional ARG_{gt} scale, then they should correlate with other variables to approximately the same degree. Blickle (1995) correlated the ARG_{ap} and ARG_{av} scales with the Big Five second-order personality factors. We reverse coded the ARG_{av} correlations with the five second-order factors. The difference between the ARG_{ap} and ARG_{av} correlations was .15 for neuroticism ($\bar{r} = -.32$), .04 for extraversion ($\bar{r} = .31$), .11 for openness to experience ($\bar{r} = .38$), .03 for agreeableness ($\bar{r} = -.07$), and .01 for conscientiousness ($\bar{r} = .18$). The average difference in the ARG_{ap} and ARG_{av} correla-

TABLE 16.2
**Average Within-Scale Correlations and Number of Items
for the ARG_{gt} Scale**

Study	N	$\bar{r}_{ws}$	N Items
Beatty et al., 1994	74	.28	20
Blickle et al., 1998 (1)	119	.28	18
Blickle et al., 1998 (2)	112	.27	18
Boster & Levine, 1988	196	.27	16
Boster et al., 1993	46	.30	13
Downs et al., 1990	148	.11	20
Infante & Gordon, 1987	131	.31	5
Infante & Gordon, 1989	146	.31	10
Infante & Gordon, 1991	216	.22	10
Infante et al., 1989	295	.22	10
Kazoleas, 1993	188	.35	12
Martin et al., 1997	276	.29	20
Prunty et al., 1990	321	.22	20
Rudd, 1996	174	.17	10

tions across the five factors was .07. That is, there was very little difference in how the ARG_{ap} and ARG_{av} scales correlated with other variables, once the ARG_{av} items had been appropriately reverse scored.

In an effort to establish the construct validity of the ARG_{gt} scale, Infante and Rancer (1982) correlated the ARG_{ap} and ARG_{av} scales with three communication predisposition scales and willingness to participate in a debate. If we reverse code the correlations of avoidance with the four scales, we find that difference in the size of the correlation for the ARG_{ap} and ARG_{av} scales is .04 for communication apprehension ($\bar{r} = -.43$), .06 for predisposition toward verbal behavior ($\bar{r} = .35$), .12 for unwillingness to communicate ($\bar{r} = -.41$), and .06 for participation in a debate ($\bar{r} = -.35$). Thus, across the four variables, the ARG_{ap} and ARG_{av} correlations were within an average of .07 of one another.

Although more data need to be collected to fully evaluate the external consistency of the ARG_{ap} and ARG_{av} scales, the current evidence indicates that the two scales are within .07 of being exactly parallel. This provides further justification for accepting the ARG_{gt} scale as a unidimensional measure. Interestingly, the average correlations across the ARG_{ap} and ARG_{av} scales are quite similar and suggestive of a negative correlation between ARG_{gt} and communication apprehension ($\bar{r} = -.42$) and a slightly smaller correlation with the more general predisposition to communicate ($\bar{r} = .35$). These correlations are consistent with ARG_{gt} as a consequence of extraversion and assertiveness.

In conclusion, the content of the ARG_{gt} scale appears relatively unidimensional with themes of argumentative skill and potentially themes of hostility, guilt, curiosity, competitiveness, anxiety over consequences, and withdrawal. The meta-analytic evidence shows that the ARG_{ap} and ARG_{av} scales are negatively correlated rather than independent as argumentativeness theorists asserted. This finding is consistent with a unidimensional ARG_{gt} scale. The limited external consistency evidence indicates that the ARG_{ap} and ARG_{av} scales are parallel when other theoretically important variables are used as the criteria. This finding is also consistent with a unidimensional measure of ARG_{gt}. The moderately strong negative correlation indicates that the majority of people belong to one of three clusters: lows, neutral moderates, or highs. A substantially smaller number of people belong to the two remaining clusters, apathetic moderates and conflicted moderates (see Fig. 16.2).

Verbal Aggressiveness

The second set of meta-analyses concerned verbal aggressiveness—its reliability and ARG_{gt} as its antecedent. The reliability of the verbal aggressiveness scale for the samples we obtained can be found in Table 16.3. The average reliability was .84, $k = 19$, $TN = 4{,}757$. There was notable variance across samples, with $SD_r = .05$, and $SD_\rho = .05$. Sampling error explained only 13% of the variance across samples, $\chi^2(18) = 143.68$, $p < .001$. The 90% confidence interval ranged from .78 to .90.

TABLE 16.3
The Reliability of the Verbal Aggressiveness Scale

Sample	N	r	N Items	Report	Intact	Item Order
Beatty et al., 1994	74	.83	20	Self	Y	Not Random
Blickle et al., 1998	153	.73	20	Self	Y	Random
Boster & Levine, 1988	196	.79				
Boster et al., 1993	46	.90	11	Self	Y	Random
Downs et al., 1990	148	.71	20	Other	Y	NR
Infante & Gordon, 1985	216	.78	5	Other	N	NR
Infante & Gordon, 1987	131	.69	5	Other	N	NR
Infante & Gordon, 1989	146	.90	10	Other	N	NR
Infante et al., 1992	181	.87	20	Self	Y	NR
Infante & Wigley, 1986	209	.81	20	Self	Y	NR
Lim, 1990	76	.85	20	Self	Y	NR
Martin & Anderson, 1995	403	.82	5	Self	Y	NR
Martin & Anderson, 1996	665	.87	10	Self	Y	NR
Martin et al., 1997	276	.88	20	Self	Y	NR
Nicotera & Rancer, 1994	175	.83	6	Self	Y	NR
Rancer et al., 1986	31	.72				NR
Rancer et al., 1992	132	.85				NR
Rudd, 1996	87	.67	10	Self	N	NR
Sanders et al., 1994	357	.85	20	Self	Y	NR
Suzuki & Rancer, 1994 (Japan)	716	.89				NR
Suzuki & Rancer, 1994 (U.S.)	763	.85				NR
Total	5,181	.84	Eta = .33	Eta = .31	Eta = .47	Eta = .38

Moderator Variables.   We explored four variables as moderators of the reliability of the verbal aggressiveness scale. The four moderators were number of items on the scale, whether the scale had respondents rate themselves or others, whether the scale had been specially adapted to a particular context, and whether the items had been randomly presented as part of a larger questionnaire. The value of the reliability coefficient correlated .31 with self-rating, .33 with number of items, –.47 with adaptation of the scale, and –.38 with random presentation of the items. There was a high correlation between self-rating and adaptation, $r = -.91$, and adaptation appeared to be the better predictor of the reliability value in a multiple regression. Hence, we did not enter the self-rating variable as a predictor of the reliability value. Excluding the relatively few participants who received a survey with the items in random order, we regressed number of items and adaptation on the reliability value. Scale reliability increased with number of items ($\beta = .22$), but decreased with adaptation ($\beta = -.43$). With the studies that adapted the scale to special contexts and those that presented the items randomly with items from other scales excluded, the reliability values were homogenous: $\bar{r} = .85$, $SD_r = .03$, with sampling error explaining most of the variance across samples.

Effect of Argumentativeness on Verbal Aggressiveness.   The correlation between ARG_{gt} and verbal aggressiveness for the samples we obtained can be found in Table 16.4. The average correlation was .16, $k = 12$, $TN = 3,397$. There was modest variance across samples, with $SD_r = .09$, and $SD_\rho = .07$. Sampling error explained 41% of the variance across samples, $\chi^2(11) = 29.10$, $p < .01$. The 90% confidence interval ranged from .07 to .25. Much of the variance was due to the Infante and Wigley (1986) study that found a correlation of –.04 between ARG_{gt} and verbal aggressiveness. This value is 3.33 SD away from the average correlation. In that study, verbal aggressiveness correlated .60 with the Buss–Durkee (BD) measure of verbal aggression. ARG_{gt} correlated .09 with the BD verbal aggression measure, which is more in keeping with the average correlation. Thus, the old BD verbal aggression measure appeared to be more valid than the new Infante–Wigley (IW) verbal aggressiveness measure. This is ironic given that use of the IW verbal aggressiveness scale has been justified on the grounds that it is more valid than the BD verbal aggression scale. Without the IW outlier, the correlation between ARG_{gt} and verbal aggressiveness increased to .17, $SD_\rho = .06$, with sampling error explaining 48% of the variance across studies.

TABLE 16.4
Correlation of Argumentativeness With Verbal Aggressiveness

Study	N	r
Blickle, 1995	153	.06
Boster et al., 1993	46	.19
Downs et al., 1990	148	.36
Infante et al., 1989	295	.22
Infante & Gordon, 1991	216	.10
Infante & Wigley, 1986 (1)	209	.10
Infante & Wigley, 1986 (2)	104	−.04
Martin et al., 1997	276	.08
Nicotera & Rancer, 1994	175	.21
Rancer et al., 1997	296	.29
Suzuki & Rancer, 1994 (Japan)	716	.09
Suzuki & Rancer, 1994 (U.S.)	763	.22
Total	3,397	.16

The Effect of Male Gender on Argumentativeness and Verbal Aggressiveness

The correlation of male gender with ARG_{gt} and verbal aggressiveness for the samples we obtained can be found in Table 16.5. The average effect of male gender on ARG_{gt} was .15, $k = 4$, $TN = 1,284$. There was notable variance across samples, with $SD_r = .10$, and $SD_\rho = .08$, $\chi^2(3) = 14.41$, $p < .01$. The average effect of male gender on verbal aggressiveness was .13, $k = 6$, $TN = 1,552$. As with ARG_{gt}, there was notable variance across samples, with $SD_r = .10$, and $SD_\rho = .08$, $\chi^2(3) = 16.52$, $p < .01$. Despite the variance, the correlations in Table 16.5 show that male gender does increase both ARG_{gt} and verbal aggressiveness, as predicted by argumentativeness theory.

DISCUSSION

The first set of meta-analyses in this chapter offered evidence that the ARG_{gt} scale is unidimensional. The second set of meta-analyses showed that the IW

TABLE 16.5
Effect of Male Gender on Argumentativeness and Verbal Aggressiveness

Study	N	ARG_{gt}	N	Verbal Aggressiveness
Dowling & Flint, 1990	113	.35		
Harman et al., 1990			308	.15
Infante, 1982	701	.12		
Infante et al., 1989	295	.04	295	.00
Infante et al., 1984			168	.18
Infante & Wigley, 1986 (Study 1)			209	.10
Infante & Wigley, 1986 (Study 2)			397	.11
Nicotera & Rancer, 1994	175	.32	175	.37
Rancer & Dierks-Stewart, 1985				
Schultz & Anderson, 1984				
Total	1,284	.15	1,552	.13

scale is a reliable measure of verbal aggressiveness, although the extent of the reliability depends somewhat on the intact presentation of the items. Adapting the ARG_{gt} items for special contexts appears to reduce the reliability of the IW scale. The meta-analyses also found that verbal aggressiveness has a positive correlation with argumentativeness. Infante and his colleagues have placed considerable weight on the argumentativeness construct, both for its role in argumentation theory and for the practical significance of its social role of improving argumentation practice (see Infante & Rancer, 1996 for a review). The meta-analytic findings presented here indicate that argumentativeness theory requires some rethinking to retrieve its usefulness.

Unidimensionality of the Argumentativeness Scale

The first issue we addressed concerned the dimensionality of the ARG_{gt} scale. Infante and his colleagues assumed that the ARG_{ap} and ARG_{av} scales are uncorrelated. This would suggest that the ARG_{gt} scale is multidimensional and that the concept of a unidimensional, general trait of argumentativeness be abandoned in favor of a two-dimensional orientation toward arguing. If the argumentativeness scale is multidimensional, then computation of argumentativeness as shown in Equation 1 is inappropriate. The difference score ignores the effect of an interaction between the ARG_{ap} and ARG_{av} scales on important criterion variables, raising the specter of averaging across heterogeneous effects.

Our content analysis of the ARG_{gt} scale uncovered a multitude of themes that suggested the possibility of multidimensionality. Meta-analysis showed that the correlation between ARG_{ap} and ARG_{av} averaged $-.28$, exposing the findings of the introductory study by Infante and Rancer as an extreme outlier. We interpreted the Infante and Rancer finding as an artifact emanating from their use of factor score correlations. Thus, the meta-analytic evidence indicates that the correlation between the ARG_{ap} and ARG_{av} scales is negative, although some question remains concerning the magnitude of this negative correlation. Recall that the proposition that ARG_{ap} and ARG_{av} are uncorrelated was patterned after the assumption that M_S and M_{AF} are uncorrelated. In fact, a meta-analysis by Hamilton and Mineo (1999) found that the correlation between M_S (as indicated by objective measures of need for achievement) and M_{AF} is positive and moderately strong. If there is linkage between the motivation to achieve and the motivation to argue, it is most likely in the positive effect of need for achievement on ARG_{gt}. Achievement motivation theory is thus a poor foundation on which to build a theory about the motivation to argue. In summary, not only is the proposition that ARG_{ap} and ARG_{av} are uncorrelated false; the rationale on which the proposition was based is false.

The meta-analysis of the average within-scale correlations (generated from reliability values) for the ARG_{av} scale found them to be homogenous across samples, $\bar{r}_{ws}, = .33$. The r would yield an average coefficient alpha reliability of .83 for a 10-item version of the scale. However, the meta-analysis of the average within-scale correlations for the ARG_{ap} scale found them to be slightly heterogeneous, with a 90% confidence interval that ranged from $\bar{r}_{ws}, = .32$ to $.45$. The r would yield an average coefficient alpha reliability of .86 for a 10-item version of the scale. To obtain the estimate of the average between-scale correlation, $\bar{r}_{bs} = -.28$, we used the correlation between the ARG_{ap} and ARG_{av} scales. We then used the average within-scale correlations for ARG_{ap} and ARG_{av}, along with the $\bar{r}_{bs}$ to produce the predicted average correlation of .32 among the items on the ARG_{gt} scale. Finally, we meta-analyzed the within-scale correlations (generated from reliability values) for the ARG_{gt} scale and found that the average $\bar{r}_{ws}$ for ARG_{gt} was .27, yielding a coefficient alpha reliability of .88 for a 20-item scale. The difference between the predicted and obtained $\bar{r}_{ws}$ for the ARG_{gt} scale was therefore only .05. This analysis provided further support for our conclusion that the correlation between the ARG_{ap} and ARG_{av} scales is at least moderately negative ($r - .30$) rather than zero.

As a final step we reviewed the external consistency of the ARG_{ap} and ARG_{av} scales. The difference in the correlation between the two scales with measures of predisposition to communicate and the Big Five personality factors was only .07. We summarize the effects of these personality variables in Fig. 16.3. If the within-scale correlation matrix for ARG_{gt} is relatively flat and the ARG_{ap} and ARG_{av} scales correlate with important variables such as predisposition to communication and personality antecedents to approximately the same degree, then the evidence for unidimensionality is quite strong. The only evidence for separating the scale into ARG_{ap} and ARG_{av} subscales came from the introductory study of Infante and Rancer (1982); we suggested that the finding of that study was due to artifact, the result of the statistical procedures used in the analysis. Thus, we conclude that the vast majority of the empirical evidence indicates that the ARG_{gt} scale is unidimensional rather than multidimensional. This led us to hypothesize that the number of people who are apathetic moderates or conflicted moderates in the argumentatives typology (see Fig. 16.2) is relatively small.

An ARG_{gt} scale that is unidimensional would be good news for argumentativeness theorists. Many of the studies they have conducted have reported statistics summarizing the relation between ARG_{gt} and other variables. Were the ARG_{gt} scale multidimensional, nearly all of the studies employing Equation 1 would have been suspect and of limited value because they would have collapsed across potentially heterogeneous effects. We suspect

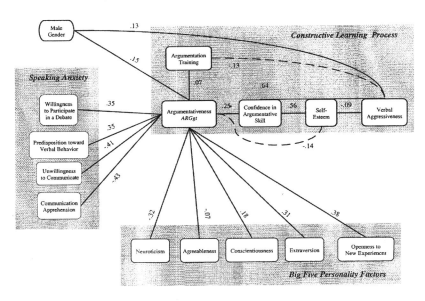

FIG. 16.3.   Revised model of argumentativeness and verbal aggressiveness.

that Infante and Rancer (1982) confused a strong–weak gradient among the ARG_{gt} items with multidimensionality. Those who have performed confirmatory factor analyses of the ARG_{gt} scale have eliminated more than a few items because those items appeared to be internally inconsistent (Blickle, 1995; Blickle et al., 1998; Boster et al., 1993; Kazoleas, 1993).

Argumentativeness and Verbal Aggressiveness

Our meta-analysis found that the reliability of the verbal aggressiveness scale increased with the number of items on the scale but decreased with adaptation of the scale from its original format. Generally, the scale showed satisfactory internal consistency with an average reliability of .85. Those who are adapting the scale for special purposes such as organizational or relational contexts should be aware that their adaptations have somewhat lower reliabilities than the original scale.

Confidence in Argumentation Skill as a Mediating Variable.

The average correlation between ARG_{gt} and verbal aggressiveness was positive, $r = .20$ corrected for attenuation. In fact, the only study to find a negative correlation between the two variables was the introductory study by Infante and Rancer (1982). The fact that this correlation is positive indicates that the constructive learning process does not operate as proposed by argumentativeness theory. ARG_{gt} appears to enhance verbal aggressiveness, although the effect is modest. The enhancing effect of ARG_{gt} on verbal aggressiveness is most likely mediated by confidence in argumentation skills. Within the context of the hypothesized model (see Fig. 16.1), ARG_{gt} should increase confidence, with confidence having antagonistic effects on verbal aggressiveness. The enhancing effect of confidence on verbal aggressiveness would need to be very large ($\rho = .64$) to explain the positive correlation between ARG_{gt} and verbal aggressiveness: $.25 * .64 = .16$. We illustrate this effect within the revised model shown in Fig. 16.3.

We suspect the large positive effect of confidence on verbal aggressiveness is due to the increased availability or appeal of negative compliance-gaining strategies. That is, as speakers become more confident in their ability to argue, they are willing to try strategies that may elicit forceful responses from their targets. Speakers who feel less competent in arguing may prefer to confine themselves to more positive compliance-gaining strategies that are not likely to generate a strong retort from their targets. The inhibiting effect of confidence on verbal aggressiveness, as shown in Fig. 16.3, would be mediated by self-esteem. Note that the enhancement effect of confidence on verbal aggressiveness (.64) is more than 10 times larger than the inhibition effect (.56 * −.09 = −.05). If true, this would disconfirm the main thesis of the theory. The social implications of this conclusion are not appealing to argumentation instructors. In the absence of additional information, it suggests that they should undermine their students' confidence in their ability to argue in the interest of squelching verbal aggression.

Male Gender as an Antecedent Variable. An alternative explanation for the positive correlation between ARG_{gt} and verbal aggressiveness is that ARG_{gt} does inhibit verbal aggressiveness, but this inhibiting effect is suppressed by antecedent variables common to both ARG_{gt} and verbal aggressiveness. We refer to this explanation as the *suppressor antecedent hypothesis*. Suppose that ARG_{gt} inhibits verbal aggressiveness, but the negative effect is suppressed at the level of the zero-order correlation by an antecedent variable such as male gender. To suppress a negative effect of ARG_{gt} on verbal aggressiveness, the product of the effects of male gender on ARG_{gt} and verbal aggressiveness would need to be positive. In fact, this is the case with male gender. The problem, however, is that both of these enhancement effects are small, and this leads to a trivial amount of suppression (.15 * .13 = .02).

The findings of the meta-analysis suggest that there is a positive effect of male gender on verbal aggressiveness that is not mediated by ARG_{gt}. As shown in Fig. 16.3, male gender would increase ARG_{gt} ($\rho = .14$), with ARG_{gt} producing an indirect effect on verbal aggressiveness of .16) for an indirect gender effect of .02 (.14 * .16). Male gender would also increase verbal aggressiveness ($\rho = .10$) without mediation from ARG_{gt}. We suspect that this direct positive effect of male gender is due to hostility. That is, male gender increases hostility, and hostility increases verbal aggressiveness. Note that despite its small size, the hostility effect is five times as large as the effect of male gender on verbal aggressiveness mediated by ARG_{gt}.

Undiscovered Common Antecedent Variables. It is possible that an as yet undiscovered variable has a strong enhancing effect ($\rho \approx .50$) on both ARGgt and verbal aggressiveness, and that this variable is responsible for the positive zero-order correlation between ARG_{gt} and verbal aggressiveness. Suppression could also occur if a common antecedent variable had strong inhibitory effects ($\rho \approx -.50$) on both ARG_{gt} and verbal aggressiveness. Negative effects of this size would suppress the zero-order correlation between ARG_{gt} and verbal aggressiveness by .25. Given the zero-order correlation of .17 obtained from the meta-analysis, a small negative effect of ARG_{gt} on verbal aggressiveness on the order of $\rho = -.08$ could be completely suppressed (−.08 +

$.25 = .17$). The personality trait of agreeableness could operate in this fashion. However, there are two more types of common antecedent variables: those that increase ARG_{gt} while decreasing verbal aggressiveness, and those that decrease ARG_{gt} while increasing verbal aggressiveness. If these latter two types of antecedents are prevalent, then we are back to the first explanation—that ARG_{gt} increases verbal aggressiveness.

The correlation between ARG_{gt} and verbal aggressiveness was fairly heterogeneous across studies. In some studies the correlation was less positive than in others. This heterogeneity is due, in part, to the fact that a number of researchers have used different subsets of the original 20 argumentativeness items in their instruments. A negative effect of ARG_{gt} on verbal aggressiveness might be possible, but operating only within a limited domain. In their review article, Infante and Rancer (1996) concluded that culture influences both ARG_{gt} and verbal aggressiveness. Suzuki and Rancer (1994) speculated that the more externalized a culture, the less likely its members will be to engage in argument and verbal aggression. They characterized this effect as a confound of external contextualization of culture with verbal aggressiveness. Actually, the effect they described is range restriction in both the ARG_{gt} and verbal aggressiveness variables. The difference between confounding and range restriction is important. Suppose that external contextualization of culture decreases both ARG_{gt} and verbal aggressiveness, resulting in skewed distributions on both variables. This would reduce the size of the correlation of ARG_{gt} with verbal aggressiveness, but it would also reduce the correlations of the two variables with the antecedent and consequence variables of ARG_{gt} and verbal aggressiveness, making the suppressor antecedent hypothesis less plausible.

The Practice of Argumentation

The meta-analyses reported here do not support the original optimism regarding the projected social effects of decreasing verbal aggressiveness by increasing argumentativeness. The results indicated that the effect of argumentativeness on verbal aggression is positive and moderately small.

Teaching argument skills may be one method of reducing verbal aggressiveness. Previous studies (Sanders et al., 1994) seem to indicate a small negative effect for argumentation training on verbal aggressiveness. More correctly, we should think in terms of retraining argument skills. In the broadest sense of skills necessary to survive disagreements, students come to the college classroom with well-honed argument skills. Verbal aggression is one such skill, as it allows these students the appearance of having preserved their position, although they do so at the expense of rational discourse and to the possible detriment of interpersonal relationships. However, there are other nonaggressive means that students use for dealing with argumentative situations, and these must be counted as part of the repertoire of argument skills they bring to the classroom. Among these are possible passive avoidance strategies (e.g., equivocation) in which people preserve their position by rendering it ambiguous enough to be immune from attack.

In the light of these alternative strategies, teaching argument skills can be redefined as teaching competence in conflict resolution through rational discourse. This amounts to providing rational strategies for resolving disagreements as an attractive replacement for the aggressive and passive strategies currently in the students' repertoire. A program for developing such competencies should emphasize argumentation in real-life contexts rather than emphasizing the formal analysis of arguments. Argumentation theory has too long concentrated on formal reasoning structures at the expense of the pragmatic goal of rationally resolving disagreements in everyday life. This misdirection has in large part been responsible for the weak effects obtained for argument instruction.

Unless teaching argument becomes more practical, students will continue to be motivated to use aggressive and passive strategies because those strategies appear effective for defending and protecting belief systems. Beyond the apparent practical effectiveness of irrational strategies, however, argument instruction must also overcome the psychological and social forces that support the use of those irrational strategies.

Verbal aggressiveness and the motivation to argue rationally are presumed to be anchored within a system of basic personality traits like extraversion and neuroticism. Aside from the questions of whether teachers have the ethical responsibility or clinical qualification to implement programs of basic motivational restructuring, such programs may be unrealistic. These personality traits are the result of a complex process of cognitive development, reinforced by social factors deeply embedded in the cultural matrix. Cultures, and the political forms that are their expression, may foster or militate against aggressiveness, assertiveness, or rationality.

Aristotle believed that the rationality of the polis could deteriorate. Far from taking the melioristic position often incorrectly attributed to him, he was ever the political realist, endorsing a form of government that would allow the rational critic to flourish, because only in such a political atmosphere could the community's level of rhetoric improve. Aristotle recognized that the process of improving the rationality of the polis depends on a slow, difficult change in the political structure, which in turn depends on cultural ideals. As long as the rational critic is free to criticize, irrational demagogues risk criticism. Such criticism leads to more rational rhetoric, which in turn leads to the encouragement of more rational critics, and so on. A rational polis is created speech by speech and criticism by criticism.

In short, the motivation to argue rationally is a personality trait that flourishes or withers depending on the cultural soil in which it is planted. By the time students reach college, their real-life argument motivations and skills are already deeply entrenched psychologically. Verbal aggressiveness is reinforced by a culture considerably hostile to rationality and prone to the use of force or threat of force, private or political, to solve problems and resolve disputes. It is unlikely that a single college course taken to fulfill a general education requirement will transform the motivations of Beavis and Butthead into those of Lincoln and Douglas. What is needed is an instructional program beginning in elementary school, when there is still a reasonable chance of affecting conflict-interaction patterns, and continuing through high school and college. Such an instructional program, however, must be informed by better understanding of the psychological antecedents of rational argumentative discourse.

Teaching competence in rational argumentation is in its infancy, if we mark its beginnings in the critiques of formalism by Toulmin (1959) and Perelman and Olbrechts-Tyteca (1958/1969). The study of the psychological antecedents of rational argumentative discourse is still struggling to be born. We hope that the meta-analytic work reported here will advance that process.

REFERENCES

References marked with an asterisk indicate studies included in the meta-analysis.

Atkinson, J. W. (1964). *An introduction to motivation*. Princeton, NJ: Van Nostrand.

Atkinson, J. W. (1974). The mainsprings of achievement-oriented activity. In J. W. Atkinson & J. O. Raynor (Eds.), *Motivation and achievement*, (pp. 13–42). Washington, DC: Winston.

*Beatty, M. J., Zelly, J. R., Dobos, J. A., & Rudd, J. E. (1994). Fathers' trait verbal aggressiveness and argumentativeness as predictors of adult sons' perception of fathers' sarcasm, criticism, and verbal aggressiveness. *Communication Quarterly, 42*, 407–415.

*Blickle, G. (1995). Conceptualization and measurement of argumentativeness: A decade later. *Psychological Reports, 77*, 99–110.

*Blickle, G., Habasch, A., & Senft, W. (1998). Verbal aggressiveness: Conceptualization and measurement: A decade later. *Psychological Reports, 82*, 287–298.

Boelkins, R. C., & Heiser, J. F. (1970). Biological bases of aggression. In D. N. Daniels, M. F. Gilula, & F. M. Ocvhberg (Eds.), *Violence and the struggle for existence* (pp. 15–52). Boston: Little, Brown.

*Boster, F., & Levine, T. (1988). Individual differences and compliance-gaining message selection: The effects of verbal aggressiveness, argumentativeness, dogmatism, and negativism. *Communication Research Reports, 5,* 114–119.

*Boster, F. J., Levine, T., & Kazoleas, D. (1993). The impact of argumentativeness and verbal aggressiveness on strategic diversity and persistence in compliance-gaining behavior. *Communication Quarterly, 41,* 405–415.

Briggs, S. R. (1992). Assessing the five-factor model of personality description. *Journal of Personality, 60,* 253–294.

Cacioppo, J. T., & Petty, R. E. (1982). The need for cognition. *Journal of Personality and Social Psychology, 42,* 116–131.

*Canary, D. J., Cunningham, E. M., & Cody, M. J. (1988). Goal types, gender and locus of control in managing interpersonal conflict. *Communication Research, 15,* 426–446.

*Dowling, R. E., & Flint, L. J. (1990). The argumentativeness scale: Problems and promise. *Communication Studies, 41,* 183–198.

*Downs, V. R., Kaid, L. L., & Ragan, S. (1990). The impact of argumentativeness and verbal aggressiveness on communicator image: The exchange between George Bush and Dan Rather. *Western Journal of Speech Communication, 54,* 99–112.

Geen, R. G. (1990). *Human aggression.* Pacific Grove, CA: Brooks/Cole.

Hamilton, M. A. & Mineo, P. J. (1999, May). *A meta-analysis of the relationship between achievement motivation and task anxiety: Implications for the study of argumentativeness.* Paper presented to the International Communication Association, San Francisco, CA.

*Harman, C. M., Klopf, D. W., & Satoshi, I. (1990). Verbal aggression among Japanese and American students. *Perceptual and Motor Skills, 70,* 1130.

Hunter, J. E. (1980). Factor analysis. In P. R. Monge & J. N. Cappella (Eds.), *Multivariate techniques in human communication research* (pp. 229–257). New York: Academic.

Hunter, J. E., & Schmidt, F. L. (1990). *Methods of meta-analysis.* Newbury Park, CA: Sage.

Infante, D. A. (1981). Trait argumentativeness as a predictor of communicative behavior in situations requiring argument. *Central States Speech Journal, 32,* 265–272.

*Infante, D. A. (1982). The argumentative student in the speech communication classroom: An investigation and implications. *Communication Education, 31,* 141–148.

Infante, D. A. (1985). Inducing women to be more argumentative: Source credibility effects. *Journal of Applied Communication Research, 13,* 33–44.

Infante, D. A. (1987). Enhancing the prediction of response to a communication situation from communication traits. *Communication Quarterly, 135,* 308–316.

*Infante, D. A., Chandler, T. A., & Rudd, J. E. (1989). Test of an argumentative skill deficiency model of interspousal violence. *Communication Monographs, 56,* 165–177.

*Infante, D. A., & Gordon, W. I. (1985). Superiors' argumentativeness and verbal aggressiveness as predictors of subordinates' satisfaction. *Human Communication Research, 12,* 117–125.

*Infante, D. A., & Gordon, W. I. (1987). Superior and subordinate communication profiles: Implications for independent-mindedness and upward effectiveness. *Central States Speech Journal, 38,* 73–80.

*Infante, D. A., & Gordon, W. I. (1989). Argumentativeness and affirming communicator style as predictors of satisfaction/dissatisfaction with subordinates. *Communication Quarterly, 37,* 81–90.

Infante, D. A., & Gordon, W. (1991). How employees see the boss: Test of an argumentative and affirming model of supervisors' communication behavior. *Western Journal of Speech Communication, 55,* 294–303.

Infante, D. A., Hartley, K. C., Martin, M. M., Higgins, M. A., Bruning, S. D., & Hur, G. (1992). Initiating and reciprocating verbal aggression: Effects on credibility and credited valid arguments. *Communication Studies, 43,* 182–190.

Infante, D. A., & Rancer, A. S. (1982). A conceptualization and measure of argumentativeness. *Journal of Personality Assessment, 46,* 72–80.

Infante, D. A., & Rancer, A. S. (1993). Relations between argumentative motivation, and advocacy and refutation on controversial issues. *Communication Quarterly, 41,* 415–426.

Infante, D. A., & Rancer, A. (1996). Argumentativeness and verbal aggressiveness: A review of recent theory and research. In B. Burleson (Ed.), *Communication yearbook 19* (pp. 319–351). Thousand Oaks, CA: Sage.

*Infante, D. A., Riddle, B. L., Horvath, C. L., & Tumlin, S. A. (1992). Verbal aggressiveness: Messages and reasons. *Communication Quarterly, 40,* 116–126.

*Infante, D. A., Trebing, J. D., Shepherd, P. E., & Seeds, D. E. (1984). The relationship of argumentativeness to verbal aggression. *The Southern Speech Communication Journal, 50,* 67–77.

*Infante, D. A., & Wigley, C. J. (1986). Verbal aggressiveness: An interpersonal model and measure. *Communication Monographs, 53,* 61–69.

*Kazoleas, D. (1993). The impact of argumentativeness on resistance to persuasion. *Human Communication Research, 20,* 118–137.

*Klopf, D. W., Thompson, C. A., & Kuparinin, A. S. (1991). Argumentativeness among selected Finnish and American college students. *Psychological Reports, 68,* 161–162.

*Lim, T. (1990). The influences of receivers' resistance on persuaders' verbal aggressiveness. *Communication Quarterly, 38,* 170–188.

Martin, M. M., & Anderson, C. M. (1995). Roommate similarity: Are roommates who are similar in their communication traits more satisfied? *Communication Research Reports, 12,* 46–52.

Martin, M. M., & Anderson, C. M. (1996). Argumentativeness and verbal aggressiveness. *Journal of Social Behavior and Personality, 11,* 547–554.

Martin, M. M., Anderson, C. M., & Thweatt, K. S. (1997, November). *Individuals' perceptions of their communication behavior: A validity study of the relationship between the cognitive flexibility scale and the communication flexibility scale with aggressive communication traits.* Paper presented at the annual meeting of the National Communication Association, Chicago.

*Nicotera, A. M., & Rancer, A. S. (1994). The influence of sex on self-perceptions and social stereotyping of aggressive communication predispositions. *Western Journal of Communication, 58,* 283–307.

*Nicotera, A., Smilowitz, M., & Pearson, J. (1990). Ambiguity tolerance, conflict management style and argumentativeness as predictors of innovativeness. *Communication Research Reports, 7,* 125–131.

*Onyekwere, E. O., Rubin, R. B., & Infante, D. A. (1991). Interpersonal perception and communication satisfaction as a function of argumentativeness and ego-involvement. *Communication Quarterly, 39,* 35–47.

Perelman, C. H., & Olbrechts-Tyteca, L. (1969). *The new rhetoric: A treatise on argumentation* (C. H. Perelman & L. Olbrechts-Tyteca, Trans.). Notre Dame, IN: University of Notre Dame Press. (Original work published 1958)

*Prunty, A. M., Klopf, D. W., & Ishii, S. (1990). Argumentativeness: Japanese and American tendencies to approach and avoid conflict. *Communication Reports, 7,* 75–79.

*Rancer, A., Baukus, R., & Amato, P. (1986). Argumentativeness, verbal aggressiveness, and marital satisfaction. *Communication Research Reports, 3,* 28–32.

*Rancer, A., & Dierks-Stewart, K. (1985). The influence of sex and sex-role orientation on trait argumentativeness. *Journal of Personality Assessment, 49,* 69–70.

Rancer, A. S. & Infante, D. A. (1985). Relations between motivation to argue and the argumentativeness of adversaries. *Communication Quarterly, 33,* 209–218.

*Rancer, A. S., Kosberg, R. L., & Silvestri, V. N. (1992). The relationship between self-esteem and aggressive communication predispositions. *Communication Research Reports, 9,* 23–32.

*Rancer, A. S., Whitecap, V. G., & Kosberb, R. L., & Avtgis, T. A. (1997). Testing the efficacy of a communication training program to increase argumentativeness and argumentative behavior in adolescents. *Communication Education, 46,* 273–286.

Roach, K. (1992). Teacher demographic characteristics and levels of teacher argumentativeness. *Communication Research Reports, 9,* 65–71.

*Rudd, J. E. (1996). Communication effects on divorce mediation: How participants' argumentativeness, verbal aggression and compliance-gaining strategy choice mediate outcome satisfaction. *Mediation Quarterly, 14,* 65–78.

*Sanders, J. A., Wiseman, R. L., & Gass, R. H. (1994). Does teaching argumentation facilitate critical thinking? *Communication Reports, 7,* 27–35.

Schultz, B., & Anderson, J. (1984). Training in the management of conflict: A communication theory perspective. *Small Group Behavior, 15,* 333–348.

*Stewart, R. A., & Roach, K. D. (1993). Argumentativeness, religious orientation, and reactions to argument situations involving religious versus nonreligious issues. *Communication Quarterly, 41,* 26–39.

Storr, A. (1968). *Human aggression.* New York: Atheneum.

*Suzuki, S., & Rancer, A. S. (1994). Argumentativeness and verbal aggressiveness: Testing for conceptual and measurement equivalence across cultures. *Communication Monographs, 61,* 256–279.

Toulmin, S. E. (1959). *The uses of argument.* Cambridge, UK: Cambridge University Press.

Trapp, R., Yingling, J. M., & Wanner, J. (1987). Measuring argumentative competence. In F. H. van Eemeren, R. Grootendorst, J. A. Blair, & C. A. Willard (Eds.), *Argumentation across the lines of disciplines* (pp. 251–261). New York: Foris.

*Wigley, C. J., III, Gayle, H. P., & Watt, M. G. (1989). Conversational sensitivity as a correlate of trait verbal aggressiveness and the predisposition to verbally praise others. *Communication Reports, 2,* 92–95.

Zillmann, D. (1979). *Hostility and aggression.* Hillsdale, NJ: Lawrence Erlbaum Associates.

17

Sexual Coercion and Resistance

Tara M. Emmers-Sommer

Smart Date is a Web site that enables women to leave a bread crumb trail, of sorts, regarding the details of a date (Temple, 1997). The purpose of the site is to provide women with a place to send their upcoming date plans to "an electronic message system that lets users document their dating plans for use by police if the unthinkable happens and they never return home" (Temple, 1997, p. 4D). The goal of the Web site is to reduce date rape and date assaults. During Smart Date's first 24 hours of service in the fall of 1997, more than 1,000 submissions were received, as were numerous supportive e-mails (Temple, 1997).

PERVASIVENESS OF SEXUAL COERCION

Sexual coercion and rape are pervasive in our society, with both men and women serving as perpetrators (Sigelman, Berry, & Wiles, 1984). In addition, both men and women are the targets of unwanted sexual advances and sexually coercive behaviors (e.g., Muehlenhard & Cook, 1988; Poppen & Segal, 1988; C.J. Struckman-Johnson, 1988). According to Poppen and Segal (1988), some studies reported as many as 75% of women being victimized by sexual coercion and as many as 63% of men having engaged in unwanted sex (Muehlenhard & Cook, 1988).

Although both men and women experience coercive situations, the statistics indicate that women are typically the targets of such acts. Becchofer and Parrot (1991) observed:

> Both males and females can be either assailants or victims of acquaintance rape. Although it is statistically unusual for males to be victims and females to be assailants, it does occur. Men report being forced into sexual encounters by other men (sometimes gangs) as well as by females. Because these types of sexual assaults are rarely reported to the police, many believe that they do not occur. The Federal Bureau of Investigation (FBI, 1982) estimated that 10% of all sexual assault victims are male, although male victims rarely report the crime unless they are physically injured. (pp. 13–14)

Other researchers concurred that few studies examine men's victimization (Poppen & Segal, 1988). Of the few studies that do, the perpetrator is typically another man rather than a woman (Muehlenhard, Goggins, Jones, & Satterfield, 1991).

The United States Bureau of Justice Statistics (1996) on victim characteristics indicated that rape and sexual assault are the only violent crimes for which women experience higher rates of victimization than men. The Bureau also reported that women are at higher risk than men for falling victim to an intimate (e.g., husband, boyfriend) for both fatal and nonfatal violence.

The majority of studies on sexual coercion in interpersonal relationships examined the man as the perpetrator and the woman as the victim (e.g., Koss, 1988; Muehlenhard, 1988). In a study with a sample of nearly 1,500, Koss (1988) found 71% of women reported their dates as perpetrators in instances of sexual contact and 85% reported their dates as perpetrating sexual coercion. Similarly, 70% reported their date as attempting rape and 57% reported their date as committing rape. The FBI's Uniform Crime Report (1992), based on reports representing 96% of the U.S. population, indicated that there were 105,593 reported rapes in 1991 or approximately one rape every 5 minutes (Kuhn, 1996). The report also indicated that between 1972 and 1991, reported rape increased 128% and there were 1.5 million women who had survived forcible rape or attempted rape. In 1994, 1 out of every 270 women was raped (Bureau of Justice Statistics, 1996). These statistics are staggering, but what we must remember is that these figures unfortunately only reflect reported rapes or rape attempts.

Although the scholarly community argues that sexual coercion is a problem, controversy centers on what sexual coercion is, specifically, and what theoretical approaches explain the profile of a sexually coercive situation. Similarly, controversy exists regarding what variables, specifically, are associated with sexual coercion and resistance. The purpose of this chapter is to review the literature regarding sexual coercion and what meta-analyses have found regarding contributors to coercion and resistance. Individual studies exist that examine a woman's perspective or a man's perspective on this issue, but only a minimal amount of research examined men's and women's perspectives meta-analytically. Meta-analysis enables researchers to statistically evaluate the individual studies cumulatively, thus reducing the potential for Type II error. First, however, theoretical approaches, definitions, and profiles of perpetrators are presented.

THEORETICAL APPROACHES

Much of the research examining sexual coercion, date rape, acquaintance rape, wife rape, gang rape, and unwanted sex approached these issues from varied, often opposing, perspectives. For example, one perspective regarding sexually coercive beliefs is that the man is just "being a guy," he was led on, was teased, was only giving in to hormonal urges, misunderstood the situation, a miscommunication between he and his date, spouse, or friend, "real men" are supposed to pursue sex, and so on. Many of these beliefs are reflected in the various scales examining accepted beliefs and attitudes toward rape. For example, in a meta-analysis on attitudes toward rape, K. B. Anderson, Cooper, and Okamura (1997) found that men held greater rape acceptance than women. Similarly, variables such as traditional gender-role beliefs, adversarial sexual beliefs, power and dominance needs, aggression and anger, and conservatism predicted rape acceptance. Items from such scales, some of which were used in the K. B. Anderson et al. (1997) study, often suggested that responsibility for the sexual act resides with the woman-that she either "asked for it" or she could and should have controlled the situation if she really wanted to.

Sexual Coercion Measures

Several existing measures assessing men's and women's beliefs focus on attitudes toward women, rape myth acceptance, and rape attitudes; particularly, men's and women's attitudes toward women who have been the target of some sexually coercive act and the men who perpetrated the act. Some of these measures include the RMA, AIV, Sexual Callousness, and the ASB scales. What follows are brief descriptions of these measures and scales and examples of questions from these indexes.

Rape Myth Acceptance Scale (RMA; Burt, 1980; Burt & Albin, 1981). Rape myth acceptance assumes little responsibility on the part of the perpetrator. Specifically, those accepting rape myths are inclined to cast the responsibility for the unwanted sexual episode on the victim and assume that the victim could have avoided the situation if she really wanted to. Examples from the RMA scale include "a woman who goes to the home or apartment of a man on their first date implies that she is willing to have sex" and "any healthy woman could resist if she really wants to" (Burt, 1980, p. 223).

Acceptance of Interpersonal Violence (AIV) Against Women Scale (Burt, 1980). The AIV assesses the acceptance of using force on a woman to obtain sex. Examples from the AIV scale include, "being roughed up is sexually stimulating to women" and "many times a woman will pretend she doesn't want to have intercourse because she doesn't want to seem loose; but she's really hoping the man will force her" (Burt, 1980, p. 222.).

Sexual Callousness Scale (Zillmann & Bryant, 1982). This scale asks participants to respond to a number of items representing callous or insensitive beliefs regarding sexual activity. Examples from the Sexual Callousness scale include, "pickups should expect to put out" and "a woman doesn't mean 'no' unless she slaps you" (Zillmann & Bryant, 1982, p. 14).

Adversarial Sexual Beliefs (ASB) Scale (Burt, 1980). The ASB contains items that examine reported acceptability of using force on females in male-female relationships and beliefs that such behaviors lead to sexual gratification. Items from the ASB include "men are only out for one thing" and "a woman will only respect a man who will lay down the law to her" (Burt, 1980, p. 222).

Although these scales and measures are certainly not an exhaustive review of measures assessing attitudes toward women, they are recognized and often-used measures in research on sexual coercion. As illustrated, items on the various scales share common characteristics: (a) Rape is not considered a serious crime, or even a crime at all; (b) men acting as aggressors are only doing what "men do" or what women "expect" or even "want" men to do; (c) women often engage in token resistance (i.e., say "no" when they really mean "yes") in an effort to preserve their reputation; and (d) if a woman does not want to engage in sex, she could get out of the situation.

Many of the arguments and explanations for sexually coercive situations just presented (e.g., the man was only giving in to uncontrollable urges, a perceived sexual invitation, societal expectations) are not adequate in explaining all sexually coercive situations, however. Stock (1991) argued:

When this approach is applied to rape, for example, it becomes evident that rape is not only the result of uncontrolled lust, exaggerated gender roles, miscommunication, or a misguided desire for sexual intimacy. These factors do not sufficiently explain why rape occurs when alternative sexual outlets are always available, including masturbation, when the aggression could be exhibited by a nonsexual attack, or where direct communication by the woman is often ignored, not misunderstood by the rapist. Rather, rape and other forms of sexual coercion can be viewed as both the expression and confirmation of male power, dominance, and control of women. (p. 62)

A feminist theoretical perspective argues that unwanted sexual situations are reflections of male dominance, power, and social reinforcement of such gendered expectations. Power inequality, then, is the base of such acts toward women. Stock (1991) argued that power inequality "is the result of and represents an attempt to maintain that imbalance" (p. 62). Such a perspective, unlike the one discussed earlier, emphasizes that the responsibility for unwanted sexual situations resides with the man. These issues are revisited when variables associated with sexual coercion are reviewed.

Another theoretical perspective explaining sexual coercion is the traditional sexual script (TSS) perspective. The TSS is regarded by several feminists as guiding and reinforcing traditional gender roles, social attitudes, and cultural attitudes that condone male sexual coercion of females (Byers, 1996). Despite more contemporary changes in dating behavior (e.g., going "dutch," the woman initiating or paying for the date), dating rituals nevertheless typically follow traditional dating scripts (Check & Malamuth, 1983).

The TSS is learned through socialization and provides the framework for very different sexual expectations for men and women in our society. Such expectations have often been associated with men's sexual coercion of women (e.g., Byers, 1996; Korman & Leslie, 1982). Cast within heterosexual relationships, Byers (1996) argued that the TSS prescribes the following beliefs:

1. Men are oversexed and women are undersexed.
2. Women's value and status are decreased by sexual experience, men's are increased. In a word, women are "promiscuous" or a "slut," whereas men are "studs."
3. Men initiate sexual situations, whereas women are the recipients. Men must pursue sexual activity to reinforce their masculinity, whereas women must remain passive and protective of their reputation.
4. Due to their supposed lack of interest in sex, women should remain reluctant to engage in sexual activity or allow it to proceed beyond

a certain point. In response to a woman's reluctance, a man is justi-fied in being coercive to get her past her anxiety. Because the TSS suggests that women often engage in token resistance (i.e., saying "no" when there is every intention to have sex), men may be more coercive to get past the "game-playing" women engage in to pre-serve their reputations.

5.   A woman's value is increased by being romantically involved. She must resist sex to preserve her reputation, but not to the degree that the man loses interest in her. Thus, the TSS promotes coyness, teasing, and promises of reward on the part of the woman if the man remains in the relationship.

6.   The TSS promotes emotionality and nurturing for women and coldness and insensitivity for men. In sexual situations, this as-sumption suggests that a woman put a man's needs before her own and that the man needn't worry how his actions affect her.

Byers (1996) tested the theoretical relevance of the TSS by examining if the TSS was the normative sexual script. She found mixed support for the theory. Specifically, although men initiated dates and sex more than women, women's initiation was not out of the ordinary; agreement about the level and amount of sexual activity was more common among heterosexual cou-ples than was disagreement; disagreement about sexual activity did not nec-essarily lead to sexual coercion; men were inclined to pursue further sexual activity if the woman refused and tended to accept her "no" as a "no." Byers concluded that the TSS provided a useful framework, but that it is not the normative dating script. Specifically, many of the assumptions of the TSS did not hold when tested.

If the TSS is not the normative dating script, then controversy exists re-garding what, specifically, predicts sexual coercion. Many of the variables associated with sexual coercion prevalence relate to the traditional sexual script (e.g., who asked and who paid, gender, location of the date, etc.). A more feminist perspective argues that men engage in sexual coercion due to dominance and power but does not necessarily explain coercion. For exam-ple, Byers's (1996) results indicated that disagreement about sexual activity did not necessarily lead to sexual coercion and that men were inclined to ac-cept "no" for an answer. Along the same lines, Mac Donald (1995) argued that "Most date rapists are motivated by a desire for sex than wanting to show their power over their victims or over women in general" (p. 52).

In an attempt to examine the various predictors cumulatively (rather than case by case) several of the aforementioned variables are tested meta-analytically later in the chapter. Prior to examining variables associated with coercion, it is first necessary to define types of coercion. Lack of consistency on definitions and operationalizations could be detrimental to the validity of a meta-analysis on the topic.

DEFINITIONS OF RAPE, ASSAULT, AND COERCION

Of all the various terms and definitions regarding sexual relations, the only form that exists and does not involve crime or violation of any sort is consensual sex. *Consensual sex* is "sexual relations with both partners desiring sex"(Parrot, 1991, p. 4). Unfortunately, many instances involving sexual behavior occur that do not involve mutual consent. Problematically, in the literature, another controversy exists regarding definitions and language used in studies on sexual coercion because various terms are used interchangeably when they do not represent the same thing (e.g., *date rape* and *acquaintance rape* are used interchangeably). The purpose of this section is to review the related terms as defined in the literature.

Rape and Assault

Several terms exist regarding sexual coercion and illustrations are provided for some of the terms here. For example, *acquaintance rape* as is often defined as nonconsensual sex between adults who know each other (Becchofer & Parrot, 1991; Parrot, 1991). An illustration of acquaintance rape follows. Sally and John are college classmates. John sees Sally at the library and offers her a ride home. Although Sally does not know John well, she feels comfortable accepting his offer to drive her home because she recognizes him from class. En route to her home, John parks his car in an abandoned lot and has nonconsensual sex with Sally. *Date rape* involves individuals who are involved in a dating relationship or who are on a date. Date rape is defined as nonconsensual sex between people who are dating or on a date (Becchofer & Parrot, 1991; Parrot, 1991). For example, Sally and John are out on a date. John drives Sally home and she invites him into her home for a drink. John has nonconsensual sex with Sally. Unlike acquaintance rape or date rape, a woman who is raped does not know her assailant. *Rape* is defined as "penis–vagina intercourse against a woman's will and without her consent" (Parrot, 1991, p. 4.) Variations of rape exist. For example, *soft rape* is "coercion used to engage a victim in intercourse against his/her will" (Parrot, 1991, p. 4). *Simple rape* is "rape without violence or force, with a single assailant or without any other accompanying crime (kidnapping, murder, assault, etc.)" (Parrot, 1991, p. 4). *Aggravated rape* is "rape which occurs with more than one assailant or in conjunction with another crime (kidnapping, murder, assault, etc.)" (Parrot, 1991, p. 4). *Sexual assault* is defined as "a forced sexual act against one's will (men and women may be assaulted according to this definition" (Parrot, 1991, p. 4).

Sexual Coercion

Coercion exists in forms of psychological or physical pressure (C.J. Struckman-Johnson, 1988). Psychological pressure is often conveyed through verbal coercion (e.g., Kanin, 1967; Koss, Gidycz, & Wisniewski, 1987; Mosher & Anderson, 1986; Muehlenhard & Cook, 1988; Parrot, 1991). Similar to the definition of soft rape, examples of verbal coercion included, "What's the matter with you? Why won't you have sex?", "If you don't give in, I'll tell everyone that you are a tease/gay," "Considering how much money I've spent on you tonight, you owe me," and "Come on, don't be afraid, you know you want to do this."

Physical coercion involves force or threat of physical force or bodily harm if the target does want to engage in sexual activity (e.g., Mahoney, Shively, & Traw, 1986; Parrot, 1991; C.J. Struckman-Johnson, 1988). Definitions of rape and assault coincide with physical coercion. Examples of physical force included, "He forced himself on me and I couldn't get away" or "I tried to stop him but he physically forced me" (C. J. Struckman-Johnson, 1988, pp. 238–239).

Nonviolent coercion exists in subtle forms. According to Muehlenhard and Schrag (1991), examples included compulsory heterosexuality, gender roles, assumptions about the nature of sex, assumptions about the nature of marriage, fear of male violence, status coercion, economic coercion, discrimination against lesbians, verbal sexual coercion, alcohol and drugs, and rape without force.

As evident from this review, many definitions exist in the literature. Problematically, researchers often interchange definitions. As noted, many of the studies reviewed and used in meta-analyses operationalize a term differently. Unless the authors clearly define how terms (e.g., *date rape*) were defined and operationalized, it is not clear to readers or those conducting a meta-analysis what, specifically, is being addressed conceptually. For example, Knight, Fabes, and Higgins (1996) cautioned against making causal inferences from meta-analyses. In their meta-analysis on gender differences in aggression, the authors observed that inconsistencies in definitions and measures of a concept (i.e., aggression) lead to problems in interpretation and conclusion. Particular to their study, "A more cautious conclusion is that the most reliable moderators of gender differences in aggression are found in the qualities of the studies themselves (e.g., how aggression is defined, measured, or both)" (Knight et al, 1996, p. 417). Thus, it is necessary to keep in mind that inconsistencies likely exist among the definitions used across studies.

The variables explored in this chapter associated with sexual coercion and resistance reflect all three forms of coercion (verbal, physical, and unspoken). As mentioned earlier in the review of the TSS (Byers, 1996), aspects of the TSS condone unspoken, verbal, and physical forms of coercion to a degree. For example, the very nature of gender itself emits a form of unspoken coercion (e.g., who asks for a date, who pays, unspoken societal expectations about male–female relationships, etc.). Similarly, according to the TSS, men are socially expected to request sex and women are expected to say "no." Finally, according to the TSS, men are socially expected to pursue sex—even if they have been denied—and such pursuits may involve some physical coercion and the line between noncriminal and criminal pursuit is a fine one.

Aspects of coercion (e.g., unspoken, verbal, and physical) encapsulate all of the various forms discussed thus far because all forms involve some or all of these aspects of coercion. Thus, for clarity and brevity's sake, such behaviors are referred to as coercive in the remainder of this chapter unless otherwise defined by certain pieces of research.

From the more physical aspect of coercion, several profiles of male sexual perpetrators exist, most of which reinforce a feminist perspective that a man's violation of a woman reflects feelings of power or anger (e.g., Stock, 1991). The following section provides an overview of the various types of male offenders. Just as various types of coercion exist, various types of perpetrators exist. Their motives and behaviors vary to a degree, but there is a consistent theme of power, violation, and degradation.

PROFILES OF PERPETRATORS

Mac Donald (1995) interviewed more than 200 rape offenders, including 10 who killed their targets, as well as targets of sexual assault. Along with information from the Behavioral Science Unit of the FBI Academy, he offered five rapist profiles. Those profiles are briefly reviewed below (see Mac Donald, 1995, for a more extensive description).

The Power-Reassurance Rapist

Such individuals are the least violent sexual offenders. This type often wants to reassure his masculinity and may be a closet homosexual. He is typically a loner, has few friends, and has difficulty relating to women. The sexual act is typically brief and the perpetrator often asks for reassurance regarding his sexual performance. This type of rapist keeps a souvenir from the scene and may keep a record of his conquests (Mac Donald, 1995). The various forms of sexual assault, coercion, and rape described earlier could fit this description (e.g., acquaintance rape, date rape, simple rape, soft rape, rape, sexual assault, verbal or physical coercion).

The Power-Assertive Rapist

This sort of man is asserting his masculinity and is more violent than the power-reassurance rapist. He often drives a flashy car, hits the bar scene, and uses a "con" approach. He will resort to verbal or physical violence if necessary and there is no distinct pattern to his rapes. Sex acts often involve repeated vaginal sex or oral sex following anal sex. Such a man is often "impersonal, demanding, threatening, domineering, and degrading" (MacDonald, 1995, p. 159). Previously described acts that fit this description include the forms mentioned earlier, as well the possibility of aggravated rape.

The Anger-Retaliatory Rapist

This rapist uses excessive violence and force and his goal is to demean and make women "pay." When he feels that an injustice has been done to him, he gets even, possibly through sexual retaliation. Often, a domestic violence or speeding report was issued to him earlier on the day of a rape. This type will use a weapon, beat the woman during the act, use a lot of profanity, and oral sex often follows anal sex. Although the aim of this attacker is not to kill, death can occur due to the level of violence and anger associated with the attack (Mac Donald, 1995). The aggravated rape definition fits the profile of this perpetrator.

The Sadistic (Anger-Excitation) Rapist

This sort of rapist is the most violent and fatality may result if the target resists the attacker. His goals include domination, control, and emotional and physical harm. According to Mac Donald (1995), "he is probably in his thirties, has a 'good marriage,' a white-collar job, and no arrest record" (p. 160). This perpetrator carefully plans his attacks and enjoyment is gained from the target's reaction to the torture. The act may be taped or photographed and levels of sex may vary, although anal sex is typically used (Mac Donald, 1995). The aggravated rape definition also fits the profile of this perpetrator.

The Opportunist Rapist

This attacker did not plan the rape and often does not commit rape again. Typically, a rape results when the man, for example, robs a home and finds a woman there. Often, the man will leave evidence at the scene and is under the influence of alcohol or drugs (MacDonald, 1995). Similarly, the opportunist rape qualifies as aggravated rape because it typically involves an unrelated crime (e.g., robbery) from which a rape will occur. Unlike the anger-retaliatory rapist or the sadistic rapist—who also qualify as enacting aggravated rape—opportunistic rapists do not set out with the intent to use excessive violence or torture against women.

To summarize, power-reassurance and power-assertive rapists hold attitudes and engage in actions that appear to be more specific to many theoretical assumptions of the TSS than anger-retaliatory, sadistic, or opportunistic rapists. That is, power-reassurance rapists typically want to be reassured of their "manliness" and often "keep score" of their conquests. Moreover, power-assertive rapists seem to follow a more extreme aspect of the sexual script. Specifically, the man is in control of the sexual situation, picks up dates and has his way with them, and exercises dominance in the relationship. The TSS prescribes that men assert their manliness, engage in multiple sexual experiences to reinforce their manliness, are justified in coercing a woman to have sex because they are men, and need not be sensitive or attentive to the woman's feelings about the situation (e.g., Byers, 1996).

One can see the complexities involved in examining sexual coercion phenomena. Specifically, definitions of sexual coercion vary, perceptions of what is "coercive" vary from both the perpetrator and the victim perspectives, and various types of perpetrators exist. Similarly, contradicting theoretical perspectives exist explaining why sexual coercion occurs.

After reviewing the various theoretical frameworks explaining sexual coercion, definitions and types of coercion, and profiles of perpetrators, we next discuss the variables identified in the literature as relating to sexual coercion and resistance. The following variables are reported often as contributors to sexual coercion (e.g., Bostwick & DeLucia, 1992; Muehlenhard, 1988).

VARIABLES RELATED TO SEXUAL COERCION

Gender

When considering gender as a variable in regard to sexual coercion, we must consider men's and women's conditioning (e.g., gender roles, attitudes) as well as men's and women's perceptions of what sexual coercion and rape are.

Embracing a gender identity of being masculine or feminine impacts perceptions of appropriate and inappropriate sexual behavior (Burke, Stets, &
Pirog-Good, 1989; Byers, 1996).

Both women and men struggle with societal expectations in terms of sex
and the personal or relational consequences of not engaging in sex (W.P. Anderson & Cummings, 1993). Even more complicated is that societal perceptions of men's and women's behavior are often diametrically opposed in terms
of acceptance. Specifically, a woman who engages in sex is often perceived as a
"slut," whereas a woman who abstains is a good girl, "frigid" (Muehlenhard &
Cook, 1988), or a "tease" in the eyes of some men (Byers, 1996). Conversely,
men who pursue women are "real men," whereas those who refrain from aggressive pursuit can be perceived as homosexual (Kuhn, 1996) or as refusing
to engage in something that is expected of them (C.J. Struckman-Johnson,
1988). In agreement with the TSS, a stereotypical dichotomy occurs: Men
who are real men have sex and women who are ladies do not.

It is not surprising that men and women often struggle with managing
sexuality and sexual boundaries in their relationships. Evidence exists suggesting that perceptions of rape differ. For example, in a sample of nearly
3,000 men, Koss (1988) found that "most men (88%) who reported an assault that met the legal definition of rape were adamant that their behavior
was definitely not rape" (p. 19). Problematically, women often engage in unwanted sexual behavior due to men's constant badgering for sex and men
may view women's giving in as willing consent (Muehlenhard & Schrag,
1991). Koss et al. (1987) reported that 44% of women engaged in unwanted
sexual intercourse due to constant pressure and arguing. According to
Muehlenhard and Falcon (1991), men who adopt traditional gender roles
are more likely to exercise verbal sexual coercion. Thus, in accordance with
the TSS, traditional men are more likely to expect sex, pursue sex, and believe that they are justified in doing so even if that pursuit involves the use of
badgering and threats.

Relational Stage and Past—Current Relationship

When we consider the act of rape, we often consider stranger rape. Koss
(1988) found that 60% to 75% of the rapes reported in the National Crime
Survey were stranger rapes; however, 84% of his sample reported that close
acquaintances or dates had committed unwanted sexual acts. Recall that
women are more likely to fall victim to an intimate's violence (Bureau of Justice Statistics, 1996). It is possible that many women do not report acquaintance or date rape to law enforcement as readily as stranger rape because the
boundaries are less clear (Becchofer & Parrot, 1991). Specifically, a woman

who is the victim of date rape may be more likely to question herself (e.g., "Maybe I asked for it? Maybe I led him on?"; Parrot, 1991) than a woman who is raped by a stranger. Although rape is rape, regardless of the relationship with the perpetrator, many women may not perceive it in this way. Women who are victimized by men they know often do not realize that rape occurred (Koss, 1985) or may see themselves as victims, "but not as legitimate crime victims" (Estrich, 1987, p. 12, cited in Becchofer & Parrot, 1991, pp. 9–25).

Research suggests that a forced-sex episode is less likely to be viewed as coercive if the woman had engaged in sex with the man before. For example, Shotland and Goodstein (1992) found that participants were less likely to acknowledge coercive sex as date rape if the woman had engaged in sex with the man 10 times prior to the episode (as opposed to once or twice). Additional research also suggests that women and men are less likely to view unwanted sex on a traditional date or a date in a closer relationship (vs. with a stranger or pickup date) as rape (e.g., Jenkins & Dambrot, 1987; Koss, 1985). Regarding sexual coercion, the findings suggest that being in a close relationship is associated with a lessened likelihood of perceiving that anything untoward occurred. Typically, as relationships advance, greater levels of trust, intimacy, and commitment develop. Unfortunately, such relational aspects may convolute what is right and wrong.

Who Initiated and Who Paid

Research regarding who initiates and pays for a date suggested that the woman is in an awkward position regardless of whether she was the initiator or receiver of the date proposal. Some men perceive a willing acceptance of a date proposal, transportation, and expenses as justification for sexual aggressiveness (Harney & Muehlenhard, 1991). Muehlenhard, Friedman, and Thomas (1985) found that if a woman allows the man to pay for the date, the man may perceive the woman as being interested in sex. Research also suggested that men perceive a woman more willing to engage in sex and are also more likely to justify their pursuing sex without a woman's consent if the man paid for the date (Muehlenhard, 1988). These findings support the notion that the man feels as though he is "owed" something or the woman may feel as though she "owes" compliance to his unwanted advances (Korman, 1983).

Conversely, findings suggested that women who initiate dates or pay for them are also often perceived negatively. Specifically, men may perceive such women as "experienced," "loose," or interested in sex. For example, Muehlenhard (1988) found that men often interpret a woman's date invitation as an invitation for sex. Muehlenhard and Scardino (1985) found that men enter into first dates with particularly high sexual expectations when the woman initiated the date. Other research supports these findings (Bostwick & De Lucia, 1992; Mongeau & Carey, 1996; Mongeau, Hale, Johnson, & Hillis, 1993). Research on who initiated and paid for the date suggests that women are in a precarious position whether or not they initiate a date or accept a date proposal. Specifically, women are perceived as owing compliance to unwanted sexual advances if they accept a date proposal and paid expenses and are also perceived as being interested in sex if they initiate or pay for the date.

Alcohol and Drugs

Often adding complications to an often already ambiguous dating situation are intoxicants. Specifically, one third to two thirds of perpetrators and victims are under the influence of alcohol at the time of the sexual assault (e.g., Koss & Dinero, 1989). Often, men will use drugs or alcohol to lower the inhibitions of their victims (Muehlenhard et al., 1991). Mosher and Anderson (1986) found that 75% of men in their sample used drugs or alcohol to persuade unwilling women to engage in sex. Levine and Kanin (1987) found that perpetrators often used being under the influence as an excuse for their behavior. Other findings supported the notion that drugs and alcohol are used as coercive tools with unwilling partners (Christopher & Frandsen, 1990; C. J. Struckman-Johnson, 1988). In a sample of nearly 1,500 respondents, Koss (1988) found that a man's use of alcohol or drugs played a role in sexual contact 35% of the time, in sexual coercion 64% of the time, in attempted rape 54% of the time, and 73% of the time in the case of actual rape. In addition, Koss (1988) found that women had been using alcohol or drugs in 29% of the sexual contact incidents, in 31% of the sexual coercion incidents, in 58% of the attempted rape incidents, and in 55% of the actual rapes. Thus, the findings suggest that for both the perpetrator and victim, use of intoxicants is related to an increased likelihood that unwanted sexual behavior will occur.

Location of the Encounter

The surroundings in which an unwanted sexual incident transpires relates to the perpetrator's perception that nothing untoward has occurred. That is, location of the encounter often contributes to a man's justification for the sexual incident. Research indicated that a man's justifiability and a woman's perceived willingness are highest when the date is at the man's apartment (as opposed to a movie or a religious function; Muehlenhard et al., 1985).

Both men and women are more likely to report a date rape as more justified if the incident occurred at the man's apartment (as opposed to a movie date; Muehlenhard, 1988). In terms of occurrence, Muehlenhard and Linton (1987) reported that date rapes are most likely to take place in the perpetrator's home, car, or in an isolated location. Bart and O'Brien (1985) reported that rapes are more likely to occur indoors than outdoors and that women have a decreased chance of getting away if the incident occurs indoors. To summarize, these findings suggest that a woman increases risk by going to man's apartment or home, has a decreased likelihood of avoiding the rape if she does go to such locations, and is perceived as more willing to engage in sex by deciding to go to the man's apartment.

Victim Resistance

Just as various forms of coercion exist (e.g., verbal, physical), several forms of resistance also exist regarding reaction to the unwanted coercive behavior. Specifically, *resistance* can take the form of verbal resistance (e.g., "No"), physical resistance (e.g., fighting, hitting, slapping), and token resistance (e.g., saying "no" when what is really meant is "yes"; Muehlenhard & Hollabaugh, 1988). Although evidence exists suggesting that both men and women engage in token resistant behaviors (Sprecher, Hatfield, Cortese, Potapova, & Levitskaya, 1994), the notion of token resistance is often focused on women. Muehlenhard and Hollabaugh (1988) reported that as many as 39% of women have admitted to engaging in token resistance at least once and 17% have admitted to practicing it regularly. Problematically, many men interpret a woman's "no" to mean "yes" (Check & Malamuth, 1983). Such behavior reflects prescriptions of the TSS or arguments that men are just "being men" and responding to women's equivocal overtures.

Findings on verbal or physical resistance to sexual coercion indicate a lack of consistent results (e.g., Atkeson, Calhoun, & Morris, 1989; Bart & O'Brien, 1985; Brady, Chrisler, Hosdale, Osowiecki, & Veal, 1991). Disagreements exist regarding whether women should resist an attack or acquiesce. Some research indicated that men or women who resist an attack are less likely to be raped (Kleck & Sayles, 1990). Other research suggested that resistance could be fatal (Mac Donald, 1995). The findings are also mixed regarding the effectiveness of physical and verbal strategies. Ullman & Knight (1993) found that physical resistance strategies were most effective, whereas others found that these behaviors instigated contact (Siegel, Sorenson, Golding, Burnam, & Stein, 1989). Siegel et al. (1989) found that verbal resistance strategies were more effective in resisting sexual coercion.

Conversely, Mac Donald (1971) found that a combination of physical and verbal strategies was more effective.

To summarize, several of these variables (e.g., gender, relational stage, who initiated or paid, location of the encounter) are related to expectations prescribed by the TSS. Other variables considered are attitudes toward women, justifiability of the coercion, perceived willingness of the victim, and actual or perceived levels of coercion used. Considering the previous review, certain patterns are expected to exist among the variables. Specifically, men are expected to have more negative attitudes toward women than women do. Initiating and paying for a date is expected to relate to justification for the sexual incident, particularly if the woman initiated the date or paid for it. Initiation and payment for the date are expected to negatively relate to perceptions that coercion occurred. Similarly, the literature suggests that if the date occurs at a more private location (as opposed to a public location), there is a greater likelihood that the woman will be perceived as willing to engage in sex. It is expected that relational level will negatively relate to perceptions of coercion occurring, such that the more advanced the relationship, the less likely one will perceive that coercion took place. Finally, the literature suggests that use of intoxicants will relate to reduced perceptions that coercion occurred. The next section involves the meta-analyses on sexual coercion and resistance. Studies on both coercion and resistance are presented and an overall discussion follows.

SEXUAL COERCION META-ANALYSIS

Studies included in this meta-analysis (see Emmers & Allen, 1995a) were initially amassed from computer searches using keywords such as *sexual coercion, sexual aggression,* and *date rape.* Computer databases utilized included Psychlit, ERIC, PSYCHInfo, Dissertation Abstracts International and library reference databases to locate books, articles, and dissertations on sexual coercion, acquaintance rape, and date rape. The purposes of the literature search were to pinpoint research that investigated this topic area and to examine the repetitive reporting the impact of certain key variables (e.g., who asked or who paid, gender) on sexual coercion across studies. Each article's, chapter's, and dissertation's reference section was examined to locate additional articles. Of the articles examined, the ones meeting the following criteria were included in this investigation:

1. The manuscript examined nonstranger sexually coercive situations.
2. The manuscript examined all or some of the independent variables previously reviewed as being potential contributors to a sexually

coercive situation (e.g., who paid, location of date, level of the relationship, etc.).

3.   The manuscript examined all or some of the following dependent variables: justifiability, willingness, and coercion.

4.   The manuscript held data involving men's or women's use of sexually coercive behaviors and reported usable statistical information that enabled an estimate between the aforementioned independent variables and justifiability, willingness, and coercion.

Finally, an effort was made to examine articles which involved both male and female perpetration and victimization. However, this condition could not be met because all studies included in this meta-analysis involved female victimization and male perpetration. It should also be noted that the majority of studies included in this investigation involved scenarios (i.e., participants' ratings of coercion based on forced-sex depictions) as opposed to reports of actual coercive situations. Nevertheless, both men's and women's perceptions are included in this analysis.

Manuscript Coding

The following section overviews the variables examined and coded for the meta-analysis on coercion. Specifically, sex, justifiability and willingness, alcohol and drugs, who initiated and who paid, location of the encounter, and relationship level were investigated.

Justifiability and Willingness.
Several studies examined justifiability for date rape or for sexually coercive behavior (the perpetrator's justifiability for the behavior) and perceived victim willingness (the victim's willingness to engage in sex; e.g., Bostwick & DeLucia, 1992; Muehlenhard, 1988; Muehlenhard et al., 1985). All three of the aforementioned studies provided two questions which were answered on a scale ranging from 1–7 following date rape vignettes. The first question addressed victim willingness—"Given this information, do you think Mary wants to have intercourse with John?" Justifiability was assessed by answering, "If it turned out that Mary did not want to have intercourse with John, would John be justified in doing it against her wishes?" (Muehlenhard, 1988, p. 23).

Coercive Strategies.
Much of the literature examines coercive strategies (e.g., Christopher & Frandsen, 1990; McCormick, 1979; C. J. Struckman-Johnson, 1988). As mentioned earlier in the chapter, coercion can take verbal (e.g., threats, requests, manipulation, profanities), physical

(e.g., forced sex, physical force), or unspoken forms (e.g., making the other feel as though she "owes" sex, making the other feel as though the relationship will be jeopardized without sex, etc.). Threats, persuasion tactics, direct and indirect requests, and explanations provided by men in an effort to gain sex were coded as verbal strategies. Pushing, hitting, holding the victim down, or physically overcoming the victim to gain sex were coded as physical strategies. Finally, unspoken coercive strategies were coded from participants' reports of the other making them feel (void of verbal or physical strategies) that they should engage in sex.

Sex.   Sex was coded according to each article's report of men and women in their sample.

Attitudes Toward Women.   Attitudes toward women were assessed by examining the various measures of attitudes (e.g., AIV, RMA) in the literature. The higher the score on the scale, the more negative the attitude toward women.

Alcohol and Drugs.   Alcohol and drugs were coded according to each article's report that intoxicants had been used by the perpetrator, the target, or both in conjunction with the sexual incident.

Location of the Encounter.   Location of the encounter was coded according to the articles' reports that the incident occurred at a private location (e.g., an apartment) as opposed to a public location (e.g., a rock concert). Overall, Emmers and Allen (1995a) had 98% coding agreement.

Statistical Analysis

Similar to other meta-analyses (e.g., Allen, Emmers, Gebhardt, & Giery, 1995), this study used Hunter and Schmidt's (1990) methodology. Briefly, Hunter and Schmidt's method is a variance-centered form of meta-analysis (Bangert-Downs, 1986). This form of meta-analysis extracts an average effect from a population of effects and sampling error is responsible for deviations from the average effect. Correlation coefficients calculated in this investigation represent effect sizes. An overall correlation was calculated for each study as well as correlation for justifiability, willingness, verbal, physical, and unspoken coercive strategies resulting from each of the predictor variables. Chi-squares were calculated to test homogeneity of groups such that a significant chi-square indicates nonhomogeneity and a nonsignificant chi-square indicates homogeneity.

Results

Overall, 19 studies were included in this meta-analysis. Results indicate positive correlations between initiation and perceived victim willingness ($N = 1,266, r = .350, k = 4, p < .05$) and perpetrator's justification ($N = 326, r = .128, k = 4, p > .05$). Thus, initiation of a date related to perceiving the victim as willing to engage in sex. Initiation of a date also related to the perpetrator believing he was justified in pursuing sex. Initiation was negatively related to coercion ($N = 326, r = -.239, k = 4, p < .05$). Overall, both men and women perceived sex as more justified if the woman initiated the date than if the man did. Also, both men and women perceived the woman as more willing to engage in sex if she initiated the date and were less likely to perceive that coercion occurred.

Who paid for the date was positively related to perceived victim willingness to engage in sex ($N = 1,653, r = .248, k = 3, p < .05$) and perpetrator's justification ($N = 1098, r = .097, k = 3, p < .05$), and was negatively related to coercion ($N = 1013, r = -.193, k = 2, p < .05$). Thus, both men and women perceived the woman as being more willing to engage in sex when the man paid for the date. Similarly, both sexes viewed the coercion as more justified when the man paid for the date and were also less likely to perceive that coercion had occurred.

Analysis of the gender variable compared men's and women's perceptions of justifiability, willingness, and coercion. Results indicated that men perceived the female victim as more willing to engage in sex than women did ($N = 1,981, r = .290, k = 5, p < .05$). Men also perceived the coercion as more justified than women did ($N = 1,576, r = .167, k = 5, p < .05$) and were less likely than women to perceive that coercion occurred ($N = 522, r = -.418, k = 5$).

Regarding relational level, both men and women were less likely to perceive that coercion had occurred ($N = 1,268, r = -.036, k = 4, p > .05$) if the couple had a relationship or had engaged in sex prior to the forced sexual episode than if the couple did not have a prior relationship or had never engaged in sex.

Drug and alcohol use also contributed to reduced perceptions that coercion occurred. Specifically, both men and women perceived forced sex as less coercive if drugs and alcohol were used by the involved parties than if the parties were sober ($N = 3,038, r = -.093, k = 3, p < .05$).

Finally, results of the location of the date indicate that going to an apartment for a date, as opposed to a religious function, movie, or rock concert, greatly contributed to the perceptions of the woman being willing to engage in sex ($N = 808, r = .58, k = 3, p < .05$) and individuals perceived the coercion as being more justified ($N = 808, r = .267, k = 3, p < .05$).

RESISTANCE TO SEXUAL COERCION
META-ANALYSIS

The literature search process for this meta-analysis (Emmers & Allen, 1995b) followed the procedure used in the previously mentioned meta-analysis (Emmers & Allen, 1995a). All articles meeting the following criteria were included in the investigation:

1.   The manuscript examined nonstranger sexually coercive situations.
2.   The manuscript examined victim resistance (e.g., verbal, physical strategies) in response to sexual coercion.
3.   The manuscript included data for male and female participants.
4.   The manuscript included data for both males' and females' resistance behaviors.
5.   The data from each manuscript had to report adequate statistical information to allow an estimate of the relation between sexual coercion and males' and females' resistance behaviors.

Manuscript Coding

The following sections overview the variables examined in the meta-analysis on resistance to coercion. Specifically, verbal and physical resistance and sex differences were examined and coded.

Verbal or Physical Resistance.   This code determined whether the strategies exercised by men or women were verbal or physical in nature. Verbal strategies involved the victim's use of threats, explanations, or persuasive strategies to resist the sexual coercion. Token resistance was not coded as a verbal resistance strategy because of its disingenuous nature. Physical strategies involved flight or some physical behavior used to halt the sexual coercion (e.g., pushing the pursuer away, removing the perpetrator's hand from the target's body, etc.).

Sex.   This variable was coded based on each article's reports of men and women in their sample. Emmers and Allen (1995b) had 100% agreement on the studies involving men's and women's resistance to sexual coercion as well as the types of strategies used.

Results

The overall analysis of the six studies with 993 participants indicated an average negative correlation $(r = -.045)$ between gender differences in resistance to sexual coercion. The effect size was homogenous, χ^2 (5) = 1.74, k = 5, $p > .05$. Gender differences $(N = 910)$ in exercising verbal resistance behaviors to sexual coercion correlated at $r = .008$ and homogenous χ^2 (5) = 2.78, $k = 5, p > .05$. Finally, the average effect for gender differences $(N = 609)$ in using physical resistance to sexual coercion was small, $r = -.146$, and was also homogenous, χ^2 (4) = 7.23, $k = 4, p > .05$.

No significant differences existed between men and women in overall strategy use or in verbal strategy use. However, compared to men, women were more likely to exercise physical resistance behaviors (e.g., fight or flight) in response to sexual coercion. Thus, although men and women might have equal choices in terms of responses to unwanted sexual coercion, the effectiveness of those choices differs between the sexes. Specifically, women in sexually coercive situations more often resort to physical resistance, whereas verbal resistance appears to be sufficient for men.

DISCUSSION

Byers (1996) found only mixed support for the TSS; however, Byers's work was not meta-analytical. Nevertheless, results of these meta-analyses suggest similar support for the TSS, specifically that mixed support for the TSS about male-female relationships exists.

Recall that the TSS argued that sexual pursuit is acceptable, even expected, for men, whereas sexual abstinence or passivity is anticipated for women. Although some of the correlations in these analyses were small, results suggested that both men and women generally perceive sexual coercion as more acceptable, the victim as more willing, and the perpetrator as more justified whether the woman follows the TSS or violates expectations. Research previously found that a man paying for a date follows a traditional script (e.g., Check & Malamuth, 1983). Results of Emmers and Allen's (1995a) meta-analysis suggested that both men and women perceive the woman as more willing to engage in sex if the man paid for the date. This finding supported previous research that found that men perceived women as more interested in sex if the men paid for the date (Muehlenhard et al., 1985) and that women may be more willing to engage in sex or feel as though they "owe" sex if the man paid for the date (Korman, 1983).

Previous research found that a woman initiating the date violates the traditional script (e.g., Check & Malamuth, 1983; Mongeau & Carey, 1996;

Muehlenhard & Scardino, 1985). Results of the meta-analysis indicated that both men and women perceived the woman as more willing to engage in sex if the woman initiated the date, consistent with Muehlenhard's (1988) contention that men often perceive a woman's invitation for a date as an invitation for sex.

Traditional dates often involve going out to dinner, a movie, a concert, or a man's apartment for the date. Muehlenhard et al. (1985) found that men perceived women as more willing to engage in sex if the date took place at the man's apartment. Findings of this study, however, indicated that both men and women perceive a woman as more willing to engage in sex if the date took place at the man's apartment. According to the TSS, a woman's involvement in a romantic relationship increases her "value" socially; she must keep the man interested without being perceived as promiscuous (Byers, 1996). One of the problems with ongoing romantic relationships is that sex is less likely to be viewed as rape if the couple has engaged in sex previously (Shotland & Goodstein, 1992). Results of this meta-analysis found that both men and women perceived forced sex to be less coercive if the couple had engaged in sex before as opposed to if they were not in a relationship or never had sex. Women are less likely to acknowledge a forced-sex incident as rape if they know the assailant (Koss, 1985; Parrot, 1991) and women are more likely to be accosted in some form by an intimate as opposed to a nonintimate (Bureau of Justice Statistics, 1996). Thus, similar to past research, the findings of this meta-analysis indicated that unwanted sex in an advanced relationship is less likely to be perceived as a violation.

Although the effect was small, results of this study indicated that both men and women were significantly less inclined to perceive that sexual coercion occurred if alcohol or drugs were involved in the incident than if the individuals were sober. These findings shed some new light on the mixture of intoxicants and sexual activity. Specifically, past research has found that alcohol is often involved in cases of unwanted sex (e.g., Koss, 1988; Koss & Dinero, 1989), is used to persuade unwilling partners (e.g., Christopher & Frandsen, 1990; Mosher & Anderson, 1986; C. J. Struckman-Johnson, 1988), and has been used by men to justify their behavior (Levine & Kanin, 1987). However, the results of this analysis found that both men and women, as opposed to only men, were less inclined to perceive that coercion had occurred if intoxicants were involved.

The findings of this study supported past findings revealing some gender differences (Emmers & Allen, 1995a). Specifically, men perceived women as more willing to engage in sex than women and the effect was moderate. Consistent with the TSS, men are expected to "see through" a woman's supposed token resistance and persist sexually (Byers, 1996). Thus, a man reads a woman's resistance as disingenuous and continues sexually with her. The effects for gender, particularly for men perceiving forced sex as less coercive than women, were particularly strong.

Consistent with Muehlenhard et al. (1985), results of this analysis indicated that men perceived forced sex as more justifiable. According to the TSS, men are supposed to pursue sex, even if the woman is somewhat ambivalent (Byers, 1996). Men who believe that women lead them on often feel more justified in exercising coercive behaviors (Goodchilds & Zellman, 1984; Muehlenhard & MacNaughton, 1988).

In examining how men and women react to sexually coercive situations, results indicated that men and women do not significantly differ in overall strategies or in verbal strategies. However, findings suggested a small, significant effect for women being more likely to exercise physical resistance behaviors than men did, as Emmers and Allen (1995b) found. Other research has found that women are more likely to be faced with physical coercion than men (C. J. Struckman-Johnson, 1988) and women may be forced to fight fire with fire by responding physically to physically coercive overtures and behaviors. These findings are not surprising, considering that the TSS suggests that men pursue sex, even if met with resistance (Byers, 1996).

CONCLUSION

The results of these meta-analyses suggest that women, in particular, risk potential negative evaluation whether they follow or deviate from the TSS. Whether converging with (i.e., letting the man pay for the date) or diverging from (i.e., the woman initiating the date) the script, a possible outcome of either behavior is the sexual coercion of women. A troubling outcome of these findings is that men and women share many perceptions regarding justifiability, willingness, and coercion. This is particularly disturbing considering that those involved in advanced relationships are less likely to perceive that anything untoward has occurred in the event of unwanted sex.

As insightful as these findings may be, limitations do exist. A main limitation is that many of the studies on sexual coercion rely on perceptual rather than experiential data. However, it may be that experiential data do not produce different results. K. B. Anderson et al. (1997) only found small effects for slightly less acceptance of rape attitudes when examining women who had been coerced or knew someone who had experienced coercion. Nonetheless, an exploration of experiential data is necessary.

Another limitation is that meta-analyses are only as good as the original investigations' methodological rigor. If each study does not carefully identify, operationalize, or attenuate accordingly, those conducting a meta-analysis on the topic may grapple with validity issues. Methodological and statistical improvements and standardization across studies are needed (Hall, Shondrick, & Hirschman, 1993; Knight et al., 1996).

Based on the findings presented here, future research should examine prevalence of sexual coercion in both heterosexual and homosexual relationships. In heterosexual relationships, particularly traditional relationships, a more predictive theoretical framework is needed to explain the sexual coercion phenomenon. Although support was found for the TSS to a degree, the findings from this study were mixed, as were Byers's (1996). In accordance with Byers (1996), the TSS is useful in explaining coercion, but a more predictive framework is desired.

Although coercion exists in nontraditional relationships, more research is needed to examine and test the various theoretical frameworks. For example, how would sexual coercion be explained by the TSS or feminist theory in same-sex relationships, in heterosexual relationships in which the woman is the perpetrator, or in relationships involving individuals who hold fewer sex-typed beliefs and engage in less sex-typed behaviors? Research examining something other than male perpetration and female victimization exists (e.g., Bureau of Justice Statistics, 1996; Mac Donald, 1995), but more research is needed for the sake of both theory and practicality. A more solid theoretical framework could better explain sexually coercive situations and aid in the practical implementation of educational and intervention programs.

Nonetheless, the results of this study offer insights salient to interpersonal relationships and several findings are particular to romantic relationships. Although we are at the start of the 21st century, stereotypes continue to exist for women who initiate or pay for dates and for women who engage in a date at a private locale versus a public locale. Specifically, it is assumed that the woman who engages in these behaviors is interested in sex and, although men's perceptions were stronger than women's, both sexes perceived the victim to be willing and the behavior as justified in such situations. Being in an advanced relationship also clouded the perception that unwanted sex occurred for both men and women. Although men and women shared many of the same perceptions regarding unwanted sexual activity, the effects for men were stronger than they were for women. In fact, the strongest effect in the analysis occurred for men perceiving that forced sex was less coercive than women did. Considering that men also perceived the woman as more willing to engage in sex and perceived the forced sex as more justified than women, this finding is disturbing. This finding may link to the result that women engage in significantly more physical resistance strategies than men. These results offer support for the necessity of communication in interpersonal relationships. Rather than relying on perceptions and social stereotypes, it is imperative for partners to negotiate sexual scripts and behavior throughout the course of the relationship such that partners are clear on what is acceptable and what is not.

REFERENCES

References marked with an asterisk indicate studies used in the meta-analysis.

*Abbey, A. (1987). Misperceptions of friendly behavior as sexual interest: A survey of naturally occurring incidents. *Psychology of Women Quarterly, 11,* 171–194.

Allen, M., Emmers, T. M., Gebhardt, L. J., & Giery, M. (1995). Exposure to pornography and acceptance of rape myths: A summary of research using meta-analysis. *Journal of Communication, 45,* 5–26.

Anderson, K. B., Cooper, H., & Okamura, L. (1997). Individual differences and attitudes toward rape: A meta-analytic review. Personality and Social Psychology Bulletin, 23, 295–315.

Anderson, W. P., & Cummings, K. (1993). Women's acceptance of rape myths and their sexual experiences. *Journal of College Student Development, 34,* 53–57.

Atkeson, B. M., Calhoun, K., & Morris, K. T. (1989). Victim resistance to rape: The relationships of previous victimization, demographics, and situational factors. *Archives of Sexual Behavior, 18,* 497–507.

Bangert-Downs, R. (1986). Review of developments in meta-analytic method. *Psychological Bulletin, 99,* 388–399.

Bart, P. B., & O'Brien, P. H. (1985). *Stopping rape: Successful survival strategies.* New York: Pergamon.

Becchofer, L., & Parrot, A. (1991). What is acquaintance rape? In A. Parrot & L. Becchofer (Eds.), *Acquaintance rape: The hidden crime* (pp. 9–25). New York: Wiley.

*Belk, S. S., & Snell, W. E. (1988). Avoidance strategy use in intimate relationships. *Journal of Social and Clinical Psychology, 7,* 80–96.

Bostwick, T. D., & DeLucia, J. L. (1992). Effects of gender and specific dating behaviors on perceptions of sex willingness and date rape. *Journal of Social and Clinical Psychology, 11,* 14–25.

*Brady, E. C., Chrisler, J. C., Hosdale, D. C., Osowiecki, T., & Veal, T. A. (1991). Date rape: Expectations, avoidance strategies, and attitudes toward victims. *Journal of Social Psychology, 131,* 427–429.

*Bridges, J. (1991). Perceptions of date and stranger rape: A difference in sex role expectations and beliefs. *Sex Roles, 24,* 291–307.

Bureau of Justice Statistics (1996). Female victims of crime. Retrieved June 8, 1998 from the World Wide Web: http://www.ojp.usdoj.gov/bjs/

Burke, P. J., Stets, J. E., & Pirog-Good, M. A. (1989). Gender identity, self-esteem, and physical and sexual abuse in dating relationships. In M. A. Pirog-Good (Ed.), *Violence in dating relationships: Emerging social issues* (pp. 72–93). New York: Praeger.

Burt, M. (1980). Cultural myths and supports for rape. *Journal of Personality and Social Psychology, 38,* 217–230.

Burt, M., & Albin, R. (1981). Rape myths, rape definitions, and probability of conviction. *Journal of Applied Social Psychology, 11,* 212–230.

Byers, E. A. (1996). How well does the traditional sexual script explain sexual coercion? Review of a program of research. In E. S. Byers & L. F. O'Sullivan (Eds.), *Sexual coercion in dating relationships* (pp. 7–26). New York: Hawthorne.

Check, J. V., & Malamuth, N. M. (1983). Sex role stereotyping and reactions to depictions of stranger vs. acquaintance rape. *Journal of Personality and Social Psychology, 45,* 344–356.

Christopher, F. S., & Frandsen, M. M. (1990). Strategies of influence in sex and dating. *Journal of Social and Personal Relationships, 7,* 89–105.

*Dull, T., & Giacopassi, D. (1987). Demographic correlates of sexual and dating attitudes: A study of date rape. *Criminal Justice and Behavior, 14,* 175–193.

*Emmers, T. M., & Allen, M. (1995a, November). *Factors contributing to sexually coercive behaviors: A meta-analysis.* Paper presented at the Speech Communication Association convention, San Antonio, TX.

*Emmers, T. M., & Allen, M. (1995b, February). *Resistance to sexual coercion behaviors: A meta-analysis.* Paper presented at the Western States Communication Association convention, Portland, OR.

Federal Bureau of Investigation. (1992, August 30). *Crime in the United States, 1991.* Washington, DC: United States Department of Justice.

*Feltey, K., Ainslie, J., & Geib, A. (1991). Sexual coercion attitudes among high school students: The influence of gender in rape education. *Youth & Society, 23,* 229–250.

*Fischer, G. J. (1987). Hispanic and majority students attitudes toward forcible date rape as a function of differences in attitudes toward women. *Sex Roles, 17,* 93–100.

*Garcia, L., Milano, L., & Quijano, A. (1989). Perceptions of coercive sexual behavior by males and females. *Sex Roles, 21,* 569–577.

Goodchilds, J. D., & Zellman, G. L. (1984). Sexual signaling and sexual aggression in adolescent relationships. In N. M. Malamuth & E. Donnerstein (Eds.), *Pornography and sexual aggression* (pp. 233–243). Orlando, FL: Academic.

Hall, G. C. N., Shondrick, D. D., & Hirschman, R. (1993). The role of sexual arousal in sexually aggressive behavior: A meta-analysis. *Journal of Consulting and Clinical Psychology, 61,* 1091–1095.

Harney, P. A., & Muehlenhard, C. L. (1991). Factors that increase the likelihood of victimization. In A. Parrot & L. Becchofer (Eds.), *Acquaintance rape: The hidden crime* (pp. 159–175). New York: Wiley.

Hunter, J., & Schmidt, F. (1990). *Methods of meta-analysis.* Newbury Park, CA: Sage.

*Jenkins, M. J., & Dambrot, F. H. (1987). The attribution of date rape: Observer's attitudes and sexual experiences and the dating situation. Journal of Applied Social Psychology, 17, 875–895.

Kanin, E. J. (1967). An examination of sexual aggression in response to sexual frustration. *Journal of Marriage and the Family, 29,* 428–433.

Kleck, G., & Sayles, S. (1990). Rape and resistance. *Social Problems, 37,* 149–162.

Knight, G. P., Fabes, R. A., & Higgins, D. A. (1996). Concerns about drawing causal inferences from meta-analyses: An example in the study of gender differences in aggression. *Psychological Bulletin, 119,* 410–421.

Korman, S. K. (1983). Nontraditional dating behavior: Date initiation and date expense sharing among feminists and nonfeminists. *Family Relations, 32,* 575–581.

Korman, S. K., & Leslie, G. R. (1982). The relationship of feminist ideology and date expense sharing to perceptions of sexual aggression in dating. *The Journal of Sex Research, 18,* 114–129.

Koss, M. P. (1985). The hidden rape victim: Personality, attitudinal, and situational characteristics. *Psychology of Women Quarterly, 9*, 193–212.

Koss, M. P. (1988). Hidden rape: Incidence, prevalence, and descriptive characteristics of sexual aggression and victimization in a national sample of college students. In A. W. Burgess (Ed.), *Sexual assault* Vol.2, pp. 3–25). New York: Garland.

Koss, M. P., & Dinero, T. E. (1989). Discriminant analysis of risk factors for sexual victimization among a national sample of college women. *Journal of Consulting and Clinical Psychology, 57*, 242–250.

Koss, M. P., Gidycz, C. A., & Wisniewski, N. (1987). The scope of rape: Incidence and prevalence of sexual aggression and victimization in a national sample of higher education students. *Journal of Consulting and Clinical Psychology, 55*, 162–170.

Kuhn, L. (1996). Exposing a woman-hating culture. In J. Andrzejewski (Ed.), *Oppression and social justice: Critical frameworks* (5th ed., pp. 335–346). Needham Heights, MA: Simon & Schuster.

*Langley, T., Beatty, G., Yost, E. A., & O'Neal, E. C. (1991). How behavioral cues in a date rape scenario influence judgments regarding victim and perpetrator. *Forensic Reports, 4*, 355–358.

Levine, E. M., & Kanin, E. J. (1987). Sexual violence among dates and acquaintances: Trends and their implications for marriage and family. *Journal of Family Violence, 2*, 55–65.

Mac Donald, J. M. (1971). *Rape: Offenders and their victims*. Springfield, IL: Thomas.

Mac Donald, J. M. (1995). *Rape: Controversial issues*. Springfield, IL: Thomas.

Mahoney, E. R., Shively, M. D., & Traw, M. (1986). Sexual coercion and assault: Male socialization and female risk. *Sexual Coercion and Assault, 1*, 2–8.

*Makepeace, J. M. (1987). Social factor and victim–offender differences in courtship violence. *Family Relations, 36*, 87–91.

Malamuth, N. M. (1993). Predicting men's antisocial behavior against women. The interaction model of sexual aggression. In G. C. Nagayama Hall, R. Hirschman, J. R. Graham, & M. S. Zaragoza (Eds.), *Sexual aggression: Issues in etiology, assessment, and treatment* (pp. 63–97). Washington, DC: Taylor & Francis.

*McCormick, N. B. (1979). Come-ons and put-offs: Unmarried students' strategies for having and avoiding sexual intercourse. Psychology of Women Quarterly, 4, 194–211.

Mongeau, P. A., & Carey, C. M. (1996). Who's wooing whom II?: An experimental investigation of date-initiation and expectancy violation. *Western Journal of Communication, 60*, 195–213.

Mongeau, P. A., Hale, J. L., Johnson, K. L., & Hillis, J. D. (1993). Who's wooing whom? An investigation of female initiated dating. In P. J. Kalbfleisch (Ed.), *Interpersonal communication: Evolving interpersonal relationships* (pp. 51–68). Hillsdale, NJ: Lawrence Erlbaum Associates.

Mosher, D. L., & Anderson, R. D. (1986). Macho personality, sexual aggression, and reactions to guided imagery of realistic rape. *Journal of Research in Personality, 20*, 77–94.

*Muehlenhard, C. L. (1988). Misinterpreting dating behaviors and the risk of date rape. *Journal of Social and Clinical Psychology, 6*, 20–37.

Muehlenhard, C. L., & Cook, S. W. (1988). Men's reports of unwanted sexual activity. The *Journal of Sex Research, 24*, 58–72.

*Muehlenhard, C. L., & Falcon, P. L. (1991). Men's heterosexual skill and attitudes toward women as predictors of verbal sexual coercion and forceful rape. *Sex Roles, 23*, 241–259.

*Muehlenhard, C. L., Friedman, D. E., & Thomas, C. M. (1985). Is date rape justifiable? The effects of dating activity, who initiated, who paid, and men's attitudes toward women. *Psychology of Women Quarterly, 9,* 297–310.

Muehlenhard, C. L., Goggins, M. F., Jones, J. M., & Satterfield, A. T. (1991). Sexual violence and coercion in close relationships. In K. Kinney & S. Sprecher (Eds.), *Sexuality in close relationships* (pp. 155–175). Hillsdale, NJ: Lawrence Erlbaum Associates.

Muehlenhard, C. L., & Hollabaugh, L. C. (1988). Do women sometimes say no when they mean yes? The prevalence and correlates of women's token resistance to sex. *Journal of Personality and Social Psychology, 54,* 872–879.

Muehlenhard, C. L., & Linton, M. A. (1987). Date rape and sexual aggression in dating situations: Incidence and risk factors. *Journal of Personality and Social Psychology, 34,* 186–196.

Muehlenhard, C. L., & MacNaughton, J. S. (1988). Women's beliefs about women who "lead men on." *Journal of Social and Clinical Psychology, 7,* 65–79.

Muehlenhard, C. L., & Scardino, T. J. (1985). What will he think? Men's impressions of women who initiate dates and achieve academically. *Journal of Counseling Psychology, 32,* 560–569.

Muehlenhard, C. L., & Schrag, J. L. (1991). Nonviolent sexual coercion. In A. Parrot & L. Bechhofer (Eds.), *Acquaintance rape: The hidden crime* (pp. 115–128). New York: Wiley.

*Murnen, S. K., Perot, A., & Byrne, D. (1989). Coping with unwanted sexual activity: Normative responses, situational determinants, and individual differences. *The Journal of Sex Research, 26,* 85–106.

*Mynatt, C., & Allgeier, E. (1990). The risk factors, self-attributions, and adjustment problems among victims of sexual coercion. *Journal of Applied Social Psychology, 20,* 130–153.

Parrot, A. (1991). *Acquaintance rape and sexual assault* (5th ed.). Holmes Beach, FL: Learning Publications.

Poppen, P. J., & Segal, N. J. (1988). The influence of sex and sex role orientation on sexual coercion. *Sex Roles, 19,* 689–701.

*Sarwer, D. B., Kalichman, S. C., Johnson, J., & Early, J. (1993). Sexual aggression and love styles: An exploratory study. *Archives of Sexual Behavior, 22,* 265–275.

*Shotland, R. L., & Goodstein, L. (1992). Sexual precedence reduces the perceived legitimacy of sexual refusal: An examination of attributions concerning date rape and consensual sex. *Personality and Social Psychology Bulletin, 18,* 756–764.

*Siegel, J. M., Sorenson, S. B., Golding, J. M., Burnam, M. A., & Stein, J. A. (1989). Resistance to sexual assault: Who resists and what happens? *American Journal of Public Health, 79,* 27–31.

Sigelman, C. K., Berry, C. J., & Wiles, K. A. (1984). Violence in college students' relationships. *Journal of Applied Social Psychology, 5,* 530–548.

Sprecher, S., Hatfield, E., Cortese, A., Potapova, E., & Levitskaya, A. (1994). Token resistance to sexual intercourse and consent to unwanted sexual intercourse: College students' dating experiences in three countries. *The Journal of Sex Research, 31,* 125–132.

Stock, W. E. (1991). Feminist explanations: Male power, hostility, and sexual coercion. In E. Grauerholz & M. A. Koralewski (Eds.), *Sexual coercion* (pp. 61–73). Toronto: Lexington.

Struckman-Johnson, C. J. (1988). Forced sex on dates: It happens to men, too. *The Journal of Sex Research, 24,* 234–241.

*Struckman-Johnson, D. L., & Struckman-Johnson, C. J. (1991). Men and women's acceptance of coercive strategies varied by initiator gender and couple intimacy. *Sex Roles, 25,* 661–676.

Temple, L. (1997, September 18). Safety site keeps tabs on women. *USA Today,* p. 4D.

Ullman, S. E., & Knight, R. A. (1993). The efficacy of women's resistance strategies in rape situations. *Psychology of Women Quarterly, 17,* 23–28.

Zillmann, D., & Bryant, J. (1982). Pornography, sexual callousness, and the trivialization of rape. *Journal of Communication, 32,* 10–21.

18

A Meta-Analytic Interpretation of Intimate and Nonintimate Interpersonal Conflict

Barbara Mae Gayle, Raymond W. Preiss, and Mike Allen

Over the last 20 years, researchers have examined gender- and sex-based differences in the selection of conflict management strategies. Yet the conditions under which women and men differ or are similar in their selection of conflict management strategies in interpersonal relationships have not been clearly delineated. The underlying stereotypical assumptions of this literature are that men use more competitive-type strategies in nonintimate interpersonal relationships and more withdrawal strategies in intimate interpersonal relationships. Similarly, the stereotypical beliefs are that women use more compromising strategies in nonintimate interpersonal relationships and more demanding strategies in intimate interpersonal relationships.

However, results do not provide consistent support for gender- or sex-based stereotypes. Some studies identify gender or sex as a salient issue in interpersonal conflicts regardless of whether the relationships are intimate or nonintimate. Even then, however, researchers do not agree on the patterns of, or situations involving, gender or sex differences in the preference for particular conflict management strategies. Other researchers suggest that men and women employ quite similar conflict management strategies across interpersonal relationship types.

A review of gender differences in interpersonal conflict management strategy selection literature reveals a fragmented body of results replete with theoretical and methodological inconsistencies. These contradictory findings hinder the ability of researchers to determine whether men and women employ unique or similar conflict management styles. The purpose of this study is to meta-analytically review the primary conflict management strategy studies in intimate and nonintimate conflicts to produce a unified perspective on the impact that gender or sex has on the selection of conflict management strategies. A brief examination of the theoretical perspectives driving this line of inquiry is followed by results of a meta-analytic review of the sex differences in interpersonal conflicts and a meta-analytic review of the sex differences in conflict management strategy selection in marital relationships. These investigations of the magnitude of gender differences in conflict management are followed by an interpretation of the findings.

LITERATURE REVIEW

Three distinctive theoretical approaches have been used to explain gender or sex differences in conflict management strategy selection. Whether researchers explore intimate or nonintimate interpersonal conflicts, the theoretical rationale focuses on either trait differences, gender socialization, or social structure expectations.

The Trait Approach

Some researchers argue that conflict management strategy selection patterns are the result of the different personality characteristics of men and women (Chanin & Schneer, 1984; Christensen & Heavey, 1990; Gottman & Levenson, 1992; Temkin & Cummings, 1986). The traits approach suggests that people respond to conflict in ways consistent with their personality regardless of the situation or other person involved. The reasoning here is that an individual's perceptions of conflict are influenced by her or his personality predispositions. For example, Gottman and Levenson (1992) argued that men are more physiologically reactive to stress and thus more comfortable with conflicts. Sternberg and Soriano (1984) argued that the way an individual perceives a conflict situation is based on the intensity of a particular personality trait.

Researchers embracing the trait approach argue that men's and women's personality traits are relatively stable, so that men more often display strong independent personality traits and women more often display more affiliative and emotionally expressive personality traits (Christensen & Heavey, 1990). Unfortunately, a consistent set of personality traits associated with male and female conflict management strategy selection has not emerged. Even the three studies investigating androgyny (Baxter & Shepherd, 1978; Nowak, 1984; Yelsma & Brown, 1985) failed to produce any consistent pattern of conflict management strategy selection based on personality traits.

The Gender Socialization Approach

Some researchers ground their conflict management strategy selection research in the ideas of Gilligan (1982). This line of reasoning suggests that women's and men's identities are developed by the societal messages they receive about being female or male (Euwema & Van de Vliert, 1994; Heavey, Layne, & Christensen, 1993; Margolin & Wampold, 1981; Ruble & Schneer, 1994). Ruble and Schneer (1994) argued that girls and boys are raised so differently that it affects their conflict management strategy preferences. Several researchers found that because girls are socialized to play with other girls and value relationships, they are more likely to be cooperative (Bond & Vinache, 1961; Linkskold & Tedeschi, 1971; Rapoport & Chammah, 1965). On the other hand, researchers posited because boys are socialized into teams, they value competition and winning, and are more likely to maximize their own self-interest in a conflictual situation (Bond & Vinache, 1961; Linkskold & Tedeschi, 1971; Rapoport & Chammah, 1965).

These differences in socialization make it more likely that men and women will differ in their approaches to conflict management strategy selection (Christensen & Heavey, 1990; Ruble & Schneer, 1994). However, results using this approach are inconsistent and do not reveal a pattern of conflict management common to females and males.

The Social Structural Approach

The social structural approach posits that men and women conform to the positions they hold in the social structure (Eagly, 1987; Jacobson, 1989). This reasoning focuses on the distinctive role men and women enact in marriage or the distinctive role women and men assume as managers at work. For example, in marital roles women carry the responsibility for maintaining family relationships, household management, and childrearing. Usually the responsibility men have in marriage is to complete home and car repairs, provide financial security for the family, and make decisions that benefit the welfare of their families (Jacobson, 1989). At work, however, both men and women who occupy a manager's role will likely succumb to the role demands of that position (Eagly, 1987). The underlying assumption is that women and men behave the way they do because of the social role they occupy, and they enact the conflict management strategies consistent with their social roles.

Kofron (1986), Ruble and Schneer (1994), Ruble and Stander (1990), and Chusmir and Mills (1989) investigated whether women and men employed different conflict management strategies depending on their roles as family members or their roles as organizational workers. The results were inconclusive.

Overall, none of the current theoretical explanations for conflict strategy selection differences between men and women provide a consistent picture of either differences or similarities. Thus, a meta-analytic review of the conflict management strategy selection literature is a necessary step in consolidating knowledge claims and providing a quantitative summary that is much less vulnerable "to biases stemming from the reviewer's own preference concerning the presence or absence of sex differences" (Eagly, 1987, p. 36).

STUDY 1: NONINTIMATE INTERPERSONAL CONFLICT MANAGEMENT

Most of the research on sex differences in nonintimate interpersonal conflicts used surveys and relied on some form of the Blake and Mouton (1964) five-factor model: avoid, accommodate, compete, compromise, and collaborate. Thomas (1988) suggested that each conflict strategy is composed of some balance between concern for self (assertiveness) and concern for others (cooperativeness). This model is based on the underlying assumption that individuals develop fairly stable preferences for certain conflict strategies regardless of situations or topics. The studies examined in this meta-analysis also assumed that gender or sex differences are a prime reason for one's preference for certain strategies. However, the research does not consistently show any differences or similarities between men and women's preferences to be aggressive or cooperative in their conflict management strategy selection in nonintimate relationships.

Method

To explore the effect of gender differences on the selection of conflict management strategies, relevant studies were located and aggregated meta-analytically into a common metric to estimate the direction and magnitude of an average effect size (Cooper & Rosenthal, 1986; Eagly, 1987; Glass, McGraw, & Smith, 1981; Hunter, Schmidt, & Jackson, 1983). The search procedure resulted in the location of 33 manuscripts with 39 studies relevant to the variables of interest (see Table 18.1). Five studies did not provide sufficient information to allow meta-analytic aggregation (Fitzpatrick & Winke, 1979; Monroe, DiSalvo, Lewis, & Borzi, 1989; Rahim, 1983; Roloff & Greenberg, 1979; Stemberg & Soriano, 1984). The remaining 28 manuscripts with 34 separate studies[1] were coded using the definitions of Blake and Mouton's (1964) five strategies. When study definitions differed, definitions were used to match those strategies with the five-factor model. In the six studies (Gayle, 1991; Putnam & Wilson, 1982; Schuekle & McDowell, 1990; Tempkin & Cummings, 1986; Ting-Toomey, 1986; Ugbah & DeWine, 1986) using a three-factor model, the nonconfrontation strategy was entered as both accommodation and avoidance, the control strategy was coded as competitive, and the solution-oriented strategies were counted both as collaboration and compromise.

Statistical Procedures. The summary statistics of each study were converted to correlations so that the magnitude of outcomes attributable to sex or gender differences in conflict management strategy selection could be quantified. A positive correlation (a randomly assigned designation) indicates that male means were higher on a particular strategy, whereas a negative correlation indicates female means were higher.

The correlations were weighted for sample size and then averaged. Each average correlation was assessed to determine if the variance in the observed sample correlations was larger than expected by random sample error (Hedges & Olkin, 1985). To detect a moderator variable, the sum of the squared error was tested using a chi-square test. A nonsignificant chi-square indicates that the amount of variability is probably the result of chance, whereas a significant chi-square indicates that the amount of variability is probably the result of some type of moderating variable.

Results

The effect size for each conflict management strategy reported in all studies is listed in Table 18.2. Overall, most findings reveal small effect sizes. The

---

[1] When authors used different samples or situations in the same manuscript and reported separate analyses, we reported all the findings. For example, Chusmir and Mills (1989) and Ruble and Stander (1990) both examined the gender differences in conflict management strategy selection between work and home. Shockley-Zalabak and Morley (1984) used a college student sample and an employee sample to investigate gender differences in the choice of conflict management strategies. Kofron (1986) looked at gender differences in choosing conflict strategies if the other person was an authority figure or a friend. Ruble and Schneer (1994) compared three different samples and two instruments looking for a gender difference pattern in conflict management selection.

TABLE 18.1

Sex Differences in Interpersonal Conflicts Information

Author (s) of Study	Year	Sample Size	Sample Type	Sex Differences	Method Used	Published
Baxter & Shepherd	1978	57	Student	Yes	MODE	Yes
Berryman-Fink & Bruner	1987	147	Student	Yes	MODE	Yes
Chanin & Schneer	1984	94	Student	Yes	MODE	Yes
Chusmir & Mills	1989a	201	Workers	No	MODE	Yes
	1989b		Workers	Yes	MODE	Yes
Euwema & Vande Vliert	1994	215	Workers	Yes	Survey	Yes
Fitzpatrick & Winke	1979	170	Student	Yes	Survey	Yes
Gayle	1991	304	Workers	No	OCCI	Yes
Goering	1986	22	Student	Yes	Survey	No
Howell	1981	52	Workers	No	MODE	No
Kilmann & Thomas	1977	205	Student	Yes	MODE	Yes
Kofron	1986a	300	Workers	Yes	MODE	No
	1986b		Workers	No	MODE	No
Konovosky et al.	1988	586	Workers	Yes	MODE	No
Monroe et al.	1989	381	Workers	Yes	Describe	Yes
Nadler & Nadler	1988	160	Workers	Yes	Scenario	No
Papa & Natalle	1989	26	Workers	Yes	Observe	Yes
Putnam & Wilson	1982	120	Workers	Yes	OCCI	Yes
Rahim	1983	100	Workers	Yes	Survey	Yes
Renwick	1977	95	Workers	No	Survey	Yes
Revilla	1984	113	Workers	No	MODE	No
Roloff & Greenberg	1979	175	Student	Yes	Survey	Yes
	1987	80	Workers	Yes	Scenario	Yes
Ruble & Schneer	1994a	211	Student	Yes	MODE	Yes
	1994b	174	Student	Yes	Survey	Yes
	1994c	198	Student	No	Survey	Yes
Ruble & Stander	1990a	62	Workers	Yes	MODE	No
	1990b	62	Workers	No	MODE	No
Scheukle & McDowell	1990	217	Student	No	OCCI	No
Shockley-Zalabak	1981	69	Workers	No	Survey	Yes
Shockley-Zalabak	1984a	61	Student	Yes	MODE	Yes
& Morley	1984b	100	Workers	No	MODE	Yes
Sone	1981	110	Workers	Yes	Survey	No
Sternberg & Soriano	1984	32	Student	No	Survey	Yes
Temkin & Cummings	1986	162	Workers	No	OCCI	Yes
Thomas	1971	253	Workers	Yes	Survey	No
Ting-Toomey	1986	303	Student	Yes	OCCI	Yes
Ugbah & DeWine	1986	175	Student	Yes	Survey	No
Zammuto et al.	1979	106	Student	Yes	Survey	Yes

Note. OCCI = Organizational Communication Conflict Instrument.

TABLE 18.2

Effect Sizes and Variances by Strategy for the Nonintimate Conflict Studies

Author(s) of Study	Effect Size and Variance by Strategy					
	Avoidance	Accommodation	Compete	Compromise	Collaboration	Covariance
Baxter & Shepherd	-.001	-.106	.394	-.106	-.106	3.49
Berryman-Fink & Brunner	-.020	-.074	.171	-.180	-.130	3.49
Chanin & Schneer	.012	.042	.064	-.297	.220	2.65
Chusmir & Mills	-.114	.028	.086	.091	-.084	3.06
	.016	.007	.040	-.102	-.010	3.14
Euwema & Van de Vliert	-.052	.007	.166	-.132	-.007	2.86
Gayle	-.106	-.055	.212	-.147	-.001	3.53
Goering	-.520	3.25				
Howell	.071	-.233	.209	-.081	-.235	3.44
Kilmann & Thomas	.069	-.069	.098	-.104	.098	2.90
Kofron	-.205	-.327	.441	-.051	.028	2.92
	-.167	-.099	.249	-.099	.007	
Konovosky et al.	-.080	-.005	-.040	-.040	2.79	
Nadler & Nadler	.153	.181	-.199	-.224	3.06	
Papa & Natalle	.016	.070	.129	.172	3.53	
Putnam & Wilson	-.013	-.013	.030	-.129	-.129	3.25
Renwick	-.155	.056	-.075	-.200	.152	3.53
Revilla	-.191	.034	.071	.028	.019	3.25
Rossi et al.	.001	-.210	2.25			

continued on next page

TABLE 18.2 (continued)

Author(s) of Study	Effect Size and Variance by Strategy					
	Avoidance	Accommodation	Compete	Compromise	Collaboration	Covariance
Ruble & Schneer	.013	-.013	.190	-.162	-.108	
	-.010	-.050	.303	-.235	-.017	
	-.066	-.114	.136	-.123	-.044	3.88
Ruble & Stander	-.082	-.019	.254	-.343	.053	
	.034	-.098	.126	-.136	.120	3.11
Scheukle & McDowell	-.002	-.002	.123	-.200	-.200	
Shockley-Zalabak	-.001	.001	.001	-.001	.001	
Shockley-Zalabak & Morley	.001	.001	.235	-.289	-.001	
	.001	-.001	.112	-.057	.001	
Sone	-.042	-.246	.157	-.172	-.098	2.38
Temkin & Cummings	-.001	-.001	.001	-.001	-.001	2.57
Thomas	-.033	-.040	.154	-.126	.044	3.06
Ting-Toomey	.001	.001	.160	-.108	-.108	3.14
Ugbah & DeWine	-.189	-.184	.059	-.189	-.184	3.14
Zammuto et al.	-.034	-.164	.261	-.017	-.164	2.87

Note. *A positive correlation (a randomly assigned designation) indicates that male means were higher on a particular strategy, whereas a negative correlation indicates female means were higher.

352

average effect sizes for each conflict management strategy are displayed in Table 18.3. Each of the five effect sizes merit separate discussion.

Avoidance. An overall frequency analysis of the avoidance strategy results reveals that five studies (16%) reported a significantly higher use of avoiding strategies by women (Kofron, 1986, sample b; Konovosky, Jaster, & McDonald, 1988; Putnam & Wilson, 1982; Ugbah & DeWine, 1986; Zammuto, London, & Rowland, 1979). Ting-Toomey (1986) reported a significantly higher use of avoiding strategies by men. The remaining 26 studies[2] (81%) reported no significant gender difference in the use of avoidance strategies.

In the meta-analysis of 31 studies employing 5,155 respondents the average correlation ($r = -.053$) was extremely small (see Table 18.3). A formal significance test revealed that the amount of variation is probably due to sampling error, $\chi^2 = 34.52, p > .05$.

Accommodation. An overall frequency analysis of the accommodation strategy results reveals that four studies (13%) reported a significantly

TABLE 18.3
Average Effect Sizes for Interpersonal Conflict Studies

	Effect Sizes			
	r	*N*	*K*	χ^2
Avoidance	−.053	5,155	31	34.52
Accommodate	−.068	4,435	30	40.36
Compete	.147	5,261	33	71.54*
Compromise	−.119	5,283	34	35.63
Collaborate	−.041	5,181	32	42.73

Note. A positive correlation (a randomly assigned designation) indicates that male means were higher on a particular strategy, whereas a negative correlation indicates female means were higher.
*$p = < .05$

[2]Baxter and Shepherd (1978), Berryman-Fink and Brunner (1987), Chanin and Schneer (1984), Chusmir and Mills (1989, samples a and b), Euwema and Van de Vliert (1994), Gayle (1991), Howell (1981), Kilmann and Thomas (1977), Kofron (1986, sample b), Nadler and Nadler (1988), Renwick (1977), Revilla (1984), Ruble and Schneer (1994, samples a, b, and c), Ruble and Stander (1990, samples a and b), Schuekle and McDowell (1990), Shockley-Zalabak (1981), Shockley-Zalabak and Morley (1984, samples a and b), Sone (1981), Sternberg and Soriano (1984), Temkin and Cummings (1986), and Thomas (1971) found no significant gender difference in the use of avoidance strategies.

higher use of accommodating strategies by women (Kofron, 1986, sample a; Putnam & Wilson, 1982; Sone, 1981; Ugbah & DeWine, 1986). Ting-Toomey (1986) reported a significantly higher use of accommodating strategies by men. The remaining 27 studies[3] (84%) reported no significant gender difference in the use of accommodation strategies.

In the meta-analysis of 30 studies employing 4,435 respondents the average correlation ($r = -.068$) was extremely small (see Table 18.3). A formal significance test revealed that the amount of variation is probably due to sampling error, $\chi^2 = 40.36, p > .05$.

Compete.   An overall frequency analysis of the competing strategy results reveals that Zammuto et al. (1979) reported a significantly higher use of competitive strategies by women and 16 studies[4] (44%) reported a significantly higher use of competing strategies by men. The remaining 19 studies[5] (53%) reported no significant gender difference in the use of competing strategies.

In the meta-analysis of 33 studies employing 5,261 respondents the average correlation ($r = .147$) was small (see Table 18.3). A formal significance test revealed that the amount of variation is probably not due to sampling error, $\chi^2 = 71.54, p < .05$. The impact of the moderating variable was difficult to assess given the variety of instruments, the various sample populations, and the variety of different instructions given.

Compromise.   An overall frequency analysis of the compromising strategy results reveals that no studies found men to use more compromising

---

[3]Baxter and Shepherd (1978), Berryman-Fink and Brunner (1987), Chanin and Schneer (1984), Chusmir and Mills (1989, samples a and b), Euwema and Van de Vliert (1994), Gayle (1991), Howell (1981), Kilmann and Thomas (1977), Kofron (1986, sample a), Konovosky et al. (1988), Nadler and Nadler (1988), Renwick (1977), Revilla (1984), Ruble and Schneer (1994, samples a, b, and c), Ruble and Stander (1990, samples a and b), Schuekle and McDowell (1990), Shockley-Zalabak (1981), Shockley-Zalabak and Morley (1984, samples a and b), Sone (1981), Sternberg and Soriano (1984), Temkin and Cummings (1986), and Zammuto et al. (1979) found no significant gender difference in the use of accommodation strategies.

[4]Baxter and Shepherd (1978), Berryman-Fink and Brunner (1987), Kilmann and Thomas (1977), Kofron (1986, samples a and b), Nadler and Nadler (1988), Papa and Natalle (1989), Putnam and Wilson (1982), Rahim (1983), Roloff and Greenberg (1979), Rossi and Todd-Mancillas (1987), Ruble and Schneer (1994, samples a and b), Ruble and Stander (1990, sample a), Schuekle and McDowell (1990), Shockley-Zalabak and Morley (1984, sample a), and Thomas (1971) found significant male usage of competing strategies.

[5]Chanin and Schneer (1984), Chusmir and Mills (1989, samples a and b), Gayle (1991), Howell (1981), Kofron (1986, sample a), Konovosky et al. (1988), Nowak (1984), Renwick (1977), Revilla (1984), Ruble and Schneer (1994, sample c), Ruble and Stander (1990, sample b), Shockley-Zalabak (1981), Shockley-Zalabak and Morley (1984, sample b), Sone (1981), Sternberg and Soriano (1984), Temkin and Cummings (1986), Ting-Toomey (1986), and Ugbah and DeWine (1986) found no significant gender difference in the use of competing strategies.

strategies and 15 studies[6] (43%) reported a significantly higher use of compromising strategies by women. Twenty studies[7] (57%) reported no significant gender difference in the use of compromising strategies.

In the meta-analysis of 34 studies employing 5,283 respondents the average correlation ($r = -.119$) was small (see Table 18.3). A formal significance test revealed that the amount of variation is probably due to sampling error, $\chi^2 = 35.63, p > .05$.

Collaboration. An overall frequency analysis of the collaboration strategy results reveals that Chanin and Schneer (1984) found a significantly higher use of collaboration strategies by men and 4 studies (12%) reported a significantly higher use of collaboration strategies by women (Papa & Natalle, 1989; Schuekle & McDowell, 1990; Ting-Toomey, 1986; Ugbah & DeWine, 1986). The remaining 28 studies[8] (85%) reported no significant gender difference in the use of collaboration strategies.

In the meta-analysis of 32 studies employing 5,181 respondents the average correlation ($r = -.041$) was extremely small (see Table 18.3). A formal significance test revealed that the amount of variation is probably due to sampling error, $\chi^2 = 42.73, p > .05$.

STUDY 2: MARITAL CONFLICT MANAGEMENT

Most of the marital conflict research focuses on the demand–withdrawal conflict strategy selection sequence using observational analysis (e.g.,

---

[6]Berryman-Fink and Brunner (1987), Chanin and Schneer (1984), Euwema and Van de Vliert (1994), Kilmann and Thomas (1977), Nadler and Nadler (1988), Papa and Natalle (1989), Roloff and Greenberg (1979), Ruble and Schneer (1994, samples a and b), Ruble and Stander (1990, sample a), Schuekle and McDowell (1990), Shockley-Zalabak and Morley (1984, sample a), Thomas (1971), Ting-Toomey (1986), and Ugbah and DeWine (1986) found significant female usage of compromising strategies.

[7]Baxter and Shepherd (1978), Chusmir and Mills (1989, samples a and b), Gayle (1991), Howell (1981), Kofron (1986 samples a and b), Kofron (1986, sample a), Konovosky et al. (1988), Nowak (1984), Renwick (1977), Revilla (1984), Ruble and Schneer (1994, sample c), Ruble and Stander (1990, sample b), Shockley-Zalabak (1981), Shockley-Zalabak and Morley (1984, sample b), Sone (1981), Sternberg and Soriano (1984), Temkin and Cummings (1986), and Zammuto et al. (1979) found no significant gender difference in the use of compromising strategies.

[8]Baxter and Shepherd (1978), Berryman-Fink and Brunner (1987), Chusmir and Mills (1989, samples a and b), Euwema and Van de Vliert (1994), Gayle (1991), Howell (1981), Kilmann and Thomas (1977), Kofron (1986, samples a and b), Konovosky et al. (1988), Nadler and Nadler (1988), Nowak (1984), Renwick (1977), Revilla (1984), Ruble and Schneer (1994, samples a, b, and c), Ruble and Stander (1990, samples a and b), Shockley-Zalabak (1981), Shockley-Zalabak and Morley (1984, samples a and b), Sone (1981), Sternberg and Soriano (1984), Temkin and Cummings (1986), Thomas (1971), and Zammuto et al. (1979) found no significant gender difference in the use of collaboration strategies.

Christensen & Heavey, 1990; Gottman & Carre, 1994; Heavey et al. 1991). This interactional process between wives and husbands "is characterized by one spouse making demands and the other spouse withdrawing" (Jacobson, 1989, p. 29). The underlying assumption has been that wives employ more demanding strategies in their quest to change relationships or seek more closeness or involvement, and husbands use more withdrawal strategies as they seek more autonomy or seek to preserve the status quo (Christensen, 1987; Jacobson, 1989). However, Roberts and Krokoff (1990) argued that reciprocity may be a more likely explanation of why women use demanding strategies. These authors argued that wives employ demanding strategies as a response to husbands who withdraw rather than initiating the strategy to fulfill their own needs. Other researchers suggested it is the issue that determines the demand–withdrawal pattern (Billings, 1979; Christensen & Heavey, 1990; Heavey et al., 1991).

Jacobson (1989) argued that power is at the core of the demand–withdrawal conflict pattern. He claimed that men's "withdrawal patterns are both a manifestation of and a factor which perpetuates their dominance" and that women's demand patterns arise "from a position of weakness" (pp. 30–31) within the relationship. Christensen (1987), on the other hand, argued it is the partners' "different needs and preference for intimacy and independence" (p. 261) that triggers the use of the demand–withdrawal conflict pattern and that gender-role socialization is most likely responsible for women seeking more relational intimacy and men requiring more independence.

Method

To explore the effect of gender differences on the selection of marital conflict management strategies, relevant studies were located and aggregated meta-analytically into a common metric following procedures employed for the nonintimate interpersonal meta-analysis in Study 1. The search procedure resulted in the location of 16 manuscripts relevant to the variables of interest (see Table 18.4). Two studies did not provide sufficient statistical information to allow meta-analytic aggregation (Nowak, 1984; Resick et al., 1981). Two other studies employed the same data set (Gottman & Carre, 1994; Gottman & Levenson, 1992), so only one study was included in the analysis. The remaining 13 manuscripts were coded using power, accommodation, cognitive, and emotional strategies. Power strategies were coded if either partner used demands, withdrawals, or rejection to exert control as Jacobson (1989) suggested. Accommodation strategies were coded if attempts were made to reconcile, resolve, or engage in the positive behavior of

TABLE 18.4
Sex Differences in Marital Conflicts Information

Author (s) of Study	Year	Sample Size	Sex Difference	Method Used	Published
Barry	1968	96	Yes	Coding audio	No
Bell et al.	1982	60	Yes	Coding interview	Yes
Billings	1979	48	Yes	Coding video	Yes
Christensen	1987	110	Yes	Survey	Yes
Christensen & Heavey	1990	124	Yes	Coding video	Yes
Gottman & Levenson	1992	146	Yes	Coding video	Yes
Heavey et al.	1993	58	Yes	Coding video	Yes
Margolin & Wampold	1981	78	Yes	Coding video	Yes
Miller	1994	100	Yes	Survey	Yes
Nowak	1984	40	No	Coding video	No
Perregaux	1971	64	Yes	Coding audio	No
Raush et al.	1974	92	Yes	Coding audio	Yes
Resick et al.	1981	38	No	Coding video	Yes
Roberts & Krokoff	1990	44	Yes	Coding video	Yes
Yelsma & Brown	1985	182	Yes	Survey	Yes

conciliation. Cognitive strategies were coded if individuals accepted responsibility or engaged in mutual attempts to problem solve or compromise. Emotional strategies were coded if appeals were made in the form of nagging, whining, or complaining.

Statistical Procedures.   The same statistical procedures were employed as in Study 1.

Results

The effect size for each conflict management strategy reported in all studies are listed in Table 18.5. Overall, most findings reveal small effect sizes. The average effect sizes for each conflict management strategy are displayed in Table 18.6. Each of the four effect sizes merit separate discussion.

TABLE 18.5
Effect Sizes for the Marital Conflict Studies

Author(s) of Study	Effect Size by Strategy			
	Power	Accommodation	Cognitive	Emotional
Barry	−.037	.065	.032	−.087
Bell et al.	.270			
Billings	−.003	.001	.095	−.075
Christensen	−.504			
Christensen & Heavey	−.125			
Gottman & Levenson	−.171	−.130		
Heavey et al.	−.154	.001	−.162	
Margolin & Wampold	−.264	−.187	−.027	
Miller	.001	.510	.001	.001
Perregaux	−.103	−.629	.011	
Raush et al.	−.140	.001	.068	−.062
Roberts & Krokoff	−.120	.136		
Yelsma & Brown	.088	−.088		

Note. A positive correlation (a randomly assigned designation) indicates that male means were higher on a particular strategy, whereas a negative correlation indicates female means were higher.

Power.   An overall frequency analysis of the power strategy results reveals that Bell, Chaftez, and Horn (1982) reported a higher use of power strategies by men and seven studies (54%) reported a higher use of power strategies by wives (Barry, 1968; Christensen, 1987; Christensen & Heavey, 1990; Gottman & Levenson, 1992; Heavey et al., 1993; Margolin & Wampold, 1981; Raush, Barry, Hertel, & Swain, 1974). The remaining five studies (38%) reported no significant gender difference in the use of power strategies (Billings, 1979; Miller, 1994; Nowak, 1984; Perregaux, 1971; Roberts & Krokoff, 1990).

In the meta-analysis of 11 studies employing 918 respondents the average correlation ($r = -.124$) was extremely small (see Table 18.6). A formal significance test revealed that the amount of variation is probably due to sampling error, $\chi^2 = 27.59, p > .05$.

TABLE 18.6
Average Effect Sizes for Marital Conflict Studies

	Effect Sizes			
	r	N	K	χ^2
Power	−.124	942	11	27.59
Emotional	−.069	682	8	2.04
Cognitive	−.035	654	7	3.72
Accommodation	.031	704	8	56.66*

Note. A positive correlation (a randomly assigned designation) indicates that male means were higher on a particular strategy, whereas a negative correlation indicates female means were higher.
$^*p > .05$.

Accommodation.   An overall frequency analysis of the accommodation strategy results reveals that two studies (22%) reported a higher use of accommodating strategies by women (Margolin & Wampold, 1981; Perregaux, 1971). Four studies (45%) reported a higher use of accommodating strategies by men (Barry, 1968; Miller, 1994; Raush et al., 1974, Yelsma & Brown, 1985). Three studies (33%) reported no significant gender difference in the use of accommodation strategies (Billings, 1979; Nowak, 1984; Roberts & Krokoff, 1990).

In the meta-analysis of eight studies employing 680 respondents the average correlation ($r = .031$) was extremely small (see Table 18.6). A formal significance test revealed that the amount of variation is probably not due to sampling error, $\chi^2 = 56.66, p < .05$. Due to the small number of studies and the vast coding differences, the moderator variable could not be thoroughly assessed.

Cognitive.   An overall frequency analysis of the cognitive strategy results reveals that two studies (25%) reported a higher use of cognitive strategies by women (Margolin & Wampold, 1981; Yelsma & Brown, 1985). Four studies (50%) reported a higher use of cognitive strategies by men (Barry, 1968; Heavey et al., 1993; Miller, 1994; Raush et al., 1974). The remaining two studies (25%) reported no significant gender difference in the use of cognitive strategies (Billings, 1979; Nowak, 1984).

In the meta-analysis of seven studies employing 630 respondents the average correlation ($r = −.035$) was extremely small (see Table 18.6). A formal significance test revealed that the amount of variation is probably due to sampling error, $\chi^2 = 3.72, p > .05$.

Emotional.   An overall frequency analysis of the emotional strategy results reveals that four studies (50%) reported a higher use of emotional strategies by women (Barry, 1968; Gottman & Levenson, 1992; Heavey et al., 1993; Margolin & Wampold, 1981; Raush et al., 1974). Two studies (25%) reported no significant gender difference in the use of emotional strategies (Billings, 1979; Nowak, 1984). Two studies (25%) found men using more emotional strategies than women (Miller, 1994; Perregaux, 1971).

In the meta-analysis of eight studies employing 658 respondents the average correlation ($r = -.069$) was extremely small (see Table 18.6). A formal significance test revealed that the amount of variation is probably due to sampling error, $\chi^2 = 2.04, p > .05$.

PUTTING GENDER DIFFERENCE RESULTS INTO PERSPECTIVE

Not surprisingly, results do not provide unequivocal support for gender- or sex-based stereotypes. Overall findings revealed small average effect sizes in both intimate and nonintimate interpersonal conflicts. These results support Raush et al.'s (1974) argument that differences between men's and women's approach to conflict accounted for very little of the behavior of wives and husbands. However, it is questionable whether a static standard can fully illuminate the complex factors involved with gender differences in conflict strategy selection.

Cohen (1977) suggested that the lack of "good experimental or measurement control or both" (p. 25) could account for the creation of small effect sizes. This is an important consideration because many conflict researchers have questioned the lack of systematic correlation between instruments, the social desirability of some instruments, the overall lack of predictive validity of the conflict management strategy selection instruments, the oversimplification of the current strategy configuration, and the fact that conflicts are initiated by events or responded to in ways that will not occur during observations (Christensen, 1987; Thomas, 1988; Weider-Hatfield, 1988; Wilson & Waltman, 1988; Womack, 1988).

Another way to assess the results involved is to use a binomial effect size display (Rosenthal & Rubin, 1982) for a more practical interpretation of how often competing, compromising, and power strategies are selected (see Table 18.7). This analysis revealed that employing compromising strategies in nonintimate interpersonal conflicts would be associated with an increase

TABLE 18.7
Binomial Effect Size Display

Strategy	r	Sex Difference	
		Male	Female
Compromising	−.119	44 56	56 44
Competing	.147	57 43	43 57
Power	−.124	44 56	56 44

in the percentage of women using these strategies from about 44% to 56%. Also in nonintimate interpersonal conflicts, employing competitive strategies would be associated with an increase in the percentage of men using those strategies from 43% to 57%. In marital conflict, the interpretation suggests that the percentage of women employing power strategies would increase from 44% to 56%. These figures may suggest that compromising, competing, and power strategies might be separate orientations more closely linked to "appropriate" gender-role behavior than processes that emerge over the duration of the conflict interaction. Therefore, females and males in some situations may act according to their prescribed gender roles. In other situations, the norms associated with the social roles they occupy (e.g., membership in an organization or family) may regulate and alter behavior (Eagly, 1987), in this case conflict strategy selection.

One might also try to clarify these findings by comparing the results to several related meta-analyses. Even though the overall effect sizes of the comparison analyses can be classified as small (compliance-gaining: $r < .07$; aggression: $r = .14$; influenceability: $r = .08$), the direction and magnitude of the effect sizes indicated a pattern of responses consistent with both meta-analyses conducted in this article. The findings that men more often select competitive-type strategies and women select more compromising strategies, parallels Krone, Allen, and Ludlum's (1994) managerial compliance-gaining meta-analysis results, in which female managers tended to use more "soft" tactics such as helping and counseling and male mangers reported using slightly more "harsh" tactics such as threats and punishments. The results of the marital meta-analysis are consistent with Eagly and Carli's (1981) meta-analytic findings that women are more impacted by influence attempts and Eagly and Steffen's (1986) meta-analytic findings that men receive and deliver more aggression.

Our results could also be influenced by the respondents' perceptions of the strategies and contexts or situations employed in the primary investigations or the observational coder's categorization schema. Margolin and Wampold (1981) argued that coders seem to describe the wife's negative behavior more pejoratively than the husband's negative behavior. These authors suggested that some gender bias may be the result of the coder's expectations or stereotypes. Thus, it may be that gender or sex-role biases embedded in the original studies could affect the results of the meta-analysis. To determine if the conflict management strategies or the contexts and situations described in the original studies elicited a gender or sex difference bias, a questionnaire was designed and an independent experiment was conducted using the nonintimate interpersonal conflict studies.

Methods

The first part of the questionnaire contained the conceptual and operational definitions of the five conflict management strategies. Using *five-step* semantic differential scales, respondents were asked to rate: (a) the perceived effectiveness of each strategy from *always effective* to *never effective*, (b) the perceived positive and negative social consequences of each strategy from *people will like me a lot* to *people will not like me*, and (c) the perceived gender bias of the strategy from *typically male* to *typically female*. The goal of this assessment was to determine whether respondents viewed any of the strategies as being more typically associated with male or female communication behavior and whether any of the strategies were viewed more positively than the other strategies.

In the second part of the questionnaire, each of the contexts or situations described in the original experiments was listed.[9] The goal of the rating in this section was to identify whether the situations reported in the original studies represented circumstances biased in favor of male or female roles. For example, if in the minds of the respondents, a situation involving a manager having to discipline a worker represents a typical "male" situation, then the direction and size of the effect should be correlated with that finding. A "male" situation should demonstrate larger positive correlations than a "female" situation. A "female" situation should produce effects that are smaller or negative.

---

[9]Not all studies provided this information or were available to be tested.

Forty-nine students from a small private college in the Pacific Northwest filled out the questionnaire. Respondents read each situation as described in the original experiment and rated those situations on a scale with the endpoints determining whether the situation was one typically encountered by males or females. The questionnaire generated a rating for each situation reported in each of the original studies used in the meta-analysis. The responses were then averaged to produce a mean value for each situation on the scale. The correlation between effect sizes for each study and the ratings of the situation for each study represented a correlation between the effect size observed and the mean rating of the situation provided by the respondents. A positive correlation indicated that "male" type situations (as rated by the respondents) were more likely to produce responses that favored the probability of a conflict style utilized by males.[10]

Results

The covariate figures calculated for each study are presented in Table 18.2. These covariates ranged from 2.25 to 3.88. The 15 t tests investigating strategy bias and respondent sex revealed no significant relation between respondent sex and perceptions of strategy effectiveness, consequences of strategy selection, and the perceived gender appropriateness of each strategy. The Pearson correlation revealed a significant relation between effect sizes and the selection of competing strategies ($r = .4099$, $p < .05$). This finding suggests that certain contexts and situations are more likely perceived as "typically male." No other conflict strategies were significantly correlated with changes in the masculine–feminine covariate.

Discussion

The significant correlation between competing strategies and contextual or situational descriptions of the original studies suggests that in certain circumstances respondents expect competitive gender-role behavior because they perceive the situation or context to be masculine. These findings indicate that some of the identifiable gender differences in conflict strategy se-

---

[10]Such a rating system contains a potential defect. The students doing the ratings are removed by more than 10 years from the actual rating of the original respondents. This creates some difficulty in that the participants view of the current applicability of the contexts or situations may not be the same as past views. Also, some of the original studies used nonstudent samples that may have had a different orientation toward the contexts or situations than the current undergraduate population. This limitation, however, should minimize the impact of the rating because the respondents are probably more sensitized to the entrance of women in the workforce and the larger number of roles available for women. The fact that such a correlation exists probably understates the importance of such effects.

lection begin with respondents' perception of the contexts or situations that are inherently male or female. Thus, gender roles are enacted in the mind of the respondent and this stereotypical thinking may influence their conflict management strategy selection. As Eagly (1987) argued, gender differences "in social behaviors are likely to be inconsistent because the definition of the situation in which the behavior occurs must be considered in order to account for the variability" (pp. 2–3).

IMPLICATIONS

Taken together, the results of these meta-analyses and the covariate analysis suggest that other extraneous variables may have an impact on the perceived gender or sex differences in interpersonal conflict management strategy selection. Results seem to suggest that the situation or context and stereotypical expectations play a distinct role in unraveling the sex or gender difference claims made in this body of literature.

Interestingly, several authors in the marital conflict literature suggested that the use of power strategies varied depending on whether the wife's issues or the husband's issues were being discussed (Billings, 1979; Christensen & Heavey, 1990). Christensen and Heavey (1990) argued that "both husband and wife were more likely to be demanding when discussing a change they wanted and more likely to be withdrawing when discussing a change their partner wanted" (p. 73). Thus, it may be the situation or context that influences conflict management strategy selection rather than the gender or social role of either individual involved in the interpersonal conflict.

It is also apparent that stereotypical expectations do play a part in the selection of conflict management behavior. Allen (1998) suggested that respondents often remember the extreme examples of a particular behavior so that their gender stereotypes have a basis in fact. He argued that these stereotypes are applied to everyone and assigned based on gender even when the stereotype is inaccurate.

Methodologically, the findings of our investigation indicate the need to consider and explore the nature of situations that people encounter and when those situations evoke strong, generalized gender-role expectations. Gender differences in any given body of literature may reflect more of a sense of appropriateness of the stimuli for the particular gender than actual behavioral indexes. Rather than exploring the nature of communication that assumes a cross-situational consistency, our results suggest the importance of establishing a situational or contextual view of gender enactment. The data in this study indicate that the respondents did in fact consider gender in their determination of the appropriate conflict management strategy.

However, their responses were linked to their perceptions of how a particular gender ought to behave in particular situations.

REFERENCES

References marked with one asterisk indicate studies included in the nonintimate meta-analysis.

References marked with two asterisks indicate studies included in the marital meta-analysis.

Allen, M. (1998). Methodological considerations when examining a gendered world. In D. Canary & K. Dindia (Eds.), *Handbook of sex differences and similarities in communication* (pp. 427–444). Mahwah, NJ: Lawrence Erlbaum Associates.

**Barry, W. A. (1968). *Conflict in marriage: A study of the interaction of newlywed couples in experimentally induced conflicts.* Unpublished doctoral dissertation, University of Michigan, Ann Arbor, MI.

*Baxter, L. A., & Shepherd, T. L. (1978). Sex-role identity, sex of other, and affective relationship as determinants of interpersonal conflict-management styles. *Sex Roles, 6,* 813–825.

**Bell, D. C., Chafetz, J. S., & Horn, L. H. (1982). Marital conflict resolution: A study of strategies and outcomes. *Journal of Family Issues, 3,* 111–131.

*Berryman-Fink, C., & Brunner, C. C. (1987). The effects of sex of source and target on interpersonal conflict management styles. *Southern Speech Communication Journal, 53,* 38–48.

**Billings, A. (1979). Conflict resolution in distressed and nondistressed couples. *Journal of Consulting and Clinical Psychology, 47,* 368–376.

Blake, R. R., & Mouton, J. S. (1964). *The managerial grid.* Houston, TX: Gulf.

Bond, J. R., & Vinache, W. E. (1961). Coalitions in mixed-sex triads. *Sociometry, 34,* 61–75.

*Chanin, M. N., & Schneer, J. A. (1984). A study of relationship between Jungian personality dimensions and conflict-handling behavior. *Human Relations, 37,* 865–879.

**Christensen, A. (1987). Detection of conflict patterns in couples. In K. Hahlweg & M. J. Goldstein (Eds.), *Understanding major mental disorders* (pp. 250–265). New York: Family Processes.

**Christensen, A., & Heavey, C. L. (1990). Gender and social structure in demand/withdraw patterns of marital conflict. *Journal of Personality and Social Psychology, 59,* 73–81.

*Chusmir, L. H., & Mills, J. (1989). Gender differences in conflict resolution styles of managers: At work and at home. *Sex Roles, 20,* 149–163.

Cohen, J. (1977). *Statistical power analysis for the behavioral sciences.* New York: Academic.

Cooper, H. M., & Rosenthal, R. (1986). Statistical versus traditional procedures for summarizing research findings. *Psychological Bulletin, 87,* 442–449.

Eagly, A. H. (1987). *Sex differences in social behavior: A social-role interpretation.* Hillsdale, NJ: Lawrence Erlbaum Associates.

Eagly, A. H., & Carli, L. L. (1981). Sex of researcher and sex-typed communications as determinants of sex differences in influenceability: A meta-analysis of social influence studies. *Psychological Bulletin, 90,* 1–20.

Eagly, A. H., & Steffen, V. J. (1986). Gender and aggressive behavior: A meta-analytic review of the social psychological literature. *Psychological Bulletin, 100,* 309–330.

*Euwema, M. C., & Van de Vliert, E. (1994). The influence of sex on manager's reactions in conflict with their subordinates. In A. Taylor & J. B. Miller (Eds.), *Conflict and gender* (pp. 119–140). Cresskill, NJ: Hampton.

Fitzpatrick, M. A., & Winke, J. (1979). You always hurt the one you love: Strategies and tactics in interpersonal conflict. *Communication Quarterly, 27,* 3–11.

Gayle, B. M. (1991). Sex equity in workplace conflict management. *Journal of Applied Communication, 19,* 152–169.

Gilligan, C. (1982). *In a different voice.* Cambridge, MA: Harvard University Press.

Glass, G. V., McGraw, B., & Smith, M. L. (1981). *Meta-analysis in social research.* Beverly Hills, CA: Sage.

*Goering, E. M. (1986, November). *Context, definition, and sex of actor as variables in conflict management style.* Paper presented at the annual meeting of the Speech Communication Association, Chicago.

Gottman, J. M., & Carre, S. (1994). Why can't men and women get along? Developmental roots and marital inequities. In D. J. Canary & L. Stafford (Eds.), *Communication and relational maintenance* (pp. 203–229). San Diego, CA: Academic.

**Gottman, J. M., & Levenson, R. W. (1992). Marital processes predictive of later dissolution: Behavior physiology and health. *Journal of Personality and Social Psychology, 63,* 221–223.

**Heavey, C. L., Layne, C., & Christensen, A. (1993). Gender and conflict structure in marital interaction: A replication and extension. *Journal of Consulting and Clinical Psychology, 61,* 16–27.

Hedges, L. V., & Olkin, I. (1985). *Statistical methods for meta-analysis.* Orlando, FL: Academic.

*Howell, J. L. (1981). *The identification, description and analysis of competencies focused on conflict management in a human services organization: An exploratory study.* Unpublished doctoral dissertation, University of Massachusetts, Amherst, MA.

Hunter, J., Schmidt, F., & Jackson, G. (1983). *Meta-analysis: Accumulating research findings across studies.* Beverly Hills, CA: Sage.

Jacobson, N. S. (1989). The politics of intimacy. *The Behavioral Therapist, 12,* 29–32.

*Kilmann, R. H., & Thomas, K. W. (1977). Developing a forced-choice measure of conflict-handling behavior: The "mode" instrument. *Educational and Psychological Measurement, 37,* 309–323.

*Kofron, C. P. (1986). *A structural perspective of interpersonal conflict management.* Unpublished doctoral dissertation, St. Louis University, St. Louis, MO.

*Konovosky, M. A., Jaster, F., & McDonald, M. A. (1988, November). *Using parametric statistics to explore the underlying structures of the Thomas–Kilmann conflict MODE survey.* Paper presented at the annual meeting of the Speech Communication Association, New Orleans, LA.

Krone, K., Allen, M., & Ludlum, J. (1994). A meta-analysis of gender research in managerial influence. In L. H. Turner & H. M. Sterk (Eds.), *Differences that make a difference* (pp. 73–84). Westport, CT: Bergin & Garvey.

Linkskold, S., & Tedeschi, J. T. (1971). Reward power and attraction in interpersonal conflict. *Psychonomic Science, 22,* 211–213.

**Margolin, G., & Wampold, B. E. (1981). Sequential analysis of conflict and accord in distressed and nondistressed marital partners. *Journal of Consulting and Clinical Psychology*, 49, 554–567.

**Miller, J. B. (1994). Conflict management and marital adjustment among African-American and White middle-class couples. In A. Taylor & J. B. Miller (Eds.), *Conflict and gender* (pp. 141–154). Cresskill, NJ: Hampton.

Monroe, C., DiSalvo, V. S., Lewis, J. J., & Borzi, M. G. (1989). Conflict behaviors of difficult subordinates: Interactive effects of gender. *Southern Communication Journal*, 54, 12–23.

*Nadler, M. K., & Nadler, L. B. (1988, November). *Sex differences in perceptions of and orientations toward conflict resolving behaviors in the organizational environment.* Paper presented at the annual meeting of the Speech Communication Association, New Orleans, LA.

Nowak, M. (1984). *Conflict resolution and power seeking behavior of androgynous and traditional married couples.* Unpublished doctoral dissertation, Michigan State University, East Lansing, MI.

*Papa, M. J., & Natalle, E. J. (1989). Gender, strategy selection, and discussion satisfaction in interpersonal conflict. *Western Journal of Speech Communication*, 53, 260–272.

**Perregaux, J. L. (1971). *Dyadal interactions: A study of disagreement resolution in the marital dyad.* Unpublished doctoral dissertation, Purdue University, West Lafayette, IN.

*Putnam, L. L., & Wilson, C. E. (1982). Communicative strategies in organizational conflicts: Reliability and validity of a measurement scale. In M. Burgoon (Ed.), *Communication yearbook 6* (pp. 629–652). Beverly Hills, CA: Sage.

Rahim, A. (1983). A measure of styles of handling interpersonal conflict. *Academy of Management Journal*, 26, 368–376.

Rapoport, A., & Chammah, A. M. (1965). Sex differences in factors contributing to the level of cooperation in the prisoner's dilemma game. *Journal of Personality and Social Psychology*, 2, 831–838.

**Raush, H. L., Barry, W. A., Hertel, R. K., & Swain, M. A. (1974). *Communication, conflict and marriage.* San Francisco: Jossey-Bass.

*Renwick, P. A. (1977). Effects of sex differences on the perception and management of conflict: An exploratory study. *Organizational Behavior and Human Performance*, 19, 403–415. Resick, P. A., Barr, P. K., Sweet, J. J., Kieffer, D. M., Riby, N. L., & Spiegel, D. K. (1981). Perceived and actual discriminators of conflict from accord in marital communication. *American Journal of Family Therapy*, 9, 56–68.

*Revilla, V. M. (1984). *Conflict management styles of men and women in higher education.* Unpublished doctoral dissertation, University of Pittsburgh, Pittsburgh, PA.

**Roberts, L. J., & Krokoff, L. J. (1990). A time series analysis of withdrawal, hostility, and displeasure in satisfied and dissatisfied marriages. *Journal of Marriage and the Family*, 52, 95–105.

Roloff, M. E., & Greenberg, B. S. (1979). Sex differences in choice of modes of conflict resolutions in real-life and television. *Communication Quarterly*, 27, 3–12.

Rosenthal, R., & Rubin, D. B. (1982). A simple general response display of magnitude of experimental effect. *Journal of Educational Psychology*, 74, 166–169.

*Rossi, A. M., & Todd-Mancillas, W. R. (1987). Male and female differences in managing conflicts. In L. P. Stewart & S. Ting-Toomey (Eds.), *Communication, gender, and sex roles in diverse interaction contexts* (pp._96–104). Norwood, NJ: Ablex.

*Ruble, T. L., & Schneer, J. A. (1994). Gender differences to conflict-handling styles: Less than meets the eye? In A. Taylor & J. B. Miller (Eds.), *Conflict and gender* (pp. 155–165). Cresskill, NJ: Hampton.

*Ruble, T. L., & Stander, N. E. (1990, June). *Effects of role and gender on conflict-handling styles*. Paper presented at the meeting of the International Association for Conflict Management, Vancouver, Canada.

*Schuekle, D., & McDowell, E. (1990, May). *A study of the relationship between willingness to communicate and referred conflict strategy: Implications for teaching communication and conflict*. Paper presented at the International Communication Association conference, Chicago.

*Shockley-Zalabak, P. (1981). The effects of sex differences on the preference for utilization of conflict styles of managers in a work setting: An exploratory study. *Public Personnel Management Journal, 10,* 289–295.

*Shockley-Zalabak, P., & Morley, D. D. (1984). Sex differences in conflict style preferences. *Communication Research Reports, 1,* 28–32.

*Sone, P. G. (1981). *The effects of gender on managers' resolution of superior–subordinate conflict*. Unpublished doctoral dissertation, Arizona State University, Tempe, AZ.

Sternberg, R. J., & Soriano, L. J. (1984). Styles of conflict resolution. *Journal of Personality and Social Psychology, 47,* 115–126.

*Temkin, T., & Cummings, H. W. (1986). The use of conflict management behaviors in voluntary organizations: An exploratory study. *Journal of Voluntary Action Research, 15,* 5–18.

*Thomas, K. W. (1971). *Conflict-handling modes in interdepartmental relations*. Unpublished doctoral dissertation, Purdue University, West Lafayette, IN.

Thomas, K. W. (1988). The conflict handling modes: Toward more precise theory. *Management Communication Quarterly, 1,* 430–436.

*Ting-Toomey, S. (1986). Conflict communication styles in black and white subjective cultures. In Y. Y. Kim (Ed.), *Interethnic communication: Current research* (pp. 75–88). Newbury Park, CA: Sage.

*Ugbah, S. D., & DeWine, S. (1986, November). *Conflict management and relational disengagement: Are the communication strategies the same?* Paper presented at the annual meeting of the Speech Communication Association, Chicago.

Weider-Hatfield, D. (1988). Assessing the Rahim Organizational Conflict Inventory–II (ROC–II). *Management Communication Quarterly, 1,* 350–366.

Wilson, S. R., & Waltman, M. S. (1988). Assessing the Putnam–Wilson Organizational Communication Conflict Instrument (OCCI). *Management Communication Quarterly, 1,* 367–386.

Womack, D. F. (1988). A review of conflict instruments in organizational settings. *Management Communication Quarterly, 1,* 437–445.

**Yelsma, P., & Brown, C. T. (1985). Gender roles, biological sex, and predisposition to conflict management. *Sex Roles, 12,* 28–32.

*Zammuto, M. L., London, M., & Rowland, K. W. (1979). Effects of sex on commitment and conflict resolution. *Journal of Applied Psychology, 64,* 227–231.

V

Meta-Analysis
and Interpersonal
Communication Theory
Generation

19

An Analysis of Textbooks in Interpersonal Communication: How Accurate are the Representations?

Mike Allen and Raymond W. Preiss

Textbooks are a source of information for the students that read them. As educators and scientists, we expect that textbook authors report relevant and accurate information. Authors review, critique, and revise textbooks to provide more accurate and understandable material. The normal course of events for textbooks is that each subsequent edition is supposed to provide an improvement in the content. Textbooks are revised for many reasons and to accomplish a variety of purposes, including clarity, addition of material, deletion of material, inclusion of topics, and simplification of material. The goal of this ongoing effort is to improve the information available to teachers and students.

As information in the sciences is updated and verified, textbooks begin to reflect the updated and more accurate information. Recently, the transition to viewing the study of human behavior as a form of science is gaining acceptance. Hedges's (1987) observation that the variability in the outcomes of psychological experiments is slightly less than experiments in particle physics suggests that human behavior can be studied scientifically. As doubts diminish about whether the investigation of human behavior can meet the rigor of science, the requirement that scholars and textbooks begin to conform to the scientific ideal becomes increasingly urgent and inevitable.

The logic of the scientific method pivots on the use of induction as a means of proof. That is, learning about a particular case or cases should provide information for understanding the next case or occurrence. When the requirement moves from certainty to probability, the information on one case or set of cases only provides an inference (based on probability) about the tendency of the next case to exhibit the same property or tendency. The basis of scientific inference involves the reliance on experience (data) to generate and help evaluate an understanding (theory) that eventually translates into improved practice (application). The progression and improvement is not linear or predictable, but the long-term expectation is that improvement is an inevitable result of adherence to the method.

THE RATIONALE FOR EVALUATING TEXTBOOKS

The logic for analyzing the textbooks in interpersonal communication is similar to that used when comparing textbooks in persuasion to relevant meta-analyses (Allen & Preiss, 1990, 1998; Allen et al., 1997). The method examines whether the representations of scientific literature in a textbook are consistent or inconsistent with a particular meta-analysis about that issue. This procedure permits an examination of the advice that scientists intend to create for textbook writers (Allen & Preiss, 1997). If a textbook author is making claims about the existence of particular relationships based on empirical evidence, then the claim can be evaluated on the basis of accuracy. In this case, the level of consistency with a relevant meta-analysis determines accuracy. Such a procedure provides the basis for eventual improvement in textbooks by creating a consensus about the information that any textbook could represent accurately.

The evaluation of a textbook requires a set of criteria that have as much to do with the style and format of the presentation as with the accuracy of the actual material. For example, the author may attempt to provide a readable and accessible text that does not fundamentally compromise the theoretical positions developed in the chapters. The textbook author wants to maintain the intellectual quality of the theory without "dumbing down" the material, but at the same time to make the information accessible to students that lack the years of experience (sometimes decades) of a professional scholar. Although the theory and the elements may not initially be understandable, a good textbook author creates a presentation that improves the student's overall comprehension of the content.

Textbook authors must also respond to the ever-changing demands of a marketplace that may require divergent sets of criteria. For example, authors must compete against rival textbooks and fight for market share. The business end of the textbook market creates marketing plans that involve Web page access, test banks, instructor's manuals, workbooks, CD-ROM supplements, videotapes, and many other types of classroom and instructional support for the course. The choice of a textbook involves not simply a decision about the representation of content, but also issues of cost, the level of support available for the material, and issues such as the match between book content and course curriculum. Here we advance accuracy of the content as another important criteria for evaluating the textbooks available in the marketplace.

Scientific findings should not be required to play a central role in all approaches to pedagogy. For example, one criterion increasingly considered is the issue of diversity. Evaluations of textbooks have considered many issues regarding the representation of a variety of groups by communication textbooks (Hanson & Lovelace, 1998; Yook, 1998), and the issue of diversity remains an important one. However, meta-analysis is focused on the ability of content to accurately reflect the research material, rather than reflect other important inclusion criteria. On this level, meta-analyses can contribute to the discussion of other criteria. In the area of self-disclosure, Dindia and Allen (1992) observed that virtually all of the more than 200 data sets were conducted in North America and that virtually no analysis specifically considered various minority groups and whether the disclosure pattern differed on the basis of race or ethnicity. The result is that any meta-analysis is limited by the diversity of the original conditions of data collection. However, any textbook author representing the literature should still provide the conclusion of the meta-analysis, decide explicitly whether or not to accept the generalizability of the conclusion, and document the rationale for an alternative interpretation.

In other pedagogical decisions, the role of meta-analysis is much more limited. For example, an issue of *Communication Education* published a symposium on "The Women's University." When examining the articles (DeFrancisco, 1996; Gregg, 1996; Houston, 1996; Jenefsky, 1996; F. Johnson, 1996; Kramarae, 1996) the expectations may not involve a high degree of requirements for scientific accuracy because the goals focus on the outcomes of empowerment and cultural transformation. The collection of articles provides a snapshot of expectations and requirements for a vision of the university. It is unclear how the scientific requirements of accuracy in representation would fall within this framework. Scientific accuracy or the need for the accuracy of depictions of material may be subordinate to other outcomes in some types of investigations. The importance of meta-analysis as an evaluative tool must be placed within the context of the particular pedagogical goals sought by the educational system. We subscribe to the notion that scientific information should be represented as accurately as possible or reasonable. This is not an endorsement or requirement for objectivity, as scientific consensus is not objective. Scientific consensus only represents agreement that the data do indicate that a relation exists.

SUMMARIZING THE AVAILABLE ADVICE

This section of the chapter provides a short summary of the previous chapters for the purposes of evaluating the various textbooks. The intent is to provide a bridge between the conclusions offered by the various meta-analyses and the treatment of the information in textbooks. Theoretically, the textbooks should offer conclusions consistent with the available research in that area. Meta-analysis, as a literature review technique, provides a systematic and comprehensive review processes that others can choose to replicate. The advantage of meta-analysis lies in its ability to handle Type I and Type II errors in a systematic fashion. When this is combined with the ability of others to replicate the procedures and outcomes, the basis of an intersubjective knowledge claim is met. That is, other scholars can verify for themselves whether the claims and outcomes can be stipulated as a result of independent summaries of the same literature.

This review is not concerned directly with theoretical evaluation, as that information, as well as a perspective on the field, is offered by Roloff (chap. 22), Fitzpatrick (chap. 21), Berger (chap. 2), and Canary and Mattrey (chap. 20) in this book. The treatment of the information in this analysis is less targeted at theoretical or methodological levels of analysis, but is pedagogical in nature. The information in the other chapters just mentioned is important and essential, but it meets different goals by providing a sense of urgency and coherency to the available information on interpersonal communication for the purpose of research and theory construction. Those four chapters set the agenda for research and theories for the scholars yet to come. This chapter provides an evaluation of current information contained in classroom textbooks.

The contents of this book, in terms of the topics considered, are not exhaustive or necessarily indicative of the corpus of interpersonal communication research. Not included are issues surrounding compliance gaining, communication apprehension, discourse sequences (action assemblies, Memory Organization Packets, or schema), dialectics, marital or family communication, uncertainty reduction, or research related to the various "stages" of relationships (this list could probably fill several pages). A lot of the "normal" material included in most textbooks is not reflected in the available research or examined in this analysis. Thus, the sample of topics used to evaluate the textbooks should not be considered a random sample of available research or topics in interpersonal communication. The diversity of topics in research programs would require hundreds of meta-analyses (and these are slowly being assembled) and are beyond the scope of this book. However, the review provided in this analysis represents a beginning of the evaluation process and systematic reassessment of research material that will be ongoing in the future.

METHOD

Selection of Textbooks

Textbooks selected for this evaluation do not represent a systematic or comprehensive inclusion of information. Instead, the choice of books was literally dictated by what was on the shelves of the chapter authors as made available by various book company representatives. In some cases, the selections were textbooks we had used as undergraduate or graduate students or as instructors. The goal of this analysis should be taken as more illustrative than definitive. The purpose is to illustrate the potential application of meta-analysis to pedagogical issues in interpersonal communication, rather than to provide an exhaustive and authoritative review of available materials. Such a review will eventually be necessary and beneficial for the field, but is not the intent of this analysis.

The textbooks were intended to represent a wide variety of books and should include authors of textbooks and titles familiar to anyone teaching interpersonal communication. As such, the textbooks represent, in a varied and inconsistent manner, a limited snapshot of the field of interpersonal communication undergraduate textbooks. The books were obtained in rather ordinary ways. More often than not, the scope of choices was dictated by which textbooks were mailed to the instructors' offices, provided as samples by publishers' representatives, or ordered at a publisher's table at a conference. The selection of the textbooks for inclusion in this analysis, in many respects, reflects the competition among textbooks in the marketplace.

Rating System

Each interpersonal communication textbook was examined and the following ratings were completed: (a) consistent with the meta-analysis, indicated by a +, (b) inconsistent with the meta-analysis, indicated by a –, and (c) failure to mention the topic in the text, indicated by leaving the space in the table blank. As demonstrated in Table 19.1, the most frequent or modal value is the failure to mention a particular topic. The majority of topics considered in this analysis do not appear in most interpersonal textbooks. This is consistent with examination of textbooks in public speaking and persuasion (Allen & Preiss, 1990; 1998) where the vast majority of research topics were not likely to be re-

TABLE 19.1
Rating of Selected Textbooks

	1	2	3	4	5	6	7	8	9	10	11	12	13
Adler (1998)			+		+		+			+	+	+	
Adler (1996)					+		–		+			+	
Anderson											+		
Berko			+				–		+			+	
DeVito			+							+		+	
Gamble	+		–				+	–				+	
Gudykunst					+					+		+	
D. Johnson												+	
Knapp			–									+	
Pearson												+	
Trenholm			+						+	+		+	
Verderber			–						+	+		+	
Wood (1996)	+						+					+	
Wood (1998)						+	+					+	
Wood (1999)								–		–		+	
Wright							+					+	

Note. Only the first author is listed; please consult the References for complete citations. The ratings reflect the complexity of the analysis provided by the author. A positive (+) indicates that the issue is mentioned and nothing was stated that directly contradicts the meta-analysis. A negative (–) appears when something occurs in the text that is clearly contradicted by the available meta-analysis.

flected in the content of a textbook. A caveat is needed because the coding may have missed information. The problem with a textbook of about 400 pages is that information may not be well indexed and issues can appear in multiple places. Every effort was made to ensure accuracy of the coding and inspection of all relevant passages; however, oversights do occur. The coding represents a human process subject to error and oversight.

RESULTS

A total of 16 textbooks were examined using the 13 meta-analyses contained in this book. That creates a total series of 208 judgments. A total of 49 codes were assigned out of a possible 208 (about 24%). This indicates only about a 24% probability that any conclusion reviewed by a meta-analysis would appear as an issue in a textbook. Three of the topics (argumentativeness, cognitive editing, and social support during divorce) did not appear in any textbook in a manner that could be coded against the conclusions of the meta-analysis. The inclusion, exclusion, or noninclusion of content was highly variable. Other than not including any of the information, no two textbooks commented exactly on the same set of issues. In other words, the exposure to particular content was not replicated in any book. This means that exposure to any particular set of information was dependent on which particular book an instructor chose.

A cursory inspection of Table 19.2 provides a sense of the scope and implication of the various findings as laid out by the authors in the respective chapters. The summary offered is only a thumbnail sketch of the conclusions and each chapter should be read for the methodological and theoretical discussion necessary to contextualize and interpret the scope of the findings. The Table 19.2 summary is only intended to provide a simple statement against which the textbooks examined could be compared. In the case of more complex representations in the textbooks, a more thorough comparison to the particular chapter was undertaken to determine the accuracy of the representation.

Of the 49 items coded, 41 (84%) of them were considered consistent and 8 were considered inconsistent with the available meta-analysis. The results indicate a more positive accuracy rate than the 63% of the persuasion books reviewed using meta-analysis (Allen et al., 1997). However, the larger number of missing entries suggests some potential areas for discussion. The problem in interpersonal research may be that the larger and more diverse terrain of content permits wider latitude in the possible inclusion or exclusion of various topics. The result is that there becomes less focus within the

TABLE 19.2

List of Results for the Various Analyses

1. AIDS and HIV—This chapter examines the degree to which persons communicating about HIV and AIDS increases the probability of the use of a condom. In addition, the comparative willingness of men and women to engage in such discussions was examined.

2. Argumentativeness and Verbal Aggression—This chapter finds that the scale used to measure argumentativeness is unidimensional. Only a small correlation exists between argumentativeness and verbal aggression.

3. Attitudinal Similarity and Attraction—The findings indicate that persons are more attracted to those with more similar attitudes.

4. Cognitive Editing of Statements—The canonical analysis demonstrates that persons are more selective in choosing appeals when the matter is relationally delicate and the target is expected to be pliable, people do not try hard to persuade a dominant target to maintain face, and finally, the persuaders consider the possible relational consequences as trade-offs against the choice of effective strategies.

5. Constructivism and Comforting—The model indicates that age predicts the level of cognitive complexity (as measured by cognitive differentiation and cognitive abstraction). In turn, cognitive complexity predicts perspective taking, which predicts the quality of the comforting message generated.

6. Gay and Heterosexual Parents—This summary finds that the sexual practice of the parent (homosexual or heterosexual) does not differentiate various outcome measures (cognitive, social, sexual orientation).

7. Gender and Conflict Strategies—Little difference exists on the choice of conflict strategy based on the biological gender of the individual. The small difference indicates that men are slightly more competitive and women are slightly more compromising.

8. Gender and Levels of Self-Esteem—Little difference exists on the basis of biological gender, except for levels of self-esteem related to body image. Females demonstrate significantly lower levels of self-esteem based on body image.

9. Gender and the Production of Powerless Language—Women produce less powerful utterances than men.

10. Self-Disclosure—Women disclose slightly more than men do, but the effect is not stable and related to the methodology of the investigation, and self-disclosure tends to be reciprocal.

11. Sexual Coercion and Resistance—Support was found for the traditional dating script for encounters between men and women. The perception of an event as coercive is related to the status of the relationship between the partners and the circumstances of the particular incident.

12. Social Skills—There is a substantial association between various behaviors as the evaluation of social skills during an interaction.

13. Sources of Social Support During Divorce—Women seek and receive more social support during a divorce than men. The exception is that men seek more support from lovers and romantic partners than women.

Note. The findings presented in this chapter are simple summaries of the major findings of the meta-analyses. The reader should consult the original chapters and published articles for additional explanations and other pertinent information.

field on core issues that are subject to voluminous research capable of accumulation and synthesis.

An examination of individual topics found only four topics mentioned in the majority of textbooks: social skills, attitude similarity and attraction, gender and conflict strategies, and self-disclosure and gender. The only topic mentioned universally was the issue of social skills or communicative competence. The issue in the meta-analysis was the ability to predict the performance of behaviors viewed as competent. Every textbook addresses some form or aspect of communication competence. For example, Verderber and Verderber (1998) specifically mentioned and emphasized the idea of skill building as an aspect of the textbook. If there is any universal topic or characteristic it is the concept of communication competence (social skills); however, the application of this concept and incorporation differs from textbook to textbook.

The discussion of gender and self-disclosure was consistent with the meta-analysis in finding that women disclose more than men do, but that difference is not particularly large. The methodological issues discussed by Dindia (chap. 10) receive little attention in the textbooks and only the general conclusion is represented. Verderber and Verderber (1998) commented on the general difference but did not acknowledge the size of the difference or the problems of observer versus self-reported measurement. The interpretation of this conclusion receives varied discussion in terms of mental health and relational issues. Gudykunst, Ting-Toomey, Sudweeks, and Stewart (1995) commented on the difference but did not contextualize the issues in terms of importance to relational development. Originally, the arguments about gender differences in self-disclosure focused on whether women would make better therapists because patients would be more likely to disclose to female therapists rather than male therapists.

The attitude similarity relation to attraction is a fundamental concern in many interpersonal textbooks because it is the basis for explaining why some people choose to form relationships. The reason for the inconsistency (4 consistent out of 7) was the use of complementarity or the notion that opposites attract. The inconsistent cases revealed that similarity leads to attraction, but then failed to point out that this research generally supports the similarity position as opposed to the opposites attract or complementary position. Verderber and Verderber (1998) stated, "The more interests people have in common, the more they are attracted to each other" (p. 88), which is accurate. However, in the next paragraph they went on to conclude that "'opposites attract' is as accurate as 'birds of a feather flock together'" (p. 88). This is similar to the statements in the Adler, Rosenfeld, Towne, and

Proctor (1998) book, which concludes that this forms the basis for much of the relational development literature. However, when Adler et al. (1988), discussed complementarity in the next section, the text states that this seems to contradict the similarity section and concludes that, "in truth, though, both are valid" (p. 280). The presentation of these positions without a clear preference for similarity as a stronger predictor is inconsistent with the meta-analysis.

The final issue involves gender and conflict strategies. The inconsistency of results (4 positive out of 7) comes from the mixing of general conflict tendencies with behavior in established relationships where the attack–withdraw pattern is prevalent. The isolation of methodological, theoretical, and contextual parameters is necessary in the meta-analysis to understand the synthesis of the available research. The tendency, when inconsistent, was to ignore the dual truths that men are generally more competitive but only for situations defined as masculine. In relationships or situations defined as more feminine, the male preference for outcome over relationships does not appear to be valid. This complicated representation was not represented in the literature; the textbooks coded as consistent usually only included one set of information and were technically not inconsistent but rather incomplete when compared to the available data. For example, Gamble and Gamble (1998) pointed out that men are more focused on the goal and what is gained by resolving the conflict and women are more relationship focused and more sensitive to interpreting moods and feelings. The next sentence, however, does point out that men are more competitive and women more compromising and accommodating, which makes the section consistent.

The other meta-analyses, powerless language and gender and the constructivist model of comforting behavior, are covered correctly but only appear in 3 of the texts (19%). AIDS and HIV, sexual coercion, and the impact of homosexual and heterosexual parents were less frequently mentioned, but were covered in either one or two of the textbooks. The only issue for which there was no agreement with the meta-analysis was the comparison of gender on the basis of self-esteem. Both books mentioning the issue stated that females' self-esteem is lower than males, which is contradicted by the evidence from the meta-analysis.

DISCUSSION

Our preliminary investigation provides information regarding the state of interpersonal communication textbooks. The results should be discussed in terms of the accuracy of the reporting, the consistency of the reporting across textbooks, and the nature of the issues not covered by the textbooks. These issues provide an initial step in assessing the accuracy of textbooks.

Accuracy of Representations

Overall, the individual textbooks did extremely well in assessing and reporting the information available in research studies, when that information was included. No indictment or endorsement of any textbook is intended by this analysis. The scope of the review is so limited that the rating system cannot be said to provide a basis for the selection or rejection of any particular text for classroom use. However, when hundreds of meta-analyses exist, the basis for a more thorough and complete evaluation of textbooks will exist. Such an evaluation, when conducted at that level, should provide a more exhaustive and credible basis to evaluate the value or accuracy of a textbook and could serve legitimately as a basis for the rejection or adoption of a particular textbook. The expectation is that as more and more meta-analyses become available and textbooks are edited for future editions, the accuracy and inclusion rates will increase.

Consistency of Representations

Individual textbooks vary in the representations of material. One common factor in the 16 books reviewed was the lack of consistency across the texts, rather than any consistent handling or inclusion of particular issues. The Adler et al. (1998) book had the most topics mentioned (five) and was consistent with the research on every topic (attitudinal similarity and attraction, constructivism, conflict and gender, gender and self-disclosure, and sexual coercion). The only books with more than one inconsistency were Wood (1996) and Gamble and Gamble (1998), with two inconsistent statements each. The Gamble and Gamble text had four relevant conclusions and two were inaccurate for a 50% inconsistency rate. The Wood (1999) book only comments on two issues (gender and self-esteem and gender and self-disclosure) and is inconsistent with both meta-analyses.

Omission of Interpersonal Topics

The most obvious conclusion is that the topics and conclusions involved in the various meta-analyses are not widely incorporated in the interpersonal communication textbooks of the field. The only consistency among the textbooks was the noninclusion of information. The failure to include material reflects the distance between research and pedagogy. The failure to include topics indicates a lack of connection between the bodies of research literature and classroom instruction about interpersonal communication. If these issues are not being taught in the classroom, the relevance of the corpulent bodies of research being produced must be questioned. To continue to conduct research that ultimately is disconnected from the pedagogical experience of our students is to deny what should be the cornerstone value of research, the improvement in the ability to increase or improve student understanding of interpersonal communication. Some of the issues, like self-disclosure, attraction and similarity, and conflict, involve content that would generally be expected to be included in textbooks. Some of the issues (like self-disclosure) were included but without reference to the particular effect (gender and self-disclosure, or self-esteem [self-concept] and gender). In the case of self-disclosure, more than 200 reports of data were not included, a surprisingly large body of research not incorporated in the textbooks. The continued bifurcation between the research and the teaching community creates an interesting paradox for graduate students. Graduate students continue to receive training in the development of information that is not reflected in course content and the research agendas embarked on by graduate students do not reflect the accepted state of knowledge evident in the classroom.

Omission of Social Issues

Perhaps the largest issue is the failure of many of the textbooks to include any information on a variety of social issues. HIV infection and the safe sex dialogue received virtually no attention in the textbooks and neither did issues of sexual coercion. The lack of inclusion of research information on these two issues is surprising, particularly because the population targeted for the textbooks is college students who are typically between 18 and 22 years old. Reasonably, a scholar would expect that the incidence of sexually transmitted diseases and the continued problem of date rape on campus would generate a rush to include such information in textbooks. Given the growth and emphasis by the research community on these issues, one would expect to find these outcomes included in introductory textbooks. The process of making interpersonal communication relevant to the lives of the students would seem to necessitate the inclusion of two issues that represent a concern to virtually every person.

The failure to incorporate information on socially relevant issues in interpersonal communication represents a large omission for a variety of reasons. Much of the research community has targeted these issues because of the social importance that these topics have for relational issues. The omission of this research from textbooks makes the study of relationships disconnected from the reality of conducting relationships for students. The possibility of HIV infection relates to relational development, intimacy, self-disclosure, trust, and a host of interpersonal communication issues (including sexual orientation). The reality of sexual coercion on campus and date rape, as well as resistance strategies, generates orientation training and crisis and counseling efforts on almost every campus. The incidence of sexual coercion includes a large percentage of the population and should therefore be an important interpersonal communication understanding. Given that coercion happens within an existing or developing relationship, as the term *date rape* indicates, this topic should certainly be incorporated as part of an interpersonal communication course. Because the research often defines this issue as involving a problem of communicating intention, sexual coercion is certainly a relevant issue to the communication discipline.

CONCLUSIONS

The logic developed in this chapter and the results of our preliminary assessment of textbooks lead to the inescapable conclusion that accuracy standards can play a vital role in communication pedagogy. Authors should routinely employ criteria for accurate portrayal of research in the discipline as they prepare manuscripts for publication. Such expectations are consistent with the norms for professionalism within the scientific community, and standards for accuracy are prudent and reasonable expectations for evaluating assertions that use scientific findings as the basis for knowledge claims. The eventual outcome will be the introduction of textbooks that advertise, as a standard practice, the degree to which the content can be verified as accurate and current. The consensus of scientific findings presented should increase the standardization among textbooks. The existence of a common body of knowledge in other fields, such as chemistry, permits textbook writers to concentrate on the best means of presenting the available information. In the social sciences, textbook authors often have to create the synthesis of information as well as find the best means of presentation for that information. Too often, the outcome of both objectives could be much more effective.

The use of standards should be viewed as simultaneously liberating and constraining. The textbook author, armed with scientific consensus, can now concentrate on the development of clear and simple understandings that improve the student's learning. This constraint happens at the level of content;

the meta-analysis provides certain restrictions on depicting the nature of that relation. To say that a relation is positive when the evidence demonstrates the relation is negative generates an inconsistency with the best available synthesis of the data. The reliance on the meta-analysis as a means of generating or validating information carries some risk, but those risks are substantially greater when considering the possibility that Type I (false positive) and Type II (false negative) errors may be bleeding into textbooks. Meta-analysis, far from constituting the optimal review method, simply represents the best available method of accumulating and synthesizing literature.

Another issue concerning textbook writing is the nature of integrating information using alternative methods of generating knowledge. Figure 19.1 displays a set of relations for knowledge based on the work of Allen and

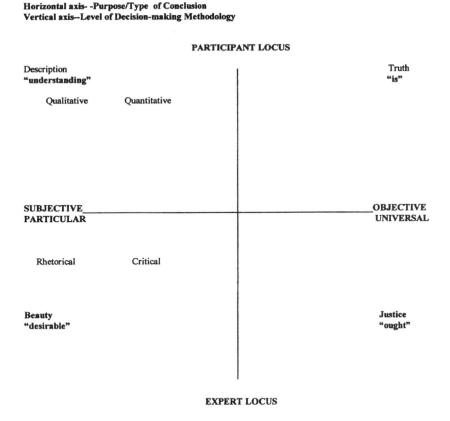

FIG 19.1.   Elements of knowledge.

Bradford (1999) that hypothesizes four divergent but necessary methodologies that must be employed. Any good textbook will, in some manner, incorporate all four elements or approaches to knowledge to provide a complete picture and understanding of information. Increased attention has been paid to the development of critical and qualitative sources of information to reflect the concerns of diversity and the inclusion of various voices as part of the pedagogy. The challenge for the quantitative methodologists is the inclusion of information that is factual and in one sense treated as objective (even though the method of generating the conclusion is intersubjective). The denial of an objective basis for a conclusion creates a fundamental challenge to quantitative methods because it denies the ability of the method to fulfill its own goal. Hypothesizing that a complete system of knowledge contains information with multiple goals and applications generated by a wide variety of methodologies redefines the problem to one that seeks to integrate rather than refute.

Similar interdependencies exist between other methods of generating information that contribute to creating knowledge. The problem is that such interdependence at the level of knowledge is countered by the independence of each method as a means of generating information that must meet the internal requirements of the method. The goal of the textbook is the synthesis and creation of some sense of integration among all the various elements. Meta-analysis contributes to this process by providing a basis for synthesis of quantitative information. The ability of this particular method to generate a synthesis permits the scientific community to generate a consensus about information that permits ease of representation and a more complete analysis.

Pedagogy does not always trail the research findings. Common sense or informed and reflected insight into the human condition may prove more accurate and often are established long before the scientific community reaches the same conclusion. One problem with reliance on rationally discussed or philosophically derived systems occurs when such systems are inconsistent with each other. When one system recommends one action or generates one conclusion and another system generates an inconsistent conclusion the problem of resolving such contradictions and inconsistencies becomes important. Scientific evidence provides empirical experience collected across a large number of diverse cases (when the body of research is properly conducted) and generates a standard for evaluation of the recommendations. If the recommendations are said to reflect an empirical reality (as opposed to some type of moral or ethical code) then the empirical evaluation is clearly warranted.

We are convinced that the examination of communication behavior can enrich the lives of students by providing a reflective understanding of practices that occur everyday. We may even be able to help students improve their interpersonal communication skills in some small but important ways. As the knowledge accumulates about interpersonal communication, theories and applications should continue to improve. The information in our textbooks constitutes a relatively accurate portrayal of research, but an incomplete and inconsistent portrayal from book to book. Heeding the call of this chapter and the other chapters in this volume should provide a basis for a general improvement in our instruction of interpersonal communication. Roloff (chap. 22, this volume) makes the case for a scholarship more situated in the lives of our society's members. Berger (chap. 22, this volume) advocates a more basic (proto) theoretical approach that provides the basis for idea unification across the segmented areas of communication scholarship.

REFERENCES

Adler, R., Rosenfeld, L., Towne, N., & Proctor, R. (1998). *Interplay: The process of interpersonal communication* (7th ed.). Fort Worth, TX: Harcourt Brace College.

Adler, R., & Towne, N. (1996). *Looking out/looking in: Interpersonal communication* (8th ed.). Fort Worth, TX: Harcourt Brace College.

Allen, M., & Bradford, L. (1999). *Creating a whole knowledge picture.* Unpublished manuscript, University of Wisconsin–Milwaukee, Milwaukee, WI.

Allen, M., & Preiss, R. (1990). Using meta-analysis to evaluate curriculum: An examination of selected college textbooks. *Communication Education, 38,* 103–116.

Allen, M., & Preiss, R. (1997). Persuasion, public address, and progression in the sciences: Where we are at what we do. In G. Barnett & F. Boster (Eds.), *Progress in communication sciences* (Vol. 13, pp. 107–131). Greenwich, CT: Ablex.

Allen, M., & Preiss, R. (1998). Evaluating the advice offered by the tool users. In M. Allen & R. Preiss (Eds.), *Persuasion: Advances through meta-analysis* (pp. 243–256). Cresskill, NJ: Hampton.

Allen, M., Preiss, R., Bielski, N., Cooper, E., Fechner, D., Henry, L., Jacobi, M., Kuhn, J., McClellan, W., & Patterson, K. (1997, April). *Examining textbooks: An analysis examining changes over time.* Paper presented at the Central States Communication Association convention, St. Louis, MO. (ERIC Document Reproduction Service No. 406 702)

Anderson, R., & Ross, V. (1994). *Questions of communication: A practical introduction to theory.* New York: St. Martin's.

Berko, R., Rosenfeld, L., & Somovar, L. (1997). *Connecting: A culture-sensitive approach to interpersonal communication competency* (2nd ed.). Fort Worth, TX: Harcourt Brace.

DeFrancisco, V. (1996). The world of designing women: A narrative account of focus group plans for a women's university. *Communication Education, 45,* 330–337.

DeVito, J. (1983). *The interpersonal communication book* (3rd ed.). New York: Harper & Row.

Dindia, K., & Allen, M. (1992). Sex differences in self-disclosure: A meta-analysis. *Psychological Bulletin, 112,* 106–124.

Gamble, T., & Gamble, M. (1998). *Contacts: Communicating interpersonally.* Boston: Allyn & Bacon.

Gregg, N. (1996). What I'd want: Communication studies in which women's university where? *Communication Education, 45,* 356–366.

Gudykunst, W., Ting-Toomey, S., Sudweeks, S., & Stewart, L. (1995). *Building bridges: Interpersonal skills for a changing world.* Boston: Houghton Mifflin.

Hanson, T., & Lovelace, C. (1998, November). *Gender sensitivity, diversity issues, and use of Internet sources in selected basic public speaking texts.* Paper presented at the annual meeting of the National Communication Association, New York.

Hedges, L. (1987). How hard is hard science, how soft is soft science: The empirical cumulativeness of research. *American Psychologist, 42,* 443–455.

Houston, M. (1996). Beyond survival on campus: Envisioning communication studies at women-centered universities. *Communication Education, 45,* 338–342.

Jenefsky, C. (1996). Public speaking as empowerment at visionary university. *Communication Education, 45,* 343–355.

Johnson, D. (1997). *Reaching out: Interpersonal effectiveness and self-actualization* (6th ed.). Boston: Allyn & Bacon.

Johnson, F. (1996). Losing the boundaries of communication study: Lessons for the academy from women's studies. *Communication Education, 45,* 322–329.

Knapp, M. (1984). *Interpersonal communication and human relationships.* Boston: Allyn & Bacon.

Kramarae, C. (1996). Centers of change: An introduction to women's own communication programs. *Communication Education, 45,* 315–321.

Pearson, J., & Nelson, P. (1985). *Understanding and sharing: An introduction to speech communication* (3rd ed.). Dubuque, IA: Brown.

Trenholm, S., & Jensen, A. (1992). *Interpersonal communication* (2nd ed.). Belmont, CA: Wadsworth.

Verderber, R., & Verderber, K. (1998). *Inter-act: Using interpersonal communication skills* (8th ed.). Belmont, CA: Wadsworth.

Wood, J. (1996). *Everyday encounters: An introduction to interpersonal communication.* Belmont, CA: Wadsworth.

Wood, J. (1998). *But I thought you meant ... Misunderstandings in human communication.* Mountain View, CA: Mayfield.

Wood, J. (1999). *Gendered lives: Communication, gender, and culture* (3rd ed.). Belmont, CA: Wadsworth.

Wright, D. (1999). *Personal relationships: An interdisciplinary approach.* Mountain View, CA: Mayfield.

Yook, E. (1998, November). *A critique of communication textbooks' coverage of diversity.* Paper presented at the annual meeting of the National Communication Association, New York.

20

How Does Meta-Analysis Represent Our Knowledge of Interpersonal Communication?

Daniel J. Canary and Michelle J. Mattrey

Originating in clinical psychology (Thomas, 1998), the use of meta-analysis has flourished in the social sciences (Wanous, Sullivan, & Malinak, 1989). As this volume documents, meta-analysis naturally has flourished in the field of interpersonal communication. Meta-analysis has influenced the way we think about interpersonal communication, the ways we go about studying it, and the credence we give to research findings.

As an analytical strategy, meta-analysis provides a wide-angle view of empirical findings. Wolf (1986) suggested that "If we view science as the accumulation and refinement of information and knowledge ... it then becomes critical to establish guidelines for reliable and valid reviews, integrations, and syntheses of studies examining similar research questions" (p. 10). He and others (Glass, 1976, 1977) contended that meta-analysis offers a powerful and systematic means of combining the results of many studies to derive reliable answers to research question. As Grob and Allen (1996) indicated, meta-analyses portray pictures in quantitative terms instead of the more traditional narrative manner. As this volume illustrates, meta-analyses provide statistical summaries and the numbers associated with those summaries are then used as a basis to make inferences and provide a better, more systematic sense of understanding the phenomenon under investigation.

Although statistics involved in summarizing the findings are not complicated, they do require a familiarity with the language of quantitative analysis. Of course, those who resist statistical analyses as a desired manner of summarizing information about communication would probably find meta-analyses doubly confusing. For those of us who find statistical analyses legitimate and even necessary to the generation of verifiable knowledge, meta-analysis represents a critical advancement in the way we know what we know about interpersonal communication.

In this chapter we discuss how meta-analysis represents our knowledge of interpersonal communication. To provide a thumbnail sketch of the topics discussed, we briefly overview meta-analytic studies that we have seen on a number of issues regarding interpersonal communication. This research also serves as one means for framing how meta-analytic findings have influenced the study of interpersonal communication. Second, we offer a set of criteria that we hope can be used to examine the knowledge claims presented in discussions of meta-analytic studies. These criteria are not meant as an exhaustive checklist; rather, they appear to us as the most important factors we found useful when reading the materials we reviewed. Next, we apply our criteria in an evaluation of a published meta-analysis on interpersonal conflict management strategies. Finally, we offer some suggestions regarding the continued use of meta-analysis as a way to build empirical knowledge about communicative behavior.

A BRIEF TOUR OF TOPICS IN INTERPERSONAL COMMUNICATION

Specific to interpersonal communication, meta-analytic research has been conducted on a massive range of topics, including social skills (Spitzberg & Dillard, chap. 6, this volume), nonverbal communication (Hall, Halberstadt, & O'Brien, 1997), persuasion (BarNir, 1998; Dillard, Hunter, & Burgoon, 1984; Hample & Dallinger, chap. 11, this volume; Johnson & Eagly, 1989), family communication (Allen & Burrell, 1996; Leaper, Anderson, & Sanders, 1998), communication apprehension (Allen, 1989; Allen & Bourhis, 1996; Allen, Hunter, & Donohue, 1989; Bourhis & Allen, 1992), sexual coercion (Emmers, 1995a, 1995b, Emmers-Sommer & Allen, 1997), sex differences (Eagly, 1994, 1995; Eagly & Wood, 1991; Hyde, 1990), gender and leaders (Eagly & Johnson, 1990; Eagly & Karau, 1991; Eagly, Makhijani, & Klonsky, 1992; Krone, Allen, & Ludlum, 1994; Wilkins & Andersen, 1991), sex differences in self-disclosure (Dindia & Allen, 1992), conflict (Gayle, Preiss, & Allen, 1994, 1997), effects of divorce on children (Amato & Keith, 1991), language use (Grob & Allen, 1996), self-esteem (Sahlstein & Allen, chap. 4, this volume), computer-mediated communication (Walther, Anderson, & Park, 1994), and comforting communication (Allen, chap. 13, this volume). These studies, which overlap with only a few of those presented in this anthology, partially illustrate the full range of meta-analyses that have been conducted regarding interpersonal communication.

In addition, meta-analysis provides an excellent tool to compare alternative hypotheses derived from competing theoretical explanations and predictions. We discuss this issue later in the presentation of criteria for the evaluation of interpersonal communication meta-analyses.

A Sample of Hypotheses Tested

In terms of communicative behaviors, meta-analysis has been used to test a number of hypotheses. For example, meta-analyses have revealed the communicative behaviors most predictive of social skill ratings (Spitzberg & Dillard, chap. 6, this volume), that subordinate people are probably deficient in their nonverbal sensitivity (Hall et al., 1997), and that when individuals are unrestricted in their opportunity to exchange messages through computer-mediated channels, they are less likely to restrict their communication to impersonal task issues (Walther et al., 1994).

Group differences in communication have also been explored using meta-analysis. For instance, Leaper et al. (1998) used meta-analysis to compare mothers and fathers in amount and type of communication with offspring. They concluded that mothers tend to talk more, use more supportive and negative speech, use less directive speech, and use less informing speech. Further, Leaper et al. found that mothers tend to talk more and use more supportive speech with girls than with boys. Allen and Burrell (1996) used meta-analysis to support their contention that there are no differences between heterosexual and homosexual parents in relation to parenting style, emotional adjustment, and sexual orientation of the children.

Persuasion (i.e., persuasive messages as well as their antecedents and consequences) illustrates another topic salient to interpersonal communication. Meta-analytic findings of persuasion research indicate that involvement is related to persuasibility (Johnson & Eagly, 1989), that foot-in-the-door and door-in-the-face strategies have small effects on persuasion (Dillard et al., 1984), and that choice shift is related to issue knowledge and issue significance (BarNir, 1998). Further, the use or suppression of possible compliance-gaining appeals is influenced by situational dimensions (Hample & Dallinger, chap. 11, this volume).

In the area of communication apprehension, meta-analysis has been conducted in an attempt to summarize the many findings of this widely researched subject. For example, Bourhis and Allen (1992) found that communication apprehension was negatively correlated with cognitive performance. Further, they found that more apprehensive individuals tend to have lower quality and quantity of communication behavior than their less apprehensive counterparts (Allen & Bourhis, 1996). Other meta-analytic research indicates that all three of the major forms of treatment (cognitive modification, systematic desensitization, and skills training) are effective in reducing communication apprehension, but combinations of the three forms prove to be the most effective (Allen, Hunter, & Donohue, 1989). Finally, in terms of assessing level of public speaking anxiety, meta-analysis confirms that self-report measurements show the most change in level of communication apprehension as a result of therapy followed by observer ratings and then physiological measurement (Allen, 1989).

Sex Differences

The research on sex differences makes extensive use of meta-analysis in attempting to draw together the findings of the many studies in that area (Dindia, 1998). The use of meta-analysis in the debate over sex differences in communicative behavior has its roots in psychology. In particular, Eagly utilized meta-analysis to support her contention that there are small but significant sex differences between men and women (Eagly, 1987, 1995; Eagly & Wood, 1991). On the other hand, Canary and Hause (1993) argued that "sex differences in social interaction are small and inconsistent ... about 1% of the variance is accounted for and these effects are moderated by other variables" (p. 140). The debate over how to interpret small or very small findings is one that plagues much of the sex difference literature, a point we elaborate later.

Of interest to many sex difference researchers is leadership. In terms of leadership emergence, Eagly and Karau (1991) argued for the presence of sex differences with men emerging as leaders more often then women, except in situations wherein social leadership is required. However, research in the communication field indicates few sex differences in choice of influence tactics (Krone et al., 1994) or managerial communication (Wilkins & Andersen, 1991). Wilkins and Andersen (1991) reported that less than .5% of superiors' message behavior is accounted for by sex differences. Eagly and Johnson (1990), however, contended that although sex differences do not appear in studies conducted in organizational settings, they do appear in laboratory experiments and assessment studies. This finding would support the argument that people may rely on stereotypes to judge leader behavior when they do not have access to other information to the contrary (Canary, Emmers-Sommer, & Faulkner, 1997).

Emmers-Sommer and Allen conducted a number of meta-analytic studies having to do with sex differences and sexually coercive behavior. These authors held that both men and women perceive the woman as more willing to have sex if she initiates the date, that previous sexual intercourse or an existent relationship make forced sex less coercive, and that sex is less coercive if drugs or alcohol are involved (Emmers & Allen, 1995a). However, they also noted that in general, men perceive forced sex as more justified, and they are more willing than women to engage in sex. This line of research further indicates that men and women do not differ in overall resistance behaviors to sexual coercion or in verbal resistance behaviors, although women engage in more physical resistance than men do (Emmers & Allen, 1995b). Finally, their findings suggest that whether a particular action is perceived as coercion or rape depends on the attitudes of the individuals making the evaluation and their perception of the situation.

A number of sex difference studies have been conducted in relation to specific communicative behaviors, and all show some differences between the sexes. For example, Dindia and Allen (1992) contended that women tend to self-disclose slightly more than do men. Similarly, Gayle et al. (1994) observed small sex differences in the selection of conflict strategies with men being more likely to use competitive strategies and women showing greater likelihood of engaging in compromising strategies. They attribute these differences to study respondents' expectations about the inherent maleness of femaleness of the test situations they encounter (Gayle et al., 1997). Timmerman (chap. 5, this volume) provided meta-analytic evidence that men tend to use powerful language more often than women, and Sahlstein and Allen (chap. 4, this volume) similarly indicate that women have slightly higher self-esteem than do men. In the face of this meta-analytic evidence of sex differences, one might conclude that small but consistent sex differences exist in human behavior, but certain caveats should be taken into account before accepting this conclusion.

In sum, the research literature reveals that meta-analysis can summarize findings in several domains relative to interpersonal communication. Perceptual and behavioral variables of many kinds appear amenable to meta-analytic synthesis. In addition, meta-analysis has been used to test various hypotheses, with research on sex differences, leadership, and persuasion offering prototypical examples of the kind of issues addressed by meta-analysis.

ASSESSING THE QUALITY OF KNOWLEDGE ACQUIRED FROM META-ANALYSES

Criteria for Evaluation

Summaries based on meta-analytic evidence provide compelling answers to important questions pursued by interpersonal communication researchers. As indicated earlier, people who are acquainted with the language of statistics and who acknowledge the veracity of statistical inference making would most likely consider as worth considering the claims made through meta-analyses. It is also clear that those with an acquaintance of statistical knowledge and a skeptical eye would not accept conclusions based on meta-analytic research if that research did not meet certain criteria. In other words, whether or not a reader accepts the results of any meta-analysis should be determined by the quality of the meta-analysis.

In this section, we offer five criteria for examining meta-analyses in interpersonal communication. Other scholars have offered similar evaluative standards with regard to meta-analysis, although we should also indicate that such standards are not necessarily unique to meta-analysis (e.g., Hunter, Schmidt, & Jackson, 1982; Wolf, 1986). Four generic standards, which are connected to each other, are as follows: (a) conceptual framework, (b) quality of sample, (c) soundness of decision rules, and (d) interpretation of effect sizes. In addition to these, we wish to add the following criterion that specifically concerns interpersonal communication: (e) explication of communication processes.

The first standard for evaluation concerns the study's conceptual framework. As with any scholarly endeavor, researchers using meta-analyses must provide a *prima facie* argument for the study and a coherent framework for conceptualizing the behavior under investigation. In other words, summarizing statistical findings without a sense of understanding what those findings represent constitutes a penultimate example of dust-bowl empiricism. It is far more desirable to provide a conceptual backdrop that lends a sense of understanding. For instance, Allen (chap. 13, this volume) uses meta-analysis to support the use of constructivist theory as a means of understanding comforting behavior. In brief, the goals of meta-analysis remain the same as any type of empirical investigation; namely, the study should help advance explanation and prediction of the phenomenon (i.e., theory).

Directly related to this criterion is the presumption that certain methods are required to make causal inferences. For instance, studies of particular types (e.g., observation or peer report) may offer significantly different outcomes than other types of studies (e.g., experiments or self-report assessments; e.g., Dindia & Allen, 1992). If one type of study was popular in the past and a different type is currently more frequently performed, it appears likely that the cause for change is due to the type of research rather than any real change in human behavior. As an example, research on gender differences in aggression has shown a decrease in sex differences over time. However, Knight, Fabes, and Higgins (1996) argued that this decrease may be due to changes in research methodology over time and not to social trends.

The second criterion we offer regards quality of sample. It is clear that meta-analytic findings are only as strong as the studies that constitute them. One criticism that has often been leveled is that meta-analysis researchers sample various studies for nonsystematic, subjective reasons. For example, establishing criteria for review, searching for relevant studies, and selecting the final set of studies all require the researcher to make judgment calls that affect meta-analytic findings. Thus, unpublished research is often not included for study because such research is simply too difficult for the researcher to access. The same contention can be made with regard to papers published in foreign languages or other countries. Additionally, researchers are reluctant to submit papers that do not support predicted hypotheses (i.e., the tests show no significant findings or findings opposite of those anticipated), and editors are less likely to publish those same types of papers (Coursol & Wagner, 1986). Such studies, of course, represent an undetermined number and quality. Accordingly, and understandably, a given meta-analysis could rely on a sample of research that does not represent all the research on a given topic. Nevertheless, the strength of the inferences drawn directly depends on the representativeness of the studies sampled, and it is the researcher's burden to report the manner in which studies are sampled.

A third criterion of meta-analyses concerns the adequacy of decision rules. As with any research, decision rules (including judgment calls regarding sampling) affect meta-analysis (Wanous et al., 1989). Wanous et al. (1989) noted a tendency for readers and authors of meta-analytic studies to adhere to the view that a given meta-analysis "produces the answer" (p. 259). They indicated that certain meta-analyses published on the same topic do not agree, contending that decisions made throughout the process of conducting meta-analyses affect their outcomes.

Providing the reader with clearly stated decision rules should assist in assessing the equivalence of findings. Several decision rules regarding sampling were mentioned earlier. In addition to these, researchers should indicate how moderating variables were coded, whether and how coders were trained, whether and how study attributes (e.g., date of publication) were coded, analytical procedures (e.g., the variance approach favored by Allen and colleagues), and bases for assessing effect sizes (e.g., reliance on Cohen's [1977] rules). In several ways, one's ability to make sense of meta-analytic findings depends on the exposition of and rationale for the decision rules that guided the study.

Fourth, meta-analytical efforts should result in a clear representation of the magnitude of the findings. In other words, authors should clearly interpret the effect size(s) for the reader. Given that meta-analyses can powerfully present statistical summaries of many studies, not to report and discuss the magnitude of the effect size appears self-defeating.

Interpreting the meaningfulness of effect size, however, is not an easy task. Hyde and Plant (1995) noted that the majority of sex difference research in psychology reveals very modest effect sizes that indicate biological sex represents a weak predictor of behavior. However, Eagly (1995) proposed that small effects due to sex are actually quite substantial, when considering the range of effects for psychological traits on behavior. Allen (1998) indicated how both camps can be correct by showing that small effects that reflect trivial differences between the sexes for most people can be quite meaningful when discussing the behavior of a minority of people, which lies at the extreme ends of the distributions.

The meaningfulness of an effect size also depends on the nature of one's theoretical assumption about the strength of the relation. Unfortunately, many people do not hold *a priori* assumptions concerning the strength of the relation being examined; most researchers appear pleased if a statistically significant finding supports the hypothesis. However, when presumed beliefs are disconfirmed, then one must take a second look at such beliefs. For instance, many vocal people argue that children suffer when gay or lesbian parents raise them. However, Allen and Burrell (1996) found that a meta-analysis of both adult and child ratings indicate that children overall are slightly more adjusted when living with homosexual (vs. heterosexual) parents. Allen and Burrell (1996) were able to conclude, "The results fail to support the assumption of widespread differences, or any differences on the basis of the particular outcome studied, between parents on the basis of sexual orientation" (p. 28). As a second example, if people hold that sex differences are large and invariant, then they would probably be puzzled or even dismayed to learn that the average of sex difference research only shows about 1% difference between men and women (i.e., $d = .23$), which is what Dindia (1998) indeed found in her meta-analysis of more than 300 studies. However, those who assume sex similarities over differences have little trouble interpreting the 1%, finding that figure corresponds to our experiences and expectations that men and women are similar creatures 99% of the time.

The fifth and final criterion concerns interpersonal interaction—the extent to which, if at all, the meta-analysis explicates communication processes. As most social scientists know, it is hard to breathe life into a correlation coefficient, especially if it is below .30. Yet, making the summary come to life is precisely the burden of the meta-analytic researcher when discussing communicative behaviors.

How one person's behavior affects another person's behavior represents the heart of the discipline of communication, and mutual behavioral influence provides a fundamental definition of interpersonal communication in particular (Cappella, 1987). According to Cappella (1987), Person B must change his or her behavior when in the company of Person A, and vice versa, beyond behaviors that Person B or Person A enact individually. Interdependence of action, then, constitutes the most rudimentary level of behavioral exchange and, accordingly, the most basic sense of observing communication as a process. All studies of interpersonal communication, including meta-analytic efforts, should reflect its processes. We are not contending that one must directly measure processes *per se*; rather, meta-analysis (especially one concerning interpersonal communication) should reveal something about the nature of symbolic exchange. For instance, Spitzberg and Dillard (chap. 6, this volume) report 12 studies that linked specific communicative behaviors (e.g., speech latency, eye contact) to perceptions of social skill. Their study clearly implies how one's behavior might affect a second person's perception of social skill—a case in Cappella's (1987) point regarding mutual influence.

Certainly, the criteria we offer are not necessarily solely applicable to meta-analytic efforts. In addition, other texts report more sophisticated, technical criteria. Still, these standards appear to us as particularly important when assessing the validity of any meta-analysis regarding interpersonal communication. The extent to which authors provide a clear account of conceptual framework, sampling and other decision rules, and communication as process signals how confident one should be in the inferences drawn from meta-analyses. The following section presents an application of these criteria to a research example regarding sex differences in managing interpersonal conflict.

Research Example: Sex Differences in Managing Conflict

As mentioned earlier, Gayle et al. (1994) reported a much-needed investigation regarding sex differences in interpersonal conflict strategies. At the outset, we want to indicate that our view of the Gayle et al. (1994) paper is quite positive in terms of what it set out to accomplish—a summary of sex differences in people's styles at managing conflict. Of course, the paper also allows us to show how particular decision rules regarding sampling can lead to very different results regarding how findings should be interpreted. As the reader will come to understand, this exercise is a bit unfair, because Gayle et al. (1994) meant to discuss styles and not necessarily behaviors. In other words, we hope this exercise is taken as instructive instead of an indictment.

Gayle et al. (1994) relied on standard indexes and abstracts to obtain their sample of studies. Moreover, the authors coded for several possible moderating factors. In the results, Gayle et al. reported a "very small" average effect due to sex differences on five conflict styles ($r = -.054$). The negative sign indicates that women more often reported the behavior. Yet two strategies—competition (i.e., direct and negative behaviors) and compromising (i.e., direct and positive behaviors) yielded larger, although still small, effects ($rs = .115$ and $-.114$, respectively). These findings indicate that approximately 1% of competitive and compromising behaviors are due to sex differences, with men being more competitive and women being more compromising.

The authors relied on expectancy theory as well as an "interaction-conflict perspective" (Gayle et al., 1994, p. 14), which concerns the contextual constraints on behavior. For this latter conceptual framework, Gayle et al. (1994) cited Eagly's (1987) social role theory among other researchers. The authors concluded:

> Thus, the findings of this study lend some credence to the idea that individuals employ stable conflict management strategies across varying situations and contexts.
>
> The conflict model that emerges suggests that compromising and competitive strategies may be separate orientations intrinsically tied to gender roles rather than processes that emerge over the length of the conflict interaction. (p. 19)

In terms of the criteria for evaluating the quality of this meta-analysis, the paper generally succeeds. In brief, Gayle et al. (1994) relied on two alternative theoretical approaches to establish the conceptual framework for the study. They used standard indexes to construct the sample. They clearly reported decision rules regarding their exclusion of some studies and how they recoded behaviors from three categories into the five-category scheme that they opted to use as a primary scheme to divide conflict strategies. To assess contextual issues, they offered and coded for moderating factors. They clearly interpreted the effect sizes to argue that men are more competitive and women are more compromising, tying their interpretation back to their original conceptual framework that indicated competing points of view.

Had it not been for several other quantitative studies and narrative reviews of these studies, we could accept this meta-analysis as an accurate summary of the literature on conflict management behaviors. Understandably, given their purpose, Gayle et al. (1994) incorporated self-reported conflict strategies (30 of 32 studies examined conflict styles operationally defined through survey data). The uncritical reader might overgeneralize the findings of Gayle et al. to include research that observes actual conflict behaviors, but such a conclusion is unwarranted.

Most important, we should note that the Gayle et al. (1994) paper does not include studies that examine conflict interactions in close relationships (for reviews, see Cupach & Canary, 1995; Gottman, 1994; Sagrestano, Christensen, & Heavey, 1998; Schaap, Buunk, & Kerkstra, 1988). For example, Margolin and Wampold (1981) found that wives engaged in more smiling and laughter, complaining, and criticizing, whereas husbands presented more excuses. Also, distressed husbands appeared more withdrawn (i.e., paid less attention to the conversation). Yet, husbands and wives did not differ on 75% of the codes, including the categories of problem solving, positive verbal comments, negative verbal comments, and negative nonverbal behaviors. Behavioral research on the demand–withdrawal pattern (e.g., Heavey, Layne, & Christensen, 1993), wherein wives more likely confront their husbands, who avoid their wives, is omitted from this meta-analysis. Moreover, other observational methodologies that document no sex differences (e.g., Burggraf & Sillars, 1987) are not included in the Gayle et al. (1994) paper.

The emphasis on the self-reported research provides no guarantee about knowledge regarding actual interaction behaviors, at least in the case of examining conflict behaviors from the conflict styles literature. Following their review of the marital literature, Schaap et al. (1988) concluded, "Women tend to be more emotional and show more negative affect, while men are inclined to be more rational and withdrawn" (p. 236). Self-reported data permit people to project themselves as they might stereotypically imagine men and women interacting, rather than how partners actually behave. For example, Markman, Silvern, Clements, and Kraft-Hanak (1993) observed actual interaction and self-reported accounts of marital partner withdrawal and demand complaints (which they called "withdrawal" and "pursuit"). As Markman et al. (1993) concluded, "In either case, the present results add to other findings that *when couples are actually observed, fewer [sex] differences emerge than indicated by their self-reports*" (p. 120, italics in original).

The omission of the observational research is certainly understandable given the authors' focus on conflict styles. At the same time, the observational literature also comes wrapped in its own conceptual framework to explain why women are more negative and confrontative in marriage. Accordingly, the theoretical points of view provided by Gayle et al. (1994) do not include theorizing regarding how men and women manage conflict in close relationships. For example, one popular explanation emphasizes biological responses of men versus women, where men experience greater diffuse physiological arousal to conflict and, therefore, more likely avoid competitive interactions with their angry spouses (Gottman, 1994). An alternative explanation is that the person who is inequitably treated is more likely to complain to the partner; because women suffer from greater inequity than do their husbands, women become more negative and forceful during conflict interactions (Heavey et al., 1993). Accordingly, the knowledge claims derived from Gayle et al. (1994) rely on self-reported behaviors that indicate predisposition toward conflict. Readers might mistakenly generalize the findings from predispositions of what people think they would say or do to actual interaction behaviors. Also, it appears that some of the conflict interaction patterns recently researched are not represented, thereby not fully elaborating on communicative processes. This suggests that whereas the Gayle et al. paper is a sound benchmark for sex differences in predispositions for behavior, the relation to how people influence each other in actual interaction is less certain.

In sum, this section stressed how five criteria for evaluation can be used to examine the knowledge claims of particular meta-analyses. These criteria—conceptual framework, quality of sample, soundness of decision rules, interpretation of effect sizes, and explication of communication processes—were then applied to an excellent paper on conflict styles (Gayle et al., 1994). This exercise shows how a choice in one standard (the definition of the sampling procedure or rules for inclusion and exclusion of studies) can affect the generalizability of the findings, as well as influence other criteria (in this case, conceptual framework and explication of communication processes). At this juncture, we turn our attention to conclusions and considerations for the future.

CONCLUSIONS AND CONSIDERATIONS
FOR THE FUTURE

Thus far, a general description of the literature and guidelines for evaluation have been offered. This final section presents some ideas regarding how we can advance the study of interpersonal communication through meta-analysis, drawing on the previous sections. First, we indicate in a concluding statement how paradoxical features of meta-analysis affect our knowledge of interpersonal communication. We do this by comparing what meta-analysis offers in light of its limitations. Finally, we close this chapter by pointing to future considerations.

Knowledge Contributions and Limitations

In this section, we consider the contributions and limitations of meta-analysis. These are cast as competing and parallel statements, with the contributions offered first.

First, meta-analysis summarizes quantitative information, which is amenable to those who have a propensity to use such information; yet it cannot presume that everyone is acquainted with the statistics used to conduct meta-analyses. From the outset, we must acknowledge that meta-analysis depends on a particular form of knowledge and is mute with regard to qualitative studies. In addition, one's understanding of the quantitative summaries directly depends on one's familiarity with meta-analytical translations of difference scores, correlations, effect sizes, and the like. In other words, the basis of knowledge does not rest only on the summary figure.

Second, meta-analysis reveals behavioral trends in an efficient manner; it does not capture processes as effectively as do other methods. Again, the summary nature of meta-analysis permits a quick and encompassing look at specific behaviors. However, meta-analysis does not permit a close inspection of how specific behaviors emerge in time. For instance, conflict researchers have uncovered various patterns of interaction that reflect how conflict evolves in time (for a review, see Messman & Canary, 1998). How partners reciprocate and compensate conflict tactics in actual interaction constitutes a complex process that has been variously defined and tested, and that accordingly resists efficient summary.

Third, meta-analysis provides systematic analysis of data, which implies that decision rules regarding sampling and other procedures should be carefully reported; but it cannot presume that objective procedures support the results. This duality underscores the idea that meta-analyses on the same topic might reveal different findings due to the many decision rules and specific analytical tools that researchers decide to use. In addition, this statement calls for careful examination of the methods that underlie the results. This statement also reminds us not to lend credence that might be placed on a given meta-analysis.

Fourth, meta-analysis can be applied to many, if not all, facets of interpersonal communication; it cannot be readily applied to minute examinations of interactions. This point differs from the second one in the sense that meta-analysis allows for the investigation of a great number of different kinds of topics more than a detailed understanding of interactional processes. For example, conversational analysis of couple interaction behavior reveals precise, nuanced, and perhaps largely idiosyncratic processes that cannot be readily examined using meta-analysis (e.g., Alberts & Driscoll, 1992).

Fifth, meta-analysis can offer compelling answers to questions debated in narrative form; it cannot presume that the summary statistic itself is persuasive. The heuristic nature of meta-analysis is both a boon and a bane. On the positive side, a summary statistic helps the scientific community make clear statements. On the negative side, eristic research is less valued than heuristic endeavors that generate more curiosity and attention. In addition, it is a mistake to presume the value of a summary statistic on others—especially on scholars steeped in alternative paradigms. In reference to this fifth point, meta-analysis is an argument that works only when delivered before one's own methodological choir.

Sixth, meta-analysis allows for discussion and debate regarding the meaningfulness of effect sizes; but it provides little guidance regarding the range of what one considers meaningful. The current debate on the meaningfulness of effect sizes in sex difference meta-analyses illustrates this point (e.g., Eagly, 1995). Another way of saying this is that objective standards for assessing the strength of effect sizes do not exist, and even the intersubjectively agreed-to standards (e.g., Cohen's, 1977) can still be used as springboards for contention.

Finally, meta-analysis presents a powerful way to test and to advance theory; it does not generate new theory. This seventh and final observation presumes that conventional uses of meta-analyses entail posttheoretical testing and refinement. Of course, given the powerful nature of meta-analysis, it could also be used to test new theory. However, whether or not it can successfully lead to bottom-up construction of theory remains to be seen. For example, only future efforts will reveal if meta-analyses can be used to generate models of interaction behavior.

These paradoxical conclusions should indicate that, given an understanding of its limitations, meta-analysis offers an important analytical tool for the advancement of interpersonal communication research. The knowledge that we acquire from such a tool is clearly an empirical abstraction, based on studies with countless variation in samples, methods, and analyses. Nevertheless, the knowledge that meta-analysis provides overrides within-study variance and offers a general map of the specific territory. Of course, the question before us concerns how we can make better use of the general map.

First, we believe that it is necessary to consider meta-analytic findings as complementing qualitative research, as well as quantitative research and narrative reviews. Because meta-analytic findings can only utilize quantitative results, one way to check the findings is to determine if they coincide with other findings. A difference in findings between two types of research would probably suggest that more than one way exists to understand any given communicative behavior.

A second consideration for future interpersonal researchers concerns narrowing the perspective offered by meta-analytic findings. Meta-analysis tends to offer a macro perspective of communicative behavior. For example, meta-analytic research on communication apprehension suggests that all three of the major approaches to dealing with communication apprehension are effective in bringing about a decrease in communication apprehension level. However, the findings do not offer a detailed understanding of the more specific, micro elements that constitute each of the approaches.

A third and final consideration for interpersonal communication research is greater concentration of the process of communication. As stated earlier, meta-analyses do not tend to explore minute communicative processes, although they could do so given carefully reasoned decision rules that help categorize various types of interaction patterns. More often than not, communication researchers concentrate on single communicative events rather than on communication as an ongoing process. Such understanding of interpersonal communication as a singular occurrence does not provide a complete picture of that behavior. It is time for interpersonal communication researchers to focus on ways that interactive processes are captured in a way that can be summarized.

REFERENCES

Alberts, J. K., & Driscoll, G. (1992). Containment versus escalation: The trajectory of couples' conversation complaints. *Western Journal of Communication, 56,* 394–412.

Allen, M. (1989). A comparison of self-report, observer, and physiological assessments of public speaking anxiety reduction techniques using meta-analysis. *Communication Studies, 40,* 127–139.

Allen, M. (1998). Methodological concerns when examining a gendered world. In D. J. Canary & K. Dindia (Eds.), *Sex differences and similarities in communication: Critical essays and empirical investigations of sex and gender in interaction* (pp. 427–444). Mahwah, NJ: Lawrence Erlbaum Associates.

Allen, M., & Bourhis, J. (1996). The relationship of communication apprehension to communication behavior: A meta-analysis. *Communication Quarterly, 44,* 214–226.

Allen, M., & Burrell, N. (1996). Comparing the impact of homosexual and heterosexual parents on children: Meta-analysis of existing research. *Journal of Homosexuality, 32,* 19–35.

Allen, M., Hunter, J. E., & Donohue, W. A. (1989). Meta-analysis of self-report data on the effectiveness of public speaking anxiety treatment techniques. *Communication Education, 38,* 54–76.

Amato, P. R., & Keith, B. (1991). Parental divorce and the well being of children: A meta-analysis. *Psychological Bulletin, 110,* 26–46.

BarNir, A. (1998). Can group and issue-related factors predict choice shift: A meta-analysis of group decisions on life dilemmas. *Small Group Research, 29,* 308–338.

Bourhis, J., & Allen, M. (1992). Meta-analysis of the relationship between communication apprehension and cognitive performance. *Communication Education, 41,* 68–76.

Burggraf, C. S., & Sillars, A. L. (1987). A critical examination of sex differences in marital communication. *Communication Monographs, 54,* 276–294.

Canary, D. J., Emmers-Sommer, T. M., & Faulkner, S. (1997). *Sex and gender differences in personal relationships.* New York: Guilford.

Canary, D. J., & Hause, K. S. (1993). Is there any reason to research sex differences in communication? *Communication Quarterly, 41,* 129–144.

Cappella, J. N. (1987). Interpersonal communication: Fundamental questions and issues. In S. Chaffee & C. R. Berger (Eds.), *Handbook of communication science* (pp. 184–238). Newbury Park, CA: Sage.

Cohen, J. (1977). *Statistical power analysis for the behavioral sciences* (rev. ed.). New York: Academic.

Coursol, A., & Wagner, E. E. (1986). Effect of positive findings on submission and acceptance rates: A note on meta-analysis bias. *Professional Psychology: Research and Practice, 17,* 136–137.

Cupach, W. R., & Canary, D. J. (1995). Managing conflict and anger: Investigating the sex stereotype hypothesis. In P. J. Kalbfleisch & M. J. Cody (Eds.), *Gender, power, and communication in human relationships* (pp. 211–233). Hillsdale, NJ: Lawrence Erlbaum Associates.

Dillard, J. P., Hunter, J. E., & Burgoon, M. (1984). Sequential-request persuasive strategies: Meta-analysis of foot-in-the-door and door-in-the-face. *Human Communication Research, 10,* 461–488.

Dindia, K. (1998, June). *Men are from South Dakota, women are from North Dakota.* Paper presented at the International Network on Personal Relationship conference, Norman, OK.

Dindia, K., & Allen, M. (1992). Sex differences in self-disclosure: A meta-analysis. *Psychological Bulletin, 112,* 106–124.

Eagly, A. H. (1987). *Sex differences in social behavior: A social-role interpretation.* Hillsdale, NJ: Lawrence Erlbaum Associates.

Eagly, A. H. (1994). On comparing women and men. *Feminism and Psychology, 4,* 513–522.

Eagly, A. H. (1995). The science and politics of comparing women and men. *American Psychologist, 50,* 145–158.

Eagly, A. H., & Johnson, B. T. (1990). Gender and leadership style: A meta-analysis. *Psychological Bulletin, 108,* 233–256.

Eagly, A. H., & Karau, S. J. (1991). Gender and the emergence of leaders: A meta-analysis. *Journal of Personality and Social Psychology, 60,* 685–710.

Eagly, A. H., Makhijani, M. G., & Klonsky, B. G. (1992). Gender and the evaluation of leaders: A meta-analysis. *Psychological Bulletin, 111,* 3–22.

Eagly, A. H., & Wood, W. (1991). Explaining sex differences in social behavior: A meta-analytic perspective. *Personality and Social Psychology Bulletin, 17,* 306–315.

Emmers, T. M., & Allen, M. (1995a, November). *Factors contributing to sexually coercive behaviors: A meta-analysis.* Paper presented at the annual meeting of the Speech Communication Association, San Antonio, TX.

Emmers, T. M., & Allen, M. (1995b, February). *Resistance to sexual coercion behaviors: A meta-analysis.* Paper presented at the annual meeting of the Western States Communication Association, Portland, OR.

Emmers-Sommer, T. M., & Allen, M. (1997, November). *Variables related to sexual coercion: A path model.* Paper presented at the annual meeting of the National Communication Association, Chicago, IL.

Gayle, B. M., Preiss, R. W., & Allen, M. (1994). Gender differences and the use of conflict strategies. In L. Turner & H. Sterk (Eds.), *Differences that make a difference: Examining the assumptions in gender research* (pp. 13–26). Westport, CT: Bergin & Garvey.

Gayle, B. M., Preiss, R. W., & Allen, M. (1997, November). *The cognitive processing of gender schema and conflict management strategy selection.* Paper presented at the annual meeting of the Speech Communication Association, Chicago, IL.

Glass, G. (1976). Primary, secondary, and meta-analysis of research. *Educational Researcher, 5*, 3–8.

Glass, G. (1977). Integrating findings: The meta-analysis of research. *Review of Research in Education, 5*, 351–379.

Gottman, J. M. (1994). *What predicts divorce? The relationship between marital processes and marital outcomes.* Hillsdale, NJ: Lawrence Erlbaum Associates.

Grob, L. M., & Allen, M. (1996, April). *Sex differences in powerful/powerless language use: A meta-analytic review.* Paper presented at the annual meeting of the Central States Communication Association, Minneapolis, MN.

Hall, J. A., Halberstadt, A. G., & O'Brien, C. E. (1997). "Subordination" and nonverbal sensitivity: A study and synthesis of findings based on trait measures. *Sex Roles, 37*, 295–317.

Heavey, C. L., Layne, C., & Christensen, A. (1993). Gender and conflict structure in marital interaction: A replication and extension. *Journal of Consulting and Clinical Psychology, 61*, 16–27.

Hunter, J. E., Schmidt, F. L., & Jackson, G. B. (1982). *Meta-analysis: Cumulating research findings across studies.* Beverly Hills, CA: Sage.

Hyde, J. S. (1990). Meta-analysis and the psychology of gender differences. *Journal of Women in Culture and Society, 16*, 55–73.

Hyde, J. S., & Plant, E. A. (1995). Magnitude of psychological gender differences: Another side to the story. *American Psychologist, 50*, 159–161.

Johnson, B. T., & Eagly, A. H. (1989). Effects of involvement on persuasion: A meta-analysis. *Psychological Bulletin, 106*, 290–314.

Knight, G. P., Fabes, R. A., & Higgins, D. A. (1996). Concerns about drawing causal inferences from meta-analyses: An example in the study of gender differences in aggression. *Psychological Bulletin, 119*, 410–421.

Krone, K. J., Allen, M., & Ludlum, J. (1994). A meta-analysis of gender research in managerial influence. In L. Turner & H. Sterk (Eds.), *Differences that make a difference: Examining the assumptions in gender research* (pp. 73–84). Westport, CT: Bergin & Garvey.

Leaper, C., Anderson, K. J., & Sanders, P. (1998). Moderators of gender effects on parents' talk to their children: A meta-analysis. *Developmental Psychology, 34*, 3–27.

Margolin, G., & Wampold, B. E. (1981). Sequential analysis of conflict and accord in distressed and nondistressed marital partners. *Journal of Consulting and Clinical Psychology, 49*, 554–567.

Markman, H. J., Silvern, L., Clements, M., & Kraft-Hanak, S. (1993). Men and women dealing with conflict in heterosexual relationships. *Journal of Social Issues, 49,* 107–125.

Messman, S. J., & Canary, D. J. (1998). Patterns of conflict and argument. In W. R. Cupach & B. H. Spitzberg (Eds.), *The darkside of personal relationships* (pp. 154–179). Mahwah, NJ: Lawrence Erlbaum Associates.

Sagrestano, L. M., Christensen, A., & Heavey, C. L. (1998). Sex differences in managing conflict. In D. J. Canary & K. Dindia (Eds.), *Sex differences and similarities* (pp. 287–302). Mahwah, NJ: Lawrence Erlbaum Associates.

Schaap, C., Buunk, B., & Kerkstra, A. (1988). Marital conflict resolution. In P. Noller & M. A. Fitzpatrick (Eds.), *Perspectives on marital interaction* (pp. 203–244). Philadelphia: Multilingual Matters.

Thomas, J. C. (1998). How science takes stock: The story of meta-analysis by Morton Hunt is reviewed. *Personnel Psychology, 51,* 476–479.

Walther, J. B., Anderson, J. F., & Park, D. W. (1994). Interpersonal effects in computer-mediated interaction: A meta-analysis of social and anti-social communication. *Communication Research, 21,* 460–487.

Wanous, J. P., Sullivan, S. E., & Malinak, J. (1989). The role of judgment calls in meta-analysis. *Journal of Applied Psychology, 74,* 259–264.

Wilkins, B. M., & Andersen, P. A. (1991). Gender differences and similarities in management communication. *Management Communication Quarterly, 5,* 6–35.

Wolf, F. M. (1986). *Meta-analysis: Quantitative methods for research synthesis.* Newbury Park, CA: Sage.

21

Better Living Through Science: Reflections on the Future of Interpersonal Communication

Mary Anne Fitzpatrick

It is reasonable to argue that this book could not have been written more than 30 years ago for two major reasons. First, the topics examined in the research on interpersonal communication would have been quite different from those pursued by the authors here. During the 1950s and 1960s, the study of interpersonal communication moved not only into the study of social and personal relationships but also into consideration of a number of different kinds of face-to-face communication events (Fitzpatrick, 1999). Current research in interpersonal communication focuses on core strategic (e.g., compliance gaining, deception) and nonstrategic (e.g., self-disclosure, emotional messages) communication processes that occur between people in a variety of contexts. Social influence and persuasion are still central areas of study within interpersonal communication although they are not the only venues for research.

Second, meta-analysis, a way to average results across studies, only became a widespread technique in the mid-1970s. Meta-analysis is a technique to review the empirical literature in which summary statistics from each study (e.g., means or correlations) are treated as units of analysis, and the aggregate data are then analyzed in quantitative tests of the propositions under consideration. According to Hunter and Schmidt (1982), most methods of meta-analysis are concerned with considering artificial variation across studies: sampling error, error of measurement, and range variation or restriction.

The promise of this volume is to advance our understanding of interpersonal communication through the use of meta-analysis. Both the topics and the technique herald a new era in the study of interpersonal communication. In my own research career, I have chosen as a topical focus the study of interaction in social and personal relationships. Like the editors of this volume, I greeted the emergence of meta-analysis with joy and optimism. My attraction to meta-analysis went through predictable stages of a romantic relationship. In the first stage, I perceived the technique as an ideal way to resolve many problems in the social sciences. Finally, we had developed a tool that could help clear away the cobwebs of sloppy, sometimes politicized thinking and help scholars make sense of a voluminous literature. Clearly, there were numerous other reasons to fall in love with this technique.

First, meta-analysis allowed a researcher to aggregate findings across studies and samples. Second, meta-analysis promised to yield more precise estimates of effects. Third, the technique examined how a method might be (mis)leading us to accept one interpretation over another. Fourth, meta-analysis considered moderator effects in the hope of resolving theoretical disputes. Fifth, meta-analysis implicitly promised that the entire research enterprise would be uplifted as old, tired questions and methods were abandoned as dead ends for understanding human behavior. Finally, the technique allowed individuals working in environments where it was difficult to conduct primary research to participate in the social science community by aggregating and making sense of the empirical work of others (however, see Burgoon, 1998, for a contrasting slant). The literature includes many examples of the power of meta-analysis. Let me discuss a few of my favorite examples of the genre and try to explicate what I find especially appealing about them.

BENCHMARKS FOR META-ANALYSIS

Oliver and Hyde (1993) examined gender differences in sexuality (see also Oliver & Hyde, 1995; Whitely & Kite, 1995) in their meta-analysis of 177 usable sources, yielding 239 independent samples testing 128,363 respondents on eight sexual attitudes (i.e., premarital intercourse, homosexuality, extramarital sex, sexual permissiveness, anxiety about sex, sexual satisfaction, double-standard attitudes, and masturbation attitudes) and nine behaviors (i.e., kissing, petting, heterosexual intercourse, age of first intercourse, number of sexual partners, frequency of intercourse, masturbation, homosexual behavior, and oral–genital behavior). The broad sampling of social actors and behaviors in this analysis was admirable, but especially enlightening were the discussions of gender differences in sexuality as predicted by Chodorow's neoanalytic theory, sociobiology, social learning theory, social role theory, and script theory. Contrary to the predictions made by most theories, and to the widespread belief in American culture that there are many large gender differences in sexual attitudes and behaviors, these authors found that most gender differences were in the small to moderate range. For example, men reported a higher incidence of intercourse ($d = .33$) and a younger age for first intercourse ($d = .38$), whereas women reported more acceptance of the double standard ($d = -.29$) and more anxiety, fear, and guilt about sexual behavior ($d = -.35$). Results indicated no significant differences between men and women in attitudes toward homosexuality or in the experience of sexual satisfaction.

Two of the largest differences in the analysis are especially noteworthy. First, men had considerably more permissive attitudes toward the acceptability of premarital intercourse in a casual dating relationship or one without emotional commitment ($d = .81$). All five theories reviewed in the article, those within a biological framework as well as the more social and cultural theories, would have predicted this difference and its magnitude. However, these theories would also predict a large difference in the number of sexual partners. Although that difference was in the expected direction with men having more sexual partners than women ($d = .25$), the magnitude of the difference was smaller than expected by theory. The authors make some interesting points about the magnitude of this difference and offer some new theoretical moves that could be forwarded to account for the unanticipated results.

Second, men had the greatest incidence of masturbation ($d = .96$). Intriguingly, only script theory predicts this difference. Indeed, Gagnon and Simon's (1973) script theory argues that early experience with masturbation leads men to view the meaning of sexuality as tied to more to individual pleasure, whereas women view the meaning of sexuality as tied to relationships. For script theory, this sex difference is the origin of most other gender differences in sexuality. What is especially strong about this piece is the constant tying of the results back to theory as well as the conclusion that gender differences of this magnitude need further theoretical explication. In the tradition of the best analyses, Oliver and Hyde (1993) reviewed a comprehensive body of empirical literature, examined the core theories underlying the research, explained the findings from the analysis in reference to those theories, and offered suggestions for future theoretical development and research.

Another example for researchers interested in the technique of meta-analysis is the original work on self-disclosure by Dindia and Allen (1992) that is updated in this volume (Dindia, chap. 10, this volume). With the publication of Jourard's (1971) classic statement, self-disclosure or the sharing of personal feelings and information about the self has become a vital area of study of interpersonal communication. Considered the hallmark of the development of a healthy personality and a relationship to others, self-disclosure has been approached as a personality trait and a process variable. As a personality trait, disclosure has been linked to race, gender, and ethnic and cultural background. As a process variable, self-disclosure has been studied as the facilitator of the development of personal relationships.

From the beginning, gender has been a focal point of study in the arena of self-disclosure. Dindia and Allen (1992) examined sex differences in self-disclosure and evaluated the major variables found to moderate the effect. Included in this list were the sex of the target, the speaker's relationship to the target, and the measure of self-disclosure (i.e., self-report inventories and self-ratings, observer or recipient ratings, objective metrics). Employing a sample of 23,702 respondents, women were indeed found to self-disclose more than men ($d = .184$).

Because the variation across studies was not solely due to sampling error, tests for moderator variables were conducted. The sex of the target did moderate the effect of sex on self-disclosure. Specifically, women disclosed more than men to same-sex partners and slightly more than men to opposite-sex partners. Although the relationship to the target did not by itself moderate the effect of sex on self-disclosure, the measure of self-disclosure did have an effect. Compared to self-reports or trained observer perceptions, individuals (i.e., respondents reporting on their partner's disclosures) clearly report that women disclose more than men.

The strength of this meta-analysis was that it carefully examined moderator variables and clearly linked these findings to directions for future research. Dindia and Allen (1992) critiqued a previous meta-analysis for not including unpublished research as well as not taking into account the various moderators proposed by extant theories. Along the same line, Collins and Miller (1994) used meta-analysis to answer three important questions about the relation between self-disclosure and liking. Of note for this discussion is how these authors link the meta-analysis findings back to an integrated model of personal relationships that views self-disclosure as part of a dynamic interpersonal system.

A third example of a well-conducted meta-analysis is that of Hall (1984, 1998), who explored sex differences in nonverbal communication. She concluded that the sex differences for smiling and nonverbal sensitivity are large and favor women. Hall (1998) made the case that we need to formulate a way to think about the size of the sex differences in nonverbal communication. One way to evaluate the size of the differences we find is to compare these differences to other established empirical findings. Her comparative approach offers three kinds of questions to frame the discussion:

1. How do sex differences compare to effects in other domains?
2. How does one sex difference (or class of sex differences) compare to other sex differences?
3. How does the magnitude of a particular sex difference compare to the magnitudes of other correlates of that same trait or behavior?

Although Hall's (1998) three questions relate to the size of sex differences in nonverbal communication, they can and should be generalized to other domains. The real value of a meta-analysis is that it yields an estimate not only of a difference, but also of the magnitude of the difference. However, the researcher must be prepared to discuss these magnitude estimates in some detail. Hall's (1998) questions can help the analyst to frame a case for whether the differences uncovered are substantial or trivial. In essence, Hall proposed some rhetorical guidelines for meta-analysts to help them frame a reasonable argument about the magnitude estimates. The basic empirical work of a meta-analysis must be supplemented with the theorist's discussion and evaluation of the magnitude of the difference. This discussion involves a consideration of the degree to which theory predicts the magnitude of the difference, the practical impact of the difference, and a contextual perspective.

For example, going back to the Oliver and Hyde (1993) meta-analysis, that article made clear comparisons among the differences they uncovered in male and female sexual attitudes and behaviors and related these differences to theory. Following Hall's (1998) advice, Oliver and Hyde's discussions of the magnitude of the differences could have been profitably framed in reference not only to one another but to other gender or social differences as well as factors other than gender that may be related to sexual attitudes (e.g., religiosity) and behaviors (e.g., physical attractiveness).

Unfortunately, like all affairs, disaffection with meta-analysis set in gradually. Perhaps I was requiring too much, asking that the technique solve too many problems. Indeed, the very structure of science works against the use of meta-analysis. In the world of Fisherian hypothesis testing, the significance test acts as an arbiter of what can be published (Dillard, 1998). Researchers trying to pull together a sample of studies on a given topic are faced with the "file drawer" problem: How could they uncover studies where a researcher found no significant differences?

The file drawer problem is often readily acknowledged: Each report discusses how this is handled so the reader can judge the efforts. For example, many researchers include a search of the Educational Resources Informational Clearinghouse (ERIC) database, and many unpublished manuscripts are included in this computerized database. Other researchers (e.g., Collins & Miller, 1994) expressly evaluate the risk of publication bias. Unfortunately, the approach of many of the chapter authors in this volume is to begin by defining studies and whole program of research as "out" of consideration rather than working to be as inclusive of as much literature, published and unpublished, as possible. Although this strategy is understandable, it leaves the authors open to criticism that important empirical findings have not been taken into consideration. A more insidious problem may be the one surrounding the organization of information and keywords in the databases that are searched for representative articles. For example Sillars's (Burgraff & Sillars, 1986; Sillars, Colletti, Parry, & Rogers, 1982; Sillars, Pike, Jones, & Redmon, 1983) or Fitzpatrick's (Fitzpatrick, Fallis, & Vance, 1982) work on sex differences in conflict in couples was ignored by Gayle, Preiss, and Allen (1994). This line of work is not included because the conceptual labels and keywords differ. The work was not included because only self-report data about conflict were used and behavioral data were not included. However, this particular decision about the criteria for inclusion leaves out research that turns the self-report data on interpersonal conflict into behavioral codes for conflict management. Ignoring highly related streams of work prevents the authors from examining potentially important moderators (e.g., type of relationship) or methods factors (e.g., self-report or behavioral codes) that may affect the outcomes. Indeed, Fitzpatrick (1991) theorized that gender differences in marital conflict were overemphasized and the ideological and conflict models were better predictors of what couples did in conflict. The chapter in this volume corrects that decision by including the behavioral data and in doing so generates a very different set of conclusions.

The narrowing of the focus in the chapter on self-esteem may work to its disadvantage (Sahlstein & Allen, chap. 4, this volume). Feingold (1994) examined gender differences in personality: self-esteem, internal locus of control, anxiety, and assertiveness. Of particular interest are his findings on self-esteem as they are related to those of Sahlstein and Allen (chap. 4, this volume). Feingold reanalyzed the classic studies of Maccoby and Jacklin (1974) and found that the mean effect size for gender differences in self esteem was .10; in Hall (1984) it was .12 and in the replication and updating of Hall's work that he conducted, the unweighted mean effect size was .16 for the sex difference in self esteem ($k = 27$, $N = 10,755$; 48% male). Men do have higher self-esteem but to a small degree. Sahlstein and Allen's figures differ in specifics with those of Feingold (1994). The Sahlstein and Allen figures for self-esteem indicate that women have higher overall self esteem (−.009); cognitive self-esteem (−.026), and comprehensive self-esteem (−.021), whereas men have higher social (.028) and physical (.201) self-esteem. Both works argue that male self-esteem seems to be on the rise. Like Dindia and Allen (1992), Sahlstein and Allen (chap. 4, this volume) need to resolve the discrepancies between their work and that of Feingold (1994).

From the stage of disaffection comes an acceptance of the good and bad points of the object of my affection. Meta-analysis is best when it is used to cumulate a clear amount of evidence on a topic (Hamilton & Mineo, chap. 16, this volume; Hample & Dallinger, chap. 11, this volume) is closely tied to theory and theoretical tests and expansions (AhYun, chap. 9, this volume); presents final data in clear, tabulated forms (Spitzberg & Dillard, chap. 6, this volume); notes any changes in results over time (Sahlstein & Allen, chap. 4, this volume); and compares its results to other meta-analytical results (Dindia, chap. 10, this volume).

One of the latent effects of the development of meta-analysis is that it provides an interesting window on the issues that preoccupy the research community. Researchers conduct meta-analyses to answer pressing questions, to weigh in on conceptual disputes, and to decide what empirical road to travel. Within this volume, there seem to be two major pressing meta-issues for the researchers in the discipline as represented in two themes. The first theme centers on what have been core questions in the study of interpersonal communication for at least 25 years. The second theme focuses on gender differences in interpersonal processes as its leitmotif. Let us take up each theme and see what it tells us about interpersonal communication as well as the field of communication study.

TRADITIONAL CORE QUESTIONS
OF INTERPERSONAL COMMUNICATION

The chapters on attitude similarity and attraction, compliance gaining, social skills manifestation, and verbal aggressiveness represent interesting attempts to deal with key issues in interpersonal communication. The sophistication of these meta-analyses represents the maturity of the conceptualizations around these core questions. In these chapters, the authors use meta-analysis in the service of improving both the research and theory.

Similarity and Attraction

A key question for the study of interpersonal communication is how we form, maintain, and dissolve (or redefine) interpersonal relationships. Clearly the role of communication is central in the process of forming and maintaining relationships. Communication is the process of developing intersubjectivity with, and impact on, a partner through the use of verbal and nonverbal codes (Noller & Fitzpatrick, 1993). Some theorists have even argued that relationships are the interaction between people over an extended period of time (e.g., Hinde, 1979), although others have viewed the constructs as discriminable (Fitzpatrick, 1988).

The study of attitude similarity and attraction was a natural move for students of interpersonal communication in the 1970s. Although there was a good deal of interest in the movement away from the study of attitude change as a dependent variable, it was easy to consider the study of attitudes as an independent variable and examine its effects on interpersonal outcomes like attraction. So, rather than developing explanatory frames for how various factors influenced attitudes, students of interpersonal communication became interested in how various attitudinal frames influenced interpersonal outcomes.

In the 1960s, a group of theorists using a reinforcement paradigm coined what was considered by many the first law of interpersonal attraction: Attitude similarity causes interpersonal attraction (see Byrne, 1997). Communication researchers argued that similarity works only if it translates into interaction. In other words, if potential partners have a chance to interact, the interaction becomes far more predictive of the relational outcome than does the initial starting attitudinal set. This insight was a powerful addition to the typical social psychological model of relationships and one that continuously echoes today in a number of chambers. Communication researchers like AhYun (chap. 9, this volume) are part of that important tradition in demonstrating the role communication plays in the attitude–attraction relation.

Compliance Gaining

Communication theory and communication researchers have been centrally interested in how individuals gain compliance from others. In the early 1970s, some of the interest in persuasion in mass media moved into the interpersonal realm as a concern for the processes of persuasion in a variety of interpersonal relationships. A feminist sociology of knowledge would say that the interest in power and the manipulation of others toward a given course of action could only have come from a male-dominated field, as men are preoccupied with control. As more female researchers rose to the forefront in the field, research questions addressed the expression of feelings, self-disclosure, and validation of the conversational partner. Whether one accepts this analysis or not, there has been a good deal of knowledge accumulated about how face-to-face interactants interact to persuade one another.

Included in this volume is a meta-analysis on sexual coercion and dating (Emmers-Sommer, chap. 19, this volume). The author grapples with important issues and their theoretical implications. Perhaps it is unusual that I have included the research on sexual coercion and resistance in this section rather than in the treatment of gender differences. Sexual coercion is about a man forcing a woman to engage in unwanted sexual activity and is usually a major facet of any consideration of gender, power, and relationships. I have grouped it with these chapters, however, because when entering this arena, the theorist is faced with the same core question as the social actor: When does seduction become rape? Is any persuasive attempt a violation of the rights of the partner? As theorists, we must grapple with these questions and what seems to be the most applied area actually requires posing essential conceptual questions.

Social Skills

The study of communication competence or social skills also emerged at about the same time. Increasingly, communication theorists became concerned with the smooth and easy flow of interaction and the manner in which communication maintained the face and line of the partner during the interaction. Conceptual distinctions had to be drawn between communication styles like assertiveness, argumentativeness, and aggressiveness. An examination of the skilled accomplishment of a conversation demanded that researchers actually focus on verbal and nonverbal behavioral exchanges during interaction.

It may be that one of the major accomplishments of the field of communication rests in the delineation of how conversation works to accomplish various ends. Involved in the careful, empirical delineation would be specific discussions of various verbal and nonverbal strategies and tactics that individuals use to accomplish their goals. The meta-analyses in this volume move us closer to this goal and allow us to begin to speak with some authority about how communication can be used to accomplish specific goals (see

Allen, chap. 13, this volume; Hample & Dallinger, chap. 11, this volume; Spitzberg & Dillard, chap. 6, this volume).

The focus of all the chapters in this section has as its underpinning the basic communication question: What works, when, and why? Whether we are discussing winning an argument without damaging a relationship or accomplishing a smooth social performance, our research has a utility to the members of the larger culture, including but not limited to, our students. The only way in which theory can become useful is when the theorist can discuss what people do under what conditions and to what effect.

In many ways, these chapters are strong additions to the social science literature because they bring a communication point of view to the foreground. These authors do not bemoan the fact that in many social science disciplines communication processes are considered error variance. Rather, through the power of their arguments and their data, they demonstrate how communication functions theoretically and how messages dramatically impact a variety of outcomes for social actors.

GENDER DIFFERENCES IN INTERPERSONAL COMMUNICATION

A number of the chapters in this book focus on some aspect of gender differences in interpersonal communication. The meta-analyses of gender differences in self-esteem, safe-sex talk, power in language, liking and self-disclosure, sources of social support, and interpersonal conflict represent core instances of an analysis of gender and power relations. It is probably not surprising that much of the intellectual energy in this book is taken up with questions surrounding gender differences. It is exciting to see communication researchers weighing in on one of the central debates in the social sciences. Questions of gender and power permeate not only academic debate, but also the culture at large. Scholars are embedded in their cultures and historical epochs and this influences the questions they pose, if not the answers they provide.

Our culture is as preoccupied with sex differences as it is with dieting and exercise. Since the 1960s, every decade has seen the emergence of popular books and articles on sex differences (e.g., Gray, 1992) and dieting (e.g., Stewart, Bethea, Andrews, Andrews, & Leighton, 1998). These books share certain argumentative features. Both offer a few simple explanations for the designated problem, develop vivid examples through personal testimony, weave in a few scientific citations, and offer simple and straightforward solutions for communication difficulties in personal relationships (e.g., when a man is in a negative state, treat him like a passing tornado and lie low) or having one's shadow grow bulkier (e.g., eat no sugar).

Communication theorists like Goldsmith and Fulfs (1999) have done an outstanding job of analyzing the claims and evidence presented in one such popular book on gender differences in communication. Spitzack (1990) critically examined the discourse of weight loss and cleverly deconstructed the messages sent to women by the popular media. Although I hope such fine critical work continues, communication scholars must also expand theoretically based, empirical research on gender differences in communication and accumulate these findings in rigorous meta-analyses.

Feminism, as one of the most important intellectual and social movements in the 20th century, has had a powerful albeit indirect impact on the communication research agenda (Wood, 1998). Eagly (1995) expressed concerns that feminism created a political climate that led to research that incorrectly minimized psychological gender differences. In response, Hyde and Plant (1995) countered that feminists did not have a uniform position on the issue (see also Wood & Dindia, 1998). In the 171 meta-analyses of psychological gender differences explored by Hyde and Plant (1995), as many feminists have argued for large gender differences as have argued for small ones.

However, a number of feminists in this discipline roundly reject neo-positivism because it relies on what they deem patriarchal models of scientific method and counting (Blair, Brown, & Baxter, 1994). According to this line of argument, women's ways of knowing are inherently unscientific and based on insight and personal experience translated through personal stories. Indeed, personal narrative is the major form of proof. Anyone can use the lens of gender, race, or class to illuminate social life, but I do not grant that being an insider gives one a better picture of social reality—different, perhaps, but not necessarily better. The wholesale move in the direction of idiosyncratic, personal insight leaves out an entire important methodological realm of the social sciences, namely ethnography and ethnomethodology.

Ethnography is a method of unstructured observational research developed by anthropologists for studying the work of groups from within. The researcher participates in the everyday lives of the groups under study. Ethnomethodology treats even the mundane aspects of social life as puzzling and tries to explain how a particular type of conduct occurs. In other words, this approach studies the everyday methods of practical reasoning used in the production and interpretation of social action. Focused as they are on the interpretation of the meaning of social actions, these approaches are very important for communication theorists who must be concerned with the development of intersubjectivity as well as the mutual influence and coordination of behavior (Fitzpatrick & Ritchie, 1990).

As a university professor and a student of interpersonal relationships, perhaps the most disturbing book I have read in the past decade is Holland and Eisenhart's (1990) study of women, achievement, and the college culture. In this fine-grained ethnographic analysis, the authors follow the lives of 23 young women in two Southern universities, one historically Black, the other White. The authors questioned past theories that attributed women's struggles with success to class resistance or academic barriers. Rather, the authors argued that a high-pressure peer system propels women into a world in college where their attractiveness to men counts most. The life of the mind counts for very little prestige; what matters is the man you attract. Any unrewarding academic experience or difficulty in a subject area leads these young women to devote more time and energy to finding, keeping, or manipulating a romantic partner. Eventually, this cycle erodes any visions of careers for these young women.

These powerful descriptions, combined with a trenchant theoretical analyses, can and should inform the development of specific hypotheses about gender and power relations in interpersonal communication. Indeed, many new insights can be gained by more in-depth understanding of the lives of our research participants outside of the laboratory. Descriptive ethnographies and ethnomethodologies can put flesh on the empirical skeleton and help us to understand the meanings that social acts and outcomes have for members of our culture. Such work, however, demands that we go beyond our own experiences and reactions.

In addition to these descriptive social scientists, many empirical social scientists reject the argument that rigorous research is by definition not feminist. Indeed, Hyde (1994) persuasively argued that the very technique of meta-analysis can make feminist transformations in social science. According to Hyde, the proper use of meta-analysis can challenge long-standing beliefs of gender differences; demonstrate the extent to which gendered behavior is context dependent and the product of gender roles; examine the intersection of gender, race, and ethnicity; and finally provide powerful data to counter assertions of difference and female inferiority that proliferate in the popular media (see Andersen, 1998).

In their meta-theoretical statement, Deaux and La France (1988) persuasively argued that gender differences are not manifest in all situational contexts. In other words, perceivers, individuals, and situations vary in the content and salience of gender expectations. Thus, after decades of research, we must specify the conditions under which we can expect gender differences and gender similarities in communication behavior. In a thoughtful treatment, Aries (1996) argued that how men and women behave in interaction depends on such moderating factors as the demands of the task, the length of the interaction, the sex composition of the group, and the relationship between the participants. These factors are, of course, the type of factors that make gender more or less salient in an interaction.

A major problem for the meta-analysis chapters on gender in this book is that they have neglected to consider larger theoretical claims as they make their arguments. The entire gender studies enterprise is now both personalized and politicized to such a degree that the accumulation of findings through meta-analyses without a disciplined concern for theory and for the assessment of the meaning and the magnitude of gender differences and similarities is doomed to failure. Communication researchers need to be at the forefront of the debates about gender, power, and human relationships, but those at the forefront must come armed with data. Both the academic community and the culture at large demand specific, documented answers to questions about how the microprocesses of language and communication relate to this central question in the social sciences.

CONCLUSION

My approach in this chapter has been a broad one. I have tried to discuss the rhetorical structure of meta-analysis and demonstrate by exemplars the best way to utilize the information gathered with this technique to advance the building of theories about interpersonal communication. My major concern centered on how scholars could best structure their arguments about the magnitudes of the differences they uncover. As I have summarized the various meta-analyses in this chapter, however, I have simply adopted the language of the authors to describe the "magnitude of the differences" they uncovered. However, there is a Mad Hatter quality to my use of this language ("Words mean what I want them to mean"). A discussion of the magnitude of these effects demands the development of arguments requiring a number of different types of comparative data. The knowledge of science, however, is the knowledge of difference and an understanding of the magnitude of the difference cannot help but make our theories stronger and capable of greater specification. In other words, I wonder if I have created another layer of interpretation that creates more questions than it answers.

Another problem for these chapters is the narrowness of some of the reviews of the literature. Meta-analysis demands that the researcher access the population of studies on a given topic. As such, the searching of databases and the consideration of key terms and words that are used in the search becomes central to the research enterprise. Everyone seems aware of the file drawer problem but authors must be diligent and not miss work that is germane to the topic under study. Too many of these types of lacunae in a meta-analysis can seriously undercut the confidence of the reader in the author's conclusions.

Finally, I have taken a rather casual sociology of knowledge approach to the topics covered in this book and divided them into two major groups. The first group grappled with gender differences and the second employed meta-analysis to examine a variety of traditional topics in the study of interpersonal communication. By choice of topic and theory testing, as well as their careful analytic work, the chapters in this volume represent a number of advances for the study of interpersonal communication through meta-analysis.

REFERENCES

Andersen, P. A. (1998). Researching sex differences within sex similarities: The evolutionary consequences of reproductive differences. In D. J. Canary & K. Dindia (Eds.), *Sex differences and similarities in communication* (pp. 83–100). Mahwah, NJ: Lawrence Erlbaum Associates.

Aries, E. (1996). *Men and women in interaction.* New York: Oxford University Press.

Blair, C., Brown, C. J., & Baxter, L. (1994). Disciplining the feminine. *Quarterly Journal of Speech, 80,* 383–409.

Burgoon, M. (1998). Social influence research: At the helm, on the edge, or over the abyss? Quod enim malvut homo verum est id potius credit. In J. S. Trent (Ed.), *Communication: Views from the helm for the 21st Century* (pp. 88–93). Needham Heights, MA: Allyn & Bacon.

Burgraff, C., & Sillars, A. (1986, November). *A critical examination of sex differences in marital communication.* Paper presented at the annual meeting of the Speech Communication Association, Chicago.

Byrne, D. (1997). An overview (and underview) of research and theory within the attraction to paradigm. *Journal of Social and Personal Relationships, 14,* 417–431.

Collins, R., & Miller, L. (1994). Self-disclosure and liking: A meta-analytic review. *Psychological Bulletin, 116,* 457–475.

Deaux, K., & La France, M. (1998). Gender. In D. T. Gilbert & S. T. Fiske (Eds.), *Handbook of social psychology,* (Vol. 2, pp. 788–827). Boston: McGraw-Hill.

Dillard, J. (1998). Evaluating and using meta-analytic knowledge claims (pp. 257–270). In M. Allen & R. W. Preiss (Eds.), *Persuasion: Advances through meta-analysis.* Cresskill, NJ: Hampton.

Dindia, K., & Allen, M. (1992). Sex differences in self-disclosure: A meta-analysis. *Psychological Bulletin, 112,* 106–124.

Eagly, A. (1995). The science and politics of comparing men and women. *American Psychologist, 50,* 145–158.

Feingold, A. (1994). Gender differences in personality: A meta-analysis. *Psychological Bulletin, 116,* 429–456.

Fitzpatrick, M. A. (1988). *Between husbands and wives: Communication in marriage.* Newbury Park, CA: Sage.

Fitzpatrick, M. A. (1991). Sex differences in marital conflict: Social psychophysiological versus cognitive explanations. *Text, 11,* 341–364.

Fitzpatrick, M. A. (1999). Racing toward the millennium: Twenty-five years of research on communication in relationships. *Human Communication Research, 25,* 443–448.

Fitzpatrick, M. A., Fallis, S., & Vance, L. (1982). Multifunctional coding of conflict resolution strategies in marital dyads. *Family Relations, 31,* 611–670.

Fitzpatrick, M. A., & Ritchie, D. (1990). Communication theory and the family. In P. G. Boss, W. J. Doherty, R. La Rossa, W. R. Schumm, & S. K. Steinmetz (Eds.), *Sourcebook of family theory and methods: A contextual approach* (pp. 565–585). New York: Plenum.

Gagnon, J. H., & Simon, W. (1973). *Sexual conduct: The social origins of human sexuality.* Chicago: Aldine.

Gayle, B., Preiss, R., & Allen, M. (1994). Gender differences and the use of conflict strategies. In L. Turner & H. Sterk (Eds.), *Differences that make a difference: Examining the assumptions in gender research* (pp. 13–26). Westport, CT: Bergin & Garvey.

Goldsmith, D. & Fulfs, P. (1999). "You just don't have the evidence": An analysis of claims and evidence in Deborah Tannen's You Just Don't Understand. In M. Roloff (Ed.), *Communication yearbook 22.* Thousand Oaks, CA: Sage.

Gray, J. (1992). *Men are from Mars: Women are from Venus.* New York: Harper Collins.

Hall, J. A. (1984) *Nonverbal sex differences.* Baltimore: Johns Hopkins University Press.

Hall, J. A. (1998). How big are nonverbal sex differences: The case of smiling and sensitivity to nonverbal cues. In D. J. Canary & K. Dindia (Eds.) *Sex differences and similarities in communication* (pp. 155–178). Mahwah, NJ: Erlbaum.

Hinde, R. (1979). *Towards understanding relationships.* London: Academic Press.

Holland, D .C. & Eisenhart, M. A. (1990) *Educated in Romance: Women, Achievement and College Culture.* Chicago: University of Chicago Press.

Hunter, J., & Schmidt, F. (1982). *Meta-analysis.* Newbury Park, CA: Sage.

Hyde, J. (1994). Can meta-analysis make feminist transformations in psychology? *Psychology of Women Quarterly, 18,* 451–462.

Hyde. J., & Plant, E. A. (1995). Magnitude of psychological sex differences: Another side to the story. *American Psychologist, 50*(3), 159–161.

Jourard, S. M. (1971). *The transparent self.* New York: Van Rostrand Reinhold.

Maccoby, E. E., & Jacklin, C. N. (1974). *The psychology of sex differences.* Stanford, CA: Stanford University Press.

Noller, P., & Fitzpatrick, M. A. (1990). *Communication in family relationships.* Englewood Cliffs, NJ: Prentice-Hall.

Oliver, M. B., & Hyde, J. S. (1993). Gender differences in sexuality: A meta-analysis. *Psychological Bulletin, 114,* 29–51.

Oliver, M. B., & Hyde, J. (1995). Gender differences in attitudes toward homosexuality: A reply to Whitley and Kite. *Psychological Bulletin, 117,* 155–158.

Sillars, A. L., Colletti, S. F., Parry, D., & Rogers, M. A. (1982). Coding verbal conflict tactics: Nonverbal and perceptual correlates of the "avoidance-distributive-integrative" distinction. *Human Communication Research, 9,* 83–95.

Sillars, A., Pike, G. R., Jones, T. S., & Redmon, K. (1983). Communication and conflict in marriage: One style is not satisfying to all. In R. Bergstrom (Ed.), *Communication yearbook 7* (pp. 414–431). Beverly Hills, CA: Sage.

Spitzack, C. (1990). *Confessing excess: Women and the politics of body reduction*. Albany: State University of New York Press.

Stewart, H. L., Bethea, M. C., Andrews, S. S., Andrews, S. S., & Leighton, S. (1998). *Sugar busters: Cut sugar to trim fat*. New York: Ballantine.

Whitely, B. E., & Kite, M. E. (1995). Sex differences in attitudes toward homosexuality: A comment on Oliver and Hyde (1993). *Psychological Bulletin, 117,* 146–154.

Wood, J. T. (1998). From isolation to integration: Gender's place in the core of communication knowledge. In J. S. Trent (Ed.), *Communication: Views form the helm of the 21st century* (pp. 184–188). Needham Heights, MA: Allyn & Bacon.

Wood, J. T. & Dindia, K. (1998). What's the difference? A dialogue about differences and similarities between women and men. In D. J. Canary & K. Dindia (Eds.), *Sex differences and similarities in communication* (pp.19–40). Mahwah, NJ: Lawrence Erlbaum Associates.

22

The State of the Art of Interpersonal Communication Research: Are We Addressing Socially Significant Issues?

Michael E. Roloff

The task of writing a "state of the art" essay focused on interpersonal communication research is a formidable one. The writer confronts multiple obstacles, the first of which is to decide how broadly to cast the review. Initially, my penchant for completeness prompted me to consider writing an omnibus evaluation of the literature. However, with a research area as diverse and large as that focused on interpersonal communication and being mindful of page limitations, there was the distinct possibility I would overlook important bodies of research, or that I would give short shrift to the key issues in some specializations. Fortunately, selected volumes of *The Communication Yearbook* (e.g., Burleson, 1995), the two editions of *The Handbook of Interpersonal Communication* (Knapp & Miller, 1985, 1994), and of course, this volume contain excellent reviews of specialized research areas that render unnecessary a single review focused on each and every one of our specializations. Hence, I chose to cast this chapter at a high level of abstraction in which I identify issues facing all interpersonal communication researchers regardless of their specialization. Although I mention specific research programs, I do so only to provide illustrations of my points rather than to imply that they embody the entirety of interpersonal communication scholarship.

My choice to focus on general trends and issues solved some of my problems but had little effect on others. Foremost in mind was how to critique our research in a manner that was not largely redundant with the criticisms raised in past commentary. Over the past two decades, communication scholars have not been shy about engaging one another over perceived problems in the conduct of our research. Lively debates have centered on the quantity of (Berger, 1991, 1998; Chautauqua, 1992; Shields, 1998) and type of theories (Benson & Pearce, 1977) that we employ. Clashes have occurred over issues related to the desirability of the ideologies implicit within our research (Burgoon, 1995; Lannamann, 1991; Parks, 1982, 1995). Moreover, scholars have disagreed as to whether or not our commitment to social scientific methods has resulted in valuable insights into communication phenomena (Miller, 1981) or has simply led to the premature abandonment of our commitment to teaching skills to undergraduates (Phillips, 1981) and has unduly fragmented the field (Chautauqua, 1990a). Finally, it is clear that researchers differ as to the types of evidence that they are willing to accept as knowledge claims (Chautauqua, 1990b; Fisher, 1977; Petronio, 1994).

Although those issues just discussed form only a partial list of critiques and controversies, it should be clear that the "state of the art" is a contestable issue. One's conclusion reflects his or her assessment of the underlying value systems of our approaches, the quantity and quality of the theoretical perspectives that inform our research, and the limitations imposed by the methods used to acquire our data. However valuable, these critiques have overlooked a critical standard for evaluating our research: To what degree does interpersonal communication research inform as to the cause and management of socially significant problems? In other words, holding aside the quality of our ideologies, theories, and methods, are we directly addressing issues that are important to and benefit individuals other than those of us conducting the research?

My concern for this issue emerged during a panel at the annual convention of the Speech Communication Association in 1995. I was part of a group of scholars who were invited to speak at a preconvention conference sponsored by the Interpersonal and Small Group Interaction Division that was entitled "Beyond 2000: Visions for the Future." Being the last speaker, I had the opportunity to ponder the messages of all of the other presenters prior to delivering my own observations. Each speaker addressed one or more issues of central importance to researchers working in a given area.

However, as I listened to each presenter, I became increasingly unsettled. Although each presentation was well crafted, reasoned, and delivered, I found myself asking the question, "Even if we settle these issues, what of social significance will be achieved?" I could easily see the contribution to scholars working in the area, but I was unclear about the benefit to anyone else. This is not to say that interpersonal communication researchers are any more self-absorbed and self-interested than are those researching in other areas of communication or in academe in general; indeed, I do not believe that we are. Instead, by and large, we have not been challenged to demonstrate the social significance of our research. Therefore, we have been afforded the luxury of setting our own research agenda and evaluating its significance. Indeed, textbooks about research methods advise young scholars to choose topics for investigation that are interesting to themselves and to the field (e.g., Tucker, Weaver, & Berryman-Fink, 1981). However, the recent economic problems plaguing U.S. universities have challenged the way we do our business. One such change is that citizens, state legislators, university administrators, and our colleagues in other departments are requiring that we show that our research is of use to individuals outside the field and the university, lest scarce resources be reallocated from us to those in more deserving or powerful specializations, fields, and disciplines (see Avery, 1995; Bach, 1997; Koester, 1996).

My objective in this chapter is to examine the extent to which research in interpersonal communication addresses socially significant issues. To do so, I first articulate the characteristics of socially significant research and then present several examples that seem to fit my conception. I end with an assessment of the problems associated with conducting such scholarship.

SOCIALLY SIGNIFICANT RESEARCH

In my view, socially significant research is scholarship that addresses issues of importance to society. In effect, such research explores the causes and solutions to problems that are on the national agenda. Consequently, socially significant scholarship is problem centered, and the problems chosen for study arise from "macro-social concerns" (Burgoon & Miller, 1990). In my view, conducting socially significant scholarship will not require substantial changes in the technical manner in which research is performed. Indeed, I suspect that researchers could employ many of the same methodological and statistical tools that are currently used. Instead, it forces us to perform research that demonstrates how interpersonal communication is linked to problems deemed by society to require action. To meet this demand, I would argue that interpersonal communication research must have four characteristics.

First, our scholarship must have a clear focus on some aspect of human interaction. One can approach social problems from a variety of perspectives, not all of which are directly related to interpersonal communication. Hence, a person unfamiliar with our area might ask, "What exactly is it that interpersonal communication researchers bring to the national conversation about this issue that is distinct from that of other scholars?" One of the most positive trends I have seen during the last two decades is a common focus on interaction processes among those researchers who identify themselves as interpersonal communication scholars (Knapp, Miller, & Fudge, 1994). Although I am doubtful that there is consensus as to exactly how to define and operationalize interaction phenomena, at least there is some agreement that the study of the linguistic and nonlinguistic behaviors enacted during an interchange constitutes our mission.

However, simply stating that we study interaction is insufficient to establish our social worth. We must also establish conceptual frameworks that inform as to the antecedents and consequences of interaction. In essence, we need to develop theories. As noted earlier, the case for vigorous theory construction has been made and debated elsewhere. I would only advance one additional argument for theory development. It is my experience that individuals outside of our field are interested not only in what we find but the principle that explains the results. They are not necessarily concerned with the metatheoretical assumptions that underlie the explanation or whether the form of the theory is propositional or not. Indeed, many are quite pleased with a story-like exposition of our arguments. Regardless of form, they do want to see a conceptual framework that informs as to our logic.

Third, we must provide relevant data. Interpersonal communication researchers have vigorously critiqued and debated aspects of our methods, including inductive versus deductive approaches to strategy development (Boster, Stiff, & Reynolds, 1985; Wiseman & Schenk-Hamlin, 1981), strategy selection versus message composition (Boster, 1988; Burleson & Wilson, 1988; Burleson et al., 1988; Seibold, 1988), representational validity (Poole & Folger, 1981), the message as fixed effects fallacy ("Colloquy," 1983, 1988; Hunter, Hamilton, & Allen, 1989; Jackson, O'Keefe, Jacobs, & Bashers, 1989), and the conceptual and operational clarity of our measures (Kellermann & Cole, 1994). Such critiques have raised important issues and probably have increased our sensitivity to the quality of our methods. However, my experience with individuals outside of our field leads me to believe that these issues are not of great importance to them. Instead, external audiences are more concerned with the relevancy of our data. By relevancy, I mean that the nature of our samples and our measures allow us to speak directly to the issue at hand. For example, if a researcher wishes to uncover the communication processes that lead to divorce, then investigating interaction patterns associated with the end of courting relationships will be insufficient. The greater legal, financial, and social bonds associated with marriage mitigate against uncritically generalizing from data garnered from individuals who are terminating their dating relationships to those who are ending their marriages. However, that is not to say that studying samples of courting individuals is never relevant. A scholar might wish to establish that communication practices that occur during courting predict subsequent divorce (e.g., Markman, 1979, 1981) and certainly, there are problems such as courtship abuse that require our attention (e.g., Stets & Henderson, 1991). Hence, I do not want to limit the scope of our inquiry to one sample. Instead, we must be prepared to demonstrate that the sample being studied can provide relevant insights into the problem.

Beyond the relevancy of our samples, we must also be concerned with the degree to which we are directly assessing the problem at hand. Interpersonal communication researchers have relied heavily on dependent measures that assess satisfaction with the relationship or the interaction, perceptions of communicator competency, attraction, mood, or understanding. From the purview of researchers in our specialization, each of these measures has led to useful knowledge about interaction. However, these measures may not always speak directly to socially significant problems. To stay with my earlier example, a researcher whose ultimate aim is to inform as to the communication processes that lead to divorce may encounter skepticism if he or she exclusively studies marital satisfaction. Certainly, marital satisfaction and the likelihood of divorce are negatively related, but not perfectly. Indeed, one can identify long-term, stable marriages in which both spouses are dissatisfied (Heaton & Albrecht, 1991; Lauer & Lauer, 1986) and some marriages end in divorce regardless of their level of marital satisfaction (Udry, 1981). Hence, interaction predictors of marital satisfaction may not completely inform as to the likelihood of divorce. Of course, one might argue that there is a path leading from interaction to dissatisfaction to divorce, but a skeptic would require that we empirically demonstrate such a sequence, which of course means including a measure of divorce along with our measures of interaction and satisfaction.

Even if we have a distinct focus on interaction that is informed by theory and we are able to generate relevant data, we still might not be deemed to be socially relevant; we also must choose some area of inquiry that is of social concern. This final requirement is difficult, for it requires the researcher to monitor the concerns of society, and we may not be accustomed to looking externally for our research agenda. Sources of such data include calls for action from societal leaders as well as legislation. In addition, the mass media constitute a rich source of such information. Although I am not advocating that we use the content of talk shows to dictate our research agendas, public opinion polls are reported that identify the important issues the nation faces. Moreover, there is evidence that media news coverage and commentary can create, highlight, or reflect the national agenda (e.g., McCombs, Danielian, & Wanta, 1995). Although not perfect indicators, the aforementioned are sources from which we might assess the issues that are socially significant.

Having described what I believe to be defensible criteria for identifying socially significant research, the next task is to determine whether there are areas of interpersonal communication research that fit my conception. I turn to that next.

SOCIALLY SIGNIFICANT INTERPERSONAL COMMUNICATION RESEARCH

In choosing exemplars, I focused on research that demonstrated a clear impact of interaction on socially significant problems. In doing so, I do not wish to imply that my list of social problems is complete, nor do I want to suggest that any unmentioned research is necessarily deficient. My sole purpose is to present the clearest examples from those areas with which I am familiar. Given that goal, I can identify four socially significant problems that are related to interaction processes: (a) divorce, (b) violent crime, (c) health care, and (d) incivility. I consider each in turn.

Divorce

In the United States, marriage affords a variety of advantages. Individuals who marry and stay married experience greater psychological well-being (e.g., Horwitz, White, & Howell-White, 1996) and lower mortality (e.g., Lillard & Waite, 1995) than do those who remain single or divorce. Furthermore, relative to children living in intact families, children whose parents are divorced or separated evidence somewhat lower levels of psychological and social well-being (Amato & Keith, 1991b) and such decrements may be greater when they become adults (Amato & Keith, 1991a). Given these patterns, it is not surprising that the populace is disturbed by a divorce rate that is estimated to be as high as 67% (Martin & Bumpass, 1989) and appears to be increasing (Gottman, 1994a). Indeed, some surveys find that many individuals believe that obtaining a divorce should be made more difficult (National Opinion Research Center, 1994), and some states have considered legislation that would do just that. However, rather than entrapping individuals in unhappy unions, it makes more sense to identify the causes of divorce and to devise treatments that would overcome them. If the marriage cannot be saved, then we must find ways to help individuals cope with the divorce.

Research demonstrates that interaction processes play an important role in divorce. When asked to identify what caused their marriage to break up, ex-spouses frequently implicate both lack of communication and prolonged arguing (Kitson, & Sussman, 1982). Although seemingly contradictory complaints (i.e., if one is arguing a great deal, there is no lack of talking), there is evidence that both of these communication problems can jointly occur and lead to divorce. In a longitudinal study of marital disruption (separation or divorce), McGonagle, Kessler, and Gotlib (1993) found that frequent arguing was positively correlated with avoiding discussion of issues due to fear of the partner's response, and those couples who argued and avoided a great deal were most at risk of relational dissolution. This pattern of concurrent arguing and avoidance is similar to that found among spouses who are emotionally separate (Fitzpatrick, 1988). Moreover, Rusbult, Verette, Whitney, Slovik, and Lipkus (1991) argued that individuals who are committed to their relationship will voice concerns over their partner's undesirable behaviors, whereas uncommitted individuals will neglect or exit the association. This implies that couples moving toward divorce may initially confront one another over problems; however, once they conclude the association cannot or should not be repaired, they are more likely to avoid or withdraw from conflict. Consistent with this notion, Courtright, Millar, Rogers, and Bagarozzi (1990) found among a sample of married couples going through counseling that those who ultimately divorced became less involved and more avoidant and indirect during their discussions of relational issues, whereas those who stayed together remained confrontational.

Perhaps Gottman (1993b) offered the clearest explanation of the link between interaction and divorce. It is clear that even individuals in happy marriages enact everyday behaviors that upset their spouses (e.g., Birchler, Wiess, & Vincent, 1975). However, the impact of such negative behavior can be offset by the positive actions that are performed by a partner. Based on empirical evidence, marriages remain stable when partners perceive a ratio of five positive actions for every negative one (Gottman, 1994a). When this ratio falls below that level, relational partners have feelings of righteous indignation and innocent victimhood, which in turn increase physiological arousal. As time goes on, negative feelings and arousal further reduce the ratio of positive to negative actions. At some point, individuals come to feel flooded with their spouse's negative affect, which results in distance and isolation from the spouse and recasting of the history of the marriage. From that point, separation and divorce follow.

Importantly, the previously cited process can be set off by an imbalance in the ratio of positive to negative behaviors enacted during marital interaction about relational problems (Gottman, 1994a). In other words, to remain stable, individuals should maintain the ratio of five positives to each negative interaction behavior. This does not mean that all married couples achieve this balance in the same way. Gottman (1993a) identified three stable marriages that have distinct ways of maintaining the balance. Volatile couples enact a great deal of negative emotional behavior during an argument but balance it with substantial positive actions such as humor and affection. Validating spouses are intermediate in their overall level of emotionality and balance their negative actions with statements that acknowledge each other's concerns. The conversations of conflict avoiders are very unemotional and often involve each person describing his or her concerns with no clash or attempted persuasion. Conversely, unstable couples are unable to maintain the balance of positive to negative interaction behavior either because their criticisms typically prompt defensiveness, or they go through cycles of mutual uninvolvement in the conversation followed by reciprocal attacks and defensiveness.

The aforementioned program of research also informs as to the contribution of sex differences to divorce. Gottman and Levenson (1988) reviewed evidence showing that men are more likely than women to respond to the negative affect that often occurs in marriage by withdrawing emotionally. In effect, men attempt to escape physiologically punitive situations. The authors speculated that this pattern is due to the greater physical sensitivity that men have to stressful situations relative to women. Because male withdrawal can be viewed negatively by women, the woman's perception of the balance of positive to negative actions is threatened. A key element in preventing the man from withdrawing stems from soothing his negative affect during the argument (Gottman, 1994a). Consistent with this view, Gottman, Coan, Carrere, and Swanson (1998) found that newlyweds are less likely to divorce when either the man or the woman engage in interaction behaviors that reduce his physiological arousal. These included the degree to which the wife employed humor, and the extent to which the husband responded to her negative affect with neutral affect, validated her position, and expressed affection for her. Indeed, the aforementioned variables predicted remaining married or divorcing in 83% of the cases.

Gottman et al. (1998) concluded that a key to predicting marital stability is the degree to which husbands accept influence from their wives. When husbands resist their wives' influence attempts, an escalating pattern of negative affect results, which in turn predicts divorce.

Although my discussion of research on divorce is brief, it indicates that interaction processes play an important role in causing divorce. Indeed, Gottman's research suggests that it is a role of sufficient magnitude that it cannot be ignored. Furthermore, if negative interaction patterns continue after a divorce, they can aversively impact the subsequent well-being of ex-spouses (Berman & Turk, 1981) and their children (Amato & Keith, 1991a, 1991b). Hence, we have clear evidence of the social significance of marital interaction.

Violent Crime

Surveys indicate that many Americans feel truly desperate about crime (Sherman, 1994), and at times, the populace view crime as the most important problem facing the country (Flanagan, 1996). Moreover, in one survey, roughly 20% reported that they worry about being murdered; 26% are concerned that they might be beaten up, knifed, or shot; and 31% fear that they could be physically attacked while driving (Haghighi & Sorenson, 1996). Although their apprehension may be exaggerated due to television coverage of violent crime (e.g., Chiricos, Eschholz, & Gertz, 1997; Haghighi & Sorensen, 1996), the physical and psychological toll inflicted on the victims of violent crime warrants concern. Hence, researchers have explored the causes and prevention of violent crimes.

There is evidence that interaction processes are one factor the lead to violence. In an early study, Luckenbill (1977) content analyzed the official documents related to 77 homicides. He uncovered evidence of a six-stage sequence that leads to a murder. Initially, the murder victim engaged in a behavior that was an affront to the murderer's image. In three quarters of the cases, the affront was an insult or a refusal to comply with a request. At the second stage, the murderer interpreted the victim's action as personal (i.e., intentionally offensive) often because the victim confirmed such an impression. Afterward, most murderers issued a physical or verbal challenge to the victim (Stage 3) and 14% killed the victim at this point. Of those cases in which no murder had yet been committed, the victim's action implied a willingness to enter into a working agreement to be violent (Stage 4). At this stage, the victim continued to engage in the offensive action, although many physically retaliated or counterchallenged the murderer. At Stage 5, the murderer accepted the victim's definition of the situation and used a weapon to perform the crime. The last stage focused on the aftermath of the murder. Most murderers fled the scene, although about 40% either voluntarily stayed or were held by witnesses. In 70% of the cases, individuals witnessed the crime and their response varied. In roughly a third of those cases, the witnesses apprehended the murderer, tried to aid the victim, and called the police. However, in 48% of the cases, onlookers helped the murderer to escape, destroyed evidence, and refused to cooperate with the police investigation. Taken as a whole, these stages constitute an interaction sequence.

Felson (1978) created an impression management theory of aggression that provides further insight into the interaction processes involved in violent crimes. He argued that aggression is a retaliatory response to an attack on one's face. By retaliating, one can demonstrate relative strength and perhaps force the perpetrator of the face attack to apologize or take back the insult. However, not all face attacks prompt retaliation. The likelihood of retaliation is hypothesized to increase when (a) the insult is perceived to be intentional and illegitimate, (b) when others observe the affront or encourage retaliation, and (c) the insult attacked an especially important part of the self-concept.

Research supports some of Felson's (1978) theory. Data garnered from records of felonious assaults, manslaughters, and homicides indicate that identity attacks occur early in a violent encounter and are often followed by influence attempts and noncompliance (Felson & Steadman, 1983). Threats appear to be used as a measure of last resort and evasion is often attempted late in the sequence (Felson & Steadman, 1983). Third parties play an important role in the sequence. Onlookers are sometimes allies of the offender or the victim or may have instigated a violent episode that required the assistance of the offender or the victim (Felson, Ribner, & Siegel, 1984). Moreover, when third parties enacted aggressive behaviors, the offender became more aggressive (Felson et al., 1984).

When analyzing a variety of disputes including some in which (a) no confrontation occurred, (b) only verbal aggression occurred, (c) hitting occurred, or (d) a weapon was used, Felson (1982, 1984) identified a three-stage sequence leading to severe violence. First, a person is observed committing a rule violation and the witness chooses to confront him or her. Typically, orders to cease the behavior are met with noncompliance and reproaches tend to escalate the conflict. However, if the rule violator offers an account for his or her action, escalation is much less likely. Second, individuals move to a stage of threats and insults that escalate to physical violence. Finally, one party submits or a third party mediates the dispute, which brings the encounter to an end short of violence. If third parties are neutral or encourage aggressive responses, then a violent outcome results.

The previously cited research suggests that violent crimes emerge from an interaction in which a person unsuccessfully attempts to control the behavior of another, which leads to identity attacks. To overcome and punish resistance as well as to restore face, aggressive responses result. Such processes are also found in episodes of domestic abuse (Roloff, 1996). Clearly then, interaction processes play an important role in violent crime.

Health Care

With increasing life span and rapidly expanding health care costs, the United States faces a problem of how to deliver affordable, quality health care to all of its citizens. This issue has occupied public officials and citizens alike and is not likely to go away. There is evidence that interaction processes are related to health care issues.

Everyday life in the United States can be stressful. When describing a recent emotional experience, more than two-thirds of the individuals surveyed described a negative event (Scherer & Tannenbaum, 1986). Among the reported aversive events were those in which the respondents felt fear or anxiety accompanied by physical symptoms such as shortness of breath, stomach cramps, shivers, changes in heartbeat, muscle tensing or shaking, and profuse sweating. Also, some respondents indicated situations involving profound sadness, which was manifested by a wavering voice, crying, and sometimes stomach cramps and shivers. Interestingly, respondents also reported that they actively tried to hide these feelings from others. This latter reaction could seriously and aversively impact a person's health. There is ample evidence that individuals who repress their emotional expression retard the ability of their immune system to combat disease (see, Petrie, Booth, & Davison, 1995).

Pennebaker (1989) offered a theory that describes the link between expression of emotional trauma and health. Essentially, individuals who actively attempt to inhibit their feelings, thoughts, and behavior arising from an emotionally traumatic event must engage in considerable physiological effort. In the short term, this effort increases the person's stress level, and if continued for quite some time becomes a significant additional stressor that makes him or her more susceptible to stress-related physical and mental problems. Moreover, by not confronting the emotional turmoil, the individual is prevented from gaining insight into his or her problem, and therefore cannot achieve resolution. In contrast, although confronting emotional turmoil may be immediately stressful, sustained confrontation reduces stress reactions and increases the likelihood of gaining self-insight into the source of the problem. Thus, confrontation may facilitate a person's psychological and physical well-being. Although not without methodological limitations, there is evidence that individuals who talk or write about their feelings concerning traumatic events in their lives show increased immune system activity relative to those who do not disclose them (see Petrie et al., 1995). Moreover, individuals who are prone to inhibit their emotional expression to stressful situations have elevated levels of muscle tension related to headaches and back pain (Traue, 1995).

Although insightful, the aforementioned research is only suggestive of the possible health-related benefits of interacting about emotional turmoil. Typically, participants in this research are asked to talk or write about their experiences in an isolated, private context (Pennebaker, 1989). Although the researchers make every attempt to create rapport with participants in the study prior to their description of their problems (i.e., they indicate concern for the participants), the disclosure occurs without anyone being present and with strong assurances that no attempt will be made to link the content of disclosure to the name of the participant. In part, researchers are concerned that more natural contextual cues such as having another person present during disclosure would socially inhibit communication, and there is some evidence in support of this conjecture (Pennebaker, Hughes, & O'Heeron, 1987). This implies that to be helpful, those who interact with individuals who have undergone emotional trauma must find ways of making disclosure easier. Indeed, individuals who have lost a loved one report that providing the opportunity to emotionally vent is one of the most helpful gestures they received from others (Lehman, Ellard, & Wortman, 1986). One means might be for the helper to also engage in emotional expression. By doing so, the helper might make the individual feel more comfortable with disclosing his or her feelings. Indeed, several studies have found that improved health outcomes are related to emotional exchange between physician and patient (Heszen-Klemens & Lapkinska, 1984; Kaplan, Greenfield, & Ware, 1989).

Although expressing emotional reactions to stressful situations seems to be an important factor in health care, it is also important that information exchange occur. Research on doctor–patient interaction finds that a patient's health improves when the physician not only provides information and advice but also successfully solicits information from the patient (see Thompson, 1994). Unfortunately, some research indicates that information exchange tends to be limited in scope. For example, Makoul, Arntson, and Schofield (1995) found that in videotaped interactions between general practitioners and patients about prescription drugs, information exchange tended to be asymmetrical, primarily flowing from the doctor to the patient and heavily focused on instructions for using the drugs, with minimal discussion of possible side effects, risks, or the patient's ability to carry out the treatment plan. Although the researchers did not include a measure of whether the patient subsequently carried out the treatment plan or whether there were any changes in the patient's health quality, the absence of such critical treatment-related information may explain why patients often fail to follow their doctor's orders (Thompson, 1994). Thus, we have evidence that a person's health can be affected by his or her interaction with others.

Incivility

In a survey of 1,000 U.S. adults, 88% felt that incivility was a serious problem facing our society and more than 80% believed incivility has the effect of increasing violence, dividing communities, and eroding moral values (*U.S. News and World Report*, 1996). Although only 28% felt that Americans speak in an uncivil manner (e.g., use rude and vulgar language), 67% believed that everyday speech has become more uncivil over the last decade. Concern over provocative speech has caused some universities and even some communities to adopt rules of civil conduct.

Research focused on the consequences of uncivil speech suggests that it warrants concern. Frequently experiencing negative interaction behaviors such as criticism, broken promises, mocking, being talked down to, and unwanted sexual advances from individuals in one's social network reduces psychological well-being (Lakey, Tardiff, & Drew, 1994; Rook, 1984). Moreover, individuals who receive inconsiderate criticism of their task performance become angry, try to avoid or resist the critic, and have lower self-efficacy than do those who receive considerate criticism (Baron, 1988). When receiving inconsiderate negative feedback from an in-group authority, individuals suffer greater loss of self-esteem and felt respect within the social system than when receiving considerate negative feedback (Smith, Tyler, Huo, Ortiz, & Lind, 1998). Even individuals who engage in uncivil speech often experience negative outcomes. Direct verbal attacks and criticism figure prominently among statements people regret having made, in part because of the personal and relational harm that they do (Knapp, Stafford, & Daly, 1986).

Although the aforementioned research focuses on individual well-being, it is possible that incivility impacts society as a whole. Tyler and Lind (1992) developed a model that posits that a person's commitment and voluntary compliance to the authorities of a social system is partially a function of the degree to which such figures treat the person with dignity and politeness. When treated in an inconsiderate manner by authority figures, the individual may feel that those in charge follow unfair decision-making procedures and do not consider him or her to be a valuable member of the group. Consequently, an individual perceives authorities to be illegitimate and has little desire to voluntarily comply with their directives. Indeed, if seen as a general pattern of inconsiderateness, a single rude encounter with an authority figure may be sufficient to reduce commitment to the social system (Tyler, Degoey, & Smith, 1996).

Because incivility can reduce the well-being of individuals and the social system in which they reside, it is essential that we identify its causes. To do so, it is helpful to define what might be considered incivility. At its core, incivility implies that a person has violated an expectation for socially appropriate behavior. One such expectation is that an individual should honor another's projected image or at least try to avoid violating his or her face (McCall & Simmons, 1978). Although the precise nature of face is complex (Lim & Bowers, 1991) and expectations for being face-supportive are not equal for all individuals (Burgoon, Dillard, & Doran, 1983), there is a general expectation that individuals should communicate in a polite and considerate manner.

In some cases, the cause of incivility resides within the speaker. For example, some individuals have a predisposition to attack the self-concepts of others (Infante & Rancer, 1996) and consequently intentionally enact a variety of forms of verbal aggression (Infante, Riddle, Horvath, & Tulmin, 1992). Alternatively, the tendency to attribute incivility to another may also vary among individuals. Hample (1999) noted that some individuals are predisposed to perceive any form of opposition to their stances and positions as an attack on their self-concepts, and hence, they may see any criticism directed toward their positions as being more verbally aggressive than do others.

It is also possible that incivility emerges out of a pattern of interaction between two people. Baumeister, Stillwell, and Wotman (1990) asked individuals to provide accounts of situations in which someone had angered them and of incidences in which they had angered someone else. The two sets of narratives suggested different outlooks on the interaction. When having been angered by someone else, individuals were more likely to perceive the situation as having resulted from accumulating provocation, attempts to avoid a confrontation on their part, and continued harm after the confrontation than if they had angered another. When having angered someone else, individuals were more likely to perceive the problem as being an isolated incident, that the confronter's anger was exaggerated and unjustified, and that the problem had been resolved after the initial confrontation than if someone had angered them. These data imply that a person might be perceived to have acted in an uncivil manner for quite some time without being aware of it. However, the victim is indeed quite aware, and after having had enough of it, angrily confronts the perpetrator, which is itself perceived to be done in an uncivil fashion. Moreover, the perception by the victim that the provocations and harm continue after the initial confrontation suggests that incivility may further escalate. Recently, Mikolic, Parker, and Pruitt (1997) found an interaction sequence that occurred as individuals tried to deal with another's persistently annoying behavior. The sequence followed these seven steps: requests to stop the annoying action, impatient demands, complaints, angry statements, threats, verbal harassment, and verbal abuse. Although completing the entire sequence is moderated by a variety of factors (Mikolic et al., 1997; Pruitt, Parker, & Mikolic, 1997), the pattern suggests that individuals initially attempt to influence others in an assertive but socially acceptable fashion, and after experiencing repeated noncompliance, they act in a manner that is increasingly verbally aggressive and less civil.

Clearly, my brief discussion indicates that the causes of incivility are complex. However, it is equally clear that as in the cases of divorce, violent crime, and health care, interaction processes are an important part of incivility. Hence, it seems reasonable that interpersonal communication researchers continue to explore these socially significant problems and to investigate new ones. However, to do so will not be unproblematic.

PROBLEMS WITH STUDYING SOCIETAL PROBLEMS

I must admit that at the outset of this project I was uncertain as to what I would find. Most literature reviews of interpersonal communication research are organized by communication phenomena (e.g., nonverbal communication, language) or by context (e.g., family communication) rather than by societal problem. Often reviewers do not even address issues of social relevancy. I was pleased and relieved to find examples of researchers who are addressing socially significant issues, and who often produce startling evidence that interaction processes play a substantial role in social problems. That is not to imply that the research I reviewed is perfect. I am sure that a more detailed analysis of the aforementioned scholarship would reveal shortcomings. Regardless, they provide plausible evidence of our social relevancy.

However, I also uncovered some bad news. The reader who is familiar with the research I cited will have noted that the majority of studies were conducted by scholars who are not in communication departments, and it is doubtful that they would label themselves interpersonal communication researchers. Although this could simply reflect a selection bias on my part, I think it actually reflects the fact that researchers outside of communication have historically done a better job addressing socially significant issues. This is not to say that our research is of low quality. Indeed, had I approached this task in a traditional way, I could identify research programs conducted by scholars in communication departments that are theoretically grounded, methodologically rigorous, and important to the field. However, this scholarship often falls short of directly addressing social problems. Indeed, to establish its significance, one must argumentatively finesse the issue of social relevancy by noting possible implications for social problems rather than by presenting direct empirical links. In my opinion, this strategy is no longer optimal. Hence, we need more research that provides such direct links.

To conduct socially significant research will not be without difficulties. I discuss six problems and challenges. First, our research will need to be interdisciplinary and collaborative. Many social problems have been the province of other fields and disciplines, and they have strong interests, extensive literatures, and methodological resources (e.g., relevant samples and measurement techniques) that can be brought to bear in conducting research. For example, the study of divorce is an important area for scholars in clinical psychology and family studies. Professors in medical schools are interested in doctor–patient interaction. Criminologists have explored violent crime. If we remain isolated from these groups, our research will be difficult to conduct and will not be visible to those who have strong traditional interests in the area. Although establishing such interdisciplinary connections can be difficult, they are a necessary ingredient for establishing our social significance.

Second, we must expand the focus of our current theory and research. Appropriately, many of our theoretical frameworks have focused on the production of verbal and nonverbal stimuli, and they have served us well. However, those frameworks stop short of drawing explicit conceptual links to social consequences. Alternatively, conceptualizations included in this review cast interaction processes as initiators of causal sequences leading to a social problem (e.g., Tyler & Lind, 1992), whereas in others, interaction processes serve as mediators between initiating events and consequences (e.g., Felson, 1984). Regardless of the role of interaction portrayed by these frameworks, they provide clarity with regard to how interaction processes influence social problems.

Third, we must shift our research designs to gather socially relevant data. I noted from the outset that we have become sophisticated with respect to methodological and statistical issues, and I do not believe that doing socially relevant research would require abandonment of our current methods. However, such a shift requires that we include direct measures of the problem we are researching and draw samples from the populations that are affected by the problem. Moreover, we may have to shift our interests from "immediate impact" effects to longitudinal research, which might uncover more serious problems. I suspect that the interaction processes that lead to divorce, violent crime, and incivility may come to a head within a single encounter, but that the nature of prior interactions heavily influenced the critical interaction. Moreover, we might find that many potentially problematic episodes do not result in socially relevant outcomes. Indeed, although domestic violence frequently escalates from a verbally aggressive act, most verbally aggressive interactions do not result in physical aggression (Roloff, 1996). Unless we study processes longitudinally, we will develop an incomplete and distorted view of the process. Such longitudinal research will be costly in terms of time, something that current tenure practices does not afford nontenured researchers. Moreover, it will require resources garnered through extramural funding, which few of us have sought (Burgoon, 1988).

Fourth, we must learn to speak to citizens, practitioners, and policymakers. Currently, our research does not seem to diffuse much further than the field. Hence, we must find ways of getting the information to interested parties. I would note that many of the researchers I cited in my review have produced books that are intended for nonacademic markets (e.g., Gottman, 1994b; Pennebaker, 1990). Furthermore, we may have to address issues related to the treatment of social problems and conduct research that evaluates such interventions. With few exceptions (e.g., Motley & Molloy, 1994), most interpersonal communication researchers have not addressed issues related to treatment and policy.

Fifth, we will need to monitor the social problems of the day and this may prove to be problematic. The national agenda is a negotiated phenomenon, and its content can change. Hence, an important topic could be rendered insignificant before a research program can be completed. Moreover, to dictate one's research agenda by the needs of society could result in becoming a servant to the interests of those groups who are able to gain the attention of the media and government. Also, privileging national issues could shift our attention from the needs of local constituencies (e.g., training undergraduates).

Although the aforementioned are serious concerns, I am doubtful that they would be significant obstacles. The social problems identified in this review have been on the national agenda for some time, and I doubt they will ever become irrelevant. Moreover, it is possible to construe societal problems in a manner that serves local constituencies. For example, to the extent that one can demonstrate that communication apprehension aversively impacts educational performance, which in turn retards employment opportunities, then one can make a strong case for implementing programs to help undergraduates overcome their apprehension.

Finally, we will need to overcome our own inertia. Most researchers, including myself, are comfortable with what they do. After all, it is what has resulted in professional and personal career success. However, it would be a mistake to suggest to young scholars and graduate students that the "tried and true" path to success will work in the future. Although I do not wish to overstate the case, I suspect that current practices will be ineffective for the next generation of scholars. External accountability pressures are increasing, and they will render less relevant field-driven evaluations of research programs. Hence, academic survival and success will increasingly depend on the ability to demonstrate that one conducts research that makes a difference to society. In doing so, we not only ensure our own survival, but we simultaneously improve the quality of our scholarship and the society in which we live.

ACKNOWLEDGMENTS

I wish to acknowledge the assistance of each of the following people in inspiring and completing this project: Professors Peter Miller, Charles Berger, Joseph Cappella, and Gaylen Paulson.

REFERENCES

Amato, P. R., & Keith, B. (1991a). Parental divorce and adult well-being. *Journal of Marriage and the Family, 53*, 43–58.

Amato, P. R., & Keith, B. (1991b). Parental divorce and the well-being of children: A meta-analysis. *Psychological Bulletin, 110*, 26–46.

Avery, R. K. (1995). Mining the mother load. *Western Journal of Communication, 59*, 246–251.

Bach, B. W. (1997). Putting an end to arrogance: Tips for climbing down from the ivory tower. *Western Journal of Communication, 61*, 338–342.

Baron, R. A. (1988). Negative effects of destructive criticism: Impact on conflict, self-efficacy, and task performance. *Journal of Applied Psychology, 73*, 199–207.

Baumeister, R. F., Stillwell, A., & Wotman, S. R. (1990). Victim and perpetrator accounts of interpersonal conflict: Autobiographical narratives about anger. *Journal of Personality and Social Psychology, 59*, 994–1005.

Benson, T. W., & Pearce, W. B. (1977). Alternative theoretical bases for the study of human communication: A symposium [Special issue]. *Communication Quarterly, 25*(1).

Berger, C. R. (1991). Communication theories and other curios. *Communication Monographs, 58*, 101–113.

Berger, C. R. (1998, April). *Are there really so few communication theories?* Paper presented at the annual meeting of the Central States Communication Association, Chicago.

Berman, W. H., & Turk, D. S. (1981). Adaptation to divorce: Problems and coping strategies. *Journal of Marriage and the Family, 42,* 179–189.

Birchler, G. R., Wiess, R. L., & Vincent, J. P. (1975). Multimethod analysis of social reinforcement exchange between maritally distressed and nondistressed spouse and stranger dyads. *Journal of Personality and Social Psychology, 31,* 349–360.

Boster, F. J. (1988). Comments on the utility of compliance-gaining message selections tasks. *Human Communication Research, 15,* 169–177.

Boster, F. J., Stiff, J. B., & Reynolds, R. A. (1985). Do persons respond differently to inductively-derived and deductively derived lists of compliance-gaining messages strategies: A reply to Wiseman and Schenk-Hamlin. *Western Journal of Speech Communication, 49,* 177–187.

Burgoon, M. (1988). Extramural funding or extracurricular research: That is the choice. A research editorial. *Western Journal of Speech Communication, 52,* 252–258.

Burgoon, M. (1995). A kinder, gentler discipline: Feeling good about being mediocre. In B. R. Burleson (Ed.), *Communication yearbook 18* (pp. 464–478). Thousand Oaks, CA: Sage.

Burgoon, M., Dillard, J. P., & Doran, N. E. (1983). Friendly or unfriendly persuasion: The effects of violations of expectations by males and females. *Human Communication Research, 10,* 283–294.

Burgoon, M., & Miller, G. R. (1990). Paths. *Communication Monographs, 57,* 152–160.

Burleson, B. R. (Ed.). (1995). *Communication yearbook 18.* Thousand Oaks, CA: Sage.

Burleson, B. R., & Wilson, S. (1988). On the continued undesirability of item desirability: A reply to Boster, Hunter and Seibold. *Human Communication Research, 15,* 178–191.

Burleson, B. R., Wilson, S. R., Waltman, M. S., Goering, E. M., Ely, T. K., & Whaley, B. B. (1988). Item desirability of effects in compliance-gaining research: Seven studies documenting artifacts in the strategy selection procedures. *Human Communication Research, 14,* 429–486.

Chautauqua. (1990a). Are rhetoric and science incompatible? *Communication Monographs, 57,* 309–332.

Chautauqua. (1990b). On the validity and generalizability of conversation analysis methods. *Communication Monographs, 57,* 231–249.

Chautauqua. (1992). A reprise of why are there so few communication theories? *Communication Monographs, 59,* 79–107.

Chiricos, T., Eschholz, S., & Gertz, M. (1997). Crime, news and fear of crime: Toward an identification of audience effects. *Social Problems, 44,* 342–358.

Colloquy. (1983). Generalizing about messages. *Human Communication Research, 9,* 169–191.

Colloquy. (1988). On generalization. *Human Communication Research, 15,* 112–151.

Courtright, J. A., Millar, F. E., Rogers, L. E., & Bagarozzi, D. (1990). Interaction dynamics of relational negotiation: Reconciliation versus termination of distressed relationships. *Western Journal of Speech Communication, 54,* 429–453.

Felson, R. B. (1978). Aggression as impression management. *Social Psychology, 41,* 205–213.

Felson, R. B. (1982). Impression management and the escalation of aggression and violence. *Social Psychology Quarterly, 45,* 245–254.

Felson, R. B. (1984). Patterns of aggressive social interaction. In A. Mummendey (Ed.), *Social psychology of aggression: From individual behavior social interaction* (pp. 108–124). Berlin, Germany: Springer-Verlag.

Felson, R. B., Ribner, S. A., & Siegel, M. S. (1984). Age and the effect of third parties during criminal violence. *Sociology and Social Research, 68,* 452–462.

Felson, R. B., & Steadman, H. J. (1983). Situational factors in disputes leading to criminal violence. *Criminology, 21,* 59–74.

Fisher, B. A. (Ed.). (1977). What criteria should be used to judge the admissibility of evidence to support theoretical propositions regarding communication research? [Special issue]. *Western Journal of Speech Communication, 41*(1).

Fitzpatrick, M. A. (1988). *Between husbands and wives: Communication in marriage.* Thousand Oaks, CA: Sage.

Flanagan, T. J. (1996). Public opinion and public policy in criminal justice. In T. J. Flanagan & D. R. Longmire (Eds.), *Americans view crime and justice: A national public opinion survey* (pp. 151–158). Thousand Oaks, CA: Sage.

Gottman, J. M. (1993a). The roles of conflict engagement, escalation, and avoidance in marital interaction: A longitudinal view of five types of couples. *Journal of Consulting and Clinical Psychology, 61,* 6–15.

Gottman, J. M. (1993b). A theory of marital dissolution and stability. *Journal of Family Psychology, 7,* 57–75.

Gottman, J. M. (1994a). *What predicts divorce? The relationship between marital processes and marital outcomes.* Hillsdale, NJ: Lawrence Erlbaum Associates.

Gottman, J. M. (1994b). *Why marriages succeed or fail.* New York: Simon & Schuster.

Gottman, J. M., Coan, J., Carrere, S., & Swanson, C. (1998). Predicting marital happiness and stability from newlywed interactions. *Journal of Marriage and the Family, 60,* 5–22.

Gottman, J. M., & Levenson, R. W. (1988). The social psychophysiology of marriage. In P. Noller & M. A. Fitzpatrick (Eds.), *Perspectives on marital interaction* (pp. 182–200). Clevedon, UK: Multilingual Matters.

Haghighi, B., & Sorensen, J. (1996). America's fear of crime. In T. J. Flanagan & D. R. Longmire (Eds.), *Americans view crime and justice: A national public opinion survey* (pp. 16–30). Thousand Oaks, CA: Sage.

Hample, D. (1999). The life space of personalized conflicts. In M. E. Roloff (Ed.), *Communication yearbook 23* (pp. 171–208). Thousand Oaks, CA: Sage.

Heaton, T. B., & Albrecht, S. L. (1991). Stable unhappy marriages. *Journal of Marriage and the Family, 53,* 747–758.

Heszen-Klemens, I., & Lapkinska, E. (1984). Doctor–patient interaction, patients' health behavior and effects of treatment. *Social Science and Medicine, 19,* 9–18.

Horwitz, A. V., White, H. R., & Howell-White, S. (1996). Becoming married and mental health: A longitudinal study of a cohort of young adults. *Journal of Marriage and the Family, 58,* 895–907.

Hunter, J. E., Hamilton, M. A., & Allen, M. (1989). The design and analysis of language experiments in communication. *Communication Monographs, 56,* 341–363.

Infante, D. A., & Rancer, A. S. (1996). Argumentativeness and verbal aggressiveness: A review of recent theory and research. In B. R. Burleson (Ed.), *Communication yearbook 19* (pp. 319–352). Thousand Oaks, CA: Sage.

Infante, D. A., Riddle, B. L., Horvath, C. L., & Tumlin, S. A. (1992). Verbal aggressiveness: Messages and reasons. *Communication Quarterly, 40,* 116–126.

Jackson, S., O'Keefe, D. J., Jacobs, S., & Bashers, D. E. (1989). Messages as replications: Toward a message-centered design strategy. *Communication Monographs, 56,* 364–384.

Kaplan, S. H., Greenfield, S., & Ware, J. E. (1989). Impact of the doctor–patient relationship on the outcomes of chronic disease. In M. Stewart & D. Roter (Eds.), *Communicating with medical patients* (pp. 228–245). Thousand Oaks, CA: Sage.

Kellermann, K., & Cole, T. (1994). Classifying compliance gaining messages: Taxonomic disorder and strategic confusion. *Communication Theory, 4,* 3–60.

Kitson, G. C., & Sussman, M. B. (1982). Marital complaints, demographic characteristics, and symptoms of mental distress in divorce. *Journal of Marriage and the Family, 43,* 87–100.

Knapp, M. L., & Miller, G. R. (1985). *Handbook of interpersonal communication.* Thousand Oaks, CA: Sage.

Knapp, M. L., & Miller, G. R. (1994). *Handbook of interpersonal communication* (2nd ed.). Thousand Oaks, CA: Sage.

Knapp, M. L., Miller, G. R., & Fudge, K. (1994). Background and current trends in the study of interpersonal communication. In M. L. Knapp & G. R. Miller (Eds.), *Handbook of interpersonal communication* (2nd ed., pp. 3–20). Thousand Oaks, CA: Sage.

Knapp, M. L., Stafford, L., & Daly, J. A. (1986). Regrettable messages: Things people wish they hadn't said. *Journal of Communication, 36,* 40–58.

Koester, J. (1996). On disciplining ourselves. *Western Journal of Communication, 60,* 285–289.

Lakey, B., Tardiff, T. A., & Drew, J. B. (1994). Negative social interactions: Assessment and relations to social support, cognition, and psychological distress. *Journal of Social and Clinical Psychology, 13,* 63–85.

Lannamann, J. W. (1991). Interpersonal communication research as ideological practice. *Communication Theory, 1,* 179–203.

Lauer, R. H., & Lauer, J. C. (1986). Factors in long-term marriage. *Journal of Family Issues, 7,* 382–390.

Lehman, D. R., Ellard, J. H., & Wortman, C. B. (1986). Social support for the bereaved: Recipients' and providers' perspectives on what is helpful. *Journal of Consulting and Clinical Psychology, 54,* 438–446.

Lillard, L. A., & Waite, L. J. (1995). 'Till death do us part: Marital disruption and mortality. *American Journal of Sociology, 100,* 1131–1156.

Lim, T., & Bowers, J. W. (1991). Facework: Solidarity, approbation, and tact. *Human Communication Research, 17,* 415–450.

Luckenbill, D. F. (1977). Criminal homicide as a situated transaction. *Social Problems, 25,* 176–186.

Makoul, G., Arntson, P., & Schofield, T. (1995). Health promotion in primary care: Physician–patient communication and decision making about prescription medications. *Social Science and Medicine, 41,* 1241–1254.

Markman, H. J. (1979). Application of a behavioral model of marriage in predicting relationship satisfaction of couples planning marriage. *Journal of Consulting and Clinical Psychology, 47,* 743–749.

Markman, H. J. (1981). Prediction of marital distress: A 5-year follow-up. *Journal of Consulting and Clinical Psychology, 49,* 760–762.

Martin, T. C., & Bumpass, L. (1989). Recent trends in marital disruption. *Demography, 26,* 37–51.

McCall, G. J., & Simmons, J. L. (1978). *Identities and interactions: An examination of human associations in everyday life* (rev. ed.). New York: The Free Press.

McCombs, M., Danielian, L., & Wanta, W. (1995). Issues in the news and the public agenda: The agenda-setting tradition. In T. L. Glasser & C. T. Salmon (Eds.), *Public opinion and the communication of consent* (pp. 281–300). New York: Guilford.

McGonagle, K. A., Kessler, R. C., & Gotlib, I. H. (1993). The effects of marital disagreement style, frequency, and outcome on marital disruption. *Journal of Social and Personal Relationships, 10,* 385–404.

Mikolic, J. M., Parker, J. C., & Pruitt, D. C. (1997). Escalation in response to persistent annoyance: Groups versus individuals and gender effects. *Journal of Personality and Social Psychology, 72,* 151–163.

Miller, G. R. (1981). "Tis the season to be jolly": A Yuletide 1980 assessment of communication research. *Human Communication Research, 7,* 371–377.

Motley, M. T., & Molloy, J. L. (1994). An efficacy test of a new therapy ("communication-orientation motivation") for public speaking anxiety. *Journal of Applied Communication Research, 22,* 48–58.

National Opinion Research Center. (1994). General social survey codebook variable: DIVLAW [Online]. Retrieved http://icpsr.umich.edu/GSS/codebook/div law.htm From The World Wide Web: 8/98.

Parks, M. P. (1982). Ideology in interpersonal communication: Off the couch and into the world. In M. Burgoon (Ed.), *Communication yearbook 5* (pp. 79–107). New Brunswick, NJ: Transaction.

Parks, M. P. (1995). Ideology in interpersonal communication: Beyond the couches, talk shows, and bunkers. In B. R. Burleson (Ed.), *Communication yearbook 18* (pp. 480–497). Thousand Oaks, CA: Sage.

Pennebaker, J. W. (1989). Confession, inhibition, and disease. In L. Berkowitz (Ed.), *Advances in experimental social psychology* (Vol. 22, pp. 211–244). San Diego, CA: Academic.

Pennebaker, J. W. (1990). *Opening up: The healing power of confiding in others.* New York: Morrow.

Pennebaker, J. W., Hughes, C., & O'Heeron, R. C. (1987). The psychophysiology of confession: Linking inhibitor and psychosomatic processes. *Journal of Personality and Social Psychology, 52,* 781–793.

Petrie, K. J., Booth, R. J., & Davison, K. P. (1995). Repression, disclosure, and immune function: Recent findings and methodological issues. In J. W. Pennebaker (Ed.), *Emotion, disclosure, & health* (pp. 223–240). Washington, DC: American Psychological Association.

Petronio, S. (Ed.). (1994). The dialogue of evidence: A topic revisited [Special issue]. *Western Journal of Communication, 58*(1).

Phillips, G. M. (1981). Science and the study of human communication: An inquiry from the other side of the two cultures. *Human Communication Research, 7,* 361–370.

Poole, M. S., & Folger, J. P. (1981). A method for establishing the representational validity of interaction coding systems: Do we see what they see? *Human Communication Research, 8,* 26–42.

Pruitt, D. G., Parker, J. C., & Mikolic, J. M. (1997). Escalation as a reaction to persistent annoyance. *The International Journal of Conflict Management, 8,* 252–270.

Roloff, M. E. (1996). The catalyst hypothesis: Conditions under which coercive communication leads to physical aggression. In D. D. Cahn & S. A. Lloyd (Eds.), *Family violence from a communication perspective* (pp. 20–36). Thousand Oaks, CA: Sage.

Rook, K. S. (1984). The negative side of social interaction. Impact on psychological well-being. *Journal of Personality and Social Psychology, 46,* 1097–1108.

Rusbult, C. E., Verette, J., Whitney, G. A., Slovik, L. F., & Lipkus, I. (1991). Accommodation processes in close relationships: Theory and preliminary empirical evidence. *Journal of Personality and Social Psychology, 60,* 53–78.

Scherer, K. R., & Tannenbaum, P. H. (1986). Emotional experiences in everyday life: A survey approach. *Motivation and Emotion, 10,* 295–314.

Seibold, D. R. (1988). A response to "item desirability" in compliance gaining research. *Human communication Research, 15*, 152–161.

Sherman, R. (1994, April 18). Crime's toll on the US: Fears, despair and guns. *National Law Journal*, pp. A1, A19–A20.

Shields, D. E. (1998, April). *Are there really so few communication theories?* Paper presented at the annual meeting of the Central States Communication Association, Chicago.

Smith, H. J., Tyler, T. R., Huo, Y. J., Ortiz, D. J., & Lind, E. A. (1998). The self-relevant implications of the group-value model: Groups membership, self-worth, and treatment quality. *Journal of Experimental Social Psychology, 34*, 470–493.

Stets, J. E., & Henderson, D. A. (1991). Contextual factors surrounding conflict resolution while dating: Results from a national study. *Family Relations, 40*, 29–36.

Thompson, T. L. (1994). Interpersonal communication and health. In M. L. Knapp & G. R. Miller (Eds.), *Handbook of interpersonal communication* (2nd ed., pp. 696–725). Thousand Oaks, CA: Sage.

Traue, H. C. (1995). Inhibition and muscle tension in myogenic pain. In J. W. Pennebaker (Ed.), *Emotion, disclosure, & health* (pp. 155–176). Washington, DC: American Psychological Association.

Tucker, R. K., Weaver, R. L., & Berryman-Fink, C. (1981). *Research in speech communication*. Englewood Cliffs, NJ: Prentice Hall.

Tyler, T. R., Degoey, P., & Smith, H. (1996). Understanding why the justice of group procedures matters: A test of the psychological dynamics of the group-value model. *Journal of Personality and Social Psychology, 70*, 913–930.

Tyler, T. R., & Lind, E. A. (1992). A relational model of authority in groups. In M. P. Zanna (Ed.), *Advances in experimental social psychology* (Vol. 25, pp. 115–192). San Diego, CA: Academic.

Udry, J. R. (1981). Marital alternatives and marital disruption. *Journal of Marriage and the Family, 43*, 889–897.

U.S. News and World Report. (1996). Special report: Civility poll [Online]. Retrieved http://www.usnews.com/usnews/news/reudpoll.htm From the World Wide Web: 8/98.

Wiseman, R. L., & Schenk-Hamlin, W. (1981). A multidimensional scaling validation of an inductively-derived set of compliance-gaining strategies. *Communication Monographs, 48*, 251–270.

Author Bios

Kimo AhYun (PhD, Michigan State University, 1996) is an Assistant Professor in the Department of Communication Studies at California State University at Sacramento. In addition to studying the effect that attitude similarity has on interpersonal attraction, his research has also focused on compliance gaining in interpersonal relationships and the persuasiveness of narrative evidence. Dr. AhYun has published in journals such as the *Journal of Applied Communication Research*, *Communication Studies*, and *Communication Research Reports*.

Mike Allen (PhD, Michigan State University, 1987) is Professor in the Department of Communication at the University of Wisconsin-Milwaukee. His more than 100 published works deal with issues of HIV/AIDS education and prevention, drug use, persuasion, and other sources of social influence. His work has appeared in *Health Education and Behavior*, *Human Communication Research*, *Journal of Personal and Social Relationships*, *Law and Human Behavior*, and *Communication Education*.

Charles R. Berger (PhD, Michigan State University, 1968) is Professor in the Department of Communication, University of California, Davis. His research interests include the roles cognitive structures and processes play in social interaction and the ways apprehension and estimates of personal risk are influenced by various features of news reports. He is the former president of the International Communication Association, editor of *Human Communication Research* and co-editor of *Communication Research*. His book *Planning Strategic*

Interaction (Erlbaum) compiled his research on plans, planning and message production, and recent articles in *Journal of Communication* and *Human Communication Research* have presented his work on threatening trends and risk perception.

Nancy A. Burrell (PhD, Michigan State University, 1987)is an Associate Professor at the University of Wisconsin-Milwaukee. Professor Burrell's research centers on managing conflict in family, workplace and educational contexts. She has published in *Human Communication Research, Communication Monographs* and *Management Communication Quarterly*. She is currently investigating the impact of workplace bullies to design dispute systems for organizations.

Daniel Canary (PhD, University of Southern California, 1983) is a Professor of Human Communication at Arizona State University. He has co-authored or edited nine books and two journal special issues. Dan has published over 50 articles, book chapters, and essays on the topic of interpersonal communication. He is the immediate Past President of the International Network for Personal Relationships and has served as a conference program planner for regional, national, and international associations. Finally, Professor Canary is the Editor-Elect of the *Western Journal of Communication* and serves as an editorial board member for several other scholarly journals.

Tara Crowell (PhD, University of Oklahoma, 1999) is an Assistant Professor at the Richard Stockton College of New Jersey. Her major areas of interests are Interpersonal, Health, and Instructional Communication. Professor Crowell continues to investigate HIV positive heterosexuals' communication, attitudes and behaviors prior to heterosexually contracting the virus, in order to link the communication, attitudes and behaviors of HIV positive individuals to those who are not infected. Her ultimate goal for this research is to motivate heterosexually individuals to start to personalize the risk of HIV and engage in safer sexual communication and behaviors.

Judith Marie Dallinger (PhD, University of Nebraska, 1984) is a professor at Western Illinois University. Her research interests fall primarily into the areas of conflict and sex differences in communication. She serves as the Executive Secretary for the Organization for the Study of Communication, Language and Gender. Her work has been published in *Human Communication Research, Communication Research Reports, Communication Quarterly,* and *Communication Reports*.

James Price Dillard (PhD, Michigan State University, 1983) is Professor of Communication Arts and Director of the Center for Communication Research at the University of Wisconsin-Madison His research interests revolve around the study of influence and persuasion with a special emphasis on the role of emotion in persuasion. In addition to the many research articles and book chapters he has authored, he is responsible for the book entitled *Seeking compliance: The production of interpersonal influence messages*. He is co-editor of the forthcoming *Persuasion Handbook: Developments in Theory and Practice*. Dillard has served as the Chair of the Interpersonal Division of the International Communication Association and currently sits on the editorial boards for five social science journals. In recognition of his research achievements, he received the Villas Associate Award from UW-Madison in 1994 and the John E. Hunter Award for Meta-Analysis in 1995.

Kathryn Dinda (PhD, University of Washington, 1981) is a Professor in the Department of Communication at the University of Wisconsin-Milwaukee. She has served on the editorial board for *Journal of Social and Personal Relationships, Human Communication Research, Journal of Applied Communication, Journal of Communication*, and *Women's Studies in Communication*. She co-edited *Sex differences and similarities in communication* and *Communication in personal relationships*. Dinda has published approximately 30 articles and book chapters including articles in *Psychological Bulletin, Human Communication Research, Journal of Social and Personal Relationships*, and *Personal Relationships*.

Tara M. Emmers-Sommer (PhD, Ohio University, 1995) is Associate Professor in the Department of Communication at the University of Arizona. Emmers-Sommer's area of research is "problematic communication" in social and personal relationships. Her work can be found in journals such as *Human Communication Research, Communication Yearbook, Journal of Social and Personal Relationships, Communication Quarterly, Journal of Communication*, and the *Journal of Sex Research*. She is also the co-author, along with Daniel J. Canary, of the 1997 Guilford book, *Sex and gender differences in personal relationships*.

Mary Anne Fitzpatrick (PhD, Temple University, 1976) is Professor of communication Arts and Dean for the Social Sciences at the University of Wisconsin. Her research interests are in interaction in personal and social relationships. She has published in numerous journals such as *Communication Monographs, Journal of Social and Personal Relationships, Human Communication Research, Communication Quarterly, Journal of Language and Social Psychology*, etc.

Barbara Mae Gayle (PhD, University of Oregon, 1989) is Professor and Chair of the Department of Communication Studies at The University of Portland. Selected as a 2001–2002 Carnegie Scholar, Gayle is published in *Women's Studies in Communication, Journal of Applied Communication, Management Communication Quarterly* and *Communication Research Reports*.

Mark Hamilton (EDD, Boston University, 1983) is a Professor at the University of Connecticut. His focus is on issues surrounding the use and impact of various forms of language in social interaction and influence. He has published in *Human Communication Research, Communication Monographs, World Communication*, and *Communication Theory*.

Dale Hample (PhD, University of Illinois, 1975) is Professor of Communication at Western Illinois University. His research interests are primarily argumentation, persuasion, message production, and conflict management. His work has been published in *Communication Yearbook, Human Communication Research, Communication Monographs*, and *Argumentation and Advocacy*.

Michelle J. Mattrey (PhD, The Pennsylvania State University, 2000) is a communication market research analyst at M&M/Mars in Hackettstown, NJ. Her research area is interpersonal communication. Specifically, she is interested in perceptions of sex/gender differences in leader behavior. Her dissertation looked at the influence of sex stereotypes on perceptions of leaders' conflict management behavior.

Paul J. Mineo (PhD, Michigan State University, 1991) is an Assistant Professor at the University of Connecticut. His research interests focus on message features and his work has been published in the *Journal of Language and Social Psychology*.

Michael E. Roloff (PhD, Michigan State University, 1975) is Professor of Communication Studies at Northwestern University. His primary research area is interpersonal influence with a specific focus on conflict management and bargaining and negotiation. He is currently is co-editor of *Communication Research* and has been the editor of the *Communication Yearbook*. He wrote *Interpersonal Communication: The Social Exchange Approach* and has co-edited four books. His articles have appeared in *Communication Monographs, Communication Research, Human Communication Research, International Journal of Conflict Management, Journal of Social and Personal Relationships* and *Personal Relationships*.

Raymond W. Preiss (PhD, University of Oregon, 1988) is Professor and Chair of the Department of Communication and Theater at the University of Puget Sound. He is a co-author *Persuasion: Advances through meta-analysis*. His work has appeared in *Management Communication Quarterly* and *Communication Research Reports*.

Erin Sahlstein (PhD, University of Iowa, 2000) is an Assistant Professor in the Department of Rhetoric and Communication Studies at the University of Richmond in Richmond, Virginia. Her theory and research focuses on personal relationships, typically long-distance relationships, from a relational dialectics perspective. She has published co-authored articles in *Communication Reports* and *Journal of Social and Personal Relationships*. She has also co-authored chapters concerning relational culture, disclosure, and relationship commitment.

Brian H. Spitzberg (PhD, University of Southern California, 1981) is Full Professor in the School of Communication at San Diego State University. His scholarly interests are in interpersonal competence, interpersonal conflict, relational violence, sexual coercion, and stalking. He has authored *Interpersonal Communication Competence* (1984, Sage), *Handbook of Interpersonal Competence Research* (1989, Springer-Verlag), and co-edited and contributed to *The Dark Side of Interpersonal Communication* (1994, Erlbaum) and *The Dark Side of Close Relationships* (1998, Erlbaum).

Lindsay M. Timmerman (PhD, University of Texas, 2001) is an Assistant professor in the Department of Communication at the University of Wisconsin-Milwaukee. Her research focuses on communication in romantic relationships and families. She has examined issues that include romantic jealousy, long-distance relationships, family secrets, and pre-marital commitment. Her work has appeared in *Communication Monographs*, *Communication Quarterly*, and *Communication Studies*.

Author Index

Subject Index

cognitive processes
  cognitive perspective and social
      interaction research, 23
  cognitive self-esteem, 413. *see also*
      self-esteem
  cognitive skill and strategy and
      marital conflict
      management, 359
  cognitive skill and strategy as
      self-esteem factor, 60, 69
  memory function and cognitive
      process research, 24
  relevant to proto-theory, 14–18
comforting behavior
  and constructivist theory and
      research, 227–242
  and relationship maintenance, 215
  as interactional process, 214
  comforting behavior domain, 36
  causal model test comforting
      message research, 236
  listener knowledge and comforting
      messages research, 228
  messages and pedagogical reference
      to, 380
  metacommunicative knowledge and
      comforting message
      research, 228
  motivation and comforting messages
      research, 228, 229
  rhetorical knowledge and comforting
      message research, 228
  Stiff model comforting messages,
      motivation for, 239
  topic knowledge and comforting
      message research, 228
commitment (relational), 429
  and messages of affection, 215
communication apprehension
  and meta-analysis, 13, 403
  apprehension as situational effect, 189
  meta-analysis findings in, 392
  public speaking anxiety, 392
communication behaviors
  and self-esteem, 50
  and self-worth conceptualizations, 49
  gender differences in, 391
  meta-analysis findings in, 392, 393, 397
communication competence
  and individual processes, 48, 52–54
  and postdivorce adjustment period, 248

  and self-esteem, 50
  communication skills, 89–104
  competence and argumentativeness
      theory, 292
  pedagogical reference to, 379
communication theory
  analysis of pedagogy in, 371–386
  analysis of research in, 423–440
  and argumentativeness promotion,
      284, 291
  and meta-analysis process, 14
  and meta-analysis results, 139–140
  research goals in, 71
  and similarity and attraction
      meta-analysis, 161
communicative satisfaction
  and attribution approach, 48
  and relational influence theory, 119
  and similarity and liking, 147
communicator style
  and power in language, 76, 83
  and self-esteem conceptualization, 60
  and and social skills, 391
  and task attraction, 113
  doctor-patient relationship and
      communicator style, 53
  meta-analysis of, 80, 81
  multidimensional components of, 53
  perception of others and
      communicator style, 53–54
  research in, 415–416
complementarity, 379
compliance-gaining strategies
  and individual-level plan, 27
  and proto-theory context, 20
  and safe sex negotiation, 268
  and situational effects, 187–207
  and URT, 115
  compliments and offers as
      compliance-gaining
      strategy, 27
  endorsing or suppressing, 189–192
  meta-analyses in, 414
  pleasantness as compliance-gaining
      strategy, 27
composure in communication
  and affinity-seeking, 52
  and self-esteem, 50
  and social skill competency, 104
comprehension
  as condition of social interaction, 15

roles
    and conflict management
        strategies, 347
    and self-esteem conceptualization,
        60, 62
    and sexual coercion, 319
    sexual coercion and resistance, 315,
        316, 325–326, 327
    meta-analysis results, 336
    sexuality
        benchmark studies in, 408–413
    socialization approach
        as conflict management strategy
            selection, 347
    theory confidence in, 10
goals and plans
    and conversational processes, 217
    and proto-theory context, 17–18, 22,
        36, 37
    and relational influence theory, 119
    children and, 31
    effectiveness in, 91
    embedded, 33
    hierarchy for, 26
    and behavior unit analysis, 29
    later recall of, 26
    long-term, 29
    non-interactive, 30
    shifts during interaction, 22–23
    significance to proto-theory, 25

H

harm
    harm-to-other criteria
        and situation effects research, 205
        as cognitive editing process, 191
    harm-to-relationship criteria
        and situation effects research, 206
        as cognitive editing process, 191
    harm-to-self criteria
        as cognitive editing process, 191
health care communication
    as social support source, 250
    and URT, 115
health and quality of social skills, 93
health and social support, 250
    social significance of research on,
        433–435
    style of, 53
hierarchy principle, 26

    and visual/written forms, 29
HIV infection
    and custody decision-making, 128
    and disclosure laws, 264
    and safe sex negotiation, 263, 271
    communication regarding
        textbook inclusion of, 382
    negotiation analysis
    lack of pedagogical reference to, 380
homosexuality
    and coercive sex, 316
    and safe sex negotiation, 274
    attitudes toward, 409
    criminalization of, 127–128

I

identity construction
    and causes of violence, 432
    in dyadic processes, 112
impression formation studies
    and disclosure-liking hypothesis, 172
    impression management behaviors,
        46, 49–50
    impression management theory, 432
inclusion *vs.* affiliation, 51
inference
    and individual processes, 47
    and long-term goals and plans, 29
information-seeking behavior, 114
    in health care interaction, 434
initial interpersonal interaction, 156, 158
    and attitude similarity studies,
        151–153
interactional processes, 46
    and attitude similarity studies, 151
    and causes of crime, 431–433
    and causes of divorce, 429
    and incivilities, 435–436
    and proto-theory context, 23–30
    and reciprocity in self-disclosure, 182
    as research characteristic, 426
    and social skills, 90
    initial interpersonal interaction, 156,
        158
    interaction sequence analysis and
        goals and plans hierarchy, 29
    interaction sequence analysis and
        limitations of meta-analysis,
        402
    mutuality of control as interactional
        process, 213, 215, 220–223